Modern Iran

The Dialectics of Continuity and Change

Edited by

Michael E. Bonine
University of Arizona

Nikki R. Keddie
University of California, Los Angeles

State University of New York Press

Albany

Published by
State University of New York Press, Albany

© 1981 State University of New York

For information, address State University of New York
Press, State University Plaza, Albany, N.Y., 12246

Library of Congress Cataloging in Publication Data
Main entry under title:

Modern Iran.

  Bibliography: p.
  Includes index.
  1. Iran—Social conditions—Addresses, essays,
lectures. 2. Iran—Politics and government—
Addresses, essays, lectures. I. Bonine, Michael
E., 1942-   II. Keddie, Nikki R.
HN670.2.A8M63   955'.053   80-19463
ISBN 0-87395-465-3

10 9 8 7 6 5 4 3 2

Contents

Illustrations

Tables

Preface

The idea for a volume on continuity and change in modern Iran originated from two colloquia on modern Iranian society held in 1977 and 1978 at the University of Arizona under the auspices of the Department of Oriental Studies and the Near Eastern Center. What emerged from the papers and discussions was that change—modernization—in the nineteenth and twentieth centuries has manifested itself in *Iranian* patterns: in the persistence of Iranian culture and society. The revolution of 1978–79 and subsequent events have stressed this endurance (and complexity) of Iranian society.

Approximately half of the essays in this work have evolved out of the Tucson conferences on Iran, while the remaining papers have been solicited and specifically written for the volume. All the articles represent recent research on Iran, with the majority of papers the result of field research in Iran in the immediate years prior to—and in a few cases into—the Iranian Revolution of 1978–79.

The colloquia on modern Iranian society were supported by funds from the Joint Committee on the Near and Middle East of the American Council of Learned Societies and the Social Science Research Council, the University of Arizona Foundation, and the Near East Center of the University of Arizona. We thank these organizations for their support.

Thanks are due to Richard Cottam and Paul English for their helpful comments on the entire manuscript, and to those whose suggestions and criticisms on individual papers are acknowledged by the specific authors. William Eastman and the staff of State University of New York Press were most helpful—and patient. Thanks also go to those who participated in the discussions without which this book would not have been possible: Constance Cronin, John Lorentz, Thomas Ricks, and Donald Stilo.

Tucson, Arizona   Michael E. Bonine
Los Angeles, California   Nikki R. Keddie
May 1980

A Note on Transliteration

The transliteration of Persian into English used in this volume is a simplified system, chosen partly to keep maximum clarity of pronunciation without any diacriticals. Consonants are as pronounced and generally follow the system adopted by the *International Journal of Middle East Studies,* but without any diacriticals. Short vowels are represented by a, e, and o; long vowels by a, i, and u; and dipthongs by ai and au. *Ain* and *hamzeh* are indicated by an apostrophe and only within a word (e.g. Isma'ili); but this is not always followed, as in the case of proper names which have become common to readers. Arabic definite articles in names and personal titles are written ol-, except for assimilated endings which then are written as pronounced (od-Dauleh, os-Saltaneh, etc.). Certain common terms, especially religious, administrative, and land tenure terms, may not follow this transliteration system (e.g. mulla instead of molla, *mujtahid* instead of *mojtahid, tuyul* instead of *toyul*). Words which have essentially entered into English usage, such as ulama and mulla, are not italicized.

Introduction

Nikki R. Keddie

The papers in this volume deal with social, cultural, and economic aspects of modern Iran, mainly from the viewpoint of a single region, social group, or cultural phenomenon. They thus represent a departure from the Tehran-centered political and elite emphases that have characterized most postwar scholarly works in Iran and attempt a more focused thorough treatment of the elements that make up the Iranian totality. Although these papers rarely concentrate directly on government-level politics or international relations, they shed new and important light on the dramatic crisis and revolution of 1978–9 that one cannot find in purely political studies. Many of them illuminate different aspects of a continuing phenomenon central to the understanding of the revolution: namely, the contradictory and dialectical nature of change which, added to the ways in which change was imposed from above, created major tensions in all areas of Iranian society. Changes that benefited some groups, especially the modernized and Westernized new middle and upper classes, often disfavored the traditional middle classes (or bazaaris, sometimes inadequately called the petty bourgeoisie) and the other popular classes. Iran, because of oil and the speed of "modernization," even more dramatically than most countries, experienced more increased tensions between the traditional classes and their culture than the Westernized classes and theirs. (These cultural tensions are shown in the Bayat-Philipp, B. Good, Hillmann, Beeman, and Naficy papers.)

The particularities of the regional studies within, and the late development of an integrated economy and national market in Iran (see Olson), warn us that generalizations about Iran past and present are subject to even more than the usual pitfalls. Nevertheless, some attempt at general background seems useful to help locate many of the individual studies within a broader framework. Several of the studies deal as a whole (Olson) or in part (Keddie, Bayat-Philipp, Floor, Garthwaite, B. Good) with pre-twentieth century developments, and some of the forces still operative in Iran are shown in these papers to go back into this pre-twentieth century period.

Most papers in this volume approach Iran via different groups and classes as they changed over time rather than through a chronological history of all Iran. Among the groups discussed are the ulama, dissident intellectuals, women, tribal nomads, agriculturalists, the urban elite, the bazaar classes, petty traders, and the working class. Also included are papers concerning cultural topics and medical change.

An important group whose roots in Iranian history go back far into the early centuries of Islam, are the educated religious leaders or ulama (literally, learned men). They are considered at some length in the Keddie and Bayat-Philipp papers, and again as parts of local elites by M. Good and Royce, and as directors of urban "toughs" in the Floor study. From Safavid times on, Iran followed the Shi'i, minority, branch of Islam, in its Twelver variety. Twelver and other Shi'a believed that succession to leadership in the Muslim community passed to Mohammad's cousin and son-in-law, Ali (Mohammad having no adult sons) and his descendants, the Imams, all of whom were theoretically infallible leaders of all spheres of life (including the political).

Twelver Shi'a believed that the infant Twelfth Imam went into hiding on earth in the ninth century and will remain hiding until the end of time, when he will return to earth as *Mahdi* (messiah) to institute the millenium of perfect equity. Although recent scholarship shows that the doctrine of the Hidden Imam was first voiced by a man who wished to avoid conflicts with the government (which might arise from having a visible Imam claiming infallibility in all spheres), the doctrine changed its role over time. Under the influence of new sociopolitical circumstances it came to have almost the contrary, antigovernmental meaning. The Safavids (1501–1722) were able to control the ulama, whose theologians they imported from Arabic-speaking lands, and who were quite financially dependent on rulers. By the seventeenth century, however, we hear of leading ulama— *mujtahids*—who claim they have more right to set policy than impious, wine-bibbing shahs. The claims and power of the ulama became stronger in the eighteenth century, when the leading ulama moved to Iraq away from the reach of Iranian rulers, which remained the center of Shi'ism until replaced by Qom ca. 1950.

The ulama had enough economic power, based on donations and

2

religious taxes taken chiefly from the bazaaris, to be quite independent of the Iranian government. In the eighteenth century a doctrine saying that all believers should follow the rulings of a *mujtahid* became dominant. In the nineteenth century there developed close religiopolitical alliances of ulama and bazaaris based on similar background and beliefs, as well as a growing common interest in combating Western penetration, which meant economic dislocations and losses for many bazaaris. Even when some merchants gained, they believed they might gain more if Western competitors lost their unfair treaty advantages. To the ulama, Western penetration meant a weakening of their power and of Islam: weakening their power when the government tried to centralize and take over new legal, social, and educational functions; and weakening Islam when Iranians began to learn Western ideas and question traditional ones. The ulama-bazaar alliance was crucial to such victories as the forced cancellation of a British tobacco concession after a mass movement in 1891–92 and the achievement of constitutional government in 1905–11; it was important in the movement culminating in nationalization of oil under Mosaddeq in 1951–53, as well as being key in the 1978–79 revolution.

As the Keddie paper indicates, even the "traditional" ulama educated in traditional schools have not been monolithic in their views over time and space; Shi'i theory has constantly evolved, and not always in one direction. To take one of many possible examples, before the twentieth century the Iranian ulama did not discuss constitutions and parliaments; in 1906–07 the majority of the leading ulama accepted, and even argued for, a constitution based on Western models, insisting only on a provision (never enforced) for a committee of at least five *mujtahids* to pass on the compatibility of parliamentary legislation with Islam. A literal return to this constitution (not observed by Reza Shah or his son) was a rallying cry of many leading ulama in the 1960s and 1970s. At first Ayatollah Khomaini's Fundamentalist position—that all necessary law was found in the Qoran and the Traditions of the Imams, which could only be interpreted by experts in Muslim law, while parliament could only see that this Islamic law was implemented—was a minority view among the ulama (although today it is reflected in the 1979 constitution, supported by most of the ulama).

If change is continual though not unidirectional even among the "traditional" ulama, there has also always been an important body of minoritarian dissenters, as discussed by Bayat-Philipp. There is both continuity and change among the dissenters she analyzes—the

3

philosophers of Safavid times, who combined rationalist, natural law and gnostic elements; the eighteenth century founder of a new religious school of Shi'ism, Shaikhism, which had many philosophical elements; and the nineteenth century Babis, whose founder began as a Shaikhi but then broke with Islam to form a new messianic and rebellious religion that expressed some of the dislocations of the early Western impact. Bayat-Philipp shows that such late nineteenth century reformers as Jamal od-Din Afghani and Mirza Aqa Khan Kermani were not as "Westoxicated" as some recent intellectuals think, but in fact had deep roots in the Shi'i past, particularly in its dissenting forms.

If we deal not only with the ulama but also with those educated in part or as a whole in Western ways, the question arises as to why in both groups in the 1960s and 1970s there was an evolution from *more* Westernized and "modern" positions to more "traditional," "Islamic," and sometimes Fundamentalist ones. (This problem, like many of those discussed, does not exist in the same way for Muslim followers of these trends, who attribute this development to the superiority and rightness of the views they follow.) For nonfollowers, however, the change toward "traditional" ideas, even though not exclusive to Iran, may appear paradoxical. A number of reasons for the growing popularity of Islam in both its Fundamentalist and reform varieties in the 1960s and 1970s may, however, be suggested. 1) Antiimperialism, specifically dislike of actions by the U.S. and Israel in postwar Iran made it difficult to borrow the ideology of those seen as imperialists and oppressors. 2) The ex-shah was seen as a Westernizer, associated with the U.S. and Israel, and also with jailings, torture, oppression, corruption, and uprooting people. The shah and those around him followed Western ideas and ways—however dressed up as ancient Iranian (and even the ancient Iranian emphasis was offensive to many believers)—and so alternative ideologies to the shah's became increasingly non-Western. 3) The shah and SAVAK managed to destroy most secular oppositional organizations, whether leftist or centrist, with the exception of student groups and small guerilla groups that were also decimated. This left the informal religious-bazaar network the only strong oppositional group. To keep alive hostility to tyranny, the age-old symbol of Ali's son Hosain dying in battle against a tyrant and similar religious stories were used repeatedly in sermons, plays, and processions. It was impossible to jail all those who led or participated in such religio-political ceremonies. 4) Even among Western-trained intellectuals there developed profound feelings of alienation as the country

4

became crowded with Westerners and old ways and structures were forcibly changed. Most twentieth century novelists and essayists were oppositional, but one may trace the evolution of this opposition from a predominantly leftist and secular one (Alavi, Hedayat, Behrangi, and others) through Jalal Al-e Ahmad (d. 1969) who, coming from a clerical family, himself went through several phases typical of his generation. He was first a Communist; then a left-liberal, increasingly disturbed by mindless borrowings of the worst things from the West—which he attacked in his famous *Gharbzadegi* (Westoxication); and finally seeking to return to Islam and making a pilgrimage to Mecca—although from his critical account of what he experienced it is unclear whether he achieved his religious aim. Most recently, there has been the wide influence of Ali Shariati, (d. 1977), also from a clerical family (as is the partly comparable figure of Abol Hasan Bani Sadr), who stressed the dynamic, revolutionary, this-wordly part of Shi'ism in ways that brought on the criticism of many of the traditional ulama during and after his lifetime. While the traditionally trained ulama appealed mainly to the bazaaris, and often voiced their complaints against the economic policies of the shah that hurt the bazaaris and helped the Western-educated bourgeoisie, Shariati appealed to students; to many, especially young people, who had physically moved from the bazaar and had some Western ideas, but still had roots in Islam; to the guerilla (later Islamic leftist party) *Mojahedin-e Khalq* whose own combination of leftism and Islam actually predated Shariati's lectures; and to many looking for an oppositionist ideology and identity that were not purely Western.

Bayat-Philipp lays forth the apparent paradox that the late nineteenth century intellectuals now criticized as "Westoxicated" were in many ways less influenced by Western thought and more within an Iranian-Islamic dissenting tradition than men like Al-e Ahmad and Shariati. In addition to her points this paradox may be partly explained by answering the question: against whom were the nineteenth century reformers fighting and against whom were the rebels of the 1960s and 1970s fighting? Except for Afghani, who was strongly against Western, particularly British, imperialism, most of the other nineteenth century reformers concentrated their opposition on traditional indigenous forces, which for many of them included both the government and the ulama. Looking at the "advanced" industrialized West, they thought that the secret of self-strengthening and of just government lay in the adoption of Western ways, notably constitutionalism. By the 1960s and 1970s, however, the ulama were no longer seen as enemies by most oppositionists; rather the enemy was the Western-supported, Westernized royal regime. It was partly because Al-e Ahmad could not attack the regime directly, that he attacked "Westoxication;" and it was largely because the ulama had showed itself in an uprising of 1963 and thereafter capable of moving against the regime that many young people who in earlier times might have been Westernizing radicals, now became Islamicizing radicals.

The above analysis has concentrated on the ideological role of the ulama and of religiously-oriented thought, but there are other equally important aspects to the ulama's position. In the nineteenth and early twentieth centuries, as Floor indicates, many important ulama had virtual private urban armies made up of "toughs" or *lutis*, who supported them by force. In this period the top ulama had a leading place in local elite structures, which added to their power and respect; this is discussed in the papers on local elites by M. Good for Maragheh and Royce for Shiraz. The relative weakness and decentralization of Qajar rule left many important powers in the hands of the ulama—virtually all education, most legal matters, most welfare and charitable matters, and important roles in local guilds and factions. The 50 year Pahlavi forced march to Westernization, partly intrinsically and partly gratuitously, took away much of the power and social position of the ulama. Schools became state-controlled and Westernized; new law codes and rules under Reza Shah took most legal roles outside personal status law from the ulama and gave them to lawyers with Western-style training: welfare and charity were increasingly under government control and so forth. The best students, even sons of ulama, mostly went abroad to be educated in Western specialties, and religious students tended to come from poorer social classes, including many who could not make it into Iranian universities—all this is a sign of transformations in the prestige structure. As with other groups and classes, interest and ideology were inextricably intertwined among the ulama: the large-scale recent return to Islamic law, courts, and education accords with *both* ulama ideology and interest.

An area heavily influenced by Islamic law and custom and important to the ulama, as it was from an opposite viewpoint to secular reformers, is that of women and the family. As on most questions, it is wrong to think that Islam has a fixed, static position on women and the family, although not enough historic research has been done to indicate what all the major variations have been. On the whole, the treatment of women in pre-modern Islamic society seems not to have been too different from that in other Mediterranean or Asian civilizations. Concern with passing on property to one's true heirs and with family honor led these societies to various degrees of male dominance, separation of the sexes, and legal and customary sanctions against a girl or woman's having sexual relations with anyone other than her husband. Popular class women worked, even outside the home, but middle and upper-class women were generally supposed to be limited to household work, although such work might cover more in the past than now. In most areas concerning the position of women, Iran and many Islamic countries have recently been more conservative than non-Islamic countries; Indian purdah and Chinese footbinding, for example, were virtually erased, while veiling persists and may even be more widespread than in the past. One reason is that some customs regarding women are found in the Qoran, believed by pious Muslims to be the literal word of God. Among these are male dominance in marriage, easy divorce for men but not for women, and polygamy (although the same *sura* of the Qoran that allows up to four wives if the husband can treat them equally says that no matter how hard he tries he will not be able to treat them equally, so that some Muslims have found reason to see the sura as an intended prohibition of polygamy).

Veiling is not mentioned in the Qoran, but existed in the Byzantine and Iranian territories early conquered by Arab Muslims, who later adopted the custom and interpreted two Qoranic suras relating to modest dress as meaning veiling, or at least covering everything but the hands, feet, and face. In Iran, travellers' accounts and Persian paintings indicate that veiling was not widespread in Safavid times, and it may be that Iran resembled Egypt and Algeria in seeing an increase in veiling and seclusion of women once Western infidels began to appear in significant numbers. After World War II, in Iran and many other Muslim countries veiling spread from the cities to many villages, which tried to imitate the bazaar bourgeoisie. Traditional treatment of women and the family was functional for those who remained within the traditional economy; for the new bourgeoisie and intellectuals, however, who increasingly wanted wives who could be companions and bring up children in ways appropriate to a modern economy and society, old ways regarding women and the family seemed bad.

On this as on other matters there was a widening twentieth century split between the "two cultures"—the modernized or Westernized culture centering on the new upper and middle classes and the traditional culture centering in the bazaar classes. Reforming authors and poets from the late nineteenth century on increasingly called for unveiling, women's education, and greater equality between the sexes, while the traditional culture resisted and increasingly put forth written arguments justifying at least a degree of inequality. Reza Shah introduced coeducation at the universities and girl's public education, and also legislated forcible unveiling in 1936. There was a backlash regarding women's dress after his 1941 abdication; bazaari and popular class women returned to the *chador,* though without a face veil, and *chadors* gradually spread to villages where they had not been seen before.

Although not intrinsically interested in women's rights, the ex-shah, Mohammad Reza (1941–79), heeded those who saw the need for women in various parts of the labor force, and he also saw that some emancipation of women, for which women's organizations had been fighting for decades, would add to his modern aura. He thus supported women's suffrage in 1963 and the Family Protection Act of 1967/75 which gave women greater equality in marriage, divorce, and child custody (formerly automatically going to the husband after a very young age). The association of such acts with an increasingly disliked shah, and of conservatism on women's position with an increasingly popular ulama created a problem for the more liberal opposition, and especially its female component. Some, like Shariati, tried to meet the problem by using the argument, popular in the Third World circles Shariati had frequented in France, that capitalism and imperialism turned women into sex objects, used in photographs or in the flesh to excite the desire of men in order to sell Western consumer products to both men and women. Shariati looked to early heroines in the Prophet's family for role-models for Muslim women. The problem with this "sex object" argument is that it is usually used apologetically and does not probe deeply enough. Like many opposi-tional arguments it was more concerned with scoring points against the regime and the West than with building a viable indigenous approach to greater equality. For while women are often sex objects in the West, in the East (or more exactly in pre-capitalist cultures and those that imitate them) they are also objects of male desires for sex and progeny, the main difference being that in recent capitalist society there is a more open and public "market," while in traditional Iranian and similar societies sex is kept more hidden and a woman can be the "property" of only her husband. While many Muslims, particularly in the traditional classes, may prefer the second to the first condition, there are no grounds for saying that under the second condition women are freer or better off than the first. Those desiring greater freedom and equality will not find real models in the past of either East or West, but must strive for something new, while working for dialog and organizational forms that involve the popular classes.

On this question as on many others, the euphoria of unity of various parties against the old regime in 1978 gave way to real differences in 1979 when Ayatollah Khomaini, true to his past writings, tried to enforce veiling, which brought on a successful women's protest; suspended the Family Protection Law, leaving Islamic law and courts operative in matters concerning marriage and the family; and supported a decree against coeducation. Regarding women as on most matters, however, there are a wide variety of past and possible future interpretations of the Qoran and Islamic tradition—as well as current models of more egalitarian treatment, not based on "Westernization" (as among many nomadic tribes), so that interpretations of Islam in 1980 (which are already variable) are likely to change further in the future.

Ulama, intellectuals, bazaar classes, and women—the groups dealt with briefly thus far—have been discussed mainly in an urban context; but there are also rural groups and classes, nomadic and sedentary, that have played a major role in Iran until today. From as far back as the eleventh century A.D., Iran came to be heavily populated by nomadic tribes, owing both to its growing aridity arising from centuries of erosion, deforestation, and salinization of the soil from irrigation, and to invasions of nomadic tribes (such as the Turkic tribes brought in by the eleventh century Seljuqs and the thirteenth century Mongols). From the tenth to the twentieth centuries all dynasties were either of nomadic tribal origin, or, as with the Safavids, were brought to power by nomadic tribes. In addition, tribal leaders often ruled their own areas, including many nontribal agriculturalists, with virtual autonomy. As Garthwaite suggests, strong tribal confederations like the Bakhtiari (as well as the Qashqa'i discussed by Beck and Barker), tended to be formed when there *was* an organized central power, like the Qajar dynasty (1796–1925), and were in a sense needed by both tribes and regime to deal with each other.

The arid, difficult Iranian terrain and the presence of large numbers of tribal peoples speaking non-Persian languages creates an ethnic and cultural diversity that both enhances Iranian life and creates problems. In periods of weak central government (the eighteenth century, 1906–21, and recently), tribal groups, among others, want to reassert as much as possible of their former autonomy, sometimes to the detriment of others; while in centralized periods, and especially under the Pahlavis (de facto 1921–79) tribal power and autonomy is so reduced as to bring great economic hardships to the tribal peoples, as shown by Beck.

In Iran, as elsewhere, changes induced by capitalism or decreed by governments have led to a trend toward a decline of pastoral nomadism. While in the eighteenth century tribal autonomy and civil war may have been abetted by tribal mastery of the horse-rifle combination, in the nineteenth century improvements in transport, communication, and government security forces, as well as growing sedentarization of tribal people when agriculture became more profitable, weakened the overall position of nomadic tribes. To these were added the forcible settlement and disarming undertaken by Reza Shah and the subtler policies of his son, the ex-shah, which contributed to increased sedentarization and the weakening and often impoverishment of the nomads—although even here there were positive trends such as tribal schools, and a few tribes that flourished (see Barker and Bradburd).

Since the 1978–79 revolution there has been a trend toward re-sumed migration, a lifestyle that makes sense in arid regions where there is insufficient pasture in one region to feed large flocks all year. How long this trend will last if a centralized government reasserts itself is hard to say. The ups and downs of tribal autonomy and tribal economy have thus followed no straight line progression, nor have the internal features of tribal life. As seen within, gains in schooling may be at the price of local culture and of tools to improve the pastoral lifestyle; tribal gains in wealth are inequitably distributed (as are non-tribal ones); and tribal migrants to cities are at least as culturally alienated as are other migrants. Pastoral nomadic peoples, who make up a part (though not as large a part as in the past) of the dissident border minorities who have put forth autonomy demands since 1979 (Kurds, Turkomans, Baluchis, Arabs) pose a continuing challenge to Iranian society. Nomads remain crucial producers of meat and animal products that cannot in Iran be produced as well as in another fashion, and so, for economic as well as cultural reasons, their way of life deserves to be studied and considered seriously for adaptation rather than abolition.

Peasants, like tribespeople, have felt a differential impact of the growth of relations with capitalist West since the nineteenth century. There was a rise in Western imports and considerable commercializa-tion of agriculture, especially for export. Exports included cotton, wool, fruits and nuts, and opium (examined in detail by Olson). As with tribespeople, the results of commercialization on peasants were contradictory, even disregarding the direct health effects of internal opium consumption. Opium was very profitable, but it took up land formerly used for food crops, which contributed to the severity of famines. Olson also demonstrates that opium profits were concentrated in the hands of a very few, and further research could show if this was and is true of other agricultural exports.

Under Reza Shah there were no significant land reforms, and the peasantry suffered from his increased indirect taxes on items of mass consumption. The three stages of land reform, a reform discussed by Hooglund, Beck and Bradburd, ended up with small benefits or even losses for most peasants and nomads. Most were left with too little land for subsistence and huge numbers had to migrate to overcrowded and unprepared cities. What happened among those who remained is shown by Hooglund, and the impoverishment of the Qashqa'is by land reform is detailed by Beck. From 1967, the old regime pushed agribusiness and farm corporation schemes of large mechanized agriculture, often with a foreign component, and encouraged export crops, creating a constantly growing dependence on food imports and increased migration to the cities by peasants displaced by mechanization. This migration, at a time when most of the regime's building and infrastructure expenditures went to the swollen military, created an alienated subproletariat that, while it could not start or spearhead a revolution, could and did provide masses of participants.

Those urban classes not yet discussed also present a mixed picture as regards the blessings of "modernization." Some benefited from it, such as those, discussed in the papers on mobility who managed to climb the mobility ladder, owing largely to such factors as modern education and good connections in Tehran. While some climbed that ladder, others fell, notably many members of local families who once held autonomous or semi-autonomous power, like the Moqaddams of Maragheh and Qavams of Shiraz, discussed by M. Good and Royce, whose local independence was seen as a threat by the centralizing Pahlavi shahs. It is striking, however, that in both cases many members of the old families retained much of their wealth and prestige as late as 1979, while they shared diminished power with officials sent out from Tehran and with rising local families tied to the modern economy and Westernized education. Both Royce and M. Good show mixtures of old and new values among the elite—a mastery of the mores and requirements of both worlds are needed, at least in provincial cities, to maintain elite status. It may be hazarded that a part of these local elites have mastered such a variety of mores and modes of discourse that some family members will be able to retain their status in post-revolutionary Iran.

The papers herein deal mainly with groups in opposite ends of urban stratification; the elite, discussed above, and the popular classes, old and new. The middle classes, old (bazaar) and new (Westernized educations and jobs) are, however, also dealt with in the papers. Among the case studies Bonine tells us about the bazaar classes. These classes, consisting of merchants and artisans centering in the urban bazaars, provided much of the financial and physical support for the revolution. Bonine discusses in detail their operation in the Yazd bazaar, showing the complex ties among artisans, merchants, and carpet and textile workers. Yet there is more to be said: The bazaar economy, centered in Tehran, has proved amazingly strong and resilient. The bazaar not only meets the retail needs of popular class Iranians, but also provides an even larger share of Iran's wholesaling and considerable credit, not only for small tradespeople but even for modern industry. Bazaar exports of major items like carpets and bazaar financial operations are important to the Iranian economy, and various governmental moves against bazaaris, notably arrests of "profiteers" since the mid–1970s, were one cause of their revolt. Several men of bazaari origins have risen to be top industrialists or have otherwise moved upward and out of the bazaar. Such people with one foot in each world were, like many students of traditional background, among the followers of Shariati and of the revolution and its leaders.

Some scholars speak generically of the "middle class(es)" and the "working class(es)" in Iran; but it is important, in a country where a "two cultures" split is so pervasive, to distinguish between the traditional and the new middle classes (even though there are transitional groups), and also between the traditional and the new (factory or skilled) working classes—as their way of life and outlook tend to differ. The new middle and upper classes, generally having Westernized education, occupying positions in the modern sectors of the economy—governmental, modern business, modern professional and white collar—under Mohammad Reza Shah tended to have a very Westernized lifestyle. To the degree they could afford it, this was complete with modern homes, automobiles, Western-dominated television, modern kitchens and a wide range of Western consumer goods. Even these classes, however, were less loyal to the regime than their prosperity would lead one to expect. Students and ex-students, including many leading professionals and intellectuals, increasingly protested against autocracy and contraventions of human rights.

The first major protests in the 1977–79 period came in the forms of petitions and complaints signed by groups of intellectuals, writers, and lawyers in 1977 against the regime's violations of such rights. In early 1978, however, the center of protest moved to the bazaar and popular classes of the cities whose mass demonstrations against the regime began as protests against the mysterious death of the son of Ayatollah Khomaini and a government-inspired violent newspaper attack of Khomaini. By late 1978, the old and new middle and working classes were all involved in opposition, but to a degree their movements had separate beginnings and represented different aspirations, although all were united against the regime. A study of opposition by the new working class, which became crucial from late 1978, makes up a part of Abrahamian's paper.

Three papers herein concern popular urban classes. Floor studies the *lutis* or urban toughs, a group romanticized by previous authors. Where others have stressed the *javanmardi* (chivalry) of this group, Floor establishes that they were often used, particularly the decentralized Qajar period, by powerful local interests (including leading ulama) as troops to fight their battles. In a period of urban factionalism and urban power diffused among landlords, ulama, and others, it is not strange that urban leaders should have such troops (much as they did in Renaissance Europe). Even in the Constitutional Revolution, Floor shows that some *lutis,* like Sattar Khan, were revolutionary leaders, while others fought on the royalist side, so that no single role can be attributed to them. *Lutis* were paid in the U.S. supported coup against Mossadeq, but since then their power has greatly declined (they must have seemed less appealing and reliable to the ex-shah than modern security forces). By coincidence, Hillmann's paper disputes an article which attributes to both *lutis* and dervishes chivalrous virtues that Floor also doubts.

Thompson deals with an almost unstudied traditional class group, the petty trader. These traders, too poor to have bazaar stalls, eke out a precarious living with urban pushcarts or by traveling from place to place. Thompson notes that they have not declined as much as might be expected with economic modernization; rather the traditional and modern sectors of the Iranian economy operate simultaneously, largely serving different groups and classes. It may be added that urban migration accelerated after the 1973 oil price rise, and left many unemployed, some of whom make small sums by selling on the streets—so there is a continual influx into the class of petty traders. While one traditional social group, the *lutis,* declined because they were not wanted by centralizing governments, another group, the small peddler, survived because they continued to meet economic needs.

Abrahamian's paper on the modern working class is, like Floor's, revisionist. Abrahamian gives a brief history of the labor movement in Iran, and concentrates on the period of major organization after World War II. He establishes the working class origin of most union leaders (which is unusual for a Third World country at any early stage in the development of the labor movement), and discusses the ties of the unions with the Tudeh (pro-soviet Communist) party. The period 1941–53 saw open activity by relatively free unions, whereas after that, free union activity became impossible—although many strikes occurred. The revival of union activity in 1978 was crucial to the decisive shutdown of Iran's oilfields late that year, which contributed crucially to the revolution's victory. The modern working class, although not now mainly tied to the Tudeh Party, is more open to Marxist influences than are the traditional popular and middle classes.

The position of Iran's minorities occasioned much comment in the West in 1979—both religious minorities, especially the Jews and Bahai's, and ethnic minorities, some of whom took action in favor of greater political and cultural autonomy. Iranians whose native tongue is not Persian probably number half or more of the population. Schooling has made Persian generally understood, but many Iranians have at least a partial non-Persian identification. A factor discouraging actual independence movements is that the oil is now concentrated in one small region of Iran, and breakoff movements elsewhere would have to do without the oil revenue on which postwar Iran has depended so heavily. It should not be inferred that the minorities would want to break off were it not for oil; in most cases this does not appear to be so, and what is sought is autonomy, not independence.

If the ethnic minorities tend to occupy whole regions, and often have a tribal basis, religious minorities are chiefly urban, as Loeb's paper notes. Loeb tells the modern history of the Jews of Shiraz, putting it in context by noting that all major scriptural monotheistic religions have tended to intolerance, with Christianity having the worst historical record in this area. As compared to past persecutions in the Christian West, disabilities suffered by Iranian Jews under Shi'i rule were not extreme, but they could be very uncomfortable. Modernist ideology, along with the regime's need for entrepreneurial and other skills, encouraged the Pahlavis to remove the disabilities of religious minorities, who had gravitated to Westernized education and hence could provide needed skills. Jews have tended to be favorably inclined toward the Pahlavis and to fear that a more religiously oriented regime would allow hostile persons to attack them. Loeb notes that although it is too early to predict the future of religious minorities, this is definitely a problem area for present-day Iran.

The final, cultural, section of this book also reveals contradictory trends. Hillmann notes the lack of communication among religiously-trained, Western-educated, and bourgeois Iranians, and also the flowery, deferential Persian politeness formulae, which he relates to despotism on the monarchical and submonarchical levels. Peterson's paper on the social use of chairs in the nineteenth and twentieth century shows how even such an "everyday" item is influenced by, and influences, social and political matters—with variation from "tradition" to "semi-traditional" to modern use patterns according to the class and location of the host and guests.

Beeman's comprehensive study of the popular theater, including both "tragic" passion plays, the *ta'ziyeh*, and comic theater, explores the socio-psychological meaning of these plays to the popular classes who watch them. Particularly new is his study of popular theater, in which the rich and mighty are brought down by the "innocent" clown who pokes fun at and undermines them. In peaceful times this expression of feeling against the rich and powerful may be mainly a chance for emotional outlet, but in times when political action occurs, it may contribute to that action, as does the *ta'zieh*, with its emotional depiction of the killing of Hosain and his just followers by unjust tyrants.

In a modern area of mass culture, Naficy shows how films were utilized by the old regime to perpetuate its "modernizing" values, but how also, for a brief period in the early 1970s a "New Wave" of young directors were permitted to express social, and indirectly critical, viewpoints. The socio-political role of even apparently apolitical films is also illuminated.

* * *

The papers herein generally support challenges now being made to post-War modernization theories, which tend to expect straight line progress, with things getting gradually better for almost everyone once investment levels in the Third World reach a certain level. Studies have indicated that, on the whole, in the Third World recently the rich have gotten richer and the poor poorer. This volume indicates that even in the nineteenth century the effects of Western trade on the life of the Iranian common people were distinctly mixed and sometimes economically negative, and that even huge oil revenues were far from an unmixed blessing for most Iranians. "Modernization" is often accomplished at the expense of a society's majority, whether through increased income distribution gaps or in terms of such phenomena as the uprooting of masses of people. Modernization creates not only a dual economy but also a dual society, in which the wealthier Westernized classes speak a different language from the traditional or popular classes and have a very different lifestyle and cultural values. Many feel caught between traditional ways and ideas and the appeal of Western modishness; this tension is certainly one factor in the Islamic revival of the 1960s and 1970s.

Iran is a very dramatic example of some of the shortcomings of modernization theory; for each step forward there is also a step backward, and almost any program of economic, social, and cultural modernization has a negative side. This comes out in the unexpected field of medicine, surveyed by B. Good, where the author shows that the modernization of medicine for a few has meant a loss of medicine for many. (Medical researchers are beginning to have more respect for traditional medical systems, and to realize that any system strongly believed in will have some medical benefits, so that undermining traditional systems, practitioners, and cures without replacing them with adequate modern care may bring a net medical loss, as do the widespread uncontrolled dispensation of antibiotics and powdered baby formula.) In Iran, as in the West, modern doctors have tended to oppose barefoot doctor and paramedic programs for the masses, and so here too large elements of the population have been hurt by "modernization."

The words "modern," "modernization," and "traditional" are in fact open to serious objections, especially if one considers the ideological way in which they have been used, and their use here is only justified by the plea that there are as yet no accepted alternatives. The notion disseminated in the Western press that in 1978–79 Iranians were revolting against modernization and for a return to the distant past is particularly unenlightening. Modernization, if it means anything, encompasses the adoption of modern technology and science, often with the assumption that Western political systems and ideas will accompany them. There are, however, many different ways of adopting, adapting, or being influenced by, modern technology and science; and to think that Mohammad Reza Shah's program is explained by calling it "rapid modernization," which then evoked a "traditionalist" response is highly simplistic. In fact, both "modernization" and "tradition" are constantly in flux, and, as indicated above and within, it was the *type* of "modernization" launched by the ex-shah, which favored the elite and new bourgeoisie and disfavored others, that contributed to his downfall.

In Iran as elsewhere there is a strong need for humane use of appropriate technology, for popular participation in decisions and processes that affect people's lives, and for cultural developments that adapt traditions to new needs rather than simply riding roughshod over old ways. The papers within were not written as policy suggestions, but many of them could serve at least the role of warning Westerners of the pitfalls of facile, Western-oriented, rapid "modernization."

I. OVERVIEWS IN TIME

Figure 1.   Revolutionary Guards in Tehran, Summer 1979.

1

Religion, Society, and Revolution in Modern Iran

Nikki R. Keddie

The phenomenon of a mass revolution largely led by heads of an orthodox religion, as seen in Iran in 1978–79, surprised most Western observers, but was less surprising to scholars who had studied the interaction of religion and politics in modern Iran.[1] The revolution of 1978–79 has no near parallel in the modern West, where leaders of orthodox religions have neither spurred mass revolutions nor claimed, as does Ayatollah Khomaini, that men with high religious positions should be direct rulers. The closest parallel to the 1978–79 revolution, in fact, is found in the Iranian revolution of 1905–11, which gave Iran a largely Western-style constitution. Paradoxically, however, although Iran was far less modernized in 1906 than in 1979, the 1906–07 constitution was more "modern" than that of 1979. In 1906–07 religious leaders did not claim the right to rule directly, but only inserted into the constitution a provision for a committee of religious leaders who could veto laws they found not in accord with the Islamic *shari'a*. Even this committee was never instituted, and the mullas were satisfied with heavy representation in parliament and the protection of Shi'i Islam as the state religion.

Unlike 1978–79 also, the religious leaders of 1906 were monarchical in outlook, as they remained until quite recently. When Reza Khan inspired a republican campaign on the Atatürk model in 1924, it was mostly ulama, led by the clerical parliamentary deputy Modarres, who opposed a republic, largely because they identified a republic with the anticlerical policies of Atatürk, who had established a republic in Turkey and abolished the caliphate and other Islamic institutions. The secularist and anticlerical policies of Reza, who abandoned republicanism and had himself crowned Reza Shah, and of his son, Mohammad Reza Shah (1941–79), created a climate ripe for the antimonarchical arguments of Ayatollah Khomaini, however.

This paper aims to outline some of the main and interacting social and ideological background elements to the 1978–79 revolution so that it should appear not as a historical anomaly but rather as a logical (if historically unique to now) outcome of a series of prior developments.

Regarding ideology one may say that, for all the research and writing in this area in recent years,[2] there has not been enough expression of two key facts: 1) "traditional" ideas and practices are always changing, and major changes over time occurred among Iran's "orthodox" religious leaders, and 2) the evolution of ideas reflects changing social, economic, and political realities, however traditional the terms of the argument may seem. I and others have pointed to the great differences between the radical "extremist" Shi'ism followed by the immediate ancestors of the Safavid dynasty (1501–1722) and the institutionalized "orthodox" Shi'ism of the Safavids after they came to power.[3] Recently two younger scholars have independently said that, contrary to some Western scholarship, Twelver Shi'is did not before the eighteenth century say that all temporal governments were illegitimate or that Shi'i religious leaders inherited some of the charisma of the Imams.[4] Though one of these scholars seems to imply that only early Shi'ism was true Shi'ism, so that the later development of the above ideas was illegitimate, and the other sometimes misreads the scholars against whom he argues, the basic point of an early Twelver Shi'ism that was politically quietist (a point that other scholars had already suggested) and a predominant Safavid Shi'i doctrine that made few political claims seems well established.[5] While a few take this as evidence that modern development of a more political Shi'ism is doctrinally illegitimate, it is more reasonable to recognize that all doctrines, and particularly which elements of a doctrine are emphasized, change—twentieth century Protestantism, for example, is no more that of earlier centuries than is twentieth century Shi'ism. All doctrines contain elements that may be rearranged, with some stressed or extended, and others pushed into the background or forgotten. The holders of a doctrine gain reassurance from believing that their version is the true and original one, as is true even of such secular beliefs as Marxism or the American belief that the Supreme Court interprets the meaning of the U.S. constitution. In the case of revealed religions the belief that one is following the meaning of revelation is particularly exigent, but even revealed religions are in constant flux. The pace of religious change varies by religion and area, and is often more rapid in cases, like Iran's, where religion is intertwined with major and rapidly changing political issues—but the fact of change is universal. Even such a useful term as "fundamentalism," which should apply to those with a literal belief in scripture, describes a phenomenon different from the early practices and beliefs of any religion and is to be understood against the background of modernization and new scientific discoveries.

The above does not imply that religious and ideological changes are *only* a response to sociopolitical circumstances, as religions and ideologies have a force and content of their own and contain elements that can most easily be changed in certain directions. For example, while we may agree that pre-eighteenth century Shi'i writings rarely stated the political claims of the *mujtahids,* this does not mean that these claims were made in the nineteenth century only for political reasons and had no base in the Shi'i past. Arjomand, who argues this point, gives too little weight to the meticulous observer Chardin's seventeenth century report that some *mujtahids* stated openly that they had more right to rule than the impious, wine-bibbing, Safavid shahs.[6] If, as some current authors say, no similar statements have yet been found in *writings* by religious figures, this may only show a discrepancy between what was spoken and what was published—a discrepancy often found under oppressive governments and known in Iran down to the present. For periods when we have no records of what was spoken we have little recourse beyond writings; but when such a strong claim is made by some *mujtahids* as that recorded by Chardin, and when it is often reiterated in later centuries by men who never read Chardin, it must be given considerable weight.

The most reasonable reconstruction of Twelver Shi'i, which after 1501 means mostly Iranian Shi'i, doctrine and its sociopolitical background would seem, briefly, to go as follows: Under the ninth century Abbasid caliphate the Shi'is of what became the Twelver line were fragmented, and became increasingly politically moderate, with many middle and upper class Shi'is supporting or entering the Government. Oppositional Shi'is were mostly of the Ismaili "Sevener" branch of Shi'ism. The doctrine that the last Imam, as an infant, went into occultation on this earth in 874 and will return at the end of time as the *Mahdi* (messiah), was first elaborated by a wealthy Shi'i in Abbasid service. It was long a convenient one for *avoiding* political conflict with the government, as it deprived the Shi'is of an Imam who could claim religious and political infallibility and might rival the caliph.[7] The Twelver Buyid dynasty in Iran and Iraq (945–1055) protected the caliph and Sunnism. The institution of the *mujtahid* who could exercise "effort" *(ijtihad)* in interpreting law and doctrine grew up gradually and the *mujtahids* at first did not make political claims. After the Buyids there were no Twelver states until the Safavids who, as noted, came to power as heads of an "extremist" Shi'i movement and claimed divinity as well as descent from the seventh Imam (meaning all earlier ones). Like such earlier dynasties as the Abbasids and Fatimids, once the Safavids came to power they began to suppress "extremists"; they also imported orthodox Shi'i theologians from nearby Arab lands. This importation, government appointment of religious officials, and their own religious aura gave the Safavids much control over religious institutions. Nonetheless, the independent income of religious leaders, from gifts of *vaqf* (mortmain) and the religious taxes of *khums* and *zakat* that Shi'i leaders collected directly, gave them an economic basis for growing autonomy.[8] Chardin's citation of *mujtahids* who claimed they had more right to rule than the shahs has been noted as a phenomenon that grew in the later Safavid period when governments became weaker and more unpopular.

In the eighteenth century, both Iran's decentralization and the abortive attempt of Nader Shah to deinstitutionalize Shi'ism and confiscate Shi'i *vaqfs* helped give impetus to a counterclaim to power by the *mujtahids,* in part reflected in the successful struggle of one school of thought, the *usuli* or *mujtahidi,* against another, the *akhbari.* Although both schools had earlier roots, the decisive conflict and definition of positions came now, with the *akhbaris* stressing reliance on Shi'i Traditions *(akhbar)* rather than on *mujtahids,* while the *mujtahidis* elaborated the victorious doctrine that every Twelver must follow the rulings of a living *mujtahid,* whose education and efforts qualified him best to interpret the will of the Hidden Imam. *Mujtahids* were not, unlike the Imam, infallible, which was one reason the rulings of a deceased one could not be followed. In practical terms this victory gave great power to living *mujtahids,* particularly those few who had the greatest following and might make pronouncements on the issues of the day. Paradoxically, the occultation of the Hidden Imam, a doctrine originally serving as a guarantor of political quietism by Twelver Shi'is, left without a visible infallible Imam to follow, became after many centuries and under different circumstances, the basis of a highly politicized religion. Sociopolitical circumstances were of major importance in this apparent turnabout. It is also true, however, that doctrines retain an influence on their own evolution.

24

⌐After the reunification of Iran in 1796 under the Qajar dynasty the political potential of the *mujtahidi* doctrine often came to the fore. It was often directed against two phenomena that were seen as threats to Islam and Iran—two entities that were often not distinguished in this the only Twelver Shi'i state: threats from the West and threats from Westernizing reformers. The first may be epitomized in the role of some leading ulama in launching the second Russo-Iranian war in ₁ 1826 (the first had resulted in territorial and other losses); in the killing of the Russian ambassador Griboyedov and his mission for acts resented by many; and in movements against British concessions—the Reuter concession of 1872 and the tobacco concession of 1890. The second is seen in active ulama opposition to the reforms of the three nineteenth century prime ministers: Amir Kabir, ₂ Mirza Hosain Khan (also opposed for backing the Reuter concession) and Amin od-Dauleh. Concessions to Westerners were seen as endangering Iran and Islam's independence, undermining the economic strength and independence of the bazaar classes, with whom the ulama were allied by family and other ties, and bringing in Westerners who might subvert Islam. Westernizing reforms were and are an economic and ideological threat to the ulama; increased governmental control over law, education, and welfare meant decreased ulama control and employment in these areas.

These dangers were also felt in other Muslim countries, but few saw strong ulama reactions; Muslim reactions tended rather to be Sufi, unorthodox, or both, as with Shamyl in the Caucasus, the Mahdist movement in the Sudan, the Sanussi in Libya, and various movements outside the Middle East. The non-Iranian (Sunni) ulama reacted less, it seems, because: 1) they had less economic independence and strength than the Iranian ulama, and nineteenth century centralizing governments like those of the Ottoman Empire, Egypt, and Tunisia were able to whittle away much of what remained; 2) the leaders of the non-Iranian ulama lived in capital cities, where their governments could pressure or control them, whereas Iran's ulama leadership resided in the Shi'i shrine cities in Iraq, uncontrolled by Iran's government; and 3) the ideological basis for the ulama's political claims developed in the seventeenth, and even more the eighteenth, century was by now widely believed in Iran.

Sociopolitical factors *alone* cannot account for the ulama's political successes and influence in the nineteenth and twentieth century; without the prior development towards a doctrine that gave the ulama political and moral claims against the government, it is hard to imagine the string of political successes scored by the Iranian ulama.

25

Whether or not the idea that the *mujtahids* partake in the charisma of the Imams had prior doctrinal justification, and whether or not the idea that temporal governments lack legitimacy had a long history, many of the ulama and their lay followers came to believe such things in the nineteenth and twentieth centuries, when temporal rulers were increasingly compared to the Umayyad killers of the martyred Imam Hosain.[9] Even those who did not speak or think of governmental illegitimacy or of *mujtahids'* partaking in the Twelfth Imam's charisma tended to have more confidence in the ulama than in the temporal government. This does not mean that there were not significant antiulama or anticlerical feelings. Many intellectuals were anticlerical, although most allied with the antigovernment ulama in 1890–1911. Old men who remembered the constitutional revolution of 1905–11 sometimes spoke to me in 1960 of oppression by the government *and* by the ulama, who were often seen as corrupt, hypocritical, narrow-minded, and restrictive in their attitudes. Nevertheless, when the chips were down, as again in 1978–79, people tended to side with sections of the ulama against the government, which was seen as the more oppressive of the two. In part, in both revolutions the ulama's antidespotic claims were believed because oppression by the secular rulers was known while what the ulama would do was unknown.

Owing to Iran's difficult topography, its distance from world economic centers, and the strength of nomadic tribes and of minorities, it was difficult to centralize—and centralization, as suggested by the cases of Egypt and the Ottoman Empire, was a necessary prelude to serious modernization. Qajar Iran remained largely decentralized, which encouraged continued power and ideological hegemony of the ulama. In the absence of government strength or armed force the ulama could help block attempts at educational, legal, and economic Westernization. Probably the Qajar government was also less shrewd than were various Ottoman and Egyptian rulers in their handling of the ulama; while Mohammad Ali of Egypt used speedy attacks and the Ottomans often followed a carrot and stick or "buying off" policy, putting some members of the ulama corps in governmental positions, and gradually bringing *vaqfs* under greater control, the Qajars were much more inclined to make unconditional gifts or pensions to some ulama or *sayyeds*, a move that did not ensure their loyalty. To be sure, ideological conditions entered, making it more difficult for the Qajars to win over the ulama than it was for their Sunni neighbors. In Iran, ulama who took positions under the monarchy were somewhat tainted and suspect;

26

once again the political situation and the doctrine of the Imam's occultation, which originally helped Shi'a to enter into doubtful (even Sunni) governments, had evolved to the point that a formally Shi'i government not guided and controlled by the ulama was considered immoral, as was service in it.

It should be remembered that Shi'a do not have unity of doctrine or any council or individual (since the occultation) who set doctrine for the future, so that the remarks herein about doctrine refer to general trends and not to unanimous opinions. Hence, some ulama can be found in the nineteenth and twentieth century who hold to older (or newer) opinions than those held by the majority, but it is wrong to take such individuals as representative of a widespread trend in their own time if their names enter into widespread discourse only decades after they wrote. Such individual citations have been made to "prove" such opposite points as the political neutrality of Qajar Shi'ism or the constitutional sophistication of the early twentieth century ulama, but in neither case is it shown than the *alim* cited had a wide following in his own time.[10]

A more useful revisionism is that stressing the importance of the big merchants in the revolution of 1905–11.[11] Most merchants were adversely affected by Western economic competition, and already took the lead in the movement against a tobacco monopoly concession to a British subject. Whereas previous concessions had been for projects not yet existing in Iran, the tobacco concession involved a widely grown, sold, exported, and profitable product, control of which was to be handed over to a British company whose representatives began arriving in Iran in 1891. Merchants saw that even should the company hire them, their independence and profits would be cut, and they took the lead in much of the protest that finally reached rebellious proportions and resulted in cancelling the concession.[12]

Similarly, merchants were key in the revolutionary movement of 1905–11, especially in 1905–06. The revolution began when sugar merchants were beaten for charging high prices. Merchants were prominent throughout, especially in organizing and leading the movement of thousands to the British legation that resulted in the formulation of demands for a constitution, which the shah was forced to grant. It is wrong, however, to understate the role of the ulama in the tobacco movement and the constitutional revolution. Although the ulama were not united, major ulama gave ideological leadership and direction to both movements, and were crucial in bringing in the participation of many of the urban masses. In the tobacco movement the climax occurred when the top leader of the Shi'a from Ottoman

27

Iraq issued (or confirmed) a decree outlawing all use and sale of tobacco, and the boycott was universally observed. In the constitutional revolution ulama gave ideological direction at all stages, and even though they were protesting at Qom when the demand for a constitution was put forth in Tehran, they were in close communication with the merchants in Tehran and approved of the demand for a constitution. Also, it was the ulama more than the merchants who gave constitutional and other demands legitimacy to large sectors of the urban populace.

As in most revolutions, including that of 1978–79, the constitutional revolution saw splits in a formerly united movement once victory had been achieved. The originally proconstitutional *alim*, Shaikh Fazlollah Nuri, split off soon after this victory, most likely primarily due to his real reservations about the Western-style constitution. There were disagreements within and outside parliament over provisions of the constitution regarding the status of Shi'i Islam as the state religion, about minority religions, and about the provision for a committee of *mujtahids* to pass on the compatibility of all legislation with Shi'i law; but these were resolved. After the coup by the new shah, Mohammad Ali, in 1908, divisions grew, and most of the ulama of Tabriz opposed the revolutionary guerilla fighters who worked with ultimate success to reestablish the constitution. In the new parliament splits increased, and a leader of the liberal Democratic party, Sayyed Hasan Taqizadeh, was forced into exile after a terrorist, with whom he was not connected killed Sayyed Abdollah Behbehani in 1910. Nevertheless, some cooperation between secularist and religious elements continued, and the revolution was abortive not so much because of internal splits as because of ultimata and invasions by the British and Russians in 1911–12.[13]

Some regional revolts in Iran after World War I, like the Khiyabani revolt in Azerbaijan and the Jangali movement in Gilan, had leaders with a religious background, but religious forces in politics generally decreased after that war. The 1921 coup of Reza Khan, largely orchestrated by the British general Ironside, was secular, and religious forces only became important in opposing Reza Khan's 1924 proposal for a republic. Promonarchic feelings by the ulama became transformed after the experience of the Pahlavi monarchy, however, and on this, as on other political points noted above we find a reversal of position made for sociopolitical reasons becoming justified as longstanding doctrine.

Reza Shah, who tried to telescope a series of nineteenth and twentieth century reforms of more centralized Middle Eastern states into two decades, lessened the power and influence of the ulama in many ways. The modern educational system and the army provided education and training for growing numbers to the detriment of the traditional Islamic system. Westernized courts, law codes, judges, and lawyers greatly reduced the legal role of those with a Muslim education. The forced unveiling of women (1936) and the entry of women into the paid labor market undermined traditions conceived as centrally Islamic. The glorification of pre-Islamic Iran and the whole trend to secularism were also resented by the religious. Under Reza Shah the recent phenomenon of "two cultures" got its real start; the traditional bazaaris, many urban workers, and rural classes remained devoted to a fairly traditional Islam, to the ulama, and to customary practices regarding women and the family; the modernized middle, upper, and professional classes largely followed Western or quasi-Western ways on the above matters, and rarely went to mosque or followed Muslim customs they considered inconvenient. (Such splits are found in many third-world countries, but in Iran may be more dramatic due to the rapidity of modernization from 1925 to 1978.)

There was some recrudescence of religious politics with the greater political freedom that followed Reza Shah's abdication in 1941. Sayyed Zia od-Din Tabataba'i's National Will party included religious elements and, like various religious movements, was supported by some who wanted to block the communist-oriented Tudeh party which was growing rapidly. There was a strong bazaar-religious element behind the nationalist and oil nationalization movement of Mosaddeq, who was premier 1951–53. The chief religious politician of this period was Ayatollah Kashani, who had a considerable bazaar following, but who after a time split from Mosaddeq, partly for power reasons.

Kashani backed the U.S.-supported overthrow of Mosaddeq, as did Ayatollah Behbehani, the chief ayatollah of Tehran and son of the (conservative) constitutional leader. Also involved in the politics of the later 1940s were the Fedayan-e Islam, a small secret group who carried out assassinations of those considered hostile to Islam and/or subservient to Western powers; these included Iran's leading secularist intellectual, Ahmad Kasravi, and the pre-Mosaddeq prime minister, General Razmara. Kashani had some relations with the Feda'iyan, and some who have studied the early works of Ayatollah Khomaini find in them similarities to the religionationalist positions of Kashani and of the Feda'iyan. (The more current group called

"Feda'iyan," the "Feda'iyan-i Khalq" are, by contrast, Marxist in-spired, and resemble the earlier group only in their pre-1978 use of individual killings.)

The *mujtahidi* doctrine that all believers must choose a single *mujtahid* to follow meant that *mujtahids* with a large reputation for learning and a considerable following became distinguished from their colleagues, and were superior "sources of imitation"—*marja'-e taqlid*. In some periods a single *mujtahid* became the final arbiter for questions posed to him on any issue; the first such man was the mid-nineteenth-century *mujtahid*, Ansari; the issuer of the tobacco boycott, Shirazi, was another; and in the 1950s Ayatollah Borujerdi occupied this position. Whereas the first two, along with other leading *mujtahids*, had lived and taught in the Iraqi shrine cities, out of the control of the Iranian government, Borujerdi lived in the chief Iranian holy city, Qom. Mostly, he was nonpolitical in his teachings, but he did issue a *fatwa* (decree) against a land reform law proposed by the government in 1960. His death in 1961 brought a return to a situation of several ayatollahs of equal rank.[14]

Already in the 1940s Ayatollah Khomaini had written a then little-known treatise in which he suggested, among other things, that those trained in religious law should rule—although he did not call for the end of monarchy. His views were stronger in his better-known *Hokumat-e Islami*, published ca. 1971.[15] It is common to speak of Khomaini as a "traditionalist" or a "fundamentalist"—the latter ap-pelation is true within certain limits—but the former is misleading. In maintaining that ulama knowing Muslim law should rule directly, Khomaini was stating neither what is found in the Qoran or in early Shi'ism, nor what is said in the treatises of the giants of postocculta-tion Shi'ism, nor even a position expressed by religious leaders in the period since 1890. At the time of the Qoran's revelation there existed no class of *fuqaha* or specialized religious leaders to rule the commu-nity; in early Shi'i theory, while the Imams were visible, it was they who were supposed to rule; and even the denigration of shahs reported by Chardin, or found among the ulama in the 1890–1911 period or after did not include a call for their deposition, but rather for their following the advice or rulings of the leading ulama when these were given.

The idea that the ulama should rule directly was accompanied by a corollary that accounted for much of Khomaini's popularity—this was that monarchy was illegitimate in Islam. Here again, the idea is a new one both in the strength of its expression and for the Shi'ism, or indeed the Islam, of the past several centuries. In those centuries nearly all theorists, Shi'i and Sunni, who discussed unjust rulers, said that, bad as they were, they were preferable to revolt, disorder, or civil war, and hence should be borne. Such theories are in the interest of traditional ruling classes. As noted, even oppositional ulama leaders like the constitutionalists, and Modarres in 1924, were not antimonarchical. Thus, in terms of the past several centuries, Khomaini put forth a new idea. On the other hand, if one looks to the earliest period of Islamic history, Khomaini may claim some fundamentalist grounds for his position. Early Islam was not monarchical; in the Sunni line the first four caliphs were in some sense "elected," and the Umayyad caliphate, though it retained some fiction of election in the dynastic line, is widely regarded as usurping—only later when local sultans arose under the Abbasid caliphate were theories developed to justify their *de facto* rule. As for the Shi'a, though political and religious power was vested in a hereditary line of Imams, these were not regarded as monarchs, and in the Twelver line, only Ali in fact ruled. There is also a Tradition of Mohammad speaking out against any "King of Kings," and this is used by Khomaini to bolster his arguments, which are not identical to the arguments presented here, although they contain some of their elements.[16]

The above and other arguments put forth by Khomaini beginning in the early 1960s were in tune with a mood shared by many ulama and non-ulama. Antiimperialist sentiment, already strongly expressed in Mosaddeq's movement, never died out; the 1954 oil agreement with an international consortium was correctly seen as maintaining foreign control and profits, and this control essentially lasted until the early 1970s. Widespread hostility to the shah and his regime was brought about by: 1) a "modernization" characterized by massive corruption benefitting especially the rich and the royal family; 2) a growing gap between rich and poor, between city and countryside, and between the two cultures; 3) the association of the dynasty with Western control and with everything unislamic; and 4) jailings, executions, tortures, and growing controls on free speech and press. It was natural that this led among many to an idealization of traditional Islamic ways and a willingness to follow religious opponents of the government. The leading role of religious opponents, which grew from the early 1960s, was also due to the difficulty of suppressing them—whereas the secular opposition could be and was suppressed by the very strong government police apparatus. Thus the local Tudeh (communist) party was almost destroyed, the guerilla Feda'iyan (Marxist) and Mojahedin (Islamic leftist) were decimated by jailings and executions, the National Front (Mosaddeqist) leadership was jailed, exiled, or quieted, and only official SAVAK-controlled unions and guilds were permitted. The ulama, however, had means of reaching the people that the government could not destroy: in a generally recognized "code," preachers as well as religious plays and storytellers dwelt upon the killing in battles by the tyrannical Umayyads of Imam Ali and of his son Hosain, drawing lessons about the need to resist tyranny. Although some ulama were arrested, jailed, or exiled, it was impossible to police every mosque or religious ceremony.

The new "religious" oppositional movement may be dated from 1963, when mass popular protests, partly instigated by the preachings of Khomaini, culminated in the shooting down of hundreds or thousands, and Khomaini's 1964 exile, first to Turkey and then to Iraq in 1965. The issues behind this movement are contested, with most pre-1978 writers following the official version that it was against land reform and votes for women, while Algar and others stress Iran's relations with Israel and a 1964 agreement giving U.S. military advisers and their families exemption from Iranian law. It seems likely that all these factors entered: Khomaini and other ayatollahs did send protests to the government against the new voting law, citing both votes for women and a provision that apparently allowed voters to take an oath on the holy book of any religion. As to land reform, although Khomaini seems only to have opposed the way it was carried out, it seems scarcely credible that a major reform, opposed in a milder version by the late Borujerdi, which was the most notable thing happening in Iran at the time, should not have elicited some of the opposition—however unfair it was to link this particular line of opposition to Khomaini.[17] Relations with Israel and the U.S. had scarcely changed, but land reform and the election law were new.

After Khomaini's exile and his settling in the holy cities in Iraq, he began to teach and write, and many of his lessons were recorded and/or published. His book, *Hokumat-e Islami,* states the position that the trained ulama should rule directly, and here and elsewhere he engaged in increasingly strong attacks on monarchy as unislamic and inherently oppressive.[18] Like many of the Iranian ulama he also showed great concern about the government's relations with Israel, seen as an enemy of Muslims, and governmental reforms in the status of women and the family. He attacked the Family Protection Law of 1967 (which made the position of men and women in marriage, divorce, and child custody more equal than it had been, and put these matters under civil law and courts) as unIslamic and invalid. A woman divorced under this law was not divorced; if she remarried she was not married, and her children would be illegitimate.[19] In sum, although some parts of what Khomaini said or wrote, notably his very important beliefs that monarchy is unIslamic and that *fuqaha* should rule directly, were *new* to the mainstream of Shi'i thought. He was not a modernist or progressive, as some who joined his movement, especially in 1978, apparently thought.[20]

Khomaini's exiled status gave him greater freedom than had his colleagues to express himself directly, while the ease of smuggling tapes and pamphlets, made at least the simpler part of his message well known in Iran. A major explanation of his popularity was also the uncompromising nature of his stand against the shah and monarchy; after the oil price rise and especially after post-1975 economic dislocations, unemployment, shortages, and unfulfilled promises led masses of people to oppose the shah and his foreign allies. In this increasingly revolutionary situation a Shi'i leader who took a constitutional monarchist position of wanting the shah as a figurehead, a position more in line with the main trends in twentieth-century Iranian Shi'ism than was Khomaini's, was likely to lose out. Even the more progressive or leftist Shi'i elements put themselves in Khomaini's camp, including the Muslim but Marxist-influenced Mojahedin and the followers of the innovative and progressive view of Islam espoused by Ali Shariati (d. 1977) and of the progressive Ayatollah Taleqani (d.1979).[21] The simplicity of Khomaini's uncompromising appeal; his refusal to be swayed into dealings with the shah or those around him; the publicity he got from exile in Iraq and France; and his forceful personality all entered into his victory.

Even after his 1979 victory, however, Khomaini's vision of Islam did not go uncontested. Not only the progressive Taleqani but also the moderate Ayatollah Shariatmadari, who comes from Azerbaijan, where he has a huge following, and lives in Qom, has differed with many of Khomaini's policies: he believed in the possibility of a figurehead king before the shah was deposed (a policy espoused by Shahpour Bakhtiar, the shah's last prime minister), and even later wanted the 1906 constitution retained minus the monarchy. He opposed deciding on a new constitution by referendum, spoke out against the council of experts to put that constitution in final shape, opposed the 1979 war against the Kurds, and says that there should not be direct rule by the *fuqaha*. To one unacquainted with recent Iranian Shi'i history these views might seem modern and liberal in a Western sense, but in fact Shariatmadari is more in line with the "tradition" of late nineteenth and twentieth century Shi'ism than are some of Khomaini's ideas. Shariatmadari's traditionalism was clear from a personal interview with him in the summer of 1979 in Qom. Regarding women, he said that women were weaker and less able than men, citing for example that even in the West where they are equal in rights, they have achieved few high positions. Hence men must be the guardians of women and have greater freedom in divorce, although here he also stressed the possibility of inserting into a marriage contract a provision that if a man takes a second wife, the first may divorce him. He did not want the government to insert this provision into all contracts, as did the 1967/75 Family Protection Act (suspended in 1979).[22]

More radical thinkers such as Mahmud Taleqani and Ali Shariati tried to interpret Islam in ways that would accommodate revolt, change, political engagement, and activism. This survey of "majoritarian" Shi'ism is not the place to go into detail about their thought, which is not now that of the mainstream of the ulama, but only to note that such men attracted liberal and radical elements to Islam who in the past, and possibly in the future, might be attracted to more secular radicalism. This they could do because of the objective situation; as the shah's regime was associated with secularist policies and with ties to the West and to Israel; as Russia and China supported the shah; and as secularist opposition had been largely crushed or contained, the popularity of the more impregnable religious opposition grew even among formerly secular students and intellectuals. During the revolution, to be sure, secularist groups like the National Front among the Liberals and the Feda'iyan among the radicals continued strong and joined a popular front with the religious opposition. The latter's support among the masses overshadowed that of the secularists, however, and helped give Khomaini the power to carry through his program for an Islamic state.

* * *

We have traced the evolution of Twelver political doctrines back to the time of the Twelfth Imam's occultation (and there were changes even earlier), showing that there have been continual changes in dominant doctrine despite Islam's hostility in theory to innovation, *bid'a*. Such changes could equally be found in Sunnism, in other varities of Shi'ism, and in other religions; in them, as in Twelver Shi'ism, major changes in religiopolitical doctrine may be traced to a combination of sociopolitical change with the elements of preexisting doctrine.

In Twelver Shi'ism, such changes have led through the centuries to virtual reversals in dominant political ideas. The earliest Shi'i politico-religious sects were predominantly messianic and totalistic—expecting their leader to establish the kingdom of God on earth. The Shi'i line that became the Twelvers became increasingly politically quietist and accepting of established rulers, a process forwarded by the development of a theory of occultation, which removed the Imam from earthly activity. (It is wrong to suppose that occultation was rendered inevitable by the fact that the Twelfth Imam had no sons; among the Isma'ilis, or "Seveners," the line of Imams was continued more than once by semihidden processes of adoption or substitution.) While acceptance of rulers remained the predominant trend through and beyond the Safavid dynasty, there also developed new claims that the *mujtahids* had a superior right to rule, although a king might be needed to act on their advice in many worldly and military matters. Such theories helped support the oppositional movements from 1891 to 1911, and again in 1924 and the 1950s. Only in the 1960s and 1970s did a leading ayatollah put forth the idea that Islam was fundamentally opposed to monarchy, and that the ulama should rule directly. With Khomaini this went with the view that no legislature was needed to make laws, as all legal needs were covered by Islamic law; the only function of a parliament was to see that Muslim law was properly interpreted and applied. Like his other political ideas, this idea of Khomaini's is new to prominent Muslim ulama; even in pre-modern times the ulama accepted some role for *urf* or secular magistrates' law, and since 1906 most ulama have been willing to accept parliamentary legislation provided it was not judged directly contrary to Islam.

Thus, as of 1980, the dominant political view of Shi'ism negates both the quietism of the first centuries after the occultation and the parliamentary constitutional monarchist view of the early twentieth century—however much it sees itself as continuing longstanding Shi'i tradition. Ironically, for reasons that probably have more to do with sociopolitical than with doctrinal factors, there is some resemblance between the situation in 1979 and that of the earliest rebellious period of Shi'ism. In its first period Shi'ism was highly messianic and rebellious, its followers expecting to bring, by victorious revolt, the rule of a messianic figure who would fill the earth with justice. Many revolts and revolutions see similar messianic expectations among their followers, especially as they often occur in times of great social disruption and discontent, and demand sacrifices that might only be made by persons expecting an almost perfect regime to emerge from their struggle. The general use for Khomaini of the title Imam, apparently adopted by analogy to some Arab Twelver leaders, but which to Iranians had meant one of the Twelve Imams, and his victory on the very eve of a new Muslim century, which often arouses messianic hopes, are among the aspects of this new messianism that witnesses have observed. On the other hand, sociopolitical realities since the victory of the revolution suggest that the last card in the history of the politics of Iranian Shi'ism is far from having been played.

Describe the aspects of rel dev which led to revn.

2

Tradition and Change in Iranian Socio-Religious Thought

Mangol Bayat-Philipp

one of Keddie's PhD offspring

اف'نی

Nineteenth century Iranian "modernist" thinkers are all too often treated by today's intellectuals with contempt and anger. This contempt is based on a belief that the ideas the nineteenth century modernists so passionately promoted were not their own but borrowed from the West and imperfectly understood, and that in their harsh criticism of their inherited value system and their endeavor to build a "new" society they promoted the destruction of Iran's traditional culture.

In this paper I shall argue that the so-called modernist thought of the turn of the century, despite its loud call for Westernization, was in spirit and in form, if not in content, deep-rooted in tradition, bearing as much the mark of the Irano-Islamic heritage outwardly rejected by some of its spokesmen, as of the European systems it strongly wished to emulate. The modernists' vision of a new society basically reflected a secularized image of traditional theological and philosophical views. I shall also show that now, several decades later, the "traditionalist" thinkers who persistently defend the "authentic" national cultural identity against the onslaught of modernism paradoxically reveal a modern mental formation which their forefathers, some of whom they scornfully refer to as the *gharbzadeh* (Westmaniac), lacked.

I do not propose in this essay to formulate a definition of "modernity," since this would involve a lengthy argument that would be, in the present volume, *hors propos*. I shall confine myself to discussing some fundamental traits of modern thought in order to

37

show two essential points, namely: 1) a characteristic feature of modernity is criticism; what is new is set over and against what is old, and 2) despite the revolutionary role played by the organized religious leadership in the twentieth century, the ideologization of religion in contemporary Iran is mainly the work of secularly educated intellectuals who are in fact upholding a centuries-long tradition of dissent in Shi'i thought against the established orthodoxy.

Dissent in Traditional Shi'i Thought

Shi'ism, the branch of Islam to which the majority of the Iranians have adhered ever since the establishment of the Safavid dynasty in the early sixteenth century, accepts the general Muslim view that the Prophet Mohammad's Revelation was final and complete, yet expects a further perfection of its interpretation through the progressive teaching of the Imams. As a consequence of the minority status it acquired from the start when, following the death of the Prophet, a group of dissidents chose to pay allegiance to the first Imam Ali, who lay claim to leadership by hereditary right, rather than to the "elected" Caliph, and of the military defeats it suffered in the successive Sunni States, the tradition of revolt and martyrdom came to characterize the spiritual cult of the Imam. However, in the eighth century, following the sixth Imam Ja'far as-Sadeq's counsel to his followers to adopt the practice of *taqiyeh* (concealment of one's true belief) as a measure of protection against the repressive policy of the established Sunni State, the alienated condition of the Shi'a living in an hostile environment was formally accepted. Similarly the Shi'i tendency to show absolute respect for esoteric knowledge was further increased.[1] When, in 874, the Twelfth Imam was declared in occultation, there developed the belief that the Qoranic Revelation will reach its utmost perfection only with his manifestation on the Day of the Resurrection, when the Imami cycle will come to an end, and the reign of pure religion will occur. Implied in this belief is the conviction that the ideal truth is beyond man's reach in the present era of occultation; and the notion that men, evil and corrupt, are not yet worthy of receiving the final perfected message of the Seal of the Prophets.[2]

Through the centuries, the Shi'i ulama (learned men in religious sciences) devoted their studies to the "external" aspects of theology, law, and jurisprudence. Such a legalistic attitude towards religion came to forbid, or at least to frown upon, any attempts made to explore further the esoteric knowledge of the Imams' teachings. As has been rightly remarked, *ijtihad* (interpretation of the religious law by a high ranking religious leader, the *mujtahid*) "which theoretically might have helped *taqlid* (following the pronouncement of a religious leader) from becoming a mere static acceptance of unexamined, even unassimilated teaching" was in this sense hardly ever used.[3]

Shi'i mystics and philosophers tried to transcend this scholastic approach to religion, and to offer instead their own *ta'wil* (spiritual interpretation of the holy texts) as an alternative or additional method to understanding its true inner meaning. The term "Perfect Man," which was coined by Ibn Arabi (1164–1240), the Andalusian born Arab Sufi philosopher, was used to refer to supposedly exceptional gifted individuals believed to appear periodically on earth, who, through mystical revelation, have direct access to *ilm* (divine knowledge), and thus are qualified to act as the mediators between God and men.[4] This title, Perfect Man, was attributed not only to the successive Prophets, from Adam to Mohammad, and to the Imams and their respective close companions, the *auliya;* but also to the spiritual heads or shaikhs of the various Sufi orders as well, and, by implication, some of the philosophers themselves. The Isma'ilis, those who seceded from the main Shi'i sect after Ja'far as-Sadeq recommended an acquiescent attitude towards the State, and chose to keep up the spirit of revolt by joining the more militant leadership of Isma'il, son of Ja'far, went so far as to assert that in time of the Imam's occultation, there are always some men chosen from amongst his followers who act as his *hujjat* (guarantor or proof). They developed the concept of evolutionary, progressive cycles of revelations, each cycle corresponding to a new historical era inaugurated by its own Saheb al-Zaman (Master of the Age).[5]

The issues of *bida* and *naskh* (occurrence and abrogation) in religion have been debated at great length by Muslim theologians and philosophers throughout the centuries. A number of Qoranic verses suggest that "God has a kind of suspended decision." Similarly, the Prophet himself had abrogated some of his earlier commands and replaced them with new ones. Although the more literalist theologians considered those verses as part of God's absoluteness, progressive schools of Islamic thought, such as the medieval Mu'tazilites, interpreted them as fitting very naturally their belief that God's purpose for His action is always the well being (*maslaha*) of the creation.[6] The Isma'ilis carried further this idea arguing that "the Imam is the ruler of religion, and gives orders with regard to whatever he thinks beneficial to the religious life or the welfare of the people" of this time.[7]

39

There are eternal truths which do not change but for the sake of the changing world there are changing "truths"

It was Mulla Sadra (d. 1640), the brilliant seventeenth century Iranian philosopher who, inspired by the various Muslim philosophical and theological ideas, synthesized the different traditions into one system, and explained his own concept of the Perfect Man in the light of his doctrine of *harekat-e jauhariyeh* (substantive movement). Claiming that existence cannot be static and that movement occurs in the very substance as well as the qualities of things, an idea which was already developed by the Isma'ilis, Sadra argued that existence moves continuously and successively through higher and higher forms of "evolutionary modes of being," culminating in the Perfect Man, the highest grade of being without whose existence the universe would be destroyed. Echoing Ibn Arabi and subsequent Muslim mystics, he defined this last stage of human perfection in terms of self-realization and awareness of the existing relationship with the Divine Being. To Sadra the Shi'i philosopher, the Perfect Man is the Prophet, each of the Twelve Imams and their respective adepts (*auliya*), and, again by implication, the philosopher. Like his predecessors and his successors who developed Islamic philosophical thought, despite the orthodox ulama's hostility to it, he insisted that Divine Truth and philosophical truth are identical and interdependent; and that true *ilm*, that is the esoteric knowledge of the Imams' teachings, is accessible only to the initiated who have to protectively conceal it from the "ordinary" man. Furthermore, consistent with his doctrine of perpetual movement, Sadra declared that, since change is imperceptibly taking place all the time in material bodies, "commands in this world have to change according to times and climes through *naskh*."[8]

Thus, in contrast to the historical determinism of the orthodox theologians who view the history of the world and of the Shi'i community in the period of occultation as going from bad to worse until corruption and injustice reach their utmost limit with the advent of the impostor Dajjal (the antichrist figure in Muslim and especially Shi'i theology), which constitutes the first sign of the Manifestation of the expected Imam; Mulla Sadra proposed a more humanist vision of the world in perpetual progressive evolution towards perfection, and a more positive faith in man's spiritual ability to perfect himself. For the belief in the Perfect Man actually offers a promise of redemption in this dark age of *ghaibat* (occultation). Moreover, the philosopher's agrument that the Imams' traditions (*akhbar*) have to be interpreted esoterically underlines his basic rejection of the theologians' belief that knowledge is already given in its entirety, and that there is nothing more to add to it until the return of the Imam.

The orthodox theologians, the *fuqaha*, waged merciless war against the philosophers and the mystics, the *urafa*,[9] threatening them with *takfir* (declaring one an infidel), and even did not hesitate to use coercive means to enforce their own views and suppress any other that might challenge their position as sole interpreters and guardians of the religious law. The *urafa*, in turn, strongly resenting their opponents' dominance over the Shi'i intellectual scene, charged them with a vulgar literalism and narrow-mindedness that stifled independent inquiry. Consequently, the *urafa* developed a self-assertive, conscious sense of independence *vis à vis* other social groups. Implicit in their idea of the Perfect Man, a neo-Platonic concept of Philosopher-king which Sadra had blended with the Sufi idea of the master initiator of the esoteric truth, is the firm conviction that a philosopher's judgment ultimately supersedes that of the *fuqaha* and of the secular monarchs. The Perfect Man ideal is symbolic of their ideal society, the heavenly "virtuous city" *(madineh-ye fazeleh)*, where pure religion reigns and where the sages rule; an ideal that clashed with, and in fact was rejected by, the established sociocultural reality of the time. Though they channeled their social idealism into religiously dedicated search for truth and did not openly revolt against the secular authority, the *urafa*'s aloof detachment, in addition to their belief in the Imam as the Supreme authority, clearly reveals their strong and conscious refusal to accept any temporal power as binding. On the other hand, towards the masses they displayed an attitude of disdain, demanding surrender and obedience. It was an attitude that reflected their view of themselves as an intellectually distinct category of superior beings, a view that upheld the general Islamic elitist conception of knowledge as the precious possession of the chosen few.

The circle of "intellectuals" in premodern Iran was polarized into two somewhat artificial and wholly theological camps. The *urafa* and the *fuqaha* did not constitute two separate classes of thinkers. From amongst the *fuqaha* there were a number of *urafa;* and the *urafa* were *fuqaha* themselves, by virtue of their training in the religious sciences if not by profession. Seen from a sociopolitical perspective, the *urafa-fuqaha* controversies appear to have been mere polemical battles over methodology, intellectual disputes over high doctrines of Shi'ism which did not relate to the daily life of the common believer.

Nineteenth Century Reform

In 1722 the Safavid dynasty fell. The centuries of relatively peaceful reign which helped bring about an Iranian cultural renaissance and witnessed the consolidation of Shi'i dogma, as formalized and formulated by distinguished theologians, on the one hand, and the development of philosophical and mystical thought on the other, came to an end. It was followed by nearly three-quarters of a century of political fragmentation and fierce power struggles which finally ended with a Turkoman tribe coming to power. With the Qajars, Iran was once more politically united under one dynastic, autocratic rule which attempted to establish a centralized government.

Unlike their predecessors, despite their adoption of the title, Zell-ollah (Shadow of God), the Qajars lay no claim to a divine right to rule. Force brought them to power, force kept them there; and little pretense was made to the contrary. Thus, the religious authority of the ulama met no serious challenge on the part of the State. However, the centuries-long polemical fight between the *urafa* and the *fuqaha* intensified as the *mujtajids,* led by defenders of orthodoxy like Mulla Mohammad Ali Behbehani, who acquired the nickname of *sufi-kosh* (Sufi-killer), were determined to erase "heresy" from Shi'i and Iranian soil, and thus ensure their total ideological domination over the nation. At this time, though, the battle proved to be bloodier as religious issues were socialized and, eventually, politicized.

Religious Reform

Shaikhism

Despite the orthodox ulama's hostility to Sadra's philosophy, his ideas and those of earlier philosophers, mystics, and Isma'ilis, greatly influenced the Iranian thinkers who ventured into the hazardous path of metaphysics and philosophy, studies traditionally considered to be the highest intellectual training, and the crown and summit of all knowledge. In the second half of the eighteenth century, a new school of Shi'i theology, Shaikhism, came into being, aiming at legitimizing some of the controversial philosophical and mystical views. Though the founder of Shaikhism, Shaikh Ahmad Ahsa'i (1753–1826),[10] was an Arab born in Bahrain, Iran provided the school with a large following, financial and political patronage, and, after the death of Ahsa'i, the leadership as well.

Shaikh Ahmad was greatly influenced by Shi'i philosophers and mystics, especially Mulla Sadra, despite his relentless refutations and denunciations of their ideas. Reminiscent of Sadra's arguments were Ahsa'i's allegorical interpretation of some of the most fundamental principles of the Shi'i dogma; his pronouncing the resurrection of the dead to be spiritual and not physical as the orthodox theologians had it; *mi'raj,* the Prophet's ascension to Heaven, a "spiritual voyage" and not physical; that the Occulted Imam exists in this world as a spirit and not physically, and that his Manifestation will occur in the intermediary world of the soul and not on earth. Moreover, Ahsa'i rested his entire system of thought on the gnostic conception of the universe as a structured hierarchy of worlds and interworlds of Reality, corresponding to the various levels of existence. Like the medieval Muslim mystics, and like Mulla Sadra and the latter's commentators, Ahsa'i conceived an intermediary world, the Realm of Images, *(alam al-mithal)* where the human soul imagines images which are as real, if not more real, than the reality perceived through the senses; a world "inaccessible to rational abstractions and to empirical materializations." For man's consciousness awakens to this Reality through his active imagination, the organ of the visionary perception. Ahsa'i, echoing his predecessors, insisted that this world, termed Hurqalya, could only be sensed by the adept, the initiated; and declared that the degree of perception of things in Hurqalya, and of the Divine, is directly proportionate to the degree of esoteric knowledge an individual possesses.

Ahsa'i thus rejected the *mujtahid's* use of *aql* (discursive reasoning) as a poor substitute for *ilham* (divine inspiration), questioned the validity of the *mujtahid's* authority, which he considered fallible since it was human and hence not binding, and denounced *taqlid* (imitation of a *mujtahid*) as contrary to the teachings of the Imams. Similarly, Ahsa'i took over the mystico-philosophical idea of the Perfect Man, which he termed Perfect Shi'i, and claimed that through the ages there has always been, and shall always be, such men, capable of "seeing things in Hurqalya," whose function is progressively to lift the veil off the esoteric truth, and thus enlighten their own restricted circle of adepts, as the Imams did in their own lifetime. They are the *babs* (gates) to the Imam's knowledge.

Whether or not Ahsa'i considered himself to be the Perfect Shi'i of his time was, and still is, a controversial question. Yet his works, and that of his successors, are full of unmistakable references to his "mission" as the initiator of the esoteric truth. The popularity he enjoyed amongst the reigning shah and his court, men of great wealth and social status, as well as amongst esteemed members of the ulama class itself, certainly testify to the enviable, prestigious position he acquired for himself as a spiritual guide.

Kazim Rashti, Ahsa'i's immediate successor to the leadership of the

Shaikhi school, further radicalized Shaikhism by accepting the Isma'ili concept of the cyclical evolution of religion. He distinguished what he termed "the cycle of apparent or esoteric precepts" of the Prophet and the Imams which would last until the "Book of Creation comes to an end within a period of 1200 years" (he was writing in 1257 A.H.); from the cycle of Perfect Man whose task is to manifest "the hidden, the esoteric things." He also asserted that "true religion" is progressively revealed in order to fit a parallel progressive maturity of mankind.[11]

The Shaikhi view of religion as progressively evolutionary played an equally dominant role in the thought of Hajj Mohammad Karim Khan Qajar of Kerman, one of the successors of Rashti, who succeeded in attracting the loyalty of the majority of the Shaikhis in Iran. He gave a historical dimension to the metaphysical conception of the fall of man into the abyss and his subsequent ascension "back to God." Depicting the world as being, from the time of the first Prophet Adam, in a perpetual, vertical, irreversible ascension, he carried the idea of *maslaha* (God's concern with His creatures' well-being), through his entire scheme, making it the moving force behind the evolutionary change that religion, and religious law, necessarily go through. "God lay the foundation of progress," he wrote, by creating man perfectable.[12] Since man's well-being differs according to time and conditions, he argued, holy laws must change accordingly. Similarly, Hajj Mohammad Karim Khan expressed a strong conviction that *ilm*, evolutionary by nature, is periodically revealed by the Perfect Shi'i, or *Rokn-e rabe'* (fourth pillar of religion, after God, the Prophet and the Imams) who must be "alive, present and commander of his time."[13] Believing that authority has to be hierarchically structured, since in plurality there is dissent and corruption, he condemned the concept of equal share in power and argued for the absolute need for one *hakim* (governor or ruler) to rule society by divine right, as God's representative.[14]

Hence, following the tradition of Shi'i philosophy, the Shaikhis rejected the orthodox ulama's basically fatalistic vision of society, which sees the period of occultation as one of decadence and corruption, and society as doomed to decline down a road paved with misery and despair—the promised hope implied in the messianic expectation not altering this fundamentally deterministic stand. The Shaikhis' view of man as in a perpetual state of steady spiritual growth, with the final manifestation of the Imam representing a "gift" for their coming of age, rather than a redemption for their long suffering, is inherently more humanistic. Like the philosophers' view, it denotes a profound faith in man's ability to progress mentally, and a conviction that man's life is potentially worthy of fulfillment in this world, and not only in the next. Furthermore, the Shaikhis' aim of rescuing the dogma from what they called the vulgar, literal interpretation of the *fuqaha*, reflects a genuine concern with the prevailing stifling and sterile intellectual milieu where religion was the major basis of all studies.

Nevertheless, despite their progressive outlook, the Shaikhis' stand cannot be termed modern; for neither is it new in Islamic thought, nor are the ideas originally innovative. Their conception of religion and society reflects a tradition of dissent in Islam. Their progressive notion of an evolutionary religious law, despite its implications, does not project a sense of commitment to social and individual progress in a modern, material way. Moreover, their theory of *ilm* does not modify the traditional view of religious knowledge as the sole monopoly of a handful of extraordinary beings. In fact, they strongly upheld the idea of a double truth, one for the adepts and the other for the public. Similarly, the Shaikhis utilized traditional Sufi doctrines in order to socialize the mystical idea of a hierarchic category of Perfect Man destined to lead the community. Despite his bold protest against established orthodoxies and despite his own heterodoxies, Hajj Mohammad Karim Khan's socioreligious thought displayed a conservative outlook. This was based on the concept of inequality, that some are born to rule, others to be ruled; that in fact all creatures of God have a definite place and rank in the structured hierarchy, from which they originate and to which they return; and that it is contrary to the Divine Order to move upward beyond one's assigned position on the scale. In fact, his proposed religious reforms basically aimed at promoting his own ambitious scheme to raise his status to that of the *Rokn-e rabe'* of his time. Thus, whereas early Shaikhism sounded progressive, and hence appealing to the minds in revolt against the prevalent intellectual stagnation, by the middle of the nineteenth century it appeared traditional and even reactionary.

In spite of Hajj Mohammed Karim Khan's call for religious change, harassed as he was by orthodox ulama, distrusted and closely watched by the court who viewed with suspicion his ideas, and, above all, put on guard by the spread of the Babi revolt led by his hated rival, Sayyed Ali Mohammad Shirazi, and the resulting violent persecution of the Babis; the Kermani Shaikhi leader was forced to refute his own extremist ideas. Under his leadership Shaikhism had become an important school of theology, yet it never realized its ultimate goal: to establish the ideal "true Shi'i" society.

Babism

Shaikhism found its most radical expression in Babism, for it was the Babis who ultimately carried the tradition of religious dissent out of the mosque and *madraseh* (religious school) into the streets.

Sayyed Ali Mohammad (1821–50),[15] a merchant from Shiraz who had become acquainted with Kazim Rashti and the Shaikhi school of thought during a two to three year stay in Kerbala, shortly after Rashti's death in 1843, proclaimed himself to be the *Bab* (gate) to the Divine Truth. Together with a small group of devoted followers, he relentlessly campaigned for his cause, and attacked the ulama for their alleged worldly corruption, spiritual ignorance and abusive use of *ijtihad*. Unshaken by the inevitable consequences that such a proclamation led to, including public interrogation, harassment, and humiliation, the *Bab* further declared himself to be the expected Imam and, when finally arrested and imprisoned in Maku, boldly asserted he was the new Prophet of the Age, and his Prophecy, superseding Mohammad's, abrogated the Qoranic Law. To a large extent echoing extremist Isma'ili and Shaikhi thinkers, in his Persian *Bayan* (his "holy book"), the *Bab* emphatically stated that Divine Revelations have no end, that each successive one, including his own, is destined to be followed by a more complete one. He also laid claim to supreme authority on earth, overriding that of shahs and governors.[16]

How much change the *Bab* was planning for the Iran he wished to guide is hard to determine. His new religion certainly aimed at severely curbing, if not eliminating, the religious basis of the ulama's power by declaring unlawful the two important functions of the *mujtahid* and of the *Imam Jom'eh*[17] (leader of the Friday Mosque prayer; a position held by high-ranking ulama). He denounced the use of arms and violence, except in case of holy war.[18] He tried to rectify the low legal and social status of women by limiting the number of wives a man can lawfully have to two (instead of four as allowed by Muslim law), the second to be taken only with the consent of the first wife and only in case of the latter's sterility.[19] He lay claim to the Iranian provinces of Azerbaijan, Khorasan, and the two Iraqs, as the official territory of the *ahl-e bayan*[20] (people of *Bayan*—that is, his scripture), yet provided no political program for it. He remained in prison until he was finally sentenced to death in July 1850 in Tabriz.

Insurrections by his followers, both before and after his death, led to the bloody massacres of the Babis, and displayed the militant nature of the movement. It produced martyrs and saints, but the new religion never achieved its aim: to establish the rule of the Sage, the heavenly kingdom on earth, that neo-Platonic ideal exalted and dreamt of by Muslim thinkers throughout the centuries. Nevertheless, the Babis, as well as the Shaikhis, inspired by the philosophers, left an important legacy to the modern Iranian: a realization that the relation of man to the conditions of his existence is complex and subject to change and development; an awareness of the distinction between conditions that are unchangeable and those that one can alter; and above all a strong conviction that religious evolution has to accompany social evolution.

Secular Reforms

Between an oppressive autocratic Qajar government and a largely illiterate, ill-treated population, there came into being in the second half of the nineteenth century a group of educated men, distinct from the ulama and *urafa* class of thinkers, who were committed to the belief that social, political, and moral problems were the central issues of life. Preaching that the truly spiritual and religious man is no longer interested in the mystery of life but in the pragmatic solution of particular problems, they rebelled against the great mystical vision of the world regarded as a "cosmos" and denounced metaphysics and theology as too barren in their abstractions. They were strongly convinced that the principal causes of the social decay, injustice, and oppression they saw in Iran lay in men's ignorance and archaic sense of values, and that only with scientific knowledge could their society liberate itself.

Professing faith in the transforming power of enlightened ideas, they conceived change as something not to be feared but to be welcomed, and saw themselves as new apostles, carrying the message of the age: that of reason, science (in nonreligious terms), liberty, and progress. They also discovered, and were irresistibly attracted to, the antitheological, antimetaphysical philosophers of eighteenth century Europe. However, given the socioreligious climate of the time, and considering the fact that, with the exception of Malkom Khan, all of those secular thinkers were first brought up in the traditional Shi'i schools of thought, it is only natural that these men, including Jamal od-Din Afghani, Mostashar od-Dauleh, Talebzadeh, Malkom Khan and Mirza Aqa Khan Kermani, either sought to accommodate Western ideas to Islam and/or called for religious reform. But, contrary to the Shaikhis and the Babis, those intellectuals focused on aspects of Islam that could be adjusted to their new views. In their attempt to adapt Islam to the social change they deemed necessary, they were greatly influenced and, to a large extent, followed, the tradition of Shi'i mystico-philosophical thought.

Afghani was echoing the Shaikhis when he was emphatically stating: "There is no doubt that in the present age, distress, misfortune, and weakness besiege all classes of Muslims from every side. Therefore, every Muslim keeps his eyes and ears open in expectation . . . to see from what corner of the earth the sage and renewer will appear and will reform the minds and souls of the Muslims . . .";[21] and that "a teacher is indispensable," "some man of high intelligence and pure soul" to help the community of the faithful find the right path.[22] His assertion that in each community there must be two groups of teachers, one to guide the intellect and the other the soul, one taking care of the spiritual and the other of the moral aspects of man's nature,[23] is reminiscent of Mohammad Karim Khan Kermani's two distinct categories of superior beings, the *nuqaba* and the *nujaba*, destined to lead and guide the people. Although Afghani quoted a Qoranic verse, "Verily, God does not change the state of people until they change themselves inwardly," which he interpreted in a truly modern sense to mean that man must rely on his own individual effort to change positively,[24] paradoxically he often expressed the traditional philosophers and Shaikhis' view that the masses, ignorant and corruptible, must be guided in order to attain a civilized stage and to control their base, animal condition. Like them, he recognized the essential role of the ulama in instructing the masses "incapable of discerning good from evil . . . (or) how to trace back causes or to discern effects,"[25] and in commanding surrender and obedience. Like them he appreciated religion as the "source of man's welfare . . . the cause of material and moral progress."[26] Also like them, he attacked the organized orthodox religious leadership, be it Sunni or Shi'i, for their antiintellectualism and its stifling effect on scientific and philosophical enquiry. In his famous "Answer to Renan" he specifically distinguished Islam from "the manner in which it was propagated in the world";[27] and Islamic science and philosophy, which made through the centuries "brilliant and fruitful achievements,"[28] despite the "heavy yoke" imposed upon them by the ulama, from the "Muslim religion" as represented by the orthodox theologians. His eloquent despair: "So long as humanity exists, the struggle will not cease between dogma and free investigation, between religion and philosophy; a desperate struggle in which, I fear, the triumph will not be for free thought, because the masses dislike reason, and its teachings are only understood by some intelligences of the elite . . ."[29] voices the centuries-long stand of the Muslim dissenters in opposition to the persecuting *fuqaha* who considered themselves the only true spokesmen for Islam.

Mirza Aqa Khan Kermani's sociological study of religion aiming at depicting it as a pragmatic, useful instrument to civilize the "savage" and control men's fear of their physical environment, reflects the unorthodox, Isma'ili, Shaikhi, Babi idea that divine revelations undergo endless evolutionary changes in order to meet the demands of a constantly changing, progressing, world. In fact, his argument that religion functions as a medical treatment for social diseases, "whether the doctor is called Docteur Muhammad, or Monsieur Issa or Mirza Musa, the purpose of the prescription is to cure,"[30] recalls Mohammad Karim Khan's own words. Kermani's fiery attacks on the ulama, like Afghani, Talebzadeh and, to a certain extent, Akhundzadeh's own anti-ulama sentiment, basically projected the *urafa's* tradition of opposition to the *fuqaha,* rather than the blunt irreligious, if not atheistic, anticlerical position of a Voltaire.

The *ilm* that the nineteenth century "modernists" spoke about so eloquently differed, however, from the *urafa's* conception of it. It was given a broader, more modern, scientific meaning. The modernists turned against the ulama's division of knowledge into a Muslim knowledge and a secular European one, and wished to see a more universal approach given to it by erasing the notion that Western science is incompatible with the Islamic faith. Yet, here again they reflected their deep-rooted traditional outlook. They argue that man's history is characterized by an unfolding of higher mental attributes and an attainment of wisdom by degree; that man, the center and summit of creation, is capable of perfectibility; and that there is order and equilibrium in the universe. These arguments, reflecting not only the seventeenth and eighteenth century European philosophers, but essentially a classical Islamic view, clashed with the more contemporary, more "modern" conception of the Positivists and the Social Darwinists who dismissed the Age of Reason ideal as an antiquated illusion. In fact, Kermani, who wholeheartedly accepted Darwin's theory, instead of adopting the ideas of the war of nature, natural selection, survival of the fittest among random variations, which make man, along with other forms of life, "the child of chance;" identified Darwinism with Sadra's *harekat-e jauhariyeh,* the substantive movement that lies behind the progressive evolution of all beings towards perfection.[31] However, whereas Sadra's moving force was man's mystical yearning for divine love, Kermani's was man's thirst for knowledge and social progress.[32]

In their attempt to define the "new society," despite their conscious or unconscious desire to emulate some of the sociopolitical practices of Western Europe, nineteenth century reformers inevitably projected the neo-Platonic view of the heavenly city on earth, the classical *madineh-ye fazeleh* of the medieval philosophers where the Perfect Man, the philosopher-king, rules over the masses; rather than the concept of a pluralistic society where the sovereignty of the people is recognized and where a representative government implements the will of the majority. Malkom Khan himself, the most modern of them all, who is considered the father of constitutionalism in Iran, and who introduced the Western concept of Law to the Iranians, adopted a traditionally elitist, paternalistic attitude towards the "people." He, Kermani, Akhundzadeh, and Afghani, thought of themselves as united by something more than mere interest in ideas; they conceived themselves as being a dedicated special category of Perfect Man, devoted to the spreading of a new revelation. They highly praised Martin Luther and his Reformation, and wished to see a similar Islamic reform movement established in the Muslim world which would usher in the age of "Islamic Renaissance;" and each one envisioned himself as the Reformer. Hence, their view of society was still a traditionally monist view, expressing a passionate longing to discover one unitary truth encompassing all existence and impregnable to attack from within and from without. Their thought, in spirit if not in content, represents a secularized form of the quest for the True Prophet, the pursuit of the prophetic philosophy which, to quote Corbin, marks the "stylization constante de la conscience Iranienne."

Their message was secular and nationalistic, in spite of their concern for religious reform. Religion was actually identified with nationalist movements of change and revolution. With the exception of Afghani, this generation of Iranian intellectuals spoke more of Iran the nation, than of Islam or Shi'ism. A careful study of *Hasht Behesht,* the commentary on the *Bab's Bayan* by Kermani and his friend Ahmad Ruhi, clearly reveals the authors' social and nationalist interest in Babism to which they had both converted. Their frankly nonreligious interpretation which, when compared with the original *Bayan,* might appear on the verge of heresy, displaced in radical fashion the central emphasis from religion to the moral and political aspects of life in society. They found in Babism the religious rationale for a humanitarian and intellectual revulsion for the autocratic fanaticism of the Qajars and some of the more corrupt Shi'i ulama a hopeful means to help bring about an Iranian cultural renaissance. Assailing with scorn the Arabs, condeming Islam as a religion fitting their "inferior" nation but not "civilized" Iran, they hailed the *Bab* as the redeemer who would liberate Iran from the "despised religion" of the Muslims. By promoting the adoption of Persian as a universal holy language; of Nauruz as the first day of an international Babi calendar; of Shiraz (the birthplace of the *Bab*) as the new Mecca; they expressed their wish to see Iran reassume its past cultural supremacy. Moreover, it is because of their ideal of a revolutionary Iran developing on purely national lines that they championed the Azali sect of Babism which, following the death of the *Bab*, kept up the spirit of revolt against the established socioreligious order; rather than the Baha'i one which adopted a pacifist, universalist religious tone.

Though most of the nineteenth century nationalist thinkers upheld the Islamic cultural identity of the Iranian nation, Akhundzadeh and Kermani sought to restore the pre-Islamic cultural legacy and attribute to it due credit for past grandeur, while condeming Islam as the cause for national decadence. In the Western racist theories of the time, they found the rationale for the contempt they felt for the Arabs, and a positive argument for their glorification of Iran "the noble Aryan nation" of the "good Aryan people of good extraction." Neither this anti-Arab sentiment, which in a sense echoes Ferdausi and the Iranian born writers of the medieval *shu'ubiyya* literary movement; nor the cult of the Zoroastrian past, found receptive ears in the nineteenth century, but they did in the twentieth century. Nevertheless, at the time they lay the foundation for a new nationalist, secular ideology which was to rival the traditional view of society, and play a dominant role in the shaping of the Pahlavis' cultural policy.

Generally speaking, nineteenth century Iranian intellectuals' part in the major political events of their time was marginal. However, they set the tone for the policy and action of the national revolt which continued through the turn of the century and climaxed with the Constitutional Revolution of 1905–11. They introduced to Iran's literary world a new genre, social criticism, which was used both as a weapon to discredit the establishment, and as a torch to enlighten their compatriots, "to awaken them from their long sleep of ignorance." With them, the Shi'i mystical ecstasy was turned to national social action and political movements.

Twentieth Century Political Activism

Much has been written about the successful role played by the ulama in twentieth century Iranian politics, and about their emergence as the champions not only of religion, but also of the nation. In fact, they are often depicted as the "national voice" of the people in revolt against the despotic government. Yet no serious consideration is given to one consequence of their collaboration with the lay revolutionaries, namely: by opting for political activism, they exposed themselves and thus proved vulnerable in comparison to the secular political groups whose modern education and world view prepared them better for social, political, and intellectual leadership. In their effort to act as guardians of the sacred, in their eagerness to save Shi'ism by whatever means were at their disposal, they fell into the trap of secular nationalism, and thus severely narrowed their horizons down to worldly considerations for which they were not, and are not, equipped. Despite some desperate attempts on the part of lay and religious thinkers to reconcile the notions of constitutionalism, representative government and sovereignty of the people with Shi'i Islam, modern Iranian political thought has followed, and is still following, a secular trend.

It was the lay intellectuals and politicians who provided the constitutional revolution with its program; and, regardless of the crucial role the ulama played in the movement, it was the very foundation of the traditional system of thought, rather than the social power structure, that was decisively shaken as a consequence. The new literature of revolt of the constitutional and postconstitutional periods was concerned not only with the corruption of the inept government but also with the social and scientific backwardness of the society. Its call for change took the form of opposition to the Qajars and to the ulama themselves. The anticlericalism of a Dehkhoda,[33] the glorification of Zoroaster and pre-Islamic Iran of an Eshqi,[34] were typical themes that dominated the new literary scene.

When Reza Shah, the founder of the Pahlavi Dynasty, came to power in the 1920s, this trend was officially encouraged and even adopted as part of its cultural and ideological policy. On the one hand, the "genius of Aryan race" was stressed as a source of pride and faith, and Zoroastrian social and artistic traditions were revived; and on the other, the position of religion and religious leadership in society were severely undermined. The blunt anti-Shi'i secular stand of Kasravi (the leading political writer of the time, whose arguments against theological and metaphysical notions, attacks upon the whole Shi'i social, political, and moral tradition, and onslaughts upon the "tyranny" of the ulama, so strikingly resemble Akhundzadeh and Kermani's) supported the official decision-makers task of secularizing Iranian society.

Despite, and perhaps because of, the obsession of Iranian thought with the problem of national identity, culture, and mission, secular nationalism has not proved to be a unifying force. It has overlooked the diversity in interests and outlook between the various sectors of the society, since it is essentially formulated and implemented by a small unrepresentative, yet highly influential, privileged group.

Religious opposition, which was severely crushed by Reza Shah's government, was allowed to surface in the 1940s and early 1950s, in the brief reign of political freedom that marked the beginning of Mohammad Reza Shah's rule. A small group of activist Muslims, known as *Feda`iyan-e Islam* (Devotees of Islam) attempted to challenge the Pahlavi secularist policies. The 1946 assassination of Kasravi by a "devotee" and the subsequent public burning of his books symbolically dramatized the *Feda`iyan's* categorical refusal to abide by secularism.

In the sixties and seventies, the emergence of a newly educated, increasingly self-aware, mainly urban middle and lower middle class onto the political scene, helped in the formation and spread of a vociferous religious opposition to the official secular policies. For it is on behalf of this segment of the population, not yet culturally uprooted but disoriented as a result of the rapid social changes taking place as well as of the secular education provided by the State (which, more often than not, teaches values that clash with the traditional socioreligious beliefs learned at home); that the leading opponents of the Pahlavi regime speak against the creation of "two cultures" in Iranian society: the modern and the traditional. Though the former is primarily associated with the Westernized affluent class, the latter can no longer be solely identified with the socioeconomically underprivileged. With the economic boom of the late sixties and the seventies, a great number of still tradition-bound, religiously oriented Iranians have rapidly climbed up the social echelons and moved into the wealthier, modern residential sections of the major towns and cities, thus coming to live next door to the despised *gharbzadeh*.

The intellectual leadership of the political and ideological battle against the regime is not provided by the ulama themselves, though Khomeini, Shariatmadari and their colleagues are giving the movement an essential religious legitimacy, but by lay ideologists of whom Ali Shariati (d. 1977) is the most influential.[35] Through their education (they have gone to Western-type, if not Western, schools) and their secular professional occupations, they are different from, and in spirit at least, opposed to the traditionally educated ulama. They are twentieth century products of the social and cultural modernizing reforms established by the Constitutional and the Pahlavi regimes; truly modern, bourgeois thinkers, who, expressing a profound disillusion and disenchantment with the West and the Westernized ruling elite, rise in defense of religion and of the "oppressed classes," of the "authentic" national cultural identity and values, and of national economic and political independence. Their message appeals to two different kinds of followers: those whose impulse is primarily religious and wish to react against the prevalent irreligious materialistic tendencies; and those who are politically minded and want to undertake a revolution.

Challenging the turn of the century intellectual leaders' faith in Westernization, blaming them for the "national wholesale sacrifice to the insistent demands of Western materialism,"[36] and condemning what the writer Jalal Al-e Ahmad scornfully refers to as *Zardosht-bazi* (playing at Zoroastrianism), they argue that "Islam, at least in our present time, is the only traditional point of unity and support which can establish a strong emotional bond. . . ."[37] Their tone, however, reflects a more utilitarian approach to religion than a genuine religious conviction. The blunt question that is often asked is not "How should I be a good Muslim?" but, "Why should one be a Muslim?" Al-e Ahmad resorts to Islam as a strategic defense-mechanism against the "threatening invasion of the materialist West,"[38] even though he could not be entirely convinced of his own faith in it. In his account of his pilgrimage to Mecca, for instance, he wonders candidly: "Why did you come here? Pilgrimage? Worship? Spectacle? Tourism? Discovery?" and honestly admits, "I feel it is hypocrisy, there is no faith. Only to be in harmony with society."[39] And when asked by one Saudi Arabian youth what religion he professes, he answers: "I wish to be Muslim."[40] Shariati, emphatically asserting that a Muslim today should first and foremost ask himself "what is Islam's usefulness and worth to the society in which he lives?"[41] conceives Shi'ism as a political ideology, a social force which would help bring about the necessary revolution. He calls for an "Islamic protestantism"; so that Shi'ism, "the religion of protest," holy war and martyrdom, "the ideology which inspires *mojaheds* (men fighting a holy war) and *raushanfekran* (the enlightened) and which creates a sense of self-awareness and a responsible leadership," as opposed to Shi'ism, the theology of *mujtahids* and ulama, is brought to light.[42] He defines *ijtihad* as "the heavy responsibility of all Shi'i individuals," as an independent research done for "the sake of the people" to keep religion alive and relevant to the changing conditions and the exigencies of time.[43] True to the tradition of the mystics' and the theosophers' opposition to the *fuqaha,* he holds the ulama who, he claims, have through the centuries neglected their duties and narrowed down their science, which is interdisciplinary, to the highly specialized field of jurisprudence, responsible for misleading and keeping the masses in ignorance of their true faith. However, instead of hailing philosophy as the "true science" that reveals the absolute Divine Truth, Shariati, the modern Western trained sociologist, proclaims that only qualified specialists can methodologically analyze religious concepts and scientifically reach the true historical, sociological, and political implications inherent in the Qoranic revelation.

Thus Shariati's aim is not so much to reform as it is to point out the potentially radical notions inherent in some basic Shi'i concepts. Once more the call for change, for revolt against the establishment, expresses itself in religious terms; once more the orthodox interpretation of religion is challenged from outside the official clerical organization. Once more, the millenarian expectation of the Hidden Imam (*entezar*) leads to political activism. To believe in the Occulted Imam, Shariati writes, is to believe in the "comeback of the Golden Age," in the revolution that will bring it about, and in the future reign of peace and justice; it is a progressive, future-oriented ideology, opposed to conservatism, to classicism, to traditionalism. "*Entezar* means futurism," *entezar* is "historical determinism," he again and again emphasizes; "the expecting man is a ready man," ready to fight the final *jehad* which will definitely take place, and revolution will triumph.[44]

Again true to the spirit of Shi'i dissent, twentieth century Iranian thinkers express a deep conviction that only the *raushanfekr* (enlightened) writer can assume the position of the Reformer, the leader. "In the twentieth century," writes Al-e Ahmad, "when a paperback is cheaper than cigarettes," and when writers are born from among the people, there is no need for divine revelations or for prophets to "reveal to mankind the bitter truths of human life. The writers are the new spokesmen."[45] Shariati depicts the function of the *raushanfekr* as that of the "torchbearer," the "scout," whose task is similar to that of earlier prophets, for he gives birth to new social movements, even new cultures.[46] Though twentieth century thinkers expressedly wish, and even attempt, to speak on behalf of the people whose conditions they want to see ameliorated, their tone reflects the same paternalistic attitude towards the masses, and the same self-image as the prophets of the day, the Redeemers, as was expressed by theosophers in past centuries. Shariati specifically declared himself against democracy and popular sovereignty, since "in a backward nation, the people are not in a position to know what is best for them,"[47] and the "principle of democracy is contrary to the principle of revolutionary change and progress. . . . Political leadership based on a new ideology that runs opposite to the thought and tradition of that society, cannot be elected nor supported by that society. Revolutionary leadership is not compatible with democracy."[48]

Shariati is overwhelmingly popular amongst the articulate, socially conscious revolté students of both secular institutions and the *madraseh*,[49] all sharing in common the same anxious desire to remain faithful to their religion and yet be modern. Basically, the growing number of educated youth in modernized Iran tend to seek the reassurance given to them by a modern, highly educated, *farangrafteh* (gone to the West) scholar who tells them it is possible to be both pious and modern; than to listen to the traditionally educated mullas who are clumsily attempting to update their knowledge of Western thought (in order to refute it better) and use a more "relevant" language. It is an ideologized Shi'ism they find supremely attractive, rather than the "liberal" ulama's concern with updating the concept and function of *ijtihad* to render it a more viable tool of the *mujtahid's* role as leader of the nation. The committed Shi'i's opposition to the sociopolitical and economic establishment displays a deep concern, not so much with the individual faith itself, as with the implications and consequences of modernization to their living conditions. If anything, Shariati's fundamental interest in religion lies in its role as a social force, a revolutionary banner that would rally the "oppressed masses" to a "holy cause." A careful analysis of his thought would show that his fundamental aim is secular: to make the individual Shi'i feel responsible for his destiny; to erase the notion that men are subject to external forces. The "alienated condition" is no longer acceptable. The "great expectation" has to be realized here and now, for this is the time when the masses, fully initiated to their rights and demands, must fight for them.

Conclusion

Imami Shi'ism, which has dominated Iranian thought for so many centuries, has proved to be an important vehicle for intellectual continuity and change. In a remarkable fashion, despite the great hostility the organized orthodox leadership displayed towards heterodox views, especially in the Safavid and Qajar periods, it has accommodated novel and radical ideas as exposed by progressive-minded men in revolt against the "stifling narrowmindedness" of the official religion. It constantly kept a door open to divergent outlooks that reflected the changing conditions and mood of the time, and thus periodically offered a more or less direct challenge to the conservative view of the sociocultural establishment.

Dissent in Iranian intellectual history almost always expressed itself in terms and fashion relevant to the sociopolitical situation of the age. In the Safavid and early Qajar periods, when individual consciousness and identity were indistinguishable from the Shi'i consciousness, both at the "mass" and "elite" levels, mystics and philosophers channeled their opposition exclusively into metaphysics and theology, aiming at the orthodox ulama's intellectual dominance. The Shaikhi reform movement, progressive as far as the dogma was concerned, was politically and socially conservative, reinforcing the traditional elitist conception of knowledge and leadership. In the middle of the nineteenth century, the Babi episode both represents the tradition of messianic revolts in Iranian history, as well as marks the beginning of radicalization and socialization of religious dissent.

By the end of the nineteenth century, when fresh ideas were gradually imported from the West, and when, simultaneously, national consciousness was aroused by contact with the same West which endangered the political and economic independence of the country, the secularization of Shi'i dissent effectively took place. Appalled by their nation's scientific and political backwardness, the late nineteenth century thinkers turned against the traditional sciences of theology and metaphysics and against its respective spokesmen on the one hand—and the corrupt, traditionally despotic Qajar government on the other. By the extreme force and vehemence of their convictions, they succeeded in turning purely literary disputes into political and social movements for change.

In the twentieth century, as the Pahlavi regime harshly and rapidly implemented modernizing and secularizing policies, opposition reverted to traditionalist, religious, Shi'i rhetoric. In the name of Islam, of the expected Imam, and in memory of the martyred third Imam Hosain, the nationalist, essentially secularist opponents of the absolute power of the government chose to unite their cause to that of the ulama, despite the latter's basically traditional views. The Iranian intellectuals have been able to play a dominant role as effective opinion makers and ideologists; yet, in the absence of organized political parties, their political action could not succeed without the support of the organized ulama leadership. Hence, the recent alliance between the secular radicals and the orthodox theologians, an alliance that might prove to be as explosive, if not more so, than the one created in the period of the Constitutional Revolution. For, despite common religious rhetoric and a common immediate political aim (the fall of the Pahlavis), contemporary Shi'i radicals, in their world outlook and in their pragmatic national program, are as fundamentally opposed to the Shi'i orthodox theologians as the *urafa* and the nineteenth century secular reformers were before them. Despite the widespread popularity of Khomaini as a symbolic figure of Shi'ism, the revolutionary mood of 1979-80, far from being fundamentalist, is for radical sociopolitical change.

3

The Transformation of Health Care in Modern Iranian History

Byron J. Good

In the nineteenth century Marx and Engels analyzed the transformation of the world order brought about by industrialization in the capitalist West.[1] Production, control of resources, and marketing had begun to be "cosmopolitan," drawing non-Western societies into new relationships with the West and initiating broad transformation within these societies. Intellectual production—including scientific and technological knowledge—had become cosmopolitan as had economic production.

The economic and intellectual transformation of the world order provided the structural context for medical change in developing nations. This paper analyzes the transformation of health care in Iran since the mid-nineteenth century. It criticizes the diffusionist model commonly employed for the analysis of medical change, and briefly outlines an alternative approach. It analyzes the relationship between changes in Iranian health care and political and socioeconomic transformations, presenting data from research in a provincial town (Maragheh). And, it describes inequalities and contradictions in Iranian health care that resulted from the structure of the evolving medical system.

A theoretical paradigm for the analysis of how medical care has changed in non-Western societies is widely shared by social scientists and specialists in world public health care. This holds that scientific medicine developed in the West and rapidly achieved dominance because of the superiority of its therapeutic efficacy. From the West scientific medicine diffused to non-Western societies, conveyed by colonial and missionary physicians, public health specialists, and local physicians trained in Western medicine. According to this paradigm, the failures of modern medicine in non-Western societies resulted from cultural conflicts, difficulties in establishing modern medical institutions, and an inability to pay the cost of modern health care. Research has focused on who introduced Western medicine (the "agents" of change), the response of the local population, how modern medical institutions developed, how they affected health, and how they may be made more effective.

Each discipline has its variant of the diffusionist model. Anthropologists focus on the interaction between conflicting medical cultures as modern medicine diffuses into small communities. Analytic terms reflect this perspective: agents of change, innovators, adopters;[2] culture brokers, role adaptation by traditional healers;[3] traditional beliefs versus medical modernization, culture conflict, cognitive dissonance;[4] and the hierarchy of resort to modern, syncretic, or traditional medicine.[5] Historians discuss the introduction of Western medical theories in non-Western societies and the response of indigenous practitioners and intellectuals. International health care planners often conceive of their task as the export of scientific medicine to societies in which health care is absent.

Diffusionist analyses of medical change involve several assumptions: that cosmopolitan medicine contributes greatly to lower mortality rates and is clearly superior to other medical systems; that because medicine is scientific, it is basically unaffected by social context and export to new settings; and that clinical medicine is truly scientific. These assumptions have been challenged by recent scholarship. First, current research shows that the rise of modern medicine had little role in the decline of morbidity and mortality rates in the West,[6] and that even the best medical efforts are relatively powerless in conditions of poverty and underdevelopment.[7] Second, studies increasingly show that medicine is fundamentally a social phenomenon, deeply embedded in the structure of social relations in a society. Historians have shown that the birth of the clinic and the asylum, as well as the development of medical science and clinical discourse, were closely linked to social and economic changes in European society.[8] Recent Marxist critiques indicate that biomedical theory and the contemporary health care industry are not value-free or context-independent.[9] There has been compelling evidence, provided by the radical transformation of health care in China and Cuba, that the "underdevelopment" of health care in third world nations is grounded in the sociopolitical structure of those societies and in their relationship to industrial nations.[10]

The work of Navarro, Althusser and others suggests alternatives to the diffusionist model of medical change. Their work indicates that analysis should focus, not on the transfer of Western medicine to economically underdeveloped societies, but rather on the relationship between societal transformations and basic changes in the structure of medical institutions. Althusser's analysis of science as a mode of production provides a conceptual framework for linking the transformation of medical institutions, considered as modes of production of medical knowledge and practice, and changes in economic and political structures.[11] The following questions are thus posed for historical analysis: What was the relationship between the transformation of the medical system and political and economic changes during critical periods in history? For both traditional and emerging forms of care, who produced medical knowledge and practice, and whose interests were served by newer medical institutions? How did patterns of domination of medical care affect the distribution of medical resources, the focus of medical research, and the emerging structure of health care? How have concepts of therapeutic power changed, and how are they related to the structure of power? How have social relationships within medical institutions—between practitioners and patients, among different categories of practitioners—reflected changes in social stratification? And how are the objects of medical attention influenced by the mode of medical production?

Critical analysis allows reinterpretation of the rise of cosmopolitan medicine in non-Western societies, focusing on the realtionship between imperialist political and economic domination and the transformation of health care. Western medicine became "cosmopolitan" in the nineteenth century, before its efficacy was significantly superior to that of the great medical systems with which it then competed. Nations such as Iran, China, and India became dependent on the imperialist powers, and this dependence played a crucial role in the transformation of their medical care. Understanding medical change in Iran requires historical analysis of the relationship among the structure of health care, the dependence upon foreign powers engendered in late nineteenth century Iran, the social and political reorganization of the society under the Pahlavi dynasty, and the interests served by the newer medical system. This paper will explore the transformation of Iranian health care and describe the contradictions within the medical system that have resulted.

Health Care in Maragheh:
Historical and Ethnographic Background

Maragheh is a Turki-speaking town in East Azerbaijan. Its population in 1974 was ca. 63,000 people. It is an agricultural center with a large bazaar and a history of wealthy landlords; it is religiously conservative with a rich tradition of dramatic ritual performances and since the 1930s it has been a bureaucratic center of a sub-province *(shahrestan)*. Maragheh has long been a medical center for the small towns and villages of the surrounding area. While Iranian villages traditionally have had bonesetters, midwives, prayer writers, and persons with special knowledge in the efficacy of local herbs, the hakims or traditional physicians, who carried on the high tradition of Galenic-Islamic medicine, were confined primarily to cities and to towns like Maragheh.

In 1974 Maragheh had a complex medical system comprising institutions of cosmopolitan medicine, folk and popular practice of Galenic-Islamic medicine, a sacred tradition of healing, and various forms of popular health care. Maragheh had two hospitals, operated by the Red Lion and Sun (the Iranian member of the International Red Cross), public health and malaria offices, a public clinic, a maternal and child health center with a family planning program, approximately 24 private physicians (most of whom also worked in the local army base or in one of the public agencies), 7 pharmacies, and a number of injectors *(pezeshkiyar*—"physician's aide").

While only cosmopolitan medicine had official sanction and government support during recent decades, older people in Maragheh clearly remember the days when the hakims were the town's doctors. The hakims were the high practitioners of "Galenic-Islamic Medicine," the classical tradition translated from Greek into Persian and Arabic and practiced for centuries in hospitals and clinics throughout the Islamic world.[12] Some hakims studied the classical texts of Avicenna or Razi, pharmaceutical texts, or traditional religious/medical texts such as *Medicine of the Prophet*[13] or *Medicine of Imam Reza;* others simply trained as apprentices. Hakims divided medical tasks with a variety of medical "auxiliaries"—herb sellers, bone-setters, midwives, specialists in cupping, and barbers who specialized in bleeding and circumcision, provided leeches, and made skin ointments. Prior to 1930, Galenic-Islamic medicine was dominant in Maragheh, and hakims were at the top of the medical division of labor. By the 1970s, while no hakims remained in Maragheh, folk specialists and popular medical practice carried on the Galenic-

Islamic tradition. Sellers of herbal medicines, traditional orthopedists, midwives, and neighborhood specialists in cupping and leeching practiced full or part-time in the bazaar and neighborhoods.

Specialists in sacred medicine also practiced in Maragheh. Writers of curative prayers *(du'a nevis)* specialize in techniques of divination based on Islamic and Indian astrology. They write curative prayers for patients whose problems are diagnosed as caused by evil *(bad nazar)*, *jinns*, intentional magic *(jadugeri)*, or "fright." Sacred medicine provides a flexible framework within which emotional or psychosocial problems are interpreted and treated.

All three of these major traditions of medicine are combined in popular medicine. The popular medical sector comprises a widely shared medical culture that shapes individuals' experience of their illness, structures care given at home, and provides the logic for resort to specialists. Popular care includes dieting, herbal medicines, religious or magical rites, vows, and visits to shrines, and is provided at home or in the sufferer's primary network of family and friends. The popular sector provides sole treatment for the majority of all illnesses.

In late Qajar Iran, the structure of health care could be characterized as decentralized, relatively self-sustaining and autonomous in small cities, institutionally centered in the bazaar, and dependent on international trade only for special herbs and spices. This structure was closely related to that of political and economic institutions in Iran, and provides the context for understanding the transformation of the health care system.

Social and Medical Transformation in Late Qajar Iran:
Political and Economic Transformation

Power in nineteenth century Iran was decentralized, with provincial areas controlled by relatively autonomous tribal leaders and governors. By the late nineteenth century, the development of markets for Iranian products began to transform economic structures in Iran, creating new bases of power behind the traditional forms and breaking down "the old local and national seclusion and self-sufficiency."[14] Self-sufficient village economies were transformed, as cotton, opium, silk, dried fruits and nuts, and wheat became valuable on international markets. Landlords and tribal khans invested in estates, and the government systematized the sale of provincial offices to satisfy their demand for cash, thus increasing tax-farming.[15] Many Iranian landlords gradually ceased to be patriarchal leaders of basically self-sufficient agrarian systems, and became instead entrepreneurs disposing of cash crops in foreign markets.[16] Villagers were increasingly subject to exploitation and the vagaries of international markets. At the same time, the government tried to acquire cash to buy arms and other Western goods by selling concessions for natural resources and exclusive rights to carry out important industrial and financial functions. As a result, Iran became increasingly subject to the interest of foreign capitalists and the imperialist powers.[17]

Medicine and Imperialism

These structural changes provide the context for developments in health care during the nineteenth and early twentieth centuries. Western medicine was introduced into Iran at a time when the West was demonstrating its economic superiority, but before the efficacy of Western therapeutics was significantly superior to that of Galenic-Islamic medicine. European physicians did not practice medicine in Iran to win the hearts and minds of the populace for purposes of colonial pacification[18] or to improve the health conditions of the indigenous labor force in imperialist enterprises.[19] But European and American physicians were an intimate part of the imperialist powers' relationship to Iran. Beginning as early as the French and British missions to the court of Fath Ali Shah in the early nineteenth century, European physicians accompanied their ambassadors. Treatment of the shah and his household not only gave the physician influence, but also inclined the monarch to look with favor upon the physician's nation and its enterprises. The British Foreign Office and the East India Company seem to have been slow to recognize this source of influence. In the mid-1830s the British envoy to Iran was forced to remind the home office of the opportunity:

> Sir John [Campbell] again and again wrote [to the East India Company] pointing out that "the presence of a medical officer, whose duties were exclusively medical and whose time, unemployed in other duties, could be devoted to the influential personages in Persian society, would be productive of solid good to British interests and would be calculated to improve and maintain the existing friendly intercourse between the English on one side and the Court and Persian peoples on the other." But no notice was taken of his letters.[20]

By the middle of the nineteenth century, with Sir John McNeill and other physician-diplomats, the British learned the value of using a trusted personal physician to the shah and the royal harem to advance their government's policies.

In addition to physicians who served their foreign services, a variety of others practiced Western medicine and helped develop new medical institutions in Iran. Physicians were employed by the British Telegraph Company and the Oil Company. European and American churches established missionary medical clinics, hospitals, and schools, particularly in areas with a large Christian population (e.g., Urumiyeh, Tabriz, Julfa). A faculty of medicine was established in the Dar ol-Fonun, the first Western technical university established in 1851, and became a focus for continuous influence by European medicine. Medical texts were translated into Persian; several generations of Iranian physicians were trained; and Naser od-Din Shah drew his medical advisers and personal physicians from the school.[21] A Sanitary Council was established in 1871 by Dr. Tholozan, Chief Physician to the shah and a professor at the Dar ol-Funun, to meet the threat of epidemic following the famine of 1869–72. Tholozan attempted to send Iranian physicians trained in the Dar ol-Fonun to the provinces to innoculate and act as sentinels for epidemics, but the Council showed little interest in the public health problems of Iran until after the victory of the Constitutionalists, when a Persian physician was named president of the Council (in 1907) and given a budget (in 1911). The Council broke down in the chaos of World War I. Finally, Western medicine was represented by the nineteenth century Quarantine Services established by the Russians on the Afghan border and the British Colonial Office in the Persian Gulf.

None of these institutions was devoted to the important health care problems of Iran. They were established in the interests of the European population, Christian minorities, or the Iranian elite. All served political as well as health purposes. For example, the Quarantine Services were established to protect European nations (not Iran) from epidemics of cholera and the plague that passed from India and the Far East.[22] They also served political functions: the Russians used a quarantine in 1906 to strangle British trade from northwest India, and the British used the Quarantine Service (especially on the Island of Hormuz) to maintain their control of the Gulf.[23]

Perhaps the most important effect of these medical institutions was to foster a cadre of Iranian physicians trained in cosmopolitan medicine. Such physicians, most of whom were from upper class families, adopted Western conceptions of the medical profession. For example, the Constitutional Assembly passed licensing laws for medicine (1911) and pharmacy (1919), requiring a diploma from a Western-style school or passage of an examination.[24] Such laws served the interests of the medical elite but were inappropriate to the needs of Iran, since practically no physicians or druggists trained in Western medicine were found in towns or villages.[25] Thus, by the early twentieth century, physicians trained in cosmopolitan medicine were recruited from the elite, practiced medicine in the major cities, especially Tehran, and supported their position through medical licensing laws.

Health Care in Maragheh

While basic political, economic and medical change was underway in Iran by the beginning of the twentieth century, provincial towns like Maragheh were only beginning to be drawn into dependence on national and international centers. Politically, Maragheh was still dominated by the independent Moqaddam governors.[16] And while some physicians trained in cosmopolitan medicine practiced in Maragheh and synthetic drugs were being added to the traditional pharmacopoeia, health care in the town was produced with relatively little dependence on national and international resources.

The hakims in Maragheh during the decades prior to Reza Shah are remembered as having several modes of practice. Older persons describe some hakims as learned men who received clients seated on carpets in special rooms of their homes. Patients would gather and sit in a circle before them. The hakim would hear their symptoms and prescribe a herbal medicine. His apprentice would then weigh and mix the herbs, and the hakim would be paid only for the drugs. Women at times would not enter, but would present their complaints and receive their medicines through a small window in the wall behind the hakim.[27]

The second mode of practice was similar to that of a bazaar shopkeeper. Some hakims' shops were in caravanserais or in a central part of the bazaar. Jars and cans of herbs—powders, dried flowers, seeds, roots—lined the walls and the counter. Patients would enter, tell their symptoms, and ask for medicine. The hakim might examine the patients briefly, would prescribe a drug, weigh and mix the herbs, and instruct the patient in its preparation (boiling, brewing, etc.) and dosage.

According to informants, the hakim's physical examination of the patient was not important. One old man remembered simply, "there was no examination in those days." Others remember a limited examination. Pulse was checked for the condition of the heart, blood pressure, and rate of heartbeat. When called for, the body, face, and throat were examined visually, and the abdomen palpated for signs of swelling or tumors. Examination and treatment were normally done in public. Fees were charged only for the drugs not for the examination.

While the normal route to becoming a hakim was apprenticeship, the history of the hakims in Maragheh indicates diverse training. Several hakims are remembered to have been religious scholars who learned medicine by reading the texts, and not through apprenticeship. (It is unclear whether they got clinical training.) Of those hakims trained as apprentices, some were boys hired to do the routine manual labor, others were real students of the master. A contemporary druggist told of his own apprenticeship. Although some 20 years later than the period we are describing, and a time when chemical drugs had largely replaced herbs, the general style of training was the same.

> R. said that his *ostad* ["master," "teacher"], Hajji Hasan, would sit at the table in his shop. People would come in and present symptoms, and he would prescribe medicine for them—usually "powders" or chemical medicines. Then the apprentices [*shagerds*] would make up the medicines for the patient. (There was one apprentice besides himself. He said hakims sometimes had two apprentices; never three.) He was trained gradually. First, he was acquainted with the various chemicals: he simply learned their names, their place on the shelves, etc. Then he was taught what the various chemicals did for the body, what illnesses they were good for, etc. As he remembered, his *ostad* did not keep pharmaceutical books in the shop. R. remained with his *ostad* for nearly 15 years.[28]

There was no clear pattern of graduation from the role of apprentice to that of *ostad*. No one declared the apprentice ready for practice or to be a master.[29] Some apprentices began their own practice when they knew very little. Others worked with their master for 15 or 20 years before beginning independent practice. A few remained loyal apprentices until the death of their master.

The hakims were diverse in status and education. Most informants characterize the hakims as being "bazaari" in status, unlike the physicians of today: "They were common people. They began as apprentices, and you know that working as an apprentice you don't make much money. Common people, not rich people, would go into this kind of thing." Several Maragheh hakims, however, were learned and highly respected. Some were even quite wealthy. The most famous, Hakim Khoylu, is remembered as affluent, modern before his time, and a philanthropist. His wife dressed in Paris fashions, and he donated money for building modern schools. Another, Hakim Hosain, was the private physician of the governor Shoja od-Dauleh. His brother and son were also hakims in Maragheh. A third well-educated hakim was the son of the *mujtahid* of Maragheh and learned to practice medicine only from books, never as a *shagerd*. On the other hand, one hakim is remembered as being of low status and a man of little learning:

> Hakim Reza Khan was a *shagerd* of an Armenian hakim in Tabriz named George. But he just "wrapped up the medicine" for him. He came to Maragheh and practiced medicine, although he didn't know anything. He was just "George's Horseman." Once a man came to call him to look at a sick child in his home. He found Reza Khan just closing up his shop. Reza Khan said, "Oh God, you know I don't know anything about medicine, only *You* give them healing!"

Thus the hakims varied in background and learning. They were not simply bazaaris, but they rarely had the status or wealth of modern physicians.

In 1921 there were approximately 13 hakims in Maragheh (see Table 1).[30] Eleven were *alafi* hakims ("herbal physicians"), three of whom were trained as mullas. Two were Armenian "surgeons," trained in Russia and specializing in treating wounds and injuries, removing bullets, and treating venereal disease in males.[31] About half practiced in their homes and half had shops in the bazaar. Several changes began to occur during the first decades of the twentieth century. First, Maragheh hakims began to use a number of new drugs discovered or synthesized in the West. These imported drugs included quinine for malaria, endemic in Maragheh, and probably included salvarsan (Paul Erlich's "606," an arsenic compound used against infectious diseases and sold in Germany from ca. 1910), emetin (an alkaloid used against dysentery), sodium bicarbonate, and aspirin.

Second, physicians trained outside Maragheh and outside traditional Iranian medicine began to practice. Russian schools, the Presbyterian missions, and the Dar ol-Fonun each trained practitioners who began to practice in Maragheh. Third, the population learned

Table 1. Physicians in Maragheh from 1921 through 1974

Year	Total	Hakims			Doctors
		Herbal [Alafi] Hakims	Traditional Surgeons	Permitted [Mojaz] Hakims	
1921	13	11	2	—	—
1930	10	7	1	—	2
1935	12	0-1	1	4-5	6
1950	8	—	—	1	7
1974	24	—	—	1	23

that Western medicine was available to patients who traveled to missionary facilities in Tabriz, Urumiyeh, or Tehran.[32] Hence, Maragheh came into contact with Western medicine. While some new elements were added to medical practice in Maragheh, these were only portents of major structural changes that occurred under Reza Shah (1925-41).

The Reforms of Reza Shah: Social Transformation and Medical Change

When Reza Shah came to power, he began to centralize political and military control over Iran and to concentrate power in his own hands. He built a strong and loyal military to challenge the autonomy of tribal leaders and provincial rulers, and he developed a centralized bureaucracy that replaced traditional institutions in carrying out many educational, legal, and other functions.

From the first years of his rule, Reza Shah supported nationalization of the health care institutions that were part of the imperialist legacy, and he undertook to establish a new system of public health care. In 1923 the Majlis passed a law that no foreigner could hold a public position in the Imperial Persian Hospital (the "English Hospital") without direct appointment by the Majlis. A few months later the last two British physicians were forced to leave, and Iranians assumed control of the hospital.[33] In 1928, after a lengthy struggle, the Quarantine Services on the Persian Gulf were wrested from British control.[34]

An embryonic public health care system existed when Reza Shah came to power, but it was poorly supported and badly run. Gilmour's report to the League of Nations gives an excellent account of the structure of public health care in Iran in the early 1920s.[35] The Sanitary Council had become the governing council and the nucleus for a Department of Public Health. The Quarantine and the Vaccination Services were under its charge. Sanitary commissions were formed in five provincial towns, and medical officers (48 in 1925) were appointed in a number of cities and towns. The municipality (*baladiyeh*) of Tehran was subordinate to the prime minister and charged with public health and medical functions. The city controlled the water supply, a beggar asylum, a nursery and orphange, a mental hospital, public latrines, public baths, an ice warehouse, and facilities for the washing and burial of corpses. A Medical Division charged its five medical officers with a wide range of inspection duties. For example, each officer was expected (rather optimistically) to "prevent the spread of malaria and infectious diseases by giving instructions concerning tanks, the water reservoirs and the privies to the owners of the houses. He must inspect the hygienic state of the quarter and prevent the spread of epidemics."[36] In addition, the Medical Division was in charge of eight public dispensaries (which saw over 95,000 patients in 1923) and a hospital. While this structure seems impressive, in reality public health received very little support. In 1925 Dr. Amir Alam, addressing the Sanitary Council as he left its presidency to become Director of Public Health, assessed the state of sanitary work in the country:

> For the last two years the general sanitary situation of the country has left much to be desired. Provincial Medical Officers of Health, having failed to receive for several months their salaries, have for the most part abandoned their posts. An indifference, a *laissez aller*, truly regretable reigns with regard to all questions of public health. Our plans, our schemes, our cries, have had no chance of finding an echo in governmental or parliamentary circles.[37]

During the 1930s, Reza Shah supported licensing regulations and developed a strong public health program that reached into the provinces. In 1927 and 1930 new procedures for licensing physicians and druggists were developed and for the first time enforced in the provinces. These required that all new physicians hold a diploma from a Western-style school of medicine, and that all physicians then practicing without a diploma pass a licensing exam if they were to continue their practice. Reza Shah established a Ministry of Health with provincial offices to enforce these standards and undertake sanitary reform. In addition, the Red Lion and Sun Society was established to provide hospitals and basic primary care along with the Ministry.

The distribution of medical resources, however, reflected the basic interests of Reza Shah and the elite. For example, in the years of intensive reforms (1928-38), only 2.3 percent of the total budget was devoted to public health.[38] Public health was secondary to health care for the military. Sir Harry Sinderson, physician to King Faisal of Iraq, noted in 1935 when Faisal visited Iran:

> The Court Physician went on to unfold an elaborate medical programme which the Council of Ministers had in view, but it appeared to me that in this the civil population was regarded as secondary in importance to the army. . . . No matter what I asked concerning military medical facilities, his invariable answer was either that they already existed or were about to be provided. With regard to the same facilities

for the civil population, his usual reply was that they were either "being considered" or "coming later."[39]

I learned from other sources that the so-called Medical School was embryonic, and the National Hospital for civilians a poor second to its military equivalent. That soldiers were cared for better than civilians in respect to medical care was obvious.[40]

Reza Shah's Reforms in Maragheh

Reza Shah's reforms, aimed at centralization and control of public services, began to affect Maragheh significantly in about 1930. Reforms were achieved through the bureaucratization of the provincial administration and police, the secularization of the courts, and the deployment of the army and gendarmerie. The autonomous political and administrative institutions of the community were dismantled and replaced with the central government's bureaucracy. The political institutions of the Moqaddam governors were supplanted, and a national gendarmerie replaced the local constabulary controlled by the Moqaddams. A secular court system replaced the religious courts between 1928 and 1936. During the 1930s and 1940s, new educational institutions began to replace the religious *maktabs* and the apprenticeship system of the bazaar as the dominant form of education. And, a professional system of cosmopolitan medicine was established, stimulated and controlled by an office of the Ministry of Health. In each of these sectors, the control of functions traditionally carried out by relatively autonomous practitioners, centered in the bazaar, was taken over by representatives of national bureaucracies. Provincial Iran lost its autonomy and became dependent upon national and international centers for the generation of knowledge, the training of "professional" practitioners, and the control of social services.

The Ministry of Health was a major institutional focus for medical change in Maragheh. A local office of the Ministry of Health was established in Maragheh in 1930, with a university-trained physician as its first director. Unlike physicians hired simply to practice in the clinics and hospitals of the Ministry or the Red Lion and Sun, the Directors of the Ministry of Health Office played an important role in local medical politics. They invited licensed druggists to establish their practice in Maragheh, directed sanitation and vaccination efforts, and initiated proceedings to control the practice of licensed and unlicensed practitioners.

Between 1930 and 1932 the Ministry of Health Office enforced the licensing regulations in Maragheh. In 1932 both physicians and druggists were given their last opportunity to take an examination and be licensed as *mojaz* ("permitted") physicians or pharmacists. The examination covered internal medicine, pharmacology, and traditional Galenic-Islamic medicine. There were approximately 11 physicians practicing in Maragheh at this time: seven hakims, two "doctors" (one trained in Russia, one in the Presbyterian Mission in Urumiyeh), one "surgeon" trained in Russia, and one man remembered as an "injection doctor." Five hakims took the examination, passed it and continued to practice with a new emphasis on chemical drug therapy. On the other hand, at least two hakims simply gave up their practice at this time. Both were mullas and had alternate sources of income.[41] A third group of hakims ignored the licensing requirements and continued their practice illegally.[42]

Licensing gave impetus to significant changes in medical practice by physicians in Maragheh. In order to pass the examination, many of the physicians read translations of European medical texts, learned to use medical instruments, and began to make more use of synthetic drugs. For example, Hakim Gholam Hosain was trained as the apprentice to Hakim Khoylu. His son described how preparation for the licensing examination affected his medical practice:

> He practiced mostly old medicine before 1930. When it was time to take the exam he went to Tabriz. There he studied with Dr. Taufiq, who had studied medicine in Switzerland. Because there were no medical books at that time in Persian *(sic)*, he used Istanbul Turkish translations of European medical texts. He studied both theory and practice. He learned from Dr. Taufiq how to use a stethoscope, how to take blood pressure, and how to do examinations of women. He then took the licensing exam and passed. This was the most important thing in changing the way he practiced medicine.

While it is impossible to judge the extent to which he learned Western medical theory, Hakim Gholam Hosain studied Western medical texts, changed his style of examination (implying a change in diagnosis), and increased his use of chemical drugs.

Thus by the mid-1930s a new mode of medical practice was emerging in Maragheh. Informants remember 12 physicians who practiced in 1935. Six were called "doktor" and were trained in Western medicine.[43] Six were called "hakim;" of these, four or five had passed the licensing exam, and one was an Armenian "surgeon" trained in Russia who practiced with the aid of an apprentice. The restriction of medical training to university medical schools marked the development of a new category of "professional" physicians. Physicians began to be recruited from a new class, because of the cost of university education. The increased status and earning power of physicians meant that sons of landlords and the elite, not just bazaaris, chose to be doctors. The change in status of the physician had profound implications for medical practice, increasing differences in status and medical knowledge between practitioners and patients and leading to physician disregard for lower-class patients.[44]

A second change in medical practice was the greatly increased use of chemical therapy. Most new drugs were in "powder" form.[45] Physicians wrote formulae, and pharmacies were developed to mix and prepare the drugs. The common drugs included quinine; salvarsan and prontosil (sulphanilamide), used as antibiotics; phenacetin, pyramidon, antipyrine, aspirin, and caffein, used as pain relievers; emetin and medicinal opium products, such as elixir of paragoric, for diarrhea; a variety of antacids; and luminal (phenobarbital), for nervous problems. During the 1930s many physicians began to write prescriptions rather than sell their own medicine. They began charging a fee for examining the patient, and the use of apprentices as aides and students declined.

These changes were accompanied by the rise of new pharmacies. Modern drugstores were opened in Maragheh for the first time between 1934 and 1936. The first was opened by the Red Lion and Sun; with the help of the first Director of Public Health, the town's first university-trained pharmacist was hired. The second drugstore was opened by the owner of a herbal medicine shop *(attar)*, who moved his shop from the bazaar to the new main street and recruited a licensed *(mojaz)* pharmacist from Tabriz. The third pharmacy was opened by a former apprentice to Hakim Khoylu. After 20 years of apprenticeship, learning to dispense herbal and chemical medicines, he opened a shop in the bazaar, worked for several years in a drugstore, and finally opened his own pharmacy on the main street. His son, who still ran the drugstore in 1974, recalled that his father practiced much as a hakim. He sat at a table, heard complaints, and prescribed medications that his apprentices prepared. Two of his apprentices eventually opened their own drugstores and were licensed as "Pharmacist's Aides."

The role of the druggist thus developed in continuity with the role of the hakim. The slow differentiation of distinct health care roles— physician, pharmacist, pharmacists' aide, physicians' aide—from the single role of hakim led to continuing conflicts among practitioners in these roles. During the past two decades, Ministry of Health officials commonly brought legal action against druggists for dispensing drugs without prescription. Druggists trained in the apprenticeship system fought the requirement that a university-trained pharmacist be paid to take legal responsibility for their practice. And, physicians sought to control any *pezeshkiyar* they suspected of selling drugs.[46]

Major changes occurred in the structure of health care in Maragheh during the reign of Reza Shah. Physicians ceased being bazaari specialists who learned their trade primarily as apprentices and who practiced in their homes, in mosques, or in the bazaar. They became professionals, elevated in status and wealth, trained in cosmopolitan learning in Iranian or foreign medical schools, given legal monopoly over medical practice, and practiced in special offices. Local health care, like education and the judiciary, lost its independence and autonomy. It became integrated into the national authority structure, dependent on national and international centers for knowledge, training, support, and pharmaceutics.

Health Care Since World War II

At the beginning of the 1950s, Iran remained a very poor nation with severe public health conditions. A study by Overseas Consultants, Inc. in 1949 estimated infant mortality to be over 50 percent, blaming poor sanitary conditions and communicable diseases. Malaria was rated the most important public health problem in the country, with an annual incidence of over five million cases in a population of about 17 million.[47] Tuberculosis, trachoma, and syphilis were ranked as widespread and serious problems (syphilis was estimated to infect 40 to 50 percent of the adult population of Tehran). The report noted that while the Ministry of Health employed 4,700 persons "none within its employ has had public health training. The health officers and other medical employees are trained only in clinical medicine."[48]

In the 1950s several steps were taken to address these health problems. Public health was elevated within national health policy and within the Ministry of Health, with vaccinations and environmental sanitation being given high priority. With the help of the American Point IV, World Health Organization, and the Near East Foundation, a campaign against malaria was launched in 1951. And, the government began to extend primary health care to the provincial towns and rural areas. Hospitals and clinics were built, and medical schools were established in Tabriz in 1946, and in Shiraz, Mashhad, and Isfahan in 1949 to train physicians to staff the new facilities. Between 1947 and 1974 the number of physicians in Iran rose from 2,300 to 9,500 (a doctor to population ratio of 1:7,500 and 1:3,470, respectively). The number of hospital beds rose from 10,280 to 40,000.[49]

Fundamental problems remained, however. In 1974 nearly half of all physicians practiced in Tehran, and one-quarter in 23 other major cities. Many hospitals and clinics were poorly staffed, and the quality of care in public facilities was often extremely low. While vaccination and malaria eradication programs included villages, neither basic public health improvements—improved water supplies, sewage and drainage systems—nor continuous primary care was available to the vast majority of villages.

The contradiction between the goal of widely distributed health care and the desire to provide curative medical facilities modeled on Western, hospital-based medicine became increasingly sharp. The debate over the relative priorities of public health and curative medicine began in the 1950s, and during the 1970s the foremost topic of medical politics was the relative merits of private enterprise medicine (including fee for service and insurance schemes) versus medical care utilizing paramedics and organized by the public welfare bureaucracy. (The relationship of this debate to the structural bases of Iranian health care will be discussed in the conclusion.)

While changes in health care proceeded slowly in small provincial towns, important developments occurred in Maragheh after World War II. Basic sanitary reforms were undertaken, including establishment of a large malaria office and development of a public health office for vaccinations and inspection of public facilities. In the late 1960s a city water and sewage system was installed, although poorer neighborhoods remained without either. In addition, the past three decades saw the continued expansion of the public sector of curative care. In 1974, Maragheh had two hospitals (one surgical, one internal medicine) under the administration of the Red Lion and Sun. The Ministry of Health had a primary care clinic, a large malaria office, and a public health center.[50] The Office of Health in Maragheh was charged with legal responsibility for supervision of all practitioners in the town. In this role it extended professional medicine's authority over the whole system of health care. After the 1950s, these health care institutions in Maragheh were in the hands of a new generation of physicians trained in Iranian medical schools.

The early 1950s were a watershed between generations of physicians in Maragheh. Most of the *mojaz* hakims, the hakims who had passed the licensing exam, had retired or moved out of Maragheh. Several Armenians left Maragheh after the war, and the physicians who remained were nearing retirement age.[51] By the late 1950s, all but one of the six physicians had died, retired, or left Maragheh. There were probably fewer physicians for the size of population at this time than at any other time this century.

In the late 1950s a new generation of physicians began coming to Maragheh. Most were trained in the Iranian provincial universities that had just been established, especially Tabriz, and many were employed by one of the new social insurance programs. In 1956 a large army base was established at the edge of Maragheh, bringing to the town a number of military doctors. They practiced on the base, but also maintained part-time private practices in town.

The pattern of physicians working part-time for the military or a social welfare agency, and part-time privately, has continued until today. In 1974 there were approximately 24 doctors in Maragheh. Of those I have information on, seven worked full-time for a public agency, eleven had public agency positions as well as a private practice, and only one solely a private practice.[52]

Major changes occurred in the structure of medical practice in Maragheh between 1950 and 1974. The number of physicians tripled from 8 to 24. Virtually all were educated in Iran and had government salaries as well as private practices. There was an increasing degree of medical specialization. However, the style of medical practice was unchanged in many respects. In the 1970s, doctors had private offices on the second story of buildings on the main streets. They had waiting rooms (sometimes separated by sex), usually attended by an old watchman who collected fees from patients (10-15 tomans—$1.50-2.00—in 1974). Patients, often accompanied by family members, would enter the physician's office and confer with the doctor briefly. The physician was expected to examine the patient, "write medicine" (i.e., a prescription), and prescribe an appropriate diet. He was not necessarily expected to explain the illness or treatment. Physicians in Maragheh kept no medical records of their patients. They would, however, make house calls in the town for an additional fee.

Along with the new generation of physicians since 1950 came the rise to professional and institutional dominance of physicians and the Ministry of Health. Folk practitioners—midwives, bone-setters, herbalists—continued to practice but were subjected to occasional surveillance and harassment. Druggists' and *pezeshkiyars'* access to chemical drugs made them a greater threat to physicians' monopoly over modern medical practice, and they were controlled accordingly.[53]

After World War II there was a rapid growth of professional, cosmopolitan health care in Maragheh. Important sanitary improvements were achieved, although poorer neighborhoods and surrounding villages were neglected. Both public and private sectors of curative medicine were expanded. And modern, professional medicine used its political power to achieve control over health care institutions in the region.

Analysis and Conclusions

Vincente Navarro argues that application of a liberal model of economic development to the understanding of medical change in underdeveloped societies is deceiving.[54] Models accounting for underdevelopment of health care similar to Rostow's theory of economic development are common.[55] Rostow holds that the critical agents of change are the "diffusion of values" and the "diffusion of capital," and that development "takes place in, is stimulated by, and is channeled through an 'enclave' of the developed, metropolitan economy within each of the underdeveloped countries."[56] Navarro argues to the contrary that excessive cultural and technological dependency and the ineffective use of capital by national and international groups that control resources lead to dual economic and medical systems and *produce* underdeveloped, marginal sectors of these systems. He argues, much as outlined in the introduction of this paper, that a diffusionist model of change should be replaced by critical analysis of the structural transformation of societies and the interrelationship of political, economic, and medical changes in underdeveloped societies.

Since the nineteenth century, medicine has entered the world market and become cosmopolitan, resulting in changes in the modes of production and consumption of health care in developing nations. Traditional health care systems have lost their seclusion and self-sufficiency and become dependent on the dominant West, and new health care structures have developed in relation to the interests served by the health care system.[57] We will use this model to make three observations about the transformation of health care in modern Iranian history.

First, changes in Iranian health care institutions over the last century are best understood as an aspect of the socioeconomic transformation of Iranian society, rather than simply as the transfer of Western medicine to a developing nation. Major medical changes were closely linked to broader transformations in political domination, economic production, and the distribution of resources. In the nineteenth century, medicine was used by foreign powers to gain access to the shah. Institutions of Western medicine, such as the Quarantine Services, were created to serve the interests of European nations rather than those of Iran. Western medicine became influential and fashionable among Iran's elite.

Medical institutions in small, provincial towns like Maragheh first underwent serious changes during the reign of Reza Shah. The production of health care by the hakims, while dependent on the high tradition of Galenic-Islamic medical sciences, was decentralized, relatively autonomous, and self-sustaining. Medical services were sold as a commodity in the bazaar by physicians of bazaari status. During the rule of Reza Shah, health care in Maragheh lost its autonomy and self-sufficiency as did other social and political institutions. Reza Shah established national bureaucracies to carry out functions previously under local control, such as security, education, the courts, and health care. The authority structure of health care was centralized, as was the rest of the bureaucracy; thus medical care in Maragheh became increasingly dependent on national and international centers. Physicians became professionals in social status, and they organized on behalf of their own interests. Landlords and wealthy merchant families in Maragheh began to send their sons to medical school as the potential for prestige and wealth through the new profession became clear. A dual system for the distribution of health care emerged, divided between the free market (fee for service) and a second-class system of public service medicine.

After World War II, the cosmopolitan health care system in Iran expanded and grew in complexity and diversity. Public health programs, insurance schemes, rural health programs, hospitals, and specialty clinics were developed by more than 70 agencies. In Maragheh, basic public health reforms were carried out and both public and private facilities expanded. Development of the medical system served, however, to heighten awareness of inequities in distribution. While Tabriz University had an open heart surgery ward, few villages of Azerbaijan had sanitary water sources. In the 1970s, inherently contradictory demands were placed on the medical system: it should be *both* comparable to health care in the West *and* able to provide equitable and appropriate care to the whole population. The dilemma faced by the medical system reflected broader contradictions in Iranian society between stated goals of socioeconomic progress for the Iranian masses and the management of resources for the benefit of the shah and the elite.

Second, problems of Iranian health care were due less to an inadequate transfer of health care technology and institutions from the West or resistance of the population to medical change than to maldistribution of medical resources and dependency on inappropriate models of health care. The basic plan for the development of health care in Iran was to establish an enclave of high-quality, Western-style medicine, and to diffuse this system gradually to the periphery until the entire nation would be served by health care equivalent to that in modern nations. The model for health care in the "modern enclave" was patterned after specialized, fee for service, hospital-based medicine of Europe and America. The American model was particularly influential, because many leading Iranian physicians were trained in American hospitals. In the 1970s, plans called for the establishment of high technology hospitals where American-trained physicians could practice in settings for which they were trained. For example, in 1975 the Iranian government asked three top American medical schools to help establish an Iranian "Mayo Clinic," the International Medical Center in Tehran, arguing that it would attract Iranian physicians to return from abroad and prevent the Iranian elite from leaving the country for their health care. The modern enclave was to include medical schools modeled on Western ones, in which clinical training would be carried out almost solely in high technology hospital settings. Diffusion of this system to smaller towns and villages was to be accomplished by public sponsorship of hospitals and clinics, by training so many physicians that competition would eventually drive some to more rural areas, and by establishing incentives to entice doctors to practice in undesirable locations.

Several difficulties resulted from this model of health care development. The conceptual model of hospital-based specialty medicine proved inappropriate and unworkable in small Iranian towns and villages. Virtually all Iranian villages lacked potable water supplies, basic sanitary improvement, or any form of continuous primary care. As a result, morbidity and mortality were very high among infants and children. Despite these basic needs, medical progress in Iran was measured in the number of doctors trained and the number of new hospital beds provided. Further expenditures on training more doctors and building more clinics and hospitals had little impact on the health conditions of rural and lower class Iranians.

Medical training in the modern enclave did not prepare physicians for medical practice at the periphery. Physicians trained to treat rare diseases in specialty hospitals found it difficult and unsatisfying to practice in the rural clinics and hospitals in Iran. Residents and recent medical school graduates who came to practice in the Red Lion and

Sun hospitals in Maragheh found the equipment and support staff seriously limited their ability to practice medicine as they were trained. Physicians assigned to the family planning clinic would travel around to the villages to dispense a monthly cycle of contraceptive pills, but were not permitted to treat medical problems of women and infants. Physicians in public clinics in Maragheh and in neighboring rural areas often saw up to 30 patients per hour. None was trained or authorized to organize basic environmental improvements or to train auxiliaries to treat the most common medical problems. Rather than reorganizing medical training to suit the needs of rural Iran, medical schools trained physicians for a type of practice that was impossible in most of the country.

Support for public health and for paramedic models of rural medical care provided a countervailing force within Iranian medical politics. After the 1950s, public health physicians were the primary critics of private enterprise medicine in Iran. Beginning in the early 1970s, programs modeled on the "barefoot doctor" program in China and on other rural auxiliary programs were tried experimentally, supported by W.H.O. and Iranian schools of public health. These programs faced great difficulties. When they were used to fundamentally criticize the structure of medical education and delivery in Iran, the medical power structure—professors and deans of medical schools, leading physician-politicians—reacted strongly on behalf of their own interests, protesting the threat to the "quality" of medical care.[58] The rural health care programs were inadequately supported and faced the resistance of physicians in the health bureaucracy both in Tehran and in the provinces. And the programs were often seen by villagers as being similar to other ventures of the national bureaucracy that led to increased domination by the central government. As a result, the programs had limited success. Resources continued to be dedicated to a relatively small sector of health care, leading to the underdevelopment of medical services for the rest of the society. This suggests our third and final observation.

The structure of Iranian health care and its distribution reflected the interests of the Iranian elite, Iranian physicians and medical schools, international drug companies, and, to some extent, American and European medical schools and health care consulting agencies. This can be demonstrated in a variety of ways. A small sector of high-quality, high-technology medicine was available to the wealthy in Iran; yet it consumed a large proportion of the country's health care resources.[59] Specialized treatment centers and private hospitals, used primarily by the upper classes, were subsidized by the government.

Two-thirds of all medical education costs went to train physicians (the rest for all other medical personnel), despite the fact that approximately 50 percent of all doctors practiced in Tehran and great numbers emigrated to the United States.[60] In addition to supporting health care for the wealthy, the financing of medical education and medical facilities subsidized physicians and hence the upper classes from which most of them came.

In contrast to the elite, the 50 percent of Iranians who lived in villages received almost none of the health care resources, and the lower classes in urban areas were provided limited public health services and extremely poor medical care. A variety of health care programs were developed for the Iranian masses: Health Corps, rural health care workers' programs, Imperial Organization of Social Services clinics, and Red Lion and Sun hospitals. These, along with insurance programs for government workers, were established to blunt political criticism of medical maldistribution and to meet popular demands for service. They did not, however, basically alter the inequity of the medical system.

Table 2. Visits to Private Physicians and Public Clinics per Household, by Class/Status Groups in Maragheh

	Professionals, High Civil Servants	High Bazaari	Low Civil Servants	Mid/Low Bazaari	Workers
MALE RESPONDENTS					
Number of Respondents	62	16	9	59	74
Percent Visited Private Doctor in Maragheh in Two Weeks	33%	25%	44%	30%	9%
Percent Visited Public Clinic in Eight Months	5%	6%	10%	13%	34%
FEMALE RESPONDENTS					
Number of Respondents	52	22	40	89	64
Percent Visited Private Doctor in Maragheh In Two Weeks	36%	45%	40%	17%	15%
Percent Visited Public Clinic in Eight Months	12%	12%	32%	33%	51%

Utilization of health care resources in Maragheh provides an example of the distribution of medical resources in Iran. Since 1960, important public health improvements were carried out in Maragheh; yet the poorest neighborhoods were not provided running water or public sewage disposal. Utilization of curative medical facilities also varied directly by social class. Table 2, reporting data from a survey carried out in 1973,[61] shows that social class varied directly with consultation of private physicians and indirectly with dependence on public health clinics. While the wealthy and the civil servants could afford to visit private physicians, the poor of the town relied heavily on the public clinics, which they knew provided inadequate care. The average consultation in the public clinic lasted less than two minutes!

The structure of health care also reflected interests of the international medical industry. The European drug trade first brought cosmopolitan medicine to Maragheh. By the 1970s, many university graduate pharmacists were employed as sales representatives of international pharmaceutical companies. They traveled throughout Iran, encouraging prescription of their drugs. Through such practices, drug companies strongly supported the excessive use of drugs in Iran, which resulted in high levels of iatrogenic problems. Much the same could be said for the role of other producers of medical technology; their interests were an important force in the development of health care structures and medical practice in twentieth century Iran.

In conclusion, this paper has outlined some aspects of the transformation of health care in Iran. It argues that a conception of medical change as the diffusion of medical values and technology from the West to medically underdeveloped societies fails to understand the extent to which medical change is embedded in basic societal transformations. Historical analysis is needed to understand how the interests of the Iranian elite and the international health care industries influenced the distribution of health care resources during the Pahlavi regime. Such analysis may help provide a basis for the restructuring of medical services to provide more equitable health care for the people of Iran.

4

The Political Role of the Lutis in Iran

Willem M. Floor

Introduction

The function and role of *lutis* (rowdies) have remained an enigma for many scholars.[1] They were often considered to be a kind of Robin Hood, essentially "good guys" who frequently turned into bands of hooligans, because "certain undesirable elements in the government sought to utilize the *lutis* in order to direct and control the public for their own end."[2]

The *lutis* and similar groups such as the *ayyar*[3] belong to the category of 'social bandits', a term coined by Hobsbawm with regard to peasant rebels.[4] Hobsbawm did not extend his thesis on social protest to the urban equivalent of the peasant rebel; for which, amongst other omissions, he has been criticized by Blok.[5] The latter in his criticism makes several illuminating and stimulating remarks, which makes the social bandit a more useful concept for sociological analysis than Hobsbawm's original social bandit.

Hobsbawm's thesis is that social banditry is a universal phenomenon and represents a primitive form of organized social protest by the peasants. The State may regard these peasant bandits as criminals, but the peasant population sees them as their champions and avengers. Social bandits, because they only want to restore the traditional order, are reformers—but not revolutionaries.[6]

Blok's criticism is that social banditry is more than just peasant protest. He states that social bandits, rather than being champions of the poor and oppressed, often terrorized the very groups from which they had originated. "Rather than promoting the articulation of peasant interests within a national context, bandits tend to obstruct or deviate concerted peasant action."[7] Although both Hobsbawm and

Blok address themselves to peasant bandits, many of the elements which they draw attention to are of importance for a better understanding of the role which the *lutis* played in Iran.

Instead of focusing mainly on the activities of the *lutis*, we shall concentrate on the place and function of social bandits within the society as a whole. Moreover, we shall examine those who protected these bandits, for history shows that without protection bandits had a very short life indeed. Based on his own experience in Sicily, Blok contends that "the more successful a man is as a bandit, the more extensive the protection granted to him."[8]

Urban Society and Structure in Qajar Iran

Qajar Iran was a preindustrial society with a broad agrarian base and illiterate population, ruled by a small elite. The literates formed a small part of the elite; because they were needed to administer the country, and because communications between parts of the country were difficult, the government had to allow a far-reaching decentralization of its patrimonial rule in favor of its supporters at the local level. Local regions were relatively self-sufficient and central authority often was only nominal. This situation led Fox to state that preindustrial states "were often less than the sum of their parts."[9] The central government was unable to control local leaders; therefore, it had to play them off against one another, maintaining a delicate balance of power. Central authority had to create a modus vivendi with local power groups to assure the collection of taxes and the maintenance of order, for which it required the cooperation of the local elite.[10]

It was this structure of preindustrial society, with its cleavages based on political and social orientation, that constituted the main cause of social banditry. Loyalties of individuals in Qajar Iran were, as far as the city was concerned, first and foremost to their city quarter (*mahalleh* or *kuy*). (Of course, family loyalty was more important, but city dwellers had this in common with all other Iranians. Here we are interested only in those characteristics that are peculiar to city dwellers.) The population of such quarters distinguished themselves from one another in a number of ways. These differences comprised one or more physical, social, economic, ethnic and/or religious characteristics. In some Iranian cities barriers were formed between various city quarters with walls and gates defining the districts. In case of disturbances and at night these gates were closed. Such action also was a last resort to prevent a mob attacking the quarter.[11]

A socioeconomic cleavage existed between city quarters of different social status. In nineteenth century Iranian cities there were low class and high class quarters. In the former the *luti* movement was always strong.[12] Ethnic cleavages were based on the fact that many quarters were inhabited by people of different geographical and/or ethnic/ language origins. This could be the difference between speakers of Persian and Arabic or of Persian and Turkish. Another type of cleavage was found in some cities like Behbehan, where the basic cleavage, which divided the city into two parts, was the existence of two groups called the Qanavatiyan and the Shahrneshinan. The former were originally mountaineers and the latter city dwellers. This distinction was an old one, but it made city life sometimes a murderous affair.[13]

The most important cleavage was one based on mutually opposing groups (with religious overtones). Practically all Iranian cities and even large villages were divided into two opposing groups (moieties), named Haidaris and Nematis, which had come into being under these names during the sixteenth century.[14] Such a two-fold division of Iranian cities is already characteristic for towns like Nishapur and Merv in the eleventh century, when the two opposing groups were simply referred to as the 'two parties' *(alfariqan)*.[15] In the nineteenth and the beginning of the twentieth century there is evidence for such a division in Tehran, Tabriz, Isfahan, Shiraz, Ardebil, Dezful, Shushtar, Hamadan, Rasht, and many other cities.[16] There were some variations as in Tabriz where the division was between the Shaikhis and the Motasharis.[17] Often, the religious content of each group was less important than its role as a point of factional identification. These factions regularly carried out bloody battles. Religious minorities, such as Jews, Christians, Zoroastrians, and later Babis, were also found in cities, often in their own districts; but they were traditionally subordinated to Muslims.

The hierarchy of loyalties for Iranian urbanites was his family, quarter, moiety, and finally, the city. The inhabitants of a city quarter formed a homogeneous group led by one or more leaders. These included the *kadkhoda* (the head of the quarter), the *pishnamaz* (the prayer leader), and other important local leaders. Some positions such as the *kadkhoda* were hereditary, allowing enmities between quarters to acquire long-term political overtones. A similar situation occurred with the ulama, who also frequently were succeeded in their religious functions by their sons or other relatives. In Shushtar, for example, each of the 18 city quarters was headed by a chief called *aqa* (master), who together were referred to as *aqavat.* They were divided into two parties, each headed by a leader who was always recruited from one family. For the Nematis he came from the Kalantar family and for the Haidaris from the Marashi family.[18] Similar phenomena can be observed in other Iranian cities.

The example of Shushtar indicates the importance of local families, who often for many generations occupied local administrative and religious positions, such as *kalantar* (mayor), *kadkhoda*, *mujtahid* (religious dignitary), *Imam Jom'eh* (overseer of the Friday mosque). Because these families retained their power even after a change of dynasty, the national government had to rely on their administrative expertise and political influence to maintain national unity and to continue the collection and payment of taxes.[19]

Lutis in Qajar Iran

Having sketched the urban social background of Qajar Iran, we may ask: who were the *lutis*? Since the term *lutis* refers to two distinct groups, I will briefly distinguish the one from the other. The first group known as *lutis* was composed of itinerant jugglers, clowns, and buffoons. This entertainment class was under the supervision of government officials. One could even distinguish two groups among the entertainment class: those belonging to the *naqqareh khaneh* (group of musicians) and those belonging to the *luti khaneh* (group of players). The group of musicians comprised the royal band, both musicians and dancers, as well as other musical performers. The group of players was composed of the other artists. In each major town a government official was in charge of these groups. This official did not only levy taxes from them, but he was also responsible for their behavior. Furthermore, this official smoothed over their differences and finally acted as a broker *vis à vis* the government for his people. This two-fold division of the entertainment class dates back to at least the fifteenth century.[20]

The second group was formed by the urban social bandits. The confusion between these two distinct groups may be explained by the fact that both groups belonged to the fringe of society. They had much in common, such as frequenting disreputable establishments and streets, having loose morals, and overlapping membership. The line between the two groups also was blurred by the fact that *varzeshkaran* (wrestlers) formally belonged to the entertainment class, but they actually were also part of the rowdies. This may also explain why both groups were referred to by the term *lutis*, which had a connotation to the supposedly homosexual relationship which existed among such socially marginal groups. (It is known that wrestlers avoided sexual intercourse with women, for this they thought would sap their strength; this belief still prevails among today's wrestlers.) Furthermore, *lutis* of both kinds had a reputation of loose sexual morals, and homosexuality was one aspect of their deviant behavior.[21]

Within certain city quarters were found the *luti* associations in the nineteenth and twentieth centuries. Here they played an important role, for it was within their own quarter in which outsiders had no business. This possessive attitude was enhanced by the fact that the *luti* associations were essentially an 'in-group' and had a very strong esprit de corps. This 'in-group' attitude was mirrored in their actions, games, ideas and outward appearance. The ideal was to make a reputation for himself, by showing off, by doing unusual and daring things. If the *lutis* did not attract attention by their actions, they certainly did with their outward appearance.[22]

Although the length of one's dress gave an indication of one's place in society, *lutis* wore their dress (*kamarchin*) shorter than anyone else.[23] They were moreover recognizable by special attributes such as a special chain made in Yazd, a brass bowl from Kerman, a silk handkerchief from Kashan, and a knife made in Isfahan. Other emblems of their membership, which they were not obliged to carry, were a pipe made of cherry wood, a shawl, and *givehs* (woven cotton slippers).[24]

Lutis also had games which were peculiar to them, which in general were all frowned upon by solid citizens and orthodox Muslims. Apart from gambling, they were basically innocent games (in Western eyes at least), such as pigeon flying, cock fighting, and ram fighting. Moreover, athletic bouts and trials of endurance in eating, swimming and the like were popular amongst them.[25] *Lutis* also made use of a lingo special to them by replacing certain vowels or consonants in normal words, and by the use of expressions which they only understood.[26]

With *lutis* from other districts they had both friendly and unfriendly fights. Duels also were fought between members of the same and opposing groups. However, opposing *luti* groups would often react together when confronted by a third force which was hostile to them.[27]

The *lutis* had their own habitual cafes or *patoq*. Here they gambled, drank alcohol, and amused themselves.[28] Another focal point in their life was the *zurkhaneh* or house of strength, where various kinds of gymnastic, wrestling, and physical arts were taught and practiced.

Apart from this sportive function, *zurkhanehs* also played an important social role and constituted a kind of neighborhood club which many of the male inhabitants of the quarter joined. Although membership was predominantly made up by artisans and bazaaris, members of the mercantile and political elite also joined.[29]

Within their own districts *lutis* aimed at making a reputation for themselves as generous men or *javanmards,* protecting the poor and weak in the neighborhood as well as by opposing too grasping government officials—for which the population gratefully remembered them. To sustain their activities they demanded money from the rich in their district.[30] In 1848 and 1849 the *lutis* under the command of their leader, Mohammad Abdollah, maintained law and order during the absence of the governor, and taxed the rich to enable them to do this job.[31]

Although *lutis* were mainly young and athletic men with strong ties and a special *zurkhaneh* (gymnasium), this did not mean that all members of this institution were *lutis*. Both the *lutis* and the other members of the *zurkhaneh* had in common that one tried to become a *javanmard*, both in spiritual and material matters. One aspired to be truthful, to stick to one's promises, and to share with one's friends.[32] One worked together in organizing all kinds of religious festivities and in other socially important events. *Lutis* even had a special shrine in Tehran to which they made pilgrimages, which was known as the Mecca of the *lutis.*[33]

The leaders of the *lutis* were men who commanded great respect, and even those *lutis* of whom everyone in the district was afraid showed humility and respect for their leader.[34]

Notwithstanding the spiritual and public-spirited elements which played a role in the *luti* associations, *lutis* as a group had no special program, ideology, or aspirations which were peculiar to them alone. To be a *javanmard,* and all that this concept entailed, was not something special to the *lutis,* for this ideal strongly appealed to all Iranians and permeated all social classes.

Apart from the more public-spirited *lutis,* there were also *lutis* who acquired a notorious reputation. This latter kind of *lutis* was called *penti* in the lingo of the *lutis.*[35] Within their own quarter these *lutis* acted with more restraint. In their own neighborhood they could acquire a reputation of men who avenged oppression by government officials and took good care of the name of their neighborhood.[36] However, it was a common practice for Muslims to take sanctuary with their *mujtahid* "when danger is apprehended either from the *looties* or from the law."[37] In the other parts of the city, however, including the bazaars and *maidans* (squares), they would pester and harass people, accost women,[38] levy taxes on passers-by, and even rob people.

Lutis also served as the executive arm of local leaders such as the *kalantar, mujtahid,* and other members of the local elite in which position they acquired great notoriety.[39] The same holds for the *tollab* (religious students) in the *madrasehs* (religious schools), who were attached to various local religious leaders. They were 'a most unruly and troublesome lot' who collected the canonical taxes such as *zakat* and *khums* by force, if threats did not work. Those persons who were bold enough to show an independent attitude, but did not command enough protection from other elite leaders, were liable to be beaten up by the *lutis* in the pay of the local elite.[40]

Because of the traditional enmity between city quarters, the fights which regularly broke out between them have received more attention than the role of intimidation the *lutis* played within their own communities. Fights between quarters especially took place during the month of Moharram, fought mainly by the *lutis*. Barricades were erected and fighting, sometimes lasting for days, was conducted with fists, stones, knives, clubs, and even guns.[41]

Although both Iranian and European sources refer to the *lutis* in negative terms,[42] one is surprised at the free rein which both central and local governments allowed these *lutis*. They were dealt with severely at times, but never in such a way that their activities were effectively curtailed. Moreover, government actions were never part of a consistent policy, but rather were incidental and ad hoc in nature. The lack of effective suppression of *lutis* was due to the political structure of preindustrial society in Iran. Local families and courtiers vied with one another for the leading role in the city. To this end they employed local supporters who were spearheaded by the *lutis*. In Shiraz, for example, at the beginning of the Qajar period the outgoing leader of the Zand dynasty, Lotf Ali Khan, relied on *lutis*.[43] Similarly, those powerful local families who backed the Qajars, like the Qavams in Shiraz[44] and the Donbolis in Tabriz and Khoy,[45] also made use of *lutis* to bolster their rule. In Tehran, *lutis* had regular contacts with court circles throughout the Qajar period.[46] In the provincial towns fights were not only waged between local contenders, but also against the governor and other functionaries appointed by the central government.[47]

Each important local leader had a band of *lutis* and other roughs at his beckoning.[48] For instance, the *Imam Jom'eh* of Tehran sheltered *lutis* in the Shah Mosque.[49] In Dezful the *mujtahid* Aqa Fattah

Mohammad Taher had about 30–40 *lutis* in his service.[50] In Isfahan, Hajji Sayyed Mohammad Baqer, the powerful *mujtahid,* had a strong grip on the *lutis.*[51] Many other examples could be cited, but these suffice to show that the *lutis* existed because of their value to their protectors. This relationship can be better understood by the following, more elaborate examples.

In 1824, one Hajji Hashem Khan terrorized the city of Isfahan with his *lutis.* At night they robbed the houses of the rich and during the day they ran an illegal tax office, extorting money from passers-by. Because Hajji Hashem Khan was a relative of the Qajar prime minister and of the governor of Isfahan, no effective measures were taken against him. But then, he had the audacity to welcome Fath Ali Shah, who had come to Isfahan to punish him and his *lutis.* He believed the shah would not touch him because of his connections and the protection he enjoyed. This time, however, he miscalculated; he was deprived of his sight and forced to return the stolen goods.[52]

In Dezful, a regional conflict between Shaikh Khaz'al and the Bakhtiyari Khans, who respectively backed the Nematis and the Haidaris, regularly led to fights between the *lutis* of the opposing parties in the second half of the nineteenth century. Here sometimes a full-scale war was waged, and the city would be immobilized for days at a time.[53]

The use of local riots and the 'spontaneous' demonstration which could escalate into a battle was a normal political weapon for Iranian notables to settle disputes or to attain particular political objectives. Surprisingly, one still finds scholars defending *lutis* as champions of the poor, when most European observers were well aware that *lutis* were used by notables, including *mujtahids,* to gain their own ends. Perkins in 1843 stated that "these desperadoes are always the instruments of violence in the hands of the fanatical Moollahs, whenever they attempt to carry a point against the laws and the rulers by the agency of a mob, which is not a rare occurrence in Persia."[54] Another observer, Baron de Bode, notes that "the government paralyzed the power of the Isfahan clergy in the successful blow that has been levelled against the *lutis.*"[55]

The *lutis* were enticed by direct payment, and by the prospect of loot and freedom to lead a licentious life. However, when their protector thought it in his interest to drop them, he did so without compunction; especially since the rank and file or the *luti*-led demonstrations were unemployed and casual laborers.[56] These individuals, stuffed with alcohol and some money (with the promise of more to come), were easy to assemble and could be sacrificed without many problems.[57]

A successful social bandit was one who obtained not only a reputation as a rowdy and the respect of his fellow bandits and quarter inhabitants, but also was one who acquired wealth. Most of the *lutis*, of course, never reached this stage of success; they were but the rank and file. However, many leaders became respected propertied men. Of the 10–15 *luti bashis* (*luti* leaders) of Tehran in 1852, it is reported that they belonged to the notables of the city.[58] In Shiraz the *luti bashi* had become a member of the local elite in the 1850s.[59] Important leaders of the Tehran *lutis* were given titles by Mohammad Ali Shah in 1908 in recompense for their part in bringing the constitutional movement to a halt in Tehran.[60]

Most famous of all Iranian *lutis* were Sattar Khan and Baqer Khan who led the constitutionalist forces in Tabriz against the royalist forces. As the last constitutionalist bulwark in the country, together with forces from Rasht and the Bakhtiyari tribesmen, they forced Mohammad Ali Shah to abdicate in 1909. Because of their courageous resistance and leadership, both *lutis* became national heroes.[61]

It must be noted, however, that *lutis* as representatives of a certain way of life did not all join the constitutional forces, either in Tabriz or elsewhere. In fact, *lutis* participated in both of the opposing parties. Their choice for either side was defined rather by negative criteria than positive ones; in each city if the Haidari *lutis* would join the royalists the Nemati *lutis* would join the constitutionalists—or vice versa. This phenomenon is to be found in all cities of Iran. In Tabriz the Shaikhi *lutis* backed the constitutional movement, and the *lutis* of the Motashara districts, Davachi and Sorkhab, joined the royalist camp.[62] In Enzeli and Rasht the partisans for the constitutionalists appear to have been mainly moved by old factional enmities. The interesting issue here was that both parties called each other absolutists and claimed to be constitutionalists; yet they fought each other.[63]

In Tehran we find *lutis* like Sani Hazrat backing the shah, while the leader of the Chalmaidan *lutis*, Abbas Beg, defended the revolution and died for it.[64] In Dezful the election for the Majlis (parliament) led to a revival of the old vendettas between Allah Yar Khan Bakhtiyari and Asad Khan Dezfuli.[65] Such old factional fights then broke out in the whole province. In Bushehr the old divisions also got the better of people, which led to the revival of tensions in that town.[66]

That *lutis* were not moved so much by patriotism and a wish for a better society, is also shown by the fact that *lutis* continued their old practices and way of life after the establishment of a constitutional government. In Taft in the province of Kerman, *lutis* were responsible for many robberies in that district in 1912. Although the governor was able to inflict some losses on them, their leaders managed to escape.[67] In Mashhad in 1912 the *lutis* were very active against the constitutionalist government and its supporters. They were able to oppress, harass, and kill people because they were protected by the Russian consul-general in that city.[68] Kasravi reports that he was harassed by the *lutis* who were backing Shaikh Khiyabani in Tabriz in 1917. When they came looking for him he went into hiding.[69] In the years prior to the establishment of the Pahlavi dynasty *lutis* remained very active, as if nothing had changed.

Pahlavi Iran

The strong and centralized government of Reza Shah neither needed nor permitted *lutis* to support or challenge the government. During his reign law and order prevailed in the cities and in most parts of the country. He also forbade such religious festivities as the 'camel sacrifice' and the passion play, activities for which the *lutis* were participants. *Lutis* may have played a role in 1934, when in Mashhad the ulama opposed the ban on wearing the veil *(chador)* for women.

The apparent disappearance of the *lutis* from the Iranian sociopolitical scene is misleading, however. The *lutis* evidently kept a low profile during Reza Shah's reign, and only showed their existence by 'patrolling' their quarter, and by continuing their unsavory activities such as theiving, pimping, and the protection racket. This we may safely assume, because after Reza Shah's abdication in 1941 the *lutis,* or *chaqu keshan* (cutthroats) as they were mainly called, reemerged. The socioeconomic structure in the cities had not been fundamentally changed by Reza Shah's rule.[70]

Especially during the hectic period of Mosaddeq's government, the *lutis* often were seen leading royalist inspired demonstrations. However, Mosaddeq's supporters also turned out *luti*-led mobs.[71] Some of the mob leaders, such as Sha'ban Bimokh, an owner of a *zurkhaneh* who led demonstrations in favor of Mohammad Reza Shah, acquired a notorious reputation. With the assistance of money and hired (or army supplied) trucks, casual laborers were brought from south Tehran towards the center of the city to demonstrate. These people sometimes even participated in opposing demonstrations on consecutive days! A very important example of such 'spontaneous' demonstrations was the one of 28 Mordad 1953 which toppled Mosaddeq and effected the return of the shah. Sha'ban Bimokh was well paid for his services and received a luxurious sports palace built by a grateful government for his services to the shah. [72]

The *lutis* again played an important role in 1963 when the shah's complaisance to Israel and the U.S. and programs for women's franchise and land reform were opposed by the ulama and landlords. [73] The mob was led by *lutis* and wrought much havoc, loss of life, and property. Among the latter was the sports palace of Sha'ban Bimokh. It is of interest that prominent in the Moharram riots of 1963 were Tayyeb and Esmail Hajj Reza'i, both rivals of Sha'ban Bimokh. Both men were *lutis* and leaders of a protection racket in the fruit and vegetable market in Tehran, which brought them an income of two million rials per day. They had already been leading mobs in the days of Mosaddeq against the National Front (Mosaddeq's party) and the Tudeh (Communist party). Because it is not clear what their motives had been in leading the 1963 riots, it has been suggested that the *lutis* had been paid by the government to organize these riots, so that the ulama could be blamed. This seems unlikely, however, since the opposition claimed that these riots were the genuine expression of a national movement. [74]

From 1963 to 1978 the use of violence and coercion has been monopolized by the government. With the creation of SAVAK (secret police) in 1957, the silencing of the opposition after 1963, and the resulting political stability, the role of the *lutis* in politics was over. They were, of course, still around in their neighborhood, in the bazaar, and running brothels and protection rackets. A research group of Tehran University observed in 1965 that the inhabitants of lower class districts in Tehran believed that 20 percent of the violence which occurred in or between districts was caused by the existence of *luti* gangs. [75]

From the political point of view, however, *lutis* were no longer important. The government had other and more effective means to control and mobilize the population—among which SAVAK acquired a reputation of its own. The population also had found other and more effective outlets for their grievances; they had acquired a greater political awareness. The growing resentment against the government's policies was not channeled and voiced via clandestine political programs, ideologies, and actions. In the new circumstances even the people had no need for such chance allies, for, although the *lutis* were always eager for a fight, one could never be sure for whom they would fight.

It is notable, therefore, that the old system of bought-mobs appears to have broken down—or at least its effectiveness and importance. During the revolution of 1978–79 the large scale demonstrations were the genuine expression of public opinion—of *political* views. Even more important, the thousands of unemployed and casual laborers who live in squalor in south Tehran could not be bought by the government—although this was tried. The government also tried in enflame passions based upon the old cleavages, such as in Kerman between the Shi'i and Sunni Muslims; but this proved fruitless as well.[76] Although some government sponsored demonstrations were staged, these were pitifully small as compared with those turned out by the opposition. Moreover, it was said that many of the participants of such demonstrations were soldiers (in civilian dress) or other privileged government employees. It was even rumored at the beginning of November 1978 that Sha'ban Bimokh would turn out a mob in favor of the shah on Friday, November 18. Before he could accomplish this, he was attacked and wounded by opponents of the shah. (His life was also threatened if he attempted to organize his mob.) Finally, it was the army who made a great weapons show for a few spectators only.[77] The role of the *lutis* as mobilizers both for and against the poor had come to an end.

Conclusion

In what has been said about the activities of the *lutis,* little can be ascribed to forms of social protest in favor of the general population. There were, of course, cases of *lutis* who acted in this way, and who were gratefully remembered for their public deeds,[78] but even then they mainly acted only as the executive arm of the local religious or administrative authorities. Even demonstrations in favor of lowering bread prices were but excuses to challenge the governor's power, or even that of the shah.[79] However, this was done at the instigation of local political opponents, or by the religious authorities.

The *lutis* lacked the organization or long term revolutionary objectives to become their own agents of change. They were only interested in making a name for themselves and, therefore, their loyalties were first and foremost to themselves, and not to the poor and the oppressed. Notwithstanding the conservative political 'Weltanschauung' of the *lutis*, which constrained political mobilization of the class from which they had sprung, they also participated in actions which were directed against the existing order, such as the constitutional revolution (1905–11). However, the *lutis* did not participate on the side of the constitutionalists because they were patriots or because they understood the significance of this constitution; the greater part of the *lutis*, in fact, supported the counterrevolutionary forces.[80] Their participation on the constitutionalist side was mainly defined by the fact that the *lutis* of 'enemy' districts joined the other side, but also because they loved a fight. Many became a *mojahed*, a fighter for the constitution, only to get a gun and ammunition.[81] There were, of course, also *lutis* who may have participated out of sincere enmity with regard to Mohammad Ali Shah, but this was probably caused by the fact that he had become very unpopular in Tabriz during his days as governor-general of that city. *Lutis* thrived on disorder, for this gave them a chance to show-off and to make a reputation for themselves. It is therefore not surprising that the influence of the *lutis* after the constitutional revolution (1905–11) dwindled as fast as it had come into being, which is not incongruent with the parochial and short-sighted objectives of the *lutis*.

During the Pahlavi period the frequency and the intensity of their action are commensurate with the extent of protection granted to them. When Iran slowly and gradually emerged from its preindustrial wrappings, with the growing power and influence of the central government, the role of the *lutis* became less noteworthy. The fast pace of development which Iran has known for the last 20 years and the growth of a politically self-conscious people, meant that the political role of the *lutis* was finished. The fact that it has been reported that the antishah forces had recruited mobs of *lutis* from the bazaar in 1979 does not change this fact. For, contrary to former days, *lutis* did not constitute the core of the demonstrations, and certainly were overshadowed by the genuine oppositional sentiments of the great number of people who participated in these demonstrations, and who were willing to risk their lives by doing so. It was these latter people who really comprised the demonstrations of 1978–79, and led to the overthrow of the Pahlavi reign.[82]

II. NOMADS AND AGRICULTURALISTS

Figure 2. Qashqa'i Woman Shepherd.

5

Economic Transformations Among Qashqa'i Nomads, 1962–1978

Lois Beck

The decline of nomadism among the Qashqa'i of southwest Iran was the most obvious and dramatic of the many alterations in their life styles in the 1970s; but it was not as significant for them as were many other aspects of political and economic change.[1] The tribal framework was dismantled and military control imposed. Pastoral production was undermined by government programs of land reform and pasture nationalization, by the spread of capitalist relations of production in rural areas, and by new market pressures. The Qashqa'i were losing their unique adaptation to the physical and social landscape and were rapidly assuming patterns found among agropastoralists and migrant wage-laborers in the region.

Almost all pastoral nomadic populations in Iran were subject to the enforced settlement schemes of Reza Shah (1925–41); many were not able to regain their nomadic patterns after his abdication. The Qashqa'i, however, quickly abandoned in 1941 the imposed settled life for a return to nomadism, and they remained nomadic for several decades. The task for this paper is to explain why the Qashqa'i—one of the last major nomadic groups in Iran—were rapidly settling in the 1970s.

The Qashqa'i are Turkic-speaking nomadic pastoralists whose ancestors came from Central Asia and the Caucasus and settled in the Zagros mountains of southwest Iran, probably around the fifteenth century. At first a small group of Turkic peoples, they expanded with the increment of other Turkic groups, as well as Lurs, Kurds, Arabs, Persians, and gypsies. A tribal confederation headed by an *Ilkhani* was recognized by the central government by at least 1818, and came to consist of more than a quarter of a million individuals by the twentieth century. There are five large Qashqa'i tribes and a number of smaller ones, most of which were headed by khans who succeeded to leadership positions by virtue of noble lineage status and sociopolitical ties. The Qashqa'i herded sheep and goats and made long-range, seasonal migrations (up to 350 miles in length) between lowlands and highlands, adjacent to and within the Zagros mountains. At the local level they were organized into flexible groups based upon ties of kinship, marriage, political alliance, and economics. Qashqa'i identity focused on political leaders and groups and on cultural, linguistic, and territorial criteria.

In the 1960s government-sponsored changes directly affected the Qashqa'i: a national land reform program was introduced, pasture-lands were nationalized, the khans' tribal responsibilities were legally removed, and control over land use and migrations was put under the military. Because of far-reaching political and economic disruption—scarcity of pasture, government control, undermining of tribal organization, national economic pressures, and capitalist penetration—a continuation of nomadic pastoralism was virtually impossible for most Qashqa'i.

The Impact of the Nation State

As soon as Qashqa'i leaders returned to power in Fars following Reza Shah's abdication in 1941, the Qashqa'i were viewed as a threat to the Iranian state. Lacking control over the large dispersed population, the government assigned responsibility for tribal affairs to the khans and used them as mediators, as it had done in the past.[2] Qashqa'i support of Mosaddeq in 1951–53, however, lost them this power and support; the three top Qashqa'i khans were exiled from Iran in 1954–56, and the title of *Ilkhani* was abolished. The government hoped that the removal of these leaders would end its Qashqa'i problems, but it underestimated tribal leadership, for other Qashqa'i khans continued handling tribal affairs. The government assigned military officers to the tribe, but this did not constitute effective control. In 1960 it abolished the title of khan and its duties and powers (tax collection, land allocation, migration supervision, army formation, dispute settlement). The military officers' functions were increased; they were now to direct tribal affairs with the khans' advice rather than to serve only as advisors. Several years passed before they had much success in handling affairs, and, in the meantime, many tribespeople continued to respond to the khans in customary fashion.

What radically changed the government's role from supervision to control was the introduction of the national Land Reform Law in 1962 and its Additional Articles in 1963. Tribal disturbances broke out in Fars province, not so much in protest against land reform as against increasing government interference in tribal affairs.[3] The killing of a land reform official near Qashqa'i territory in 1962 was interpreted by the government as a direct attack on its reform efforts, and Minister of Agriculture Arsanjani ordered the immediate implementation of land reform in Fars. The government saw the disturbances as impediments to land reform and came down heavily on the Qashqa'i; it confiscated their firearms and demanded that the khans be removed from tribal affairs. The severity of punishment, in contrast to the level of disturbance, suggests that the government was using the occasion to counter the threat of tribal power in Fars.[4] It depended on the quick implementation of land reform to prove the sincerity of its efforts to alter rural land tenure, and it could not tolerate opposition. Other social groups, such as the religious and bazaar classes and university students, also used the occasion of land reform to make general protests against the government. The "tribal problem" was the one, however, that could be handled most easily.

Tribal khans, who saw that government policies were not likely to be soon reversed, and who were increasingly cut off from tribal functions, adjusted their economic activities to compensate for losses in tribal revenue from land rents and herd taxes. With changes in land tenure in operation or anticipated, they turned their efforts to orchards and mechanized agriculture.[5]

Tribespeople see the early 1960s as a time of freedom, when the khans no longer taxed them or interfered in land use, and when the government exerted little control. In 1963 military governorship over the Qashqa'i by the army was deemed ineffective, and authority was passed to Disciplinary Officers (Afsaran-e Entezamat) of the gendarmerie.[6] An officer was assigned to each major Qashqa'i tribe, and gendarme posts were set up in towns near winter and summer quarters for the policing of tribal activities. The major functions of these forces, other than political and military control, were land allocation and regulation of migrations, tasks formerly supervised by Qashqa'i khans and headmen. This force was not immediately effective, but most tribespeople found it increasingly difficult to use pastures other than those formally assigned to them. Entezamat set the commencement date for each tribe's seasonal migrations, and gendarmes, stationed in small camps along the routes, policed Qashqa'i movements. Migration schedules were determined by political rather than ecological factors, and flocks suffered accordingly.[7] Length of encampment on the migration was restricted to forty-eight hours in a single location and was enforced by the gendarmerie. From the mid-1960s, Iran's repressive secret police— SAVAK—had increasing surveillance over Qashqa'i activities.

Land reform's effects were drastic for the Qashqa'i, for no provision was made for the seasonal use of pastureland by nomads. Only individuals who had permanent occupancy of land (and who met other requirements) were considered qualified for land distribution.[8] Qashqa'i nomads lacked year-round, regular occupancy of specific units of land and hence could not claim land under the new laws. (The majority of Iran's villagers were not provided for through land reform either.)[9] Qashqa'i who remained in one seasonal pasture area all year usually lacked the necessary verifying documents. Of the Qashqa'i and non-Qashqa'i who cultivated in winter and summer pastures, it was generally the settled non-Qashqa'i who understood land reform procedures, who first registered the land in their own names, and who received title to it. Land reform officers often visited land when the Qashqa'i were in other seasonal pastures, and again they lost out in land registration.[10] The Qashqa'i report that bribery of land reform officials was prevalent during the reform's early years.[11] The absence of active Qashqa'i political leadership was crucial, for the khans could have prevented many abuses and loss of lands.

The abortive land reform of 1960 had suggested forestalling measures which were utilized by many landowners, even after the 1962–63 laws had gone into effect. Violations were difficult to prove. Owners subdivided landholdings and titles among family members to prevent confiscation. Since orchards, gardens, mechanized agricultural lands, woodlands, and areas serviced by motor pumps were exempt from land reform, some owners pre-dated their efforts in these directions. Especially detrimental to the Qashqa'i were those who rushed to plow large tracts of land.[12] This was illegal, and the land was often not theirs even by customary right. But due to military control of the Qashqa'i and their migrations, these practices went largely unnoticed and unprevented, until the land had been deeded to those who mechanized. Since this land, with its vegetation and topsoil turned under, was often never planted, wind erosion worked quickly, and natural pasturage was destroyed.

Land reform encouraged the widespread expansion of cultivation at the expense of grazing land in all Qashqa'i areas. Previously uncultivated land outside the range of existing village water supplies was opened for distribution by land reform officials, and many individuals received rights to cultivate new land. Their efforts were facilitated by the availability of new agricultural technology (implements, chemical fertilizers, motor pumps). Many Qashqa'i lost their best land and were left with inferior, arid tracts. New cultivation often occurred in areas unsuited to agriculture, and especially after dryland farming was attempted soil erosion resulted. For the neighboring Boir Ahmad area, the "mindless conversion of valuable pastures to less profitable farm plots" is considered the most damaging aspect of land reform there.[13] In the Qashqa'i area new motor pumps lowered the water table and had other degrading environmental effects. That agricultural expansion was allowed indicates the importance the government placed on a settled, agricultural rather than a nomadic, pastoral life. Cultivation of Qashqa'i pastures also led to conflict between field owners (generally non-Qashqa'i) and animal owners (Qashqa'i), and authorities tended to favor the formers' claims over the latters'.

The effects of land reform were combined, to the further detriment of Qashqa'i pastoralism, with those of the Forest and Range Nationalization Law of 1963.[14] All natural rangelands now belonged to the government, except those surrounding villages.[15] Included were almost all Qashqa'i pastures. The Forest and Range Organization of the Ministry of Agriculture was made responsible for allocating and controlling national rangelands, and was aided by the newly-established Ministry of Natural Resources. The reservation of lands marked for government programs for range improvement, wildlife conservation, and watershed protection also affected some Qashqa'i areas, notably the Dasht Arjan area west of Shiraz, established as a hunting preserve sponsored by the shah's brother and off limits to traditional users—both villagers and nomads. These programs either restricted livestock numbers and periods of use, or totally excluded them from the areas concerned.[16] Improved rangelands were not reopened for use, because the Forest and Range Organization believed it could not enforce range-management regulations on the original users. It favored the establishment of corporations, "to whom large blocks of grazing land can be allocated on a fixed-term contract."[17] Commercial and state-owned enterprises and capital-holding groups were favored over individual pastoralists.

Until the early 1960s, the Qashqa'i held and defended land collectively. Although some agricultural land was formally registered in khans' names, control over almost all Qashqa'i territory depended on political and military strength rather than written deeds. The khans allocated winter and summer grazing lands to the subtribes on a seasonal or longer-term basis. Individuals and groups secured rights to tribal land through tax payments and other expressions of political loyalty to tribal leaders. Well-organized groups with effective leaders were able to increase land and members. Groups could change political affiliations and territories, and land beyond tribal borders could also be utilized. The viability of nomadic pastoralism hinged on such flexible arrangements in land use, and tribal leaders were essential in the overall pattern of land use and in negotiating land disputes.[18]

The removal of top tribal leaders, the annexation of Qashqa'i land by non-Qashqa'i cultivators, and the nationalization of rangelands changed these patterns. Qashqa'i nomads were now required by law to obtain land rights through government channels rather than through traditional tribal rights and customs. The government, realizing difficulties in dealing with the vast dispersed population, used the tribal headmen as its mediators. Headmen, who formerly had mediated between supporters and khans, now became more indispensable for the negotiation of land and migration rights and for government relations. By the mid-1960s each headman was receiving land use and migration schedules for his subtribe from the gendarmerie Disciplinary Officer (Afsar-e Entezamat) assigned to his tribe to administer government policies. In most cases customary winter and summer pastures were recognized. The headman was required to submit the names of the land-using households in his section, and he was issued a deed for the land in question. (This deed later became the legal basis of land use.)

There were difficulties. Entezamat authorities fixed the use of one winter and one summer pasture and prohibited use of alternative pastures, which greatly threatened pastoral production. Households had always used other pastures prior and subsequent to residence in favorite pastures; alternative pastures were needed in case of poor ecological conditions in the customary areas. The authorities fixed the identity and number of households using each section, which disrupted formerly flexible patterns. Headmen could add individuals at their own discretion, but subtracting them was more difficult, since those removed could appeal for gendarme support. Some headmen registered land in their own or in relatives' names, which allowed them to exert political force over dependent households. In time, household proliferation—resulting from normal processes of household division—put pressure on already limited pastures.

The main purpose of the Disciplinary Officers and their gendarme posts was not land allocation but military and political control over the Qashqa'i, and in 1975 highly placed government officials determined that, since the "tribe" no longer existed (they felt), there was no longer need for these overseeing forces, which were summarily removed. From the government's view, the Qashqa'i were henceforth to be considered as any rural folk, under regular gendarme authority in case of political disturbances and land conflicts. There were immediate results. Control of migration schedules and routes ceased, and the Qashqa'i once again could move according to ecological and economic needs instead of government whim. However, expanding cultivation, agribusiness ventures, irrigation projects, and paved roads increasingly blocked their migration routes.

Other consequences of Entezamat's demise were not helpful to the Qashqa'i. Nomadic households, which had been acquiring land through tribal structures, were now required to secure individual land-use permits from the government. Headmen were stripped of their recently-acquired authority. Entezamat records were passed to the Ministries of Agriculture and Natural Resources, where permits for seasonal use of pasturelands were issued to requesting households.[19] Rights to particular areas were determined by previous usage under Entezamat control. Many nomads could not secure permits, because their names and locations had not been formally recorded. Ministry officials visited some seasonal pastures to assign land and record boundaries on the basis of herd size. Grazing permits were issued "on the basis of a quick look at the area and common sense."[20] Only "grazing land" *(marta)*, defined as land above water channels, was available for permits. Land below this level was classified as cultivable land *(mazra'eh)* and was denied to the nomads, even though it had often been grazed and cultivated by them. Instead, it was deeded through land reform to non-Qashqa'i villagers. Occasional grazers and those who were not of the location's dominant kinship group were forced off the land.

Another detrimental change caused by the new regulations concerned settlement. In the past, Qashqa'i nomads had built houses, cultivated, planted orchards, and established seasonal or permanent residence on their tribal land.[21] However, the new permits prohibited these activities, allowing only *seasonal* and *pastoral* use of land. No cultivation or construction was allowed. Since agriculture would preserve land claims in the face of encroachments and would allow new market demands to be met, this regulation was economically crippling. The nomads were not even permitted to buy these lands for permanent use.

Government policies of the 1960s and 1970s denied land to many Qashqa'i and restricted the land use of all. Aside from "tribal containment," government policy aimed to restrict the number of animals using rangelands. Policy-makers in Tehran, many of whom had never visited the countryside, and who were unaware of land-use patterns among pastoral nomads, stated that Iran was being rapidly denuded of vegetation—and that it was the pastoralists' fault.[22] Programs for rangeland use emphasized desertification, not the needs of pastoral populations. Policymakers were often guilty of cultural prejudices concerning rural and especially tribal people— which should be seen in the context of the increasing gap in the rates of socioeconomic change between urban and rural areas in Iran.[23] Communication between them and rural people was poor.

Government concern about environmental degradation, especially overgrazing, was particularly misplaced in light of the resulting *increased* pressure on pastoral resources due to the impact of land reform, land nationalization, and removal of tribal leadership. Although many Qashqa'i practiced careful range management, those having insufficient land to support their herds put increased pressure on existing resources and overgrazed. Ungrazed vegetation was often carried away for future use. Those who received land deeds in 1975 attempted to conserve resources, despite the increased herd sizes needed for economic support, while those denied deeds ceased to care much about conservation. Their sense of ecological responsibility was reduced and the element of personal investment removed.[24] Some Qashqa'i rented grazing land to compensate for pasture shortage, despite a 1971 law prohibiting the practice. Renters lacked long-term interest in the tracts and tended to misuse them. In a matter of a few years, land rents and new regulations had turned formerly tribal, corporate land into private property with explicit monetary value.

Military control over the Qashqa'i opened tribal lands to non-Qashqa'i pastoralists, which further depleted vegetation available to Qashqa'i herds and increased overgrazing. Commercial stock raisers were the first to enter Qashqa'i pastures. Wealthy merchants and landowners invested in flocks and hired nontribal shepherds to graze them in Qashqa'i pastures. Grazing patterns differed from those of the Qashqa'i; the newcomers entered pastures before and after Qashqa'i occupancy, which ensured that there was little vegetation for Qashqa'i animals. Disarmed, under military control, and lacking government support, the Qashqa'i were not able effectively to challenge these armed herders. A 1971 law which prohibited use of nationalized land by herders without grazing permits and with flocks of over 200 was not enforced, and few Qashqa'i could guard their seasonal pastures all year against trespassing herders. Large commercial herds were a major factor in the impoverishment of pastoral resources and in the settlement of many Qashqa'i.[25]

Second to enter Qashqa'i pasturelands were village pastoralists, who were reasonably confident that their flocks would no longer be raided. The Qashqa'i depended on seasonal use of specific areas, but village pastoralists used the same areas almost all year, so that on the Qashqa'is' arrival, little vegetation remained. Villagers traditionally owned a few animals, but as the countryside became militarily secure they increased their flocks and then had to seek grazing beyond the village periphery—which resulted in further encroachment on Qashqa'i pasturage. The reliance of Qashqa'i flocks on the stubble of harvested village fields was also jeopardized, and nomads were forced to produce and buy dry fodder, which consumed money and time and involved transport difficulties. Third to enter Qashqa'i pastures were those Qashqa'i and non-Qashqa'i pastoralists who had no legal land rights; they sought temporary grazing wherever possible. All these "illegal" grazers decreased the chances that even Qashqa'i nomads with legal land rights would find adequate pastures.

Changes in the Household Economy

The basic economic unit of the Qashqa'i—the unit of production and consumption—was the nuclear or extended family household. It owned and herded its own animals and relied on its members for the many necessary tasks that sustained the unit.[26] Households joined together in seasonal camps and during the migrations for protection of property and personnel and for mutual aid. Most households were self-sufficient in herding and other labor, although households with large herds or at early stages of development could hire other Qashqa'i as shepherds. Households with inadequate capital in animals could acquire animals through loan or contract, engage in nonpastoral activities, or hire out one or more members as shepherds. However, the economies of most households centered on raising herd animals, producing and selling pastoral products, and cultivating grain.[27]

These patterns altered in the mid-1960s. The new laws, programs, and practices discussed above generated many changes in the household economies of the pastoral nomadic Qashqa'i. Many households were no longer self-sufficient in herds or workers and turned to a diverse set of economic contracts and alliances, nonpastoral pursuits, and altered forms of production and consumption to meet changing household needs.

One major response was livestock contracting, which became widespread. Households with insufficient sheep and goats herded animals on contract for others, who were usually nontribal persons such as urban merchants and moneylenders.[28] The household was given sheep and goats (mostly female) to herd for two to seven years; when they were sold the income was divided. Half the income of the animals' clarified butter and wool/hair was paid to the contractor on a yearly basis. Under a short-term contract, male lambs were herded for several months and then sold. Prior to the 1960s animal contracts were uncommon; nomads could live on fewer animals and could add animals through theft. As more money was needed, they sought contract animals to enlarge their herds and increase production. With good pastoral conditions, this was a profitable venture, but by the 1970s it took on a new dimension. Nomads indebted to merchants and moneylenders were forced to transfer part ownership of their animals to their creditors. Half the animals' value was subtracted from the debt, and the nomad then herded them for a set period, sold them, and gave his creditor half the income. Because of pasture shortage and rising herding costs (grazing rents, supplemental feed), the contract period often ended with the herder owing the contractor money.

Another change in herding involved hired shepherds. Animal contracts meant no change in status, residence, or choice of companions. The animals herded were simply owned in part by others and were absorbed into the herder's flock. Shepherding contracts, however, required the shepherd to join the employer's household and encampment and to follow his land use and migration patterns.[29] Hired shepherds had lower social and economic status than those who herded their own (or contracted) animals. They were paid in cash, animals (one lamb or kid yearly), clothes, and food; they barely earned a subsistence. Capital accumulation and economic mobility were rare. By the mid-1970s, shepherds had become fewer because needy nomads sought urban wage labor where wages were higher than shepherding remuneration. Herd owners were forced to compete with urban labor conditions if they wished to retain shepherds.[30] However, due to pasture shortage hired shepherding did continue in Qashqa'i areas; Qashqa'i who lacked grazing permits got access to employers' pastures and combined their herds with their employers'.[31] And, capitalist herd owners who sought Qashqa'i shepherds paid twice the regular wage. Camel driving, another wage activity for Qashqa'i, paid poorly and required supplemental income. When Qashqa'i settled or migrated by truck, they sold their camels, and camel drivers were out of work.

A third change in herding involved group members and relatives and had less potential for exploitation than animal contracting or shepherding. As household males became increasingly unable to herd because of other economic activity (see below), households merged herd animals, which freed some male workers.[32]

Other major changes in the Qashqa'i household economy involved a diversification of economic activity, especially in nonpastoral pursuits. Prior to the 1960s, many households cultivated grain in winter and summer pastures, but in insufficient quantities to satisfy yearly needs. With increased demands for supplemental animal feed and rapid increase in market grain prices, households sought ways to produce more and to acquire cash for its purchase. Household personnel and time were increasingly expended in agriculture, and one or more members lived separately from the family in order to cultivate crops. Some households coordinated their pastoral and agricultural economies. Those assuming pastoral functions maintained the pack animals, permits, and contacts necessary for pastoralism, while those in charge of agriculture bought or rented land and equipment and expanded urban and market ties. Such Qashqa'i were adapting more successfully to economic and political change than those who did not diversify their economies.[33] Needs for agricultural products and accompanying changes in labor and residence were pressures for sedentarization. Many families planned to build houses where they secured or hoped to secure cultivation rights.

Investment in land for fruit orchards involved other changes in household economy and labor, and those who established orchards tended to settle nearby. Only wealthier Qashqa'i could afford orchards, since large initial and long-term capital investments were required before a marketable crop was produced. The government's Agricultural Bank offered low-interest loans, as did new cooperatives established by the government in a few tribal areas, but few nomads possessed the means or networks to secure them. Loans from some cooperatives had to be repaid in six months, an inhibiting factor for those without a cash inflow.

Hired agricultural labor, an activity rarely found among the Qashqa'i before the 1960s, even among the poor, became an important source of cash income. The expansion of agriculture and orchards into Qashqa'i pastures brought jobs closer to the nomads. Opium production, which had been an extremely lucrative activity, was strictly controlled by the last Pahlavi government.

Tribal khans traditionally had retinues of servants and workers; most of them had sought livelihoods in the khans' service because of poverty or political trouble. Economic conditions changed more quickly than the khans' inclination to pay cash salaries to their workers, and most sought employment elsewhere. Associated with the Qashqa'i were gypsies and others who performed specialized labors and services, and they too benefited from such nonpastoral jobs as coppersmithing and woodworking. With economic conditions altered, they moved to urban squatter settlements and took on new jobs. Musicians were the only group still economically viable within tribal territory. Smuggling and caravan trade, found in some other Iranian tribes, were not important for the Qashqa'i. Some highway robbery and raiding of village flocks and fields had existed but virtually ceased under conditions of government control.

Other nonpastoral work was done primarily by Qashqa'i in the lower economic levels and had been a means to ensure continuing nomadism. Even those with as few as five goats could continue to migrate and reside with kin in traditional pastures. The natural environment was utilized for gathering, preparing, and selling natural substances, including charcoal, gum tragacanth, nuts, and saps. Pasture nationalization and land use regulations outlawed or made difficult many nonpastoral subsistence efforts, and most nomads who subsisted on them were forced off the land. Because of their poverty and their already close contacts with the marketplace due to the sale of nonpastoral commodities, these were the first Qashqa'i to take on urban wage labor. However, with the area under military control, the rural nontribal poor no longer feared expulsion by tribal occupants, and they increased their own efforts to exploit natural resources. Thus, change in the economic and political climate generated two new movement patterns: Qashqa'i migrations out of tribal territory and countermigrations of non-Qashqa'i (nonpastoral workers, commercial and village herders, agriculturalists) into the area.

An important economic diversification for the Qashqa'i was wage labor in towns and cities and on construction sites, which substituted for hired shepherding and nonpastoral tasks within the tribal territory. Jobs were low status and salaries were poor by urban standards, and the rapidly increasing numbers of unskilled, unemployed, and underemployed workers in Iran—in addition to the many foreign workers (Afghans, Pakistanis, South Koreans)—ensured job scarcity. Living expenses were high, and workers could not accumulate much cash. Uncongenial working and living conditions, absence from kin and tribe, and a new subordinate and low status added to Qashqa'i dislike of urban jobs. Some Qashqa'i followed patterns established by other Iranians and left Iran (often illegally) to seek seasonal or longer-term work in the Gulf states,[34] where salaries were high compared with similar work in Iran. It was still too soon to assess the economic and social impact of labor emigration on the Qashqa'i when the revolution of 1978–79 occurred.

Better job opportunities were found among young Qashqa'i men (and some women), who, in rapidly increasing numbers, were acquiring specialized or semiskilled training and seeking jobs with higher pay and better working conditions. Included were graduates of the tribal teacher training school in Shiraz; those with experience in the army, a veterinary program, and the national Literacy, Health, and Rural Extension Corps; and high school graduates. The key to these opportunities was the tribal school program, which brought education up to the fifth grade to children of nomads.[35] Few in these training and work programs anticipated a life of herding, and their absence caused changes in household division of labor and expenditure. School children no longer contributed as much labor to their households, some families hired shepherds, and female labor substituted for male labor. School children, especially those who went on to attend town high schools, had heavy expenses. Many parents expressed their determination to support education, even when it clearly made for lower standards of living at home. Once offspring had salaried jobs, they provided financial help to their parents and younger, school-attending siblings.

Household productive activity changed rapidly in the 1960s and 70s. Production increased and more products were market-oriented than home-consumed. Households marketed more animals per year than previously. Average household herd sizes had tripled in these two decades to meet increasing cash and market demands, but pasture scarcity since the late 1960s encouraged fewer and smaller

herds. Gifts of cash rather than animals accompanied marriage transactions in order to conserve household productive capital. After
animals, clarified butter was the most profitable market item, and
households restricted consumption in order to sell more. Wool
brought high prices, and men wanted to sell it for cash, while women
sought to convert it into yarn and woven goods. Woven goods, which
in some Qashqa'i tribes rarely went to market, were increasingly sold;
women wove for the market and its desires for designs and styles
rather than household needs, dowries, and religious offerings. Some
weaving was conducted through a "putting-out" system, with urban
merchants providing the wool and setting the items' size and design.
Some woven goods were foresold to pay off debts. Carpet merchants
from urban bazaars began to travel to encampments for purchases.
Some carpet workshops in Firuzabad were established by nontribal
entrepreneurs, who paid women weavers a nominal wage and who
sold finished products in Tehran or abroad. A weaving school in
Shiraz helped some tribal girls to refine their skills. Weaving activities, which were once controlled by women, were increasingly
interfered with by males of the household, and women were losing
out in one area where they had acquired prestige and status.

Until the 1960s, Qashqa'i households had as primary economic
concerns animal care and grain cultivation, but land restrictions and
cash and market demands transformed their strategies. Recent political and economic change meant change in relations of production;
kin-based relations were penetrated and undermined by capitalist
relations. Individuals who were paid wages by sources outside the
household no longer contributed directly to pastoral production.
Household productive activity was increasingly regulated by, and
geared toward, market and capitalist forces. Vertical, asymmetrical
economic relations with moneylenders, merchants, urban employers,
and capitalist stock raisers increasingly had more impact on Qashqa'i
households than did kinship and tribal ties. Economic differentiation
among the Qashqa'i increased as tribal institutions were disrupted, as
households and groups responded differently to new conditions, and
as pastoralism was abandoned for other livelihoods. Patterns of
economic stratification were in flux. For example, hired shepherds,
who formerly were locked into asymmetrical, contractual relations
with their employers, now had chances for well-paying jobs, partly
because the wage relations in herding facilitated their proletarianiza-
tion in urban areas. And, women doing commercial weaving could
purchase agricultural land, regardless of their former socioeconomic
and tribal status.

The Impact of the Market

Until the 1960s, the pastoral nomadic economy was based upon the periodic exchange of pastoral products for agricultural and manufactured products from villages and towns. Pastoral products included herd animals, meat, wool, dairy products, draft and riding animals, woven goods, goat hair, and animal skins. Those without pastoral goods for sale marketed charcoal, gum tragacanth, and other nonpastoral commodities. Those marketing grain did so under financial duress. Goods acquired from villages and towns included foodstuffs, animal feed, clothing and cloth, jewelry, felt rugs, metal and leather goods, lanterns and kerosene, and miscellaneous items such as tobacco and medicines. Wealthier households could afford more items than poor ones, although there was a homogeneity in goods needed by all. Difficulties in getting to town and transporting goods back to camp and on migrations were factors in restraining impulses for material goods. Nomadic life precluded too many bulky non-necessities.

The most valued pastoral product—herd animals—was traded once a year, but needs for market products were constant; trading relationships helped to balance sales and purchases. Until the mid-1960s, "village friends"—small producers and local merchants—were important in this capacity. Pastoralists and agriculturalists exchanged products. Village merchants offered agricultural and manufactured products, while village craftspeople sold specialized goods and did repairs. Animals unable to migrate were left with villagers, and nomads reciprocated by taking some village animals on their migrations. Nomads stored winter equipment with merchant friends in winter pastures. Itinerant peddlers made the rounds of nomadic camps, exchanging small items for pastoral products or cash.

Localized economic exchange was due in part to the often turbulent times in southern Iran and in the lack of security in travel to distant markets through the territory of rival tribes and government military posts. Dealing with villagers in winter and summer pastures was safer and more convenient. Harmonious relations between the Qashqa'i and the Persian or Luri villagers often depended on the political climate of the times. Raiding of village crops and animals was related to economic deprivation, government harassment, and intertribal disputes.

Economic relations changed considerably in the 1960s and 70s. New contacts between Qashqa'i nomads and urban markets almost totally eliminated exchange with local villagers, and peddlers rarely appeared in nomadic camps. The urban merchant's demand that his debtors trade *all* their products with him was a major factor in the decline in these relations, although improved roads and minibus and truck service also discouraged local exchange. The many urban services requiring or tempting the nomads' presence made it more likely that they would avoid the village and concentrate their business in towns and cities.[36] The prices of village merchants and peddlers were higher than those of urban markets, and the selection and quality of goods poorer, so it paid the nomads, who went to town anyway, to buy goods there. In addition, the inclusion of pastoralism in village economies eliminated the reliance on nomads' products. Most economic exchanges now involved urban markets, where economic relations were asymmetrical and exploitative. The most common link between nomad and market was the moneylender-merchant, who owned a shop, did wholesaling, and profited by offering goods on credit and money on loan.[37] In its simplest form, the moneylender-merchant received the nomad's sale animals or the cash they brought, and in exchange allowed the nomad to take goods from his shop throughout the year.

Until the 1960s, few nomads had become ensnared in such relationships. Contact with urban markets was less frequent and involved fewer exchanges, while animal theft lessened economic problems. However, by 1971 it was common to find nomadic households of average size and wealth (six members, 160 sheep-goats) $20,000 in debt. Pasture scarcity meant pasture rents, crop damage payments, decreased pastoral production, and increased reliance on purchased supplemental feed. Demands for cash in these and other areas (changed patterns of consumption, bribes, education, town visits) accelerated and created greater reliance on moneylender-merchants. Because of high interest rates on goods and money (30–100 percent a year), the moneylender-merchant easily came to control the nomad. The merchant paid low market prices for pastoral products—often buying them at low prices months before they were delivered—and charged high market prices for his goods. Afshar Naderi notes that these two modes of exploitation combined to deprive Iranian nomads of over half the value of their production.[38] As debt grew, nomads were forced to trade on increasingly unfavorable terms *all* their products with their creditor and borrow money *only* from him. When payment was impossible, the only option was to transfer partial ownership of flocks to the merchant, which allowed him further inroads in the production process. He made frequent supervisory visits to camps where he owned part interest in flocks. The moneylender-merchant justified these practices by the favors and services he provided the nomad, which included continued credit and loans and urban contacts. The nomad lacked alternative ways of acquiring market goods and cash.

Moneylender-merchants increasingly influenced the regional meat market by personally entering into commercial animal-raising. They acquired herd animals on default of debts from nomads, to contract them out to other nomads, or to sell. They speculated in animals, buying at certain seasons for marketing in Tehran, where prices were higher. They made the rounds of camps just prior to the migration, cheaply acquiring animals unable to migrate. Nomads who lacked the capital in animals or the mobility to engage in similar activities were increasingly subject to the prices and conditions these middlemen set.

Rapid inflation in Iran in the 1970s contributed to these difficulties. The goods nomads brought to market were not equivalently inflated in price to the goods they bought, partly because of their obligations to merchants, but also because the government allowed the importation of meat and dairy products from abroad under cheap tariff arrangements and subsidized market prices. Since 1968 the government's Meat Organization controlled the purchase price of herd animals through regional slaughterhouses, and it kept the national demand for meat from reaching a fair market price.[39] The prices gained by the nomad in meat and dairy sales were considerably less than the prices paid by consumers; middlemen gained the difference. Butchers, not pastoralists or consumers, benefited from meat subsidies, since they bought meat cheaply from government slaughterhouses (which purchased animals at the low, fixed price) and sold it expensively to customers.[40] In this fashion, the government undercut the economic base of its own pastoralists, destroyed the country's domestic meat production, and forced dependence on foreign meat suppliers to grow. Until 1977, the livestock sector of the economy was increasing at a much slower annual rate than were the demand for meat, rate of population increase, and gross domestic production rate.[41]

The marketplace filled with cheap industrial goods and consumer products, and the Qashqa'i increasingly competed for status by seeking out material goods. Horses and guns, which had been the main symbols of male status, were replaced by such industrial products as radios and motorcycles. All demanded cash and new or expanded efforts to secure it. The greatest drain on cash, however, concerned land: purchase, rents, and bribes to government officials responsible for land use. Due to land shortage and speculation, land prices increased at a much faster rate than the prices of pastoral products.

New market demands on the Qashqa'i created greater needs for effective mediators and useful market contacts. Moneylender-merchants were mediators of sorts, but indebtedness created unsatisfactory relations for nomads. Before 1962 they could rely on tribal khans and headmen to supply economic contacts, information, and often actual services, but they lost this aid. It was no longer in the khans' or headmen's interests to offer favors. In areas where the forces pushing for sedentarization operated much earlier than among the Qashqa'i, tribal entrepreneurs—petty traders, merchants, animal and weaving contractors—emerged to play important economic and political roles.[42] This was rare among the Qashqa'i, except near the oil fields, where they have settled since the 1930s. Settled Qashqa'i did serve as mediators, as have, more recently, tribal school teachers, whose literacy, mobility, urban sophistication, and extra-tribal contacts made them increasingly indispensible to the people of their assigned sections.

The Transition to Settled Life

The nature and supposed interconnections of nomadism, pastoralism, settlement, and tribalism are still confused in the literature, despite many corrective studies. Pastoralism—subsistence from the products of domestic animals—is not necessarily affected by the exchanging of a nomadic for a settled life. A "tribe," sometimes defined as a sociopolitical response to external political powers,[43] is a group often sharing a common name, cultural heritage, and presumed agnatic descent. It does not cease to exist, nor do tribal affiliations necessarily weaken, simply because its members change their residence or occupation. Instead, explanations for changes in patterns of nomadism, pastoralism, or tribalism must be sought in a complex set of political, economic, social, and cultural factors and must be placed into historical perspective. Forces "pushing" nomads away from nomadism—such as pasture scarcity and government harassment—and "pulling" them toward settled life—such as job opportunities and land availability—vary according to circumstances. Decisions to settle are made individually and by groups. Some nomads are forced to settle by government decree while others settle "voluntarily." Barth suggests that settlement occurs among the poor and the wealthy of a nomadic population,[44] but other studies show that nomads of all economic strata settle, and that the process is much more complex than he outlined.[45] For any nomadic population, settlement and, to a much lesser degree, nomadization are ongoing processes. What happened as revolutionary conditions in Iran unfolded (see below) is an excellent example of the latter.

At the beginning of the 1960s, the majority of Qashqa'i were nomadic and pastoral and lacked permanent settlements. They spent approximately four months in lowland winter pastures, two months migrating in spring to highland summer pastures, three months residing in summer pastures, and three months migrating back again in the fall to winter pastures. While occupying seasonal pastures, households made a series of local moves. Diversity in livelihood and life style was common, for households regularly adjusted their patterns to household development cycles and other factors. Flexibility was essential to viable economies and to the continuing survival of the Qashqa'i. Some Qashqa'i lived in houses in winter and summer pastures and migrated in the spring and fall; some lived in tents and did not migrate; and some lived in villages in winter and in tents at higher altitudes in summer. A few Qashqa'i lived in tents and practiced only agriculture; others lived in houses and practiced only pastoralism. Some Qashqa'i families were split into sedentary and nomadic parts, others into agricultural and pastoral parts. And, a few Qashqa'i migrated who owned no sheep and goats at all.

The changes of the 1960s and 70s undercut such flexible patterns, forced the end of large-scale migration, and led to the predominance of three patterns: 1)sedentarization in villages; 2)continuation of impoverished nomadic pastoralism; and 3)migration to towns and cities for wage labor. Most Qashqa'i settled or made plans to do so, and subsisted by combining flock raising with agriculture. Some Qashqa'i, usually owing to poverty, continued in year-round nomadic pastoralism without immediate plans or the needed capital for settlement. They had small herds which usually belonged partially or totally to others, and they did seasonal wage labor and other nonpastoral work. Other Qashqa'i settled individually or with families in towns and cities. This too was a response to poverty; they performed low-paid work and lived and worked in oppressive conditions. These Qashqa'i blended into the underemployed populations of every town and city of the region, and their residences were part of large, crowded squatter settlements.[46]Many lived in tattered tents, shacks, and underground holes covered with cardboard and tin.

Most Qashqa'i settled near traditional winter or summer pastures, in villages consisting of previously-settled tribal people or in settlements they created. Some Qashqa'i settled individually, but most settled with relatives and in groups. Location depended on land availability, prior local affiliations, and forms of production. Winter and summer pasture areas presented different but serious climatic problems; the ideal location, halfway between the two areas at middle altitudes, was already heavily populated and expensive.

Under Reza Shah, almost all Qashqa'i were forced to settle in unsuitable locations. (Some nomads secured government permits during this time to migrate between seasonal pastures, but complete households could not accompany the herds.) With his abdication, most Qashqa'i returned to full nomadic pastoralism, with the exception of oilfield workers. In times of economic and political hardship since 1941, many Qashqa'i temporarily or permanently settled again. Severe droughts in 1959–64 and again in 1970–71 led to some settlement. Subtribes changing territories over time left a few settlers in each former location. However, as the government gained control of tribal land use, such mobility was forbidden, and settling subtribes were often forced to stay near their last location. By 1978 Qashqa'i territory contained hundreds of tiny settlements, usually consisting of a few stone or mud-brick houses set down like tents in an encampment.

Some Qashqa'i who settled before 1970 have successfully adjusted to the end of nomadism. At first they sharecropped or rented agricultural land. Later, they bought land from the government or from large holders who were anxious to sell at prices higher than would be received through land reform.[47] Many created cooperative groups for grain cultivation, orchard formation, construction, and machinery purchase. They continued pastoralism by sending herds to higher altitudes in the summer or on the full migration. Many lived year-round in tents erected by their houses, which they used for storage and weaving. For some, summertime brought temporary residence in tents at higher altitudes.

The tempo and patterns of settlement, however, recently underwent a marked change. Many Qashqa'i, pressured by the forces described above, wanted to settle, but were unable to find affordable land. Under duress and lacking other options, they bought small house plots in established non-Qashqa'i villages or towns near winter or summer pastures. Construction materials were expensive and subject to national shortages, and some who could afford land purchase could not afford the additional expenses. How these new settlers intended to survive was not clear, and was a vocal concern of many Qashqa'i. Some expected to earn money as agricultural workers, following previous settlers, but the proliferation of available workers meant that many remained unemployed or were forced into low-paying urban wage labor. Some intended to continue pastoralism by sending someone on the migration with the herds. Most hoped eventually to buy land for agriculture and orchards, but as land prices rapidly escalated, this became more difficult.

The government's Office of Tribal Settlement (under the Ministry of Housing and Development) in Shiraz offered no real assistance. Government loans were supposedly available for settlement, but securing them was virtually impossible for most, and formal requests took years to travel through channels. Acquiring government help hinged on effective mediators who had official contacts, cash and favors for bribes, and time to spend in the city. Some tribal headmen used their networks and political sophistication to find land for their groups, and some financed the purchase of agricultural machinery. Other headmen were unwilling or unable to function in this manner.

Migration patterns for many Qashqa'i changed. Fewer complete households migrated. Women and young children of settling families tended to remain in one place all year, while several males migrated with the herds. They carried minimal supplies and slept in canvas pup-tents. These herders were aware that their life had changed dramatically. They lamented that, "We are just shepherds now. We have left our 'life' behind." A transitional phase for many Qashqa'i involved motor transport and the elimination of the long migration through the Zagros mountains. The herds continued the regular migration at a quickened pace with one or more adult males, while other family members and household equipment were transported by rented minibuses and trucks to new seasonal pastures in a day or two. Sometimes herd animals were moved by truck, which was expensive and unproductive, since premature arrival at seasonal pastures meant insufficient grazing and water. The separation of households and herds during the spring migration meant that families were cut off from milk products as a food supply and an important market item. Milk flow is at its heaviest level in the spring, but the few men and boys who accompanied the herds could not possibly milk and process dairy products, and baby animals were allowed to drink their fill of mother's milk.

Qashqa'i who no longer migrated also lost out in the collection of natural resources and wild foods. Dry vegetation provided fuel, and hardwoods supplied the raw material for equipment; commercial fuels and manufactured products were expensive substitutes. Gathered plants and minerals were used in dyeing wool, but Qashqa'i women increasingly relied on expensive, inferior chemical dyes. Much food eaten during the migration or stored for later use was gathered from passage through different ecological zones. This particularly affected young girls and women who were not usually fed as well as males. The migration had also provided access to wild game, although the government's confiscation of most firearms in 1963 made game meat less available. Since most milk products were market-oriented rather than home-consumed, the lack of gathered and hunted food was an additional loss. Increasingly, foodstuffs were purchased from the market, which demanded an increased cash inflow.

Since pack animals were no longer needed and their continued upkeep was expensive, households sold most of them.[48] Yet, without pack animals, households had a difficult time returning, temporarily or permanently, to nomadism. The flexibility once possible in the now-settled, now-nomadic, lifestyle seemed to be gone.

The Iranian Revolution, 1978–79

The recent dramatic turn of events in Iran has had great impact on the countryside, especially on populations affiliated by tribal ties.[49] With loss of government control, tribal groups are asserting their autonomy and in particular their rights to use traditional pastures. Land reform and pasture nationalization, which detrimentally affected nomadic pastoralists, are associated with what is seen as the illegal, corrupt regime of the shah, and many individuals and groups are reclaiming their land. Groups formerly armed and well organized under leaders are best prepared in this regard. Many nomads who had severed their connections with the land have now returned. Many who had sedentarized are now migrating, and urban wage laborers are back in the mountains. Naser Khan Qashqa'i, the paramount tribal leader who was exiled in 1954 for his support of Mosaddeq, returned to Iran shortly before the shah's departure, in order to reestablish political power and authority.

The Islamic Republic's goal is to make Iran as self-sufficient in food as possible, which entails the difficult task of restoring and reorganizing domestic production. However, food imports have continued. Imported frozen meat was initially proclaimed to be unclean and was ordered destroyed by the Ayatollah Khomaini, but foreign suppliers are now said to be following proper Islamic procedures in animal slaughter. For Iran's agriculturalists, whose links with the land had been broken, return to production is difficult. Many irrigation systems are ruined, land is abandoned and no longer cultivable, land tenure systems disrupted, and kin-based relations of production undermined and altered by urban wage migration and the penetration of capitalist relations of production into rural economies. But for nomadic pastoralists, long organized in political groups and accustomed to periodic disruptions by state authorities, a quick resumption of production is more likely. Their return to the land does not appear to be hindered. Tribal leaders are redistributing flocks and land to aid the economic survival of tribal members, as they had done following previous political crises. If permitted, Iran's pastoral nomads could be extremely important in helping the nation meet its immediate demands for meat and dairy products, as well as in facilitating indigenous production. The alternative is a continuing, deepening dependence on foreign food suppliers.

Relations of production—such as those between nomads and moneylenders, or between hired shepherds and employers—have also rapidly changed. With the Islamic Republic's appearance, interest-taking was forbidden, and religious authorities and Revolutionary Committees enforced the nomads' demands that their debts be renegotiated so that only the actual value of borrowed goods and money needed to be repaid. Many nomads were able to discharge their total debts in the new regime's first months. In the absence of government control and in light of the great national demand for meat, many poor and middle-range Qashqa'i are now able to assume economic independence. Control of land was the major factor creating differential access to it; once the control is decreased—as it is under current revolutionary conditions—former pastoralists can easily locate pastures for their flocks. What will happen as government control gradually reasserts itself is not as clear.

Conclusions

This paper has detailed the effects of government sponsored change on the Qashqa'i of Fars. At least for this tribal population, the once much-heralded reforms of the shah resulted in debilitating economic conditions. Without leaders or functioning tribal structures, the Qashqa'i became extremely vulnerable to political and economic change at the national level. With the collapse of the state, however, their political institutions rapidly resumed effectiveness.

In many ways the Qashqa'i had been resisting the political and economic pressures that encouraged them to settle and assimilate into Iranian culture and society. Of utmost importance in understanding continuity and resiliency in Qashqa'i society and culture is the nature of tribalism and the significance of tribal identity for the Qashqa'i. Among some settled pastoral nomads, the tribe as a functioning political and symbolic unit is said to cease to exist. Among others, tribal units not only continue to play important political roles, but actually take on increased political significance after settlement.[50] Qashqa'i identity used to focus on tribal leaders, especially the khans and *Ilkhani,* who had the ability to unite them in the face of opposition, and who gained dominance in the region for them. Although these leaders were removed from office, tribal and ethnic identities remained strong. The tribal school system played a role in the rekindling of Qashqa'i identity, and some Qashqa'i viewed the education program's director as *the* tribal representative and as mediator between tribe and state in ways that the *Ilkhani* and khans once were.

All Qashqa'i are aware of a common heritage and history, which centers on the opposition of Qashqa'i and non-Qashqa'i—variously defined as the state, foreign powers (especially the British), settled agriculturalists, or urban moneylender-merchants. The identifying labels of "Qashqa'i" and "Turk" (which in Fars is virtually synonymous with Qashqa'i) clearly take precedence over an "Iranian" identity. The Turkic language is an extremely important mark of identity, as is the sharing of territory, especially because of competition over land. Qashqa'i dress—the men's two-eared felt hat and the women's multi-layered, colorful dress—is also an obvious identifying feature. Finally, commonly-shared values and customs, especially in marriage ceremonies and hospitality, are important.

As viewed in 1978, the tenacity of the Qashqa'i sociocultural system over past centuries seemed to offer hopeful evidence that their identifications would continue to be meaningful, regardless of political and economic change. During the events of 1978–80, this has indeed been the case.

6

Size and Success:
Komachi Adaptation to a Changing Iran

Daniel A. Bradburd

Introduction

This paper examines changes which have occurred in the lives of
Komachi nomads from 1950–75, due to transformations of political
and economic conditions in Iran.[1] The discussion is focused upon two
problems: 1) the effect of increased state control over tribal hinter-
lands; and 2) the effect of economic development in Iran in those
regions.

There is considerable literature on these problems,[2] but in general,
these accounts have all considered the effects of the Pahlavi government's intervention into the affairs of large, powerful and (sometimes) politically important tribal groups. This paper, however, presents something of a contrast, for the Komachi are small, weak, and
politically insignificant. Thus, while many of the larger tribes were
victims of government programs aimed specifically at them, the
Komachi had to deal only with vague programs haphazardly administered from a distance. While the larger tribes suffered as a result of
government policy, the Komachi did rather well on 'benign neglect.'

This paper attempts to show how and why the Komachi prospered.
It proceeds in the following fashion: 1) an overview of tribes and their
place in Kerman; 2) a brief description of the Komachi; 3) a description
of some of the changes which befell the Komachi over the last
twenty-five years; and 4) a consideration of the implications of these
developments.

Tribes in Kerman

There are many large and famous tribes in Iran: the Lurs, Qashqa'i, and Bakhtiyari of the west, the Baluchi of the southeast, and the Turkoman of the north. Kerman, in south-central Iran, has no famous tribes. In 1975, the largest group, the Afshar, numbered less than 1,500 tents and, while there were several other tribes which were nearly as large (the Qaro'i, Luri, and the Sulemani each claimed 1,000 tents), the majority of tribes in Kerman were very small. The Komachi numbered barely 100 tents, and several of their tribal neighbors had as few as 30–40 households. These low figures do not appear to be an effect of recent circumstances. Sykes records figures for Kermani tribes in 1902 which are quite similar in magnitude to 1975 figures, as does Field for the mid-1930s.[3] Although past estimates of nomadic population are not entirely reliable, Field's figures show nearly 20,000 tribal households in Kerman Province. (However, this represents a compilation of figures which were gathered over 40 years, and in addition, many of his nomadic tribes were, in fact, villages.) In mid-1975, the director of the Office of Tribal Affairs of Kerman estimated that there were about 10,000 nomadic households in the province.[4] If this figure is accurate, then tribes represented approximately 5 percent of the total population of Kerman. By way of contrast, the Qashqa'i alone appear to number well over 100,000 persons,[5] and Barth suggests that until the latter half of this century nomadic tribes comprised 25 percent of the population of Fars Province.[6]

The individual tribes of Kerman are not only small, they also appear to lack any significant political organization. Although the larger tribes such as the Qaro'i, the Sulemani and Afshar have khans, most of the smaller tribes like the Komachi have no internal political hierarchy at all. In addition, while large confederations of tribes appear to have been common in western Iran, there is little evidence that meaningful tribal confederacies have existed in Kerman in recent times.[7] It is not entirely clear why there are both fewer nomads and few instances of political hierarchy in Kerman, but two related sets of factors appear to be involved. Barth and Salzman have suggested that the underlying cause is ecological: the tribal areas of Kerman are considerably drier than the Zagros region of western Iran;[8] therefore, it is argued, the land is unable to support such large concentrations of tribesmen as are found in the west. Salzman, especially, considers population density an important factor in determining political organization. In contrast, Garthwaite has suggested that elaborate tribal hierarchies may be the result of the interplay of tribal populations with the state.[9] In the case of Kerman, it seems quite likely that the larger political context for tribal hierarchical stratification was just as lacking as were the necessary ecological conditions. In either event, the tribes in Kerman are both small and poorly organized for concerted political or military action. As a result, while the Qashqa'i, Khamseh, and Bakhtiyari have played an active role in regional and national affairs,[10] Kermani tribes appear to have had little effect at the national level and, in fact, even relatively little impact on local affairs.

A testimony to the relative lack of importance of the tribes in Kerman is the fact that the Komachi and their neighbors claimed to have been untouched by the forced settlement schemes which were imposed on the larger and more powerful tribes during the reign of Reza Shah. Indeed, the Komachi reported that not only were they never settled, but that at various times they were given weapons by the government to protect themselves and their territory.

The Komachi

The Komachi are a very small tribe of nomadic pastoralists in south-central Kerman Province who numbered only 550 persons (just over 100 households) in 1975. They lack any formal political organization—there are no chiefs or headmen. There is no single person with any actual political power; in discussing Komachi politics it is best to speak of influence and paths of influence rather than anything more formal.

In the fall of 1975, the 100 households were divided into 18 camps. Centered about particularly wealthy and important men, these camps are the basic residential unit of the tribe and also the largest clearly bounded social unit. There is no hierarchical ordering of camps and no formal structuring of relations between them—relations between camps *qua* camps are determined by the relations between their heads.

While camps are the basic residential unit, the tribe can be more accurately seen as an aggregation of nuclear family households. Each of these households carefully guards its own independence, and almost all significant decisions are made to protect and further the narrowly-defined interests of the household.

The tribe is a body built by agglomeration and accretion. It has a core of three patronymic groups which claim radically different geographic origins: Fars, Khorasan, and Baluchistan. These groups became intertwined through marriage. Attached to this core are several smaller patronymic groups and various individual households. The best historical information available—which is meager—suggests that the process of agglomeration has been taking place since the beginning of this century and that, as a coherent body, the Komachi have existed for no more than 75 years.

There is no segmentary descent system that could account for all Komachi tribal organization, nor is there any single genealogy into which all tribesmen can be neatly placed. In practice, the tribe has functioned as a collection of overlapping egocentric networks of heads of camps.

In spite of the absence of any single overarching kinship system, the Komachi perceive the tribe to be a community of kin. They assert that all Komachi are linked to each other by kinship ties and, for the purpose of reckoning tribal membership, kinship is very broadly and generally calculated. (I was told, for example, that one man was Komachi because his son had married a girl who was Komachi.) Kinship is the idiom and the metaphor for all 'in-tribe' social relations and is the ideological marker of tribal unity and identity.

The Komachi belief that they are a tribe of kin is not simply a fiction. First, because kinship is so broadly reckoned, it is indeed true that everyone is closely related to at least someone—and through that one link, ties can be traced to other members of the tribe. Second, many members of the tribe, particularly those who are wealthy and members of the core patronymic groups have, in fact, large numbers of close kin in the tribe. One man, for example, had 112 close kinsmen (including 64 first cousins and 48 siblings, children, aunts, uncles and grandchildren) in a tribe with only 550 members; there are other men with nearly as many close kin. These large networks of close kin overlap considerably, and thus among the wealthy there are dense networks of kin ties joining individuals in multiplex ways. This is not the case for poorer members of the tribe. In a sense then, the tribe is truly a community of kin, but it is more clearly a community of close kin for the wealthier members of the tribe.

Animals are the primary wealth of the Komachi. Most herd goats, though some wealthier Komachi also have sheep. The 100 households owned a total of approximately 14,000 animals in 1975, roughly two-thirds of which were goats. Each household owns its own flock. There is considerable variation in family holdings; in September 1975, the wealthiest household owned 840 animals while the poorest had about 20. Under the economic conditions of 1975, a household of four needed a flock of over 60 animals to be economically self-sufficient—that is, to be able to support itself by consuming and selling its herd's produce. Yet, there were many households which fell below that figure. Such households had to supplement their incomes. Traditionally, these poorer households worked as hired shepherds for the wealthier families. The conditions of employment in this situation were openly exploitative, and the relationships were characterized by a great deal of tension centered particularly around demands for uncompensated female labor.[11]

The Komachi economy was based on production directed toward consumption.[12] This was so even though there was a detour in the distribution of pastoral production—a significant portion of Komachi production passed through the marketplace. The bulk of the conversion in the market was a direct exchange of pastoral produce for those nonpastoral goods needed for domestic consumption: wheat, tea, barley, clothing, sugar, rice and other items the tribesmen could not produce. Almost all Komachi exchanges for these materials took place in the bazaar of Kerman City. The exchanges were made with semipermanent trading partners, *taraf*, who extended the Komachi credit and who also acted as intermediaries with the outside world.

The Komachi in a Changing Iran

Pacification of the Countryside

The Komachi claimed that the most important change in their lives had come about through the establishment of 'law and order' in the Iranian countryside. A small and weak tribe, the Komachi appear never to have been predators but rather always to have been the prey of larger, stronger tribes or settled populations. For example, early in this century, the Buchaqchi, whose home territory is southwest of Sirjan, frequently attacked the Komachi in their summer quarters near Shirinak and Giborj. They were reported to have taken all the animals and personal property which they could find. In their winter quarters near the villages of Jaghin and Manujan, the Komachi and their tribal neighbors were harassed by both raiders from Baluchistan and by local strong men (see below). In addition, the Komachi said that during the annual migration they were so afraid of theft that they left the bulk of their valuables (except animals) in the houses of their patrons in the town of Qaryaitalarab. They migrated dressed in rags so they would look poor. To protect their animals they would attempt to sneak past certain dangerous areas in the middle of the night. Despite these tactics, they were frequently attacked and robbed. Older men and women reminiscing about the past often told about the time when the man who is now the wealthiest member of the tribe was waylaid, robbed, and stripped naked; or the time when the

Buchaqchi attacked a Komachi camp and stole all the rifles the government had supplied for their protection.

From the early 1950s to 1975 the areas of Kerman Province in which the Komachi dwell became progressively more secure. Predation was no longer a problem—the government disarmed marauding tribes (and peaceful ones as well), and it maintained patrols in all regions of the province. The removal of the threat of potential attack had a profound effect on the Komachi; it enabled them to exploit areas of the province that were formerly closed to them, especially in the winter quarter area. As mentioned above, the local strongmen in the winter quarters as well as tribesmen were involved in brigandage. The local leaders were petty warlords who dwelt in fortified residences near small date palm oases with bands of armed retainers. These strongmen attempted to steal whatever they could or to extract 'protection' money from whomever was unfortunate enough to pass nearby. Tribes like the Komachi had to pay to use certain pastures along their migration route as well as for the use of winter quarter pastures. [13]

In some cases, the Komachi were so fearful of "hungry khans" that they, and other tribes, avoided certain areas. Thus, large areas of potential pasture were closed to the Komachi due to unsettled or pernicious local conditions. With the establishment of government authority in the 1950s, the areas opened up. The Komachi moved to their current winter pastures in the area of Jaghin and Manujan in the early 1950s only after the area had been pacified. In this case, pacification benefited the Komachi in two ways: 1) they were no longer forced to make onerous payments to local leaders; and 2) they were able to move into areas which nomads had avoided for a considerable period of time. It is important to note that these areas had not been overgrazed—as many of the more secure areas had been—and hence the Komachi found themselves possessing reasonably rich pasture. The establishment of peace in the countryside benefited small tribes like the Komachi who, previously, had been the victims of anyone who possessed greater force. [14]

Barth has suggested that in extremely arid regions of Iran like Kerman and Baluchistan, settled populations will dominate nomads rather than the reverse. [15] Komachi accounts of their relations with settled leaders in their winter quarters support this view as did their accounts of former relations with the more important local landlords (khans) in their summer quarters. Although relations with summer quarter khans were not as oppressive nor as capricious as those with leaders in winter quarters, the Komachi were still under the control of these men. The khans controlled the pasture and water rights in the valleys surrounding their villages. To assure themselves access to resources the Komachi became the clients of these khans. In return for guaranteed access to resources in areas controlled by local khans, and for whatever protection the khans could provide, the Komachi supplied them with animals and dairy products.[16]

With land reform in the 1960s, the khans greatly reduced their interests in the marginally productive villages in the Komachi summer quarters. Their property was largely distributed to peasants, and concern with regulation of access to resources such as pasture and water passed from the hands of the khans to the state. Thus, where the Komachi once gained access to pastures surrounding villages through the manipulation of patron/client ties, they later gained access from permits granted by the government.

Beck documents the changes which have taken place among the Qashqa'i as a result of the institution (and abuse) of the permit system.[17] Again, the Komachi case provides an interesting contrast. As was the case among Qashqa'i, not all Komachi obtained government permits granting them access to pasture. In general, only the wealthiest Komachi, men who were heads of camps, received them. The permits were, in addition, rather broadly drawn, giving each holder access to a considerable amount of territory. However, while among the Qashqa'i the permits were used to restrict access or to fix access, this was not the case among the Komachi. All members of the tribe continued to have access to the territory 'controlled' by the permit holders. Members of the tribe who did not have permits (the poorer nomads) were assured access to land through their residence in camps with wealthier men (camp leaders) who did have permits. No direct economic remuneration was required of them in return for pasture. This was true even though it was quite clear to all Komachi that there was insufficient pasture for them in their summer quarters.[18]

In one sense, the structure of the relationship which existed when khans controlled access to pasture persisted even when the khans were replaced by government permits. Previously, wealthy Komachi maintained client relations with settled patrons, paying them in goods and services to ensure access to resources. Poorer Komachi got access to resources by being clients of wealthier Komachi—there was a pyramid of patronage. Even though the top of this pyramid was amputated by the state's assumption of control of pastoral resources, the bottom of the pyramid functioned as it once did. Wealthy Komachi ensured the tribe access to resources through ties to external authority—first the khan, then the state—while poorer Komachi were assured access to these resources through ties to the wealthier Komachi. Unlike the situation among the Qashqa'i, the structure of tribal relations was preserved.

The Komachi, in fact, benefited from this change in two ways: 1) they were relieved of the burden of maintaining client ties to khans in the area;[19] and 2) government regulation of access to pasture was strikingly casual. The permits guaranteed the Komachi access to their pasture *vis-à-vis* other tribes but placed few real restrictions upon the Komachi with regard to utilization of the resources. Once again, as with the control of raiding and the pacification of the countryside, the Komachi benefited from the passive application of government programs directed not at the Komachi but at other sectors of the rural population. These nomads were able to turn the effects of these programs to their advantage.

Land Reform

While the land reform program benefited the Komachi in general, there were some Komachi whom it has harmed as well. Specifically, there were a few relatively wealthy Komachi who owned agricultural land in summer quarter villages. The amounts they owned were rather small—the largest single holding was a one-fourth share of a very small *qanat*.[20] Nevertheless, this land supplied the Komachi owners with an important supplement of both cash income and goods for household consumption. Furthermore, it represented a fund of stored wealth. The Komachi never worked this land themselves, but employed local peasants on a sharecropping basis.

The general inadequacies of Iranian land reforms have been pointed out;[21] Dillon has shown how unevenly and haltingly it was applied in Kerman. He claims that during the first phase of land reform fewer than one-third of Kerman's villages were affected, and that during the second phase of land reform only one-half of one percent of the peasants in the province received property "distributed on the basis of former cropsharing agreements."[22] However, after the third phase of land reform, which began to be implemented in 1969, undistributed lands were divided between landlords and tenants and, without exception, every Komachi who owned agricultural property in the summer quarters had his property relations materially affected by land reform; in the vast majority of cases land reform meant the division of property on the basis of sharecropping arrangements. Thus, most Komachi property owners ceded outright one-third of their small holdings to the peasants who had worked them. These same peasants continued to work the holdings remaining in Komachi hands at the previous one-third/two thirds sharecropping rate. As a result, in the total division of crops after land reform, the peasants' share increased from three-ninths to five-ninths produce, while the Komachi share was down from six-ninths to four-ninths. Given the small size of the original holdings, this loss significantly affected the material well-being of several Komachi households. Essentially, it reduced the return on agricultural lands held by the Komachi to the point that their contribution to household operations was minimal. As one Komachi lamented, "I don't get breakfast from my land," Komachi land thus became, more than ever, a fund of stored wealth rather than a vital element in their domestic economy.

Economic Development

The Komachi tribe has been for many years integrated into the larger national and international economy. Barth long ago pointed out the extent to which Southwest Asian pastoralists have been dependent upon exchange with settled peoples for most of their needs, and the Komachi are no exception.[23] The staples of their diet—wheat, tea, sugar and rice—are produced by settled peoples, and the Komachi acquire access to these commodities only through the exchange of pastoral products. Being integrated into the larger market system has meant that Komachi production and consumption are strongly influenced by forces external to their domestic economy. The historical effects of capitalist penetration into the domestic economy of tribes in Kerman has been discussed elsewhere.[24] It need only be pointed out here that the external market extracted wealth from the Komachi domestic economy, and that this situation promoted the development of significant differences in wealth among tribesmen.[25] At least among the Komachi and their nomadic neighbors, it set the stage for exploitative shepherding contracts and, ultimately, an unstable social order.

In the short term, however, changes in marketing conditions—based in large part on internal development of the Iranian economy—had beneficial effects on the Komachi. The Komachi and other nomads in Kerman were traditionally producers of *kork* (the soft underhair from Kashmir goats) and to a lesser extent of wool.[26] In the 1960s and 1970s, however, the market in both of these natural fibers were depressed. *Kork,* which 20 and 30 years ago brought $10.00 per kilogram, dropped in price during the early 1960s to only $2.35 per kilogram in 1975. Wool prices rose in the same period from a price range of $2–$2,50 per kilogram to approximately $3.75 per kilogram in the early 1970s. Then, however, that price remained stable in the face of a better than 30 percent rate of general inflation.

During the same time period, however, the demand for meat in Iran skyrocketed. This resulted from the general increase in wealth in the country, leading to increased demand for what had once been a largely luxury item.[27] Demand increased so greatly that domestic production (which was certainly hampered by the government's policy towards nomads in most regions of the country) was not adequate; frozen meat was imported into Iran at subsidized prices. However, in Kerman province the demand was met almost exclusively with animals from the local nomadic tribes.[28] The demand for meat led to considerable increases in its price: from early 1974 to late 1975, lamb rose from about $2.35 to nearly $3.70 per kilogram. The average market price for a lamb or goat rose from about $7.50 per animal in the late 1960s to roughly $37 in 1975.

The Komachi and neighboring tribes responded to the dramatic price increase of meat by radically shifting their production from *kork* and wool to meat. This shift involved a significant modification of the composition of their herds. When producing for wool or *kork*, the Komachi favored herds of adult male animals. These larger animals were the heaviest wool producers and, in addition, the Komachi believed that since males do not breed or nurse, their fleece is longer and finer. Since there was no market for meat, and there was a market for wool and *kork*, the Komachi had no incentive to sell their male animals. Hence, their herds were very large and included a large proportion of adult male animals which required little care other than herding and their need for an annual (or biannual, for sheep) shearing.

By contrast, meat production was directed toward the growth and sale of kids and lambs, for there was definite economic advantages to marketing the younger animals. They had the highest market price; they reached a good market weight fairly rapidly; and, they did not have to be maintained over the winter or late summer (Komachi females drop in the late fall). Since they were sold immediately after their peak growth, there was a fairly high return for the feed and care required. Older animals, although they brought a greater absolute price due to their larger size, entailed greater costs, and it was questionable whether the relative value of price to input of capital was as high. Hence, economic circumstances changed herd composition; tribesmen kept relatively few adult animals and herds came to be composed almost entirely of breeding stock and, during winter and spring, kids and lambs being fattened for marketing in summer. Overall, the number of animals decreased, while the number of females and young increased. The development of a large market for meat allowed the Komachi to concentrate production on a commodity whose value rose fast enough to keep them well ahead of the pace of inflation.[29]

The Komachi sold their animals on the hoof to butchers from Kerman City. The Komachi nominally received the fair market price per kilogram on the estimated dressed-weight of the animal. The butcher's profit theoretically was based only on the sale of the animal's organs and hide. But, in fact, the butcher's estimate of dressed-weight (a matter of intensive bargaining) was likely to leave him an additional margin for profit. Nevertheless, the Komachi were making an excellent return on their animals. Their meat income was supplemented by the sale of wool, *kork,* and dairy products. A Komachi household with a herd of roughly 200 animals marketed products worth up to $2,500 in a good year, while they also were able to reserve dairy products for their own use. Households with large herds often had sufficient income to send their children to school in Kerman City, to hire shepherds to care for their flocks, and to purchase luxury items—such as a motorcycle. What debts they had were short term. In fact, even poor Komachi households did well enough for their employers to complain that "no one wants to work; our shepherds aren't hungry anymore."

The increase in the price of meat in Iran not only made the meat production quite profitable for the Komachi, but it also enabled many of them to supplement their incomes by acting as brokers for tribes near Esfandagheh in the interior of the province. The Komachi, who had long-established relations with several Kerman City butchers, bought animals from tribes who had little direct contact with the urban market. Animals were bought on either a cash or credit basis during the early spring. The Komachi drove the animals to their own territory in summer, fattened them for market, and sold them with their own animals. In a good year, one man reported making nearly $750 profit on capital of $4,500, a group of three men made $3,100 serving as brokers for 600 animals.

Brokerage was a speculative venture, and one could incur losses. However, the constant spiral of inflation made it most unlikely that animals bought in early spring would not allow the buyer to show at least a paper profit by late summer.[30] The Komachi who entered into these ventures were generally younger men with fairly large herds relative to their needs. They had some capital to spare and liked the 'adventure' of both the traveling and the gamble. Their enthusiasm for ventures of this type was not shared by all Komachi; brokers were often referred to as "peddlers" behind their backs.

The burgeoning meat market which increased the flow of wealth into Komachi society and led to changes in herd composition (and perhaps to labor demands), however, appeared to have had no marked effect on the internal structure of the tribe or on the nomads' domestic economy. Rather, it seemed to act as a barrier between the Komachi and the inflationary pressures of the external economy.

Other changes, however, did lead to significant modifications of the Komachi lifestyle. First, small-scale carpet manufacture was introduced in the summer quarters region. As Dillon has pointed out, the carpet industry in Kerman was not a traditional cottage industry but was the rural sector of an urban and capitalistic system.[31] Traditionally, the capital for weaving was supplied and controlled by the urban elite. Yet, with the initial flow of petro-dollars into Iran and the corresponding boom of the economy, much of the large-scale urban capital moved out of the carpet industry in Kerman and into more lucrative investments in other sectors of the economy. Smaller urban investors and the rural bourgeoisie stepped into this void, and they provided capital for carpet weaving. This influx of capital led to the establishment of many new carpet workshops in rather isolated villages where labor was readily available and where wages were low.

In the Komachi *sarhad,* the influx of rural capital led to the establishment of ten new workshops in the villages of Shirinak and Giborj over three years (1973–75). The workshops were small operations; each had one or two looms, employed a pattern caller, and had from three to eight weavers. In Shirinak the weavers were all young children and, indeed, many of the pattern callers were children as well. The weavers were paid on a piece work basis, 15 rials per *pud* (warp), amounting to roughly $150 per year. The pattern caller received a fixed wage of between $15 and $22.25 a month.[32]

Many of the carpet workshops in the Komachi *sarhad* were run by Komachi who had recently settled. The new workshop bosses were nomads who had had fairly large herds, 150 animals or more, but who had abandoned pastoralism to invest their capital in carpets. Generally, they put up a small fraction of the overall investment, forming partnerships with members of the rural bourgeoisie of the town of Quaryaitalarab. The former nomad was overseer of the operation but drew no direct salary from it. In theory, after the workshop had been in operation for several years, it was to be signed over to the nomad in lieu of his salary. Significantly, the men who settled to run workshops were men with many children—usually many daughters.

In the traditional tribal economy, daughters were responsible for much of the family's work, but there was no way to convert excess female labor into cash income.[33] With carpets, female labor became convertible. Men who settled put their daughters to work in their own workshops; although they drew no salaries themselves, they received their daughters' incomes directly from their partners as part of the concern's operating expenses. For men with many daughters, carpet workshops were an excellent proposition. All labor was supplied by their family so that the labor costs were returned to them as salary; their daughters earned an income not possible under traditional circumstances; and the men had some capital and a great deal of free time which they used to speculate on animals and other merchandise. Usually, households disposed of their herds when they settled. They did not practice multi-resource extraction, nor did they enter into cooperative arrangements with nomadic households.[34]

Carpet workshops were an important innovation; before their establishment the Komachi did not settle. Although the number of Komachi who could settle as entrepreneurs was limited, their sedentarization had important ripple effects among other tribesmen. Workshops were run on child labor and the work was highly labor intensive. To meet this demand for labor, the Komachi bosses tried to hire children, particularly the daughters of poorer migrating Komachi, who provided little direct input into their family's production in the traditional tribal economy. The income which they were able to bring in from carpet weaving supplemented the family income and paid for the education or early marriage of their brothers.

Given these conditions (and assuming no radical changes), certain new problems seem likely to arise. First, tribesmen who settled to capitalize on their daughters' labor must ultimately lose that source of free labor as their daughters marry. The profitability of the venture must then diminish as salaries are paid to nonfamily laborers. The effect this will have on the settled families is difficult to predict, but could be significant. One possible solution might involve making the new son-in-law a partner; this would represent a major social change, for the basic unit of the traditional Komachi economy is the nuclear family household. Second, there is the problem of marriage for the girls weaving carpets; as long as they are unmarried they bring income into their natal homes; it seems likely, therefore, that there may be some pressure for delaying the marriage of these girls. Third, there is the question of what girls who have worked in carpet workshops will do after they marry. Will they return to migrating, or will their husbands seek to settle and make use of their income?

One final development that markedly affected the Komachi was the growth of irrigated cash cropping in the *garmsir*. With the expansion of reasonably good roads and increased consumer demand, it became feasible and extraordinarily profitable to grow winter crops of cucumbers, tomatoes, and citrus fruits in the Komachi *garmsir* for transport to northern markets. Landowners in this region, and speculators from other regions of Iran, attempted to drill wells throughout the area and to change pasture into agricultural land. Although the Ministry of Environment was supposed to regulate this process, in the Komachi *garmsir* anyone who had sufficient capital to invest in such agriculture had enough wealth to secure the proper permission through bribery. As a result, there was significant agricultural encroachment on Komachi pasture. In fact, it was the best pasture—the most fertile land—which was lost first. While there were still large amounts of poor pasture available to the Komachi, the agricultural development of the regions put additional pressure on these resources. The reduction of grazing area meant that in bad years tribesmen had to buy fodder rather than move to alternative pastures. Continued agricultural development in the region would severely affect the Komachi domestic economy.

Conclusion: The Komachi Future

In this chapter I have argued that the Komachi generally benefited from the political and economic changes that took place in Iran from 1950–75. Government control of the countryside relieved them of the fear of predation from stronger groups, opening up territories that were previously too dangerous to exploit. Land reform removed some of the expenses that were incurred in assuring access to pasture, but did not disturb the nomads' traditional usufructory rights. The growth of the national economy opened new and lucrative markets for pastoral products—markets which helped the Komachi keep ahead of inflation—and promoted the development of a carpet industry which provided an alternative source of livelihood for these nomads. Indeed, the Komachi frequently claimed that things had never been better.

Why have the Komachi prospered while throughout Iran the larger and more powerful tribes have suffered terribly? The reason seems to have been the very small size of the Komachi tribe and the geographic isolation of the region they inhabited. While the larger and more powerful tribes were faced with the direct and often hostile presence of the central government, the Komachi were not. The government was always there, of course, but its programs were not specifically directed at the Komachi. As a result, these nomads were free to take advantage of opportunities brought about by the economic changes in Iran. Their relative success was evidence that pastoralism remained a viable and, indeed, a potentially very successful mode of existence—even in the midst of rapid national development and 'modernization.'

One can also see, however, the fragility of that success. The Komachi lived in constant fear that they would be forcibly settled, that their herds would be lumped together as part of a meat cooperative, or that their access to pasture would be restricted. Any one of these changes, any direct application of the government power to restrict severely the tribesmen's ability to respond flexibly to changing conditions, would mean disaster for their way of life. The Komachi and their nomadic neighbors had, as of 1975, escaped the fate which has fallen on other Iranian tribes. They prospered by luck and through a form of governmental "benign neglect." If that neglect has continued, the Komachi and their neighbors are likely to still be successful; if it has not continued, they will inevitably suffer the same fate as other Iranian tribes.

7

Tent Schools of the Qashqa'i:
A Paradox of Local Initiative
and State Control

Paul Barker

For the students of the tribal tent schools in prerevolutionary Iran, the greatest event of the academic year was the *ordu*.[1] It was a gathering of all of the tent schools in an area to be examined by Mohammad Bahmanbegi, Director General of Tribal Education, and/or other officials of his Shiraz office. Often visitors from other ministries and even foreigners attended. These guests never failed to be impressed with the irrepressible enthusiasm of these students to answer questions, with the speed and usual accuracy with which they solved long mathematical problems, and with their total lack of stage fright in reciting poems and performing skits. After one such performance a visiting army general congratulated Bahmanbegi, adding that he was amazed that the children of *yaghis* (rebels, highway robbers) could become such outstanding students. Bahmanbegi replied, "I'll tell you something which will make you even more surprised: I'm the son of a *yaghi* who became a Director General!"[2]

Bahmanbegi's depreciation of his father's good name aside, in the two and a half decades separating the fall of Mosaddeq and the 1978–79 revolution, Tribal Education programs created widespread literacy among the tribal populations of southwestern Iran and provided these people with tools to compete for jobs in rapidly modernizing Iran. The schools also peddled the shah's version of Iranian nationalism and contributed to the undermining of some of the bases of tribal society. Unique in the manner in which it arose and in the success it achieved, Tribal Education in Iran was a paradox of the possibilities of local initiative and the problems of state control in prerevolutionary Iran.

Tribes, National Goals and Education

Nomadic tribes throughout the Middle East have frustrated and slowed the efforts of numerous central governments to modernize their societies, centralize their power, and develop national consciousness among all segments of their populations. Indeed, Reza Shah thought the black tents of tribal nomads epitomized the forces of ignorance and backwardness that stood in the way of his ambitious modernization plans. His response to this perceived obstacle was as brutal as it was effective. Yet, no Iranian tribe emerged from the trials of his reign as cohesively as did the Qashqa'i.[3]

Public education is the tool with which governments hope to inculcate their youth with the skills and dogmas which will enable the states to pursue goals established by their leaders. The educational system established in Iran under the Pahlavis was broad in scope (its goal was 100 percent literacy), but it was severely encumbered by old Iranian educational traditions, inappropriate educational theories, and national ideologies which restricted the development of inquisitive, free-thinking minds through insistence on memorization, shah worship, and blind acceptance of the evolving points of the shah-people revolution. It would, therefore, have been only natural to expect tribal leaders to resist the imposition of government educational systems as being contrary to tribal values of freedom and independence. It is amazing that an educational system should evolve out of a period of great crisis for the Qashqa'i, a system which was enthusiastically accepted by most tribespeople, a system which, many would argue, has been the most excitingly successful educational experiments in modern Iranian history.

Before 1953, literacy in Qashqa'i society was a rare skill of limited economic importance, although literacy skills were to a degree associated with social status. There were few functions within tribal society which demanded the services of literate persons. Khans and other wealthy tribespeople employed scribes to carry on their correspondence. Marriage and other rites of passage encouraged the presence in each *tireh* (clan) of at least one tribesman with enough education to be able to copy his own marriage contract and substitute the names of the new couple in the appropriate places.[4]

In order to meet these minimal demands for literacy, three different educational systems were operative. Scribes, in addition to their secretarial duties, were expected to teach the sons of their employers. Following a few years of elementary education in this manner, the sons were often sent to live with relatives in Shiraz or towns along the migration route in order to continue their education in public schools.[5] The second kind of schools among the Qashqa'i were the *maktabs,* or Qoran schools, run by non-Qashqa'i mullas.[6] The third educational system was that of fathers teaching their sons what little reading, writing and mathematics they had been able to learn.[7]

Within the economic and social framework of Qashqa'i society a more elaborate system of formal education made little sense. The Qashqa'i learned within the tribal context all they needed to know in order to continue nomadic pastoralism. The educated khans and scribes served as mediators between tribespeople and government. Literacy was sufficiently widespread that essential rites of passage could be adequately documented and ritualized. A system of oral promises before witnesses combined with a high sense of honor made written transactions between tribespeople unnecessary. By the time that children were old enough for school, they were also mature enough to make a positive contribution to the economic well-being of the tent, the basic production/consumption unit of Qashqa'i society. The sedentary school models of contemporary Iran were totally inappropriate to the lifestyle of a people who spent up to five months each year traveling between winter and summer pastures. In addition, the tribal elite had a vested interest in maintaining a highly illiterate population over which to rule, a population whose world view and tribal identity were uncompromised by excessive contact with nontribal peoples and ideas.

Given the apparent contradictions between the social, economic, and political interests of the Qashqa'i, and the values and goals represented by government educational programs, how are the origins, let alone the phenomenal success, of the schools to be explained?

Historical Context

Accounts of Qashqa'i history have usually failed to make a distinction between the arena of the khans' interests and activities and the concerns and perspectives of the rest of the Qashqa'i population. They usually imply that Qashqa'i social organization was far more rigid and that the authority of the khans was far more absolute than a critical treatment of the sources would justify. The allegiance of

141

Qashqa'i clans to tribes and tribes to the confederation has always been fluid and dependent on a great variety of factors, ranging from ecological issues of pasture quality and availability, to questions of the relative charisma of the leaders of various tribal units, and occasionally to regional, national and even international political issues.[8]

The last third of the nineteenth century was a period of weak Qashqa'i leadership and decreasing central government authority in the affairs of rural Fars Province. In the midst of mounting anarchy at the turn of the century, Saulat od-Dauleh pressed his claim for Qashqa'i leadership against two half brothers and against the branch of his clan which had held the *Ilkhani* title for three generations. Following a brief rule in 1902, he was recognized as *Ilkhani* by tribespeople and the government for most of the years between 1904 and 1933, when he died in a Tehran prison. It was during his reign that the nature of the confrontation between the Qashqa'i leadership and the central government, which reached its climax in the early 1950s, began to take form.

Saulat od-Dauleh was still consolidating his power when he was forced to take a stand on a new national issue: the constitutional revolution. It is likely that his support of the constitutional movement was based, not so much on a love of democratic and nationalist values, as it was on the exigencies of coalition power politics in Fars; his arch-enemy, the acting governor of Fars, supported the monarchy. This decision set a precedent for the way in which Saulat and his sons would respond to the nationalist challenges posed by Reza Shah and Mosaddeq.[9]

Although the *Ilkhani* mustered occasional shows of strength on behalf of constitutionalists, he was either unable or unwilling to exercise sufficient control over tribal populations to stop raiding along the Shiraz-Bushehr road. This raiding, coupled with similar disruptions in other provinces between 1908 and 1911, isolated the provinces from Tehran, helped defeat the hopes of constitutionalists to create a liberal democracy, and helped pave the way for British and Russian intervention in Iran in order to secure their interests.[10]

It is doubtful that Saulat od-Dauleh could have exercised more restraint over Qashqa'i and other raiders along the caravan route. The government and the British, however, were convinced that he could, and Saulat used this conviction as leverage to press demands that he be recognized as the autonomous ruler of all districts bordering the road as the necessary price of guaranteeing trade security.[11]

The Iranian government and the British refused to accept such a price for a questionable return. Events led inevitably to a confrontation between the Qashqa'i and a British-organized army, the South Persia Rifles, during the First World War. With the aid of the German agent, Wilhelm Wassmuss, the Qashqa'i were for a time able to seriously disrupt British interests in Fars. However greatly the deeprooted anti-British and antiprovincial government sentiments of Saulat od-Dauleh may have influenced his actions during the war, it is noteworthy that his public justification of his actions used the idiom of Iranian nationalism.[12]

No segment of Iranian society suffered more under the reign of Reza Shah than did the tribes. Yet, in the early years of his rule Reza Shah was enthusiastically supported by Saulat od-Dauleh, who considered him a champion of Iranian nationalism. In 1926 the *Ilkhani* and his eldest son, Naser, were made deputies to the Majlis and willingly went to Tehran to assume their seats. They were forbidden to leave Tehran and, in 1927 both were arrested without charges.[13]

With the Qashqa'i leadership safely imprisoned in Tehran, Reza Shah proceeded to inflict on this tribe the same oppressive military administration that he had imposed on other tribes throughout Iran. There had been no major Qashqa'i attacks against commercial and governmental interests since World War I, but Reza Shah would tolerate no challenges, real or potential, to his absolutist ambitions. As the army assumed administrative responsibilities in Qashqa'i lands, the predatory desires of the soldiers to supplement their meager salaries knew no limits. In 1928 tribal dress was outlawed and offenders caught were fined or imprisoned or some were even shot on the spot. An additional factor contributing to Qashqa'i discontent was the massive conscription of young tribesmen to serve in the national army in far corners of the country. The 1929 Qashqa'i rebellion led to a temporary redress of these grievances, but soon after peace was restored, oppression resumed with increased intensity.

The consequent 1932 rebellion proved even more disastrous for the Qashqa'i. The government instituted a brutal policy of forced sedentarization. Crucial mountain passes were blocked by the army. Tribes caught in winter pastures suffered tremendous human and flock losses in the summer due to lack of water and pasture and endemic malaria, while those forced to remain in summer pastures were decimated by the winter's cold. Sometimes by daring night passage through bottlenecks, and sometimes by bribing soldiers with a percentage of their flocks, some tribespeople managed to keep migrating, though in increasing poverty.[14]

By 1941, when British and Russian forces occupied Iran and forced

Reza Shah into exile, the Qashqa'i were ripe for the chance to redress past grievances. Saulat od-Dauleh had died (or been murdered, as the Qashqa'i claim) in prison in 1933, but his son, Naser, escaped from Tehran and was able to establish his claim to be *Ilkhani*. He successfully encouraged a redistribution of Qashqa'i flocks in order to deal with poverty and promoted a policy of rearmament for a coming conflict with British occupying forces. He had contact with General Zahedi's anti-Allies resistance movement within the Iranian military, and attracted a German military mission of sorts under the command of Berthold Schulze-Holthus. Naser Khan seems to have been motivated both by a desire to reassert Qashqa'i power and autonomy and by Iranian nationalist resentment of the occupying powers. In the event of a German victory he would have been in an excellent position to push a claim for national leadership.[15]

German defeat in the war precluded Naser Khan from achieving his more ambitious goals. His military exploits during the war had, however, reinforced his claim to nationalist credentials and secured for his tribe a period of relative autonomy.

Naser further cultivated this image in the tribal rebellion of 1946. Having captured all of Fars Province and surrounded Shiraz with warriors, he pressed demands for greater autonomy for Fars; for trials of officials who had exploited the tribes; for health, education and road projects for Fars; and most importantly, for the replacement of certain leftist (Tudeh Party) members from the cabinet. The government found it prudent to give in to his major demands.[16]

During the next eight years the Qashqa'i enjoyed unprecedented peace and prosperity. The khans actively tried to promote a progressive image among foreigners. They endeared the Qashqa'i to the fumbling American Point Four program by ordering four of the ten jackasses the program had imported to improve Iranian breeding stock—a project which had made Point Four the brunt of endless jokes. Later, in 1953, the Qashqa'i rescued the Shiraz staff of Point Four from angry mobs and sheltered them in Bagh-e Eram, the *Ilkhani's* garden, until the anti-American passions had subsided.[17]

The climax of the Qashqa'i struggle for autonomy coincided with the birth of the Tribal Education program. The interests active in this phase of Qashqa'i history were complex and included: 1) a powerful nationalist movement built around the figure of Mohammad Mosaddeq; 2) American fears that the world's largest proven oil reserves might fall into communist hands; 3) the farsighted dreams of an idealistic young tribesman; and 4) the ambitions of a young shah to consolidate his control over a divided and rebellious country.

The politics of Dr. Mosaddeq, Iran's nationalist prime minister from 1951 to 1953, agreed with many of the biases of the "Four Brothers" (as Naser and his three brothers were called). Mosaddeq was remembered as a popular governor of Fars in 1920; he was an impeccable symbol of Iranian nationalism; he had strong antiforeign and especially anti-British leanings; and perhaps, most importantly, he was a strong and viable alternative to the shah and the danger that the latter might return to the oppressive antitribe dogmas that had so devastated the Qashqa'i during the reign of his father.

Mosaddeq's attempted move to establish his full powers failed in August 1953 with the shah's countercoup. The Four Brothers returned to Qashqa'i summer quarters from Tehran, and for a period of time were recognized as the most powerful potential leaders of a pro-Mosaddeq movement. According to one source, the Qashqa'i khans held a war council, all agreeing in advance to accede to the decision of the majority. The Four Brothers were not given voting power. The vote was nine to eight against going to war. The authority of the Four Brothers was irreparably compromised. In the course of the next two years the shah was able to peacefully exile the Four Brothers from Qashqa'i lands.[18]

For the United States, Mosaddeq posed a very different challenge. Even before his rise to power, American officials had feared that instability in Iran could result in that country's oil wealth ending up in Communist hands. Negotiations had been opened with the government of Prime Minister Razmara to create in Iran, America's first technical aid program to a developing country. Despite numerous administrative and name changes through the years, the program was always popularly referred to as Point Four, or in Persian, *Asl-e Chahar*. The American directors of the program were convinced that the most pressing needs of Iran were not industrial monuments but rural education, agricultural extension programs, community development projects, and institution building.

The Educational Division of the Point Four Program was created in July 1951. It recruited the core of its American staff from Brigham Young University, including Glen Gagon who, in 1951, was assigned to Fars Province. Drawing on a variety of sources, the Division analyzed the major problems plaguing the Iranian educational establishment as: massive illiteracy, a bias favoring urban education at the expense of rural education, an overcentralized bureaucracy in the Ministry of Education, outdated and inappropriate educational theories, inadequate supervision of teachers, and an abundance of Communists in the ranks of the teachers. The projects developed by the Education Division were designed to combat these perceived ills.[19]

To summarize, in the early 1950s there were three major powers competing to influence the course of Qashqa'i history: the Qashqa'i leadership, especially the Four Brothers, pursued their dreams of tribal autonomy and a progressive image; the shah and his government pressed demands that all Iranians accept the Iranian nation as their ultimate source of patriotic allegiance; and the Point Four program struggled to find ways to make a positive impact on rural Iran. Despite the often conflicting goals of these three forces, one tribesman was able to draw on the resources of all three to create an innovative tribal school program. His name was Mohammad Bahmanbegi.

Mohammad Bahmanbegi

Bahmanbegi was born about 1920, the son of a retainer of Saulat od-Dauleh. He had received a few years of education from his father's scribe before his family moved to Tehran to join the exiled *Ilkhani*. Mohammad was enrolled in a public school. Due to his tribal background, he was at times humiliated for his ignorance of things which city children took for granted. Nonetheless he proved himself to be a gifted student. By the time he graduated from Tehran University with a degree in law, he had become almost as fluent in French as he was eloquent in his second language, Persian (Qashqa'i Turkish being his first language). He took a job with a Tehran bank for six months, but longed for the free life of the tribes.[20]

Just how Bahmanbegi spent the war years is not entirely clear. According to the story he and his relatives now tell, he inherited his father's position as *kadkhoda* (headman) of the Bahmanbeglu *tireh* of the Amaleh *tayafeh* (tribe). According to this version, when he returned to the Qashqa'i, he and his brother Nader set about building up a prosperous herding business with hired shepherds. He spent leisure time studying law and teaching himself English and German as well as hunting. Monteil, on the other hand, claims that Bahmanbegi was the translator for the German agents at Naser Khan's court.[21]

In 1945 Bahmanbegi wrote *Orf va adat dar ashayer-e Fars* (Customs and Traditions among the Tribes of Fars). The majority of the book is an eloquent and entertaining description of the customs (marriage, inheritance, criminal law, etc.) of the various tribes of Fars. It was based on the author's extensive firsthand knowledge of the tribes and interpreted through the perspective of his French oriented education. This book reflects the author's appreciation of the implications of current historical trends for the tribes. The core of the book is a plea for a more enlightened government policy towards the tribes. Bahmanbegi explains Qashqa'i history in such a way that blame for tribal conflicts with the government falls neither on the leaders of the tribe nor on those of the government, but rather on short-sighted government policies, corrupt government administrators and a volatile tribal nature. He argues that misunderstandings have led to unnecessary and tragic confrontations. He is adamant in his belief that tribespeople are more intelligent than their sedentarized counterparts, and that, if given positive reasons to do so, they would readily redirect their loyalties in favor of the government. Bahmanbegi makes a strong argument that an enlightened government policy to achieve this end would consist of providing the tribes with health care, roads, schools, a guaranteed and respected general amnesty, and, lastly, collecting tribal guns. Bahmanbegi realized that while guns were tools which guaranteed tribespeoples' freedom from oppression, they were also used for turning disagreements into bloodshed; that although guns were great sources of a tribesperson's prestige, they in addition absorbed great amounts of the limited cash income. In sum, Bahmanbegi argued that the new government policy should, "understand that these simple, wild, unfortunate, hungry people are worthy of mercy and training, not fighting and war."[22]

Orf va adat also provides a surprisingly comprehensive view of tribal society in Fars on the eve of the birth of Tribal Education programs. It divides Qashqa'i society into five social classes: 1) the *Ilkhani*'s clan of Shahilu; 2) the *kalantars,* chiefs of the major *tayafeh* or tribes of the confederation; 3) *kadkhodas,* heads of the *tireh* or clans; 4) the *ro'aya,* "subjects," the bulk of the tribespeople; and 5) the lower class of camelherders, artisans, and other peoples who have attached themselves to the Qashqa'i economy and migrations. *Orf va adat* claims that social interaction between the classes was considered shameful, and therefore limited. For example, although women could marry into a higher class, only in the most exceptional of circumstances could they marry below the class of their birth. The authority of the khans and the status of tribespeople in general was based not so much on the amount of wealth possessed or fear commanded as it was on generosity, kindness, riding and shooting ability, eloquence, calligraphic skill, and lineage. The author wrote with pride and pity concerning the status of women. He was proud of the great respect given women by tribesmen and proud of the

Qashqa'i tradition of monogamy, but he pitied their heavy workload in contrast to the leisure activities of tribal men of the higher classes, and he felt it an injustice that Qashqa'i women should forfeit their rights to inheritance and *mahrieh* (divorce payment, the amount of which is negotiated in the marriage contract). He noted that enlightened fathers were beginning to insist on *mahrieh* rights for their daughters. [23]

The First Tent Schools

In the years following the publication of his book, Bahmanbegi almost accidentally began experimenting with a prototype tribal school.

> I saw my poorer relatives walking miles to have letters written for them, or getting into difficulties because they couldn't read or understand regulations or instructions. I began to teach those close at hand to read and write. Then I taught their neighbors when they came and asked me to, and then neighbors from farther off.
>
> As droughts and loss of land hurt worse, I saw that giving education was the best way to work for a better future for my people. I started a class for older children in 1952, in the shade of our traditional white guest tent. When the families moved to grassier spots, the tent was folded and taken along. I found I could teach them to read and write in the eight months of summer and winter camp. [24]

As requests for schools increased, Bahmanbegi realized that he would need outside support in order to be able to expand his experiment. He requested aid from the Ministry of Education but received no immediate answer.

Previous interest of the central government in education for the tribes had been half-hearted at best. In 1948 construction of three boarding schools for tribal children had begun in Fasa, Firuzabad, and Shiraz, but it had stopped in 1950 due to budgetary cuts. [25]

In 1951 Glen Gagon of Point Four's Educational Division arrived in Shiraz. Influenced by the 1949 report of Overseas Consultants Inc., he began thinking about the possibilities of creating moving schools for the nomadic tribes. Bahmanbegi's search for support for his tent schools led him to Gagon. The two men began making plans for strengthening and expanding Bahmanbegi's experiment. They de-

---

Figure 3. Tribal Tent School in Fars.

signed a school that could be carried by one camel. It consisted of a circular white tent, a small blackboard, textbooks, notebooks, chalk, pencils, equipment for soccer and volleyball, small wooden desks for each student, and a latrine tent.[26]

Point Four was prepared to provide the experiment with equipment, transportation, technical advice, and to include Bahmanbegi as a salaried member of its staff; it was not willing to pay the teachers' salaries. The Ministry of Education was not willing to pay them either, but it did offer to provide instructors for a training program for any teachers whom Bahmanbegi could recruit. Bahmanbegi had to turn to wealthy tribespeople for financial support and was able to convince 117 of them to assume responsibility for paying one teacher's salary each. Gagon encouraged this arrangement, believing that the more that tribespeople had invested in the program, the more they would feel determined to make the program a success.[27]

Opposition to the project was limited to a few khans who felt uneasy about any challenges to the status quo. They questioned the need for mass education and perhaps feared the possibility of further governmental encroachment into tribal affairs. They refused to contribute to the teachers' salaries, and as a result their tribal groups were among the last to receive tent schools.[28]

Bahmanbegi's next problem was to recruit teachers. He realized that in order for the program to be a success he would have to draw exclusively on tribespeople and a few villagers with long and close association with the tribes. Only they could be able to survive the rigors of nomadic life and command the respect of tribal people. He had a healthy (and in the Iranian bureaucratic context, unusual) contempt for the superficiality of qualifications based on certificates alone. Most of the candidates he found had only a few years of formal education, others were largely self-taught. Even with such low academic demands, he was only able to recruit 109 applicants for the 117 positions.

On 1 August 1953, these 109 applicants began a six-week teacher training course in Shiraz, which had already been once delayed by the reluctance of Ministry of Education officials in Tehran. Of these, 105 completed the course and by January 1954, 73 tent schools had been opened. By September 1954, the program had grown to 78 schools and a total of 1,164 students.[29]

The main reason for the delay in opening the schools and the reduction of their number was the unrest in Qashqa'i lands following the fall of Mosaddeq, and the widespread belief that the Qashqa'i would stage a major revolt in an effort to force the shah to reinstate the fallen prime minister. As the crisis in Fars grew, the provincial governor requested Point Four to give Bahmanbegi a leave of absence to travel to summer quarters and dissuade the Qashqa'i leadership from confrontation. Bahmanbegi met no initial success. At the council of war, however, despite his lower birth and because of his acknowledged intelligence, and in order that there be an odd number of voters, Bahmanbegi was given voting power. The fact that his vote proved decisive in the Qashqa'i decision not to go to war alienated him and his school program from the now militant segments of Qashqa'i leadership. Consequently the establishment of tent schools in Shishbeluki, Amaleh and Farsimadan areas was largely delayed until after the exile of the Four Brothers from Qashqa'i lands. On the other extreme, Ziad Khan of the Darrehshuri and Elias Khan of the Kashkuli became outspoken supporters of the shah's government and gave warm support to tent schools in their tribes' lands. Owing to tribal unrest, not only were many tribal leaders no longer willing to support schools financially, but a number of the newly trained teachers, including all of those of village origin, refused to serve.[30]

The success of the tent school experiment depended on support from three different sources: the Iranian government, the American Point Four program, and the Qashqa'i khans. In 1953 many of the khans had supported a powerful and losing figure (Mosaddeq) in a struggle for control of the national government. The American government had played a decisive role in that loss. It is a credit to Bahmanbegi's diplomatic skills that he was able to emerge from the crisis with his embryonic school experiment relatively intact.

For two years, Bahmanbegi's hectic schedule was divided between efforts to maintain good relations with his diverse sources of support and extensive field trips as a sort of supervisor/in-service-trainer for his inexperienced teachers.

In spite of, or perhaps in part because of, the success of the first two years of the experiment, certain khans began to complain of the financial burden which the arrangements placed on them. Why should they pay so much for the education of their children while in the rest of the country this burden was assumed largely by the government? It is noteworthy also that 1955–56 was the period in which the Four Brothers were exiled from Fars and much of their property was confiscated. As long as they had ruled in relative autonomy, an educational system largely sponsored by the tribal elite was a source of pride and a partial justification of their autonomy, even though the school curriculum was that of the national schools. With the increasing erosion of Qashqa'i independence, there was little reason for khans to continue assuming financial burdens which they felt belonged to the government. Gagon seems to have been almost alone in his belief that the long-range interests of the program were best served by keeping tribespeople responsible for payment of at least half of the teachers' salaries, preferably in kind rather than cash.[31]

In 1955 Bahmanbegi was able to arrange for a group of officials from the Ministry of Education to view a demonstration of a prize tent school class. They were favorably impressed, and shortly thereafter the Ministry agreed to undertake the payment of the teachers' and Bahmanbegi's salaries. It set a condition that all teachers be properly trained graduates of a teacher training school. But this meant the firing of all tribal teachers who had struggled to make the first two years a success and their replacement by "properly" qualified teachers, all of whom had city backgrounds.[32]

This phase of the Tribal Education experiment quickly ended in failure. The new teachers could not tolerate the hardships of a rural nomadic life and deserted their posts within the first two months. Nor were they able to establish any rapport with the tribal people, whom they tended to regard as primitive and backward.

The third year of the tent school program having thus ended in disaster after two very promising years, Bahmanbegi presented the Ministry of Education with an ultimatum: either support him in establishing a Tribal Teacher Training School or cancel the program altogether. The school was opened in Shiraz in October 1957 and recruited only tribespeople for its one year training program. Admission to the school was on the basis of literacy and general ability. In the first years even a sixth grade certificate was not required, although later it was.[33]

Encouraged by the promising results of the experiment in Fars, Point Four and the Ministry of Education attempted to establish similar programs in other provinces, especially among the Bakhtiyari in Isfahan Province. In addition to the Tribal Teacher Training School in Shiraz, five others were opened in four other provinces. Those established outside of Fars floundered, however, and by 1965 only the Shiraz school was still serving its original purpose.[34] The reasons for the failure of the programs in other provinces may be speculated upon; a more difficult issue is to explain the causes of the impressive acceptance and growth of Tribal Education programs among the tribes of Fars.

The vitality of the Tribal Education experiment in Fars is reflected both in the constant growth in enrollment of the Tribal Teacher

Training School in Shiraz and by the increase in the kinds of programs pioneered by the Shiraz based Office of Tribal Education. In 1967 a tribal boarding school was established in Shiraz. Its first class of 40 students and all future students were chosen by competitive examination from among graduating tent school sixth graders. This school grew into Tribal High School which, by the time of the 1978–79 revolution, had a total enrollment of nearly 1,000 students in Shiraz and had started a new campus at Ab Barik, 20 kms. north of Shiraz. In 1971 a Tribal Carpet Weaving School was opened near Shiraz. It accepted 50–70 teenage girls per year from *tirehs* in which carpet weaving was not practiced. It trained them for one year and then provided them with enough equipment and wool to begin weaving for themselves upon their return to their families. Although the majority of these students were from non-Qashqa'i tribes, the carpet designs were exclusively Qashqa'i, mostly from the Kashkuli *tayafeh*. In 1972 Tribal Technical School was opened in Shiraz. Programs to train paramedics and midwives for the tribes were initiated in 1973. Finally, in recent years, the Tribal Education Office experimented with roving stores, to free tribespeople from the extortions of itinerant peddlers and town merchants.[35]

Despite the diversification of programs run by the Office of Tribal Education, the primary focus of its energies has always been the primary tent schools and, as the tribes settle, tribal village schools. It is these schools which have had the most far-reaching impact on Qashqa'i society and whose success deserves explanation.

Analysis of Tent School Success

No one person could be solely responsible for the growth of an organization as large and complex as the Office of Tribal Education, but neither could this organization have come into being without the vision and abilities of Mohammad Bahmanbegi. His tribal origins and intimate knowledge of tribal customs and problems made him uniquely able to communicate with tribespeople. Some might disagree with the wisdom of some of his ideas and fear their implications for tribal identity and lifestyle, but only a few khans, in part apprehensive about the implications of mass education to their privileged position and resenting the success and prosperity of a lower class tribesman, questioned the sincerity of his motives.

Bahmanbegi's thorough understanding of tribal "psychology" enabled him to appeal to tribal values in order to sell his programs to the tribes. For example, in the early years of the experiment some tribespeople objected to girls attending tent schools. The objections were raised again in 1962 when women entered the Tribal Teacher Training School. Bahmanbegi replied that the Qashqa'i had always had the highest respect for women and their purity, and that this must be maintained at all costs. Indeed, their position must be enhanced by giving them the tools of education so that tribal hygiene, diet, and living standards might be improved.[36]

A second major factor promoting the acceptability of the tent schools to the Qashqa'i population at large was that the program was built on and around tribal traditions, timetables, and values. The schools made deep appeals to tribal pride and encouraged in the students the image of the "new tribal warrior," whose shield was a book, whose bullets were chalk, and whose enemy was whatever kept the warrior from attaining a dignified position in the emerging Iran.[37]

Another tradition of tribal warfare upon which Bahmanbegi drew was the war camp or *ordu*. In previous generations the *ordu* had been a large gathering of khans and warriors to make war preparations. In the Qashqa'i collective memory these were times of great excitement and tribal pride. Under Tribal Education, *ordus* underwent a metamorphosis and became a sort of education inspection festival. School children from a large radius were bused to the white tent camp so that the students might be tested by Tribal Education officials, participate in dancing, and share in the large meals and general excitement.

Both the annual and the daily schedules of the tent schools were built around the demands of a nomadic lifestyle. Annual vacations for the tent schools fell during the spring and fall migrations, rather than during the summer. The daily schedules of individual tent schools showed more deference to weather and the seasonal demands of a pastoral lifestyle, than they did to the tyranny of clocks.

An insistence on high standards contributed greatly to the impressive results of the schools. The teachers knew that Bahmanbegi was as apt to humiliate a poor teacher in front of his students at an *ordu* as he was to praise a good one. They believed him when he said that he would beat any teacher who beat his students. When the boarding school was opened in Shiraz it was called *Chehel Nafari* (forty people) until Bahmanbegi was satisfied that it was worthy of the "holy name" of *Dabirestan-e Ashayeri* (Tribal High School). In 1973 he attempted to repeat the high school experiment in Sanandaj for Kurdish students, but when he examined the students at the end of the first year he was dissatisfied and closed the school.

The quality of students and study environment have contributed significantly to the success of the schools. There is no question but that Qashqa'i children are healthier, due to exercise, environment and diet, than their sedentary and urban counterparts of comparable socioeconomic levels. Although nomadic children do not have to face frivolous urban distractions (cinemas, street corner loitering, etc.) their before and after school chores at home are, if anything, more demanding of their time, and make their scholastic accomplishments all the more impressive. The support of tribal parents, who are giving up economically productive members of the household to the schools for over 36 hours per week, cannot be overestimated.

Another factor of crucial importance to the success of the program was the quality of the people whom Bahmanbegi was able to recruit as teachers and administrators. The appeal of Bahmanbegi's charisma, the opportunity to participate in a vision of building a new tribal society, and the reality of being able to hold a respectable and reasonably well-paying job within tribal society, all contributed to the ability of the Office of Tribal Education to enlist many of the most capable young men and women of a generation.

Impact on Qashqa'i Society

Closely tied to a discussion of the reasons for the impressive growth and success of Tribal Education programs is a need to discuss what this success has meant for the Qashqa'i—what impact these programs have had on Qashqa'i social, economic and political structures. Any discussion of this impact is complicated by the fact that the Office of Tribal Education was but one of many forces which actively reshaped tribal society.

The years since the 1955–56 exile of the Four Brothers saw a steady decline in the political power of the traditional tribal elite, and a corresponding increase in central government involvement in matters of Qashqa'i migration patterns, land use, and administration. This, coupled with a variety of economic pressures, altered the fabric of Qashqa'i social and economic organization and put tremendous pressure on Qashqa'i to settle.[38]

One of the most obvious changes in Qashqa'i society in the past quarter century has been the creation of new occupations within the framework of its nomadic society: those of tent school teacher and supervisor and, at a more removed level, driver, administrator, and other employees of the Office of Tribal Education. While only a small percentage of the total Qashqa'i population was actually employed by the Office (in 1977 roughly 1 percent of the Qashqa'i were teachers), teaching was the profession and the route of economic mobility desired by a large percentage of tent school children. As teachers they could raise their incomes by increasing the number of class levels they were qualified to teach, by teaching in new tent schools in distant corners of the country, and by becoming supervisors. The problem of teacher attrition was nonexistent up through 1965, but the lure of easier urban employment has taken its toll in more recent years.[39]

It could be argued that a new tribal administrative structure came into being, for the power and authority of the Office of Tribal Education went far beyond that implied by its name. Tent school teachers usually commanded a great deal of respect in the communities where they lived and taught; they and their supervisors were called upon by tribespeople to serve as mediators with the government when that function was largely abolished for the tribal elite. On another level, Bahmanbegi was refered to as "Mohammad Khan" by admiring tribespeople. Whereas in former years National Geographic writers called at the tent of Naser Khan, in the 1960s and 70s they knocked at the office door of Mohammad Bahmanbegi. The Office, which could not have the same political ambitions as the khans, nonetheless in several ways effectively assume the role of guardian of tribal interests.

The impact of the teachers' salaried incomes on tribal society has been significant. Many teachers were assigned to their own *tirehs* and were often able to live with their own families. The addition of their incomes to the families' incomes allowed many to more easily withstand the financial strains brought by the developments of the past two decades. It helped numerous families buy land, build gardens, and in other ways diversify their incomes.

One of Bahmanbegi's original concerns was to improve the status of women in the tribes. By 1973, 270 women had graduated from the Tribal Teacher Training School, and each year 50 more graduated from the Carpet Weaving School. With these skills these women had far greater economic value in their natal and marital families. From available evidence, marriage patterns do not appear to have yet been greatly affected by the new status of educated women (most marriages are still arranged to kin).

Although teachers' salaries may keep some families financially solvent and able to migrate, there is no doubt but that the overall impact of the schools has been to encourage settlement. Other than teaching, there are few jobs associated with the nomadic lifestyle which specifically require formal education. The schools do not give the students tools with which to become better managers of a livestock-based economy, but rather those which they will need in order to successfully make the transition to a settled life and urban employment.

The cumulative effect of the tent schools on tribal identity is difficult to assess. One of the chief reasons for the widespread acceptance of the schools in the first place had been their use of tribal symbols and values. But the tent schools taught Iranian history in Persian, not Qashqa'i history in Turkish.[40] The curriculum was that of all Iranian schools with only a few modifications for the special circumstances of the tribes. The ideology which the students memorized was that of Iranian nationalism. However much Bahman-begi and other officials may have strived to preserve and glorify tribal culture and identity, the net impact of Tribal Education programs was to facilitate the integration of the Qashqa'i into the Iranian nation, the transition to a settled life, and the erosion of the social and economic bases of the nomadic society it set out to serve.

While some may not approve of the role of an educational system in transforming a distinctive nomadic culture, it should be remembered that a multitude of forces converged in the second half of the twentieth century, all of which contributed to the erosion of that culture. The significant aspect of Bahmanbegi's dream was that it eased much of the pain and uncertainty of the transition process and gave tens of thousands of tribespeople tools to compete for respectable jobs in the encapsulating society.

A central strength, and ultimately the crucial liability, of Bahman-begi's program was its ability to attract generous government support. The price of this support was the indoctrination of a new generation of tribespeople with nationalist dogmas as interpreted by the shah's government. Bahmanbegi's close association with the shah left him vulnerable to the revolutionary anger of 1978–79. In January 1979 the new government accepted Bahmanbegi's resignation as Director General of Tribal Education. With the excitement of the return of Naser Khan from exile in the United States, angry tribal mobs attacked Bahmanbegi's house, forcing him and his family to flee Shiraz.[41]

8

Khans and Kings: The Dialectics of Power in Bakhtiyari History

Gene R. Garthwaite

Mention of the great tribal confederations in Iran always sparks interest. The designation of Shahpour Bakhtiar as prime minister in early 1979 immediately raised the question as to whether his appointment signaled the return of the Bakhtiyari to national politics. Bakhtiar is a member of what has been the Bakhtiyari ruling family, but one of its cadet branches. His selection, however, as prime minister owed nothing to his tribal affiliation, but instead stemmed from his Tehran-Paris education and legal background, membership as an undersecretary in Dr. Mosaddeq's government, long and public opposition to Mohammad Reza Shah, and willingness, despite this, to work with the monarch within the 1906–07 Constitutional framework. Consequently, Bakhtiar emerged as a compromise acceptable to the shah and army.

If Bakhtiar had, in fact, been identified as a tribal leader, he would have been unacceptable, not only to the shah and the army, but to most Iranians who have come to accept the centralized nation-state that dates back to Reza Shah. In the first decade of his reign, 1925–35, Reza Shah undercut the military and political power of the tribes by destroying their confederational political structures, imprisoning and executing leaders, confiscating pastures and lands, attempting to implement forced sedentarization, and replacing indirect administration by direct rule. Reza Shah's success in destroying tribal power resulted from his establishment of a modern army and bureaucracy.[1] He won the support of the urban population for his policies, because they had traditionally regarded the tribes as a threat and increasingly came to view them as anachronistic and out of keeping with contemporary Iran.

Pahlavi centralization contrasts with nineteenth century Qajar decentralization. The Qajars not only tolerated tribal confederations as autonomous, administrative entities, but even created them to counterbalance established powers in key provinces. Moreover, the Qajars relied on tribal leaders and their military contingents to perform military and administrative functions rather than take on the expenses and challenge of a standing army and centralized bureaucracy. The shift from decentralized, autonomous, and even "tribal" Iran to the centralized Pahlavi state, and with it the political and military demise of the great confederations, demonstrates the hypothesis: within an organized state the potential for tribal confederation is inversely proportional to the degree of bureaucratic centralization.[2]

This paper starts with that hypothesis, and asserts that Bakhtiyari leaders accepted the values of the traditional state and functioned within them. Consequently, Bakhtiyari leaders were instruments of change only within the traditional state's parameters for autonomy; for example, the formation of the Bakhtiyari confederation in 1867. Khans who attempted to go beyond the limits of those traditional parameters faced the loss of their power base in the Bakhtiyari, whose sociopolitical dynamics opposed concentration and centralization of power within the confederation. On the other hand, khans lacked the necessary resources and organization to build a base of support outside the confederation—not to mention the active opposition that they faced from urban populations, provincial magnates, and neighboring tribal confederations. In attitudes toward, and use of power, little differentiates the Bakhtiyari khans from other leaders, including those with a base in sedentary society.

This paper describes the nature of Bakhtiyari sociopolitical structures and history, and their relation to the state and traditional values. It asserts that the family-*tayafeh,* the family's ultimate extension, defines the limits of economic, social, and political activity and identity; next in importance in terms of these same factors is the greater Irano-Shi'i framework of the state; and last in effectiveness is the Bakhtiyari confederational structure, which includes a geographic area, an administrative category, and the basis of identifications by the state, for the great khans, and those outside the Bakhtiyari. The family-*tayafeh* unit was essentially conservative, and the confederational structure was largely dependent upon the state; with Pahlavi centralization the confederation was destroyed, but the basic unit remained relatively unaffected. The Bakhtiyari administrative entity continued, while pre-Pahlavi political ties were given new meaning in terms of internal *tayafeh* alignments.

Structural Organization of the Bakhtiyari

Historically, the term "Bakhtiyari" first denoted a *tayafeh* (tribe) that had entered Iran from Syria along with some thirty other such groups in the thirteenth century.[3] In Safavid sources[4] the name refers both to a geographic area and an administrative unit, an area of some 20,000 square miles straddling the Zagros mountains between Isfahan and Khuzestan, as well as to its inhabitants. Since the late nineteenth century, "Bakhtiyari" has acquired an ethnic, occupational, and political emphasis through the prevailing assumption that the great tribal confederation ruled by the *Ilkhani* (paramount khan) and khans included only Bakhtiyari-speaking pastoral nomads. In actuality, however, and at least within the past century, but perhaps earlier, the Bakhtiyari have counted in their number Turkic and Arabic speakers, sedentary agriculturalists, and those Bakhtiyari resident in cities such as Shushtar, Isfahan, Qom, and Tehran.[5] The nomads themselves were dependent upon cereals planted in both summer and winter pasture areas as well as their flocks of sheep and goats. The Bakhtiyari, even as an administrative entity from the central government's perspective, was often politically fragmented, and seldom functioned as a unit except during the last decade of the rule of the first and most powerful *Ilkhani,* Hosain Qoli Khan (d. 1882), and during the Constitutional Revolution. Nevertheless, Bakhtiyari legend supports notions of a common origin and unity, and group formation is rationalized in the Bakhtiyari patrilineal framework.

The Bakhtiyari structure came to consist of two major, interrelated components: first, the confederation of the whole of the Bakhtiyari, which emerged in the mid-nineteenth century and which the great khans, *khavanin-e bozorg,* administered; and second, tribes, *tayafeh,* that constitute named, major units, encompassing lesser ones in a segmentary pyramid, but which long predate the confederation. The confederational framework has been more subject to change because of the political competition among the great khans for dominance within it, the interjection of state politics and policies, and the somewhat ambivalent role of the great khans who served as intermediaries between the state and the Bakhtiyari, and who faced the dilemma of contradictory goals stemming from interests and ambitions peripheral to, or even beyond, the Bakhtiyari. The form of the tribes—the *tayafeh* level and below—on the other hand, has been more persistent and less affected by external developments, for their function derives from basic pastoral and agricultural structures.[6]

Briefly, the Bakhtiyari *tayafeh* component begins with the nuclear family *(khanevadeh,* or sometimes *vargeh* [lit. tent]—classification and terminology follow Digard's).[7] Extended or related, families come together as *oulad,* or *tash,* approximating a descent group, which functions as a camp *(mal)* of from three to twelve tents and shares common herding, migrating, and defense interests. The *tireh,* roughly subtribe, forms the next level and are represented by *kad-khodas.* Tirehs come together to form *tayafeh,* some of which number 25,000 individuals, and are headed by *kalantars* appointed from the group by the khans. Pasture rights derive from membership in the *tayafeh,* which exists as a named group with its own identity and, probably, as an endogamous unit. Even though it may not always act as an entity, the *tayafeh,* indeed even the Bakhtiyari confederation, provides a conceptual framework for organizing people politically and attaching them to leaders.

Continuing with the segmentary pyramid, all *tayafeh* are a component of one of eight *bab;* each *bab* has a dominant lineage from which khans are chosen. The *bab* are grouped in one of the two moieties *(bakhsh* or *boluk*[8]) of the Haft Lang or Chahar Lang, and finally the confederation *(il)* of the Bakhtiyari after 1867, whose leadership has since been dominated by the *khavanin-e bozorg,* or great khans.

The *khavanin-e bozorg* were members of the ruling Haft Lang lineage of the Duraki from which the *Ilkhani,* paramount khans, were to be chosen by the shah after 1867. In the early eighteenth century the great khans possessed major land holdings in Chahar Mahall; functioned as government officials and military leaders there; and represented major Bakhtiyari components (and after 1867 all the Bakhtiyari). These great khans were part of a tribal/pastoral/nomadic world as well as a nontribal/agricultural/sedentary one.

Perhaps surprisingly, the *khavanin-e bozorg,* even the powerful Hosain Qoli Khan, had little direct control over the Bakhtiyari economic base of pastoralism and agriculture, which was regulated within the *tayafeh* system. The great khans exercised indirect control of the Bakhtiyari economic base through the juridical-political aspect of their intermediary role as judges, military leaders, and civil administrators. Ideologically, but within the Bakhtiyari, *khavanin-e bozorg* and their descent groups played a critical symbolic role, for they completed the Bakhtiyari hierarchical world view of God, the Imams and saints, the shah, the *Ilkhani,* the khans, and the Bakhtiyari commoners—thus fitted it into the greater Iranian ethos. In addition, the khans not only reinforced but justified and legitimized the lineage principles underlying internal Bakhtiari relationships and their integration into the traditional state system.

Within the Bakhtiari, the family unit—the most exclusive group—takes on the key and enduring ideological role, forming the basis for everyday activity and giving rise to most demands and conflicts. In addition, the family provides the conceptual basis for the process of group formation ending in the *tayafeh*, and ultimately the confederation. The farther a group moves from the family, the weaker the commitment and the identification with that level of organization. The *tayafeh*, composed of autonomous segments, hence a microcosm of the Bakhtiari itself, constitutes the terminal unit of the "family's" functional limits, in which internal factors such as herding of flocks, pastures, water, and migration assume primary importance in group formation. From the *tayafeh* to the whole of the Bakhtiari confederation, groups function within an essentially negative framework and align and define themselves through interaction with external factors—neighboring tribes, the state, or the broader ambitions of the khans. Consequently, the basis for loyalty and identification depends less on kinship, even though it may serve as the organizational principle, than on economic, political, and moral expediency. Groups were capable of significant expansion and contraction; specific group configurations were of short duration except as they reflected immediate self-interest. The confederation constitutes the most inclusive group, but exerts the fewest actual demands on its members. Nevertheless, after the confederation's formation in the mid-nineteenth century, it provides the framework for the total world view, including integration into the Irano-Shi'i system. In earlier periods, that function may have been accomplished through the moieties of the Haft Lang and Chahar Lang,[9] or possibly that of the *tayafeh* itself. In the latter case, the general term "Bakhtiari" may have been substituted for the specific name of a *tayafeh* from that larger geographic or administrative area; this substitution may explain the relative absence of references to *tayafeh* in written sources.

Even though the confederation—and earlier the Haft Lang and the Chahar Lang or possibly individual *tayafeh*—provided for integration into the greater Irano-Shi'i system, it seldom furnished more than a vague, administrative identity. Moreover, those larger units did not unite the Bakhtiari components in pursuit of common goals, and the khans made little appeal to followers as Bakhtiari. Possibly this identity was assumed or articulated only orally, but the absence of effective units argues against such an identity. Even when the Bakhtiyari formed a common front,[10] a Bakhtiyari identity was peripheral to the factors underlying that unity. Appeal for action was based on personal ties and self-interest, as in the case of the khans' personal retainers and kinsmen, institutionalized in the *bastagan* system,[11] on the promise of reward of pastures or booty to a whole *tayafeh* or its components, or on a call to defend traditional religious and political values.

The reasons for the khans' inability to rally the tribes on a Bakhtiyari basis are several. Possibly the family-*tayafeh* nexus perceived the confederation, or the moieties or *tayafeh*, as a threat and as potentially exploitative: it constituted the unit of taxation and conscription, and the focus of the great khan was often outside the Bakhtiyari, increasingly so after the Constitutional Revolution. The great khans' own backgrounds were that of landlords and government officials, which reenforced their role as a link between the state with its culture and the Bakhtiyari. As a result, however, they could not articulate a viable alternate ideology without threatening their position either with the state or the tribes. Possibly, too, they utilized the common Irano-Shi'i values as a means of broadening their bases outside the Bakhtiyari in order to consolidate their control of it or their relationship with the government. Finally, alternate values may have been seen as potentially disruptive by both khans and tribesmen; for example, Marxism attracted only a very limited Bakhtiyari following in the tumultuous period following World War I. When new ideas appeared, such as nationalism and notions of the nation-state during the period of the Constitutional Revolution, the khans, notably Hajji Ali Qoli Khan Sardar As'ad, responded as Iranians and not as Bakhtiyari.

Kings and Khans: Irano-Shi'i Ties

Expression of the great khans' Irano-Shi'i values are to be found both in their sentiments and actions. The khans maintained shrines, made major contributions to those in Kerbala, undertook pilgrimages to Mecca and Shi'i shrines, developed ties to urban ulama, and observed standard Shi'i practice. One striking example of espousal of general political and religious values is seen in the exhortation of Ali Morad, a mid-eighteenth century Bakhtiyari, when he appealed to leaders of the Haft Lang, Chahar Lang, and Lurs of Khorramabad in an attempt to recruit additional followers for his ill-fated attack against Nader Shah:

If I decide to become king, I shall cast coins in my name and have the khutbeh said in my name. All of the leaders of the army from Iraq [Ajam], Fars, and Hamadan are loyal to the Safavids. They will follow me, and after I end Nader's rule, I shall go to Khorasan, and I shall free Tahmasp who is now in prison there. The Royal Name is a great name, and if God is with me the people will follow me. Shah Tahmasp will be satisfied with only Iraq [Ajam] and Khorasan, and I shall be content with Hamadan, Fars, and Kerman.[12]

With these words Ali Morad demonstrated an acute awareness of the nature of both power and authority in post-Safavid Iran as a whole; there is, however, no appeal to a Bakhtiyari identity and nothing particularly tribal or nomadic about either the concepts expressed or the language in which they are couched. The appeal is to the values of the traditional Iranian system that owed its genesis to the Safavids and earlier dynasties.

The Safavid system, which persisted through the Qajar period but for one major modification, had a dual ideological basis[13] for its authority. This centered on the ruler who claimed descent from Musa al-Kazem, the seventh Imam, and who also claimed to represent God's choice as temporal ruler, the wielder of the sword of state. It was believed that the Safavid ruler was, therefore, representative of the will of the Imams on the one hand, but also *Zellollah* (Shadow of God), and thus heir to the far earlier tradition of divine right of rule, on the other.

Neither Nader Shah nor his own line of successors—the Afshars, Ali Mardan Khan, Karim Khan Zand, subsequent Zand claimants, and the Qajars—were in a position to assert the authoritative link to the Imams, except through Safavid puppets or collateral ties (e.g., Shahrokh, who was Nader's grandson—but also the son of a Safavid mother). The inscription on the seal of Abbas III—Nader's second puppet—unduly emphasizes Abbas III's relationship to the Imams and his descent from Shah Safi (the Safavids' eponymous ancestor who founded their Order), Abbas the Great, and Tahmasp.[14] By the time Abbas III died (1148/1736), Nader had so consolidated his power that no Safavid could successfully challenge him. He pushed his own authority on his de facto power as victor. Possibly as the result of the weakness of his claim to rule, the continuing challenge to his legitimacy by the Shi'i ulama and Safavid pretenders, and to further disassociate himself from the Safavids, Nader sought election and the replacement of Shi'ism by Sunnism.[15] With this forced, but futile, abandonment of Shi'ism, Nader perhaps hoped to unite all Muslims under his eventual rule; but more immediately and importantly, he sought to please his army, the base of his power, which was composed chiefly of essentially Sunni Afghan and Turkman tribal contingents. Despite this break with two centuries of Shi'i rule, further symbolized by the shift of the capital from Isfahan to Mashhad—Khorasan being Nader's home province and close to his political and military base—the Afshars emphasized continuity through administrative and military procedures and practices—land usage and grants, titles, and military recruitment of tribal contingents.

All subsequent rulers in the eighteenth century based their claim to rule on traditional Shi'i political-religious values and on the backing of their own tribal cores—Bakhtiyari, Zand, Afghan, and Qajar. None was able to establish an army with state or dynastic loyalty. Even as late as 1194/1780 the Zands appealed to Safavid sentiments in the inscriptions of their seals;[16] whereas Nader had sought to establish his independence from Safavid authority by linking himself directly to the Prophet: "The Seal of State and Religion [i.e., Mohammad] having been displaced, God has given order to Iran in the name of Nader." Except for Azad Khan, subsequent rulers, even though Sunni, appealed to the populace on essentially a Shi'i basis; ironically, in Shi'i political thought all government—in the absence of the Imam—is in some sense illegitimate. Shahrokh, for example, who continued Afshar rule in Khorasan, albeit with the support of Ahmad Shah Durrani—from 1163/1749–1211/1796—tied his name with Ali's on his seal: "Shah Rukh restored order to the world of Religion and State through the benevolence of the lineage of Mortaza Ali." Both Ali Mardan Khan, a Bakhtiyari of the Chahar Lang, and Karim Khan Zand were Shi'a. None of Ali Mardan Khan's seals survives, but on the coins struck during his regency for Isma'il III, he refers to himself as "bandeh-ye Isma'il," or the slave of Isma'il, the Safavid puppet supported by Ali Mardan and Karim. Ali Mardan used the title "Vakil-e Ro'aya," regent for the people. (Customarily, the title had been "Vakil od-Dauleh" regent of the state.)[17] In addition, Ali Mardan appealed to Haft Lang for support on the basis of Bakhtiyari unity. Karim formally deposed Isma'il III in 1172/1759, but neither bothered to replace him nor to take the title of shah for himself. The underlying assumption of Karim's long rule, 1163/1750—1193/1799, was that he was directly appointed by God. The succeeding Qajars (1208/1794—1344/1925) emphasized the same legitimizing principle, though it was weakened by Qajar acquiescence to Anglo-Russian imperial aims and by ulama attacks on them for their acquiescence.

Shi'i ideology and the pattern of the great king persisted from the

Safavids onwards without serious challenge. None but Nader Shah in the case of religion and Karim Khan Zand in the instance of the throne, departed from the Safavid precedent established by Shah Isma'il. This would suggest wide support and identification with an abstract, distant but attractive ideal; Ahmad Kasravi some years ago noted the charismatic appeal of the Safavids in eighteenth century Lurestan.[18] No model other than kingship was likely; rule patterned after that of tribal khan was a possibility, but a khan's government was too personal and decentralized for dynastic continuity in the state. Furthermore, the role of a tribal khan, such as the Bakhtiari great khans, was but a weak one within the tribal confederation, unless the khan had significant external support or opposition; outside support was necessary to overcome internal resistance to concentration of power, and opposition reinforced a sense of cohesion. (This was a factor of the state level, as well, where external threats such as the Ottomans, Uzbegs, Russians, or British allowed the shah to manipulate Shi'i identity and to hold out promise of reward from successful battle.)

The Safavid model represents a modification of the Turkish military patronage state system,[19] and a linking of the great king tradition, including its implicit if not explicit centralization, with a diffusion of power and regional autonomy. Autonomy was checked by the appointment of provincial and regional governors, often close kin, responsible for military levies, taxes and order, and by the control of the state's agents with appointments, *tuyuls,* exemptions, divide and rule policies, and retention of family members as hostages at court. Political identity was thus linked with the center on the one hand or the smaller tribal units, the *tayafeh,* on the other. Even confederational identity, in the case of the Bakhtiari was shaped by state activity with the recognition of an *Ilkhani*. Moreover, the state had ready access to reserve military units without having to bear their direct cost, and the degree of mobilization was determined by the perceived nature of the threat—the very same principle and system used at the tribal level.

Throughout the Safavid, Afshar, and Zand eras there is this interplay of tribal power but evanescent confederations with persisting symbols of religion and authority, and the attempt to accommodate these to the great king tradition and to maintain the state. All of these matters touch on the Bakhtiari, who emerge in the eighteenth century as important military and civil leaders, as dissidents both on the national and local scene—outside the Bakhtiari in Khorasan and Qom—and as *tuyul* holders, and landlords.

Military, tribal, and civil appointments—including governorships of major provinces; awards of title and land; and recognition of Bakhtiyari power—characterize the emerging roles, responsibilities, and rewards of the Duraki khans during the Afshar and Zand periods. This historical process stretches back through the Safavid era; the eighteenth century marks an expansion of the Bakhtiyari role, not only in central and southwestern Iran, but in the whole of the empire. Official eighteenth century documents clearly indicate that the Haft Lang was treated as an administrative unit, but do not delineate the relationship between these Bakhtiyari and their khans.

The official documents add little to our knowledge about Bakhtiyari commoners and the lesser khans, except their organization into small groups and segments headed by *rish safid, kadkhodas,* and *kalantars*—with an interdependence between these leaders, the khans, and the great khans, with the latter, at least in the Haft Lang, ultimately responsible to the government for the good administration of the whole. The Bakhtiyari economic contribution and military roles are noted, and that they fought not only for their leaders but against them as well. Consequently, the government sought to control them through governors and by resettlement in Khorasan and Qom. The Bakhtiyari tribes and their khans, Haft Lang as well as Chahar Lang, seemed to have shared the prevailing Iranian ethos of the eighteenth century, especially as it related to authority. The Bakhtiyari supported various Safavid pretenders or those who upheld their legitimacy throughout the eighteenth century. Bakhtiyari support for the Safavid and Shi'i cause sprang, no doubt, from both religious fervor and political opportunism—hence the willingness of some Bakhtiyari to support Nader and Azad Khan. The Bakhtiyari often defied the rulers of the Afshar and Zand eras, but they never challenged existing political and religious ideas and institutions by offering new ones. Moreover, whoever sought to rule central and southwestern Iran had now to contend with the strategic region and the newly expanded role of its Bakhtiyari inhabitants.

The Qajars and the Paramount Khans

In the nineteenth century the Qajars, who possibly emulated a much earlier practice, invested leaders with the title and office of *Ilkhani,* which gave its holders authority and power to act on behalf of the central government as official administrators of what were thus formally created and recognized as autonomous administrative units by Tehran. This occurred in 1818 for the Qashqa'i[20] and 1867 for the

Bakhtiyari.[21] The Khamseh confederation came into existence during Naser od-Din Shah's reign; and even though its head never held the title of *Ilkhani*, he functioned as such. The dates for the first appointment of an *Ilkhani* for the Qajar confederation (possibly early nineteenth century) and of the special status given its relationship to the ruling dynasty and the Zafaranlu of Qochan are not as yet known. None of the other Kurdish leaders possessed the title, nor did the Arab shaikhs who held similar offices as administrators for their respective areas.

The great confederations in Iran came about as the result of designation, amalgamation, or a combination of these two. In designation, the central government possibly sought to centralize or to limit tribal autonomy, when it would select a leader, not necessarily from within the group, as the one responsible for order, taxes, and conscripts. The Khamseh, formed by order of the Qajars and directed by the Qavams, a Shiraz merchant and landlord family, is an example of this type.

Confederations also emerged through a process of amalgamation, when a leader forged successively larger and more effective units, relying on a variety of leadership skills and symbols and manipulating the basic kin structures to achieve goals beyond those associated with the smaller groups. Over a period of time, corporate interests would be identified with the confederation, but would be weak in comparison with the corporate interests of the smaller units. The Qashqa'i provide but one successful illustration of this variation; they constitute a Turkic-speaking minority and their migration takes them through thickly-settled agricultural regions in close proximity to urban areas. Although this second model was commonly attempted in Iranian history, given the difficulty of obtaining outside support without threatening the central government, most tribal leaders failed because of internal and external rivalry and opposition, especially in times of a strong central government. Even with the Qashqa'i, shahs elevated the deposed *Ilkhanis* in ineffective attempts to control that confederation. Examples of failure to form such confederations are common in Bakhtiyari history up to the mid-nineteenth century and Hosain Qoli Khan Ilkhani. He exemplified the third process, a combination of designation and amalgamation, in which the central government capitalized on a khan who was in the process of forming a confederation, and by assisting him with resources and thus retaining a degree of control over him, turned a potential threat to its own advantage. Government action probably meant little to the people, who continued to respond to their own recognized leaders of the smaller units. Significantly, Ilkhani and his progenitors possessed large landholdings and held government offices that provided them with incomes and political support for the amalgamating process—in sharp contrast to Ilkhani's immediate predecessor of the mid-nineteenth century as the most powerful single khan, Mohammad Taqi Khan, who did not have such resources, and therefore failed to unite the Bakhtiyari.

Even a cursory examination of historical data relating Hosain Qoli Khan Ilkhani (d. 1882) to political-juridical, economic, and ideological roles reveals the extent to which a Bakhtiyari khan resembles a nontribal magnate and shares traditional Iranian values. The proto-elements of the traditional state—army, bureaucracy, and legitimacy —are found in Ilkhani's Bakhtiyari of 1862-82. Ilkhani, whose power impelled Naser od-Din Shah to order his death, possessed an undifferentiated and personal bureaucracy larger than but similar to Aqa Mohammad's when he established Qajar rule at the end of the eighteenth century. Ilkhani employed five *monshis,* or agents, and, in addition, one of his brothers served as his executive and another functioned as his finance minister. Ilkhani's sons served him in a variety of military, diplomatic, and administrative roles. Ilkhani was attended by his *yatim* (lit. orphans, essentially non-Bakhtiyari clients), who served as his household, and his *basteh* (sing. of *bastagan*), armed retainers primarily from the Ahmad-e Khosravi. With this core his army and cavalry could be expanded as he manipulated the Bakhtiyari segmentary structure. With such a base he performed his primary functions as *Ilkhani* and could write to Naser od-Din Shah in 1295/1878:

> It is now thirty years that I have served and labored dutifully night and day, and I have transformed the unruly Bakhtiyari into the likes of the peasants of Linjan. I have collected and submitted 31 taxes from the Bakhtiyari; the clearance of accounts are in hand, and I do not have 31 qirans outstanding on the tax account. I spend six months each year on the Isfahan side of the Bakhtiyari busy maintaining its order and collecting its taxes. The other six months I am in Arabestan and Lorestan in the service of the governor with armed Bakhtiyari cavalry.[22]

Ilkhani derived his income from extensive landholdings, from *tuyuls,* and from various tribal dues; his capital surpluses were entrusted to urban merchants for investment. Ilkhani maintained personal ties with the Vali'ahd in Tabriz, Zell os-Soltan in Isfahan, Amir Alam Khan of Birjand, shaikhs in Khuzestan, Amir Hosain Khan Shoja od-Dauleh of Qochan, the Isfahan ulama, and commercial ties with the British. Ilkhani's *"Ketabcheh"*[23] is replete with references to cash agriculture and animal husbandry (especially horses and irrigation), relations with the Qajars, interaction with Qashqa'i and Arabs, and family matters—but surprisingly little about what are popularly regarded as tribal, or even Bakhtiyari, matters. By no means was Ilkhani the exception in the Bakhtiyari; predecessors with similar interests include Abol-Khalil Khan, Ali Mardan Khan, and Elias Khan of the eighteenth century, and Mohammad Taqi Khan Chahar Lang of the nineteenth. Ilkhani's son, Ali Qoli Khan Sardar As'ad II, and grandson, Ja'far Qoli Khan Sardar As'ad III, were to play significant Bakhtiyari and national roles; both attracted the attention of the British who considered them likely regents on two different occasions.

Pahlavi Centralization

Changes in the traditional Iranian system and the structure of the state began with Reza Shah and were continued by Mohammad Reza Shah. These include centralization of power and authority, emergence of the nation-state, and an expanded state role calling for economic and social progress. Even before Reza Khan was crowned as Reza Shah, the great khans—especially Khosrau Khan Sardar Zafar—perceived him and his policies as a threat to their autonomy and power. Their challenge to him, however, failed, because it followed essentially traditional lines, while he utilized both the methods of the traditional Iranian system and of the new nation-state. Tehran successfully identified the "feudal" Bakhtiyari leadership with the decadent past and with foreign domination. The new nation-state of Iran need not share authority and power; it had its own army, bureaucracy, policies integrating Iranians into the national economy, and promotion of an "Iranian" identity through education and new national symbols.

Despite Pahlavi centralization, the form and function of the *tayafeh*, and levels below, have been more persistent and less affected by external developments, for their function derives from basic pastoral and agricultural structures. Some 500,000 Bakhtiyari still follow traditional social and economic patterns, including the migration.[24] Even today the *tayafeh* structure continues to provide the framework for traditional internal, sociopolitical activities, because the symbolic role of the great khans continues. Despite the state's assumption of their juridical and administrative functions, the *tayafeh* continue to align themselves into one of the great khan moieties of either the "Ilkhani" or the "Hajji Ilkhani."[25] (The former is identified with Hosain Qoli Khan Ilkhani's lineage and the latter with Imam Qoli Khan Hajji

Ilkhani's; Imam Qoli was Hosain Qoli's full brother and successor as *Ilkhani* in 1882. Even during Hosain Qoli's life the division between Haft Lang and Chahar Lang had lost much of its importance.) Pahlavi tribal policy of continuing to treat the Bakhtiyari as an administrative unit has possibly resulted in a more precise delineation of internal and external social and physical boundaries. This may have strengthened both Bakhtiyari identity as a social unit with a given territory and the Ilkhani/Hajji Ilkhani framework for social, economic, and political interaction. The state's general economic and political policies, especially of the 1970s, have probably had an accelerating impact on change in the Bakhtiyari, especially with the attraction of the oil fields and new industrial centers adjacent to that region—but the impact has probably been less far-reaching than on the Qashqa'i,[26] given the relative Bakhtiyari isolation. In spite of Pahlavi centralization and modernization, then, those within the Bakhtiyari family-*tayafeh* structure enjoy a degree of autonomy, because they are peripheral to the nation-state and its economy; those who permanently leave the region, however, become integrated into it.

9

Persian Gulf Trade and the Agricultural Economy of Southern Iran in the Nineteenth Century

Roger T. Olson

During the nineteenth century, the agricultural economy of southern Iran gradually was transformed from one designed to satisfy the needs of local consumption to one which, to a great degree, was devoted to the production of cash crops designed to meet the demands of Indian markets.[1] The most important factor in that gradual transformation was the influence of the trade between Iran and India which was carried on through the Persian Gulf port of Bushehr. This article will examine the way in which Persian Gulf trade affected the agricultural economy of southern Iran by concentrating on the role it played in the introduction of opium cultivation.

Opium cultivation was by no means the only change which Persian Gulf trade induced in that economy during the nineteenth century. In fact, it probably did not have as great a direct economic effect on the region as did growing exports of southern Iranian grain to India during the same period. However, opium cultivation is a particularly suitable subject for such an investigation for two reasons. First, the large-scale production of opium was unknown in southern Iran before the nineteenth century, although the drug itself had been known there for centuries. Thus, the development of opium production is relatively easy to trace, and its relation to other economic developments is fairly clear. Second, opium cultivation was the virtual antithesis of subsistence cultivation. The cultivation of opium was a laborious and time-consuming process which could be carried out economically only on the best lands in the region. It was not the sort of cultivation which peasants could undertake on marginal lands in order to supplement their normal incomes. Consequently, the substitution of opium cultivation for subsistence cultivation on a large scale is an extremely good indication that major changes were occurring in the economic, as well as the social and political, structure of southern Iran during the nineteenth century.[2]

The Agricultural Economy of Southern Iran in the Early Nineteenth Century

Despite climatic and other environmental variations, the pattern of agricultural production was essentially the same throughout southern Iran at the beginning of the nineteenth century. The most important unit of production was the peasant village. Each village functioned as a distinct unit whose primary goal was to grow the food needed for its own survival.[3] Because of their similar objectives, each village tended to cultivate much the same assortment of crops. In the *garmsir* (warm lands) cultivation was limited to wheat, barley, and dates. In the higher *sardsir* (cool lands), and in agricultural districts which lay on the border between the two zones, a somewhat more extensive array of crops was grown. During the crucial winter growing season, the land was devoted to wheat and barley, just as in the *garmsir*. In the summer however, a wide variety of fruits and vegetables, as well as a certain amount of rice, was cultivated. Such crops were valuable supplements to the region's food supply.[4]

There were three exceptions to the subsistence-oriented pattern of cultivation which characterized southern Iran in the early nineteenth century. Tobacco was grown in fairly large quantities on the Kazerun plain and in several areas around Shiraz. Grapes for wine making were grown on the hillsides west and northwest of Shiraz. Finally, a very small quantity of opium was grown, primarily around Kazerun. However, the cultivation of such crops did not alter the fundamental nature of agriculture in southern Iran. The peasant villages which carried on that cultivation functioned as units. They devoted some of their land to the production of tobacco or grapes, while reserving the majority of it for food crops. That was particularly true with grapes, which were grown on slopes not suited for grain. Furthermore, tobacco was sown in the summer whereas the crucial grain crops were sown in the winter. Although opium cultivation did not share those advantages, it was done on such a small scale that it did not detract from the peasants' ability to grow their own food.[5] Finally, all those crops played an important role in local patterns of consumption. Tobacco in particular was virtually the only luxury item available to the peasants. Consequently, those who grew such crops had little difficulty in exchanging them for whatever other locally-grown commodities they required. The cultivation of crops such as tobacco, and even opium, merely supplemented the peasants' subsistence agricultural production. It did not compete with it.

During the early nineteenth century, the market-oriented aspect of the southern Iranian economy was based primarily on the distribution of surplus crops produced by the peasants. However, the peasants had very little control over the system of distribution. The bulk of their produce was committed in advance in fulfillment of obligations incurred in the course of production. The most important of them was the obligation to pay rent to the landlord in return for the right to cultivate the land.

Generally, the rent owed by the peasants was assessed as a portion of their crop payable in kind after the harvest. However, landowners often could demand part of it in cash or compulsory labor. On land owned by the government (*divani*), the peasants theoretically surrendered half their crop to the government agent after a deduction was made to provide seed for next year's crop. Thus, they retained about 30 percent of the total crop. On privately owned land (*arbabi*), the peasants often gave four-fifths of the crop to the landlord, who set one of those fifths aside as seed, and retained one-fifth of it for themselves. In return, the owner theoretically was obligated to furnish the seed, water, and animals that the peasant needed to grow a crop.[6]

Such a system of land tenure effectively gave the landowners (of which the government was the chief) control over virtually all of the region's surplus production. The peasant cultivators retained enough of their crops to survive during the year, but little else.[7] The theoretical difference between the portion of the crop retained by peasants farming *divani* land and that retained by peasants farming *arbabi* land was of little or no significance in that respect. Generally, it quickly was consumed by "extraordinary" or "irregular" imposts and contributions levied on the peasants.[8]

However, the position of the landlords was not entirely secure, for they also had obligations to groups which claimed rights over the land. The most important was the obligation to deliver part of the crop grown on their land to the government in the form of taxes. At the beginning of the century, the government claimed one-tenth of the crop after a portion was deducted for next year's seed. During the reign of Fath Ali Shah (1797–1834) however, the portion claimed by the government was doubled to one-fifth. By the 1850s, although the assessment theoretically remained at one-fifth, the actual value taken by the government amounted to more like one-third of the crop. At the same time, the government was beginning to demand that taxes be paid in cash rather than in kind.[9]

However, the most important economic effect of the government's revenue policies lay not in the way taxes were assessed but in the way they were collected. The Qajar shahs considered Fars and its dependencies to be among the most important regions of their empire. Unfortunately, the region's importance was based almost exclusively on the substantial revenues it could provide the central government. The shah generally gave the post of governor of Fars to a prominent member of his own family, granting him complete control over the internal affairs of the region on condition that he maintain order—and thus minimize expense—and forward the approprite sums annually to the shah's treasury.[10] The Qajars, however, were outsiders in southern Iran and their administration was not able to rely on the services of a large body of local supporters. They also were unable to develop a professional bureaucracy capable of administering the region directly. As a result, the Qajars found it necessary to administer southern Iran indirectly through well-established local leaders. They did so through a widespread application of the *tuyul* system.

In theory, the term *tuyul* referred to a temporary grant, usually of land, although it could be virtually anything, made by the government to a subordinate in return for loyalty and the performance of stipulated tasks. The revenue derived from the grant enabled the recipient to perform those tasks adequately, and lasted only as long as he did so. However, the *tuyul* system practiced in southern Iran operated more as a sophisticated form of tax-farming than as the *tuyul* of theory. The provincial government in Shiraz granted the right to exercise administrative authority over a particular area to a private person in return for a cash payment. The amount of the payment was determined by a process of competitive bidding in which the highest bidder received the grant and the power that went with it. Once he had paid the agreed sum to the government, the holder of the *tuyul* (*tuyuldar*) was empowered to recoup his investment and make as much of a profit as he could manage by collecting tax revenues from the districts under his control—as long as he maintained order in them. If he chose, and most did so, he also could grant authority over all or part of that area to subordinates on similar terms. The area which a *tuyuldar* could control generally was limited only by the amount of the payment he could afford and by the strength of his competitors in the bidding.[11]

The possession of a *tuyul* enabled its holder to gain control of a large portion of the surplus agricultural produce of the area under his control. The obligations of the *tuyuldar* essentially were fixed. Once he had made the initial cash payment necessary to obtain his position, he was relatively immune from government exactions, although a prudent *tuyuldar* provided his superiors with liberal *pishkesh* (presents). At the same time, his ability to extract revenue from the area under his control was limited only by what the local economy would bear and by his own needs. A *tuyuldar* generally was given wide administrative powers over his district. In the case of *divani* lands, he collected the entire share of the crop owed to the government as rent. More importantly, he had the power to determine the exact amount of the tax—and occasionally the manner in which it was to be paid—due from each village or estate in his area. Since the productivity of most land in southern Iran had never been assessed formally, that power became very significant. A *tuyuldar* easily could assess his own property and that of his friends at a very low rate, while making ruinously high demands on property which he desired to acquire or which belonged to his enemies.

Because of the power which it conferred, the position of *tuyuldar* was a very desirable one. Virtually every landowner in the region sought to obtain a *tuyul* over at least his own possessions in order to keep his rivals from destroying him.[12] At the beginning of the nineteenth century however, the nature of the region's economy tended to limit the degree to which any single local figure could gain control over the land through the *tuyul* system. The major landowners, merchants, and tribal khans who were competing with one another all drew their economic power from the same basic source—the production and distribution of locally-grown staple crops. The revenues which they derived from these sources usually were sufficient to secure them the *tuyul* over their own districts. However, it was very seldom that any one of them was able to amass so much more money than his rivals that he could both secure his own district and gain control over theirs.

The effects of the *tuyul* system, the system of land tenure, and the nature of agricultural production in southern Iran combined during the early nineteenth century to create a social system in which both political and economic power was concentrated in the hands of a "local gentry" class. The members of that class often combined the functions of landowner, tribal leader, and occasionally merchant with the crucial function of *tuyuldar* in a way which gave them virtually complete control over the economic activity of the region. Although some members of that class lived in Shiraz or in Bushehr, most lived in the smaller Persian Gulf ports or in the agricultural towns of the hinterland which dominated the areas on which they based their power. As long as control over the production and distribution of the region's staple crops remained the only significant source of power, that system was secure.[13]

The Effect of the Trade with India: 1800–69

At the beginning of the nineteenth century, two distinct commercial systems were functioning within southern Iran. The first, and most important, was the extensive "country trade" based on the agricultural economy described in the previous section. Although information on the exact movement of goods involved in that trade is rather scanty, it appears that the trade was made up of three components. First, there was a fairly extensive trade between Shiraz and some of the agricultural district around it in order to supply the city with food and other items of local consumption. Second, a certain amount of trade took place among the principal agricultural towns of the region. Tobacco, which was exchanged for a number of foodstuffs, played an important part in that trade although a few locally-produced handicrafts also were involved.[14]

The third, and largest, component of the "country trade" at the beginning of the nineteenth century was the trade between the agricultural towns of the *sardsir* and the various ports of the Persian Gulf coast. The hinterland towns exported fairly large quantities of grain, fruits, vegetables, and dairy products to the Persian Gulf ports, with each port tending to draw such produce from a particular district.[15] A portion of the produce brought down from the interior was retained for sale in the ports, which often were unable to grow enough food to satisfy their needs. The rest was exported by local craft throughout the Gulf. Some of it was shipped as far as India although such trade generally was carried on via lower Gulf entrepots such as Bandar-e Lengeh or Muscat. In return, the upper Gulf ports imported dates, ghee, spices, and Indian piece goods from Bahrain, Bandar-e Lengeh, and other places. Most of those products were shipped back to the towns of the *sardsir* where they were consumed, although some were retained in the ports themselves. Although the quantity of goods involved was small by later standards, the "country trade" of southern Iran was quite profitable at the time. Its importance can be seen in the observations of Francklin who, in 1786, found economic conditions in both Shiraz and Bushehr to be quite good and the caravan traffic between them to be flourishing, despite the fact that all trade with the British in Bushehr had ceased.[16] However, it also possessed characteristics which were seriously to affect its subsequent development.

The most important of those characteristics was the nature of the participants in the trade. The "country trade" of southern Iran was a trade among towns and urban merchants. It was not a trade among villages and farmers. The foodstuffs and other products involved were drawn from the surplus crops which were accumulated in the form of rents or tax revenues by landowners and officials in the towns. They in turn relied on townbased merchants to dispose of whatever they did not consume themselves.[17]

The second commercial system which functioned in southern Iran at the beginning of the nineteenth century was based on the activities of the British East India Company, which possessed an official monopoly over much of the foreign trade of India. The East India Company had maintained a Residency at Bushehr since 1763, and Shiraz served as a major transshipment point on the routes connecting it with the interior of Iran. However, the nature and volume of the East India Company's trade during the early nineteenth century tended to minimize its influence on the local economy of southern Iran.

From the southern Iranian point of view, the trade of the East India Company was purely a transit trade. British goods, primarily woolens and hardware, were imported into Shiraz through Bushehr. Although small amounts of those goods were sold locally, the great bulk of them were sent farther north to markets in Tabriz, Tehran, and other northern cities. In return, raw silk and silk fabrics from northern Iran were brought to Shiraz. From there, they were sent to Bushehr and consigned to the representatives of the East India Company, who exported them to India or even Britain. Thus, the centers of production and consumption which were involved in both the import and the export trade associated with the East India Company were located outside of southern Iran.

Within the region, the trade with the East India Company was handled by a relatively small number of Iranian merchant families living in Shiraz. The profit that such merchants made on each item of British merchandise which passed through their hands could be considerable. However, during the first few years of the century, the total volume of such traffic and hence the total profit involved was rather small. Between 1770 and 1790, only one East India Company vessel per year called at Bushehr. The average cargo handled by the Company's agents there amounted to only 60–100 bales of goods (about £2,500) annually. Although the Company's trade began to expand after 1790, it still amounted to only about 600 bales of goods per year by 1809.[18]

During the first years of the century however, the rise of the cotton textile industry in Britain began to affect both the volume and the nature of the Company's trade with Iran. At first, the effect was primarily negative. Competition from the growing volume of cheap, machine-made cotton textiles quickly destroyed the British market for Indian silks. The demand for Iranian raw silk also was reduced substantially in both India and in Britain.[19] Furthermore, British industry began to export increasingly large quantities of cheap cotton goods to India. Such goods dominated the Indian market and eventually ruined the local Indian textile industry. Its collapse had a detrimental effect on the "country trade" of southern Iran, a significant portion of which had been devoted to importing Indian piece goods.

At the same time, British cotton fabrics quickly replaced woolens as the chief commodity in the East India Company's trade between Britain and Iran. Such textiles were both cheap and well suited for Iranian markets. By 1817, the value of European goods imported into Iran through Bushehr had risen to slightly over £40,000 (557,915 krans) per year. By 1823, it had reached a figure of over £160,000 (2,191,391 krans) annually.[20] Although trade fluctuated after the early 1820s in response to changes in conditions affecting the Indian market, it generally increased. Between 1825 and 1870, the value of European imports roughly quadrupled although there were some periods—notably during the American Civil War—when it temporarily reached far greater figures. Between 40 and 50 percent of those imports were cotton fabrics or piece goods imported from Britain.[21]

The rapid and substantial growth of British trade with Iran during the first two-thirds of the nineteenth-century affected southern Iran in several ways. First, the volume of imports brought into Iran became far greater than ever before. Merchants handling those imports soon found that they could not dispose of all their goods in former markets, and they began to seek new ones. As a result, southern Iran's role in the trade gradually shifted from that of a transit area to that of a center of consumption. Travelers observed only very small quantities of British goods for sale in the region before approximately 1820, and those were confined to the bazaars of Shiraz and Bushehr. By 1860, however, such goods were being sold in the bazaars of most of the agricultural towns of the region.[22] The competition which British cotton goods offered in those markets destroyed the already moribund cloth industries of southern Iran. By 1870, one can fairly state that most of the region was dependent on imported British cloth for its basic clothing needs.[23]

The growth of British trade also presented the merchants involved in it with a serious balance of payments problem. While imports from Britain and India were increasingly rapidly and gaining an ever more important role in Iranian consumption, Iranian exports via the Persian Gulf were not growing at a corresponding rate. The silk trade which previously had supported the rest of Iran's trade wtih India was no longer able to do so, and the demand for other Iranian products in India was not great. Although there was a demand for such products in Europe. the high costs of transportation and the very long shipping time around the Cape of Good Hope made it impractical to seek to satisfy that demand via the Persian Gulf. Most Iranian products exported to Europe were produced in northern Iran and exported either via Tabriz to Trebizond or to Russia. Again, high internal transportation costs kept southern Iran from participating profitably in that trade.

Iranian merchants sought to meet their difficulties in two ways. First, they used cash derived from other forms of trade, such as the trade with Russia, to pay for imports from Britain and India.[24] At the same time, Iranian merchants sought to improve the terms of their trade with India by developing new exports. Horses were exported to India on a far larger scale than ever before. By 1857, the value of horses exported to India from the Gulf region was estimated to exceed £40,000 per year, with the great bulk of it coming from Bushehr. There also is evidence that the production of tobacco was organized for export on a far more intensive scale during the period. The town of Jahrom became a center for the sale and distribution of Iranian tobacco throughout Turkish Iraq, the Arabian Peninsula, Egypt, and even India. Kazerun also was involved in that trade. However, such observations must be made with care due to the particularly poor quality of earlier data concerning the tobacco trade.[25] Finally the period saw the first attempts by southern Iranian merchants and landowners to develop an export trade based on opium.

The first known southern Iranian attempt to develop such an export trade was made by Shaikh Abd or-Rasul of Bushehr in 1823–24. The shaikh put together a shipment of twenty chests of opium and shipped them to Canton for sale. The venture was not particularly successful for, although Persian opium sold well enough, the cost and inconvenience of shipping it to China made long-term trade unfeasible. Opium production in India was a jealously guarded monopoly of the East India Company and, after the Company's demise in 1858, the British government. Consequently, prohibitively high duties were charged on the product at all ports in British India. Although such ports could be avoided by shipping the opium directly to China or to one of the Dutch-controlled ports of Indonesia, the cost of doing so was too great for most Iranian merchants.[26] As a result, the opium trade did not take root in southern Iran, although it is possible that the existing production of Kazerun was expanded slightly. It did become important in northern Iran, but the opium produced there was exported via Trebizond or Central Asia rather than the Persian Gulf.

Finally, the growth of British trade during the first two-thirds of the nineteenth century altered the fundamental basis of the social and political system of southern Iran. Trade introduced wealth into the region in previously unknown amounts. Furthermore, the nature of that trade tended to concentrate that wealth in the hands of the relatively small number of people who participated in it rather than to disperse it among a number of local landlords, officials, or even peasants. Consequently, those who were engaged in that trade, and those who had access to its wealth, gained a preponderance of economic power over those who were not. The *tuyul* system provided them with an ideal way to convert that economic power into political power.

During the nineteenth century, the *tuyul* system in southern Iran was characterized by two simultaneous developments. First, the price of individual *tuyuls* rose steadily throughout the century. Around 1800 at Bushehr, the *tuyul* was granted to the local shaikh for 4,000 tomans—plus an equal amount of unofficial presents. By 1850, the amount had risen to 22,000 tomans. By 1882, the right to collect customs duties alone was valued at 60,000 tomans; and by 1889, it was granted in return for a payment of 91,000 tomans plus a present of 5,000 tomans.[27] After the 1850s, local shaikhs were unable to raise such funds, and they were superseded. The value of other *tuyuls* also tended to rise, but those involved with trade rose more rapidly, and those which gave their possessors some measure of control over the trade with India rose most rapidly of all.[28] Such rises reflected the increasing importance of British trade in the region's economy.

At the same time, a marked tendency developed for powerful

individuals to obtain control over larger and larger districts. The men who were able to expand their control in such a manner generally had some sort of connection with the Indian trade. For example, in 1800 the principal ports of the Persian Gulf coast were each controlled by a local shaikh who purchased *tuyul* rights over the town and its immediate environs directly from Shiraz. By the middle of the century however, the shaikh of Bushehr had been able to gain control over the *tuyul* rights of many of those ports. He in turn farmed them out to local residents.[29] However, the expansion of the shaikh of Bushehr's influence was overshadowed by that of powerful figures in Shiraz, the chief of whom were Mirza Ali Mohammad Khan Qavam ol-Molk and his supporters. The Qavam ol-Molk gradually was able to use the wealth which he obtained through trade wtih India to gain control over Shiraz (where he occupied the position of *kalantar*) and its surrounding areas.[30] He also was able to obtain the leadership of the Khamseh Confederation, an artificially formed grouping of nomadic tribes whose pastures lay east and southeast of Shiraz. By 1852, he was able to use his wealth and influence to replace the shaikh of Bushehr with one of his own sons.[31]

The Introduction of Opium Cultivation

During the first two-thirds of the nineteenth century, the growth of trade with British India affected the political and economic structure of southern Iran in several ways. However, the system of agricultural production on which the region's economy was based remained relatively unaffected by those developments. It continued to be based on the efforts of local peasant villages to grow the food they needed for their survival.[32] In general, only the way in which the surpluses resulting from that cultivation were distributed and used had been changed. Even the introduction of steam navigation in the western Indian Ocean and the Persian Gulf in the late 1850s did not lead to significant alterations in the agricultural patterns of the region; although it did fundamentally disrupt the economies of the commercial communities of the Gulf itself.

The opening of the Suez Canal in 1869, however, had an intense influence on the agricultural economy of southern Iran. It did so primarily by "revolutionizing" the trade of India. When combined with the already existing steamship lines in the Indian Ocean, the Canal greatly reduced freight rates between India and Europe. The lower rates were so advantageous to trade that by 1875, about 70 percent of India's imports were brought in via the Canal route. By

1895, the figure had risen to 88 percent. In part, such figures merely represent a diversion of India's import trade from the Cape route to the Suez route. However, they also represent a vast rise in the volume of goods imported from Europe, which in time rendered other sources of imports statistically insignificant. Indian markets were flooded with goods imported from Europe, and merchants in India were forced to develop new exports in order to pay for them.

The expansion of India's export trade, particularly that with Europe, also was aided by the opening of the Canal. Again, the drop in freight rates was important, but the reduction in shipping time between India and Europe was equally so. Until 1869, it was difficult to ship many agricultural products, particularly foodstuffs, from India to Europe, because ships took months to cover the Cape route and spent a large part of the time in the tropics where such products were likely to spoil. Once the canal route had been opened, the combination of low freight rates and short shipping times combined to stimulate an intense demand for Indian agricultural products in Europe. India could satisfy such a demand only at the expense of local consumption and its export trade to other markets.[33]

Such changes in Indian trade affected the southern Iranian economy in two ways. First, the quantity and variety of European goods imported into Iran through Bushehr increased sharply. Indian firms found it very profitable to reexport European goods to Iran, usually via Aden. Between 1875 and 1878 for example, the total value of imports at Bushehr rose from 3,466,503 rupees per year to 7,395,000 rupees per year. In part, the figures represent an absolute rise in the volume of goods imported into Iran from Europe. They also, however, represent the effects of a diversion of trade from the Trebizond-Tabriz route to the Persian Gulf. It had become more profitable to ship goods from Britain to northern Iran via Suez and Bushehr, than it was to ship them from Britain to Tabriz via Trebizond.[34] Although the exact figures fluctuated from year to year between 1878 and 1900, the value of Iranian imports generally continued to rise. The bulk of the trade consisted of cotton goods produced either in Britain or the mills of Bombay, but other articles were becoming increasingly important.[35] By the 1890s, Iran was dependent on Europe for a wide variety of necessary items of consumption.

The rise in the volume of European imports after 1869 further emphasized the earlier difficulties which Iranian merchants were having in paying for their imports. By the 1870s, the old sources of exports clearly were insufficient to pay for the new volume of imports. At the same time, however, an intense demand for agricultural products was rising in the Indian market as a result of the changes taking place in India's trade. Many of the products for which a demand was developing were crops which already were being grown on a large scale in southern Iran such as wheat, barley, and dried fruits. But the crop for which demand was greatest and for which profits were potentially highest was opium.

The production and export of opium offered a number of economic advantages to the merchants, landowners, and tax farmers who controlled the region's economy by 1870. Opium was a high value, low bulk commodity which could be prepared and shipped to market with a minimum of investment in special equipment or in transportation facilities. The demand for opium to use in British India's rapidly growing trade with China was so great that those who controlled its production had no difficulty in disposing of their crops, often at great profit. It was estimated that a piece of land planted in opium poppies would yield its owner three times the profit of an equivalent amount planted in grain. Equally important however, was the fact that by cultivating opium, the complex system of distribution which gave shares in the crop to several different groups could be circumvented. Opium was not an item of local consumption. Instead, the entire crop was sold by the landowner for a cash payment, and the cultivators were paid a fixed sum, from which they could then buy what they previously would have grown for themselves. The remainder, regardless of the portion of the total value of the crop it represented, was the landowner's share.[36]

Although the advantages of opium cultivation had been evident for years, they did not become fully operative in southern Iran until after 1869, when changes in shipping patterns, the rapid expansion of Chinese markets, and the general reduction in oceanic freight rates made it feasible to export opium on a large scale via the Persian Gulf. Once the steamship traffic between Europe, India, and China via the Suez Canal became well established, southern Iranian merchants found that they could send opium to Aden and transship it there for China duty-free. When the authorities in Aden began charging a duty on opium, the merchants shifted their activities to Suez. Eventually, the merchants of Yazd found that they could ship their opium to ports in Ceylon, which also were duty-free and much more convenient.[37]

After 1870, the amount of opium exported from Iran via the Persian Gulf increased dramatically. During 1871, 870 chests of opium valued at 696,000 rupees were exported through the ports of Bushehr and Bandar Abbas. By 1880, the figure had risen to 7,700 chests valued at

8,470,000 rupees. By that time, the export of opium made up well over 50 percent, by value, of all exports from southern Iran. During the remainder of the century, the amount of opium exported increased gradually, although its value fluctuated considerably in response to changing conditions in both the Chinese and Indian markets.[38]

Much of the opium exported from the Persian Gulf was not produced in southern Iran. Isfahan and Yazd both produced very large quantities, which generally were exported via Shiraz and Bushehr. However, southern Iran's share in the production rose considerably after 1870. Between 1870 and 1880, extensive lands which previously had been devoted to the cultivation of grain were converted to the cultivation of poppies. By 1880, the opium poppy had become a major crop in ten administrative districts in southern Iran and a minor crop in three more. With the exception of Kazerun, its cultivation had been unknown in all those districts before 1870.[39] The districts involved primarily were those of the *sardsir*, which previously had grown the bulk of the region's food supplies. Most of them were in the lands east and southeast of Shiraz, which were controlled by the Qavam ol-Molk and his supporters.

The introduction of large-scale opium cultivation in southern Iran temporarily eased, although it did not eliminate, the problems faced by Iranians in paying for the increasing volume of European and Indian goods imported into the region. Furthermore, the profits derived from the export of opium tended greatly to enhance the power and status of those who were in a position to control it. For example, the Qavam ol-Molk was able to use the increased revenue gained from his role in the opium trade to extend his control over nearly all the land around Shiraz; the plains to the north, east, and southeast of it—and the Persian Gulf coast around Bandar-e Taheri.[40]

However, the introduction of opium cultivation on a large scale had several additional effects which eventually proved highly disruptive of the agricultural economy of the region. Merchants and landowners who could not participate in the opium trade found it difficult to compete with the new power and wealth available to those who could. In many cases, the former were ruined or forced to move to other cities.

The situation of the region's peasant farmers was more complex. Although opium cultivation offered many advantages to the landowners, it was not entirely in the interests of the cultivators. A village engaged in the large-scale cultivation of opium seldom retained a sufficient amount of land or labor to grow its own food. Yet, there does not appear to have been much initial resistance to the idea of cultivating opium on the part of the villagers. That was due primarily to the tremendous range of inducements available to landowners, merchants, and tax farmers. In some cases, tax farmers offered to reduce or even eliminate the collection of taxes on land devoted to opium cultivation. In other cases, merchants advanced loans on relatively easy terms to the debt-ridden villagers in return for their agreement to grow opium for them.[41] If other means were ineffective, the landowner could always raise the tax assessment of the village and threaten the peasants with eviction if they did not comply. However, such measures were seldom necessary at first, since the villagers generally responded quickly to the prospect of short-term cash profits.

By the mid-1870s, however, the attitude of the villagers tended to become more negative as the long-term effects of vastly increased opium cultivation made themselves felt. Villagers involved in opium cultivation were transformed into virtual wage laborers, who had to buy food on the open market rather than grow it for themselves. Of course as long as food supplies were plentiful and prices remained low, such an arrangement actually was advantageous for the villagers. But expanding opium production tended to take increasingly large amounts of land out of grain production. As a result, the region's total food supply was reduced and grain prices rose. This affected the villagers in two ways. First, in years when for any number of natural reasons the harvest in the region was bad, famine was quick to strike. It also was more difficult for the region to recover from such famines, since much of the land was no longer devoted to food production. Furthermore, the villagers increasingly were forced to compete with British and Indian merchants involved in the growing grain trade between southern Iran and India for limited supplies of grain. They seldom could match the purchasing power of such buyers.[42]

As the position of the villagers—and the region's urban poor who were even more affected by such trends—deteriorated during the 1870s and early 1880s, resistance to the idea of opium cultivation began to develop. In order to forestall serious outbreaks of popular unrest, the provincial government sought to limit the growth of opium production by imposing restrictions on the amount of land which could be devoted to poppies at the expense of grain.[43] But neither popular discontent nor administrative restriction was particularly successful in limiting the growth of opium production. The profits to be gained from it were too great, and it was too easy for landowners to avoid compliance. In fact, by 1880 neither the villagers nor the central government had the power to resist for long the demands of men who combined the positions of landowner, tax collector, merchant, and moneylender.

Conclusion

During the nineteenth century, the agricultural economy of southern Iran changed from one designed overwhelmingly to meet the needs of local consumption to one which, to a large degree, was geared to meeting the demands of expanding foreign markets. The exact nature of the change was determined primarily by the impact of growing trade relations between Iran and India on local social, economic, and political structures, and was not necessarily identical to changes occurring in other parts of Iran at the same time. Merchants, landowners, and officials gradually found that it was more profitable to trade with British India than it was to engage in local commerce, and they began to devote an increasingly large share of whatever economic resources they controlled to that trade. At the same time, participation in the trade with India gave such individuals access to sources of economic power which were far greater than any others available within the region. As a result, those who were involved in the trade with India eventually were able to extend their control over most of the southern Iranian economy.

During the first two-thirds of the nineteenth century, such developments did not affect the system of agricultural production in southern Iran significantly, although they did affect the way in which the region's surplus crops were used. The opening of the Suez Canal in 1869, however, fundamentally changed the nature of Iran's economic relationship with India and with it, the agricultural economy of southern Iran. Iranian markets were flooded with cheap imported goods. At the same time, the opening of the canal stimulated a great demand for Indian agricultural products in Europe. Products which previously had been consumed locally or exported to markets in Africa or Asia were quickly diverted to European markets to meet that demand. That, in turn, gave rise to an intense demand for certain southern Iranian agricultural products in India, as Indian firms sought to preserve their local or regional trade while taking advantage of new opportunities in Europe.

Iranian merchants, landowners, and officials sought to cash in on that demand by converting increasingly large amounts of agricultural land in southern Iran from the cultivation of staple crops to the cultivation of cash crops such as opium. This would both satisfy the demands of the Indian market and provide them with the funds necessary to pay for the growing amount of goods imported from Europe and India. They were able to do so because the profits which they had obtained from their previous participation in the trade with India had enabled them to extend their control over the bulk of the agricultural land in the region. Thus, the Persian Gulf trade provided both the incentive and the means to transform the agricultural economy of southern Iran from one based on staple crops to one based largely on cash crops.

10

Rural Socioeconomic Organization in Transition: The Case of Iran's Bonehs

Eric J. Hooglund

Iranian villages experienced significant socioeconomic changes during the last 17 years of the Pahlavi dynasty.[1] These changes transformed many of the traditional patterns which had prevailed in village society and economy throughout the first half of the twentieth century. The primary catalyst for these changes was external: government policies specifically aimed at effecting rural social and economic change. The single most important government program of active intervention in agricultural affairs remains land reform, which was initiated in 1962 and implemented in four distinct stages over the course of a decade. Even though its actual results were somewhat short of original expectations, land redistribution had an important impact on rural Iran. While the consequences of the reform have been examined in detail elsewhere, a review of some of the more salient effects is necessary in order to understand the changes which this paper will address.[2]

Land redistribution was a major goal of the land reform program, and undoubtedly the most positive aspect of reform was the termination of the feudal relationship that formerly existed between landlords and peasants.[3] However, large and absentee landownership was not ended and rural poverty remained. The ways in which the redistribution were implemented virtually insured these results. For example, large landlords were not required to relinquish all their holdings. Initially, only those owning more than one village had to sell their "surplus" villages. This phase, however, applied to less than 25 percent of all villages. Under subsequent stages of the reform, landlords were permitted effectively to keep an amount of land equivalent to the share of the harvest they had customarily received. The result was that in nearly 50,000 of the country's 66,000 villages, on the average half the land was exempted from redistribution.[4]

The land which was affected by land reform legislation was neither distributed equitably nor given to all peasants. Under the terms of the law, only those sharecroppers who possessed traditional cultivation rights *(haqq-e nasaq)* were entitled to buy land that landlords were obligated to sell. Consequently, nearly half the peasant families who did not have these rights were automatically excluded from the benefits of the reform. Those who were able to obtain land generally acquired only a fraction of the land they formerly had cultivated, due to the great amount of land exempted in an overwhelming majority of villages. About 65 percent of all peasants who received any land got less than 12 acres. If we consider peasant holdings between 12 and 25 acres, the number of proprietors who had less than 25 acres rises to 84 percent of all peasants who received land under the reform.[5] Additionally, since landlords could choose which part of a village to retain, the land left to be divided among the peasants often was of inferior quality, distant from or without access to irrigation water, and fragmented into several scattered plots. As a result, the majority of peasant proprietors remained subsistence farmers who, increasingly in the 1970s, experienced difficulty eking out a livelihood from their holdings.

The consequent need to find supplementary sources of income led to widespread sale of holdings and abandonment of cropland to pasture, fallow, and uncultivated waste.[6] One practice that became fairly common throughout Iran was for peasants to work as laborers in the fields of their former landlords. While in the first few years following land reform daily or monthly wages were the typical form of remuneration, by the mid-1970s sharecropping arrangements—whereby the peasant agreed to perform all the work in return for a share of the harvest—had become common in many areas. Ironically, the very situation that land reform was intended to end was reinstituted.

Excluded as beneficiaries of land under the reform law were those villagers who did not possess the traditional cultivation rights. Known as *khoshneshin,* in the early 1960s they accounted for 40-50 percent of the total rural populations.[7] While some *khoshneshin* families, especially in larger villages, were prosperous traders, the great majority were very poor people who depended upon agricultural labor and low-status service jobs for their livelihood. Their work frequently was irregular, as they were employed mainly during those peak periods in the agricultural year when the number of peasants possessing cultivation rights was insufficient for the tasks at hand. Consequently, the position of the majority of *khoshneshin* was insecure, and they constituted a virtual rural proletariat. Their situation worsened as poorer *khoshneshin* lost out in competition with peasant proprietors for the limited available work.[8]

In the early 1960s there was general optimism among specialists, who thought that land reform would lead to a dramatic rise in agricultural production. There was general confidence that private proprietorship would provide peasants with an incentive to engage in profitable farming. However, since the overwhelming majority of peasants acquired only subsistence plots, they were not able to produce for markets. While studies have found that productivity per acre was higher among small proprietorships than in fields of more than 25 acres, this did not contribute to overall increased market production, since small peasant holders had to use virtually all their crops for family consumption.[9] The larger landowners with holdings in excess of 25 acres, on the other hand, devoted less and less land to the production of essential grain crops such as wheat, barley, and rice; instead, they invested in cash crops such as cotton, sugar cane, cattle fodder, and fruit orchards. The result was an absolute decline in the production of basic food crops. Consequently, a once self-sufficient Iran had become a net importer of grains and other foodstuffs by the early 1970s.

Iran's agricultural development problems were compounded by government policies. For example, while there were programs designed to provide credits for various agricultural projects ranging from animal husbandry to water resources, the primary beneficiaries of government loans were the large owners. Lending practices tended to favor borrowers who were considered good risks, i.e., the commercial farmers.[10] Among numerous Iranian officials there was a collective inability to comprehend that the problems of small peasant owners stemmed from their poverty. It was generally believed that ignorance, resistance to change, and laziness were the root of rural problems. An excellent example of official insensitivity to peasant needs was wheat prices; the government maintained a ceiling but no floor price. In both 1977 and 1978 this price averaged about five rials (seven cents) less per kilogram than it cost farmers to grow wheat.[11] Consequently, many farmers became discouraged and increasingly were reluctant to cultivate a crop which was cheaper to buy than to plant (because of price controls and subsidies given to wheat imports).

In addition to purely economic policies such as credits and pricing, between 1962-78 the former government devised and implemented various projects to promote general rural development. While plans emphasized providing villages with access roads, primary schools, health clinics, electricity, and piped water, the actual capital expenditures were small compared to Iran's needs. Thus, as late as 1978 an overwhelming majority of villages still lacked any serviceable road to the nearest town, let alone amenities such as schools, clinics, potable water, or electricity. Meanwhile, the expectations of the rural population had been raised by the promises and propaganda of the "Great Civilization." However, the government's poor performance in the provision of basic social services and in its other policies, including land reform, led to widespread dissatisfaction among villagers.

The process of socioeconomic change after 1962 can be better understood by isolating various village institutions and examining their adaptations to the situation created by redistribution. In this regard, a significant institution for study is the *boneh*. Essentially, *bonehs* were peasant workteams responsible for specific sharecropped plots within landlord-owned villages. Since *bonehs* constituted the primary socioeconomic organizations of many Iranian villages before 1962, the transformations that they have undergone as a result of land reform provide useful insights into the process of change in rural Iran during the past 15 years.

The discussion of *bonehs* which follows will be divided into four parts. First is an historical overview of *bonehs* and an analysis of their socioeconomic role in villages. Second, in order to provide necessary background for understanding how *bonehs* have changed since 1962, the operation of a "typical" *boneh* on the eve of land reform will be described. Third, examples of two types of *boneh* transformations which had occurred by the mid-1970s will be presented. Fourth, some of the implications for Iranian agriculture suggested by the changes in the *bonehs* will be examined.

Role of the Bonehs in Iranian Villages

In the early 1960s *bonehs* existed in many villages throughout central, southern, and eastern Iran.[12] Their primary *raison d'etre* was the cooperative management of agricultural production. In any one village there were several *bonehs*, each of which usually had an equal number of members. Yet, the size of these teams varied from village to village; in some cases *bonehs* had only three men, in other instances as many as fourteen. Although their purpose was the cultivation of crops, the fact that village life and agriculture were so intimately intertwined made it inevitable that *bonehs* affected all aspects of rural society. Since almost all village income derived directly or indirectly from agricultural production, those peasants who were members of a *boneh*, and consequently had rights to a share of the harvest, had a certain elevated social status *vis à vis* villagers who were not *boneh* members. In addition, since the *bonehs* were the principal source of work in the villages, nonmembers were dependent upon them for their own welfare.

The role of *bonehs* began to be understood only in the 1960s with the development of serious studies about rural Iran.[13] Coincident with the implementation of land reform, villages in general and *bonehs* in particular became subjects of intensive scholarly inquiry. Particularly important for elucidating the structure of *bonehs* has been the work of Javad Safi-nezhad whose village monograph, *Talebabad*, documents the existence of *bonehs* and provides extensive detail about their functions.[14] Since this pioneering study, Safi-nezhad's continuing work on *bonehs* has focused upon three areas: 1) historical evolution of *bonehs*; 2) comparative study of *bonehs* in different regions; and 3) the transformation of *bonehs* since the initiation of land reform. With complementary studies undertaken by other scholars, there now exists a considerable body of knowledge about how *bonehs* operated in the past and how they have changed. Some of these findings are summarized below.

While the historical origins of *bonehs* remain obscure, available evidence indicates that they were well institutionalized by the late nineteenth century, and probably were a Qajar inheritance from the Safavid period.[15] Some scholars, including Safi-nezhad, believe the *bonehs'* origins lie in ancient Iran.[16] While such antiquity is only conjecture, recent research has lent support to the hypothesis that *bonehs* have existed at least for many centuries. In this regard, Abbas Garrousi of Tehran's Institute for Peasant and Rural Studies has discovered Arabic manuscripts of the late Abbasid period (twelfth century, A.D.) which describe agricultural work teams in the Baghdad area that were remarkably similar to twentieth century descriptions of *bonehs*.[17]

Although the origin of *bonehs* cannot be established, the more important consideration is their specific occurrence within Iran. There are essentially two different scholarly interpretations regarding the

195

location of *bonehs*. The first view maintains that *bonehs* represent a unique form of cooperation necessitated by extremely harsh climatic conditions; thus, *bonehs* were prevalent in areas where irrigation is mandatory for successful agricultural production and, conversely, rare or absent in regions where dry-farming was practiced.[18] In contrast, the second view holds that *bonehs* were utilized throughout Iran for the most efficient production regardless of the nature of the climate. Since research on *bonehs* has focused primarily upon the more arid areas of Iran, it is not possible to evaluate satisfactorily the validity of either hypothesis at present. My own investigations, however, have turned up evidence of *bonehs* in both Azerbaijan and Kurdestan, two regions which normally receive considerably more than 300 millimeters of rainfall per year.[19]

In addition to the paucity of scholarly research on the villages of western Iran in comparison to those of the arid east, another major impediment to ascertaining the extent of *bonehs* has been the bewildering variety of terms used. While *boneh* has become generally accepted by scholars, the term tends to be restricted to the Qazvin-Tehran-Varamin regions. A variety of other words are utilized elsewhere: *sahra* in Khorasan; *harasih* in Fars; *dang* in Arak; *pagav* in Sistan; and *darkar* in the Kuhgiluyeh area, for example. In western Iran where Turkic, Kurdish and Luri languages predominate, a linguistic problem compounds the semantic one. Nevertheless, it has been established, at least with regard to eastern Iran, that the various terms essentially refer to similar structures.

Whether or not *bonehs* were found throughout all Iran, they were important in many villages for at least several generations. Their role began to change in the 1960s, and by 1978 *bonehs* were fundamentally different from 10 to 15 years previously. Land redistribution had a major impact on the *bonehs*, even though initially the government was largely ignorant of their existence. There are two major schools of thought concerning the effects of land reform on *bonehs*. Safi-nezhad represents the view that land reform had an overall negative effect on the *bonehs* and contributed to their decline. The other school of thought contends that *bonehs* were representative of village cooperation; new forms of cooperation—in which *bonehs* tended to be involved—arose, while other activities no longer required cooperation. The *boneh* thus transformed itself to meet the new needs.

With this background, we can now examine the operation and function of *bonehs* as was typical in the early 1960s. Such a discussion provides the basis for understanding the changes which have taken place.

The "Typical" Boneh Before Land Reform

In order to understand the role of *bonehs* in traditional Iranian agriculture, it is first necessary to examine exactly how *bonehs* operated. For this purpose it is useful to postulate a hypothetical village—Aliabad—located on the central plateau. We should consider conditions in the village as they may have existed in the early 1960s, prior to the effect of land reform. For the sake of simplicity, let us assume that the whole village belonged to a single landlord. The number of *bonehs* required to cultivate the village fields depended upon the areal extent of land, quantity of available irrigation water, and draught animals. With respect to land, let us assume the area attached to Aliabad was 1,000 hectares (2,471 acres). The actual extent, however, was not as important as the acreage which could be irrigated, since it was the quantity of available water which determined the amount of land which could be cultivated. Since all agricultural production was dependent upon irrigation, the crucial question for this village would be: given a fixed amount of water for irrigation, how much land could be cultivated?

To answer the foregoing question properly, it is necessary to know what crops were cultivated and what were their water requirements. Under the complex irrigation technology that has evolved in Iran over the centuries, the minimum quantity of water for each variety of crop has been calculated. For example, wheat, the most important and ubiquitous crop in Iran, needs a minimum of 24 continuous hours of water per field once every 12 days. Assuming that wheat was the principal crop in Aliabad and that all of the village's irrigation water was supplied by one *qanat* with sufficient water to irrigate about 200 hectares every 12 days (16⅔ hectares/day), then the villagers could not sow more than 200 of their 1,000 hectares. Since the quantity of water available could cover only 200 hectares before one irrigation cycle was completed (12 days), it was necessary to repeat the cycle over again or risk certain—perhaps irreversible—damage to crops. Thus, no matter what the quality of the "surplus" land, insufficient water prevented bringing it under cultivation.[20]

Knowing 200 hectares were cultivated annually, we can proceed to examine how this work was undertaken. The first consideration was field preparation in advance of the actual planting of crops. Ploughing constituted the most important preparatory work, and in Iran fields traditionally were ploughed with oxen—this is still the predominant mode in many areas despite the significant degree of mechanization in the past decade. The normal practice was to yoke two oxen, called a *joft-e gav*, to a shallow "nail" plough. The land was measured by the amount which an oxen team could plough in one day. The number of times the soil had to be turned over before it was considered sufficiently ploughed as well as the total number of days allocated for field preparation were determined by the particular crop to be planted. In the case of wheat, normally one oxen team could plough seven hectares prior to the fixed date for sowing of seed. Thus, to plough the total 200 hectares, the village required about 30 *joft-e gav*.

While ploughing was of primary importance, there also was a diversity of other essential tasks. For example, seeds had to be sown and covered, manure spread, boundaries marked, fields irrigated, plants weeded, and crops harvested. Much of this work had to be completed according to fixed schedules. Given the number of hectares and the time constraints, it was imperative that several persons cooperate to accomplish the required work. Hence, men farmed in teams, each team having responsibility for a certain number of hectares. In Aliabad there were ten such teams or *bonehs;* five men worked together in each *boneh* to cultivate about twenty hectares with the aid of three *joft-e gav*. Effectively then, *bonehs* represented the institutionalization of cooperative work efforts in agriculture.

Each *boneh* was headed by a peasant chosen by the landlord upon the basis of experience and demonstrated expertise, especially in irrigation practices. The chief responsibility of each *boneh* head was to supervise all work connected with crop production on the land assigned to his *boneh*. Various privileges were derived from the status of *boneh* head; most significantly, his share of the harvest usually was more than that of other peasants, and he received an annual bonus from the landlord.

One member of each *boneh* was considered the assistant to the *boneh* head. The principal responsibility of *boneh* assistants was to help supervise the work. This could be an important function since each *boneh* cultivated about 20 hectares (ca. 49 acres) of the total 200. Furthermore, assuming Aliabad's field pattern assignment typical, each *boneh's* 20 hectares was dispersed in five or six separate plots among lands of varying productive quality.

The main burden of *boneh* work fell upon the three other members. From the initial ploughing to the final harvest (a period of some eight to ten months for crops such as winter wheat), these men were responsible for performing most of the labor. Their most important task was to care for and supervise the oxen teams. Typically, one man is in full charge of each *joft-e gav*. We may assume that in Aliabad the oxen were owned by the *boneh* members. However, this was not necessarily always the case; in some areas the oxen were provided by the landlord; in others certain villagers who did not farm held a monopolistic ownership of oxen, which were rented out to the *bonehs* for either a cash payment or share of the crop.

The *bonehs* were reformed annually at the beginning of the fall. The actual *boneh* contract was between the *boneh* head and the landlord. Although all *boneh* heads were chosen directly by the landlord, normally they were free to choose the other members from among those peasants possessing cultivation rights. (In Aliabad there were 50 such men, including the *boneh* heads.) This system permitted any peasant who was not on friendly terms with a particular *boneh* head to seek membership in a more congenial team.

The most important benefit of *boneh* membership was the right to share in the harvest, which was divided between the *bonehs* and the landlord. There were five customary production inputs, each of which received a fixed percentage as a share. The ideal division allotted 20 percent of the harvest to each of the following: land, water, plough work, labor, and seed. In practice, however, this ideal scheme rarely worked perfectly, and shares commonly were computed in fourths, thirds, or other fractions. For Aliabad, however, we may assume a more or less "ideal" crop division in which each *boneh* received 40 percent of the harvest based upon its contribution of plough work and labor; the landlord reserved 40 percent as rent for land and water, while the remaining 20 percent was stored away as seed for the next season.

The 40 percent of the crop that each *boneh* received was not a net profit. Before the *boneh* could distribute its harvest among its members, claims had to be deducted for various individuals who had rendered services to the *boneh* throughout the agricultural year in return for a share of the *boneh's* share of the crop; for example, the blacksmith who provided the oxen's iron shoes and necessary metal tools; the carpenter who made new yokes, handles, and other wooden implements; and *khoshneshins* who worked for the *bonehs* as agricultural laborers during peak activity seasons, as at harvest time. The claims of all of these individuals could amount to as much as 10 percent of the total share of each *boneh*. Thus the *bonehs* were left with 36 percent of the total crop to divide among their members.

Although the division of the harvest within the *boneh* may be equal, it already has been suggested that in Aliabad the *boneh* head received an 8 percent share, while each of the other four *boneh* members received 7 percent. Even these small amounts were not free of certain customary dues since each *boneh* member was expected to give

a portion of his personal share as payment to people such as the barber and bathhouse keeper who had rendered him personal services throughout the year.

The nature of the crop distribution demonstrates an important feature of *bonehs:* villagers who did not belong to any of them still had a relationship to them. Since the economies of villages such as Aliabad were based upon cultivation, and since the *bonehs* were the basic units of agricultural production, it was inevitable that a major source for all livelihoods originated with the *bonehs*. The principal beneficiaries of the *bonehs* naturally were the peasant members. Accordingly, their social status in village society reflected the direct economic advantages they derived from participating in the *bonehs*. Those villagers who did not belong to *bonehs* generally occupied a lower status than the sharecroppers.

The description of *bonehs* presented above has been hypothetical and represents the situation before land reform. Probably no *boneh* functioned exactly like the one described for Aliabad, which represents a composite—albeit simplified—of scores of *bonehs* this writer has investigated in Iranian villages. Yet, Aliabad fits a general pattern of annual *bonehs* cultivating primarily wheat and barley. There were, in addition, many other varieties of *bonehs*. Some, for example, are formed only for summer crops, or even for special cash crops; still other *bonehs* were for the management of livestock.[21] Whatever their specific function, however, all *bonehs* shared in common the feature of being indigenous work cooperatives.

The Transformation of Bonehs

The implementation of land reform in the villages during the 1960s caused changes in the organizational structure of *bonehs*. Under the landlord-peasant sharecropping system, *bonehs* were controlled by the owner who could determine the number needed, the amount of land each would cultivate, which crops would be grown, how many *nasaqs* (peasant cultivation rights) were necessary, and who might become members.[22] Once village lands had been redistributed, however, the peasants acquired complete freedom to make their own decisions, including whether or not to continue participation in a *boneh*.[23]

The practical effect of land redistribution was to divide the formerly collectively worked land among *boneh* members. That is, each peasant

Figure 4. Agricultural Work Team in Central Iran.

received title to a portion of the land assigned to his *boneh* in the most recent allotment prior to the land reform program. As newly established private proprietors, the peasants immediately were confronted with a decision as to whether they would continue to farm in cooperation with their *boneh* partners, or whether they preferred to cultivate alone. Several factors influenced peasant attitudes towards this question. One was the method by which land was redistributed. In certain villages, for example, the peasants received an equal amount of land in terms of both areal extent and productive quality. In others, the peasants acquired ownership rights to unspecified land, the actual location of which continued to be determined by annual lottery. In still other places, land was redistributed inequitably with the result that some peasants obtained much larger holdings than others.

A second factor which has affected the role of *bonehs* has been the fragmentation of land holdings. In virtually all villages, peasants benefiting from redistribution received their land in several separate plots rather than in one contiguous section. The rationale for this procedure was to ensure that all peasants had equitable access to lands of variable productive quality. However, since large landowners retained the most fertile areas in a majority of villages, this rationale became virtually meaningless with the very implementation of land reform. Consequently, most peasants tended to consider the dispersion of the fields at the very least a nuisance.[24]

The particular phase of land reform to which a village was subject was a third factor affecting *bonehs*. Only in phase one was redistribution of all village land among the sharecroppers required; in subsequent phases landlords retained the option to keep or sell that part of their land equivalent to the share of the harvest which they customarily received. As a result, in nearly 80 percent of all villages the land available for redistribution among the peasants was adequate to provide a majority of them only with subsistence plots.

How peasants, individually and collectively, perceived the problems resulting from the inequality of land holdings, the dispersion of fields, and the subsistence character of farming has influenced strongly their attitude towards the continued utility of cooperative agriculture. For example, in those villages where land distribution was equitable and each peasant received an adequate amount of land, the benefits to be derived from group farming would be more obvious than in those villages where the division left a few persons owning most of the land and the majority of peasants with small plots. Naturally, however, social and psychological considerations also have a role in shaping attitudes towards the retention or abandonment of *bonehs*. In this regard, we may reasonably assume that if peasants were to elect to keep *bonehs*, then their traditional setup whereby *boneh* heads enjoyed special privileges *vis à vis* other members, would have to be abandoned. That is, for *bonehs* to adapt to the different conditions posed by peasant proprietorship, they would have to be transformed into genuine partnerships of peasants sharing resources, labor, expenses, and profit upon an equal basis.

Since there was a well-established tradition of working together among peasants, immediately following land reform there was a strong tendency in most villages for *bonehs* to remain functionally intact.[25] Changes were instituted, however, in the terms under which *bonehs* operated. Most notably, the privileges which had previously resulted in an inequitable distribution of both labor and income (from the share of the harvest) were abolished.[26] Nevertheless, the newly-independent cultivators generally failed to establish satisfactory group farming requirements.

Consequently, throughout the 1970s *bonehs* underwent major transformations. At least two observable patterns had emerged by 1978. The first pattern was one in which peasants gradually abandoned *bonehs* completely in favor of individual farming, while the second pattern features the survival of the *boneh* for specific agricultural activities. At the present time, there is insufficient evidence available to draw definite conclusions regarding which of the above two trends has been most prevalent.[27] Nevertheless, the research undertaken to date does provide some insights into possible reasons for these changes.

The decline of the *bonehs* has been most thoroughly documented by Safi-nezhad.[28] He has observed that their gradual but steady dissolution during the past decade has followed a similar model in several villages. Initially, *bonehs* in a typical redistributed village were reconstituted in relatively the same size and number as existed prior to land reform. In the second and third seasons, there is a numerical expansion of *bonehs* as larger teams divide up into two, three, and four-man units. This division continues in successive seasons as peasants decide to work on their own rather than in partnership with others. Consequently, the number of real *bonehs,* that is those in which at least two men farm the land jointly, declined. The village of Talebabad provides an excellent illustration of this process: whereas in 1965-66 all 60 peasants worked in 15 four-man *bonehs,* by 1975-76, all the four-man *bonehs* were gone and 39 of 60 peasants worked alone.[29]

While the motives for peasant reluctance to continue working in *bonehs* undoubtedly were complex, economics probably were an important underlying cause. In this respect, the size of peasant holdings was significant. About 50 percent of all rural families obtained land after 1962. However, two-thirds received less than 12 acres, while only 16 percent obtained more than 25 acres.[30] This inequality in size of land holdings has had several implications. First, the majority of peasants farmed subsistence-size plots and thus could normally manage their land adequately through the use of family labor. Under these circumstances, there was no obvious advantage to be gained through cooperation with other peasants. Second, when peasants whose holdings were of unequal size formed partnerships, friction developed over the amount of labor to be contributed by each and the methods for dividing the harvest.[31] Third, for the minority of peasants who received large-size land holdings, cooperation with smaller holders was less practical than hiring agricultural workers.

While economic considerations may have encouraged or at least reinforced a trend towards *boneh* dissolution, other factors operated to preserve, at least partially, the tradition of cooperative agricultural efforts. For example, in those instances where kinship bonds existed among members, *bonehs* often maintained their essential pre-land reform structure for several successive seasons.[32] Even in villages in which large *bonehs* have broken up into smaller teams of two or three men, the splits usually have been based upon family ties.[33]

There is evidence which indicates that in certain villages *bonehs* have survived quite well, albeit in greatly modified form.[34] Mustafa Azkia contends that the difficulties of farming in Iran's arid climate necessitate some form of cooperative effort, especially in regard to the management of irrigation water. His study of the village of Fardis demonstrates how *bonehs* have been adapted by the peasants following land reform. The original 12 *bonehs* remained intact. However, their purpose was solely cooperation in irrigation. For example, each of the *bonehs* received one complete 24-hour period of water every 12 days. On the day scheduled for water delivery, the *boneh* members worked together constructing, breaking up, and rebuilding earthen barriers and channels to help conduct the water to appropriate fields. The end of their period of water terminated the *bonehs'* work, and the members then separated to work on their own fields individually.[35]

The reason why modified *bonehs* functioned successfully in some villages and not in others needs to be examined thoroughly. It may be related to economic incentives. For example, in the village of Fardis, discussed above, there was a much more equitable distribution of land than in many other villages. In such a situation, the potential for disputes over the distribution of labor can be minimized. Fardis also was a relatively small village—50 families—although there yet is no clear evidence regarding the effect of village size on the fate of *bonehs*. [36]

Conclusion: Bonehs and Agricultural Production

The role of *bonehs* prior to 1962 and their transformation after land reform have been described. Essentially, the above discussion demonstrates a dramatic decline in peasant willingness to participate in collective agricultural work efforts as extensively as in the past. It is suggested that a primary motivation for this reluctance probably was economic considerations, arising from the subsistence nature of the overwhelming majority of peasant land holdings. Since *bonehs* formerly were one of the most important socioeconomic institutions in villages (where they existed), it is now appropriate to inquire into the effects, if any, their decline has had for Iranian agriculture.

The most significant fact about Iran's agriculture during the 1970s has been the general stagnation in the production of basic food crops. [37] Indeed, by the mid-1970s annual yields of such essential commodities as wheat and rice had become insufficient to meet domestic demand. In sharp contrast, there has been steady growth in the production of cash crops for the industrial and export markets. Although the reasons for this situation obviously are complex, it is significant to note that the bulk of food crops are grown on subsistence farms which produce little marketable surplus, while cash crops are grown primarily by larger landowners interested in profitable farming. This difference is important when one considers that the main beneficiaries of the former government's agricultural programs were the commercial farmers, not the subsistence peasants. [38]

At this point we can question how the generally poor performance in agricultural production relates to the decline of the role of *bonehs*. It is not my intention to claim that the dissolution of *bonehs* has caused stagnation in agriculture. Rather, both of these developments have been the consequence of government policies. The transformation of *bonehs*, in particular, presents an example of the effects, albeit often unintended, of rural development plans devised and controlled by urban based authorities insensitive to the real problems and needs of villagers. Since government officials were unaware of the *bonehs'* role in the management of agricultural production at the time land reform policy was being formulated, no strategies were devised to utilize their existence in positive ways. Ironically, a concern about the reform program was that the peasants lacked sufficient managerial skills to farm successfully as independent proprietors. This general opinion was the principal motivation for the formation of rural cooperative societies that were to provide peasants with the necessary aid in the postreform period.[39]

Even after the nature of *bonehs* had been widely publicized through the research of Safi-nezhad and other scholars, an appreciation of their function remained poorly developed among senior officials involved with agricultural policy.[40] This meant that not only were policies aimed at the potential preservation or even revitalization of *bonehs* not conceived, but also no substantive programs were initiated to make the cooperative societies—the natural successors to *bonehs*—into genuine peasant partnerships. Rather, the cooperatives became agencies for exercising bureaucratic control of rural affairs. Consequently, the peasants tended to be suspicious of their managers and reluctant to cooperate with their programs.[41]

The essential point of the above discussion has not been to argue that villagers would be in a better position if the *boneh* structure had remained intact, but to demonstrate first, that *bonehs* no longer serve the central role they did in the early 1960s; and second, that no village-level institution has replaced the function of the *bonehs*. The transformations of the *bonehs* may have been less fundamental if policies of the former government had recognized the position of *bonehs* and tried to accommodate them within the general framework of land redistribution. That the government did not exemplified official attitudes towards Iranian agriculture which prevailed under the Pahlavi dynasty—attitudes characterized by paternalism, the desire for central control, the subordination of rural plans to urban policies, and insensitivity to village views and needs. These attitudes resulted in short-sighted policies, the consequences of which included stagnation in agricultural production and the decline of *bonehs*.

From the above discussion it is obvious that the fate of *bonehs* in particular, and agriculture more generally, was not positive under the final years of the *ancien régime*. The revolution of 1978–79 affords an opportunity to reverse some of the negative policies of the past. Certain changes, especially with respect to land tenure, already have been occurring, albeit without the official sanction of the Islamic government. In villages where peasants had long resented their "benefits" from land reform there have been popular expropriations of land belonging to large, absentee owners. Interestingly, these properties have been cultivated collectively pending final decisions regarding the legitimacy of the confiscations and methods for redistribution. If the Islamic government decides to accept these *faits accomplis,* then the majority of peasants would be able to acquire sufficient additional land to raise their holdings above the size of subsistence plots. The resulting potential for profitable farming would improve peasant morale and could encourage the survival of *bonehs* as rural cooperative networks benefiting not just the peasants, but the whole country. In the long run, however, healthy agriculture in Iran will require supportive government policies. These can only be formulated effectively if there is a fundamental transformation of the attitudes which prevailed among agriculture policy makers prior to the revolution.

III. URBAN GROUPS AND CLASSES

Figure 5. Women at a Tehran Friday Prayer, 1979.

11

The Strengths and Weaknesses of the Labor Movement in Iran, 1941–1953

Ervand Abrahamian

Introduction

The period between the destruction of Reza Shah's autocracy in August 1941 and the construction of Mohammad Reza Shah's autocracy in August 1953 provides a rare opportunity to examine the social conflicts of modern Iran. These years permit the social scientist to look below the political surface into the social structure, observe the main internal cleavages, and trace the complex ties between political forces, especially organized parties, and the major social forces, particularly the socioeconomic classes. In short, these thirteen years enable the social scientist to write a political sociology of modern Iran.

Of the many political parties that challenged the status quo in these years, the most effective was the *Hezb-e Tudeh-e Iran* (Party of the Iranian Masses) and its labor affiliate, the C.C.F.T.U. (Central Council of Federated Trade Unions of Iranian Workers and Toilers). Beginning in 1941 as a small circle of Marxist intellectuals, the Tudeh grew rapidly in 1941–45 to become the party of the masses in fact as well as in name. By May Day 1946, it could organize rallies of over 40,000 in Isfahan, 50,000 in Tehran, and 80,000 in Abadan, and, having established branches in almost every town, recruited more than 40,000 members and unionized as many as 355,000 blue and white collar workers.[1] The British ambassador warned the Foreign Office that the Tudeh was "strong enough to nip in the bud any serious opposition" because it was the "only coherent political force in the country" and enjoyed "complete control over labour throughout Iran."[2] After a series of mass arrests, defections, and other setbacks in 1947–49, the Tudeh revived after 1951 to become again a major challenge to the establishment. By mid-1953, its demonstrations in Tehran drew over 100,000, its branches had some 325,000 members and sympathizers, and its labor affiliates surpassed their 1946 peak. One foreign journalist wrote on the eve of the 1953 coup that the Tudeh was gaining so many adherents every day, especially among workers, that it would "sooner or later take over the country without even the need to use violence."[3]

Although the Tudeh was the main revolutionary challenge to traditional Iran, few scholars have studied its social bases, especially its labor movement.[4] The present paper has three major aims. First, it will trace the birth of the labor movement between 1941 and 1953. Second, it will examine its rapid growth between 1941 and 1953. In doing so, it will focus on its strengths and weaknesses, and thereby throw light on why the traditional power structure survived during the turbulent 1940s. Third, it will illustrate these strengths and weaknesses via the dramatic strike of 1946 in the oil industry. Even though this strike did not shatter the power structure, it did provide Iran with a dress rehearsal not only for the oil crisis of 1951–53, but also for the Islamic Revolution of 1978–79.

Historical Background: 1921–41

Although skilled workers, particularly printers in Tehran, organized unions as early as 1910, unskilled workers, especially dockers in Enzeli, struck for higher wages in the 1910s, and migrant laborers in Baku participated in the Russian revolutions of 1905 and 1917, it was not until 1921 that the first significant labor movement appeared in Iran. In that year, the recently-formed Communist and Socialist parties brought together nine existing unions in Tehran to create the Central Council of Federated Trade Unions.[5] The nine, each with representation on the C.C.F.T.U., were the Unions of Printers, Pharmacists, Shoemakers, Bath Attendants, Bakery Assistants, Construction Laborers, Municipal Employees, Tailors, and Textile Workers in Tehran's only modern mill. In the following three years, the C.C.F.T.U. published a paper named *Haqiqat* (Truth); organized May Day parades; won over the existing Union of Teachers and Union of Post and Telephone Employees; led strikes among printers against censorship, and among teachers, postal clerks, bakery assistants, and textile workers for higher wages; and helped organize twenty-one new unions in different regions of the country. These consisted of the

Union of Dockers in Enzeli; Carpet Weavers in Kerman; Textile Workers in Isfahan; Oil Workers in Khuzestan; Teachers, Porters, Tobacco Workers, and Rice Cleaners in Rasht; Teachers, Tailors, Shoemakers, Office Employees, Carpet Weavers, Confectioners, and Telegraphers in Mashhad; as well as Cooks, Carpet Weavers, Carriage Drivers, Domestic Servants, Carpenters, and Tobacco Workers in Tehran. Thus the early labor movement reflected the economic backwardness of the country: of the thirty-two unions existing in 1925, twelve represented bazaar wage earners, workshop employees, and traditional craftsmen; eight represented clerks, professionals, and technicians; six represented unskilled workers, such as porters, laborers, and domestic servants; and only six represented modern wage earners, such as printers, mill hands, and oil workers.

Despite early successes, the growth of the labor movement was cut short by Reza Shah. Crowning himself in 1926, Reza Shah dissolved the C.C.F.T.U., banned trade unions, outlawed the Communist and Socialist parties, imposed heavy sentences on anyone advocating socialism, and arrested over 200 labor organizers. Five of these organizers, including the leader of the Printers Union, "died" in prison. Although in the short run Reza Shah retarded the labor movement, in the long run he unwittingly helped it by modernizing the economy and creating an industrial working class. He started the Trans-Iranian Railway; built new ports; constructed 12,000 miles of road; and, most important, introduced modern factories. In 1925, Iran had fewer than 20 modern industrial plants. Of these, only 5 were large, with over 50 workers. By 1941, however, the country had over 346 modern industrial plants.[6] Of these, some 200 were small—silos, distilleries, tanneries, and electrical power stations. But the other 146 included such major installations as 36 textile mills, 11 match factories, 8 sugar refineries, 8 chemical plants, 2 modern glassworks, and 5 tea and tobacco processing plants. As a result of this industrialization drive, the number of workers employed in large modern factories increased from less than 1,000 in 1925 to more than 50,000 in 1941.

The industrial proletariat further expanded in part because the oil labor force grew from 20,000 to nearly 31,000, and in part because many small workshops, especially shoe factories, carpentry stores, and tailoring shops, merged to form larger workshops employing over 30 workers. Thus by 1941 wage earners in the large modern factories and the oil installations, along with some 10,000 in small modern factories, 2,500 in the Caspian fisheries, 9,000 in the railways, 4,000 in the coalfields, 4,000 in the port docks, and a large number in seasonal construction, totaled over 170,000 workers. A modern proletariat had been born.

In addition to being new, this working class was intensely exploited. Hours were long, wages low, consumer taxes heavy, and factory conditions, in the words of a British observer, "resembled slavery."[7] Lacking unions, workers expressed their discontent through underground activities and wildcat strikes. For example, on May Day in 1929, 11,000 workers in the Abadan oil refinery struck for higher wages, an eight-hour day, paid vacations, company housing, and independent trade unions. While the oil company granted the wage demands, the British navy dispatched gunboats to Basra, and Iranian authorities arrested over 500 workers. Five strike leaders remained in prison until 1941. Similarly in 1931, 500 employees of the main textile mill in Isfahan stopped work, demanding better wages, pay for Fridays, and an eight-hour day. Although the workers won a 20 percent wage increase and a cut in the work day from ten hours to nine, the strike organizers were imprisoned and a few remained in jail until 1941. Finally in 1937—only two years after the completion of the first stretch of the Trans-Iranian Railway—800 railwaymen in Mazandaran organized a successful strike for higher wages and better work conditions. Their main leaders, however, were still in jail in 1941. A British consul viewed the labor situation as follows:

> We are in a transitional stage between old and new. The employee is losing his personal association with his employer and much of his pride in the finished product. There is as yet no adequate provisions for injury or unemployment to replace the moral responsibility of the old type employer. The government has broken down a structure without building in its place a new one. Reza Shah has, rather dangerously perhaps, dismissed Allah from the economic sphere and set himself instead in the moral ethics of industry.[8]

The Growth of the Labor Movement: 1941–53

The Anglo-Soviet invasion of August 1941 destroyed Reza Shah's dictatorship, and, opening the prison doors, released over 1,250 political prisoners, including many veteran labor organizers and a group of young Marxist intellectuals, famous as the "Fifty-three." A few days after their release, these labor organizers and radical intellectuals formed the Tudeh party and set out to revive the trade union movement. During 1942, they focused their energies on the factories and workshops of Tehran, the coalfields nearby, and the textile mills of Mazandaran and Gilan. During 1943, they turned their attention to winning over independent unions that had sprung up in Tabriz, Mashhad, Rasht, and, most important, among textile workers in Isfahan. Describing the Isfahan situation as a classic example of "class conflict," the British consul reported that the Tudeh successfully recruited many of the 10,500 mill workers:

> Under Reza Shah, the land and millowners—who are mostly ignorant, believing that money can do everything, reactionary to a degree, and solely interested in making as much money as possible—reigned supreme in Isfahan with the help of the central Government. But with the change of regime in 1941 and removal of the ban on communist propaganda, the British-backed Tudeh began to develop by taking advantage of this struggle between labour and capital. As present Isfahan is the center of this struggle.[9]

By May 1944, the Tudeh labor organizers felt strong enough to announce the formation of the C.C.F.T.U. Adopting the name of the earlier labor organization, the C.C.F.T.U. invited all workers, regardless of political views, to join, but stressed that only those intellectuals whose past proved their concern for the labor movement would be welcome. The C.C.F.T.U. program avoided political issues, focusing on economic concerns, especially an eight-hour work day; Friday pay; double pay for overtime; two weeks paid vacations; pensions, sick pay, and unemployment insurance; equal pay for men and women doing the same jobs; ban on child labor; safety measures; safeguards against arbitrary dismissals; and the right to strike, form unions, and bargain collectively. These remained the main goals of the labor movement for the next decade.

Almost all the leaders of the C.C.F.T.U. were either members of the "Fifty-three" or veteran labor organizers.[10] Reza Rusta, the C.C.F.T.U.'s first secretary, was probably the most important figure in the history of the Iranian labor movement. The son of an Azeri-speaking farmer in Gilan, Reza Rusta grew up in Rasht where he studied agriculture, taught literacy courses organized by the Socialist party, and, joining the Communist party, helped establish the first teachers union. In the late 1920s, he migrated south, found employment as a factory worker, and set up underground cells in the new industrial plants of Isfahan, Tehran, and Bandar Abbas. Arrested in 1931, he spent the next decade in prison where he met the "Fifty-three."

Ebrahim Mohazeri, the C.C.F.T.U.'s second secretary, was a lathe worker employed in the army munitions factory near Tehran. The son of an Azerbaijani radical killed in the constitutional revolution, Mehazari had migrated to Gilan to seek work and had spent much of the 1930s in prison because of his labor activities. Reza Ebrahim-zadeh, the third secretary, was a railroad worker who had been arrested in 1931 for organizing the first railway strike. A native of Azerbaijan, he had fought in the 1921 revolt in Tabriz and then migrated to seek work in Mazandaran.

Among the other nine on the Central Committee of the C.C.F.T.U., there were two railwaymen, two white collar workers, one professor, one lawyer, one cobbler, one carpenter, and one tailor. Of the twelve, eight had been born in lower class families and four in lower middle class families. The leadership included one Armenian and six Azeris, reflecting the large number of Azerbaijanis working in Tehran, Gilan, and Mazandaran. Thus, the leadership of the C.C.F.T.U. disproves the conventional notion that Iranian workers are too passive to head their own organizations and that the labor movement of the 1940s was no more than an artificial creation of the radical intelligentsia.

Having set up a central office in 1944, the C.C.F.T.U. spent the next two years strengthening its provincial network. By mid-1946, it claimed to have 186 affiliated unions and a total membership of 335,000—90,000 in Khuzestan, 50,000 in Azerbaijan, 50,000 in Tehran, 45,000 in Gilan and Mazandaran, 40,000 in Isfahan, 25,000 in Fars, 20,000 in Khorasan, and 15,500 in Kerman.[11] Having unionized 75 percent of the industrial labor force, it had cells in almost all of the large modern plants and in many of the smaller workshops and factories. The 186 affiliated unions encompassed most sectors of the urban economy. They included unions of industrial wage earners such as oil workers, textile workers, railwaymen, tobacco processors, and coal miners; skilled nonindustrial wage earners, such as printers, garage mechanics, and truck drivers; skilled traditional craftsmen, notably carpet weavers; relatively unskilled wage earners—for example, construction workers, dockers, municipal road sweepers, and house painters; service employees, especially restaurant waiters, clothes cleaners, and cinema attendants; professional and white collar associations, such as the Syndicate of Engineers and Technicians, Association of Lawyers, and Union of Teachers; wage earners in the bazaar workshops, particularly tailors, carpenters, and shoemakers; and even some shopkeepers, such as the pharmacists, confectioners, and newspaper sellers.

The labor movement reached a peak in 1946. In the summer of that year, a Tudeh leader became Minister of Trade and Industry, pro-Tudeh workers took over some of the textile mills in the Caspian provinces, and the C.C.F.T.U. organized successful strikes, not only in the oil fields but also in many of the main urban centers. Meanwhile, the Communist-led World Federation of Trade Unions recognized the C.C.F.T.U. as the "only genuine labor organization in Iran."[12] The anticommunist International Labour Office in Geneva described the C.C.F.T.U. as the "only organization with a national network,"[13] and admitted that "trade unionism in Iran owed its existence to the Tudeh Party."[14] A report issued by the U.S. Congress warned that the Tudeh "exercised effective control over labor."[15] Similarly, a government book published after the 1953 coup argued that the Tudeh had subverted the working class, especially "simple minded and inexperienced workers," by disseminating such foreign concepts as "the people," "the reactionary ruling class," "the struggle against imperialism," and "the need to prevent the recurrence of another dictatorship."[16] Finally, the British ambassador, who was by no means a friend of the Tudeh, described the achievements of the C.C.F.T.U. in these words:

> In Persia we are clearly at the beginning of a new era and are seeing the rise of a new social movement. The advantages which the workers have won are considerable and they will certainly continue to make the employers feel their newly discovered power. . . . When the first signs of resistance made their appearance, the factory owners and the government had no understanding of their importance. They feared Soviet Russia and worried that their factories would fall prey to the allegedly communist ideas now spreading among the workers. Moreover, they feel outraged that such important persons as themselves should be treated disrespectfully by mere workmen. They are motivated by fear and injured dignity. To these may be added greed—for their sole thought is money and more money and the thought of losing any of their enormous profits to the workers is unpalatable to them. They find the whole topic of labour disputes distasteful, and usually take the line that disputes are mere work of agitators and that workers are too ignorant to exercise responsibility.[17]

The labor movement, however, suffered a major setback in late 1946. In the autumn of that year, the government suddenly turned to the right, dropped Tudeh leaders from the cabinet, formed its own unions, and arrested over 360 labor organizers in Isfahan, Khuzestan, Gilan, and Mazandaran. The C.C.F.T.U. retaliated by calling for a one-day general strike in Tehran on November 12, 1946. According to the Tudeh, the strike was 100 percent successful with the vast majority of the 50,000 union members in Tehran staying away from work.[18] But according to the British embassy, the strike was only 50 percent successful since the government arrested 150 union leaders, occupied the C.C.F.T.U. headquarters, closed down its newspaper, used army trucks to crash through picketlines, hired unemployed workers to replace strikers, and offered an extra day's pay to all employees who came to work.[19] The drive to repress the labor movement continued through 1947–48, and intensified in February 1949 when, after an assassination attempt on the shah, the government outlawed both the Tudeh and the C.C.F.T.U.

Despite the loss of its organizational effectiveness, the C.C.F.T.U. retained most of its working class appeal. The British consul in Isfahan warned that the Tudeh "nucleus remained intact within the mills,"[20] and added that the Tudeh would continue to have appeal as long as employers "displayed little interest in work conditions" and anticommunist unions acted like "government puppets."[21] Similarly, the British embassy, in a report on "Labour Conditions in the Anglo-Iranian Oil Company," admitted that the vast majority of the oil workers had supported the Tudeh and the shop steward system introduced by the C.C.F.T.U.[22] It stressed that the workers "hope the Tudeh leaders will return to complete their work." Also a U.S. Congressional Report stated in 1949: "A.I.O.C. officials estimate that some 95 percent of the Iranian employees in Abadan are members of the (Tudeh) unions, and as long as they are denied an increase in real wages and improvements in housing, transportation, and work conditions, the possibility of a Tudeh comeback must be reckoned with."[23]

The relaxation of police controls after 1950 paved the way for the expected comeback. Using the cover name of the Coalition of Workers Syndicates, the C.C.F.T.U. strengthened its provincial affiliates, led strikes among silo workers and railwaymen in February 1951, and during the next month burst into the political arena by organizing a series of dramatic strikes in the oil installations. The new crisis began on the eve of the Iranian New Year, when the A.I.O.C. announced immediate cuts in wages, travel allowances, and housing subsidies on the grounds that the cost of living had fallen. The following day, port workers struck to protest this "New Year gift." Three days later, they were joined by workers at the pipelines, at the company repair shops, and at the Agha Jari oil fields. By April 1, most of the company's 45,000 employees were on strike, the government had imposed martial law on Khuzestan, and, as usual, the British had strengthened their Gulf fleet. Shaken by the strike and pressed by the government, A.I.O.C. rescinded the cuts and beseeched employees to return. The settlement, however, was short-lived, as the day after the workers returned the company managers declared that strikers would not be paid for the three weeks they were absent. Reacting quickly, the unions called a general strike throughout Khuzestan, demanding not only the three weeks' back pay but also immediate nationalization of the entire oil industry. The economic demands of the C.C.F.T.U. had been joined to the political demands of both the Tudeh and Mosaddeq's National Front.

The call for a general strike was heeded by over 65,000, including truckdrivers, railwaymen, road sweepers, shopkeepers, craftsmen, high school students, as well as the 45,000 oil company employees. Although the general strike began peacefully, violent clashes took place when the police surrounded the union headquarters to arrest the labor organizers, and, in the tense situation, panicked and fired into an angry crowd, killing four men and two women. The strike persisted for another two weeks, ending only when the company agreed to give back pay, the Majlis nationalized the oil industry, and Mosaddeq, the new premier, warned that workers' intransigency could invite a British invasion. In summarizing the whole strike, *Ettela'at-e Haftegi* (Weekly News), a conservative Tehran paper, claimed that the workers had been "too ignorant" to understand the "real issues," but did admit that the workers had proved to have "strong feelings of unity and solidarity."[24]

The crisis of spring 1951 was not limited to Khuzestan. As soon as news of the street killings reached Isfahan, the pro-Tudeh unions organized sympathy strikes in the main textile mills, in the smaller factories, and even in the bazaar workshops. *Ettela'at-e Haftegi* reported that the strikes involved over 30,000 workers and were the most impressive in the city's history.[25] To contain the strikes, the military placed machine guns, tanks, and armored vehicles around the mills and the working class districts. Despite these precautions, one worker and one policeman were killed as some 10,000 demonstrators tried to make their way from the mills to the city's central square.[26]

The C.C.F.T.U. followed up the Isfahan and Khuzestan strikes with a conference of its Tehran affiliates. Convening 350 delegates from all the major plants in the capital and 20 observers from the provinces, the conference elected a new leadership to replace those who had been forced into exile in recent years. In the following two years, the pro-Tudeh unions waged an aggressive campaign to raise wages, obtain government recognition, and exact written contracts from their employers. They also held large meetings in July 1952 to commemorate those who had died during the 1946 oil strike; even larger demonstrations in October 1951 to demand collective bargaining and removal of military personnel from factories; and yet even larger demonstrations in 1952 and 1953 to celebrate May Day. By the summer of 1953, the labor movement had surpassed its 1946 peak.

Not surprisingly, the revival of the labor movement shook the establishment. *Ettela'at-e Haftegi* exclaimed that the "fire" which had almost consumed Iran in 1946 had suddenly reappeared to threaten not only industry but also the whole country.[27] *Tehran Mosavvar* (Tehran Illustrated), the only major weekly, warned that "subversive" labor organizers had infiltrated the factories and displayed utter "contempt for the authorities."[28] One senator proclaimed: "Foreign-paid agitators are misleading our workers. Every time they exact concessions, they demand more. The net result is demonstrations, street battles, strikes, and more strikes. The agitators will not rest until they have dragged the country into an atheistic revolution."[29] And a Majlis deputy argued that the Tudeh was daily gaining ground in the factories because it fought aggressively for higher wages and better conditions, because the other parties lacked interest in the labor movement, and because the government unions had proved to be "corrupt" and "ineffective."[30]

Meanwhile, Mosaddeq's administration tried to stem the Tudeh tide. Khalil Maleki, who led the socialist wing of the National Front, warned that in national emergencies economic strikes were as dangerous as political sabotage.[31] Ayatollah Kashani, who headed the religious wing of the National Front, appealed to Muslim sentiments to draw workers away from the pro-Tudeh unions. His colleague, Mozaffar Baqai, tried to form unions to counter the C.C.F.T.U., and hired armed thugs *(chaqukeshan)* to terrorize labor organizers. Finally, Mosaddeq, to fight inflation and cut expenditures, decreed a Law for Social Stability restricting wage increases, scrutinizing union organizations, and threatening prison sentences to those "inciting strikes."[32] These attempts, however, came to little, and by late 1952 a prominent member of the National Front admitted that his organization had lost the war for the working class:

> Our country is being torn apart by strikes, demonstrations, and labor disputes. What can we do about it?. . . . In most factories, there are three distinct groups: first, the communists who hammer away with the propaganda that the rich in our country are corrupt and own everything while the workers own nothing; second, the patriots who support the National Front; third, the neutrals who follow the lead of any organization that will represent their economic interests *vis-à-vis* the managers and the factory owners. . . . We must admit that at present the initiative lies with the first group. The communists lead the neutrals, and, consequently, control the vast majority of the urban working class.[33]

Strengths and Weaknesses

The C.C.F.T.U. derived its strength from two major sources: the economic grievances of the working class; and the willingness of the Tudeh to represent these grievances through not only petitions, newspapers, and parliamentary speeches, but also strikes, protest meetings, and other forms of militant action.

The economic grievances, already intense under Reza Shah, were drastically intensified after 1941 by spiraling inflation. According to the National Bank, the cost-of-living index rose from 100 in 1936–37 to 163 in 1940–41; jumped dramatically during the war to reach 1,030 in 1944–45; dipped slightly in the postwar years to 946 in 1949–50; and jumped again during the oil crisis to hit a new peak of 1,047 in late 1953.[34] As employers invariably let wages drag behind consumer prices, employers had little choice but struggle for better wages by participating in unions, protests, and work stoppages. In fact, the number of major industrial strikes (involving more than 50 workers) closely corresponded to fluctuations in the cost-of-living index. There were 3 major industrial strikes in 1941; 37 in 1942; 28 in 1943; 57 in 1944; 44 in 1945; 183 in 1946; 8 in 1947; 5 in 1948; 4 in 1949; 5 in 1950; 42 in 1951; 55 in 1952; and 71 in the first eight months of 1953.[35]

Inflation not only sparked industrial disputes, but also drove a wedge between bazaar employers and employees. As an electoral survey submitted to the prime minister in 1951 showed, class lines divided almost all the craft and trade guilds of the Tehran bazaar.[36] For example, the shoe manufacturers backed a pro-British politician, but their 5,000 workers sympathized with the Tudeh; the owners of barber shops supported Mosaddeq and Kashani, whereas their employees leaned towards the Tudeh; the 400 bathhouse owners favored the *Imam Jom'eh*, while many of the 4,000 bath attendants were affiliated with the C.C.F.T.U.; the 250 clothes manufacturers helped conservative candidates, but their 8,000 tailors backed the Tudeh; and the 1,914 coffeehouse keepers endorsed Mosaddeq, Kashani, and the *Imam Jom'eh*, whereas their 4,500 assistants and waiters favored the C.C.F.T.U. Inflation had destroyed the political unity of the traditional guilds.

The labor movement was also helped by the organizational machinery of the Tudeh. Party branches collected contributions to help striking workers. Party lawyers formed legal aid societies to defend labor organizers. Party intellectuals set up literacy courses in factories, helped publish *Zafar* (Victory), the organ of the C.C.F.T.U., and aired labor grievances through a large array of left wing newspapers. While helping the C.C.F.T.U., the Tudeh scrupulously avoided political strikes so as not to strain the allegiance of rank-and-file union members. Except for the general strike of November 1946 and two nationwide strikes in support of Mosaddeq in 1952 and 1953, all the other work stoppages focused on bread and butter issues. Moreover, the Tudeh used its influence within professional groups, the legal structure, and even the police system to protect strikers and labor organizers. For example, the C.C.F.T.U. admitted that in 1945 it had won a major labor dispute in the Tehran sugar mill by threatening to call a sympathy strike among the plant's engineers, technicians, and white collar employees.[37] The British consul in Yazd reported that in 1946 the local authorities did not even bother to arrest demonstrating workers, for they knew that the "local courts were controlled by the Tudeh."[38] The consul in Bandar Abbas wrote that in 1946 a strike in the town's textile mill had been successful mainly because the plant manager was a Tudeh sympathizer.[39] The Shiraz consul described how the police broke up a strike in the city's electrical plant by arresting all the ringleaders, but the local courts promptly released them and thereby encouraged the workers to strike again.[40] Similarly, the Zahedan consul reported that the Tudeh protected the local unions by bringing together against the region's main landed magnate a broad coalition of groups including judges, teachers, policemen, and even gendarmerie officers.[41]

If the labor movement thrived in periods of inflation and political freedom, it declined in years of mass unemployment and police repression. Unemployment was particularly detrimental during the postwar recession when the Allies dismantled their bases, the A.I.O.C. adjusted to peacetime needs, and many manufacturers, unable to compete with foreign imports, reduced production. With thousands outside the factory gates searching for work, those inside were certainly in no position to bargain for union rights and threaten industrial action. This trend was not reversed until 1951–53 when the oil crisis drastically decreased imports and encouraged local manufacturers to increase production.

・Police repression was also detrimental to the labor movement. This can be seen both in 1947–49 when martial law was imposed on the major industrial centers, and after 1953 when Tudeh and C.C.F.T.U. leaders were arrested or forced into exile. Without freedom to function, trade unions could not organize. Without the freedom to organize, the labor movement was impotent. This is best illustrated in 1947–49 when the combination of repression and mass unemployment reduced the number of major strikes from 183 in 1946 to 8 in

1947 and 5 in 1948. Thus, the ups and downs of the Tudeh are tied not—as previous historians have claimed—to Soviet activities but to economic and political fluctuations within Iran.

In addition to these temporary problems, the labor movement suffered from two structural weaknesses. First, the trade unions were no match for the armed forces which contained as many as 100,000 men, remained loyal to the shah, and, with substantial American assistance, recovered quickly from their 1941 defeat. In head-on collisions with the army, as occurred in November 1946 and again in August 1953, the labor movement had no chance. Second, the urban working class, totaling at most 10 percent of the adult population, was an oasis of radicalism in a desert of widespread conservatism. The peasantry, for a variety of complex reasons, remained passive and outside national politics.[42] The nomadic tribes, many of whom were armed, continued to follow their traditional chiefs and actively intervened in late 1946 to help the army against the Tudeh. Moreover, the bazaar petty bourgeoisie—especially small merchants, shopkeepers, and workshop owners—opposed the communist-led unions, partly for religious reasons, and partly from fear of militancy among their own employees. Alienated from the rural masses and the urban bourgeoisie, the labor movement found allies only among radical segments of the intelligentsia.

The 1946 Oil Strike

The strengths and weaknesses of the labor movement can be illustrated by the development of trade unions in the oil industry. Although Tudeh organizers first appeared in the oil installations in early 1943, they soon withdrew when the local authorities clamped down and party leaders decided to keep out of the vital industry until the war against Fascism had been won. Avoiding the oil industry, pro-Tudeh organizers in Khuzestan formed other unions, especially among road sweepers, irrigation cleaners, taxi drivers, cotton spinners, and bakery assistants. Meanwhile, some 200 A.I.O.C. employees in Abadan, disappointed by the decision to avoid the oil industry, formed their own Union of Iranian Workers, and in May 1945 helped a wildcat strike of 1,200 workers in the Kermanshah refinery. Although the C.C.F.T.U. condemned the strike and intervened to end it, the British ambassador claimed that the pro-Tudeh unions had "engineered" the whole crisis.[43] He also advised the A.I.O.C. to improve housing and medical facilities to "deprive the Tudeh of legitimate grievances."[44] The A.I.O.C., however, replied

that such criticisms were unwarranted, and argued that the pro-British Arab tribes of Khuzestan should be armed to deal with "communist subversion."[45]

Pro-Tudeh labor organizers moved into the oil industry as soon as the war ended. Establishing a provincial branch of the C.C.F.T.U., they won over the Union of Iranian Workers, and on May Day 1946 organized in Abadan a massive parade of over 80,000. At the parade, speakers demanded higher wages, better housing, Friday pay, an eight-hour day, and a comprehensive labor law. A woman orator described oil as the "jewel" of Iran, and, accusing the British of spending more on dog food than on workers' wages, demanded nationalization of the A.I.O.C.[46] This was probably the first time that the call for oil nationalization had been heard in the streets of Abadan.

The oil unions were led by three Tudeh members: Hosain Tarbiyat, Ali Omid, and Abdollah Vafaizadeh. Tarbiyat, a member of the "Fifty-three," was an office employee of the British Imperial Bank. From a middle class family, he had been the headmaster of the main high school in Abadan at the time of his arrest in 1937. Omid, an effective speaker, was an oil worker who had been imprisoned after the 1929 oil strike. Vafaizadeh, also an oil worker, had likewise participated in the 1929 strike. Their assistants in the oil unions were, according to British accounts, mostly skilled workers, especially "drivers, fitters, and plant attendants."[47]

Having formed the Oil Workers Union, the C.C.F.T.U. led a series of well-organized strikes. On May 2, 1946, 250 artisans and laborers at the Abadan distillery stopped work, demanding higher wages and shorter hours. The company met these demands on May 9 when employees at the local asphalt plant and locomotive repair shop threatened sympathy strikes. On May 10, the entire labor force of 2,500 at the Agha Jari oilfields struck, requesting contracts similar to those won recently by Isfahan textile workers—higher wages, Friday pay, and better overtime rates. At first the company dismissed the requests as "unreasonable," and cut off the water supply to Agha Jari. But it reluctantly came to the negotiating table three weeks later when the C.C.F.T.U. threatened a general strike in Abadan, collected contributions for the strikers, compared the plight of the Agha Jari workers to that of Imam Hosain in the desert of Kerbala, and pressed the prime minister to send a mediation committee to Khuzestan. In the eventual settlement, the company was forced not only to meet

Figure 6. Oil Workers in Khuzestan.

many of the initial demands, but also to give back pay for the three-week strike and implement labor legislation to be drafted by the central government. The London *Times,* unfamiliar with Isfahan conditions, commented that "it was unprecedented in Iranian history to give seven days pay for only six days work."[48] The British consul in Khorramshahr wrote that the company accepted the unfavorable settlement and treated the union leaders as the proper workers' representatives, because it was alarmed by the extent of communist influence and feared the spread of the strike to the Abadan refinery.[49] Similarly, the British embassy reported that the A.I.O.C. had no choice but to negotiate, since the Tudeh was in "an extremely strong position" having enrolled in its unions some 75 percent of the oil workers.[50]

By mid-June 1946, the Tudeh organization in Khuzestan paralleled, rivaled, and even overshadowed the provincial administration. In the words of the British consul in Ahwaz, "the effective government of the province has passed into the hands of the Tudeh."[51] Its unions represented workers' grievances before management, collected funds for future emergencies, organized an extensive shop-steward system, and opened 45 clubhouses in Abadan alone. Its party branches set food prices, enjoyed the support of local fire brigades, and controlled the communication networks, especially the trucking system. Moreover, its militia patrolled the streets, guarded the oil installations, and impressed observers by quickly transporting some 2,500 volunteers from Abadan to Khorramshahr to build an emergency flood wall. The British authorities reported that during the flood warnings: "The Company admitted that they could not, nor could the Persian authorities, have commanded the Abadan workers in the numbers organized by the Tudeh. It was certainly an impressive illustration of Tudeh power over the worker."[52] The British ambassador added: "It is indeed true to say that at the present time the security of the refinery and fields, and the safety of the British personnel, depends on the good will and pleasure of the Tudeh Party."[53] Similarly, the British military attaché reported in mid-June:

> The present situation in Abadan and Agha Jari, though quiet on the surface, is precarious. The Tudeh is in complete control of labour at the refinery and is gaining ground in the fields. The Anglo-Iranian Oil Company's management exists only on sufferance. At any moment, at any reason, a strike could be called which would bring production to a standstill. Hitherto the Tudeh leaders have used their power to maintain order. Although inciting to violence in theory, they have discouraged it in practice. The Tudeh has constituted itself the de facto representative

of labour in Persia and the management is discussing with it, in that capacity, the organization of the trade unions contemplated under the new labour law. By doing so the company can maintain some sort of contact with the representatives of labour and production in the fields, but few will believe that such a course of action will result in anything more than a short respite.[54]

The expected confrontation came on July 10. The confrontation, however, was instigated not by the unions but by the authorities. On July 10, the company rescinded its promise of Friday pay, the provincial governor-general declared martial law, and the military commander of Agha Jari arrested local labor leaders whom he had invited for negotiations. Responding quickly, the Tudeh and the C.C.F.T.U. endorsed a spontaneous strike that had broken out in Agha Jari, and called upon all employees throughout Khuzestan to stay away from work on July 13 and to remain absent until the government removed the governor-general, lifted martial law, released the labor leaders, and guaranteed Friday pay. The call was heeded by over 65,000, making it the largest industrial strike in Iran and one of the largest in the Middle East. It involved not only 50,000 manual and clerical workers in A.I.O.C.; but also 200 Indian artisans at the Abadan refinery; thousands of firemen, truck drivers, roadsweepers, and railwaymen, textile workers, and high school students through Khuzestan; hundreds of shopkeepers, craftsmen, and small traders in the Abadan bazaar; and even cooks, chauffeurs, and domestic servants employed by Europeans. The British consul in Ahwaz wrote that the strike "was enforced with great efficiency."[55] The Khorramshahr consul reported that in Abadan the strike began with "an orderly procession directed at the military authorities."[56] Likewise, the British military attaché noted that the general strike started peacefully and "immediately gave the Tudeh complete control over the industrial regions of Khuzestan."[57]

Although the general strike began peacefully, it turned violent when oil workers were attacked not only by army contingents but also by local Arab tribes. From the day the C.C.F.T.U. entered the ethnically diverse region of Khuzestan, it had made a special effort to recruit workers from different religious, regional, linguistic, and tribal backgrounds. It had remarkable success among unskilled workers from Isfahan, Shiraz, Kerman, and Bushehr; among skilled workers, especially welders, artisans, and mechanics, from Azeri, Persian, Armenian, and Assyrian backgrounds; and among migrant laborers from the Bakhtiyari, Luri, Khamseh, and Qashqa'i tribes. But it had

227

failed among the Arab population. Three factors explain this failure. First, the Arabs, unlike the Khamsehs, Qashqa'is, and Bakhtiyaris, remained within their own communities. Consequently, while the others had escaped the jurisdiction of their *kadkhodas, kalantars,* and khans, the Arabs continued to live under the watchful eyes of their shaikhs and tribal chiefs. In short, the Arabs remained bound by kinship ties, whereas the others had escaped, even if temporarily, from these hierarchical and conservative networks. Second, the Arabs associated with the oil industry were hired not as individual wage earners but as members of construction teams led by private contractors, many of whom were Arab chiefs. As contract workers, they remained dependent on their shaikhs, received pay for piece work instead of day work, and therefore did not share with the vast majority of oil workers the burning concerns over higher wages, shorter hours, and Friday pay. Third, the Arab leaders had political, economic, and social reasons for resisting the Tudeh. The British consuls frequently reported that the Arab chiefs looked upon British as their traditional protector;[58] that the Arab landlords were fearful of unions influencing their villagers;[59] and that the Arab businessmen had been shaken by the sight of Tudeh "policemen and street guards wearing arm bands, ordering people in the streets, controlling the buses, and giving orders to bakers about bread prices."[60]

The Arab opposition to the Tudeh first surfaced in early July when the tribal chiefs, at the urging of the governor-general, formed a Farmers Union and promptly changed the name of the Arab Union on the grounds that "they were a martial race not a bunch of farmers."[61] The pro-Tudeh organizations immediately charged that the so-called Arab Union was receiving arms from the A.I.O.C. and was scheming to separate Khuzestan from Iran.[62] The British consul in Khorramshahr wrote that the opening of the Arab Union in Abadan created concern among average citizens since the urban population had been traditionally fearful of tribal attacks.[63]

These fears turned into panic on the second day of the general strike when news reached Abadan that armed Arab tribesmen had surrounded Agha Jari, cut off the water supply, and threatened to march on Abadan. The British consul reported that he advised the Arab leaders to keep their men out of Abadan, but that there were "strong rumors the Governor had instructed them to bring their men and burn down the Tudeh offices."[64] The consul also reported that he suspected the governor had turned to the Arabs since the army garrison could muster no more than 250 soldiers.[65] As rumors of a tribal attack spread, angry crowds gathered outside the offices of the

Arab Union. And when the police panicked and fired, the angry crowd attacked the offices and thus began a nightlong riot which left 19 dead and 338 hospitalized. Among the dead were 12 Arabs, including their leading contractor and richest merchant. Contradicting the evidence sent by the local consuls, the British embassy in Tehran informed the Western press that the whole crisis had been carefully engineered by "Tudeh hooligans."[66]

The riots lasted until the following morning when an emergency delegation arrived from Tehran. The delegation included representatives of the prime minister, the Tudeh, and the C.C.F.T.U. After six hours of intense negotiations, the delegation imposed a settlement on the warring parties. By the accord, the unions agreed to end the general strike, drop the demand for the removal of the governor-general, and cease making inflammatory denunciations of the A.I.O.C. and the Arab Union. In return, the military authorities released the union leaders, the Arab Union withdrew from Abadan, and the oil company agreed both to pay for Fridays and to raise the minimum wage. Thus the oil workers had won their basic economic demands.

Once the workers returned to work, Mr. Noel Baker, a member of the British cabinet, confidentially told his fellow ministers that the entire crisis had been caused by the company's "intransigence on Friday pay."[67] Similarly, an anonymous British official of the A.I.O.C. complained to the foreign office that the four-day general strike had been instigated by "diehard company leaders" who failed to appreciate workers' problems and whose knowledge of trade unionism was "limited to the repetition of worn-out jokes that went out with crinolines."[68] Meanwhile, a British delegation sent to investigate the crisis was so impressed by the C.C.F.T.U. that it reported "the trade union movement [in Khuzestan] is a genuine one and we recommend winning over Tudeh unionists to British ideas."[69] Reading the report, a member of the British cabinet noted: "I cannot get it out of my mind that the Tudeh Party, although admittedly revolutionary, may be the party of the future which is going to look after the interests of the working man in Persia."[70] Finally, the British consul in Ahwaz, concluding his memorandum on the general strike, warned that the economic gains had strengthened communist unions and that workers continued to insist that the "Tudeh represent them in their negotiations with the oil company."[71]

Despite the victory of July 1946, the basic weaknesses of the oil unions became apparent in October 1946 when a conservative reaction, spearheaded by tribal chiefs, swept through the southern provinces. The reaction began when the Qashqa'i khans, supported by the Bakhtiyari, Khamseh, and Boir Ahmadi chiefs, raised the banner of revolt and accused the central government of helping the "atheistic" Tudeh Party. The revolt quickly spread when the military governor of Fars, General Zahedi, sided with the rebels against the central government. And it further spread as the rebels were joined by the Arabs of Khuzestan, the Mamasanis of Fars, the Tangestanis of Bushehr, the Afshars of Ardalan, and the Kalhur Kurds of Kermanshah. Forced to choose between the unarmed Tudeh unions and the armed tribes, the central government sided with the latter. It purged the cabinet of Tudeh members, closed down party organizations in the central and southern provinces, reimposed martial law on the oil regions, and deported over 120 labor leaders from Khuzestan. Meanwhile, the A.I.O.C. fired 813 strike organizers, and discharged, on grounds of "absenteeism," over 1,000 workers who had been arrested by the military authorities. Deprived of union organizations and judicial protections, the labor movement in the oil industry, as in the rest of the country, entered a period of decline that lasted until the political upheavals of 1951–53. The general strike of July 1946 had definitely shaken the establishment; but it had not even come close to sparking a nationwide social revolution.

Conclusions

The 1953 coup easily defeated the labor movement; for the armed forces remained royalist. The ulama, speaking on behalf of the traditional middle class, waged an intense anticommunist campaign. The Tudeh, for a variety of reasons, failed to forge an alliance with the National Front. The rural masses remained passive or acted on behalf of their conservative landlords. Moreover, the urban working class by itself was too small and too isolated to initiate a revolution. Thus, the shah won the 1953 struggle hands down.

In the years after the coup, the Tudeh and the labor movement bore the brunt of police repression. Forty Tudeh militants, including labor organizers, were excuted. Other labor leaders were imprisoned or forced into exile. Over 3,000 union organizers and members were jailed until they publicly recanted. The C.C.F.T.U. was dissolved again and all its affiliates were meticulously rooted out. State factories were placed under the management of retired army officers. The newly-created secret police, SAVAK, obtained an omnipotent presence in the factories and directly supervised the state-run trade unions. As one student of the labor movement has stated, "the efficiency and ruthlessness of the Pahlavi regime [was] far greater than that of, for example, the Czarist state in the 1890s and 1900s."[72] Not surprisingly, the labor movement ceased to be a political force.

The labor movement, however, reappeared as a decisive force during the latter part of the Islamic Revolution. The revolution began in mid-1977 as a protest movement of the modern middle class—of university students, lawyers, judges, writers, journalists, and intellectuals denouncing the regime for its unconstitutional activities.[73] The protests rapidly expanded in early 1978 as the ulama and the traditional middle class joined the agitation, organizing demonstrations, leading bazaar strikes, and accusing the regime of undermining Islam. By mid-June 1978, it was clear that the regime and the middle class opposition had reached a stalemate. The former could use force to clear the streets, but could not compel the bazaars and the universities to reopen. The latter, on the other hand, could embarrass the regime, but lacked the clout to destroy it.

What broke this stalemate in the second half of 1978 was the intervention of the industrial working class. As state power weakened, as SAVAK shifted focus from the factories to the bazaars, and as government planners imposed austerity measures to cope with spiraling inflation, working class opposition reemerged. As first, strikes broke out in the textile mills of Mazandaran, in the machine tool factories of Tabriz, in the car assembly plants of Tehran, and in the power stations of the major cities. Then strike committees appeared in most large factories and government enterprises.

Finally, in October 1978, the oil workers struck demanding higher wages, better housing, free trade unions, end of martial law, return of the 1906–07 Constitution, amnesty for all political prisoners, and equal pay for men and women doing the same job. To coordinate this oil strike, workers in the refineries, pipelines, oilfields, repair shops, and company offices formed not only local strike committees but also a central strike committee. According to reliable sources, many of these local strike committees were led by Tudeh sympathizers, and as much as 35 percent of the central strike committee represented the Tudeh and other left wing elements.[74] The legacy of the 1946 and 1951 general strikes had survived. But this time, the oil workers, supported by the middle classes and fully aware of their stranglehold over the economy, demanded not just economic concessions but the removal of the whole royalist regime. As one strike leader told the press, the workers would not "export oil until they had exported the shah."[75] In 1953 the labor movement by itself had been too weak and too isolated to prevent the military *coup d'état*. In 1979, however, the same movement was strong enough and crucial enough to transform the middle class rebellion of 1977–78 into a joint middle class-working class revolt of the Islamic Revolution.

12.

Shops and Shopkeepers:
Dynamics of an Iranian Provincial Bazaar

Michael E. Bonine

Introduction: The Traditional Iranian Bazaar

The Iranian bazaar is a concentrated complex of craftsmen, retailers, and wholesalers which traditionally was the commercial focus of the city and its hinterland.[1] This central market comprises many linear, vaulted passageways, lined with small stalls on each side for the craftsmen and retailers; while large, open caravanserais for wholesaling fill in the spaces behind and between the branches.[2] Types of trades and sellers often are grouped together, especially craftsmen such as coppersmiths, blacksmiths, and goldsmiths. Most crafts and retailers were organized into different guilds *(senf)*.

In late Qajar times, each guild was headed by two or three *ostads* (masters), who represented the group in the citywide organization of the *senfs*, the *heyat-e asnaf*. This group discussed and tried to solve problems mutual to the bazaar, although several representatives of the government, such as the *darugheh* (market superintendent), *muhtasib* (market inspector), and *kalantar* (mayor), had some control over the marketplace in various capacities.[3] Taxes had to be paid to the government by each guild as a corporate body, and one of the main functions of the guild leaders was to collect taxes equably from their own members on the basis of income.

In practice, the *ostads* served as a buffer for their members against the government and its myriad officials and demands. Disputes and problems were preferably solved within a particular *senf* or the *heyat-e asnaf*, as decisions by government officials often involved expense and corporal punishments. Such duties as price fixing, guaranteeing the quality of a good, granting permission to open a shop, or insuring correct weights and measures were dealt with either by the guilds or the government officials—the exact mix of duties varying among cities and time periods. Generally, the weak central government of the Qajars enabled the bazaar to have a degree of self-regulation; the government officials overseeing this marketplace were local persons and the central government was interested mainly in getting its revenues.

The Iranian bazaar was not simply the locale for shopping and business activities, but was also the focus for the economic dominance of the surrounding region. Absentee landlords often sold part of their agricultural surplus through the bazaar system. Crops also were brought to the city by peasants, although many peasants had little surplus to market or were so far in debt that foreselling of their crop was common.[4] Such debt was facilitated by the many moneylenders in the bazaar, for this market was the traditional center of credit and banking. Although their loans often were short-term ones to wholesale merchants for completing transactions, the moneylenders' exorbitant rates perpetuated the debt of many peasants and urbanites.

Bazaaris constituted one of the main elements of the bourgeoisie in traditional Iranian society. Along with bureaucrats and the ulama these groups comprised the middle classes—below the ruling class, but higher in status and power than the masses of peasants, nomads, and urban laborers.[5] Bazaar merchants often allied themselves with the rest of the bourgeoisie, and with the ulama, in opposing governmental policies inimical to their livelihood and beliefs. Bazaaris often were trained in the traditional educational system, which emphasized religious values.[6]

As in any social class, variations in status occurred among the bazaaris. Wholesale merchants generally were at the top, and some individuals in the wealthier crafts or trades were also influential. Depending upon the status of specific occupations within a city's bazaar, such men might be clothsellers, carpetsellers, candymakers, coppersmiths, dyers, goldsmiths, vegetablesellers, or others. The leaders of each guild were among the wealthiest members of their trade. For some crafts, the more prosperous bazaaris had other members producing articles for them for wages.

Religious minorities in Iran often were engaged in (or limited to) specific occupations, both in and outside the bazaar. Jews, besides being moneylenders, often were clothsellers and peddlers; Armenians were silversmiths and goldsmiths; and, at least by late Qajar times, Zoroastrians became wholesale merchants in some cities. Although some minorities were relatively wealthy, their non-Muslim status generally has kept them outside the mainstream sociopolitical and religious role of this marketplace.

The religious schooling of bazaaris promoted traditional, conservative values, and so the bazaar was a major bulwark of Shi'i Islam. The bazaar itself was entwined with mosques and religious schools (*madraseh*), and usually much of this marketplace was religious endowment (*vaqf*) for these buildings—or for support of particular religious activities, students of *madrasehs*, or the ulama.[7] The bazaaris largely conducted their business in a framework of Islamic economic morality,[8] and wealthier merchants often had made the arduous pilgrimage to Mecca. The presence of these *hajjis* imparted one more element of religiosity to this commercial area. Religious gatherings were sometimes sponsored by individual guilds—although activities such as mourning ceremonies or processions also were frequently organized by neighborhoods or quarters.

The support of the religious establishment by the bazaaris went beyond just symbols and financial support, however. The bazaar has been a political arena in which bazaaris and ulama supported each other's complaints against the government. The Tehran bazaar especially has been a center of opposition, which, for instance, manifested itself in the constitutional movement of the early twentieth century (as well as the revolution of 1978-79). Bazaars often closed down to protest government policies, a protest that was quite effective as commerce ground to a halt.

When Reza Shah took control of Iran, one of his policies was to emasculate the strength and power base of the ulama, tribes, or any other groups who might not provide primary loyalty to his regime. This included the guilds and the bazaaris, and so the Pahlavi dynasty kept a strict control over the merchants. Meetings of the guild or the *heyat-e asnaf* were either prohibited or closely supervised, and the composition of the guilds and their relationship to the government underwent a number of changes over the half century of Pahlavi rule.[9] In essence, the central government took over the control of the bazaars, and local initiative and decision-making were minimal.

An even greater impact on the economic position of the bazaar resulted from the development and modernization programs of the Pahlavis. Reza Shah had straight, wide streets constructed through the compact Iranian cities, creating new avenues for commercial development. In some instances part of the main bazaar was destroyed by a new avenue, and in all cases the streets provided

235

possible new locations for shops—locations which became more and more important as the use of motor vehicles spread.

The bazaar began to lose its dominant position in the commerce of Iranian cities. Shops spread along the avenues and industrialization and economic development brought new forces, international in scope, which were outside the range of the traditional marketplace. With the growth of the economy came the expansion of cities. As cities doubled and tripled in size the bazaar became less and less accessible, and the commercial structure began to focus on the avenues. Although a center for handicrafts, the bazaar economy was not part of the new, large-scale industrialization being established in Iran.

The bazaaris also became less important as a socioeconomic force in the Pahlavi era because a new professional middle class began to control and reap the benefits of the changing economy of Iran. The product of a modern educational system, including universities within and outside Iran, this new class included engineers, doctors, civil servants, and many other occupations which require considerable skill or talent.[10] Investment in large-scale workshops and factories, often using foreign capital, created a new group of industrialists and bankers outside the traditional bazaar system; and they soon became a more powerful, influential group than the bazaaris. The most important wholesale merchants became involved in modern shipping and trucking, connected to the new factories and large warehouses—most of which has bypassed the bazaar.

But the central bazaar has not died. It has not been abandoned by shopkeepers for the avenues; it has remained a viable commercial center. The bazaar is no longer the predominant economic focus of the city—but neither have the modern factories and avenues usurped all its commercial functions and role. Although many types of new retail businesses, such as modern household appliances, auto-related products, and large banks are on the avenues, the bazaar remains the center for many traditional crafts and retail shops. The bazaar is especially important for textiles (carpets, cloth) and metalwork (coppersmiths, goldsmiths), with tourist items significant in some of these markets.

The bazaar also has retained its traditional religiopolitical orientation, despite Pahlavi policies. Especially since 1963 Mohammad Reza Shah supported large industrialists and businessmen at the expense of the bazaaris. The tax structure, banking system, and myriad government regulations all favored the new, modern economic sectors. Price controls, fines, and arrests for profiteering and hoarding were directed at the small retailers-bazaaris, rather than the big industrialists.

The government's neglect of—and hostility to—the bazaar economy meant that the shah had no support from the bazaar during the events of 1978-79. Traditional bazaari support of the ulama strengthened—the bazaar bankrolled the revolution of 1978–79. The bazaar closed down for long periods, effectively leading the nation in a general strike and causing the economy to grind to a halt.

The bazaar had emerged in the Islamic Republic greatly strengthened, both politically and economically. The alliance with the ulama had given the bazaaris a voice in the government—not only because of their support during the revolution, but also because of their Islamic values and orientation. The disarray of the banking system had returned many moneylending and currency exchange functions to the bazaar. But by 1981 the bazaaris had become hostile to the new government because of decline in trade and many new regulations. Yet, incessantly adaptable, the bazaar has survived. This adaptability is one of the main themes of the following pages.

The Traditional Economy and the Role of the Yazd Bazaar[11]

The main bazaar of Yazd traditionally provided most of the material goods for the inhabitants of the city, especially those "specialty" items which were needed only occasionally. Small local bazaars (*bazarcheh*) were scattered throughout the residential quarters and many of the everyday foodstuffs and other frequently needed goods and services were found in these markets. Individual, separated shops, such as bakeries or small groceries, also were scattered among the residences.

Villagers also patronized the main bazaar. In the late Qajar period many peasants came to the city every couple of months to buy some provisions. Protected by a rifleman to guard against bandits, the other settlements were avoided and contacts were made directly with the bazaar of Yazd. Flour, salt, sugar, and tea were some of the more frequent purchases, although copperware, cloth, and other expensive items might sometimes be acquired.

Agricultural produce, especially more valuable dried fruits and nuts, were sometimes brought to the bazaar by the peasants. But the more bulky produce for the city, generally, came from the immediate vicinity of the city (five-ten kilometers). Wheat also was imported by caravans from outside the region, especially from Fars Province. Sheep and goats often came from Fars as well, for Yazd and its hinterland in most years had a deficiency of grains and meat.

The bazaar controlled the exports of the city and its region. Cloth was one of the most important exports; Yazd for many centuries has had a reputation as a major textile center.[12] Elaborate, expensive Yazdi silks and brocades were famous throughout Iran. Many kinds of ordinary cloth, however, also were woven in the city. Thousands of wooden handlooms were in the city, some in homes but many in small workshops *(karkhaneh)* with three or four looms. These were concentrated in the old city, specifically in Mahalleh-ye Fahadan. In some instances a weaving workshop was associated with one of the local *bazarcheh*.

The produce of the weaving workshops was controlled by the merchants of the bazaar.[13] Some clothsellers owned looms, while other merchants contracted with the weavers for the cloth. There also were many middlemen *(dallal)* dealing in cloth, often without a shop themselves, who sold the material to the retailers and wholesalers on a commission basis. The more expensive silk and brocade weaving was controlled by a few of the wealthier merchants.

Traditional handlooms for cloth weaving have declined drastically in Yazd, although hundreds of looms still existed in the early 1970s. Over the last several decades many of these have been replaced by electrical looms that run on house current. Many homes have acquired such looms as well, and this weaving provides a supplemental income to the family.[14] Most of this cloth is still handled by the bazaaris, with similar relationships as to the handwoven material.

Rough cotton cloth in the past was woven by most village and lower class urban women for their own household use.[15] Although such looms are now less common, a number of villages in Boluk-e Rustaq, the rural area northwest of Yazd, now produce considerable amounts of this cloth. Most of these looms have been established within the last thirty years and, as in Yazd, many are operated by men in small workshops. Some looms are family-owned, while others are owned by a local middleman. Most of this cloth is sold through the Yazd bazaar, either by wholesalers for export or by retail shops which often are owned by one of these villagers.

The reputation of Yazd for textiles has been partly responsible for the establishment of many large, modern textile mills in the city. The first such mill was opened as early as the mid-1930s, and by the end of the Pahlavi era about 25 large spinning or cloth weaving factories were in the city.[16] Although a few of these cloth weaving mills have specific retail outlets (agents) in the bazaar and on the avenues, the vast majority of the produce of these large plants bypasses the bazaar (and the avenues). Cloth, blankets, and yarn are sent directly to Tehran and the other cities of Iran.

Carpets traditionally were not an important part of the economy of Yazd. Although there was a specific Yazdi design in the early twentieth century, not many carpets were woven in the city or its region. Before World War II there were only 20–30 looms in Yazd, but this had expanded to about 200 looms by the end of the 1940s.[17] Most of these carpets were of Kerman design, the result of Yazdi merchants importing Kermani designers and even some weavers.[18]

In the 1960s, the carpet industry began to mushroom in the region. Whereas the older carpet weaving was largely an urban phenomenon, thousands of looms were soon established in the villages. In the beginning most of these looms were owned by the Yazdi carpet merchants, several of whom had over a hundred looms each (scattered in several villages). Villagers soon realized how profitable carpet weaving could be as a supplemental income (the labor being provided by females), and so, by the mid-1970s thousands of looms were owned by the villagers themselves. In 1977, the carpet merchants estimated that at least 50,000 looms were operating in the Yazd region. Most of the carpets being woven in the area are now of the Kashan pattern—and, secondarily, the Kerman and Isfahan styles. There are Na'in patterns woven in villages in the northwestern part of the province, but these very fine, partly silk, carpets are marketed through Na'in itself, or directly to Tehran.[19]

Most of the carpets woven in the Yazd region are funneled through the city to Tehran, where many become part of Iran's exports.[20] On the other hand, more carpets are being sold in Yazd itself, and the number of carpet merchants has increased from about 45 in 1971 to 240 (members of the carpetsellers guild) in 1977. Since extensive carpet weaving is a recent development, the bazaar and the avenues share in the provision of raw materials and the selling of this traditional handicraft. Within the bazaar there are a number of wholesale carpet merchants in the caravanserais, although, until the 1970s there were few carpet retailers in the bazaar (see below). Cordagesellers (twine for the warp and weft), woolsellers, and dyesellers also are found in the bazaar.

Dyers have always been an important part of the traditional economy because of the weaving industry. In fact, in the late Qajar period the dyers were one of the most powerful and wealthiest guilds in the city. But the decline in the cottage cloth weaving industry has seen a concomitant decline in this traditional craft; and the importation of foreign, predyed threads has meant even less business for the dyers. The dyer workshops require a large space, and even though a few are associated with *bazarcheh* or the main bazaar, most are separate establishments scattered through the city. The workshops usually specialize in particular types of dyes or material, such as silk, cotton yarn, or wool. Only the latter dyers *(pashmkar)* have increased or prospered, due to the growth of the carpet industry (although some predyed wool is imported into the city).[21]

Other textile specialities occur in the Yazd region, and the bazaar traditionally was the focus for the purchase of these items by the urbanites, as well as the center for exporting such items out of the area. The town of Mehriz, south of Yazd, is the most important locus for the manufacture of cloth shoes *(givehs)*. Most of the Yazd *giveh*-sellers (or their fathers) are from Mehriz. Meybod, Ardekan, and the nearby villages of these two towns are the centers of weaving *zilus*, a cheap cotton floor covering.[22] Numerous shops in the Yazd bazaar sell *zilus*. Although some of the looms are under contract by Yazdi merchants, most of the *zilus* are controlled by merchants in the two towns, who export the rugs to many Iranian cities.

Economic activities besides textiles also can be found in Yazd's hinterland. Lead mines east of the city have been exploited for centuries, and during the last several decades mines have been developed for exporting lead and zinc. With Russian technology an iron ore mine has been established in the same area, the mine being the source of the ore for the new steel mill near Isfahan. All these mines have affected the town of Bafq more than Yazd itself, although the city certainly has benefited.

Many other minor economic activities occur in the villages and towns, and, in toto, these specialities were a significant part of the traditional economy of the region. Many of the settlements have a reputation for specific handicrafts or occupations; besides the textile crafts mentioned previously, villages or towns are known for their pottery, blacksmith, carpenters, raising of silkworms, bakers, ropemakers, *qanat* diggers *(muqanni)*, porters, knives, gardeners, particular fruits or crops, and so forth.[23]

The city of Yazd is renowned for its cloth; other traditional specialities include the refining of sugar into cone loaves and the making of sweets by confectioners. Although several of these establishments are located in the main bazaar, most are now on the avenues. Yazd also has been a center for milling henna, which is shipped from the town of Bam, southeast of Kerman.

Yazd's own hinterland has been rather inadequate for providing many of the raw materials for its traditional manufacturing and processing. Cotton, wool, silk (or silkworms), sugar, and henna all had to be imported into the city. Yazd was a major processing center—not due to its hinterland—but because of the industriousness of its inhabitants and its role as caravan city on major trade routes within Iran. Yazd was especially an important trading node during the Qajar period, because of its location between the port of Bandar Abbas and Tehran, although significant separate trade routes also existed between Yazd and Mashhad, Kerman, Shiraz, and Isfahan.

Contemporary Yazd continues to be a center for textiles with its many large mills. A few other "modern" factories have been established within the last several decades, including such diverse industries as flour mills, ice plants, brick kilns, and factories for packaged cookies, loaf bread, plastic bags, nails, sugar cubes, oxygen, tile, and even whiskey (the latter closed by 1979). Most of these establishments employ only 5 or 10 persons, although a few do have 20–30 employees. The bazaar economy does not participate in these newer ventures.

Although the large textile mills may dominate the local economy of Yazd today, the major commerce of the city itself is still composed of thousands of retailers and craftsmen, traditional and modern, and located both in the bazaar and on the avenues. It is to this section of the economy which we now must turn.

Commercial Shops and Districts: A Statistical Mélange

Major changes have occurred in the form and function of the Yazd bazaar within the twentieth century due to the construction of avenues through the city. The first major avenue in Yazd was Pahlavi Avenue, constructed in the early 1930s; while Kerman and Shah Avenues were established in the late 1930s.[24] The latter avenue had the most effect on the commercial structure because it was built right through the bazaar (Figure 7). Although many of the shopkeepers, whose shops had been destroyed by the new avenue, located on that street, most of the other bazaaris remained in their location, and the avenues became a place for apprentices in the bazaar to have a shop of their own, or even for previous nonshopkeepers to open one. Newer avenues, such as Iranshahr (established in the early 1950s) and Sorayya (established in the mid-1960s), have fewer establishments and are not as commercially important as the previously established avenues.

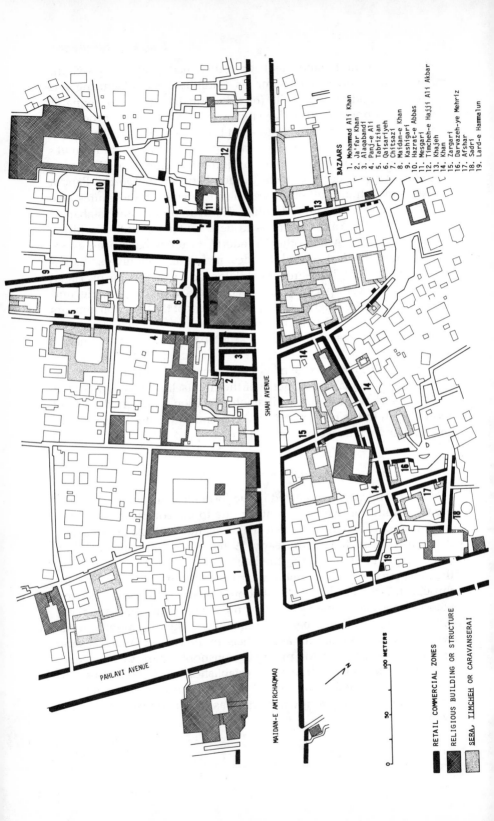

PAHLAVI AVENUE

MAIDAN-E AMIRCHAQMAQ

SHAH AVENUE

RETAIL COMMERCIAL ZONES

RELIGIOUS BUILDING OR STRUCTURE

SERAI, TIMCHEH OR CARAVANSERAI

N

0   50   100 METERS

In 1971 approximately 3,500 commercial establishments were occupied in Yazd—located in the main bazaar, on newly established avenues, in small neighborhood *bazarcheh,* and as scattered, separate shops.[25] The distribution of shops by location and major category types (Table 3) indicates that the avenues contain about half of the shops, while the bazaar constitutes a quarter, and the *bazarcheh* and separate shops the remaining fourth. Hence, even though the shops may be rather different, it is significant that half of the commercial establishments in Yazd still are not located on the new avenues. There has been no great abandonment of the traditional retailing and craft sectors for the new commercial zones.

Almost one-third (30 percent) of all the occupied shops are for foodstuffs and half of these are on the avenues and one-fourth in the *bazarchehs*—the paucity of foodstuffs within the bazaar indicating other specializations. As in the bazaars of Kermanshah, Shiraz, and Tabriz, the main specialization is textile-related shops.[26] Clothsellers are by far the largest single type (150 shops) in the Yazd bazaar, and textile shops constitute 37 percent of the bazaar's 861 occupied shops. In fact, about half (47 percent) of all the city's textile shops are located in the bazaar. Bazaar-e Khan is the principal cloth bazaar, although Bazaar-e Qaisariyeh is also mostly clothsellers. These retailers also can be found scattered among most of the other bazaar branches. Other textile-type shops found principally in the bazaar are thread and ribbonsellers, cordagesellers, sellers of *zilus,* yarn and woolsellers, carpetsellers, quiltmakers, donkey-bagmakers, felt-hatmakers, *giveh*-makers, and dyesellers. Tailors, on the other hand, are mainly on the avenues; only 23 of 123 tailors are found in the bazaar.

Metalworkers are a second specialty of the Yazd bazaar (19 percent of the bazaar shops). Coppersmiths (59 shops) and goldsmiths (48 shops) are the major types, and it is significant to note that the former is important in the Shiraz bazaar and the latter is a major group in the Kermanshah bazaar.[27] Neither of the metalworker groups, however, is of relative importance in the Tabriz bazaar.[28] These traditional craftsmen in the Yazd bazaar are concentrated in those branches named after their craft: coppersmiths in Bazaar-e Mesgari and goldsmiths in Bazaar-e Zargari, although the former spill out into Bazaar-e Maidan-e Khan and the latter have been expanding into Bazaar-e Khan. Half of the blacksmiths (24 of 49) are also in the bazaar, concentrated in Bazaar-e Kashigari, and all six brassworkers of Yazd are in the bazaar.

Figure 7. Yazd Bazaar and Central Commercial District

Table 3. Numbers and Categories of Occupied Shops in Yazd

Category	Avenue No.	Avenue +	Avenue *	Bazaar No.	Bazaar +	Bazaar *	Bazarcheh No.	Bazarcheh +	Bazarcheh *	Separate No.	Separate +	Separate *	Total No.	Total +	Total *
Foodstuffs															
Retail	435	.24	.54	78	.09	.10	222	.27	.27	73	.26	.09	808	.23	1.00
Craftsmen	109	.06	.44	47	.05	.19	50	.20	.20	43	.16	.17	249	.07	1.00
	544	.30	.51	125	.14	.12	272	.47	.26	116	.42	.11	1,057	.30	1.00
Textile															
Retail	167	.09	.39	256	.30	.60	2	#	—	1	#	—	426	.12	1.00
Craftsmen	93	.05	.36	62	.07	.24	53	.10	.21	48	.17	.19	256	.08	1.00
	260	.14	.38	318	.37	.47	55	.10	.08	49	.17	.07	682	.20	1.00
Metalworkers	230	.13	.51	163	.19	.36	48	.09	.11	8	.03	.02	449	.13	1.00
Wood, Stone, Leather															
Retail	38	.02	.93	1	—	.02	1	#	.02	1	#	.02	41	.01	.99
Craftsmen	86	.05	.40	51	.06	.23	69	.13	.32	11	.04	.05	217	.06	1.00
	124	.07	.48	52	.06	.20	70	.13	.27	12	.04	.05	258	.07	1.00
Personal Goods (R)	192	.11	.83	23	.03	.10	11	.02	.05	4	.01	.02	230	.07	1.00
Household Provisions (R)	65	.04	.72	6	.01	.07	15	.03	.17	4	.01	.04	90	.03	1.00
Personal Services	183	.10	.59	22	.02	.07	27	.05	.09	77	.28	.25	309	.09	1.00
Motor Vehicles															
Repair (C)	39	.02	1.00	—	—	—	—	—	—	—	—	—	39	.01	1.00
Retail	54	.03	1.00	—	—	—	—	—	—	—	—	—	54	.02	1.00
Misc.	31	.02	.97	—	—	—	1	#	.03	—	—	—	32	.01	1.00
	124	.02	.99	—	—	—	1	#	.01	—	—	—	125	.04	1.00
Wholesale Traders	37	.02	.32	76	.09	.67	1	#	.01	—	—	—	114	.04	1.00
Storage	33	.02	.23	76	.09	.52	29	.06	.20	8	.03	.05	146	.04	1.00
TOTAL	1,792	1.00	.52	861	1.00	.25	529	1.00	.15	278	1.00	.08	3,460	1.00	1.00

+ = Percentage by location; * = Percentage by category; # = Totals .01; C = Craftsmen; R = Retail

Metalworkers and textile shops together comprise 56 percent of the Yazd bazaar (compared to 27 percent of the avenue shops and 20 percent of all shops), and it is this specialization that contributes to distinguishing the bazaar from the rest of the commercial areas and districts of the city. On the other hand, the majority of the personal services, such as doctors, dentists, barbers, and banks, are found on the avenues (59 percent). Also, the great majority of retail personal goods (83 percent) and household provisions (72 percent) occurs on the avenues, reflecting the growing number of modern-type retail stores and services.

The neighborhood *bazarcheh* contains principally local needs and daily necessities. About 60 of these small bazaars are scattered throughout the residential areas, especially in the older sections of the city. These may consist of a cluster of only four to five shops, although 15–20 and even more shops may occur. Half of all these shops (47 percent) sell basic foodstuffs, such as a grocer, vegetable seller, butcher, or baker. The great number of these *bazarcheh* in Yazd is one reason why in the past and today few foodstuffs are found in the main bazaar—unlike many other Middle Eastern bazaars.[29] (As previously noted, the majority of the shops selling foodstuffs in Yazd are located on the avenues.) Certain craftsmen can be found in the *bazarcheh,* especially carpenters, blacksmiths, cobblers, carders, and dyers; while in the old city the workshops of traditional cloth weavers are sometimes part of the small bazaars (although these workshops are not included in the shop totals).[30] A few speciality shops, such as a tinsmith, coppersmith, watch repairer, or carpet designer, can be found in one or more of the *bazarcheh,* but these establishments are rare in the small markets.

Single establishments are represented by 278 units. Bakers, public baths, and small grocers comprise many of these establishments, although there also are doctors and dentists (associated with their residences). Many of these small grocers also are part of a residence, often representing only a part-time activity. Because of the great number of *bazarcheh* and the other main commercial areas, separate shops are not as (relatively) common in the city as in the villages around Yazd, where the majority of the shops usually are noncontiguous establishments.[31]

The degree of shop or craft specialization differs for the avenues, bazaar, and *bazarcheh*.[32] Most of the bazaar branches have fewer types of shops (grocers, coppersmiths, and so forth) per number of establishments than the avenues or *bazarcheh,* and, hence, are more specialized. Some of the branches are predominately one type of

shop, such as coppersmiths in Bazaar-e Mesgari, blacksmiths in Kashigari, goldsmiths in Zargari, and clothsellers in Qaisariyeh and Khan. The avenues tend to have a great mixture of types, while even the small *bazarcheh* often have as many types as number of establishments until they reach a size of 10–12 shops.[33]

If the Yazdi shops are classified as pure retailers or craftsmen (although the latter also retail their products), the avenues are predominantly retail establishments while craftsmen comprise the majority in a number of the bazaar branches. Even some of the *bazarcheh* have a majority of craftsmen; although foodsellers are the largest single category the various craftsmen, when taken together, may form a majority.

Shops and Shopkeepers: Continuity and Change

Shopkeeper Characteristics

Commercial districts are composed of individual shopkeepers, and we now turn to some of the characteristics of these entrepreneurs and how their attributes are related to the commercial area. Tables 4 and 5 compare several characteristics of the shopkeepers on the avenues and in the bazaar. The shopkeeper in the bazaar is, on the average, slightly older (47.4 to 43.8 years) and has occupied his shop longer (15.9 to 13.3 years), but data on place of birth, previous employment outside the city, and being a *hajji*, show essentially the same percentages for both the bazaar and the avenue. In both locations about one out of five shopkeepers was born outside of the city, has worked outside the Yard area, and is a *hajji*.

Both in the bazaar and on the avenues non-natives of the city of Yazd are not common. In fact, the majority of those from a village or outside the Yazd region came to the city when they were young (usually with their parents), and they became shopkeepers only after being apprentices for many years. The main exception are the blacksmiths in Bazaar-e Kashigari, who often do come directly from a village (or the town of Taft). The lack of outsiders indicates that either too much capital is needed to open a shop, or that the social milieu makes it difficult for outsiders to establish and maintain a successful business.

Employment outside the Yazd region by younger men has become common within the last several decades, and the accumulation of

---

Figure 8. The Cloth Bazaar in Yazd.

Table 4. Characteristics of Shopkeepers on the Avenues

	Mj	P(Ia)	P(Ib)	P(II)	P(III)	P(IV)	Mir	S(I)	S(II)	S(III)	K	Sor	Total	
Length Occupied (Mean Years)	12.0	14.9	18.2	18.6	14.7	7.8	11.0	13.4	10.1	7.3	11.9	3.3	13.3	
Age (Mean Years)	46.0	38.3	48.9	46.4	43.8	35.6	43.4	41.6	49.3	40.8	41.8	45.6	43.8	
													No.*	%
Place of Birth														
Yazd	7	13	24	24	16	14	5	14	20	14	23	12	186	81
Village	1	1	2	6	3	1	3	6	—	10	1	2	36	16
Other	1	—	—	—	1	—	—	—	1	—	1	2	6	03
													228	100
Employment														
Yazd	5	6	9	15	15	10	5	11	16	16	14	3	125	79
Other City	1	3	4	1	3	2	—	2	1	5	3	3	28	17
Other Country	—	—	—	1	—	—	—	1	1	—	2	1	6	04
													159	100
Hajji														
No	5	9	18	23	17	13	6	13	13	17	20	15	169	81
Yes	2	5	5	2	3	1	2	5	7	3	3	1	39	19
													208	100

Avenues: Mj=Mojassameh, P=Pahlavi, Mir= Mirchaqmaq, S=Shah, K=Kerman, Sor=Sorayya
( ) = Sections of Avenues
* = The total numbers of each category are not the same because not all information was obtained from each informant

capital by working in Tehran, Bandar Abbas, Abadan, Shiraz, Kuwait, Bombay or other cities provides the financial means for opening a shop upon returning to Yazd.[34] Often the outside employment is in a different occupation than the type of shop opened in Yazd. In Kuwait, for instance, most Yazdis are bakers or grocers, while in Bombay they are usually associated with a restaurant. Upon returning to Yazd, they may open up a cloth shop, miscellaneous goods shop *(kharazi)*, or other retail shop. The fact that many of these persons are opening up shops in the bazaar, as well as on the avenues, indicates that the Yazd bazaar is still perceived as a viable economic location.

Rotblat has shown the importance of the manifestation of religiosity in the Qazvin bazaar, and that the title *hajji* is one of the most overt religious symbols possessed by the merchants.[35] If this title may be used as an outward sign of religiosity (as well as wealth), it appears that in Yazd, due to the similar percentages of *hajjis*, the same value systems operate on the avenue as in the bazaar.[36] Hence, it may be incorrect to consider the bazaar as the derelict, traditional commercial area and the avenues as the progressive, modern zone. (During some religious holidays, however, the stalls and passageways of the bazaar are decorated in celebration—or mourning—which, generally, is not replicated on the avenues.)

Even though characteristics of shopkeepers in the bazaar and the avenues are on the average similar, these aggregate statistics do mask important differences *within* each commercial area. Certain sections of the avenues and bazaar branches have rather different orientations (Tables 4 and 5)—such as almost total native-born Yazdis, many non-natives, few outside workers, many *hajjis,* no *hajjis,* and so forth. The patterns that emerge show similarities in both commercial zones. Native Yazdis (i.e., born in the city of Yazd) are in the higher rent (and key money)[37] areas, a greater percentage of persons have worked outside the city in such locations, and more *hajjis* occur in these areas. The mean age and length of occupancy show less consistency. Generally, the lower rent areas on the avenues have lower mean values, indicating a younger and newer occupant, while the less expensive bazaar branches have either lesser or greater means than the one for the entire bazaar. This indicates that younger men are moving into the bazaar and the avenues via the lower rent areas. Yet, it also points out that the most viable bazaar branches, such as Khan, Zargari, or Qaisariyeh, are changing, and only in some of the less expensive bazaar branches are the more aged shopkeepers able to survive.

Table 5. Characteristics of Shopkeepers in the Bazaar

	M.A.K.	J.K.	Alq.	P.A.	Tab	Qa	Ch	M.R.	M.K.	Kas	H.A.	M	Kh	Z	Af	Sad	Total	%
Length Occupied (Mean Years)	15.4	17.3	15.5	15.7	14.5	15.5	21.3	23.9	18.0	13.9	18.0	21.7	15.4	16.7	5.8	8.8	15.9	
Age (Mean Years)	45.1	53.1	50.9	48.1	50.0	46.8	53.3	54.6	52.1	38.0	47.8	52.1	46.1	47.6	46.2	38.1	47.4	
																	No.*	%
Place of Birth																		
Yazd	13	12	9	31	8	21	9	13	35	10	15	11	35	38	3	15	278	82
Village	3	2	—	4	1	5	1	5	7	12	6	1	5	2	1	3	58	17
Other	—	—	—	—	—	—	—	—	—	—	—	—	—	1	3	1	5	01
																	341	100
Employment																		
Yazd only	10	9	6	14	2	11	4	9	24	15	12	4	19	28	1	6	174	77
Other City	1	2	2	7	1	3	—	2	3	1	3	—	6	4	3	3	41	18
Other Country	—	—	—	—	—	1	—	3	2	1	1	—	—	—	1	3	12	05
																	227	100
Hajji																		
No	2	12	6	24	7	18	7	11	28	17	13	7	28	26	7	17	230	78
Yes	4	7	4	6	1	7	—	2	8	—	1	2	9	11	—	1	63	22
																	293	100

Bazaars: M.A.K.=Mohammad Ali Khan, J.K.=Ja'far Khan, Alq=Alaqabandi, P.A.=Panj-e Ali, Tab=Tabrizian, Qa=Qaisariyeh, Ch=Chitsaz, M.R.=Masjed-e Rig, M.K.=Meidan-e Khan, Kas=Kashigari, H.A.=Hazrat-e Abbas, M=Mesgari, Kh=Khan, Z=Zargari, Af=Afshar, Sad=Sadri

* = The total numbers of each category are not the same because not all information was obtained from each informant

Table 6. Locational Changes of Shops, 1951-1971

Avenue Shops			Bazaar Shops		
Previous Shopkeeper	No.	%	*Previous Shopkeeper*	No.	%
Closed (or New)	74	45	Closed (or New)	34	20
Died	18	11	Died	57	34
Retired	4	02	Retired	6	03
To Same Avenue	21	13	To Same Bazaar	18	11
To Diff. Avenue	5	03	To Diff. Bazaar	7	04
To Bazaar	2	01	To Avenue	15	09
To *Bazarcheh*	5	03	To *Bazarcheh*	1	01
To Diff. City	11	07	To Diff. City	8	05
To Diff. Country	3	02	To Diff. Country	3	02
To Village	1	01	To Village	3	02
To New Occupation	20	12	To New Occupation	15	09
Total	164	100	Total	167	100
New Shopkeepers	No.	%	*New Shopkeepers*	No.	%
Apprentice	22	16	Apprentice	18	10
Father's Shop	5	04	Father's Shop	37	20
From Same Avenue	28	21	From Same Bazaar	35	19
From Diff. Avenue	19	14	From Diff. Bazaar	29	16
From Bazaar	17	12	From Avenue	19	10
From *Bazarcheh*	18	13	From *Bazarcheh*	1	01
From Diff. City	8	06	From Diff. City	12	06
From Diff. Country	5	04	From Diff. Country	4	02
From Village	1	01	From Village	4	02
From Diff. Occupation	12	09	From Diff. Occupation	26	14
Total	135	100	Total	185	100

Locational Changes

The shopkeeper comparisons stress the need to understand the mechanism of shop occupancy. What types of shop changes occur? Where are shopkeepers specifically coming from and going to? And what type of movements exist between the bazaar, the avenues, and the *bazarcheh*—is there a concerted movement to the avenues? Insights into these questions are provided by a survey of shop occupancy changes for the 20 years prior to 1971, including the former location of the new shopkeeper and the new location of the former shopkeeper (Table 6).

Data on the new shopkeeper reveals that on the avenues 35 percent of the shopkeepers had been on the same or another avenue at their previous location and only 12 percent came from the bazaar and 13 percent from a *bazarcheh*. In the bazaar the majority came from within the bazaar system itself, only 10 percent coming from the avenues. A larger percentage in the bazaar than on the avenues came from nonshopkeeping occupations, mainly a reflection of former weavers becoming clothsellers in Bazaar-e Qaisariyeh and Khan.

Comparisons of data on the previous shop or shopkeeper also show major differences between the avenue and bazaar. Almost half (45 percent) of the avenue shops had been permanently closed or were new, mostly the latter due to the construction of establishments on the new avenues. The majority of shop changes in the bazaar was due to the death of the former shopkeeper (34 percent), although even 20 percent of the shops in the bazaar were closed before the new person took the shop.[38]

The pattern that emerges from these comparisons is that most movements are minimal. For both new and previous shopkeepers who moved, the greatest percentage were within the same bazaar or the same avenue, and secondarily to another bazaar or another avenue (which usually were the adjacent bazaar or avenue). As in Herat, for instance, "the shops and shopkeepers of the bazaar [= the entire commercial area] are perpetually changing as some men grow wealthy and move closer to the center of the bazaar, and others less fortunate move outward to the margins."[39] Persons are not making major moves in Yazd, however, and neither do they tend to move from or to areas differing greatly in rents or key money. The length of occupancy (Tables 4 and 5) has shown that shops generally are occupied for many years, and it takes an unusual and major opportunity—or disaster—to engender a move.

Most moves are for short distances because the shopkeeper needs to keep the same clientele he has accumulated over the years (even on the avenues the vast majority of customers are still pedestrians). The distance of moves is short also because those individuals within a bazaar or a section of an avenue learn about the possible vacancy of a shop before "outsiders," and they have the first opportunity to acquire that shop. Even after the death of a shopkeeper (whose death must be publically advertised for settling the estate), the heirs tend to deal with individuals who had been acquainted with the former shopowner. When a shopkeeper wants to move he may sometimes use an agent (*dallal*) to help him find a shop, but the request usually is to find a nearby location.

Further insight into the changing character of the Yazd bazaar is provided by another survey by the author in 1977. Changes in the bazaar from 1971–77 (Table 7) reveal the dynamic changes in this traditional commercial zone. Although two-thirds of the shops and

Table 7. Changes in Yazd Bazaar Shops, 1971-1977

Bazaar Branch	A	B	C	C	E	Total
Mohammad Ali Khan	38	2	2	16	3	61
Ja'far Khan	19	2	1	8	2	32
Alaqabandi	10	1	0	4	4	19
Panj-e Ali	35	8	3	17	5	68
Tabrizian	19	0	0	4	3	26
Qaisariyeh	26	1	1	2	1	31
Chitsazi	15	1	1	2	2	21
Masjed-e Rig	13	3	2	6	1	25
Maidan-e Khan	66	3	7	6	2	84
Kashigari	38	2	0	8	1	49
Hazrat-e Abbas	30	0	2	12	1	45
Mesgari	35	0	4	12	2	53
Khan	103	10	2	29	6	150
Zargari	42	2	4	6	3	57
Afshar	7	4	0	11	1	23
Sadri	28	2	0	11	0	41
Hajji Gambar	21	1	3	3	1	29
Others#	34	2	0	14	3	37
	579	44	32	171	41	867*
	67%	5%	3%	20%	5%	100%

A = Same man and same shop type (includes storage and closed shops where status has not changed).
B = Same man but changed shop type.
C = Different man but same shop type (includes several instances of sons taking over their father's business).
D = Different man and different shop type (includes shops becoming storage and cases when closed shops have been occupied).
E = Closed shops, but occupied earlier.
# = Fringe areas of the main bazaar, but not in one of the principal branches.
* = Total does not equal the number of shops in 1971 (954) because wholesale traders and shops in *serai* were not surveyed in 1977, and a few shops have been subdivided or demolished.

shopkeepers had not changed status, the fact that in a six-year period, one-third of the shops had undergone some change, indicates a very fluid economic situation. A different shopkeeper occupies about one-fourth of the shops compared to six years earlier, while 5 percent of the shopkeepers changed their line of work or selling. The great number of changing shop types (by new individuals as well as the same shopkeepers) stresses the variability of shop types which can occur in some locations.

A number of trends have been responsible for many of the changes taking place in the bazaar. The most evident is the great number of carpetsellers which has emerged. Within the bazaar the carpetsellers have increased mainly in Bazaar-e Mohammad Ali Khan, Ja'far Khan, and Panj-e Ali. These three branches had 19 carpetsellers in 1971, and this had increased to 50 by 1977. (Of course, the increase of carpetsellers on the avenues had been as dramatic.) Several shopkeepers have switched from cordage, twine, *zilus*, wool, or cloth to carpets. The decline of *zilus* and increase in carpets reflect the great increase in consumer buying power and demand; more and more Iranians are replacing their cheaper *zilus* with carpets.

Another trend which manifests itself in the bazaar is the continued decline of many of the traditional crafts. Blacksmiths, coppersmiths, *giveh*-makers and sellers, tailors, and leatherworkers have decreased in numbers—replaced by retailing shops. On the other hand, along with carpetsellers, the clothsellers have increased. Selling modern "factory" clothing also is more common; in fact, a number of tailors have switched to this product as the profits of their trade declined. One traditional craft which has increased is goldsmithing. The following section contrasts these craftsmen with the coppersmiths, a trade on the decline.

Two Traditional Trades in Yazd

Coppersmiths: Decline of a Traditional Craft: The coppersmiths of Yazd for at least the last several centuries have been concentrated in the coppersmith bazaar (Bazaar-e Mesgari), as well as having expanded into adjacent branches such as Maidan-e Khan. Many of the present coppersmiths have a long family history of this trade, and some of the stalls have been occupied by many generations of the same family.

In 1971, of the 36 stalls in the main branch of Bazaar-e Mesgari only 6 shops were not coppersmiths—and one of these was a tinner for copper *(messefidkon)*. With the stalls in the nearby branches, a total of 59 coppersmith shops were in the bazaar in that year. Since some shops contain partners or several workers, a total of approximately 80 coppersmiths were in these stalls. There also were 34 coppersmith shops located on the avenues. A few of these opened on Pahlavi Avenue soon after its construction in the 1930s, or on Shah Avenue at the end of that decade. There was not, however, an exodus from the bazaar to the new streets. Only a few moved to the avenues, and most of these had been apprentices in the bazaar. But the majority of the present coppersmiths on the avenues actually were apprentices on the avenues.

Two rather distinct economic and even social networks of coppersmiths have evolved in Yazd. Within the bazaar many of the coppersmiths are wage workers *(mozdkar* or *kargar)* for several of the more prominent bazaaris of this craft. A similar system works on the avenues, but these *mozdkar* are in avenue shops working for coppersmiths on the avenues. Two kinship systems also exist. Within the bazaar at least 30 of these shops have one or more relatives who are coppersmiths in the bazaar.[40] Only 6 of the 59 shops have any coppersmith relative on the avenues. A separate kinship network exists among the coppersmiths of the avenues—especially among those on Pahlavi Avenue.

Another difference between the coppersmiths of the bazaar and the avenues is that most of the bazaaris of this trade live in the same quarter of the city, Mahalleh-ye Poshteh Bagh. This neighborhood is one of the newer and better traditional quarters (before modern residential areas established during the Pahlavi era), and is located in the southwestern part of the city.[41] This type of residential pattern, which is not characteristic of most of the other craftsmen or retailers of the city, resulted partly from the extensive kinship network (which undoubtedly was even more prevalent in the past). This network kept the craft among relatives in the quarter once they had begun to reside there. The pattern also was facilitated by the fact that an apprentice, when not a relative, often was a neighbor's son—who then stayed in the quarter after marrying. Even in those cases where an apprentice came from another quarter, the coppersmiths would help find him a house in Mahalleh-ye Poshteh Bagh when it came time to set up a household (and such an apprentice often was marrying one of the girls of a coppersmith). Within the last several decades a number of the bazaari coppersmiths have relocated in newer residential areas, although a majority still do live in the one quarter. On the other hand, the coppersmiths of the avenues live scattered in various quarters of the city and have never been concentrated residentially like the bazaaris of this craft.[42]

Despite two rather separate systems of interaction, the shops, work, and coppersmiths themselves are similar in both the bazaar and on the avenues. Like most traditional craftsmen in Iran they work in small stalls, and, except for those working for wages, the coppersmiths are retailer-producers, making various copper bowls, trays, and utensils and selling directly to the public. Although small margins of profit are made, such as one or two tomans[43] per kilogram, a few of these craftsmen are considered to be rather wealthy (although such status is partly a legacy of better times). Many of the older coppersmiths are *hajjis*, both in the bazaar and on the avenues, and a few have gone several times to Mecca.

There is one difference between the work of the coppersmiths of the bazaar and the avenues. Because of several individuals, it can be stated that the bazaar is slightly more specialized than the avenues. A few of the bazaari coppersmiths specialize in particular items, such as trays, ewers *(aftabeh)*, "antique" pitchers *(golabgir)*, or specific utensils.[44] The craftsmen on the avenues, like the majority in the bazaar, work on a variety of items—although in neither area are tourist items extensively produced (as can be found in Isfahan or Shiraz).

The coppersmiths of Yazd were once a thriving and powerful group; along with the dyers, the guild was one of the most prominent in the city in late Qajar times. But today these craftsmen are on the decline. In 1977 in Bazaar-e Mesgari, there were only 23 coppersmith shops, seven fewer than in 1971.[45] The decline is basically due to the decrease in the use of their products. During the last several decades customers have been replacing copper bowls and utensils with items made of aluminum, plastic, and other materials. Although often not as durable, the new articles are cheaper.[46]

Another obvious sign of the decline of this craft is the lack of young apprentices among the coppersmiths. Most of these craftsmen are middle-aged or older, and teenage apprentices are not to be found. Coppersmiths do not want their own sons to be in a trade which they consider moribund; if possible, their sons go into more modern occupations and professions. And even though these merchants mention that apprentices are very difficult to find today because of kids attending school, not even the coppersmiths themselves would encourage a boy to enter their trade.

Goldsmiths: Ascendancy of a Traditional Craft: One of the few traditional crafts that has grown in Yazd during the last few decades is goldsmithing. Centered in the goldsmith bazaar (Bazaar-e Zargari), these craftsmen have recently expanded into the adjacent cloth bazaar, Bazaar-e Khan. There were only 5 or 6 goldsmiths in Yazd in late Qajar times,[47] but by 1971 there were 48 goldsmith shops in the bazaar and another 27 shops on the avenues. From 1971 to 1977 goldsmith shops had increased from 29 to 33 in Bazaar-e Zargari, and the total in the bazaar had reached 66 shops.

A goldsmith's shop is a small stall with glass display cases for the predominantly gold bracelets, rings, chains, and other jewelry. The back of the shop may be the workshop area, or an upstairs workshop is above the retail shop. In a few instances the workshop is in a separate location or even in the master goldsmith's house. Although traditionally the goldsmiths made most of the items they sold, today only some of the jewelry is made locally. Much of the gold jewelry being sold is made by larger firms in Tehran or Isfahan, and similar articles tend to be sold by all the shops, not only in Yazd, but in other Iranian cities as well.

Unlike the coppersmiths, the goldsmiths have never been concentrated in one predominant residential quarter. They are scattered in the various neighborhoods, although some kinsmen certainly do tend to live in the same quarter. More recently, a number of the more affluent goldsmiths have moved into some of the new residential areas to the west and south of the older sections of the city.

The more prestigious and wealthier goldsmiths are found in Bazaar-e Zargari, and the better locations are those closer to Shah Avenue. Several goldsmiths in that bazaar have moved toward the avenue when a shop became available, although the key money payments for such shops had reached many hundreds of thousands of tomans by the mid-1970s. The spread of goldsmiths into Bazaar-e Khan and even onto the avenues has resulted principally from apprentices in the goldsmith bazaar seeking their own shops. Indeed, unlike the coppersmiths, there are many youths learning this lucrative craft. One master may have five or six apprentices, including one or more of his sons or other male relatives.

As with the coppersmiths, there is an extensive kinship network among some of the goldsmiths. There are not two separate systems, however, because Bazaar-e Zargari has remained the center of activity for all the goldsmiths. These craftsmen on the avenues often have numerous relatives in the bazaar. For example, one master on Shah Avenue is the son of a goldsmith in Bazaar-e Zargari, and nine of his *amu* (paternal uncle) are goldsmiths—more than half located in the bazaar.[48]

The wealth of the goldsmiths also is illustrated by the master on Shah Avenue mentioned above. He is a *hajji* (going to Mecca in the late 1960s); has a house in Tazirjan, a mountain village used for summer homes by the traditional elite; owns a Land Rover; and owns a shop which sells modern shoes (also located on Shah Avenue, at the site of his previous goldsmith shop). Such wealth is common for an established goldsmith, although it is rare for the coppersmiths. Several of the goldsmiths even have children studying in Europe or the United States, and so doctors and engineers are more common among the sons of these craftsmen.

Conclusion

The Yazd bazaar is a viable commercial zone of the city. It remains more specialized than the avenues, especially as the center of textiles and traditional metalworkers. Several of the branches are very esteemed locations for shops. With a quarter of Yazd's shops, the bazaar is a dynamic business center which continues to change in complexion to adjust to changing economic conditions. It is true that many types of modern goods are not available in the bazaar, but it is a mistake to think that Iranians have abandoned traditional goods and services for new ones—they have incorporated both into their contemporary life styles.

Similarities between shopkeepers in the bazaar and on the avenue point out that divisions between the old and new, the traditional and modern, may have been drawn too finely. This study, however, has shown that there is not a great amount of interchange of shopkeepers between the bazaar and the avenues; that basically they remain as two separate systems. But there also is little interchange even between parts of the bazaar—or between avenues. The moves usually are within the same bazaar branch or section of one avenue. Yet, the significant pattern is that the shopkeepers of the bazaar are not leaving; that this marketplace remains a productive and profitable place for these Iranian entrepreneurs.

This paper has shown that the traditional bazaar structure is able to survive. Small stalls, extreme specialization of products, branches of similar shops, craftsmen retailing their products, and many other features represent the traditional system. And, even though individual trades and crafts may decline or even disappear, other types of shops replace them. The extensive changes in shop types which occurred in the Yazd bazaar from 1971–77 indicate that the bazaar is continually changing, that this market place is dynamic and adaptable—even under the impact of what some call modernization.

The avenues represent an extension of the bazaar system. Although there is less specialization and even some Western-type stores, a similar linear arrangement of small stalls, shopkeeper characteristics, and many other traditional facets characterize the commercial zones of the avenues. In many respects, the avenues are as traditional as the bazaar is modern.

13
Petty Traders in Iran
C. Tom Thompson

Introduction

Petty traders in the Middle East have scarcely been studied.[1] Meillassoux, as well as Bohannon and Dalton, has edited a volume on the markets of sub-Saharan Africa; S. Tax, G. Foster, S. Mintz and others have published on the petty traders of Latin America; and A. Dewey, C. Geertz, and C. Belshaw have written of the markets of the Far East.[2] In contrast, social scientists working in the Middle East, when they have worked in the markets at all, have concentrated on merchants in the urban bazaars, giving special emphasis to the bazaar's intricate social structures, which are often held together by the presence of well-organized guilds.[3] The small vendor, whether urban or rural, who operates outside the structure of the urban bazaar and the protective umbrella of the guilds, has been largely ignored.

Considering the high degree of interest in itinerant vendors in other parts of the world—especially North Africa[4]—the lack of studies of petty traders in Iran and the rest of the Middle East is surprising.[5] This paper proposes to examine the position of the petty traders in the traditional marketing system of Iran and to identify the conflicts being faced in what is generally considered to be a changing market economy.

In Iran, as in other Middle Eastern countries, petty traders are ubiquitous.[6] They are found in cities as street vendors or traveling peddlers, or as owners of hand lorries; in rural areas, they are found as itinerant peddlers or as traveling merchants who go from village to village often as participants in periodic markets. The terms petty trader, small marketer, itinerant peddler, street vendor, or peasant trader can be applied to a wide spectrum of market participants, ranging from those with only a few items to sell and having no fixed locations to those having an arrangement with municipal authorities or property owners where they conduct their business on a regular basis. In this paper, the terms apply to those traders who have no, or very low, overhead, and include full-time as well as part-time traders. The terms do not apply to or include those marketers who own, lease, or rent a room in a building; or who operate with municipal licenses or guild memberships (e.g., operators of magazine and newspaper kiosks, of cigarette wagons, or nut and candy vendors).

Petty traders can be part-time or full-time buyers and sellers of agricultural produce, handcrafts,[7] and/or inexpensive manufactured items. They are generally typified by a high degree of task specialization and role duplication, and they invest a great deal of time in their activities. The nature of the marketing system allows traders to enter or leave at will or to change products (albeit with limitations on the type of change) either because of seasonal constraints or because of consumer tastes. There are virtually no qualifications for new participants except for a limited amount of capital or goods as well as a great deal of time to expend on marketing activities. In rural areas, the traders serve the needs of peasants (indeed may be peasants themselves) and in urban areas, the needs of low-income, possibly peasant, workers. While there are sometimes defined areas (e.g., marketplaces) in which the traders operate, the group is characterized by high mobility.

While realizing that small marketers are influenced to different degrees by the urban bazaar system and, in some respects, represent an extension of that urban system, I intend here to demonstrate that the participants share a core of socioeconomic traits which distinguishes them from, and keeps them outside, the more formal structures shared by the merchants of the bazaar system.[8] The traits include a subsistence-level income, an underdog status with regard to the more powerful merchants, a position outside the formal structure of the bazaar, an emphasis on cheap goods having high turnover, an absence of innovation, low level of literacy, and a fragile social network which is not dependable over time.

I will deal first with the urban (Tehran) and rural (Mazandaran) traders separately. Secondly, I will discuss the challenges and threats facing traders as a group, and finally, I will take up the question of continued viability of the group.

The Urban Trader—Tehran

There is a plethora of small traders in Tehran, ranging from sidewalk vendors who always occupy the same spot and stall owners in traditional *bazarchehs* to traveling peddlers with handcrafts or agricultural produce who come to the city only occasionally when they have something to sell.[9] The traders have manufactured items which they buy in the main bazaar, handcrafts, secondhand items such as housewares and clothing, or food items such as tea, cookies, cakes, fruit punch, ice cream, farm produce, or cooked foods. While most of these petty traders are at least nominally tied into the distribution system in the city as the last link before the consumer, a large number of them are either independent producers (e.g., prepared foods and handcrafts) or middlemen (used clothing buyers who buy from homes and sell to traders in the bazaar).

Sidewalk vendors are scattered throughout the city, but their highest concentrations are on or near several *maidans* (traffic circles) or traditional marketplaces (called *bazarchehs,* to differentiate them from the main Tehran bazaar) where there is a dense concentration of pedestrians. Items sold by these traders are purchased in the wholesale fruit/vegetable markets in the case of produce vendors, in the main Tehran bazaar from wholesaler/retailers by other vendors, directly from small workshops, or in the case of used items, from middlemen or households.

Pricing by street vendors is based upon their expenses, but the rule of thumb is *caveat emptor,* with both buyer and seller bargaining dilligently.[10] However, if a trader has an immediate need for cash, he/she will sell at a loss, hoping to make it up the next day. Overall, there is a surprising consistency among the various traders in estimating daily cash needs. In 1973, fruit vendors needed 1,200 to 1,300 rials (1973, 67.5 rials = US $1.00) daily for purchases and averaged a daily net profit of 200 to 300 rials. Novelty item traders and clothing vendors usually had 2,000–3,000 rials invested in their merchandise and averaged 300–500 rials net profit daily. Prepared food vendors averaged less, 200–400 rials daily. Handcraft traders/producers and middlemen buying and selling used items did not always have a daily turnover, since time had to be allotted for production and/or collection of items. If a daily income is computed, however, from the estimated monthly incomes of these traders (6,000–12,000 rials), a net profit of 200–400 rials daily was common.[11]

Petty traders are dependent upon short-range cash needs operating on a daily, or at most a weekly, income. Vendors of perishables must make daily purchases in the wholesale markets for their fruits or vegetables. After the licensed shopkeepers have made their purchases, the vendors move in for their produce. Although a few vendors indicated that they might be able to buy on short-range credit from wholesalers who knew them well, most pay cash for their purchases.[12] If there is produce remaining after the regular vendors leave, the wholesalers will provide a hand lorry and produce to other part-time vendors, who receive a wage or percentage of the day's income.

Petty traders selling new clothing, household items, and novelties make their purchases weekly. Again, although a few individuals indicated they might be able to receive credit from wholesalers, the majority of purchases are paid in cash. The question of small amounts of credit is less clear for middlemen buying and selling used items, for handcraft producer/sellers, for prepared food vendors, or for villagers entering the city to sell produce or handcrafts. The middlemen obviously work on a cash basis when buying used items from householders; the others make use of lines of petty credit sometimes only indirectly related to their business transactions.

Competition and Cooperation

Although the petty traders in Tehran say they have a high degree of mobility and can go anywhere in the city, in actual practice they group together in specific areas—anywhere there is a concentration of pedestrian traffic, and most often in low-income neighborhoods. In these areas they can provide some help to one another and become part of a social group (but see below). For example, in the Sayyed Ismail Bazarcheh near Cyrus Avenue, there is a strong sense of friendship and cooperation among the traders. Much of this has developed during the 15–25 years the traders have been conducting their businesses in the *bazarcheh*.

All of the traders are heavily dependent upon a daily cash income for their own needs and for their business operations. Daily fluctuations in selling for each trader have brought about a high degree of cooperation and lending when cash is needed. Traders who do not want to buy a particular item will refer the seller to other traders. Likewise, if a trader needs to buy some particular item to build up his stock but lacks the necessary cash, he will turn to a friend in the *bazarcheh* for aid. The lender of the cash or the informant for the merchandise will receive a tip of about 10 percent of the value of the item(s) for his aid. Traders sometimes receive goods from brokers (middlemen) without making payment until the merchandise is sold.

Traders also cooperate with one another by exchanging goods at cost.

If a trader needs to borrow a large amount of money, which fellow traders are unable to lend, he usually goes to one of the nearby shopowners. Since most of these men are religious and observe the letter of the Qoranic prohibition of interest, they use methods which have been developed since early Islamic times. The trader needing money will buy something—e.g., a room heater—from the shop-keeper agreeing to pay a set amount (e.g., 2,000 rials over a four or five month period.[13] The shopkeeper then buys the heater back from the trader for 1,800 rials cash. The trader receives 1,800 rials immediately and pays the shopowner 2,000 rials in monthly install-ments. Traders are very careful to maintain good relationships with the shopkeepers in order to have emergency sources of cash, which would otherwise be unavailable to them.

Although the above examples seem to indicate a well-developed and stable social network for the traders in the *bazarcheh,* in actual fact the relationships are very fragile and subject to changes and/or breakdown at any time. The cooperation is a result of necessity more than any real sense of altruism. The Sayyed Ismail Bazarcheh traders also have had the advantage of long-time association. Other petty traders less permanently located and more mobile cannot perhaps depend even on these ties. Petty traders are at one and the same time independent entreprenuers having considerable freedom in the way they conduct their affairs, and vulnerable individuals subject to the whims of the marketplace. Both factors account for the instability of their relationships with other traders.

The Rural Traders—Mazandaran

Around the city of Babol in central Mazandaran there are two cycles of periodic markets,[14] operating in much the same manner as peasant markets described, particularly by geographers, in the growing litera-ture on cyclic marketing systems.[15] It is difficult to date the origins of this system. J. K. Thorpe writes that "the presence of the Islamic seven-day market week in Gilan [to the west of Mazandaran] is of great antiquity, introduced into the region following its gradual colonization after the Arab conquests;" but he gives no source for that information.[16] H. Rabino noted the weekly market of Aliabad (now Shahi) when he traveled through the Babol area in the early twen-tieth century,[17] and local informants state with some authority that the markets were in existence in the nineteenth century. It is plausible that periodic markets in the Caspian are quite old; however, since individual travel in the Caspian regions was more difficult in the past—even dangerous—it would seem unlikely that extensive traveling by traders was undertaken before there was sufficient security in the area.

For obvious reasons, urban based traders traveled as a group from Babol to a different market each day of the week. There they traded retail merchandise and/or foodstuffs for handcrafts, or raw materials (in particular, silk, cotton, linen, and jute). Whereas trade was once conducted primarily by barter, cash is now the basis of exchange in these weekly markets, and the products handled by the traders are almost exclusively retail items from Tehran. A few traders continue to buy handcrafts, which they then sell in both the weekly markets and in the urban bazaars. It seems that peasant agricultural produce was never of great importance.[18]

Trader participants travel to the cities or villages on specific market days; in this manner, they can conduct business on every day of the week if they so desire. There are several participant types who are active in the cyclic marketing system—full-time traders, part-time traders, prepared food vendors, service vendors (blacksmiths, tinsmiths, cobblers, barbers), crafts traders, middlemen, beggars, and religious specialists. Each type is present to a greater or lesser degree in each market, although not all service vendors are in every market. In addition to the traveling peddlers, there are small-scale traders who sell only in one or two of the periodic markets or in the bazaars of Babol and Shahi.[19]

In addition to the traders in the cyclic marketing system, there are traveling peddlers who go from village to village either on foot or by horse, bicycle, or moped. These traders carry salt, housewares, cloth, clothing, pottery, and the like. They rarely have food items to sell but sometimes take village produce in exchange for their retail items.

Typical of the average trader is Shir Mohammad Kerbali who sells village-woven linen and cotton sheeting, cheap cotton prayer rugs from Turkey, headscarves, and assorted odds and ends of silver jewelry and trinkets. He began selling and buying village-made cloth some twenty years ago and has gradually added the factory-made cloths and other items. He has well-established contacts with village weavers (all women) who sell primarily to him and, in some cases, he provides raw materials to weavers to whom he pays a wage for completed work. In addition, Shir Mohammad has a trading partner relationship with a man who buys and sells woolen cloth and knitted woolen items in the mountainous areas of Mazandaran. Shir

Mohammad receives woolen cloth and knitted items such as scarves, caps, and mittens, in exchange for the cotton and linen cloth which he buys in the Babol area.

Shir Mohammad goes to five markets each week and travels to villages to buy cloth from the weavers on the other days. He varies the kind and the amount of merchandise he carries to each market according to his estimate of what he can sell there. Shir Mohammad estimated that the two largest village markets he attends average 1,000 villagers as customers, and the other two village markets have about half that number. He also attended the urban bazaar of Shahi each week, but his sales there were lower because of the competition from the urban merchants. By 1978 Shir Mohammad had given up the weekly trip to Shahi.

In the early 1970s, Shir Mohammad felt that his activities as a trader in the weekly markets were very profitable. He estimated that on good days, he grossed as much as 10,000 rials (about $150); however, his average gross income was somewhat lower, probably nearer 6,000–7,000 rials per day (a net profit of 600–1,000 rials per day, five days a week). Buying and selling in the rural areas, however, is a time-consuming job, and Shir Mohammad sometimes thinks of the possibility of opening a small shop in Babol. But the costs of opening a shop are high. In 1973, a location some distance from the bazaar area and not on a "heavy traffic" street would probably have cost about 300,000 rials for a 20-meter square building, including key money and guild licenses and memberships. In the bazaar, a shop and land would have cost between 50,000 and 100,000 rials, while key money would be about another 1,000,000 rials. In addition, Shir Mohammad felt he would need approximately 1,000,000 rials in capital goods investment. In contrast, the trader said that he can make a good living in the rural markets with a *total* capital investment of only 60,000 rials.

Shir Mohammad represents one of a group of traders who are relatively secure in their trading activities. While there are a few traders, particularly cloth merchants, who have a large investment in goods and who can act as moneylenders to other traders and villagers, a vast number of them share the pattern of daily cash needs of their urban counterparts. Incomes are at the subsistence level (net profits of 100–500 rials per day in 1973), and they have few channels through which to borrow money or to buy goods on credit. They have few skills other than selling, and no united group (such as a guild) to which they can turn in time of need.

Challenges and Threats

Petty traders, whether they are sidewalk merchants in an urban bazaar, middlemen, traveling merchants, itinerant peddlers, village producers, service vendors, or food vendors, share a common trait with all subsistence oriented groups—lack of access to the sources of power. Without membership in a guild or licenses from the municipalities, the petty traders are, in effect, disenfranchised; they occupy the lowest rungs on the ladders of social, political, and economic power. As a group, the traders share several traits: 1) largely rural origins; 2) a low level of literacy; 3) a low level of skills other than selling; 4) little capital to invest; 5) a need for a daily cash income to cover expenses; 6) little or no security in marketing activities; 7) a sense of isolation both economically and socially in relation to the larger bazaar structure; and 8) a need to invest a great deal of time for a subsistence-level income.

Low purchasing capabilities and dependence upon seasonal demand and production also characterize petty traders. Since they do not have storage facilities, access to credit facilities, or large amounts of capital to invest, they cannot make investments on future production or availability of production during a period of low cost in order to sell later at a higher profit. For those traders dependent upon the production of handcrafts from households (such as Shir Mohammad) or cottage industries, the availability of particular goods might have little to do with the market demand but will fluctuate according to extra-market factors such as social commitments, economic situations, or pressing household duties of the *producer*. Petty traders also are dealing largely with a populace which has a low and erratic purchasing power, since peasants and lower income urban residents live close to the subsistence level themselves.

Whereas urban bazaar merchants are united not only through guilds and credit networks but kinship ties as well, the traders on the periphery of the bazaar are characterized largely by the absence of any significant ties or social networks.[20] The petty trader has only the fragile good will of his similarly impoverished fellow traders upon whom to depend in time of need. With perhaps some exceptions in the rural areas, petty traders as a whole indicated that they did not depend upon an extended kin network—according to one informant: "Who can afford relatives?".

The prices of goods sold by peasant traders are never fixed, but instead, fluctuate. In the case of those traders who purchase their goods in the urban bazaar, the cost of each item is known and an attempt is made to gain the highest profit possible. Selling price, however, is also geared to the cash needs of the trader for that day and merchandise or produce will sometimes be sold for a loss in order to gain necessary cash. Dealers who sell below cost hope that they will make up the difference in the near future. Those who are selling their own home crafts or produce try to have an estimate of the market value, but price depends not only on costs of materials but also whether or not the time and labor involved in production is considered to be a priceable commodity.

Traders who buy their merchandise from the urban bazaars can rarely do so on credit, and they receive only slightly lower prices than customers who make single purchases. In order to make a sale (and profit), the traders charge prices only slightly higher than the retail prices of the same items in the bazaar. Customers who buy from petty traders must be able to rationalize the time and expense of going to the main bazaar versus the slightly higher prices they must pay for the convenience of immediate purchase. This is as true for the urban resident living in Tehran as it is for the villager in Mazandaran.[21]

Fruit and vegetable vendors are at the mercy of seasonal availability. Other traders combat the vagaries of production by having as many suppliers as possible and/or by carrying related products such as cloth, socks, scarves, and sundries or novelties. Traders who enter the market only occasionally might have a different product each time. Generally speaking, however, traders specialize in a particular type of product and are very reluctant to change even when demand decreases. Their reasons for conservatism are that they know their products, have suppliers—who might give them limited amounts of credit—and they continue to hope that demand will increase. Their limited amounts of disposable cash also act as a restraint in their ability to try out new products. With no new stimuli or alternatives within the system to which to respond, petty traders have no choice but to remain with the products they feel they know best.

Traders usually acknowledge they have aspirations other than trading for their sons, indicating its low social status. The role of petty trader continues to be one open to men and women who have few other usable skills or who find the rigors of factory labor or other time-consuming employment not to their liking. The feeling of being free to do what one wants should not be underestimated as a perceived advantage of being a trader; the low income is as good as that of other employment for unskilled and semiskilled labor in any case. The incomes mentioned previously were common for unskilled labor in 1973. In 1978 factory workers in Shahi were earning between 15,000 and 17,500 rials monthly (1978: 70 rials = US $1.00). Incomes of petty traders, where I have information, had nearly matched and sometimes exceeded these figures.

Conclusion

Petty traders are important in an era of restricted economic alternatives in an economy of low purchasing power and low productivity. In such economies, the petty trader fulfills the function of distributing goods, combining a plentiful resource—labor—intelligently with a scarce resource—capital.[22] In Iran, itinerant peddling and trading have historically been utilized to earn or augment a subsistence income. The periodic markets in the rural areas of Mazandaran appear to be decreasing in importance,[23] because peasants have become more mobile and travel to cities, and urban authorities have instituted greater controls over the activities of traders in *bazarchehs* and sidewalk vending areas.[24] Yet, the inflation accompanying economic development has wiped out much of the real or imagined gains of peasants and workers, and so petty traders continue to serve consumer groups with low purchasing power.

Obvious infrastructural changes such as new transportation networks and facilities, storage facilities, the standardization of production and prices in some sectors, and a growing middle class of technocrats with high salaries and purchasing ability might lead one to conclude that a rapid change would also occur in the traditional bazaar system. There are no studies, however, which indicate that real and meaningful changes are being made in the traditional bazaar economy structure in Iran or in the role of the petty trader. Instead, it appears that there has been a development of a newer economic sector separate from, but not totally independent of the well-established bazaar structure. This new sector is in the realm of international marketing and available only to the upper strata of Iranian society. Peasants and workers derive some peripheral advantages from this new sector (use of infrastructure, some low-level employment, and the like). However, until there is real structural change in marketing practices and greater equality between the poorer and richer classes, the role of the petty trader will not go away. Petty traders will continue to fulfill their subsistence needs and to respond to the daily needs of low income groups on the periphery of the bazaar system.

14

The Changing Status and Composition of an Iranian Provincial Elite

Mary-Jo DelVecchio Good

Introduction: Social Processes and Changes in Elite Status

Most studies of elites in Iranian society have focused on the national political elite, especially the prestigious families and tribal leaders associated with the Qajar or Pahlavi dynasties.[1] Although the sources of wealth and political power of these elites frequently originated in provincial areas, the families and individuals most commonly discussed resided in Iran's major metropolitan centers such as Tehran, Isfahan, and Shiraz.[2] Much less effort has been directed to the analysis of families and individuals whose social prominence has been largely confined to provincial centers. It is important to understand the changing characteristics of elites in provincial regions in Iran, especially in light of the political revolution and social disruptions of 1978–79 that have involved the smaller provincial centers as well as major metropolitan centers.

This paper explores the meaning and structure of elite status in provincial Iran and examines the changes in the status of provincial elites that occurred over the last half century during the rule of the Pahlavis. Social histories of two groups of traditional elite from Maragheh, a *shahrestan* (subprovince) capital in East Azerbaijan, will be presented to illustrate these changes. The first case concerns the Moqaddam notables, who were the town's ruling and military elite for over a century, from ca. 1800 to 1925. The second case concerns several of the major families of landed gentry, the *arbabs*, who resided

in Maragheh. Until recently, especially prior to the implementation of
land reform in the province, the major landed families were important members of the town's elite. Since land reform in 1963, their
status has been less secure, although some were still considered
members of the older, established elite by the townspeople in the
1970s.

The meaning and structure of provincial elite status underwent a
major transformation in twentieth century Iran. Changes were evident in the characteristics of elites, in the resources that enhanced
social status, and in the position of provincial elites *vis-à-vis* the rest of
the community's social heirarchy. These changes were in part a
response to internally and externally generated social processes, often
termed modernization, that affected the structure of social hierarchy
in all Iranian communities.[3]

These processes include: first, the centralization of political administration and authority during the Pahlavi regimes, which led to
greater control over the provinces by the central government and a
concomitant loss of autonomy for provincially-based elites. Members
of the national political and military bureaucracy became increasingly
important in provincial affairs. Specific central government policies,
such as the appointment of high-level provincial administrators who
had no local power base or ties to provincial elite families, and the
implementation of land reform, tended to dislodge the historical
provincial elites from their monopoly of politically and economically
influential positions.

Second, the transformation of economic and occupational structures led to the establishment of new criteria of social prestige and the
emergence of new roles and social groups in provincial communities
such as Maragheh. Thus, the contemporary system of social stratification of the town exhibits a dualistic hierarchial structure of traditional
and modern social groups.[4]

Third, the cosmopolitanization and expansion of educational institutions introduced a new evaluative criterion of social prestige to
provincial communities. In order to acquire a higher education and
thus a modern status-enhancing resource in provincial towns, students competed on a national level for university placement, and
enrolled in universities usually located in major centers.

These processes of social change had a major impact on the provincial elite of Maragheh. They led to a shift in the distribution and
concentration of power, wealth, and prestige. The model of elite
status that prevailed during the late nineteenth and early twentieth
centuries of an independent, autonomous and powerful group of

local landed notables was clearly altered. One former landlord made a telling comment in 1974 that encapsulated the change: "Before Reza Shah, everybody was a king. But after Reza Shah came to power, he controlled all of us." The two cases discussed below will illustrate this transformation.

Provincial Elites in Contemporary Maragheh

In the early twentieth century, the elite of Maragheh included the provincial ruler (the Moqaddam notables), major landowning families, major merchant families, and the prominent ulama. Some landowning families were involved in commerce, and many merchant families owned orchards and villages. Except for the Moqaddam notables, members of each of these social groups continued to constitute the town's traditional elite in 1974.

Although the focus of this discussion is on the historical elite, it is important to note that new social groups emerged and gained prestige in Maragheh during the Pahlavi regimes. These newly prominent groups, who were often in conflict with members of the traditional elite over local issues and policies, included university-educated professionals, physicians, high-level bureaucrats, administrators and politicians. Some were native to the town, others were Azerbaijanis who settled in Maragheh but identified with local interests and community-oriented institutions. These included school principals, physicians with the Red Lion and Sun hospitals, and local court officials. Other new elites were transients, whose status was a function of official positions of power within the government and bureacracy. Prior to the 1978–79 revolution, the elite status of government functionaries such as the military commander, police chief, and governor, was often precarious and partial because some groups within the town only grudgingly recognized their power.[5]

Status Enhancing Resources of the Provincial Elite

For both traditional and modern groups in Maragheh, elite status was attained through the possession of a constellation of unequally distributed resources that were highly valued by the community. The inhabitants of Maragheh characterized the town's former elites of the Qajar and early Pahlavi periods and the current members of the town's contemporary elites as possessing variants of *parti, pul,* and *pilau* (influence and power; money or wealth; and rice). *Pilau,* or banquet rice, symbolized the ability to perform patronage roles; one acquired supporters or clients, and therefore prestige, through the distribution of favors and largess. Personal characteristics, such as being a believer *(mo'men)*, pure *(tamiz)*, and religious learning, also enhanced social prestige, especially for those in the religious ranks. As the town's occupational structure became more cosmopolitan, higher education, specialized knowledge, and professional skills were added to traditionally-valued resources that marked elite status.

The acquisition of these various resources distinguished one's place in the social hierarchy as a member of the provincial elite. In more analytic terms, these resources may be categorized as follows:

1) Influence *(parti)* implied closeness to national and/or provincial political centers. *Parti* enabled the elite to exercise power within the local government, and on occasion, to acquire positions in the national government. Politically influential positions also led to heightened prestige in other areas of provincial affairs and to key patronage roles in the community. In Qajar times political positions increased opportunities to acquire wealth in the form of villages, and in recent decades political roles enabled some politicians to increase their personal wealth.[6] Historical circumstances continue to alter the composition of those who possess *parti*.[7]

2) Wealth *(pul)* appears to be an essential criteria of elite status, except perhaps for the religious elite. The wealth of the traditional elite consisted primarily of village lands and commercial enterprises in town, and in the past, led to opportunities to purchase influence within the local government. Ownership of villages also implied domination and patronage of the peasant population. Commercial wealth gave one prestige and influence in the bazaar community. Community expectations of the wealthy meant that patronage roles and obligations to perform civic deeds within the town frequently accompanied positions of wealth; fulfillment of such roles enhanced one's prestige.

3) *Closeness to sacred community symbols* through patronage of religious rituals, especially during Moharram, the civic works (establishing *auqaf* and aiding secular charities) enhanced the social prestige of the secular elite, past and present.[8] The sacred knowledge and religious roles of the ulama led to positions of moral authority and political power and influence, particularly within the bazaar community. The resources also contributed to the ulama's prestige in town society at large.

4) *Education* and *skills* are status enhancing resources that underwent substantial changes after 1921. Many of the elite of the Qajar and early Pahlavi eras were among the town's best educated individuals, and it was their children who first took advantage of higher

education and professional occupations. In recent times, higher education and professional roles were almost a prerequisite for inclusion in the new elite of Maragheh. Yet, neither accomplishment was sufficient to secure that status.

5) *Family tradition* could contribute to one's social prestige. Membership in one of the town's historically prestigious families often conferred elite status when combined with other resources. Ascribed elite status rarely appears today, and it is questionable whether it was of much importance in the past.

The Moqaddam Notables: A Provincial Governing Elite

The Moqaddam notables were among the elite of Azerbaijan for over a century, from the Qajar era to the mid-twentieth century. The social history of this family illustrates the historical bases of elite status in Azerbaijan, and the changes that occurred in the twentieth century. Members of the Moqaddam family governed Maragheh and its environs for over a century, from about 1800 to 1925.[9] Their domination of the region coincided with the reign of the Qajar shahs, and their demise as provincial rulers and landed notables coincided with the growing strength of the Pahlavi dynasty and the centralization of political authority. Because of their consistent and lengthy involvement in top positions of local government, the history of this family differs somewhat from that of other elite families in the region. Yet, the processes that contributed to their loss of status as "provincial nobility" also contributed to the diminished status of other elite landed families in the area.

The Moqaddams epitomized the model of provincial elite status in Qajar Iran. Family members were locally powerful, both politically and economically, and the Moqaddam governors ruled the region in an autonomous fashion with little interference from the Qajar shahs for over a century. The family's origin is unclear, but townspeople as well as Moqaddams remaining in Maragheh trace the origin of the governing household to Ahmad Khan Moqaddam, the family patriarch who ruled Maragheh in the early nineteenth century. The family apparently migrated to Azerbaijan from the Caucasus in the late eighteenth century and were leaders of a tribal group who settled in the area. The Moqaddams, by the early nineteenth century, were mostly settled, and they owned vast numbers of villages in East Azerbaijan.

Khan Malek Sasani, a Persian historian who writes on the Qajar era, claims that the Maragheh branch of the family were always faithful servants of the shah. He notes that Ahmad Khan's father, Ali

Khan Moqaddam, came to the aid of Nader Shah in India with infantry and cavalry from Maragheh. Ahmad Khan was named Beylerbey of Azerbaijan and was sent as the Vali of Erevand to quell the Armenian revolt during the reign of Fath Ali Shah.[10] In 1818, James Morier described Ahmad Khan as the wealthy governor of Maragheh who owned the house in Tabriz in which the English ambassador and his party resided during their visit to the Crown Prince Abbas Mirza.[11] Although Ahmad Khan's village holdings were primarily in the area of Maragheh, his family's land and governing role extended to neighboring regions, including Hashtrud and Saraskand.

The Moqaddams' authority was derived in large part from their ability to maintain sufficient troops to ensure the security of the villages, cities, and caravan routes in areas over which the royal court had little or no control. Although the crown prince seated in Tabriz occasionally sent troops to execute particular tax policies in the area, it appears that the bulk of governing duties were relinquished to the Moqaddams.[12] The duties of a provincial governor were to maintain security, a prerequisite for the collection of taxes and the stability of trade and commerce, and to farm his province for his own profit, that of his prince, and of his landed clients. These duties were carried out by the Moqaddam governors for five generations, in Maragheh from ca. 1800 until 1925, and at times in Zanjan, Ardebil, Tabriz and Urumiyeh.

The Moqaddam family's functions—as provincial governors, military leaders, and landed notables—were reflected in the family's kinship organization. According to the genealogies given by three family members who resided in Maragheh in 1974, and by other townspeople familiar with the family's history, the Moqaddams divided into two provincially based *tayafeh* or branches in the early nineteenth century. These are currently referred to as the ruling or "government" (*hokumat*) *tayafeh* and the landlord (*arbab*) *tayafeh*. Members of each *tayafeh* were referred to by their titles, with military or government assignations for the ruling branch, and the title of *aqa* (and the label *arbab*, landlord) for most members of the landlord branch of the family.

Ahmad Khan, the family patriarch, allegedly had two sons, who became the patriarchs of the two *tayafehs*. Hosain Pasha Khan Mir Panj headed the ruling *tayafeh* based in Maragheh, and Hajji Imam Qoli Aqa became a patriarch of the landlord *tayafeh* based in Maragheh and Hashtrud. All of the male members accounted in the ruling *tayafeh*, from Hosain Pasha's generation through the next three generations, to those born in the 1920s, were military officers, government administrators and/or politicians. The daughters tended to marry military officers, high-level government administrators, or prominent men from the Tehran court, although three married into *arbab* families in Azerbaijan. The male members of the landlord *tayafeh* over the same generations continued to be referred to as *arbabs* and titled *aqa*. Only one male from this entire lineage was designated a military man as well as an *arbab*, and one also served the local Moqaddam governor as a purchaser. The women were married to men from landlord families.

Positions of provincial rule, such as governorships and military leadership, were inherited through patrilineal kin in the ruling *tayafeh*. Although members of the landlord *tayafeh* occasionally participated in governing the province, it appears to have been only on an *ad hoc* basis. Both *tayafehs* owned numerous villages in the region; however, members of the ruling *tayafeh* resided in Maragheh, whereas the members of the landlord *tayafeh* frequently lived in the villages surrounding Hashtrud and Maragheh. A third *tayafeh* of the ruling family was established in Tehran in the early nineteenth century by Hosain Khan Moqaddam, a cousin of the family's patriarch, Ahmad Khan.[13] The members of this branch became prominent military figures in the Qajar court, and the family acknowledges that one of its Tehran members was involved in the death of the dismissed reformer, Prime Minister Amir Kabir in 1852.

The functional differentiation of the provincial Moqaddam notables into military-political *tayafeh* and a landlord *tayafeh* is indicative of the differentiation in the social status of the family members. In Maragheh in the 1970s, remaining members of the ruling *tayafeh* had more prestige than did those of the *arbab tayafeh*. Numerous status-enhancing resources provided the basis of the ruling *tayafeh*'s elite status and political authority in Maragheh during the nineteenth and early twentieth centuries. Tribal chieftainship and leadership of armed troops enabled Ahmad Khan to consolidate his position as Beylerbey of Azerbaijan. The Moqaddams' positions as patriarchs, rulers, and military commanders were enhanced by their ability to maintain household and tribal troops. These troops were necessary not only to maintain security in the region of Maragheh, in particular to keep the rebellious Kurds from encroaching on Moqaddam territory, but also to provide troops to assist the Qajar shahs in their various battles within and outside Iran. Ownership and control of large numbers of villages (directly and indirectly through ties to the *arbab tayafeh*) provided resources to maintain and recruit troops and to enhance the family's personal wealth. The Moqaddam governors also maintained extensive patronage networks and family ties with other landed notables in the region in order to support troops. Similar ties with the urban population, particularly the bazaaris, were enhanced through their support of Moharram and other religious rituals. This support helped place the Moqaddam rulers at the center of the town's sacred life.

Finally, the Moqaddam notables had a special, ongoing relationship with the Qajar royalty. For example, not only did the Tehran branch of the family continue to support the court, and to take on military, governmental, and diplomatic positions, but the Maragheh-based governors continued to supply troops and military leaders to the court, when necessary, throughout their reign. And, during the constitutionalist period the ruling household supported the Qajars against the constitutionalist forces in Maragheh and Tabriz.[14] This special relationship may have been strengthened through the marriage of Ahmad Khan's descendants to lesser princes and princesses of the Qajar family.[15] Yet, the fact that the Moqaddams were allowed extensive autonomy in provincial affairs for over a century, even within the crown prince's province, suggests that their loyalty to the Qajar shahs was unquestioned. Perhaps more significantly, it attested to their ability to maintain security.

The elite status of the Moqaddams underwent dramatic change with the rise to power of the Pahlavi dynasty. Although the family pledged its loyalty to the new regime, the ruling *tayafeh* was unable to sustain its political independence in provincial affairs. The last Moqaddam patriarch in Maragheh, Eskandar Khan Sardar Naser, ruled as governor from 1911 to 1925. He was then appointed Majlis representative by Reza Shah, and served in parliament from 1925 to 1949. This clever move by Reza Shah contributed to refocusing the family's political ambitions toward Tehran and the central government. As individuals other than the Moqaddams were appointed local governors, the family lost its combination of provincial political offices and its autonomy in local political affairs. The family no longer commanded or recruited their own troops, and although many still owned villages in the province, most became absentee landlords residing in Tehran. Only one Moqaddam from the male line of the ruling *tayafeh* held political office in the local administration of Maragheh while the Pahlavis were in power. His position as mayor was considered a low-status political office.

The ruling *tayafeh's* reorientation to national politics during the Pahlavi regime was exemplified by the political activities of Eskandar

Table 8. The Moqaddam Governors of Maragheh: Qajar Era

Qajar Shahs	*Moqaddam Governors*
Fath Ali Shah (1797-1834)	Ahmad Khan (ca. early 1800s, in 1815 known as Rishsefid (White Beard) of Azerbaijan)
Abbas Mirza Crown Prince in Tabriz	
Mohammad Shah (1834-1848)	Governor of Hashtrud (ca. 1815)
Naser od-Din Shah (1848-1896)	

Under Ahmad Khan:

- Governor of Hashtrud (ca. 1815)
- Hosain (Pasha Khan Mir Panj) Governor of Maragheh during Mohammad Shah and Naser od-Din Shah

Qajar Shahs	
Mozaffar od-Din Shah (1896-1907)	Eskandar Khan (Governor of Maragheh under Naser od-Din Shah; family claims he was governor of Rezaiyeh and Tabriz in various periods.)
Mohammad Ali Shah (1907-1909)	
Ahmad Shah (1909-1925)	

Under Eskandar Khan:

- Fathollah Khan known as Sardar Moayyed, Governor of Zanjan for 15 years Military Commander under Mozaffar od-Din Shah
- Samad Khan Shoja od-Dauleh Governor of Maragheh ca. 1890s to 1911. Governor General of Azerbaijan 1911-1914 (no children)

Pahlavi Shahs

Reza Shah (1925-1941)

Mohammad Reza Shah (1941-1979)

Under Fathollah Khan (Sardar Moayyed):

- Eskander Khan Sardar Naser, b. 1880s d. 1949. Married to Zekineh Shahzedeh, Granddaughter of Fath Ali Shah; Governor of Maragheh ca. 1911-1925; Majlis Representative from Maragheh ca. 1927-1949. Appointed by Reza Shah.

- General Moqaddam, b. 1890s. Married to Qajar Royal Descendent, Head of National Police circa 1950s.

- Rahmatollah Moqaddam Maraghehi b. 1921; 20th Majlis Representative from Miandoab (1958); Human Rights Activist 1977; National Front Member; Head of Radical Party 1978-1980; Participant in Assembly of Experts to draft a new Constitution in 1979; brief appointment as Governor General of Azerbaijan during Bazargan government; forced underground because of political conflicts with Islamic militants, and Khomaini government officials in December, 1979.

Khan's younger brothers. One, Rahmatollah Moqaddam-Maraghehi, initially served as deputy from Miandoab in the Twentieth Majlis (1960). Cottam notes that Rahmatollah Moqaddam's political career in government-sanctioned activities was cut short because he made a speech critical of the regime while in parliament.[16] Nevertheless, he remained active in nationalist dissident politics and resurfaced as a political leader with national and Azerbaijan regional support during the early phases of the revolution in 1978–79. He headed the progressive Radical Movement party, participated in the Assembly of Experts to draft a new constitution, and briefly held the post of governor-general of East Azerbaijan under Bazargan's administration. During the clashes in Tabriz between Khomaini and Shariatmadari supporters in December, 1979, over the issue of constitutional provisions for regional autonomy and local rule, Shariatmadari supporters of the Muslim People's Party proposed that Rahmatollah Moqaddam be appointed the next governor-general of East Azerbaijan. Moqaddam's regional support and his identification with Shariatmadari appeared to be political liabilities. He was accused of pro-American ties and forced to abandon his political role by the new revolutionary government.[17] Thus it appeared that the Islamic Republic was attempting to reassert central government control over the province by opposing the reemergence of strong political leaders with independent regional bases of power.

As the Moqaddams' political base shifted from Azerbaijan to Tehran, and from provincial politics to national politics, they found themselves competing with numerous other provincial notables for recognition by the court. The changes in the functional role of the ruling *tayafeh* during the early decades of Pahlavi rule reflected changes at the societal level that had begun to restructure the relationship of the central government to the provinces, and that were part of the modernization of most institutions. The ruling *tayafeh* was transformed from a group of relatively independent provincial notables, administrators, and traditional military commanders with their own local power base and troops, into military and political bureaucrats whose authority was a function of their position within the national government. All the younger brothers of Eskandar Khan and many of their sons joined Reza Shah's new military as officers. Most of the women married into military or bureaucratic families in Tehran. Other family members became civil servants in Tehran or in provinces other than Azerbaijan. Preparation for these new roles involved formal education at universities and military academies in Iran and abroad, and in advanced secondary schools such as the American school in Tabriz. All of the men in Eskandar Khan's generation had such training, as did 74 percent of male and female children of the next generation of Moqaddams from this family branch. This is in marked contrast to the landlord *tayafeh*. None of the *arbabs* of Eskandar Khan's generation, and only 30 percent of the next generation, received formal high school or university training.

The distinction between the two branches of the family has been marked by place of residence. In 1974, of all the living members of the ruling *tayafeh*, only two women resided in Maragheh, most others lived in Tehran. In contast, most of the offspring of the *arbab tayafeh* lived in Maragheh, or in other places in Azerbaijan (Tabriz, Rezaiyeh, villages). Only one had a permanent residence in Tehran, and he maintained a home in Maragheh as well. However, some of the current generation of students were attracted to Iran's metropolitan centers for university education.

The elite status of the *arbab tayafeh* also underwent changes after World War II. As noted, most of the Moqaddams who remained in Maragheh after the war were from the landlord *tayafeh*. These family members lost much of their prestige and local political influence with the increasing disintegration of the ruling *tayafeh*. Many who remained in Maragheh worked as civil servants in the lower echelons of the *shahrestan* and municipal bureaucracies. An additional factor in the decline of the Moqaddams' status as provincial political and landed elite was the especially thorough implementation of land reform in Maragheh in 1962. Land reform effectively destroyed the remaining provincial economic base held by Moqaddams of the ruling *tayafeh* who were absentee landlords living in Tehran. Most members of the landlord *tayafeh* still living in Maragheh lost portions of their villages, although some managed to mechanize their holdings or to expand their commercially profitable orchards—in order to insure exemption from land reform. In 1974, the agricultural wealth of the Moqaddam provincial landlords appeared to be flourishing once again; however, their dominance of the peasant population was apparently curtailed.

The decline of the Moqaddam notables as a provincial elite was directly due to the disintegration of their provincial bases of power and wealth and to their loss of a wide range of resources that had formerly assured the family a large measure of autonomy from the central government. It was also due to broad societal changes that restructured provincial political administration and the relationship of the central government to provincial communities. The factors in their decline as a local provincial elite may be summarized as: 1) a shift in their political base from the provinces to Tehran, and integration into the national military and political bureaucracies; 2) a loss of personal troops recruited, maintained, and commanded independently of the crown; 3) a loss of control over village lands as absentee landlords, and the fractionalization of lands among numerous offspring; 4) an adoption of new roles dependent upon cosmopolitan education which provided impetus to leave the provinces and seek outlets for talents in metropolitan centers; 5) competition in Tehran with members of other prestigious families—a kind of levelling process; 6) a decline in status of the *arbab tayafeh,* in part because of the ruling *tayafeh's* shift to Tehran; and 7) land reform, which diminished the provincial economic base for both *tayafehs,* and which altered the relationship between peasants and *arbabs.*

Landlords as Provincial Elites

The second group of the historical provincial elite to be considered are the major landowning families who resided in Maragheh during the late nineteenth and twentieth centuries. These families included the Fotuhis, Kabiris, Hamidiyehs and Mosavis, and they acquired their land by various means. Several of the families migrated as tribal groups to the environs of Maragheh in the mid to late nineteenth century. Others originally came as merchants and purchased their land. Some received their first land grants in the area from the Qajar crown princes for whom they provided various services, most often as scribes to the court. All maintained patronage ties and mutual security relationships with the ruling Moqaddams. There was some intermarriage between these families.

The elite status of the landowners was a product of their ownership of vast tracts of land, their monopoly of the agricultural sector, and their association with the ruling and royal households. Of the elite families in this group, most owned over twenty villages, and prior to the land reform in 1962, several extended families owned over sixty villages each. As rural patriarchs, they also dominated large segments of the peasant population. Landlords who lived in Maragheh were often involved in commercial as well as agricultural activities. Many were central figures in urban patronage networks and sponsors of community activities.

The power and influence of these families began to be diffused during Reza Shah's reign. Their more adventurous and successful children went to Tehran and abroad for schooling. Many remained in the capital and became involved in national politics and modern professions. While the power base of many families shifted to Tehran or Tabriz, some remained powerful provincial notables. Reza Shah appointed several of the most prominent local family members as Majlis representatives, governors of various subprovinces in Azerbaijan, and military commanders. In addition, throughout the first half of the twentieth century, the landed elite continued to amass villages, buying them from absentee and lesser landlords. Until the early 1960s the landed elite continued to wield great influence over the urban courts and political and government offices. Although their power, prestige, and influence sharply diminished after the successful implementation of land reform, declining status for many landed families had begun earlier with the fractionalization of land holdings, and since the 1930s the tendency of children to leave the town.

The decline in the prestige of these elite landed families in Maragheh appears to be a function of the same processes that led to changes in the elite status of the Moqaddam notables: political centralization, modernization of educational and economic institutions, migration to cosmopolitan centers, and land reform. The land reform program of 1962–66 in the villages around Maragheh was in part a sign of the earlier diffusion of elite status that had already occurred as a response to various centralizing trends, and in part a precipitating event that led to further decline of the landed elite's status in the community. An examination of the genealogies of several elite landed families offers examples of contrasting patterns of change in provincial elite status.

The Fotuhi family was among the town's most prestigious families up to World War II. The family's patriarch was born in Tabriz in the middle of the nineteenth century, was a scribe to the crown prince, and came to Maragheh in the 1890s. He was awarded a village for his service to the prince, and expanded his holdings to 35 villages before he died in the 1930s. His three sons added to their father's village holdings during the ensuing decades. They were not merely landlords; all were educated and held important political positions in town society. Two received secondary school diplomas from Russia. The oldest received a *maktab* education and served as scribe to the crown prince during his youth. He was involved in the constitutionalist movement, and under Reza Shah was the Majlis representative from Maragheh for ten sessions. A younger brother started the first government school in Maragheh and was director of education for the town under Reza Shah. Their sister, who also received a *maktab* education, married into a prominent Tabriz family and moved to Tehran. It is not surprising that the next generation of children, who all received university education in Tehran or abroad from the late 1920s to 1940s, opted for professional positions in metropolitan centers of Iran or in the United States. Only one son of this last generation of the Fotuhi elite returned to settle in Maragheh after World War II to continue to manage the family's villages with his father and paternal uncle. When the land reform program was first announced, the family decided to sell all of their approximately 60 villages to the government. They kept their profitable orchards and continued to expand them to take advantage of the growing demand for cash crops in the metropolitan areas of the country.

In 1974, only one Fotuhi patriarch remained in Maragheh. He was considered by the townspeople to be a member of the community's elite, because of his wealth, his family's historical prestige, his educational attainments and personal qualities, and his position in various community civic organizations. However, he was no longer an *arbab*, a landlord. His influence in town affairs, particularly in local politics, was far less than the influence of the previous generation of Fotuhi landlords.

This first pattern of change in family occupation and source of wealth illustrated by the Fotuhis was common for many landed families in Maragheh, including the ruling branch of the Moqaddam notables. Clearly, the most successful families, whose children received higher education and sought new professional occupations that could best be practiced in more cosmopolitan centers than Maragheh, no longer hold claims to high status, or to powerful and influential positions in the provincial community. And, although many were successful professionals in Tehran or Tabriz society, few became recognized members of the national elite.

A second pattern of decline in elite status of the traditional landlords of the town also emerges from the genealogies and family histories of several families. Some elite families appeared to maintain their provincial orientation and residence, in contrast to the family discussed above. Although a few family members of these more provincially oriented groups left Maragheh for education and professional lives elsewhere, most remained in Maragheh for education and professional lives elsewhere, most remained in Maragheh to manage their village lands and commercial interests. Furthermore, their influence in town politics was extensive until the post-land reform era. These families, in particular, experienced land reform as a harsh blow to their prestige in the community. The loss of their village lands continued to be discussed with distress by some of the former *arbabs* (men and women in their forties, fifties, and sixties). One of the largest landowning families claimed they lost 80 percent of their holdings due to land reform and were only paid one-tenth of what the villages were worth. Although many of these former landowners continued to own parts of villages and orchards, many turned to commercial fruitgrowing and to investments in new manufacturing enterprises. Others, dispirited, remained too fearful to invest in anything new. They lived off their government remunerations, the profits from their small orchards, and the rent from their buildings in the town.

After land reform, a number of the former landlord elite were characterized by the townspeople as pursuing a decadent lifestyle, and as squandering their remaining resources on gambling, women, and opium. One former *arbab*, still highly respected by the townspeople, felt that part of the declining prestige of the landed elite was due to this decadent life style, to bad management of orchards and lands still in their control, and to their reluctance or inability to pursue higher education and enter more prestigious newer professions. Ironically, it was higher education and professional pursuits that encouraged the children of the landed elite to abandon the *arbab* role and the provincial life of the town.

The situation of the landed elite after land reform redefined their status in the town's social hierarchy. On the whole, most of the former elite maintained their upper class economic positions through commercial enterprises and real estate investment, but they lost much of their political influence and privileged status. They shared their elite economic status with many newcomers, and were no longer regarded as the most enterprising of the town's wealthy. The ideological campaign waged against the *arbabs* by the government in the early 1960s enabled the town's common people to express their hostility and disdain for the landlords who had "lived off the labor of others." Comments such as "*arbabs* are no more," "they have fallen from power" were common. As the Pahlavi government became less beholden to the landed elite for political support, the town's new bureaucratic and professional elites were freer to check the former *arbabs*' attempts to mold local government policy to their own interests. While reflecting on changes since World War II in the composition of elite families in Maragheh, one former *arbab* also noted that "the same families are not always the most powerful or wealthy. There is always change." He noted that prior to World War II, there were only few wealthy elite families. Since then there has been a proliferation of wealthy people, many replacing the old elite.

Positions that required local recognition and selection by the central government were rarely filled by members of the former landed elite in recent decades. From Reza Shah's first parliament up through the Twentieth Majlis in 1960, Maragheh's representatives were either from the town's resident landed elite or were the sons of the landed elite. Beginning with the Nineteenth Majlis (1957–60), the region's representatives included professionals and civil servants who had no kinship ties to the landed elite. This pattern of political recruitment in Maragheh was typical of other Iranian provinces.[18]

In town government, new faces emerged. In 1960–62, the last Moqaddam of any local importance served as town mayor. After land reform, the office was filled by young professionals who had connections with the new political professionals. The remnants of the landed elite condescendingly referred to these "upstarts" from the bazaar class as "our little mayors." The town's mayor from 1972–76 was a young lawyer whose father was a *chelokebabi* (small restaurant owner). Only one member of the former landed elite was on the town council in 1974.

One need not fill an official political position to exercise political power or influence. Yet, by the early 1970s, the influence of the former *arbabs* on officials of government was very much diminished. For example, one young prosecutor of the *shahrestan* court noted: "Before land reform, the courts, the police and the gendarmes were under the influence of the *arbabs*. It's not merely so extensive today. Even A— Khan, who is a really bad man, does not have the power he had in the past. He still gives trouble to the farmers, though. His land was divided, but he still takes over part of the farmers' land. I threw one such person out of my office recently. He went to the director. The director said, 'Those times are passed and finished.' " In another case, one of the town's former landlords tried to have his land taxes reduced. He attempted to bribe the tax official who was a young man from a bazaari family with no great appreciation for the *arbabs*. Efforts to bribe him were repulsed.

In spite of these changes in the power and influence of the former landed elite, their loss of overall status was gradual and tempered by a long tradition of family prestige and political and economic dominance of town affairs. It was clear from local politics that control over local and provincial political affairs had not fallen solely to the professionals or government bureaucrats. In fact, several individuals who had prominent bureaucratic and civic positions in town, or who were influential professionals, were kinsmen through marriage of the former landed elite.

Conclusion:
Traditional and Modern Elites in Prerevolutionary Maragheh

Changes in elite status within the provincial community have been illustrated by the preceding cases of historically elite families. By 1974 both the Moqaddam notables and the former landed families had lost many of their resources that formerly supported their status in provincial Maragheh. Most of the Moqaddam ruling *tayafeh* migrated to cosmopolitan centers and thus relinquished their provincial roles. Those who remained, largely the Moqaddams of the landlord *tayafeh*, were no longer active or notably influential in provincial or national politics. The Moqaddams in Tehran, who continued to have political connections, had slight contact with the family who remained in Maragheh. Much of the family in Maragheh lost its village-based wealth *(pul)*, although a few became commercial farmers. By 1974, religious patronage roles were no longer filled by the Moqaddams; thus, the family was no longer identified with the community's sacred symbols. Furthermore, the stance taken by one of the Moqaddam governors against the ulama who supported the con-stitutionalist movement was not readily forgotten. Some of the family who remained in town acquired professional roles and higher educa-tion, and their social prestige appeared to be derived largely from their new resources and achieved status.

The former elite landed families had a similar experience. Their *parti* diminished considerably in local politics, although several were involved in municipal and national party politics. None appeared to have politically influential connections in the central government. Most of the former landlords lost their extensive agricultural re-sources. Those still considered elite, however, were among the town's wealthiest people. The traditions of religious patronage, such as giving religious meals and supporting the Moharram rituals, were still practiced; and those who continued to be patrons of civic or religious activities maintained their elite status by their identification with sacred community symbols.

The best educated of the former landed elite who returned to the town tended to be among the most socially prestigious. Those families who had university-educated relatives or children who were professionals living elsewhere pointed out the new achievements of their kin in order to be associated with these new resources for social prestige. The former landlord elite no longer monopolized the status-enhancing resources of town society.

The preceding cases suggest only some of the complexities in-volved in the changes and continuities of elite status in provincial

Iranian communities such as Maragheh. It is evident that the system of social prestige was far more complex in the late Pahlavi era than it was in Qajar Iran. The criteria of elite status in the provinces had been altered and expanded with political and economic modernization in Iran, and although one still required some constellation of the three "P's" (influence, wealth, patronage), the system clearly became more flexible and open to newcomers.

Yet, the openness of the system to include newcomers as members of the community's elite suggested that elite status carried less political and economic power at the end of the Pahlavi era than during the Qajar era or even in the Pahlavi period prior to land reform. The traditional model of an independent, autonomous and powerful local elite as exemplified by the Moqaddam notables, was clearly passé. And the model of the politically influential and economically powerful provincial landlord had been considerably eroded.

In 1974 no single group possessed the concentration of resources formerly held by the town's historical elites. What appeared in the late Pahlavi period was a multiplicity of elites. Groups of competing elites or individuals of high status represented the interests of factions, classes, and status groups that were frequently in conflict over political, cultural, and economic issues that concerned the community. The presence of bureaucrats of the national government in the town also had an effect on the status of local elites. Although the policies of these bureaucrats were often influenced by local elites, various bureau heads, judges, and administrators checked the power and independence of local community leaders. This structural change in provincial political administration was extremely significant in altering the meaning of elite status in provincial communities.

The provincial elites of Maragheh in the mid-1970s may be categorized by distinguishing between historical/traditional and newly emergent/modern elites, and between native or locally-based elites and "official" transient elites sent to govern the *shahrestan* by the central government. Local traditional elites included large merchant and some former landlord families. The source of their prestige was their wealth, and their patronage roles in the bazaar, in the community, in civic organizations, and in religious rituals during Moharram. The Pahlavi government tried to utilize the prestige of this elite by involving them in government-sponsored institutions and policy implementation such as the Chamber of Guilds, the *Shahrestan* Society, the Red Lion and Sun Society, and the city council. Not all the local elites were willing to participate in these government-sponsored activities, as many wished to avoid being identified with the central regime. Notable among these were prominent ulama. The ulama's prestige was derived from their religious scholarship, reputation, and the number of their followers, rather than from any official religious position. One local religious leader commented in 1974 that he had more prestige than the secular governor, the *farmandar*. He claimed that when the governor invites 100 guests only 10 come, but when he invites 100 guests, 1,000 come. His statement was not an idle boast, but rather an indication of the prestige of the religious elite—and perhaps a foretelling of the role of the ulama in the revolution of 1978–79.

Local modern elites included many of the town's professionals, especially the physicians who maintained permanent residences in Maragheh. The source of their prestige was their university education, profession, wealth, and for a few, their family traditions or personal qualities. Although some were involved in local civic organizations, or in political parties, their political positions were of slight importance in conferring elite status. Many of the professional elite were children of the historical elite from the town or region, which suggests that selected old elite families continued their elite statue in new guises.

In addition to the professionals, the newly-emergent local elite consisted of politicans and high-level government administrators and technicians. Their elite status was also a function of their university education, professional or technical skills, wealth, and political positions. Some of the politicians and bureaucrats (such as the mayor and the Majlis representative) were in positions that allowed them to play patronage roles, and thereby to maintain good relations with the bazaar and religious communities.

New non-local elites consisted of high officials of government and the military who were temporarily assigned to positions in the town. These individuals, such as the *shahrestan* governor, the police chief, the military commanders of the nearby base, and heads of various bureaucratic offices, were granted social prestige in town society because of the power of their official positions. Although some officials attempted to establish patronage ties to the local community, others remained aloof, and on occasion, in opposition to the interests of the community. For example, in 1974 the governor was supportive of the Moharram rituals and was a close friend of the local political elite, whereas the police chief attempted to curtail the Moharram rituals, resulting in vociferous community opposition. The social position in the town of this newer nonlocal elite was precarious. As representatives of the central government, their prestige was largely subject to the fluctuation of its strength. The 1978–79 revolution places in doubt the positions of all central government officials.

The very highest status positions of the past in which economic and political power were concentrated no longer existed as part of the contemporary structure of the town's social hierarchy. The integration of Maragheh into the national political and economic community led to the diffusion of status-enhancing resources and to the proliferation of provincial elites. This was a function of a broader distribution of resources among the town's population, and of the increased assumption of decision-making power over provincial and town affairs by the central government. While the town's elites proliferated in the contemporary era, each has had less influence and power in town affairs than did the notables of the Qajar and early Pahlavi eras.

15.

The Shirazi Provincial Elite:
Status Maintenance and Change

William R. Royce

Introduction

The following is an investigation of the major characteristics of the elite families of Shiraz, those families who possess social, economic, and political influence and power and prestige.[1]

In Shiraz, at the present as in the past, there are two almost mutually exclusive groups who constitute the local elite: 1) the transients: government officials appointed from Tehran (military commanders, governors, etc.); 2) the permanents: members of families who regard themselves, and are recognized by the public, as Shirazis.

This study will be limited to the second category, the permanent Shirazi elite. We shall not attempt to name every family which might belong to the present elite; rather, we shall concentrate on two families and one individual who are illustrative of the basic characteristics and tendencies of this social group.

During his visit to Shiraz in 1888, E. G. Browne, the British Orientalist, had an opportunity to become acquainted with members of the elite families of the city. In the account of his stay in Shiraz,[2] he mentions the following: 1) the Qavam;[3] 2) the descendants of the early nineteenth century poet, Vesal-e Shirazi;[4] 3) the *Ilkhani* (paramount chief) of the Qashqa'i tribe and his family;[5] 4) the Navvab family;[6] and 5) several brothers, descendants of Hosain Ali Mirza, Farmanfarma, an early nineteenth century Qajar prince who served as *vali* (governor) of Fars.[7] Today, both the Qavams and the Vesals are firmly established elite families. The Qashqa'i *Ilkhani* family maintained elite status, in spite of Reza Shah's attempts to destroy its power and influence, until it was militarily and politically defeated by the central government in the 1950s. While some descendants of Hosain Ali Mirza and members of the Navvab family still reside in Shiraz, they no longer possess the social, political, and economic power which would grant them elite status.

Thus, in the past century there has been both continuity (in the case of the Qavams and Vesals), and change (in the case of the Qashqa'i *Ilkhanis*, Navvabs and Qajars). Some families have survived and others have not. Furthermore, new families have entered the ranks of the elite.

With this historical perspective in mind, we feel that the most important questions to ask regarding the contemporary Shirazi elite are the following: 1) What are the bases of their elite status? 2) What actions were taken to maintain this elite status?

The Bases of the Elite's Power

A combination of the following factors confer elite status on a family. In some cases, all five are present, while in others, we find only one or two. The first three factors constitute what one usually refers to as prestige.

An Historical Tradition: the role previous members of the family have played in the social, political, economic, cultural, and religious life of the city and nation. Iranians, provincial Iranians in particular, place great importance on family history and background. "Good family" is synonymous (at least on the surface) with good breeding. The historical tradition of a family is possibly more important in the smaller urban centers where family histories (both good deeds and skeletons in closets) are public knowledge, than they are in the bustling and more socially and economically mobile metropolis of Tehran. As a corollary of the above, it is usually more difficult for an individual without family background to enter the elite in a provincial town than in the more anonymous society of Tehran.

Individual Traits: These include the following, often interrelated characteristics: 1) education and scholarship; 2) eloquence in expression; 3) artistic talent (as one might expect in Shiraz, the city of poets, the most esteemed artistic talent is poetry); 4) *javanmardi*, an Iranian concept usually translated as chivalry, which encompasses championing the underdog, personal courage, generosity, loyalty and the ability to forgive; 5) piety, a necessity for the religious elite and an advantage for the secular elite *vis-à-vis* the lower and middle classes.

Civic Action and Public Works: donation and maintenance of schools, orphanages, hospitals, and mosques through *auqaf* or pious foundations. Members of the elite are expected to share their wealth with the less fortunate segments of society. This factor is an outgrowth of the basic Islamic concept of *zakat,* or charitable donation, based on the premise that those blessed by God with wealth should share it with society, in order to demonstrate their gratitude to Him. Social pressure for those with wealth to share it through civic action and public works seems to be greater in the intimate atmosphere of provincial towns than in Tehran.

Wealth: this enables one to have the leisure and finances for education, the funds for public works, and even the means to purchase power and influence.

Political Influence: the power, ability and willingness to represent local interests and individuals *vis-à-vis* the national government and its representatives, both in the provinces and in Tehran.

Maintenance of Elite Status

In order to maintain their position and insure elite status in the future, the following actions must be taken by members of the elite. If they are neglected, the family may revert to obscurity, as many have in the past.

1. Members of the family must live up to its historical tradition.

2. The necessary individual personality traits must be developed.

3. The tradition of civic action and public works must be continued.

4. The family's wealth must be maintained, or better, increased. In the 1970s, times of inflation and land reform, this often required investment in urban real estate and industry, sometimes outside the home city and province.

5. Members of the provincial elite must preserve the old and cultivate new ties with the national government and the national elite by such means as marriage alliances, placement of members of the family in government positions in Tehran, and development of close friendships with Tehran-appointed officials in Shiraz.

Case Studies: Three Types of Elites

Below we will look at one example from three types of Shirazi elite families from the vantage point of the factors presented earlier. The three categories which will be investigated are:

1. *The traditional secular elite:* families who have had elite status in

Shiraz for at least two generations, with background in government service, commerce, and the arts, and in some cases, a combination of these.

2. *The elite families of the ulama* (clergy, literally the learned ones). At this juncture we would like to emphasize that the ulama are not now, and have never been, a monolithic group. Under the general heading of ulama, there were traditionally such diverse groups as the *Imams Jom'eh* of the major towns, then royally appointed religious representatives of the shah, scholars and teachers in theology, religious law and philosophy, custodians of mosques, whose major responsibility was to lead public prayer, and finally, preachers. Ulama families tend to have long continuity for many reasons, the most important being the maintenance of high educational standards and continued income derived from administration of public pious foundations and from personal *auqaf*.

3. *The new elite,* those individuals or families whose status was acquired in this generation.

The Qavam, A Traditional, Secular Elite Family

Qavam oral tradition traces their ancestry back to Hajji Qavam od-Din (the pillar of religion), a fourteenth century *vazir*, who had the distinction of having been mentioned in a poem by his contemporary, Hafez.[8] Local tradition, however, has it that they were originally Jews, and this assertion is repeated in a secret British *Who's Who of Iran* compiled in the 1890s.[9] The present-day Qavam family can document their ancestry to Hajji Mahmud, an early eighteenth century Shirazi merchant, who was the founder of the family fortune.[10] His son, Hajji Hashem (after whom the family was often referred to as the Hashemiyyeh in nineteenth century sources), was the first of the family to hold office.[11] He served as *kadkhoda* (headman or ward-boss) of five of Shiraz's ten Muslim quarters (the eleventh quarter was the Jewish *mahalleh*).

The first member of the family to achieve national political prominence was Hajji Ebrahim,[12] son of Hajji Hashem, *kalantar* (mayor)[13] of Shiraz under the later Zands, whom he betrayed to Aqa Mohammad Khan, the first Qajar shah, and was rewarded by being named chief minister. He brought his family to Tehran, and soon, according to Mirza Hasan-e Fasai, "the governorship of the whole of Persia was held by the brothers and sons of Hajji Ebrahim Khan."[14] The pattern, frequently observed in Iranian history, that the acquisition of too much power by a subject in an absolute monarchy is a risky and often dangerous move, proved true: Fath Ali Shah retaliated in 1801 by having Hajji Ebrahim killed, and his brothers and sons either killed, blinded or castrated.[15]

Ali Akbar Khan (1789–1865),[16] Hajji Ebrahim's fourth son, who was very young and was thought to have been dying of cholera, was spared Fath Ali Shah's revenge. He survived, returned to Shiraz, became very popular with the inhabitants of the city, and at their request was named *kalantar* of Fars by Fath Ali Shah in 1812.[17] Over the years he received additional honors and posts; in 1829–30 he was awarded the honorific title Qavam ol-Molk (the Pillar of the King-dom), on which the family name is based;[18] and in 1864–65 he was named administrator of the Shrine of Imam Reza at Mashhad.[19]

Hajji Ali Akbar Khan was succeeded as *kalantar* by his fourth son, Ali Mohammad Khan (1829–83),[20] who also inherited the title Qavam ol-Molk.[21] In all, five members of this family held the title[22] and the post of *kalantar* until Reza Shah abolished the office in the 1930s, and Ebrahim Khan, Qavam ol-Molk V (d.1969), and his immediate family were forced to leave Shiraz. They settled (or one might say, were settled) in Tehran. Fath Ali Khan, Saheb Divan (1820–96),[23] another son of the first Qavam ol-Molk, went to Tehran in the 1830s, married a daughter of Fath Ali Shah, and entered the central administration. He served as governor of many provinces, and was named the shah's chief minister in 1873.[24] Nasir ol-Molk (1821–93),[25] another son of Ali Akbar Khan, remained in Fars, and served as governor of Bushehr, Lar, and Bandar Abbas, regions where the family still maintains influence. In short, the Qavam historical tradition in Shiraz is one of wealth, political power and authority. Many old Shirazis have told me, "Before Reza Shah, Qavam was shah here."

Today there are three major branches of the Qavam family: 1) the Qavam, all in Tehran, sons and daughters of Ebrahim Qavam; 2) the Qavami, descendants of Nasir ol-Molk; and 3) the Saheb Divani, descendants of the Saheb Divan, both in Shiraz.

Even though he had been exiled from Shiraz, Ebrahim Qavam was able to maintain his family's status. His son Ali married Princess Ashraf, sister of Mohammad Reza Shah. Their son, Prince Shahram, is therefore the grandson of both Reza Shah and Ebrahim Khan, Qavam ol-Molk V. I have often heard Shirazis remark, "Shahram is not just a Pahlavi. He's a Qavam." After divorcing Ashraf, Ali Qavam married a sister of the shah's close associate, Asadollah Alam,[26] who in turn married one of Ebrahim Qavam's daughters. Another daugh-ter married Dr. Abol-Qasem Nafisi, a Tehrani physician, from an old established medical family. Ebrahim Qavam, himself, became senator from Fars under Mohammad Reza Shah.

The best-known members of the Qavami branch are three brothers: Abdollah; Azizollah, and Abol-Qasem. Abdollah is a large landlord in Fars, and plays the role of local head of the family. He is married to a daughter of one of the sisters of Ebrahim Qavam. Azizollah has done well in land and agricultural investment. He was first married to a member of an important Shirazi ulama family. His present wife is a member of the Tehrani elite Hedayat family. Azizollah has served as a special aide to the shah, and was elected to represent Shiraz in the Twenty-fourth Majlis.[27] The third brother, Abol-Qasem, the best educated, is a Swiss trained physician and served as vice-chancellor of Pahlavi University, now the University of Shiraz, for many years. His wife is the daughter of Dr. Abol-Qasem Nafisi. The Saheb Divani family is no longer so important as the other branches, but still has some wealth and influence.

Individual Traits of Leading Members of the Family. The first three Qavam ol-Molks were examples of the Iranian concept of *javanmardi* in that they constantly defended the interests of the city against Tehran-appointed governors. The third and fourth Qavam ol-Molks, however, were unpopular locally, because they strongly supported British interests in Fars. While the nineteenth century Qavams were educated, the family did not produce any poets or artists. In the sphere of piety, both Ali Akbar Khan, Qavam ol-Molk I, and Fath Ali Khan, Saheb Divan, served as administrators of the Shrine of Imam Reza.[28] Abdollah Qavami, who prides himself on his generosity, continues the *javanmardi* tradition of the early Qavams. The current member of the family best known for his intellectual gifts and accomplishments is Dr. Abol-Qasem Qavami.

Public Works. Almost wherever one steps in the older quarters of Shiraz, one encounters *madrasehs* (traditional theological schools), *hosainiyehs* (theaters for the Shi'i passion play, the *ta'ziyeh*), and mosques built by the Qavam family. They also constructed *caravanserais* outside the city and *abambars* (water cisterns). One of the family residences, now the Asia Institute, was presented to Pahlavi University by Prince Shahram. Khorshid Kolah Khanom, Leqa od-Dauleh, sister of Ebrahim Qavam, built the first orphanage in the city, and also served on the boards of several charitable organizations.

Wealth. The eighteenth century family fortune, originating from commerce was wisely invested in some of the most choice lands of Fars. The family also acquired a number of villages and gardens all over the province from grants by the Qajar shahs. Many estates were also reportedly gained by confiscation. When Ebrahim Qavam was brought to Tehran in the 1930s, Reza Shah took title to his personal estates in the Shiraz area and granted him lands on the Caspian in exchange. The Qavami and Saheb Divani lands do not seem to have been touched by Reza Shah.

Political Influence. Before Reza Shah, the holder of the title Qavam ol-Molk was the chief representative of the people of Shiraz *vis-à-vis* the central government. During the last years of Pahlavi rule, although the family no longer possessed the formal, direct political power of the past, its members continued to have great influence at court.

Have the present generation of the family been able to maintain themselves as an elite family? What is the outlook for the future?

Historical Tradition. With the absence of the main Qavam branch from Shiraz, the family's historical tradition has been maintained by the Qavamis, who fill the traditional roles of public service. Abdollah, especially, attempts to maintain an almost princely life style. Azizollah has been associated with the imperial court and represented Shiraz in the Majlis, and Abol-Qasem served as second in command at Pahlavi University.

Individual Traits. Abdollah Qavami continues the *javanmardi* tradition of the early Qavam ol-Molks. Also, the Qavami brothers have taken great care in seeing to their children's education. Abdollah's eldest son studied political science in the United States. The other Qavami children are still in primary and secondary school.

Public Works. This is a field in which the current generation of the family does not seem to have been active. The Asia Institute is an exception.

Wealth. The estates of Abdollah Qavami, the eldest brother, have been considerably reduced by personal extravagance and land reform. Azizollah, however, was one of the first Shirazis to invest in mechanized agriculture, both in Fars as well as in Jiroft in Kerman province, and as a result became one of the city's wealthier citizens. As a physician and vice-chancellor of the university, Abol-Qasem was well off.

Political Influence. Until the fall of the Pahlavi dynasty in 1979, the Qavamis had more influence in Tehran than any other Shirazi family due to their connections by marriage to Alam and Prince Shahram. All the brothers, but especially Abdollah, also continually maintained close relations with what were the five most powerful central government representatives in Shiraz: the governor-general, army commander, gendarmerie commander, chief of SAVAK; and the chancellor of the university.

From the above analysis, we conclude that during the final years of Pahlavi rule the future of the Qavam-Qavami families appeared to be bright. Azizollah, especially, was a very wealthy man, and most important of all, the family was well connected at Court. What effect the change of regime in 1979 will have, it is too soon to predict.

The Imami-Shirazi, an Ulama Elite Family

Historical Tradition. Since the latter part of the eighteenth century, the post of *Imam Jom'eh* of Shiraz, the leader of public prayer at the *Masjed-e Jom'eh* (Friday or cathedral mosque), and royally appointed chief of the city's ulama was in this family, which originated in the Jazayer region between Shushtar and Basra.[29]

The chief of the family during the last decade of Pahlavi rule was Naser osh-Sharieh, the *Imam Jom'eh* of Shiraz. His brother, who is not a member of the ulama, headed the local bus company and had served on the city council. The *Imam Jom'eh*'s sons both resided in the U.S., and a daughter was the principal of one of the largest girls' schools in Shiraz, and was working on an M.A. in English literature at the local university. Her husband, Mr. Mohammad Mo'ayyedi, also from a Shirazi ulama background and a grandson of the author of the *Farsnameh-ye Naseri*, is a retired civil servant who at one time served as *farmandar* of Shiraz. Their sons are studying or have studied in California, and their daughter, a high school English teacher, pursued graduate degrees in English at Pahlavi University.

Individual Traits. As official chiefs of the Shiraz ulama, the holders of the title *Imam Jom'eh* have all had a thorough religious education. No theological scholars of renown, however, seem to have been produced by this family since the eighteenth century. The *Imams Jom'eh* have also been known for their piety, a trait which must be possessed by the bearer of this title and office.

Public Works. The family has traditionally been generous to the poor of the city. Pious foundations have been set up to provide public distribution of food during the holy months of Ramazan, Moharram, and Safar.

Wealth. During its long history of prominence in Shiraz, the Imami family has amassed large tracts of valuable urban real estate and some of the most fertile villages around Shiraz. Many individual members of the family also have private incomes from pious foundations.

Will the Imami family be able to maintain its position as an ulama elite family?

Historical Tradition. The primary traditional role of the family in the life of the city has been that of royally appointed chief of the clergy. This tradition was maintained by Naser osh-Sharieh. His brother, sons, and son-in-law, none of whom are members of the ulama, will not be able to succeed him.

Individual Traits. The characteristic traits of this family, religious education and piety, have been maintained by the present *Imam Jom'eh*. While familiar with the principles of Shi'i Islam, his brothers, sons, and son-in-law have received "modern," secular educations. The same applies to his grandsons. The emphasis on education is there, but its direction has changed.

Public Works. Naser osh-Sharieh continued the charitable acts of his predecessors, and his daughter and son-in-law have continued the tradition of social service.

Wealth. The *Imam Jom'eh* has added to the family fortune by developing Rahmatabad, his former summer estate outside Shiraz, into one of the city's best residential areas. His brother has many business interests in the city and his son-in-law is actively engaged in mechanized farming.

Political Influence. The *Imam Jom'eh* served, as had his predecessors, as the shah's religious representative to Shiraz and Shiraz's official religious representative to the shah. Since there are no members of the clergy in the immediate family, it seems unlikely that this unique type of political influence with the central government will remain. Naser osh-Sharieh's brother and son-in-law, because of their relationship to him as well as because of their own personal qualities, also have possessed political influence, but of a very different nature from that of the *Imam Jom'eh*.

From the above analysis, we conclude that the future nature of the Imami family's elite status, if it is maintained at all, will be very different from its traditional role. A shift has taken place from ulama to secular, and there is reason to believe that this change was a conscious one. No member of the family seems to have been designated or trained for the position of *Imam Jom'eh*. If the post continues, it will most likely be confered upon someone outside the immediate family. Furthermore, one generation, the *Imam Jom'eh*'s sons, now reside outside Iran. Their wealth, prestige, and influence may enable the *Imam Jom'eh*'s brothers, nephews and cousins to maintain their elite status, but this remains to be seen. Undoubtedly, the family's close connection with the monarchy will prove to be a liability in the Islamic Republic—yet another challenge to their survival as members of the elite.

The Abtahi, a New Elite Family?

Analysis of our concluding case study will concentrate on the career of one individual, Ja'far Abtahi, emphasizing the means by which he joined the ranks of the elite and observing how he has attempted to establish his family within the Shirazi elite.

Historical Tradition. Abtahi has no tradition as a member of the Shirazi elite. He is a Lur, not of a Khan family, from the Massani region of Fars, who showed promise as a young boy and was sent to high school in Shiraz where he was an outstanding student. Upon graduation, he went on to obtain a law degree at Tehran University. In the early 1950s he was associated with leftist circles in Shiraz, but repented and was forgiven (along with several other Shirazis, who thanks to strong support from Alam obtained important posts in the ministry of court: Dr. Baheri, Rasul-e Parvizi (d. 1977), and Jalal-e Jahanmir). Abtahi is recognized by almost everyone in Shiraz as the best lawyer in the city. His wife is from a family with small landholdings on the fringes of the elite. He possesses a great sense of loyalty to his lateral and nuclear family, financing the education abroad of his brother and cousin, both physicians. His eldest son has studied at M.I.T. and Harvard Business School.

Individual Traits. He prides himself upon his *javanmardi,* and is held in high respect by the lower classes because of this quality. Also, in addition to his legal education, he has a broad general culture, both traditionally Iranian and Western. To insure the establishment of his family as a member of the elite he has also, as has been mentioned above, seen to the education of his eldest son, his brother, and cousin. Abtahi envisages a political future for his second son, a teenager still in high school.

Civic Action and Public Works. Abtahi's charities, for the most part, seem to be limited to support of his family's education, yet he contributed generously to the Qir-Karzin earthquake relief.

Wealth. According to rumor he has amassed great wealth in his legal career, but he denies this, claiming that he has spent all he has earned on the education of his family. He does, however, have a fine home and spends great amounts on lavish entertaining.

Political Influence. Political skill, and its resulting influence, is one of Abtahi's strongest points, which he hopes will be continued by his second son. He had close connections, through Baheri and Jahanmir, with the Pahlavi ministry of court in Tehran.

From the above, it seems quite likely that the Abtahi family has become, within the short span of 30 years, one of the city's elite families. Ja'far Abtahi possesses the important individual traits, wealth, and at least up to the fall of the Pahlavi regime in 1979, had friends in the right places to secure political influence. In addition, he is an excellent lawyer. His sons are being trained to follow in his footsteps.

Conclusions

Broadly speaking, the experience of both the Qavam and Imami families in Shiraz has been characterized by continuity. They established their prominence in the late eighteenth century and have maintained it down to the present, in spite of radical political, social, and economic change, by constantly adapting to new environments. Of the elite characteristics we have isolated, wealth, political influence, and education are outstanding. In all these areas both the Imamis and the Qavams have demonstrated an amazing talent to adapt, to channel their energies in these fields according to the demands of the times. The Qavam fortune, founded on commerce, was invested in agricultural lands, which were, in turn, mechanized in the twentieth century. Likewise the present *Imam Jom'eh* has converted an estate into luxury housing and his son-in-law is involved in mechanized agriculture. Education of members of both families has also shifted from the traditional bureaucratic preparation (in the case of the Qavams) and theological training (in the case of the Imamis) to more modern disciplines such as medicine and engineering. Wealth and education are constants but the nature and bases of each have changed.

The key element to local political power has always been influence at the center, and this influence was maintained despite the change from the Qajars to Pahlavis by virtue of marriage alliances and placement of family members in positions in the national government. What we have characterized as individual traits should not, however, be slighted, since they are essential to preserve that local respect for the families which in turn enhances their national political influence, since through it the ruler hopes to gain a measure of local control.

Yet, as the case of Ja'far Abtahi has demonstrated, although the society is dominated by the old families, if one is aware of the key elements which grant elite status and manipulates them well, he can attain it.

Continuity among the elite is, however, more prevalent in Shiraz than in Tehran. The greater economic opportunity in the capital stands out as a key factor in this regard, but it is by no means the only element. The chance that one's wealth might be confiscated by the shah, or whoever holds supreme power, a frequent happening in Tehran under both the Qajars and the Pahlavis, is less likely in the provinces. Furthermore, the elite's local power base in the form of influence among the local population also frequently served as a shield against interference from the center. Finally, in the smaller towns the importance of having a family tradition and the population's knowledge of each other's backgrounds also served to make it difficult for new individuals to enter the elite.

The fall of the Pahlavi dynasty in 1979 and its replacement by the Islamic Republic poses a definite challenge to the adaptability of the Shirazi elite. All three families are now at a great disadvantage because of their connections with the Pahlavi regime, which is anathema to the Islamic Republic. The Imami family's shift from ulama to secular may harm them initially, but at least they have the pious family tradition to fall back on. Personal piety will doubtlessly be essential to prosperity within the new system. Yet the Qavams, the Imamis, and Ja'far Abtahi are all survivors. The supreme test of their adaptability will be to see if they can weather the storm and survive the current transformation of the Iranian political system.

16

The Religious Dimension of Modernization Among the Jews of Shiraz

Laurence D. Loeb

During the 2,500 years of Jewish settlement in Fars, extensive changes have taken place in the community's life style and socioeconomic condition.[1] In no period have changes been so fundamental as during the fifty years of Pahlavi rule. This paper examines the role of religion in the traditional past and at present, focusing on those complexes that appear critical in shaping the Jewish community of present day Shiraz.

The Religious Dimension

The major scriptural monotheistic religions, Judaism, Christianity and Islam, have traditionally discriminated in various degrees against representatives of other religions living in their territories. This may be a logical result of their ideas of correct orthodox belief, which makes unbelievers inferior in some sense; on these matters religions like Buddhism and Hinduism are much more tolerant. Historically, among the scriptural monotheistic religions, Christianity has had the most intolerant record; the treatment of Jews by Christians from the Middle Ages to modern times, has included pogroms, forced conversions, and numerous expulsions of Jewish communities. Jews have rarely been in a ruling position that would allow them to discriminate violently against others, but one might speculate that were strict orthodox Jews to govern Israel, the position of some religious minorities might be uncomfortable.

In this context, the problems experienced by Jews in Muslim

territories are not exceptional, and Jews have probably suffered less intensive discrimination over time in Muslim lands than in Christian ones. Pervasive discrimination against Jews in the Christian West waned in recent centuries due to capitalism, the Industrial Revolution, and Enlightenment and French Revolutionary ideology which undermined religious orthodoxy and favored a system of free exchange and markets and a "career open to talents" that broke down many traditional barriers and prejudices. Similarly, the tolerance shown minorities by the Pahlavi regime was, in part, a response to the rquirements of economic and ideological modernization.

Other anthropologists have written about the importance of religion in contemporary Iran.[2] However, most of the published material deals only with the dominant Shi'i Muslim community, paying little attention to minorities. While some minorities in Iran are primarily linguistic or ethnic, one marker of considerable antiquity—religion—remains a major classificatory means of bounding minorities. Religion serves to segregate the community of Muslim believers (*umma*) from nonbelievers and also provides the minority with a structure and ideology for continued survival.

In the present study, religion, examined from the perspective of one minority community, is viewed both as an internal force and external constraint. For analytic purposes, external religion is treated largely as monolithic, as it is generally perceived by the minority. Shirazi Judaism, on the other hand, is analyzed in terms of its major components: (1) an action/activity system, (2) ideology, (3) symbolic system, and (4) temporal/locational structure. Dichotomization is a major component of the Jewish world view,[3] and hence the "we"/ "other" perspective which pervades this study is intentional, and is necessary in order to place modernization into the Shirazi Jewish framework.

The Setting

Shiraz is a fast-growing urban center in Iran's important southern province of Fars. Its population rose from approximately 100,000 in 1945 to about 600,000 in 1978. The city has dominated the affairs of Fars since its founding at the end of the eighth century C.E., and urban centers in nearby Istakhr and before that near Persepolis suggest that this has been a critical location since at least Achaemenian times.

Travelers such as Eldad the Danite[4] and Istakhri[5] suggest that large numbers of Jews in Fars were once rural, many of them apparently pastoralists. According to oral tradition the first Jewish settlers of Shiraz were villagers. Pastoralism among Fars Jews seems to have largely disappeared by the Mongol period, but agricultural pursuits continued until the Safavid period.[6] Since the eighteenth century there is no further evidence of direct participation in farming. The rural Jewish population of Fars, which may have totaled more than 4,500 in 1930,[7] resided in towns and villages, where they engaged in crafts, peddling, and other services to the rural population. Once important centers of Fars Jewry in Lar, Jahrom, and nearby towns and villages were abandoned in the early part of this century when their Jews were expelled.[8] In 1968, I counted only 82 Jews in rural Fars. In 1977, a few families residing in Firuzabad were the sole remnant of Fars rural Jewry.

The major vector of movement for Fars Jewry over the centuries was towards Shiraz. During the twentieth century the tendency towards urbanization increased dramatically. The Jewish population of Shiraz peaked at some 17,000 to 20,000 in 1949,[9] perhaps 20 percent of the city's total population. Due largely to emigration to Israel, the Jewish population dropped to about 8,500 by the mid-1950s, stabilizing through 1968 when Jews in Shiraz were about 3 percent of the total. In 1977, informants' population estimates ranged from 7,000 to 10,000—less than 2 percent of Shiraz's total population. Only between one-quarter and one-third of the Jews of Shiraz resided in the older sections of the city.

The Religious Context of the Premodern Period

Through the thirteenth century, Fars Jewry was under the religious and communal control of the Exilarch *(Resh Galuta)* of Babylonia, who administered that distant province through the *Sar Shalom*, his representative in Isfahan. A linguistic gap evolved over the centuries, as Mesopotamian Jewry continued to use Aramaic, which was gradually replaced by Arabic. In Fars, Jews spoke Persian, forgot Aramaic, and never learned Arabic. The language drift may have contributed to a developing cultural gap between the two communities. After the Mongol invasions, from the fourteenth to the seventeenth centuries, Shirazi Jews seem to have been largely cut off from foreign coreligionists. Social and cultural isolation during this period reduced contacts with other Iranian Jews, with consequent linguistic drift, decline of Hebrew competence, and the development of local traditions. Contact with the outside was tentatively reestablished in the Safavid period, with emissaries bringing knowledge of other traditions from Baghdad and Palestine. But significant contact with foreign Jewry was only restored in the late nineteenth century Qajar period.

Little is known about Iranian Jewish life in Mongol and Turkic times. The lack of folklore about the period and absence of chronicle poetry about major calamities suggest possible tranquillity for Shirazi Jewry. Under the early Safavids, Jews prospered in the improved commercial conditions under this dynasty. Qazvin, and later Isfahan, reemerged as important centers of Iranian Jewry.

One significant change effected under the Safavids was the shift from Sunni Islam to Imami Shi'i Islam as the state religion. Although Shi'ism, like Sunnism, regards Jews as a protected people, it appears that the growth in power of the Shi'i ulama, some of whom encouraged moves against the Jews, meant that life was often more difficult for Jews under the Safavids than it had been previously. Widespread persecution of Jews, including forced conversion, took place during the reigns of Abbas I and II. A restrictive code, the *Jam Abbasi*, was directed towards all of the protected minorities.[10] The code, as applied to Jews, included dress, residence, building and travel restrictions, as well as circumscription of public social intercourse with believers. A "law of apostasy" was promulgated allowing converts to Islam to inherit the estates of most of their close kinsmen.[11] This rule was viewed by Shirazi Jews as a real threat to community stability until its removal in the twentieth century.[12]

The Qajar Period (1795–1925)

Shirazi Jews, like coreligionists elsewhere, were not well treated under the Qajar dynasty, despite the probability that Hajji Ebrahim, the first Qajar Qavam ol-Molk, was a Shirazi Jew who converted to Islam. Travelers' descriptions depict exploitation and public degradation of Iranian Jews.[13] Most of the Shirazi Jewish community converted to Islam in the mid-1820s to escape oppression,[14] although some continued to practice the Jewish religion and to identify themselves as Jews. Jews were otherwise restricted and forced to suffer indignities under new applications of the *Jam Abbasi*, designed to prevent ritual contamination of Muslims through physical contact.

Under the Qajars, the ulama were both active and powerful. In Fars, they were implicated by informants and sources in the harassment of Jews,[15] strict application of the *Jam Abbasi*, the expulsion of Jews from Lar and Jahrom, the liquor prohibition of 1904,[16] public degradation of Jews,[17] and riots and synagogue burnings in the 1890s. They also were instrumental in helping stage the riot of 1910 in which Qashqa'i tribesmen were lured into attacking the Jewish quarter, leaving 15 Jews killed and thousands homeless.[18]

Shirazi Jews consider the Qajar period to be among the most difficult in their history. Some of the leading pietists sought to escape altogether by emigrating to Palestine as early as 1815; large numbers arrived between 1886 and 1919, where they formed an enclave in Jerusalem. Among the departing pietists were the leading scholars of the period; for more than two generations, until the early 1970s, Shirazi Jewry was bereft of strong religious leadership.

Jewish life during the Qajar period serves as a baseline for comparison with the contemporary period. Older informants had little difficulty recalling their style of living and the problems they faced in late Qajar times. According to informants, farming by Jews was forbidden although they had been active in silk farming in late seventeenth century Lar.[19] Jews were gradually forced to sell their farmlands and then restricted to commercial rather than subsistence occupations. Even in Shiraz, they were restricted to their own residential quarter, the *mahalleh,* and for ostensibly religious reasons forbidden by the ulama to dwell outside of it.[20]

During this period, Jews no longer engaged in international commerce and were discouraged from any occupation which would bring them into direct competition with Muslims, unless it was so necessary that exceptions could be made. Islam prohibits profit on the sale of gold and silver to the faithful,[21] so many Jews in Shiraz became silversmiths or goldsmiths and moneylenders. Since liquor making and selling are forbidden to the faithful, Jews competed with Armenians to manufacture and sell wine and *araq.*[22] Music, acting, and dance, associated with licentious behavior, were activities providing income for Jewish professionals. Other *dhimmi* occupations exploited by Shirazi Jews included healing, fortunetelling, peddling, masonry, merchandizing, spinning, and warpwinding. There were, of course, a few occupational opportunities provided by the nature of Jewish communal life, e.g., teaching, prayer-reading, custodianship of synagogues, and butchering. In general, however, the traditional occupations tended to be those largely inappropriate to Muslims for religious or other reasons.[23]

Shirazi Jews traditionally avoided all forms of conspicuous consumption that might make known their wealth to the Muslim community. Only within the privacy of the synagogue was any show of wealth possible.[24] Much Jewish wealth was taken out of direct circulation by moneylending and by hiding for unforeseen circumstances.

Charity was limited, since too much largesse would expose the donor to exploitation not only by the needy, but perhaps by non-Jewish neighbors as well.

The relative poverty of Shirazi Jewry is attested to by informants and most nineteenth century travelers, though no evidence is given showing Jews as worse off than contemporary urban Muslims. Nevertheless, through expropriation,[25] taxfarming, extortion,[26] debt default, and theft, Shirazi Jews were often compelled to contribute to the financial needs of almost every element of the population.

Typically, the Jewish community tended to be insular, avoiding all forms of contact with authorities. Therefore the traditional political structure was of a dual nature. The political *elite,* including wealthy and influential men selected by the authorities, as well as volunteers, formed a council, the *ene ha'eda* ('eyes of the group'), whose main function appears to have been external relations. Decision-making was by consensus and most often no decision at all would be rendered on a particularly touchy problem. The *ene ha'eda* were all known to the authorities; they were often called before them to explain decisions and were occasionally selected to be tortured as a vicarious pressure on the rest of the community.[27] Hence, one response to external pressure was avoidance of responsibility.

A second structure, dubbed the "council of the pious," consisted of the religious elite, whose pious concerns and lower visibility *vis-à-vis* the authorities made them far less reluctant to take action on behalf of the whole community. The "council of the pious" imposed taxes on ritual slaughter and accepted responsibility for the distribution of relief monies.

Jewish communal structure was largely self-contained. A ranking system of differential prestige formed as a product of occupation, family wealth, and piety, was the operant structure in Shirazi Jewish life. This ranking system was critical within the framework of public behavior, regulated by the rules of *ta'arof* (formal polite behavior). It was significant in arranging marriages and in forming economic alliances. However, one's rank in Jewish society was not necessarily relevant to one's status in Iranian society at large, and honor provided by coreligionists was not necessarily a correlate of prestige in Iranian society.

Informants report that they were generally excluded from meaningful interaction with the Persian population at large by means of ritual and social segregation. Jews, like other *dhimmis,* could not eat with Muslims nor drink from their cups. Muslims would refuse Jewish food when offered.[28] The pietists would not even sit on the same carpet with an unbeliever and would insist on proper deference. Ritually polluting Jews, in order that believers might avoid pollution, were forced to wear distinctive identifying dress, forbidden to handle sale-merchandise (especially food) and were beaten if they ventured out into the rain which could run down their bodies into the street and possibly contaminate the faithful.[29] During Ramazan and Moharram, many of the faithful avoided Jewish businesses, while on Ashura, some Jews considered it dangerous even to appear on the street. Given their low status, even with respect to the generally exploited urban Muslim masses, few Jews had illusions about their prestige and influence in Iranian society as a whole. Jews were an outcaste, whose cultural response I have labeled "pariah culture."[30]

In sum, the treatment of religious minorities by Islam in Iran has fluctuated, and while nineteenth century problems resulted in part from strict views about ritual pollution, the Iranian-Islamic defensive reaction to incursions by clearly non-Muslim and increasingly threatening Westerners, was likewise significant.

The First Steps Toward Modernization

Modernization for Shirazi Jews has involved accommodation and resistance to both Iranian and non-Iranian ideas and values. Change has occurred in almost every aspect of Jewish life at an increasing tempo, as has been the case among Iranians generally.

The first impetus for change was the reestablishment of contact with the outside Jewish world in the late 1870s. While communications had never been totally severed, the influx of British and French consuls to Shiraz led to direct interest in Fars Jewry by European coreligionists. The Alliance Israélite Universelle set up a coeducational school in 1903, and its director became a kind of "consul" for Shirazi Jews.

Before the arrival of the Alliance, Jewish education in the *maktab* (school) was restricted to boys and was wholly of religious content. Few pupils attained functional literacy in Hebrew. The Alliance introduced French and Persian as well as other secular subjects into the curriculum. Elite Jews pushed their children (girls as well as boys) to Alliance schools, and thus secular education began to have prestige value for Jews even before the onset of the Pahlavi dynasty. The 1906–07 Constitution seems to have had no direct impact on Shirazi Jews, but it did set the stage for later participation in national politics, albeit in a limited way.

The Reza Shah period, beginning in 1925, signalled a major change in conditions and opportunities for Shirazi Jewry. The dress code was finally eliminated; employment restrictions were officially lifted; and residence restrictions were no longer applied. Public primary education was supported by government funds, and the authorities took the opportunity to supply civil teachers to the Ibn Sina school, which replaced the defunct Alliance system in Shiraz during the 1930s. The first Jews to live outside the Jewish quarter were a number of Jadid ol-Islam[31] from Mashhad who immigrated to Shiraz in the 1930s, and set up their own synagogue; they persisted in not identifying themselves openly as Jews until the late 1940s. By World War II only about 40 households were established outside the old Jewish quarter (less than 2 percent of the Jewish population). Political life continued along traditional lines, excepting the innovation of Jewish participation in electing a Jewish deputy to the Majlis.

Already primed by Alliance, Shirazi Jews were far better prepared for universal education than the Muslim urban masses. The new economic opportunities available through literacy were well appreciated. More than 80 percent of the young men remaining in Shiraz in 1968 who had grown up during the pre-World War II period, as well as 25 percent of the women, had obtained some secular education. Due to de facto hiring bias, some of the occupational opportunities failed to materialize until the late 1950s, but the motivation nevertheless persisted.

The Pahlavis, interested in economic development, provided lucrative investment opportunities. For generations Jewish real estate investment was restricted to the Jewish quarter, but when these restrictions were no longer enforced, Jews bought large tracts to the immediate north and west of the old city. Later, Shiraz's main thoroughfares were cut through these tracts, and this real property became extremely valuable. Other Jews, active in the export of gum tragacanth *(katira)*, bought up orchard tracts far from Shiraz to protect their supplies. Still others, who took village property as collateral on large personal loans, became absentee landlords upon default.

World War II had a great impact on Iranian Jewry as it did on Jewry throughout the world. The extent to which Reza Shah flirted with Nazi Germany has been a source of controversy among scholars, but according to informants, many of the local population made no effort to hide their support of Hitler and to intimidate local Jews. Emissaries from the *Yishuv* in Palestine made an effort to stimulate the Persian Jewish conscience by asking for their immigration as well as for financial support.

The Contemporary Period

In the years following World War II, the pace of change increased rapidly. Several factors were instrumental in these developments:

Mohammad Reza Shah

Without a doubt, the shah, in his struggle to find himself and to coerce Iran into becoming a modern country, was critical for Shirazi Jews. In a brief trip to Shiraz in October 1977, I learned that the basic positive Jewish assessment of the shah had undergone no substantial change in the previous ten years. He was still viewed as a benefactor of Jewish society. His maintenance of commercial and diplomatic relations with Israel and relative aloofness from the Arab-Israel conflict instilled a favorable disposition toward all of his policies. There was no hindering of emigration to Israel, though active Zionism was inhibited. More importantly, as official educational and economic bias declined, Jews swiftly moved to reap the benefits of development.

Post-Holocaust Jewry and the State of Israel

Jews throughout the world tended to refocus their attention in the post-World War II period on the immediate concerns of Jewish survival, physical and socioreligious. Every Jewish population that could be reached was given active attention by Jewish aid organizations for local development as well as immigration to Palestine.

Iranian Jewry was strengthened directly by organized Jewry through the introduction of three institutions:

Otsar Hatorah: a Polish Jewish war refugee, Rav Levi, reportedly disappointed by the poor quality of Jewish education throughout Iran, began a school in Tehran. After World War II, he was able to convince Otsar Hatorah, an American Orthodox Jewish education movement, to take responsibility for religious education throughout Iran. In Shiraz, schools were purchased and developed, which served about one-half of the Jewish school children. A teacher's Yeshiva was established and for a number of years provided religious teachers for Jewish schools throughout Iran. The impact of Otsar Hatorah on Jewish religious life, though largely indirect, has been marked, and lately has given impetus to new religious developments (see below).

American Joint Distribution Committee: provided major relief monies in the late 1940s and 1950s. Long before Shiraz as a whole enjoyed such services, the Jewish *mahalleh* had an effective sanitation program, a modern clinic, active preventive medicine and disease control, pre and postnatal supervision, and a feeding program for school children. A summer daycamp in cooperation with Otsar Hatorah was extremely popular. For many reasons, most of these programs were closed down or curtailed,[32] but their impact was significant.

The Jewish Agency: handled Shirazi emigration to Israel until 1979. Its programs in education were quite limited and operations generally small-scale; but over the years, perhaps 12,000 Shirazi Jews emigrated to Israel, which attests to the importance of the organization.

Leadership

The absence, for the most part, of charismatic leadership within the community, secular or religious, has had important consequences. Lack of secular leadership has allowed the community to be relatively unresponsive to government pressures for an active if limited local autonomy. In short, until recently the Jewish community had made little progress in directing its own development. Religious leadership, largely absent in modern times, was provided by a dedicated outsider during the late 1950s. He was responsible for encouraging Shiraz's first dynamic religious leadership in several generations, whose importance will be seen below.

Changes in the Contemporary Period

Emigration to Israel, coupled with new mobility, greatly decreased population density in the *mahalleh*. By 1967, fully half of Shirazi Jewry had relocated to the northwest quadrant of the new city, mostly close to the old Jewish quarter. By 1977, only one-fourth of the Jewish population still resided in the old *mahalleh*, and most of those had moved into improved housing. Few people were still living in the mud/straw housing that had been prevalent in 1968. Two hundred families moved to the Bagh-e Eram area, where a new synagogue and Yeshiva were being constructed in 1978. Since few Jews now live in the *mahalleh*, a new ritual bath has been constructed as part of the Jewish school complex in the new city.

While most of the traditional occupations continue to involve Shirazi Jews, fewer are entering them. Large numbers have become professionals, and even the shopkeepers found new forms of merchandising (Table 9).

There has been relatively little Jewish investment in industry, although there has been some effort to obtain sales franchises and to

Table 9. Jewish Occupations in Modernizing Shiraz

Old Occupations	New Occupations
peddler	teacher
goldsmith	engineer
silversmith	doctor
mason	dentist
musician	civil servant
dancer	banker
actor	landlord
moneylender	photographer
healer	shopkeeper
merchant	haberdasher
spinner	appliance seller
warpwinder	technician
fortuneteller	
prostitute	
liquor maker	
butcher	
prayer reader	

enter hostelering. The overall economic status of the community improved dramatically. On the one hand, large numbers of the destitute emigrated to Israel, while, on the other, relief efforts and education allowed others to give up poverty-bound occupations. By 1977, fewer than 80 families (2 to 3 percent) were receiving any kind of community or foreign relief. Certainly Shiraz's industrial boom was of great importance to this continuing economic improvement. In 1978, few Jews lived in the conditions of poverty that were widespread ten years earlier.

Despite modern banks, moneylending continued to be very important. Land speculation, rural and urban, provided some Jews with large sources of capital, which still tend to be "invested" in traditional ways.[33] But musicmaking, acting, liquormaking (except for private consumption), and warpwinding all but disappeared. The occupations that were favored served to integrate Jews economically into the national life, with fewer Jews servicing the needs of the Jewish community alone.

The many economic and political changes which culminated in intense technological development affected important attitudinal changes throughout Iranian society. The consequent social change for Iranian Jewry was substantial.

After generations of strenuous effort to maintain low visibility, thwarted by dress codes, residence and occupational restrictions, and religious stricture, Shirazi Jews achieved this long-sought goal.

Names have been disguised, and ethnic giveaways such as linguistic markers have been gradually eliminated through language standardization in the schools. While Jews tend to live close to one another, neighborhoods are mixed. The government, too, fostered minority rights with official support for equal opportunity at all but the highest governmental levels. However, this imposition of social equality from above met resistance from several directions in the society at large.

The ulama largely opposed the policies of the shah and, according to informants, many continue to use the epithet of "ritual pollutor" against Jews. Likewise, feeling a common pan-Islamic bond against Israel, some link local and world Jewry in their pronouncements on the Arab-Israel conflict. In times of crisis, as in the 1967 and 1973 wars, sermons have resulted in widescale boycotting of Jewish businesses. During the crisis periods of the religious calendar, Ramazan and Moharram especially, there is anything but good will expressed by some of the ulama, and this still affects the behavior of many believers at those times.

Informants describe a new "antisemitism," somewhat reminiscent of the genre which existed in the 1940s in the United States, by and large replacing the kind of Jewish-Muslim relations found in the traditional past. It was suggested that commercial jealousy may play some role in this evolving relationship.

Political opportunity was never a reality for Shirazi Jewry, so that voting for the Jewish deputy, who was invariably from Tehran, was given a good-natured nod but little active participation. The Anjoman central committee, established in the mid-1960s, was dominated by the "old-guard" elite and operated in the manner of the old *ene ha'eda*, i.e., avoiding all controversial decisions. In 1977, for the first time, there were open elections overturning the old elite. Cynics felt that changing the membership of the Anjoman would have no real impact on the substance of its activity. The "council of the pious" continued its existence, but with greatly reduced impact. In short, the above conditions, coupled with a continuing reluctance to deal with the authorities, resulted in relatively little internal political activity. Whether by their choice or otherwise, Jews are almost never active in the political affairs of non-Jews.

As alluded to in earlier research,[34] the process of national integration began in the 1960s with tentative contact between the elite (Jewish and non-Jewish) and later extended to the emerging middle class moving into new mixed neighborhoods. These contacts are greatest among the youth and include some young marrieds. Cross gender socializing has not become extensive, though informants report a noticeable difference since 1967. Among some of the elite, contacts with Muslims have an inverse relationship to the intensity of religious education and observance in the home.

In any case, from the Jews' perspective the fact that the larger society opened up, if only slightly, to permit social contact with non-Jews, was viewed as a very positive development. Unfortunately, it was still not clear in 1977 whether Jews' high status within their own community afforded them a like measure of respect outside, thereby implying a certain amalgamation of Jewish society into the greater whole.

The emerging middle class did extremely well economically despite inflation. Shirazi Jews report they did not suffer much from the meat shortages of 1976. Goldsmithing, which was dominated by Muslims in the late 1960s, saw Jews again manufacturing gold jewelry in 1977. Despite the competition from new stores of all kinds, Jewish merchants, who have now left the bazaars, were doing very well, partly due to the population boom and national prosperity.

New-Found prosperity and sophistication led to increasing rejection of foreign Jewish intervention. Prior to the revolution the operations of the Joint Distribution Committee were on the brink of closing down and largely in local hands. Otsar Hatorah gave up much of its control over Shirazi schools to local people. Joint's clinic was no longer important since most of the Jews lived far from it. Their day camp no longer operated. The school food program, while heavily subsidized, was given progressively greater support by parents who payed more than a token share of its cost. Jewish Agency operations were quiet, and no new organizations moved into Shiraz.

Educational opportunities allowed many Shirazis to go to other cities and to the United States for study. Military service and civil employment exposed a generation of Jews to life outside of Shiraz. The attractions of Tehran and elsewhere contributed to a demographic imbalance; the emigration of young men left an ever-growing surplus of marriageable females. Dowry prices to attract potential grooms soared, but there had been no noticeable increase of intermarriage such as has been reported in Tehran. While Persian literacy among the young approaches 100 percent and many go to the university, few seem possessed of any sophisticated awareness of the outside world. The momentous news events of the world and of Iran were not well understood by my Shirazi informants. Provincialism and ethnocentrism are still significant.

Traditional Shirazi Judaism

Shirazi Jews have long shared a sense of community and ethnic identity strongly reinforced by aspects of the Jewish Great Tradition. Sentiments of solidarity have grown over time, even as modernization has eroded some adherence to the ritual tradition.

Action/Activity System

Great Tradition Judaism places a heavy emphasis on practice as contrasted with Christianity, or even Islam.[35] The hundreds of commandments to be performed are classified as positive and negative. Men are expected to perfrom nearly all of both categories while women are freed from the responsibility of all but a few of the positive commandments. During the Qajar period, when Shirazi scholars were still issuing responsa, ritual observance was reportedly strict. Functional literacy in Hebrew was probably not high even during this period, but it dropped further after the emigration of leading scholars near the turn of the century. Many Jewish men, however, attended worship daily, reciting some prayers by rote and observing the Sabbath within the limits imposed by unfamiliarity with the law. The dietary laws were observed by all. The rules concerning the ritual purity of women were known and practiced strictly by everyone; women attended the ritual bath monthly as required. The calendrical rituals were by and large observed in accordance with Great Tradition requirements, though often with some local modification. Shirazis added a Little Tradition holiday, *Medak,* a kind of secondary Purim, commemorating the downfall of the apostate villain Abol Hasan Lari.[36] Critical rituals, e.g. circumcision, marriage, and death, were marked by elaborate procedures. Public gatherings occasioned blessings over the many kinds of foods, spices, and fruits and were often highlighted by creative sermonizing by the more learned. Some of the pious engaged in collecting and distributing charity while meeting the needs of the community for *maktab* education. Shirazi Jews instituted several local customs including a communitywide animal sacrifice *(kappara)* on each New Moon.

Temporal/Locational Structure

The central institution of Shirazi Judaism was the synagogue. There were at least a dozen scattered around the *mahalleh*. Many men went there to pray three times per day. Some men wound phylacteries in the morning, but these seem to have always been in short supply. All of the men had participant roles at some time or other leading worship, reciting blessings, purchasing ritual honors (or at least bidding for them), touching the Tora, and kissing the prayer shawl of the priests. Women came to hear the recitation of blessings and to see the Tora. Synagogue functionaries were hierarchically organized. Regular animal sacrifices took place in the courtyards.

A second Jewish institution was the ritual bath, though attendance there was not normally a social event.[37] The cemetery was the third important religious institution. During the year of mourning, kinsmen visited the cemetery monthly. There were no Jewish religious shrines in Shiraz or its vicinity, but some visited Serah bat Asher at Lenjan (near Isfahan) for the forty days preceding Yom Kippur, while others went to Hamadan, where the tomb of Esther and Mordecai is found. Some even traveled to Jewish holy sites in Iraq—a journey lasting several months. The hardy, taking over a year to return, went to Jerusalem, thereby attaining the status of *Hajji*.

Traditional Jewish schooling in the *maktab* used to begin for children at age four or five. Classes were held in a synagogue under the direction of a mulla, whose pedagogy relied heavily on rote memorization and the encouragement of a long stick. The curriculum consisted of prayer book, Tora, the prophetic portions read on Sabbaths in the synagogue, and for the astute, Mishna. By age nine or ten, most boys had completed their education, and began working as apprentices to their fathers or other close kinsman.

All of the critical rituals required extensive preparation and were communal "rites." But the Sabbath, above all, stood out as a most important consecration of time. It was a day of great familial interaction, a day whose events differed in almost every way from the workday week. Informants report strict observance of the Sabbath in conformity with Great Tradition. Friday evening and Sabbath morning were spent in synagogue. After breakfast the literate would usually study. On Sabbath afternoons, men used to gather in the synagogues to chant sections from the fourteenth century Judaeo-Persian poetic bible commentary of Shahin. In sum, the temporal element in Shirazi Judaism closely follows the Great Tradition.

Shirazi Judaism in the Contemporary Period

Action/Activity System

The changing economic and social circumstances in the contemporary period have had considerable impact on ritual observance among Shirazi Jews. Rituals most affected are those that are time-bound, especially the prohibitions (e.g. negative commandments). As more

Jews entered civil service and white collar professions, they found Iran's Saturday through Thursday workweek conflicted with the observance of the Sabbath and holidays. Children attending government schools could not be absent on Saturdays. Attendance at work or school frequently necessitated riding, writing, the use of money, and other acts forbidden on the Sabbath. Traditional Sabbath observance became circumscribed for perhaps a majority of Jewish men as well as some women. While the rest continue to observe Shabbat more or less as in the past, there are few households that are not torn between Sabbath observers and violators.[38] The violators for the most part evince considerable guilt and often complain over the circumstantial necessity to behave in this manner. They have made considerable efforts to observe positive Sabbath commandments, and the community has tried to accommodate them. All of the men, increasing numbers of women and a large proportion of teenagers of both sexes attend Friday night Sabbath worship, at which time sermons/study lessons are presented in some synagogues. Many males arise early on Saturday morning to attend an early quorum at many of the synagogues, beginning before 6 A.M., fulfilling the worship and Tora study commandments before leaving for work or school. One pious violator confided that he takes biblical study texts to work, avoids writing as far as possible, and leaves his phone off the hook for long periods in order to make the Sabbath a special day at work. The High Holidays are observed by nearly everyone, but the other festivals, Passover, Pentecost, and Tabernacles are dealt with like the Sabbath.

One important impact of the foreign based Otsar Hatorah schools has been to raise the general level of Hebrew and ritual knowledge among those born after 1950, while concomitantly raising the quality of observance of the Sabbath and *kashrut* (dietary law). Even that majority of young people who attend state schools have been strongly influenced in these areas by peers and by supplementary religious schooling, about which more will be said. Young females have a better understanding of Great Tradition dietary laws and special Passover taboos than did their mothers. There does not appear to be extensive violation of the dietary laws.

Whereas Sabbath and festival synagogue attendance have not slackened to an appreciable degree, attendance at weekday worship has dropped. Furthermore, a Shirazi Little Tradition has emerged in the contemporary period wherein daily prayer is recited only if there is a quorum. For the illiterate, communal prayer was always a necessity, but for others it could be described as merely highly meritorious. In modern Shiraz, it is rare to find an individual praying without a quorum—its lack precludes fixed prayer altogether.

Wedding ritual has been greatly curtailed—elaborate prenuptial ceremonies have been largely eliminated.[39] Henna application is rare, festivities at the bath curtailed, and so forth. Several changes have occurred in the wedding ceremony itself. A *tallit* (prayer shawl) is held over the bride and groom during the ceremony as a *huppa* (canopy), a custom possibly borrowed from European Jewry, probably via Israel. New is a postwedding drive to the spring of Saadi, a custom apparently borrowed from Muslim elites. Circumcision and funeral customs have changed little since the 1930s.

Temporal/Location Structure

The central institution of Shirazi Jewish life remains the synagogue. On weekdays only a few synagogues are in use. In 1968 four or five were open daily in the Jewish quarter and one outside. By 1977, only two were regularly open inside the Jewish quarter and two outside. In recent years there clearly have been fewer people attending daily worship than in the past, but there has been a considerable increase since 1968 of attendance by young people. Since the mass emigration of the 1950s, the number of synagogues/sanctuaries has remained about the same. As the old Jewish quarter population drops, attendance at synagogues in newer areas increases. By 1977, several synagogues were on the verge of closing, while a new one was under construction in Bagh-e Eram.

Jewish schools changed dramatically during the Pahlavi period. The *maktab* was replaced by the Alliance and government-run schools, with some Jewish content. After World War II, Otsar Hatorah schools catered to hundreds of boys and girls with both secular and religious courses. A Yeshiva was established in Shiraz in the late 1950s to train religious teachers and ritual slaughterers. Its successful operation was terminated by Otsar Hatorah in 1968, and part of its program shifted to the Otsar Hatorah high school. In 1977 a new Yeshiva, under private auspices, was being constructed.

The framework of all of the Otsar Hatorah schools was to provide both a measure of Judaic knowledge as well as an adequate secular education to Jewish school children. It is not clear whether Otsar Hatorah has been successful on either count, but its impact is unquestionable. The majority of Jewish children did not go to Jewish schools, and they suffered from vastly inferior Judaic skills. This handicapped them in a society whose primary public institution is the religious sanctuary. Efforts at remedial help through afterschool and summer classes were successful during the 1970s.

The only public ritual bath in the *mahalleh* in 1968 had fallen into serious disrepair by the mid-1970s. A large proportion of women, still scrupulous and meticulous in their observance of "family purity" laws, were using the ritual bath infrequently or not at all.[40] In 1977, Rabbi Y. Baal Hanes collected communal funds and constructed a new *miqve*, ritual bath, adjacent to the Kosar girls school. He hoped that modern facilities would encourage women to regularly use this ritually proper *miqve*.

Symbolic System

The symbols of Shirazi Judaism are, by and large, those of Great Tradition Judaism. Many of the symbols appear to have undergone no significant change over the years either in meaning or in frequency of use. Symbols of identity, e.g. the *mzuza* scroll found on the inside entrance doorpost of each house,[41] the observance of the dietary law, and the observance of the Sabbath as a distinctive day of rest survive intact. For some Jews, however, guilt over nonobservance due to secularizing/modernizing pressures may be more significant than the symbols themselves. Ignorance with respect to Great Tradition meaning of the symbols has abated, so that proper dietary rules for Passover, separation of meat and milk, and other ritual practices have taken on new importance. Little Traditions, e.g. *kappara* (animal sacrifice), special mourning practices, the 2 A.M. feast on Purim Night in one's wife's father's house commemorating Esther's feast for Haman and Ahaseuros, and the celebration of *Medak*, among other customs, are observed primarily by those in their forties and older.

New Little Traditions have been added, such as visiting the tomb of Saadi on the wedding night. Other Little Traditions, such as waiting outside the *hejle* (where consummation of the wedding is to take place) for the display of the bride's "token of virginity," are on the wane or have been totally discarded. Younger people under the impact of Israeli emmissaries and visits to Israel are inclined to stress the oriental Sfardic Great Tradition over local practices.

Some Great Tradition symbols never taken up in Shiraz, have still not caught on. The wearing of *pe'ot* (side curls) does not seem to have been common at any time for Shirazi Jewish males; no one follows this tradition in contemporary Shiraz. The covering of the head at all times, customarily observed by pious Jews throughout the world, has not been observed for at least several generations by Shirazis. Other

Great Tradition symbols have been newly integrated into Shirazi Judaism. Thus, the *huppa,* the marriage canopy, has become a common symbol at the contemporary wedding. Kabbalistic writings on synagogue walls and Sfardic prayer books have replaced older indigenous traditions.

In sum, while the basic symbols remain intact, new ones are being added and others discarded, some in the name of Jewish solidarity, others in keeping with the growing appreciation of "Western" values. The kinds and extent of change to the symbolic system in the modern period are far more important than changes in the past. Religious functionaries have been successful, so far, in limiting these changes and their consequences, but only one, who shall be discussed later, has attempted to organize and manipulate religious change and the mechanisms of symbolizing to attain specific socioreligious objectives.

Ideology

For Jews as well as Muslims, fatalism is a significant factor in shaping a world view. The Jewish worldview is further influenced by a pervading premise of communal and personal guilt, seen as the root cause of the harsh exile *(galut)* long experienced by Shirazi Jews. The sins that gave rise to this include: refusal to respond to Ezra the Scribe's command to return to Judaea in the fifth century B.C.E.; baseless interpersonal hatred *(sinat hinam)*; sexual immorality (real or imagined); and lack of honesty with one's fellow Jew. Shirazi Jews look towards Israel as a symbol of God's restoration of favor toward the Jewish people, but any optimism is tempered by the calamities suffered by the Jewish people the past forty years, reinforcing negative aspects of fatalism. Lack of desire to change one's life style, or emigrate—or ostensible inability to do so for social, economic, or medical reasons—are seen as arising from divine providence.

Jewish ethnic chauvinism, partially compensating for continued low social status, is a strong component of the modern Shirazi Jewish worldview. Judaism as a way of life is continually contrasted and compared with Iranian non-Jewish alternatives and is always found to be superior. Pride in continued Shirazi adherence to the ritual tradition is contrasted with the trend to secularism among other Iranian Jews.

Group identity, belief in and adherence to the commandments of the God of Israel, and the acceptance of messianic redemption, have been augmented in the contemporary period, if not actually supplanted, by Jewish political redemption symbolized by creation and success of Israel. Israel has become the source of renewed Shirazi spiritual vitality. Its leaders have become Shirazi Jewry's chief "culture heroes"; many have gone to Israel as tourists or on educational seminars. Israel's concerns and tribulations are second only to Shirazi's Jewry's own physical survival. From the onset of the Iranian political crisis in 1978, to the end of 1979, more than 30,000 Jews had left Iran temporarily or permanently; more than 75 percent went to Israel; many were Shirazis.

Charisma and Revitalization

Whereas there has been no dearth of lay religious leadership among Shirazi Jews over the past 75 years, the absence of an educated, ordained clergy has been sorely felt. Although Shirazi scholars were consulted from afar in the nineteenth century, in this century Shirazi Jews have referred all important questions of Jewish law to outside authorities. Whether the departure of the most important scholars at the turn of the century is sufficient cause for the absence of significant scholarship and spiritual leadership during the twentieth century is not clear, but the episodic founding of the Otsar Hatorah Yeshiva and the inspiration of its director, created the basis for pervasive religious revitalization of Shirazi Judaism. Doubtless, the Iranian government's decision to foster relations with Israel indirectly had a major impact on this development. Open travel between Iran and Israel allowed rabbinical emmissaries from Israel in the 1950s and 1960s to aid the Yeshiva program, providing new religious direction as well as bona fide scholarship.

As an adolescent in the 1950s, Yitshaq Baal Hanes was disturbed by the unavailability of adequate religious studies through the Otsar Hatorah school system. He campaigned to have Otsar Hatorah and the Joint Distribution Committee sponsor a boys' Yeshiva in Shiraz. A building was donated for Yeshiva use in a new Jewish residential area, dormitory and board were provided by Joint Distribution Committee funds, and Otsar Hatorah brought in emmissaries from Tehran and Israel to help provide the proper educational framework. Through relatively intensive study and the cameraderie of living together, high *esprit de corps* was developed and maintained. Eventually Baal Hanes succeeded to the directorship of the Yeshiva. He provided scholarly direction for the students, but more importantly, imbued them with a sense of purpose, a comprehension and appreciation for the need to reform Little Tradition practices, while making religious life more meaningful to young and old. Early Yeshiva graduates became teachers throughout the Otsar Hatorah/Alliance

320

Israélite Universelle schools of Iran, staffing all of the schools of Shiraz, but also those in Sanandaj, Yazd, Isfahan and Tehran. The Yeshiva was the only institution in Iran offering training in ritual slaughter and graduates of that program were in great demand throughout the country. The early graduates came under the influence of Natan-Eli, an Iranian scholar of Hamadani origin who was sent to coordinate the Yeshiva program in the early years. The later graduates, with few exceptions, developed a close relationship which evolved into a discipleship of Baal Hanes. The Yeshiva was phased out by Otsar Hatorah in 1968 and closed down the following year ostensibly for cost reasons, but possibly also due to its great success and popularity. There were too many graduates for the limited number of poorly paying teaching positions.

Baal Hanes became a teacher in the Otsar Hatorah high school, but together with former students continued developing a religious service program for the Shirazi community. Over the years, he gradually assumed the spiritual leadership as preacher and cantor of the city's most prestigious Rabizadeh synagogue. His disciples and friends provided supplementary afterschool Hebrew and Judaic study for those boys and girls not going to Otsar Hatorah schools. An intensive summer Hebrew study program was successfully promoted year after year. In the early 1970s, Baal Hanes finally persuaded Otsar Hatorah to sponsor his formal study for the rabbinate in Israel and he became the first orthodox ordained Rabbi in Iran in several generations.

Upon his return to Iran after nearly four years absence, he simply reentered his previous positions and performed the same roles. He was not invited to serve the community as *dayan* (judge), although it was obvious that he was the only qualified Shirazi for the position. It is conceivable that the traditional community leadership who respected him and even liked him were nevertheless afraid that he would emerge as too powerful a figure. Informants supplied no reason for this policy, but Baal Hanes evinced no resentment about this state of affairs when I asked him about it in 1977.

His disciples had, in the meantime, continued the education program in his absence, developing an enthusiastic group of several hundred young people, male and female, who participated weekly in the Sabbath worship. Ever increasing numbers of young men attend the morning worship at Baal Hanes' synagogue, and there were noticeable modifications in the Little Tradition in the several synagogues I visited. In 1977 he succeeded in raising funds for completing the renovation of a new ritual bath. A new synagogue going up in the Bagh-e Eram area was to house a new private

Yeshiva, about which young people interviewed were very enthusiastic, as were the members of the Council of the Pious.

His Friday night and Saturday afternoon preaching at Rabizadeh synagogue seems to have struck the proper balance of oratory, scholarship, and relevance to have made him an "attraction." Baal Hanes exudes no charismatic aura and his strength of character seems to arise primarily from his determination to strive to complete the task of providing spiritual leadership. His total command of the social-prestige system and flair for manipulating it for his purposes, have enhanced his overall success.

Conclusions

The impact of the changes wrought by Baal Hanes and his friends and disciples have radically transformed the religious picture of Shirazi Judaism. Secularism which had made some inroads in the 1960s was halted. The new religious emphasis is not a nativistic return to old practices, but a syncretism of traditional Shirazi Judaism with a neoorthodoxy modeled on trends discernible among oriental Jews in Israel. The thrust of reform is directed at the young, but is given moral support by major elements of the community. Shirazi Jewish life in the late 1970s is thus viewed optimistically as contrasted with Tehran and elsewhere. Shirazi Judaism was better informed, more literate, more creative, and better led than at any time since the turn of the century. How conditions in the Islamic Republic might change this assessment is difficult to predict.

IV. ASPECTS OF CULTURE

Figure 9. Taz'iyeh Performance near Isfahan, Festival of Popular Traditions, 1977

17

Language and Social Distinctions in Iran

Michael C. Hillmann

One of the most famous of all Persian short stories is Mohammad Ali Jamalzadeh's *"Farsi Shekar-ast"* [Persian Is (as Sweet as) Sugar] (1921), an anecdotal tale narrated by an apparently middleaged, worldwise Iranian just back from Europe who is inexplicably detained in a customs-house cell at the Caspian port of Enzeli.[1] There are two other persons in the cell with the narrator: a young Iranian male whose dress and manner make it obvious that he is returning from school in France; and a bearded, turbaned mulla. Suddenly, a fourth person is thrown into the cell, a young man called Ramazan, whose accent and dress mark him as a native of the Caspian province of Gilan.

Upset at the injustice of being jailed for no apparent reason, Ramazan rants and raves for some minutes. When he calms down, he turns to the mulla and begs for an explanation of their incarceration. The mulla replies at some length, beginning with *jazakum allah, mu'min,* "may God reward you, O believer," and *al-sabr miftah al-faraj,* "patience is the key to comfort," and, with the Arabic phrases and allusions punctuated occasionally by a Persian verb or noun, thoroughly confusing Ramazan, who understands nothing of what is said to him. Stunned by the mulla's reply and now desperate to fathom what is going on, Ramazan turns to the Frenchified Iranian student and says: "Sir . . . this sheikh is obviously a jinn and an epilectic who doesn't understand our language . . . he's an Arab . . . so, would *you* please tell me why they've thrown us into this tomb?" To this, the student warmly replies, his explanation full of terms such as *possibilité, despotisme,* and *décadence,* all of them equally incomprehensible to Ramazan, who thereupon cries out for help, begging

327

the guards as fellow Muslims to torture or to do whatever they wish to him, if only they will get him "out of the clutches of these madmen . . . who do not even understand human speech."

Naturally sympathetic to Ramazan's plight, the narrator now steps forward and begins talking to Ramazan who becomes almost ecstatic at hearing Persian that he can understand. In a paternal tone, the narrator explains to Ramazan that "these other two people are not mad or jinns; they're Iranians and fellow Muslims." Ramazan begins to laugh and begs the narrator, "Please, sir, don't put me on. If they're Iranians, why do they speak these languages that don't even slightly resemble human speech?" The narrator starts to tell Ramazan that the mulla and the student *were* speaking *Persian*; but he realizes that Ramazan would never believe him.

At this point the four cellmates are released. As they leave the customs house, guards are bringing in another person who, in a thick Azerbaijani accent with numerous Turkish words and phrases, is begging his captors to listen to him. Ramazan overhears the conversation and remarks to the narrator how amazing it is that on this particular day every imaginable lunatic is being sent to Enzeli. The narrator thinks better of explaining to Ramazan that the newcomer, obviously from Khoy or thereabouts, is just as much Iranian as anyone else, and that what he speaks is also Persian. The story draws to a close with the narrator, the mulla, and the student sharing a carriage to Rasht. Ramazan says goodbye to the narrator and marvels at his courage in his choice of traveling companions.[2]

Over a half-century later, the cast of characters in "Persian Is Sugar" is still very much a part of the Iranian scene, with the Iranian educated in the United Kingdom or North America the most important indigenous addition to it. And these characters and their interaction serve well to identify significant aspects of the subject of language and social distinctions in Iran or, in other words, significant facts about Iranian society that are indicated by the language Iranians speak, how they speak it, and the sorts of terms that are peculiar to it. The purpose of this essay is to illustrate how fruitful sociolinguistic research into Persian can prove in offering either insights into Iranian culture and society or evidence corroborating insights derived from other disciplinary *foci*.

What "Persian Is Sugar" first provides is a sort of *caveat* to any generalization that one might make about Iranians. In other words, the characters in the story seem not to have much in common but their plight; whereas, in American academic, government, and business views of Iran, the assumption that there is an Iranian national character or that Iranians as a group exhibit significant shared traits is common.[3] For example, anyone even casually acquainted with Iran has surely heard, or has the impression, that Iranians are individualistic as opposed to team-oriented; shrewd and opportunistic as opposed to straightforward; pessimistic and fatalistic as opposed to optimistic and confident; lazy and emotional as opposed to industrious and rational; and indecisive as opposed to decisive.[4] Interestingly, such characterizations often seem basically negative stereotypes, with only lipservice to alleged Iranian "hospitality," "friendship," and family closeness balancing the picture. The story "Persian Is Sugar" seems, first of all, to suggest that generalizations about characteristics and traits of Iranian are likely to be false.

As an introduction to the subject of language and social distinctions in Iran, "Persian Is Sugar" draws attention to at least six aspects of the question. First, there are the social distinctions related to whether one's mother tongue is Persian, Azerbaijani Turkish, Kurdish, Gilaki, Armenian, Arabic, or another language. Second, there is the issue of the relative prestige of the particular Persian dialect spoken, for example, Tehran, Isfahan, Shiraz, Mashhad, Kerman, and Hamadan. Third, there is the distinctiveness of the Persian spoken by native speakers of other languages in Iran such as Turkish or Armenian. Fourth, there is the issue of formal education distinguishing the Persian of the villager from the Persian of the bazaar merchant, the government clerk, and the university graduate. Fifth, there is the significance of exposure to languages spoken beyond Iran's borders, e.g., Arabic, English, French, and German. Sixth, there are the interrelated issues of levels of politeness, formality, and familiarity which are communicated differently through different dialects and styles of Persian. All of these factors are at play even in as simple a tale as "Persian Is Sugar," in which the narrator, who knows Arabic and French, and speaks Modern Standard Persian with appropriate politeness and graciousness, is the *one* character who can without difficulty deal linguistically with any situation.

In view of this, among facts about language and social distinctions in Iran which "Persian Is Sugar" suggests are: (1) that the Persian language *(farsi)* and Persian *(fars)* Iranian culture (as opposed to Turkish Iranian culture, for example) are dominant in Iran; and upward mobility is almost nonexistent for individuals unable to deal in the Persian Iranian cultural context with the Persian language; (2) that Persian spoken by the educated people of Tehran is Modern Standard Persian, i.e., the standard dialect in relation to which other dialects of Persian sound more or less provincial; whether it is one's dialect or not, one has to be able to adjust to or use it in order to make use of radio, television, the press, and of Tehran, the center of nearly everything in Iran; (3) that, insofar as sophistication in speaking the Tehran dialect of Persian depends in part upon and increases with amount of exposure to formal education, functional literacy in Persian in indicative in one's speech of social status; and (4) that the world beyond Iran's borders is naturally open only to Iranians who can operate linguistically in it, which mean through English—since that world, as it were, invaded Iran in general during the sixties and seventies. In places such as Tehran and Isfahan in particular, an Iranian's status, upward mobility, and power within Iran can depend in part on being comfortable with English texts and speakers. In short, the narrator of "Persian Is Sugar," at least relative to the persons interacting with him in the story and presumably in other situations, is a member of that enviable minority of Iranians whose speech reveals them as: male, middleaged, urban(e), prosperous, Muslim, literate in Persian, Arabic, and English (French at that time), conversant in English (at that time French), and educated speakers of Modern Standard Persian. In other words, sex; age; religious orientation; geographical, ethnic, and family origins; level of education; wealth; occupation; ability to speak a foreign language such as English; and an ability to speak a language of an Iranian minority are all important factors that are reflected in one's speech and that reflect significant social distinctions.

Without underestimating the significance of these factors or of languages other than Persian spoken in Iran and aspects of social distinctions within those non-Persian linguistic contexts, this brief essay focuses exclusively on the Tehran dialect of Persian, that is, Modern Standard Persian, in its consideration of language and social distinctions in Iran.

Reference to Modern Standard Persian does not imply a single way or style of communication either in speaking or writing. For, Persian features two distinct levels or styles: *ketabi* (literary) and *mohavereh'i* (colloquial or conversational). Ability to use the literary style of standard Persian presupposes exposure to formal education, reading, and the middle and upper class activities where it is used. Literary Persian is thought of as "correct," "proper," and "formal," and its use leads to an impression of education, cultivation, sophistication, or status—although everyday conversation even among the most literate Persian Iranians is generally carried out in colloquial Persian—and colloquial Persian has for several decades now been a literary vehicle in hundreds of contexts.[5] In any case, it is within the spectrum of literary and colloquial Persian that perhaps the most obvious set of variations in Modern Standard Persian involving social distinctions is revealed, the terms *basavad* "literate," and *bisavad*, "illiterate" emphatically used to describe an impression relating to sophistication in speech among speakers, all of whom may be in a literal sense, literate. Sophistication in Persian speech is also communicated through aspects of diction that have little to do with the literary-colloquial spectrum, one of which is linguistic borrowing, a superficially complicated and revealing feature of Modern Standard Persian. Hardly an aspect of Modern Standard Persian has been immune to significant linguistic borrowing. It is observed in Persian grammar, phonology, style, and particularly vocabulary, where from Arabic, French, and English there are thousands upon thousands of loanwords, loanblends, loanshifts, loanshift extensions, and loanshift creations. Prestige, foreign education, translations, and necessity have been cited as causes or reasons for the borrowing, the term necessity, in this context, referring to the need for or a lack of certain cultural phenomena, objects, ideas, or social and political institutions that stimulates the borrowing.[6]

The most obvious and pervasive linguistic borrowing in Persian has been from Arabic, with more than 60 percent of the vocabulary in Modern Standard Persian of Arabic origin. One result of this is to highlight the prevailing Islamic tone of life in Iran, where significant minorities of Armenians, Assyrians, Baha'is, Jews, and Zoroastrians have always had to participate linguistically in a Shi'i Muslim cultural context; the significance of which seems to have been underestimated in Iran and abroad for years, even before the dramatic reminders provided by the civil strife and clamor for political reforms in accord with Shi'i principles throughout 1978, and the subsequent establishment of the Islamic Republic of Iran. The amount of Arabic in Persian *vis-à-vis* the more recent linguistic borrowing from French and English is one aspect of the conflict of past and present, religion and secularization, and tradition and modernization continuing in Iran: the Arabic of the past *versus* the English of the future, as it were, with the Persian core modulating the conflict. At the extremes there are pejorative terms such as *mota'asseb*, "fanatic, usually with respect to religious attitudes," and *gharbzadeh* 'Weststruck' or 'Westoxicated,' i.e., referring to someone whose ideas, ideals, and lifestyle, often including manner of speech, are imitative of the West." In this religious and cultural context, the calls for linguistic reforms in Iran during the past half-century, such as reduction of the number of loanwords in Persian or the introduction of the Latin alphabet, have obvious

331

religious and political implications and identify the views of their proponents toward modernization, secularization, Westernization, nationalism, traditional values, and the like.

But the nature and extent of linguistic borrowing, as significant as it is, do not seem to offer as much insight into the essence of distinctively Iranian social distinctions as other, broader aspects of stylistic variation.

Stylistic variation in Persian, in linguistic terms, involves morpheme alternants, phonetic variants, morpheme substitutions and variations in vocabulary and syntax. For example, in the context of differences between literary and colloquial Persian there are morpheme alternants, such as the colloquial *miram*, "I go/am going," *vis-à-vis* the literary *miravam* (the colloquial Persian present verb stems of a dozen or more very common simple, i.e., one-word verbs, show a sound reduction in comparison to literary stems); an example of a phonetic variant is *Tehrun* in colloquial *vis-à-vis Tehran* in literary Persian (the /ā/ of the latter often changing to /u/ in the former when followed by /n/ or /m/); as for morpheme substitutions, *ferestadan*, "to send," is a most common verb in colloquial and literary Persian; but *ersal dashtan* is a specifically literary synonym. As for syntax, word order often varies in colloquial as compared to literary Persian; e.g., the colloquial Persian sentence *miram Tehrun*, "I'm going to Tehran," appears in literary Persian as *be-Tehran miravam*, (prepositions often omitted in colloquial Persian in unambiguous contexts are regularly used in literary Persian, and the colloquial Persian option of placing the goal or indirect object after verbs of direction is not available in literary Persian where the normal sentence word order of subject, object, and verb is adhered to).

But, again, it is not in the context of literary and colloquial Persian usages, as significant a feature of Persian as they constitute (insofar as inability to deal with spoken literary Persian is as limiting as being unable to deal with the written word) that distinctively Iranian social distinctions are apparent.

These distinctions arise in the area of so-called "politeness levels," as termed by Carleton Hodge in "Some Aspects of Persian Style" (1957), the first linguistic attempt at systematic analysis of stylistic variation in Modern Standard Persian.[7] The simplest instance of the "politeness levels" occurs in second person pronouns and deferential substitutes for "you," i.e., *to* "familiar you, used in addressing children, servants, intimate friends and family members, and God, and in insulting people"; *shoma*, "polite singular you, also plural, although when ambiguity might occur *shomaha*, /ha/ being the commonest

332

plural marker in Persian, is used," *jenab-e 'ali,* "*deferential* singular you, used more often by and to males, with *sarkar* more often used for females," and *a'la hazrat* "*royal* you,: masculine elative of *hazrat-e'ali,* often a synonym for *jenab-e 'ali,* with *'oliya hazrat* the feminine form used exclusively for and to the monarch's wife." According to Hodge, the uses of *familiar, polite, deferential,* and *royal* forms identify the strata of Iranian society, there being:

> stratification of society with regard to the usage of the politeness levels. One stratum consists of professional people—doctors, lawyers, engineers, professors, specialists (such as economists), teachers, military men of the ranks from captain to colonel. These use *polite* speech to each other and to the next stratum down (the business men), but *deferential* speech to the next stratum up (such as government officials on higher levels). The business stratum— owners of firms such as stores, factores, plantations, landlords, real estate people—use *deferential* speech to each other and to the professional stratum, but *polite* speech to the bazaar (tradesman) stratum, which is the next one down. The bazaar stratum includes both merchants of considerable holdings, with offices in the bazaar, and the bazaar shopkeepers and artisans. These use *polite* speech to one of their own group older than themselves, *familiar* speech to an equal or to someone of the lowest stratum, and of course *deferential* speech to the strata above them. The lowest stratum includes the peddlars, the newspaper vendors, and, at the very bottom, the porters. These use *familiar* speech to each other and, when their education is adequate, *deferential* speech to the strata above.[8]

Although this description is oversimplified in categorization and elimination of shadings, it is nevertheless instructive in providing a feel for the very palpable social distinctions that the sorts of stylistic variations associated with politeness levels reveal about interaction participants speaking Modern Standard Persian.

In any case, the question here is whether or not the so-called politeness levels actually indicate such social stratification, there being no question but that such stratification in Iranian society exists; and Hodge is not alone in assuming that they do. For example, Donald Wilber in "Language and Society: The Case of Iran" (1967) talks about "the formal courtesy which pervades speech" in Persian and argues that "degrees of formal courtesy and behavior identify the fixed rank of the individual in Persian society."[9]

It can be argued that the use of politeness levels does intimate something of the rank or stature of the person speaking. Insofar as the use of politeness levels involves linguistic sophistication, including the ability to manipulate a varied and studied diction, some of it relating to literary Persian, that style which comes usually from formal education or extensive reading. But, without asking right here

333

if individuals really have "fixed" rank in Iranian society, there is another way of looking at politeness levels that seems to demonstrate that the person manipulating their linguistic signals, and the persons so addressed or referred to, are not thereby automatically identified in terms of fixed social rank or position. And that is the fact that two or more Persian Iranians in an interaction situation who are of the same sex, age, background, economic and social class, and position may employ the different politeness levels among themselves; in so doing, they can hardly be indicating social stratification or hierarchy among themselves that is relevant to facts beyond the immediate interaction situation.

What the meaning of such interaction situations is has been considered by William Beeman in two articles: "Status, Style and Strategy in Iranian Interaction" and "The Hows and Whys of Persian Style: A Pragmatic Approach" (1976).[10] Assuming that "in any interaction, status of participants can be non-equal or equal, with these two status dimensions . . . intersecting with dimensions of intimacy and nonintimacy," Beeman sees interaction as a four-cell pattern "which is reflected in both linguistic and nonlinguistic behavioral variation": (1) unequal, nonintimate relative status, (2) equal, nonintimate relative status, (3) unequal, intimate relative status, and (4) equal, intimate relative status. Beeman focuses attention on the first and fourth so-called cells. In the latter regard, he argues that equal, intimate relative status encourages interaction partners to be free as opposed to restricted expression, to use the forms of the so-called "familiar" politeness level, and to exhibit stylistic variations such as deletion of /h/ and /'/ in all but word-initial position, neutralization of /r/ in wordfinal position, and deletion of certain final elements within consonant clusters.[11] Hodge, by the way, in his discussion of *ketabi,* (literary) and *mohavereh'i,* (colloquial or conversational) Persian styles, discerns two substyles within colloquial Persian: deliberate and casual.[12]

One reservation comes to mind concerning the specific instances of sound reduction that Beeman discusses. An illiterate Persian Iranian conversing with a Persian Iranian physician might illustrate the three specific sorts of sound reduction because he or she might know only that conversational style. Yet, the interaction situation would involve unequal, nonintimate relative status; further, the physician might reply in kind to make his or her patient feel comfortable. This does not mean that two persons of equal, intimate relative status might not use "casual," colloquial Persian forms; it just means that their use does not necessarily reveal their relative status.

334

As for Beeman's analysis of unequal, nonintimate relative status situations, it is, in one sense, a rebuttal of the view of Hodge and Wilber that politeness levels intimate or have reference to fixed rank or stratification of individuals in society. For Beeman argues that in Iran "status is relative for individuals in different interaction situations . . . and as a result of this relativity rights and obligations shift constantly with changes in one's social environment."[13] Specifically, according to Beeman, terms referring to politeness levels are often a strategy in interaction whereby one person, even with nonintimate, equal status to another, attempts "to move to a status-unequal relationship to get on with business," two typical ploys being (1) "to aim for a lower relative status position and defer to another person"; and (2) to redirect an "offer in hopes that it will eventually devolve on oneself." In such interaction situations, the person "cast in higher status position" becomes obligated to "grant favors, give presents, or gratuities, [and] practice *noblesse oblige*," while the person who has achieved lower relative status concomitantly relieves him or herself of such responsibilities and can await the magnanimity of the other party.[14]

Again, a reservation. The sorts of Persian stylistic variation employed in situations such as the ones which Beeman describes are largely lexical substitutions that may merely communicate to interaction partners a recognition of equal relative status and a desire to maintain nonintimate status. Or a general might use such terms to a shopkeeper, for example, merely as an indication of good manners and good will; and in the expression of deference, the general actually reminds the person so addressed of his obvious superiority. Or, for example, common polite, deferential substitutes such as *lotf kardan*, *marhamat kardan*, and *mohabat kardan* for *dadan*, "to give"; *farmudan* for *goftan*, "to say"; *tashrif bordan* for *raftan*, "to go"; *tashrif avordan* for *amadan* "to come," and *tashrif dashtan* for *budan*, "to be present," of themselves do not imply lower relative status for the person who uses them. The reservation could be put another way. Beeman's argument seems speculative. He observes a situation and evaluates it, choosing one of the real possibilities; but although the language shows a capacity for x, y, or z to happen, it will be nonlinguistic aspects of the interaction situation that will usually tell an observer that x, rather than something else, is going on.

There is a specific and much discussed Persian term with which all of the linguistic and nonlinguistic behavior relating to politeness levels is described. In fact, it is the term that Hodge is freely translating when he uses the term "politeness levels." The word is *ta'arof*, which

Wilber calls "formal courtesy" and which Beeman defines as "the active, ritualized realization of differential status in interaction." Solaiman Ha'im in *The One-Volume Persian-English Dictionary* (1969) defines it as: "compliment(s), ceremony, offer"; and he gives as the denotations of the verb *ta'arof kardan:* "to offer, to stand upon ceremony, to make a present of." In the Aryanpurs' *The Concise Persian English Dictionary* (1976) *ta'arof* is defined as "compliment, offer, gift, formality, good manners, honeyed phrases, respect"; and the verb *ta'arof kardan* is defined as "to use compliment, to stand upon ceremony, to make present of, to speak courtesy." In Mohammad Mo'in's monolingual *An Intermediate Persian Dictionary* (1963–1973), *ta'arof* appears with four meanings: (1) *yekdigar-ra shenakhtan,* "to know one another," (2) *khoshamad goftan be yekdigar,* "to greet/welcome one another," (3) *pishkesh dadan,* "to offer a present," and (4) *ezhar-e ashna'i,* "expression of acquaintance/familiarity."[15]

In conversation, when the term *ta'arof* appears as the nonverbal element of the compound verb *ta'arof kardan,* "literally: to make/do *ta'arof,*" two different meanings are ordinarily communicated: (1) in a sentence such as *azizam, chera chizi be-ishun ta'arof nemikonid,* "my dear, why don't you offer him/her something," which a host/hostess might address to his/her spouse, the sense of the term is the physical offering through words and/or proferring of something to someone; and (2) in a statement such as *Aqa-ye Kermani, khahesh mikonam, sham bemunid, ta'arof nemikonam,* "Mr. Kermani, please stay for dinner, I'm not *ta'arof*ing," which a host might make to a guest who has arrived shortly before the dinner hour, the *sense of the term* is a verbal offer one neither literally means nor expects to be accepted; and, of course, *the sense of the utterance* is that the speaker sincerely wants the guest to stay. In this sense of the term *ta'arof,* there is an adjective *ta'arofi,* used in statements such as *Aqa-ye Shirazi khayli ta'arofi-yeh,* "Mr. Shirazi is very *ta'arof*ish," which is to say that he is always making verbal offers or accepts an invitation only after much polite and deferential conversation. Also in this sense the noun *ta'arof* is used in expressions such as *man ahl-e ta'arof nistam,* "I'm not a devotee of *ta'arof.*"

The definitions and examples of *ta'arof* given here merely scratch the surface of the linguistic and nonlinguistic dimensions of the behavioral system that *ta'arof* constitutes. But they provide sufficient evidence to question two popular views of the system prior to a presentation of the view to which this discussion is leading. The first view, which has its most recent exposition in an article by M. C. Bateson, J. W. Clinton, J. B. M. Kassarjian, H. Safavi, and M. Soraya called *"Safa-ye Baten:* A Study of the Interrelations of a Set of Iranian

Ideal Character Types" (1977), views *ta'arof* as, in part, a symptom or manifestation of a "constellation of negative traits" observed in Iranian behavior by Iranians and "foreign commentators" alike, resulting in an image whose "central element may be recognized as a hidden purpose, a discontinuity between behavior and intention."[16] In contrast with these traits and the image they evoke is the quality of *safa-ye baten*, which is "a certain integrity and simplicity of action and motivation . . . inner purity . . . sincerity." This virtue of *safa-ye baten*, according to Bateson *et al.*, is exemplified in *lutigari*, "tough, manly chivalry," and *darvishi* "spirituality and detachment from material things." The *luti* and the *darvish* are presented as ideal Iranian personality types that share a "common contrast with the image of the constantly calculating, maneuvering individual"; they embody "a lack of hypocrisy, a consistency between feeling and behavior, and a lack of ambivalence." More important in the present discussion is the assertion by Bateson *et al.*, that "*darvishi* and *lutigari* have special relationships to the courtesy system *(ta'arof* = 'expressed courtesy')*. Ta'arof* is used literally by the *luti* and scorned by the *darvish*," who, "courteous to all, avoids *ta'arof*."[17] To be sure, Bateson *et al.*, unlike many naive Western observers, admit that aspects of *ta'arof* are "sincere"; nevertheless, their description of *lutigari* and *darvishi* implies that the *ta'arof* system is something that real or imagined ideal Iranian personality types either would not use or would use in a way far different from its actual use, with even less noble actual Iranians wishing that they could somehow break themselves of the *ta'arof* habit (younger, Western-educated Iranians often express strong criticism of the *ta'arof* system, especially to Westerners). The facts seem to suggest that even the *luti* and *darvish* use *ta'arof*. Bateson *et al.*, seem to be mistaken in asserting that the *darvish* "courteous to all, avoids *ta'arof*," which seems to be a contradiction in terms. The facts also suggest that the *ta'arof* system might atrophy in both linguistic and social senses did it not constitute an efficient means by which customary sorts of interaction might be carried out in the best interests of all participants.

The second view of the *ta'arof* system as represented by Beeman sees it as a linguistic reflection of differential status in Iranian society at large and as a strategy for establishing differential status in specific interaction situations so that interaction can be productive and efficient. Surely this is the case in some interaction situations; but many features of the *ta'arof* system, among them greetings, leavetakings, the predictable verbal behavior of hosts and guests, and various other situations in casual conversation seem not to involve relative status issues except insofar as the ability to use *ta'arof* expressions adeptly, as suggested earlier, may itself imply a certain status resulting from presumed background, education, and manners. And there is no denying that many Iranians on some occasions employ *ta'arof* expressions out of a sincere desire to be "cordial, warm, hospitable, respectful, and mindful of others."[18]

What is needed is a view of the *ta'arof* system that avoids any a priori or hypothetical characterization of Iranian character and that accounts for both the strategic use of *ta'arof* as Beeman sees it and those other manifold instances of it that do not readily fit that pattern.

Perhaps the most obvious fact of social and political life in Iran is that Iranians in public generally have to be ready to behave as subjects *vis-à-vis* the head of state and his representatives and institutions. Yet, frank views about this fact have traditionally not been presented in public, even though naturally the whole question has seemed, at least during the 1953–77 Mohammad Reza Pahlavi period, an almost obsessive concern on the part of many educated urban Iranians, of which their much discussed pessimism, cynicism, and distrust seems to be symptomatic.[19] Although the events of 1978–79 seem to have indicated the beginnings of perhaps a new process in contemporary Iranian political life, much of what happened, even where open participation of the Iranian people occurred, seems to fit the traditional pattern. On the one hand, when the monarch wished to demonstrate that things were under control during the second week of November 1978 the foreign press was invited to observe not the streets of Tehran but a reception at which all the participating Iranian officials were given the opportunity to bow and otherwise demonstrate the proper behavior of subjects *vis-à-vis* the monarch—a demonstration that the monarch apparently assumed was a sign of his control over things. On the other hand, in the streets, the popular demonstrations against the shah did not involve the clamor for a new role for the people in political life as individual Iranians, but rather the destruction of images of the monarch along with cries for his death and the substitution of a new image, that of Ayatollah Ruhollah Khomaini, toward whom demonstrating masses seemed and still seem prepared to behave as subjects *vis-à-vis* a leader with near absolute powers.

In any case, the system of *ta'arof* seems central to the participation by Iranians in, and their feelings about, the traditional political system in Iran. On the one hand, as Wilber says,

> . . . the proper formulas [of *ta'arof*] serve to protect the individual from the corrosive demands of the world; they serve to isolate him from direct involvement in the affairs of others. They serve to preserve his identity.

In being well mannered and in deliberately refraining from causing trouble to others, he wins respect, regardless of his social position.[20]

Beyond the privacy of one's intimate family circle and home, many Iranians, at least during the 1953–77 period, seem to have much appreciated this affirmation of a sense of self-respect, even if it has often been a ritual performance, because in public situations on Pahlavi Street, at Pahlavi Square, at Pahlavi Club, in Pahlavi Hospital, at Bandar Pahlavi, at Pahlavi University, at Pahlavi Foundation, at Pahlavi Dezh there seems to have been a constant, subconscious, gnawing sense of lack of individual self-esteem. And the bowing has been real and obligatory; the headline in *The Iran Times* on January 12, 1979, published immediately after the formalization of the short-lived civilian government headed by Shahpour Bakhtiyar, read: "New Cabinet Doesn't Bow to Shah," an indication of how much political meaning is attached to the use or failure to use aspects of the *ta'arof* system in its representation of expected ruler-subject relations.

This ruler-subject dimension of *ta'arof* and the ruler-subject relationships behind it seem to be enacted throughout Iranian society—family elder, father, husband, landowner, landlord, professor, manager, general, and the like—everyone verbally falling into the pattern in *ta'arof*, with each individual given more or less frequent opportunities to play the role of the ruler. Of course, it is neither theater nor a game, because Iranians interacting with *ta'arof* expressions and gestures have often been playing out the reality of their situations.

The *ta'arof* terms used to refer to oneself in conversation seem also to reflect an appreciation of the reality of ruler-subject relations, terms such as *bandeh*, "slave," a substitute for *man*, "I, me"; *qorban-e shoma* "(may I be) your sacrifice" for *mersi*, "thank you," among other things; *pishkesh*, "the statement made in response to favorable comments about a personal possession, i.e., 'here, take it, it's yours' "; *ested'a mikonam* and *tamanna mikonam*, "I beg, implore" in place of *lotfan* or *khahesh mikonam*, "please"; *eta'at misheh*, "it will be obeyed," in place of *basheh*, "okay, so be it"; and *'arz mikonam* "I petition," in place of *migam* "I say." These are a few among hundreds of expressions that foreign learners of Persian often find "insincere." But, literally, when would one "petition" instead of "talk," automatically proffer one's possessions in response to a favorable comment, and "beg" instead of "request?" In the presence of absolute authority, which it is being suggested here Iranians are always psychologically mindful of.

The politics of the situation has been, very simply, survival. And the capriciousness of politics in Iran has been such that one has had to be able to play both roles in the ruler-subject spectrum that the *ta'arof* reflects and provides the verbiage for. At the same time, in anticipation of unforseen future twists of fate or turns of the wheel of fortune, one can at least verbally protect oneself by behaving always, as suggested above, as if one's interaction partner(s) might someday wield the utmost power. This obviously makes this aspect or function of the *ta'arof* system as "insincere" or "excessive" or "decorative" as endowment-65 life insurance policies. At the same time, if the view represented here is correct, it implies that aspects of *ta'arof*, that is, the particular expressions and gestures that pertain specifically to the interaction roles of ruler-subject relations, should fall into disuse if the nature of the political system in Iran and the attitudes of Iranians toward it change radically. This does not mean simply the dissolution of the monarchy because in early 1979, after the departure of the shah, many Iranians began treating Ayatollah Khomaini and his representatives in the same manner as the monarch and his representatives had been treated, with the special title Imam serving as the equivalent for the royal politeness level expression *a'lahazrat*. [21]

The most expressive aspect of Modern Standard Persian in terms of social distinctions seems to be the *ta'arof* system, which seems to reveal basic facts about classes and relationships in Iranian society, one of which has to do with ruler-subject relations. Of course, during the 1953–79 years, there was only one person in Iran whose status was immediately perceived through the use of *ta'arof* expressions; ironically, he was the one person who never used them. Perhaps his inability to use them or unwillingness to participate in an environment where they would either no longer be used or not exclusively used with him were subconscious, psychological considerations in his decision to leave Iran without ceremony in January 1979. Ultimately, he must have realized that he was neither *shahanshah* nor *a'lahazrat*. It remains to be seen whether or not Ayatollah Khomaini and his followers realize that he is not an Imam.

18

Cinema as a Political Instrument

Hamid Naficy

Feature film in Iran, rather than exploring the principal indigenous social, ethical, and psychological developments, has mainly been used by Iran's rulers both to impose a false "modern" image of Iran and to manipulate Iranians into believing in the desireability and inevitability of modernization along Western lines. These policies suited the world view and aspirations of many educated Iranians in the first half of this century, who perhaps with reason, felt many aspects of Iranian traditional life to be inferior to the progressive aspects of Western ways of life.

Infatuation with the West soon led to the imitation and assimilation of its cultural products. The growth and development of the Iranian film industry serves as a prime example. The government of Iran, with foreign support, embarked under the Pahlavis on the Westernization of Iran, using film and television as major purveyors of this policy. This arrangement suited the aims both of foreign interests and the Iranian regime. Foreign interests, especially American, could thus pave the way for the creation of a captive consumer market in Iran, including the motion picture and television program market; the Iranian government received in return a handsomely packaged, pre-produced, persuasive modern image for Iranian audiences to emulate.

This essay will give a brief history of feature film in Iran, and then focus on the particular themes presented by Iranian films since their inception. The last section analyzes briefly the relationship of these elements to the evolving social and political fabric of Iran.

Brief History of Cinema

The development of feature films in Iran can be divided into five periods.[1]

The Beginnings (1900–26)

The birth of cinema in Iran is attributed to the fascination of Mozaffar od-Din Shah Qajar (1896–1907) who while in Paris in 1900 saw newsreels for the first time, and subsequently noted in his diary: "We ordered our photographer to purchase all kinds [of cinematographic equipment] and bring them to Tehran so that, God willing, we could make and show films to our servants."[2] The real impetus for the early development of cinema, however, was supplied by a few enterprising individuals who had learned their trade in Western countries, primarily Russia and France. These were Mirza Ebrahim Khan Akasbashi and Mehdi Rusi Khan (who filmed royal ceremonies), Ebrahim Khan Sahhafbashi (who opened the first cinema in Iran in 1905) and Khan Baba Motazedi (who produced some entertainment films as well as newsreels).[3]

These filmmakers had to make do with inadequate equipment, facilities, technicians, and talent. In addition, social conditions were not conducive to the growth of cinema. Iran was economically and socially backward. The majority was illiterate. The religious establishment was against movies and women could not attend cinemas. Because of these adverse conditions, there was no local production to speak of. Most films shown were newsreels or comedy and adventure films from Europe, Russia and the U.S. From the beginning, local film production became the domain of royalty and the upper classes and was often limited to newsreels about royal activities.

Early Feature Films (1930–37)

During the early Pahlavi period, technical problems persisted. The government did not support feature films, and private investment in film was meager. Social conditions continued to militate against the development of a film industry, and the unchecked inflow of foreign films and the difficulties and expenses accompanying the advent of sound brought about a situation in which local producers could not compete.

Attempts were made to establish film training schools. A Russian Armenian, Avans Ohanian (Oganians), made the first Iranian feature film, based on a Danish comedy, called *Abi and Rabi* (1930). Ohanian's second film, *Hajji Aqa, the Movie Actor* (1932), for the first time presented the dichotomy between traditional religious attitudes and the more modern ones current among the upper classes. Ebrahim Moradi directed *The Capricious Lover* (1934), in which the themes of capriciousness of the wealthy, the lure of modern cities, and their corrupting influence on the villagers were illustrated.

Amid such beginnings, Abdol Hosain Sepanta, a creative Iranian poet living in India, injected a short-lived ray of light. Unburdened by the difficulties which beset his colleagues in Iran, he produced the first Persian language sound film, a musical love story *The Lor Girl* (1934), which was well received in Iran. Before returning to Iran in 1937, he produced several other successful films, most of which were based on popular Iranian folk tales.

The Dormant Era (1938–65)

World War II put a stop to the production of local films. The motion picture industry was limited to importing and exhibiting foreign films, 60 percent of which came from the U.S., and the rest from Germany, France and Russia. This situation persisted for a decade, until in 1948, Esmail Kushan produced the first Persian language sound film in Iran, *The Tempest of Love*. This and other sentimental melodramatic love stories, such as *Disgraced* (1949), began a trend which survived up to the present.

During this period, censorship assumed a powerful role *vis à vis* the media in Iran, and very few socially conscious films were produced. Among them were Farrokh Gaffary's feature *South of the Town* (1958), a realistic portrait of the slums of Tehran, and Ebrahim Golestan's *Mudbrick and Mirror* (1963), a realistic portrayal of the life of average people.

Television was introduced in Iran by a Bahai businessman, Iraj Sabet, and was patterned after the U.S. commercial system. Its programming was based on entertainment, and its schedule contained few locally produced shows, but was heavily stocked with MGM features and NBC series.

The Development of a Film Industry (1966–77)

In this period, the shah, supported by the U.S., consolidated his power. Censorship and repression increased. Serious sociopolitical criticism in all media was silenced; and in its place a cacaphony of panegyrics was carefully orchestrated, in which the Western media

343

also participated. Gradually, however, a growing number of under-ground antigovernment groups began to lay the foundation for a revolution against the Pahlavi regime and royal dictatorship.

Movies and television, the most popular arts and sources of enter-tainment, and the instruments of manipulation and image making for the regime, flourished. Many factors contributed to the emergence of a national film industry in this decade: the establishment of a single strong government controlled TV network, the Ministry of Culture and Art, film schools, film festivals, film clubs, semigovernment film production companies, the emergence of foreign trained Iranian filmmakers, the cooperation of socially conscious writers with filmmakers, the acclaim and awards received by Iranian "New Wave" filmmakers in international festivals, and finally the royal sponsor-ship of the arts and the new Iranian cinema.

Many themes popular with mass audiences emerged during this decade; among them, modern life in *The Eighth Day of the Week* (1974), family revenge in *Qaisar* (1969), sex and violence in *Prostitute* (1969), village vs. city in *Mr. Gullible* (1970), the poor against the rich in *Man from Tehran* (1966), mistaken identity in *Salute to Love* (1975), muscle power in *The Song* (1971), and Western influence on Iranians in *Golnesa in Paris* (1974).

At the same time, a growing number of young progressive filmmakers began presenting a more realistic and less cliched portrayal of Iranian society. Daryoush Mehrjui's *The Cow* (1968) gave impetus to this New Wave in Iranian cinema, which eventually led to the formation of the New Film Group in 1974. A number of these films expressed realistic and sometimes critical views of Iranian society and its government, such as *Downpour* (1970) by Bahram Baiza'i and Mehrjui's *The Cycle* (1974).

But after a brief flurry of activity and growth, the New Wave filmmakers found it almost impossible to work in an atmosphere frought with repression and heavy-handed haphazard censorship. In addition, inflation and other economic and social ills contributed to a gradual slowdown and decline in national film production. Finally, competition with imported films and stereotyped local TV shows (supported by the government) helped to bring what had been a burst of rapid development for the Iranian cinema to a virtual standstill.

Decline (1977–79)

As political unrest widened, sporadic strikes and demonstrations by the workers, the poor, students, and merchants gained momentum, and in 1978 broke into a full blown revolution culminating in the departure of the shah in January 1979 and the establishment of an Islamic Republic. During this period, few feature films of significance were released. In fact, the industry, which in the previous decade had produced more than 480 feature films, produced fewer than ten films in the period under discussion. Inflation, censorship, the lack of protection against a flood of foreign films, the unavailability of financing for New Wave and other films, and the national revolt all contributed to the decline in Iranian film production.

The Expression of Social Themes in Feature Films

Drama, melodrama, comedy, crime, and adventure films have been the principal genres of films produced in Iran, and most of these originated in the first two periods of the development of cinema, during which Iranian filmmakers copied the formulae of the foreign film products then saturating the Iranian market. Of ten feature films produced during the first and second periods of development (1900–37), there were three comedies, six dramas and one adventure film. A survey of approximately 290 films produced in the third period (1938–65) reveals that 51 percent of the films were drama and melodrama, 27.6 percent comedy and 12 percent adventure/crime films. In the fourth period (1966–77), of 480 films produced, 62 percent were drama and melodrama, 19.3 percent comedy and 12.3 percent crime and adventure films.[4]

Initially, these film genres represented an effort on the part of the novice Iranian filmmakers to imitate the superior imported films. Unfortunately, competition from technically superior foreign films, widespread censorship, and various socioeconomic factors forced Iranian filmmakers to maintain this essentially imitative stance throughout.

Popular Themes With Large Traditional Component

Films with these themes basically portrayed and/or lauded values and customs consistent with those found in traditional Iranian society. Some of these are briefly outlined and discussed below.

The Family: The family is represented in films as an important, enduring institution, often worthy of the sacrifice of one's own rights. Relationships among family members are intricate. The mother-son tie is very strong, almost oedipal. There is subservience of the son to the father, but there is also rivalry for mother's love. The father is the strong man in the family, and rules it with an iron hand. The women

345

must remain pure, self-sacrificing, resigned, decent and generous. They must keep the family together and forgive the men for their intrasigence and waywardness. There are "other" sexy and amoral women outside the family who seduce husbands and sons and endanger the family's unity and stability. These women, and their tempted victims, are inevitably punished, and in the end the family grants forgiveness to its transgressors and accepts them back. *Expectant* (1959) and *The One Hundred Kilo Bridegroom* (1962) are examples of this theme.

Strong family ties often create an obligation to seek revenge. In many films, a member of the family (usually a female), is wronged, forcing other members of the family (most often the males) to embark on a revengeful adventure, leading to the death or punishment of the culprit. For example, in *Golnesa* (1952) and *Rape* (1972) the fathers avenge their daughter's seduction and corruption. In *Qaisar*, the brother takes revenge; in *Sadeq the Kurd* (1972) it is the husband who takes revenge. In a few films the women seek revenge. *Tehran Nights* (1932) is a film in which a mother must avenge her daughter's dishonor. In most films, crimes of passion are justified, since the culprits have stained the honor of the family.

Arranged Marriages: This partially traditional theme also appeared very early, in *The Tempest of Love*. In this film the two protagonists, Nahid and Farhad, fall in love. Nahid's father opposes their marriage and arranges his daughter's wedding to a wealthy businessman. Farhad is forlorn; however, he works hard, excels in his profession, and becomes successful and wealthy. Many fateful adventures ensue which bring the original lovers together at last. In a few films, such as, *The Outlaw* (1953), the girl defies the rule of the family and tradition, but in the end is forced to relinquish and repent. As time passed and Western influence on Iran increased, this motif of defiance by both women and men was seen more and more frequently; the traditional theme was transformed and evolved to the point of displaying free choice of the marriage partner and premarital sexual relationship. Examples are, *Thirsty Ones* (1974) and *Honeymoon* (1976).

Seduction of Females: Numerous films depict women as weak in the face of a seducer, especially a seducer of means. Almost always, women submit. The result is shame and an inexorable slide into prostitution, sin, and singing and dancing in nightclubs (the latter, signs of modern influence). Sometimes, as in *Disgraced*, the seducer is punished; in other cases the girl is punished by a long period of imprisonment, as in the case of the heroine of a 1953 film *Mother*.

Bad Company: Men also are susceptible to seduction, but this is due to the bad company they keep. Happy family men are goaded by their "bad" male friends (or occasionally by sexy women) to leave their families, gamble, drink, and become involved in crime. These vices, while not inherently Western, are nonetheless depicted in Western style and thus constitute Western influence. The protagonist in these films loses not only his family but his wealth, and is punished by suffering poverty and degredation or imprisonment. Often years later, in a chance meeting, he is reunited with his family who accepts him immediately. *Vagabond* (1952) and *Neglect* (1953) are early examples of this theme.

Village vs. City: This early motif appeared in *Disgraced,* the story of Maryam, a simple peasant girl with a village fiancé, who is seduced by a man from the city named Ahmad. Ashamed, Maryam leaves the village for the city, where she becomes a famous singer. Fate and perseverence pay off in the end, and the village fiancé is able to revenge himself on the culprit, after which the long lost lovers return to the village and wed happily. Many variations of this theme were developed through the years, but the basic message remained praise of indigenous values (the innocence, purity and simplicity of rural life) and condemnation of Western values (the moral corruption rampant in city life). Other recent examples of this theme are *Mr. Gullible* and *Baluch* (1972).

The Poor vs. the Rich: Many films took as their subjects the differences between the poor and the rich (usually in urban setting), but almost none of them dealt deeply with the economic and social bases of these differences; instead, they were a framework around which to weave an intricate melodramatic or comic nexus of relationships and adventures. *Return* (1954), *The Stars Shine* (1961) and *The Bride of Tehran* (1967) provide variations on this theme.

Stringent censorship prevented any realistic treatment of such issues, and led to a barren artistic and intellectual atmosphere. The situation, however, permitted filmmakers to laud the qualities of the poor and abhor or ridicule those of the rich. For the most part, the poor are honest, simple, religious, hard-working, and ethical; while the rich are dishonest, lazy, materialistic, unhappy, cruel and unethical. Many of the latter qualities were associated also with modern and Western influence.

The class differences between the peasants and the landlords also were submerged in plots and intrigues, like those whereby a landlord would prevent the marriage of his daughter to a peasant. Sometimes,

347

however, the peasant through hard work would achieve a measure of wealth and qualify to marry here. *The Nightingale of the Farm* (1958) provides an early and popular example.

In a few films, such as, *Aras Khan* (1963) and *Farman Khan* (1967), the villagers who are fed up with the village head or the tribal chief's cruelty and oppression are mobilized by a heroic villager, take their lives in their own hands, and successfully fight their oppressors. Other films involve individual vindication as the motive behind the uprising against the power of the landlords, such as *Gol Aqa* (1967).

Another perennial social conflict commonly interpreted as personal conflict by filmmakers was that between the cruel and lascivious factory owner and the worker and his family. These stories were usually resolved in favor of the workers, in such films as, *Sin City* (1970) and *The Starless Sky* (1971).

These films in which the average peasant or worker was successful against the pitiless landlords and bosses appeared while the shah's White Revolution was being planned and implemented. Two of the well-publicized provisions of the revolution called for land reform and the granting of common shares to factory workers.

Mistaken Identity and Fatalism: These are very widespread traditional themes, as indicated by a cursory survey which showed that since the early 1950s more than 40 films have featured one form or another of mistaken identity and fatalism. Basically, the heros and heroines by an accident of fate or for reasons beyond their control, are separated and when they meet many years later, they do not recognize each other. They persist in their error until a chance event or encounter reveals to them their true identities, resulting in their reunion. *A Waif* (1954), *Morad and Laleh* (1965) and *Trees Die Standing* (1972) are examples of the mistaken identity theme.

Vagabond is an early popular example of the fatalism theme. Naser lives happily with his family, but he is pulled into a life of crime and corruption to the extent that he must sever his ties with his family. After 17 years of tortuous and painful existence (his due punishment), he encounters his family once again and starts life with them anew.

Power: According to Iranian films, both traditional and modern, power emanates from two principal sources: money and muscle. Money corrupts and forces men and women, young and old, to resort to crime—and a variety of other evils. *Long Live the Aunt* (1953), *The One Million Toman Man* (1956) and *Tunnel* (1968) are examples of this theme.

Muscle power, often represented by the boisterous and heavy-handed behavior of neighborhood toughs, has alternately provided protection to the poor, the weak, and the wealthy. *The Generous Tough Guy* (1959), *Man with the Felt Hat* (1961), *Neighborhood Tough Guy* (1964), and *The Song* all show variations on this character and theme. In early films the "tough guy" character was often protrayed as a helpful, selfless individual, inclined to support the weak against the powerful interests; in later years, he has developed into a more of a hooligan, prone to drinking, fighting, and rabble-rousing. The former portrayal is in line with the traditional view of the toughs and their role in Iranian society, while the latter may be interpreted to represent symbolically the government and its modus operandi.

Modern Western Themes

The Western themes in Iranian films presented attitudes and values imported by Iranians who had traveled abroad and by the Westernization policy of the government and its foreign supporters. While a number of films using themes described earlier, such as female seduction, bad company, the poor, the villagers, and the workers against the ruling class, depicted Western values along with Iranian values, during the initial periods of development in Iranian cinema (1900–37), films seldom wholeheartedly advocated Western values— and at times even condemned them. Increasingly in the third and fourth periods of development (1938–77), however, films focused on showing a modern way of life taking hold in Iran and indirectly urged its further adoption. The most popular modern themes are briefly described below.

Traditional vs. Modern Living: This theme was launched in one of the first feature films produced in Iran, *Hajji Aqa, the Movie Actor*. This film tells the story of a religious and traditional man, Hajji Aqa, who is firmly opposed to cinema. In the course of a number of adventures, set up by a film director, who wants to use Hajji and his daughter in a film, Hajji changes his mind about cinema and finally acquiesces to the participation of his daughter and her fiancé in the movie. A reviewer in the daily *Ettela'at* proclaimed that the movie had, ". . . many shortcomings. It was dark, the faces were dark, and from a technical standpoint, the film was not satisfactory."[5] Apparently, the reviewer did not consider it sufficiently important to comment on the fact the film had for the first time set up a conflict between the traditional, religious stance and the emerging "modern" point of view, which was gaining hold among the upper class of Iran.

The traditional, religious way of life, as represented by many "Hajji Aqa" types throughout the history of film, was backward, closed-minded, inflexible, filled with greed, and the character was fanatical, irrational, ridiculous, capricious and even lascivious. This particular stereotype appeared as a standard element in feature films both early and recently, in films such as *The Grass is Greener* (1975).

Other films sought to depict, with differing degrees of realism and insight, the modern life style in Iran; for example *Accusation* (1955), *Wild City* (1970), *The Eighth Day of the Week* and *Report* (1976). These films are set in the city, and the lives portrayed are basically those of young, upwardly mobile individuals, who are often affected by Western influence, including a touch of loss of identity and alienation.

Nightclubs: Song and dance are two of the earliest and most enduring features of Iranian films. They were employed in the first Persian language sound film, *The Lor Girl*, and with variations, continued until 1979. The overwhelmingly positive response to these elements in the movies seems to have encouraged filmmakers to find, by hook or crook, a place in their movies for a few sequences devoted to revealingly clad women singing and dancing lasciviously (which are signs of Westernization and are considered sinful by Muslims). From the 1950s onward, these motifs were expanded to include entire movies about cabarets and night life, female singers, strongmen bouncer types, and the corruption, money, sex, and violence which are part of life in that world. Examples are *A Ray of Hope* (1959), *Luck, Love and Chance* (1962), *Prostitute* (1969), and *Penance* (1972).

These films are devoid of realistic plots, and exist only as an excuse for displaying sex and violence. For audiences as religious and traditional as most in Iran, these films must have proved vicariously exciting. Indeed, a survey of young audiences in Tehran in 1966 showed that 37 percent of them were tremendously influenced and excited by sexy scenes in the movies.[6]

As for the reaction that these kinds of films evoked among the religious populace, the available accounts indicate vehement opposition to sexy films and to the display of physical expression of sexual love and lust. A writer in 1935 in a series of articles in a religious magazine, calling sexual attraction a "raging fire" and a "savage force," announced that movies were responsible for youth falling prey to such a fire and force.[7] Some years later, in 1953, a young college student in a book on culture and sociology lauded the educational and informational values of movies, but lamented that importers and exhibitors of foreign films had chosen to expose youngsters to lewd and amoral song and dance films. He further complained that Iranian youth, instead of learning from the lives and works of Marie Curie and Jeanne d'Arc, are taught to imitate Western modes of dress, makeup, and conduct; that is, Douglas Fairbanks' mustache, Cornel Wilde's hair style, Charles Boyer's romantic glances, and Dorothy Lamour's posing.[8]

However, as official "modernization," "Westernization," and "progress" gained momentum in Iran, so did the magnitude and tempo of the production, importation, and exhibition of softcore films. In 1978, the daily newspaper *Kayhan* reported that the majority of the sexploitation films shown in Tehran theaters came from Italy and the U.S., and continued by stating that of 120 movie houses in Tehran, 67 were showing "sexy" films. The Ministry of Culture and Art, which was responsible for overall cultural policies (including censorship of movies), announced in 1978 that it would ban the production, importation and exhibition of sexploitation films.[9] These intentions, however, were highly suspect in so far as they had been voiced previously with little effect, and in the light of the flagrant flouting of the already existing and fairly explicit laws against the exhibition of such "sexy" films. The ministry's sincerity was never put to the test, however, since revolutionaries chose theaters as one of their primary targets, burning down a great number of them before significant alterations in the programming could be effected.

The Police: The police and security forces are almost always portrayed as alert, rational, efficient, humane individuals working to right the wrongs and bring criminals to justice. *The Shadow* (1960), *The Night of the Hunchback* (1964), and *Sergeant Ghazanfar's Family* (1972) demonstrate the positive and humane qualities of the police and the security forces during a decade which was marked by ever widening activities of the secret police (SAVAK), and the establishment of an oppressive and unjust police and judicial system.

Western Influence: In the 1930s, educated Iranians living abroad saw Leon Poirier's travelog, *Yellow Cruise* (1934), which included scenes of the horsedrawn streetcars in the streets of Tehran. They reacted negatively, especially because they thought the film had shown Iran to be a backward country. This reaction was exemplified by a letter written by an Iranian living in Belgium and published in the daily newspaper *Ettela'at* in Tehran, in which he stated:

> The thing that attracted everyone's attention was the horsedrawn street car in Tehran. To the foreigners this appeared so ridiculous that it saddened and embarassed every Iranian. . . . Before, it was the dress, and hats and the varicolored turbins worn by Iranians, who resembled

characters in a masked ball, that attracted the foreigners' attention. Fortunately, this great defect has been overcome, but the thing that now destroys the prestige of our country is this horsedrawn streetcar.[10]

The apparent inferiority complex illustrated by the Iranians' reaction to such films,[11] and the concomitant tendency to want to appear modern and progressive at the expense of denying one's own tradition and reality, has persisted in Iranian culture and has plagued the motion picture industry throughout all stages of its development.[12]

As far as feature films are concerned, in a review of the first Iranian feature, *Abi and Rabi* in 1931, the reviewer in a Tehran daily urged an increase in the production of local films and their export to other countries, because this exchange of films with other nations could constitute, ". . . the best means of propaganda for the country and the best way of showing our country to European society."[13] A few years later, the same paper reviewed the first Persian language talkie, *The Lor Girl*, declaring: *"The Lor Girl*, in addition to fine cinematography, accurate depiction of the Eastern [Iranian] spirit, and beautiful scenery, contains another element which met with enthusiastic audience applause and that was the showing of the progress made [in Iran] during the last few years."[14]

As Iranian contact with Western countries increased (especially, through students' travels abroad), and those countries' domination of the Iranian culture and economy increased, foreigners (especially Western characters or Westernized Iranians), began to appear in films. One character frequently shown was the "foreign bride" who, unaccustomed to Iranian culture, sometimes represented a comic element. In most cases, despite many traditional and religious objections to the marriage between a foreigner and an Iranian, the love existing between the Iranian and his foreign bride, prevailed. *Play of Love* (1960), *The Foreign Bride* (1961), *Gift from Abroad* (1967), and *Mehdi Meshki and the Hot Pants* (1972) all employ variations of this theme.

Some films involved references to Western countries, others showed Iranians who had returned from study or business trips to the West or depicted Iranians in foreign countries. *Hajji Jabbar in Paris* (1961), *Swallows Return to their Nests* (1963), *Three Rabble-rousers* (1966), *Ricardo* (1968), *It Happened in USA* (1971), *An Isfahani in New York* (1972), and *Golnesa in Paris* (1974) provide examples of this theme. In general, these films tended to emphasize the early infatuation with and admiration of Western behavior and superficial trappings which affected both a portion of the Iranian people and the media.

Iran's Progressive Image: The government sought to force the establishment of a progressive modern image of Iran in the movies by limiting the situations, locations, topics, the mode of dress, and the character types that could appear in films. In the 1940s, revolutions, riots, indecency, pacifism and anti-Islamic films were censored.[15] In the early 1970s, sequences showing, ". . . hooligans' revenge, pigeon flying by pigeon fanciers, gambling on sidewalks, slums, actors with torn clothing, and sexual relations," were banned.[16]

Most Iranian film stories take place in an urban environment, despite the fact that most of Iran's population is rural. This may simply reflect the overwhelmingly urban population of movie goers,[17] or may, on the other hand, be another indication of the government's determination to stress the modern image of Iran. Without a doubt the regime intended to project an untroubled, stable, and modern image of a country in which, in fact, inequality, injustice, and poverty were widespread.

Official effort to present Iran as an "island of stability" led to a situation in which the government in the late 1970s via film and television introduced, ". . . every dissident as a spy, a saboteur, a drug addict or a carrier of arms and explosives."[18] The unfortunate result of the total control and manipulation of media and other forms of cultural and artistic expression, can be pointed out by quoting at length from an English version of an open letter dated June 13, 1977, written by 40 Iranian writers and addressed to the prime minister, Amir Abbas Hovaida:

> Mr. Prime Minister, in our society, culture and intellectural and artistic creativity are at a standstill and stagnate. . . . All the articles of the Constitution . . . have been for some time totally suspended and abrogated by the State and organizations under its control. . . . The existence of these liberties (of thought, association and the press) for several hundred years has led to the cultural movement and the intellectual, political and social development and maturity of people of various countries throughout the world, whilst today we have become the consumers of their material and intellectual products as a result of the suspension of freedom and the consequent intellectual stagnation, and have thus been afflicted by a total cultural sterility.[19]

New Wave Themes

During the third period (1966–77), while the general feature film industry was producing an ever growing number of formula films featuring one or more of the popular themes, a small but articulate movement was growing whose goal was the emancipation of Iranian cinema from its socioeconomic and artistic bonds. The New Wave filmmakers were able to win the support of the various governmental filmmaking organizations and produce an impressive number of films which realistically portrayed Iranian life.

A number of these filmmakers were themselves writers, poets or dramatists, such as Ebrahim Golestan, Feraidun Rahnema, Naser Taqva'i and Bahram Baiza'i. Other directors in their search for indigenous topics and stories, adapted recent Iranian novels and short stories, producing such films as, *Ahu's Husband* (1966), directed by Davud Mollapur based on a novel by Mohammad Ali Afghani; *The Song*, directed by Masud Kimiya'i based on Sadeq Hedayat's story *Dash Akol; Tangsir* (1973), directed by Amir Taheri based on a novel by Sadeq Chubak; *The Earth* (1973), directed by Kimiya'i based on a short story by Mahmud Daulatabadi; and *The Divine One* (1976) by Khosrau Haritash based on a story by Bahram Sadeqi.

Another group of New Wave filmmakers collaborated closely with writers and poets in adapting their stories to screenplays. For instance, the script for *The Cow* was written by Daryoush Mehrjui and Gholam Hosain Sa'edi; that of *Tranquility in the Presence of Others* (1971) was written by Taqva'i and Sa'edi; the one for *Prince Ehtejab* (1974) was written by Bahman Farmanara and Hushang Golshiri; that of *The Cycle* (1974) was written by Mehrjui and Sa'edi; and finally, the script for *The Tall Shadows of the Wind* (1978) was written by Farmanara and Golshiri. Almost all of the writers whose works formed the backbone of the New Wave films, were socially conscious, politically active, antigovernment writers who had been jailed and/or harassed for their political views. The cases of Daulatabadi, Sa'edi and Golshiri are clear examples.

The New Wave films by and large did not deal with the themes previously mentioned which had flooded the Iranian market, or if they did, they utilized realistic plots, character development, situations, and dialogues; and their superior technical quality added force to their message. A number of these films etched out portraits of the village and city life in harsh realism; for example, *The Cow*, and *A Simple Event* (1973), and *Still Life* (1974), all directed by Sohrab Shahid Saless; *The Report*, directed by Abbas Kiarostami; and *Broken Hearts* (1978) by Ali Hatami. Some films resorted to symbolism, a form of subterfuge practiced throughout the history in Iranian arts (especially poetry), in times of political and social oppression. *Tranquility in the Presence of Others*, and *City of Fables* (1972), directed by Manuchehr Anvar and written by Bizhan Mofid, and *The Stranger and the Fog* (1974) by Baiza'i, all utilized symbolism of one sort or another to depict and criticize the social and political system.

A number of filmmakers, some of them trained in the West, focused on the devastation of the indigenous cultural values and institutions by Western countries or by Westernized Iranians, and the resulting economic and moral bankruptcy and alienation. *The Postman* (1970) by Mehrjui, *The Earth,* and *The Mongols* (1973) by Parviz Kimiavi, *Far From Home* (1975) by Shahid Saless, *The Journey of Stone* (1977) by Kimiya'i, and *O.K. Mister* (1978) by Kimiavi are all examples of this theme. Royal and social corruption were the motifs of *Prince Ehtejab* and *The Cycle.* In *Downpour* by Baiza'i, the themes were social conditions and government suppression; and in *Tangsir* individual revenge evolved into a one-man armed insurrection against the powers that be.

Many of these films won awards and acclaim in international film festivals. The government found that its financing of the New Wave filmmakers brought fame and prestige in international circles. But the filmmakers themselves were not satisfied with their heavily compromised statements. Usually their bolder social scripts and completed films were subjected to censorship or withdrawal from distribution. *The Cow, Tranquility in the Presence of Others,* and *The Cycle,* for example, were each banned for one or more years. Gradually, the government preferred to channel their extensive financial support into coproduction film projects with foreign firms requiring financial backing, which enabled it to avoid dealing with thorny censorship problems and at the same time gave the regime a progressive world image as a financier of prestigious film projects. Thus, the Iranian New Wave and the relative tolerance of the government for the expression of fresh and relevant social film themes came to an end.

Analysis

Briefly reviewed above have been those themes most frequently presented in over seventy years of Iranian feature films. The seven decades discussed were very eventful, seeing the rise of a modern dictatorship backed by its foreign allies and the reemergence of Iranian nationalism. In a society on its way towards Western-style modernization, all traditional values and customs are questioned and often carelessly discarded. This can cause trauma and confusion unless the old discredited value system is replaced with a viable new value system. It seems that the Pahlavi regime deliberately set out to make use of communication media in social and political development. Through heavy-handed official censorship and through the perpetration of a system of terror and of individual and artistic insecurity, the expression of real issues in arts and media was effectively suppressed. While, during periodic slackening of official censorship, writers and poets were able to produce significant socially conscious poems, short stories, essays and novels, movies and television were scrutinized incessantly and mercilessly by the board of censors to prevent the expression of themes antithetical to the official government policy or royal position.

Since all scripts *and* all completed films had to be reviewed by the censors before receiving a production permit and a certificate of exhibition, the government had at its disposal a sure means of infusing films with what it considered to be proper social norms and values. A review of the themes and characters presented by Iranian feature films suggests a complex set of social and moral values that faithfully reflects the government's modernization and Westernization policies. Not that the complex social and moral values expressed through cinema fall neatly into one category, solely urging modernization and Westernization; a few films condemned indiscriminate Westernization, and some lauded traditional Iranian values, while many others criticized them. The set of values and attitudes which emerged from the offices of the censors then, contained a mixture of values, indigenous and modern, but more often than not they ridiculed and disparaged the traditional values and urged their abandonment in favor of more modern Western attitudes.

Thus, traditional and religious values and characters were ridiculed and considered backward. Religion, although not openly condemned, was often disparaged via derogatory plot structure and ludicrous, stupid, unreasoning and fanatical caricatures. Modern life, characterized by urban living and portrayed as a combination of freewheeling relationships among attractive, upwardly mobile groups on the one hand, and socially unacceptable behavior such as gambling, drug use, sex, money and violence on the other, were displayed endlessly. Clearly, similar vices existed long before Western influence were felt in Iran, but insofar as Westernization represented a falling away from traditional Iranian virtues, it tended to be associated with the "fast" or "seamy" style of life. It should be noted that despite the apparently negative nature of the antisocial modern behavior, it can be argued that incessant recurrence of any behavior via film and television in fact contributes to a greater acceptance of it, whether it is ostensibly condemned or not.

The police and all other government agents were portrayed very positively, always working to right wrongs. The judicial system was portrayed as fair and efficient. Criminals met with bad ends, at the hands of the police or the courts.

Landlords, village chiefs, and others representing the old feudalism with whom the shah was in conflict, were portrayed as arbitrary, cruel, greedy and lascivious. The rich often did not fare much better. On the other hand, the peasants, the workers, and the poor were shown as simple (sometimes to the point of stupidity), honest, and hard-working. The conflict between the poor and the rich was represented crudely, often immersed in a milieu of sex and personal revenge motifs. These films, although they identified the schism, ignored the economic and political bases of class conflict. Instead, the audience was presented with intricate sentimental love-revenge formulae, to the detriment of any real understanding of the issues involved, participating vicariously in the victories against the rich and powerful, drawing solace and venting frustration and hostility in a safe and ineffectual manner. Two purposes were served by this silver screen class warfare. One effect was to mollify and pacify the mass of poor people who continued to exist in varying degrees of deprivation and exploitation. On the other hand, it helped maintain the high level of mistrust and contempt between the modern, educated elite and the masses, so that no bond of shared purpose or ideals would be formed, since such a coalition would have constituted a threat to the absolute power of the shah and his regime.

While all these popular themes were being presented in films, many socially significant issues were ignored. Poverty, the destruction of agriculture, migration of peasants to town slums, oppression, police terror, censorship, the plight of tribes and the ethnic minorities, inequality, injustice, social and royal corruption, exploitation of the dispossessed, disruption of indigenous culture, the undermining of religion, and inflation were not considered or explored in the Iranian cinema.

Thus, indigenous cinema never assumed the function of a social barometer, reflecting the people's needs, problems and aspirations, but it clearly served as an indicator of the government cultural policy. Films imported from the West supported the government's political use of cinema. These films, which constituted the majority of films shown in Iran, often carried the motifs of sex and violence and of the modern way of life much further than their Iranian counterparts, owing to the double standards of censorship in which native Iranian films received by far the harshest treatment.[20]

The reaction of Iranians to this mosaic of their society in films was not uniform. The country was modernizing rapidly, the validity of many traditional values had come into question, and a few had already been discarded. An evaluation of movies by the audiences in the provincial city of Yazd in central Iran in 1974 points to the two contrasting and conflicting value systems coexisting both in the Iranian populace and on the Iranian movie screens. One, represented by the older and the less educated, defended the traditional values; while the other, represented by the younger and the more educated, advocated contemporary values.[21] The statistics indicated that 27.2 percent of the respondents considered the overall effect of movie viewing to be that of entertainment and relaxation, while 22.1 percent considered it to be one of corruption of character.[22]

Also, the influence of television in purveying the state's cultural policy into the home should be taken into consideration. In 1974, for example, 40 percent of the televised programs consisted of foreign imports.[23] A survey of popular programs on the National Iranian Radio and Television (NIRT) is shown in Table 10.[24]

The preponderance of the U.S.-made serials among the best liked programs is staggering, indicating the share of foreign products' participation in the cultural colonization of Iran. Even locally produced TV serials (controlled by a small group of individuals) were essentially parodies containing a variety of Western style characters, while those Iranian elements which remained were often manipulated in accordance with Western values and formulae in such a way

Table 10. Popularity of Programs on Iranian Television

Program title	Percent naming program among top five choices
Morad Barqi (local serial)	75%
Days of Our Lives (U.S. serial)	49%
Zir Bazarcheh (local serial)	45%
Feature film (basically imported)	30%
Tarzan (U.S. serial)	20%
Variety show	18%
Science program	15%
News	14%
Ironside (U.S. serial)	14%
Young Lawyers (U.S. serial)	12%
Salhaye bi Panahi (local serial)	12%
Variety show	12%
The Sixth Sense (U.S. serial)	11%
Marcus Welby, M.D. (U.S. serial)	9%
Colombo (U.S. serial)	8%

as to distort and subvert the traditional values held by the majority of the audience. These "Westernized" local series represented not only the embodiment of the government's cultural policy, but also reflect the least desirable aspects of the value system of the Iranian intelligentsia and artistic elite who produced them.

The effects of this media-transmitted cultural policy were far-reaching, given the huge amount of time Iranians spent watching movies and TV programs. Audience research studies conducted in different cities in the 1960s and the 1970s have shown that movie going and TV watching were the most popular leisure activities of the population. A survey of audiences in 1969 in the city of Rezaiyeh showed that 39 percent of the respondents spent their leisure time going to the movies and 42 percent spent it watching television.[25] A survey conducted in Tehran in 1973 showed that movie going was the most popular leisure time activity of university students.[26] Yet another survey carried out in the city of Yazd in 1974 indicated that 70 percent of high school students chose movies as their favorite pastime, and a study of film audiences in Tehran in 1977 indicated that 35 percent of them went to the movies once a week.[27]

The images projected by the media then, were among the more powerful measures used to undermine both traditional and progressive values, leaving little intact or sacred other than royalty and its policies. Eventually, the divisive stereotyping and distortions used to deepen mistrust and polarization within society, became a weapon in the hands of the victims. The media images offered were generally unreal, unattainable, and undesirable. Neither the rich nor the poor could find in the screen images a reality, an identity, or an integrity to which they might aspire. As the activities of the regime and the media which carried its messages became increasingly aggressive and pervasive, the rapid erosion of traditional Iranian values and the absence of any viable progressive alternatives provoked a response from the Iranian masses, who resisted state policies and cultural attitudes, and brought their ultimate collapse. It is not surprising that during the 1978-79 revolution cinemas were chosen as one of the principal targets of revolutionary destruction, considering the role they played in the cultural dissolution wrought by those who sought to manipulate Iran for their own benefit.[28]

19

A Full Arena:
The Development and Meaning
of Popular Performance Traditions in Iran

William O. Beeman

Introduction—Iranian Performance Traditions:
Vital Social Institutions

The study of folk performance traditions is a topic not typically confronted directly by social scientists, judging from the extreme paucity of literature on it.[1] A reason for this lack of attention may lie in the difficulty of obtaining historical documentation and field data—certainly very real obstacles—but the real reason may well be that social scientists feel that such matters as folk theatre, narrative, dance, and ceremonial religious drama are somehow peripheral to the central core of social phenomena.

The typical treatment of performance traditions, particularly popular theatre, within social science is to relegate them to secondary mention in accounts of the fine arts of a nation or region, and to treat them in a purely descriptive manner. Even anthropologists, who should find this material of the greatest interest, have dealt seriously with performance traditions in only a handful of studies.

The most serious attempts in social science at interpretation of traditional performance rarely go beyond relegating performance to a kind of residual category of social activities. Often it is seen, as Natalie Davis points out, as having the function popular view attaches to the ancient Roman circus: something that keeps the population occupied, and lets them blow off steam and excess energy on occasion.[2]

The study of folk performance in Iran, and indeed, throughout the

Middle East, suffers from inattention for these reasons and for others relating to the peculiarities of research on the Islamic world. A surprising number of persons have either flatly denied the existence of theatrical tradition in the Middle East, or have denigrated its importance in Middle Eastern cultures.[3] With increasing research, fortunately, such notions are beginning to be corrected as the wealth of complex and interesting folk performance traditions throughout the region are gradually made known to the world.

In this discussion, I wish to counter both the notions cited above. I hope to demonstrate that traditional performance is now, and has been, a vital and meaningful element in Iranian cultural life for centuries, having preserved its significance through several changes of regime; surviving war, bad economic conditions, and political suppression. Further, I hope to show that Iranian traditional performance forms have been able to survive and retain a degree of vitality because they are important to the lives of the people who support them; not just as a kind of residual "escape valve," but as part of the complex of cultural institutions which provide the meaningful symbolic material helping the public to deal with the realities of their own situation in the idealized past, the harshly real present, and the uncertain, variable future.

In Iran two principal popular performance traditions have thrived at the folk level for a long time—perhaps many centuries. The first is the Shi'i Muslim passion drama, commonly known among Orientalists as *ta'ziyeh*.[4] This performance tradition has attracted the bulk of attention among both casual observers and scholarly researchers. As a dramatic tradition it is one of the most powerful in the world, utilizing culturally appropriate dramatic conventions and devices designed to engage spectators in a deeply moving emotional experience.[5] The subject matter for *ta'ziyeh* is most commonly, but not exclusively, the events leading to the martyrdom of Hosain, grandson of the Prophet Mohammad, and third Imam of Shi'i Muslims. Hosain was killed on the plains of Kerbala in present-day Iraq in 680 A.D. in the Islamic lunar month of Moharram. Performances of *ta'ziyeh* are enacted on an epic scale, and are performed in the open (or in a special structure [*hosainiyeh* or *tekiyeh*] built for the purpose) as part of the general mourning ceremonies taking place during the month of Moharram. Performances take place throughout present-day Iran, and are also seen in Iraq, Bahrain, and southern Lebanon, where extensive Shi'i communities are to be found. *Ta'ziyeh* has been called "Islamic opera," and although it is somewhat vulgar to refer to it thus, this is what it must seem like to many Western observers. The principal "sympathetic" characters chant their parts in lines of elegant verse to traditional classical Persian musical modes, while the "villainous" characters declaim their lines in exaggerated speech contours. For Western observers the most striking aspect of *ta'ziyeh* is the sight of thousands of spectators openly weeping at the sights reflected in the performance. The drama is intended to produce this weeping—indeed, to weep under these circumstances is thought to be a sacred duty—and it is highly successful in this regard. Because the performance takes place during a formal period of religious mourning, it takes on the character of religious ritual.[6]

The second popular performance tradition in Iran has no single name throughout the country. I refer to it as "traditional comic improvisatory theatre" to distinguish it from the scripted *ta'ziyeh* tradition, but it is known by various other names, the most common of which is the urban term *ru-hauzi* or *takht-e hauzi* theatre.[7] These appellations have now become current in referring to the performance tradition as a whole, in all of its forms, and so I will continue to use the term *ru-hauzi* throughout this discussion—although it is not strictly accurate, especially when referring to these forms as seen in rural areas.

Ru-hauzi theatre is found throughout Iran, principally in areas having a settled agricultural economy; although a more professional form is found in public theatres in the cities of Tehran, Isfahan and Mashhad. Most players are also musicians, and the theatrical performance is part of an extended entertainment program performed for traditional wedding and circumcision celebrations. Performances are usually, but not always, riotously comic in nature, and the measure of the success of a performance is the amount of laughter produced among spectators.

In the discussion that follows, I have attempted to give a short sketch of the historical development of each of these two performance forms, and show how each is carried out in Iran today. Additionally, I attempt to give a brief picture of the way in which each performance form is received and understood by spectators. In the final section of the discussion I return to the question of the significance these performance forms continue to have for Iranians at a cultural and cognitive level, and draw some tentative conclusions about the role of performance in human society.

Ta'ziyeh

Although relatively few scholars are currently engaged in research on *ta'ziyeh*, controversy rages among them over the question of the origins of this performance form. I will not detail the various arguments, but theories range from claims that *ta'ziyeh* is a direct borrowing from ancient Greek theatre; to assertions that it is an entirely native form deriving from mourning ceremonies for the pre-Islamic Iranian hero Siavush; that it is a Byzantine theatrical form; that it was borrowed from European traditions variously during the Medieval, Renaissance, Classic or Romantic eras; and other theories too numerous to mention.[8] Most of these theories are necessarily based on speculation, since so little documentary evidence exists of *ta'ziyeh* performances before the beginning of the nineteenth century. Earlier travelers' accounts indicate mourning ceremonies during the month of Moharram which consist of religious processions with effigies of various figures associated with the martyrdom of Hosain—but no dramatic performances.

The first account of *ta'ziyeh* as a clearly dramatic performance is probably that of Adrian Dupré, who was attached to the scientific body accompanying the French Mission to Persia in 1807–09.[9] Dupre offers an account which is essentially a description of *ta'ziyeh* as it is seen today. Many experts doubt that the full dramatic form could have developed suddenly as late as this. This doubt comes first from the fact that Dupré's report is of a fairly highly evolved form, contrasting sharply with accounts of simple processions during the Safavid era. It seems that a long incubation period would have been needed to have produced something so complete. The second reason to doubt that Dupré's account represents the first instance of *ta'ziyeh* in full dramatic form is that manuscripts of *ta'ziyeh* texts exist from the early nineteenth century and before, which are extensive, complete literary works—indicating a full-blown tradition in existence, not a newly evolving form.[10]

The most widely accepted theory of the development of *ta'ziyeh* accepts the existence of pre-Islamic mourning ceremonies. It next picks up reports during the Buyid period (late tenth century A.D.) of officially accepted mourning ceremonies in public for Ali, the Prophet Mohammad's son-in-law, and heir; and his descendants, including Imam Hosain.[11]

Ritual mourning for the death of Imam Hosain is reported regularly by Arab and European travelers through the Safavid era (1501–1722 A.D.). The elaborateness and size of the ceremonies increased over time, changing from simple public mourning to the use of costumed figures in processions, to simple enactments of the individual events of the martyrdom story, until the full dramatic forms of the early nineteenth century during the Qajar era are finally documented.

It is during the Qajar era that *ta'ziyeh* as a dramatic form reached full flower. By the time of Naser od-Din Shah (1848–96) they were a regular feature of court life. Foreign ambassadors were invited along with thousands of others to the enormous productions at the *Tekiyeh-ye Daulat* in Tehran, and the shah had a *ta'ziyeh* "director" as part of his royal household.[12] Gradually, according to Krymsky, drawing from reports of Russian writers living in Tehran at the end of the nineteenth century, the season for production of *ta'ziyeh* extended to the following month of Safar—and even beyond, until finally *ta'ziyeh* players could count on employment for most of the year.[13]

Ta'ziyeh had then moved from being a simple mourning ceremony in the tenth century to a full-fledged dramatic tradition on the eve of the twentieth. The reason for its ascendency during this period is difficult to judge, but there is no question but that as a ceremonial act dramatizing the central historical event upon which the Shi'a base their claims to distinctness within the brotherhood of Islam, it was a ceremony of unparalleled historical and emotional importance. The earlier Moharram mourning ceremonies found their greatest support in the Shi'i Buyid and Safavid dynasties, reaching an evolutionary pinnacle in the theatrical form so widespread during the Qajar period. Thus, in a real sense, *ta'ziyeh* had become far more than a religious ceremonial observance. It was on the verge of becoming a national dramatic tradition embodying exclusively Iranian elements of music, poetry, mythic and religious history.[14] Its performance had become a state activity with strong Iranian cultural overtones.

Predictably, it suddenly went into rapid decline with the dethronement of Mohammad Ali Shah in 1909. Krymsky reports the following from K. Smirnov:

> The mystery plays have survived until very recently, but unfortunately the event is beginning to lose ground. . . . In the reign of Mohammad Ali-Shah, the *ta'ziyeh* as the mystery plays are called, was still preserved [here K. Smirnov describes the majesty with which the royal government supported the *ta'ziyehs*]. After his dethronement the plays were suppressed. . . . It is true, however, that the first days of Moharram cost tens of thousands of tomans; but nevertheless it is a pity that in the future, a tradition which has existed from the tenth century up to our time is disappearing. . . . At the present [1916, in the midst of the conflagration of the world war] only in Tehran can the remnants of the mystery plays be seen—this is in the coffee houses; it is understood that the populace has little interest in the spectacle.[15]

The fall of the Qajar dynasty itself cannot be the only reason for the decline of *ta'ziyeh*, however. The performances had never been popular with the ulama,[16] the more sincere of whom believed the

365

performances to be involved with the forbidden representation of images, and the less sincere of whom probably believed that the elaborate and expensive performances took away from their own income as *rauzeh-khans* (reciters of the events of Imam Hosain's martyrdom) at private ceremonies, for which they were paid. The state, weakened and impoverished by war and revolution, could ill-afford public support for the massive spectacles commissioned by the Qajar shahs. Moreover, Reza Shah himself viewed *ta'ziyeh* performances as decadent and backward—not at all in keeping with his image of a modern state. He therefore officially forbade their performance.

Under the reign of Mohammad Reza Shah Pahlavi the fortunes of *ta'ziyeh* were variable. Officially disapproved, *ta'ziyeh* was nonetheless allowed to continue in an underground fashion at the popular level. Performances in villages, small towns, and even in certain quarters of large cities continued unabated—disapproved, but tolerated.

Ta'ziyeh continued to be appreciated among the intelligentsia as an art form, however, and was presented on several occasions under state support. The first such presentation under Pahlavi rule was in 1965 (Majles-e Abdollah-e Afif) at the 25th of Shahrivar Theatre under the direction of Parviz Sayyad. A second production (Ta'ziyeh-ye Khorr) was staged by Sayyad and theatre scholar Khojasteh Kia in 1967 at the first annual Festival of Arts in Shiraz. Two badly staged productions at the Festival of Arts in 1970 and 1971 were followed by a series of ten performances in 1976 held in the Hosainiyeh-ye Moshir in Shiraz and also in the village of Kaftarak outside Shiraz using traditional performers selected from active troupes from throughout the nation by actor, director, and theatre researcher Mohammad Bagher Ghaffari.[17] These performances were immensely successful, drawing Iranian crowds of ten thousand and more from hundreds of miles away and from all segments of society. A program of non-passion cycle *ta'ziyeh* (see n. 14 above) was also presented at the Festival of Popular Traditions in Isfahan in 1977. Following these Festivals an attempt was made by Festival of Arts director Farrokh Ghaffary and director of National Iranian Radio-Television Reza Qotbi to lift the government ban on *ta'ziyeh* performances in rural areas. In this attempt the aid of the queen was enlisted. She approached her husband on the matter, and he in turn consulted SAVAK. By that point the religious oppositionist fervor leading to the revolutionary events of 1979 had begun to make itself felt, and SAVAK recoiled in horror at the thought of hundreds of *ta'ziyeh* performances involving millions of persons being brought to an emotional pitch in a highly moving religious spectacle. Moreover, they wished to pacify the conservative mullas opposing the government. Therefore, SAVAK sternly advised the shah not to lift the ban, and for the months of Moharram and Safar in 1977 a strict prohibition against *ta'ziyeh* performances was again announced.

But despite the prohibition during the Pahlavi dynasty, *ta'ziyeh* continued to be performed—continually, regularly, and without interruption throughout the country in city, town, and village.[18]

The rise of *ta'ziyeh* as an officially sanctioned performance form and its subsequent decline following the Qajar era did nothing to diminish its ability to move the people emotionally. Although the number of *ta'ziyeh* troupes has grown smaller, many are still active throughout the country. Young men and boys are still recruited to the ranks of performers through the traditional system of giving them first children's and women's roles, and allowing them to "graduate" to the more mature roles as they gain experience over the years. *Ta'ziyeh* is an income producing activity for the most professional troupes, and although it is unlikely that anyone today earns his whole income through *ta'ziyeh* performances, many are able to supplement their incomes from other work in this way.

Ta'ziyeh has become institutionalized as part of the normal cycle of annual ritual practice in many rural areas of Iran. Many villages have their own performance tradition, using natives of the village in *ta'ziyeh* roles. Whether the performers are drawn from the village or town itself and perform gratis, or whether the performance is given by a hired troupe, all the events surrounding it are a cooperative community venture. Money is collected from throughout the community for the performers' fees, tea and cigarettes for performers and spectators, and meals for both performers and the community as a whole (especially on the two days of Tasua and Ashura, the ninth and tenth days of the month of Moharram), and for the purchase and upkeep of clothing, properties, and the playing arena. It is not uncommon for a *ta'ziyeh* performance to be paid for entirely by one rich man or family in fulfillment of a religious vow (*nazr*). In some areas, the annual performance of *ta'ziyeh* is actually supported by endowment.

There is no doubt whatever that *ta'ziyeh* performance continues to constitute a powerful religious and emotional experience for the spectators that support it today. It continues despite official prohibitions, because local officials do not dare to stop it. Many have adopted the attitude of turning a blind eye to the event when it occurs in areas

367

under their jurisdiction. In some rural areas, gendarmes or soldiers from military outposts near a performance site have been actually assigned duty to perform in the spectacle as trumpet and drum players, mounted warriors, or foot soldiers—with the knowledge and tacit approval of high ranking military chiefs.

Ta'ziyeh performance gains in power by being coupled with other demonstrations of public mourning. Often a performance is proceeded by, and leads directly into a public procession with breast beating, self flagellation, and chanting on the parts of organized groups of men.

All mourning ceremonies, including *ta'ziyeh*, invite the spectators to project their own personal troubles and woes onto the event of the martyrdom of Hosain (and Ali). In a sermon in the city of Shiraz in 1972 on the anniversary of the death of Ali, I once heard a clergyman exhort his listeners: "Weep, weep all of you! But do not weep for Ali! He is in heaven. Weep for the injustice of his death, and weep for yourselves, you poor unlucky sinners. Weep for the misery of your own condition!" For many, participation in these ceremonies serves a therapeutic purpose as well as a religious one. Many families have had regular ceremonies of *rauzeh-khani* in their homes on a set day every month for decades. The *rauzeh-khan* is often a clergyman, and he receives a fee.[19] For the most famous of these orators, fees can reach thousands of dollars during the month of Moharram, or on other religious holidays. The best of the *rauzeh-khans* deliver sermons based on contemporary events, to which they append an emotional rendering of the events leading to the martyrdom of Imam Hosain, exhorting the people to weep. One family in Shiraz where I used to attend *rauzeh-khani* several times during the year told me that: "Weeping for Hosain helps us to deal with our own problems, since we remember that his suffering and the suffering of his family was so much greater than our suffering now."

Oratorical skill in *rauzeh-khani* involves the ability to make the events of Hosain's martyrdom seem immediate and relevant to the audience. One *rauzeh* widely distributed on cassette tapes during the fall of 1978 when the revolution in Iran was in full swing was delivered by the late Ayatollah Kafi of Mashhad. In this *rauzeh* he calls Imam Hosain on the telephone, and cries out to him to quit the plains of Kerbala, because the greater enemy is in Iran in the person of the shah's regime. In this he duplicates the kind of telephone conversation that must take place between separated relatives in Iran all the time. The pathos of the plea to Imam Hosain is accentuated by the contemporary setting given to the message.

Ta'ziyeh utilizes many of the same devices in presenting the story of the martyrdom. In one separate dramatic episode Fatemeh, daughter of Mohammad, wife of Ali, and mother of Hosain and his brother Hasan is seen washing the clothing of the children while they are still young. As she takes each small piece of clothing out of the washbasin, she identifies it and bemoans the fact that the child who wears it will one day be tortured and killed in the most horrendous way. She ends fainting in grief, her children's clothing spread around her. The scene is immensely moving, combining as it does the deep symbolism of the death of Hosain with the most commonplace activity a woman undertakes in managing a household. Needless to say, this scene touches all persons deeply, but women are especially affected, and are sent into uncontrolled fits of weeping. In 1978 in Tehran, one woman spectator, whose own son had died just days before in a street-battle with police during a political demonstration, had to be removed from a performance of this *ta'ziyeh* episode for fear she would physically injure herself in a paroxysm of grief.

Ta'ziyeh further presents stereotypes and symbolic characterizations which have meaning within Iranian cultural context far deeper than the historical events they portray. The male characters are idealized forms of heroic figures of a type which pervades Iranian literature and folklore; they probably have roots in pre-Islamic mythic history. Female characters are likewise ideal wives, mothers, and daughters. All characters are not only ideally heroic, but ideally religious as well, submitting to the fate ordained for them. Again and again it is shown that Hosain, Ali, and other characters know full well what will happen on the plains of Kerbala years in advance of the event. Hosain is offered help from many quarters and refuses it, preferring to obey the will of God, as Islam prescribes.

The unsympathetic characters are by contrast, supremely, ideally bad. They are shown inflicting cruelty for its own sake, murdering helpless children, and denying water to those dying of thirst. They are, furthermore, deaf to the pleas of holy men and persons of virtue. They ignore holy scripture, and indeed, make fun of it; they are shown drinking, womanizing, thieving, and living entirely sinful lives. The contrast constitutes a virtual mirror image of the picture presented by the sympathetic characters.

Ta'ziyeh, as has already been mentioned, also embodies highly meaningful artistic elements characteristic of Iranian civilization. Music and poetry in classical modes and meters are the most clearly identifiable elements, but the costumes are also reminiscent of the glories of the historical past, and the content of many of the *ta'ziyeh*

369

texts contain direct quotes from the greatest Iranian authors.

To sum up, *ta'ziyeh* is a performance tradition which presents spectators with:

1. All that is meaningful and inspiring in Iranian life represented in symbolic form: an ideal hero undergoing an ideal supreme test of his ability to submit to the will of God, surrounded by an ideal set of male and female relatives and companions acting in perfect faith.

2. All that is abhorred and despised in the ideal Iranian life, presented likewise in an ideal form: horrible villains who murder the faithful, deny virtue, destroy the family, war with God and his messengers, and act throughout in bad faith.

3. A drama designed to bring the import of this cosmic struggle to the level of the common people. Heroes and villains alike perform the events of the martyrdom in a setting which includes the humble trappings of everyday life. Performance takes place in a ritual mourning setting, making it one with other mourning observances such as *rauzeh-khani* in which spectators are invited to project their own sorrows, difficulties, and concerns into the tragedy of the events at Kerbala. Therefore, much of the power of the drama lies in the heavy degree of *association* which the audience feels with the events they witness.

4. A drama which is in a very real sense a symbolic presentation of Iranian civilization. As *ta'ziyeh* evolved and rose to prominence in a period when Shi'ism became the state religion in Iran, and the fortunes of Iran were high, it is not surprising that this should be so. Once the form had fully evolved, received royal patronage, and become a prominent event in Iran's national life, it is likewise not surprising that the best of Iranian art, music, architectural skill and craftsmanship have made themselves felt in the form.

Ru-hauzi

The origins of comic improvisatory theatre in Iran are even more obscure than those of *ta'ziyeh*. If *ta'ziyeh* attracted only the casual attention of travelers and historical commentators, comic theatrical traditions were almost completely ignored. It is only through the barest of clues that we can piece together a few guesses at their history.

One way to get information is to compare the theatrical traditions of Iran today with others of a similar nature in Europe and Asia. We find that the distribution of comic improvisatory theatrical forms similar to those in Iran today is extremely wide, ranging from Indonesia *(ludruk)* and Malaysia *(boria)* to India, Afghanistan, and Turkey.[20] It seems likely that there is a connection between all of these forms and both *commedia dell'Arte* of the late Italian Renaissance, and northern European comic carnival plays based on similarity of performance themes, character types, costumes, and performance conventions.

The extremely wide distribution of these comic forms at least leaves the possibility open that they share a single origin of great antiquity. The connection between Iranian performance and the performance forms of India has been suggested many times, and several historical accounts exist of migrations of musicians and dancers from India. Amanallahi cites numerous historical sources documenting the migration of gypsies across Iran during the Sassanian period, and he also quotes the well-known passage from Ferdausi's epic, the *Shahnameh*, in which Bahram-Gur, the legendary Sassanian king, orders the importation of ten thousand musicians, dancers, and performers from India to Iran.[21]

The principal historical reports of performers in Iran entertaining in a comic mode occur in general accounts of court life down through the centuries. The Sassanian king, Khosrau Parviz is said to have supported actors.[22] Writers in the years following the Islamic conquest of Iran provide very little material on this subject, but the reign of Shah Abbas (1585–1628 A.D.) marks a resurgence of information about popular performers. The court clown, named Enayat, received the title "Kachal" (lit. bald) from Shah Abbas himself. A miniature painting by Soltan Mohammad Naqqash from this period (1621) shows performers entertaining in what seems to be a court setting. One of the clowns wears a tall hat, and others are clothed in goatskins.[23]

Beza'i reports that musicians from this period used to give comic performances when called on to entertain in the court and the homes of the wealthy:

> These programs consisted of: several dances . . . one or two stories produced in dance form (one in particular known as *Qahr va 'Ashti* "getting mad and not speaking, then making up") is known to us, and one or two short "curtain raisers" in which a dialogue in question and answer format: sometimes romantic, sometimes humorous; were presented in song. As these "curtain raisers" become more elaborate, they took the form of short humorous stories in song with two or three performers. These stories usually ended with the characters beating each other followed by a chase. Itinerant performers, because of their intimate acquaintance with the desires of the people may have taken on this story form sooner. The humor of these performers was much freer than that of the performers who entertained in the homes of the wealthy, who were bound to protect the dignity of the gathering.
>
> *Taqlid* (lit. "imitation"), which soon began to be found in the humorous

371

presentations of the itinerant entertainers had much longer stories and a distinct singing aspect. Songs were sometimes sung separately during parts of the performance where they were appropriate, but the dialogue was not sung. The number of performers was the same, but since the dialogue was not sung, the story was much freer. Entertainers in *taqlid* would normally imitate the accents and personal characteristics of well known people in the town and villages in which they performed. These people would be seen meeting and greeting each other. After a short while they would fall to arguing and making fun of each other's accents and behavior, and the story would end with the two characters fighting and chasing each other.[24]

As will be seen below, the *taqlid* form is in all essentials the same basic comic improvisatory comic theatrical form seen in Iran today.

Comic performance continued to be a feature of the court during Qajar times. The most famous of the Qajar court clowns was Karim Shire'i (*shireh* = sugar syrup or treacle), clown in the court of Naser od-Din Shah. Karim Shire'i was not only personal jester to Naser od-Din Shah, but also personally responsible for all court entertainment. Some of his own productions were truly elaborate, and although only one of his productions has been recorded for us to see today, from accounts contemporary with his times, it seems he was highly thought of as a truly gifted comedian and clown. Many jokes and witicism are attributed to him.[25]

Perhaps the most important point to note concerning Karim Shire'i is the degree to which he was allowed to satirize the court and its officials. In this regard he carries on the tradition of ridicule Beza'i speculates existed in the earlier *taqlid* form. This license to deal humorously with members of the court seems to have given Karim Shire'i a degree of power and influence, also allowing him to receive "presents" from members of the court to be spared from his wit.

The single example we have of Karim Shire'i's comic wit in dramatic form is the play: *Baqqal-bazi dar Hozur* (Grocer play in the [Royal] Presence), printed in a slightly expurgated version by Jannati-Ata'i.[26] The original text reportedly comes from a nineteenth century handwritten manuscript now reputed to be in the United States.[27] An example from a speech in the play itself will serve to illustrate the liberty allowed Karim Shire'i:

> . . . Go away you miserable beggar, dont you see that you can't trust anyone in the world! Hajji Mirza Bey, the poor man, died and left an inheritance of 80,000 tomans. Every person of influence made all sorts of excuses, and finally stole every bit of the money. They first took the 10,000 tomans that was to be spent for the funeral. The minister of science and trade took 2,000 tomans for his own wife, and finished it

buying her clothes and baubles. The rest was taken by Mirza Issa Vazir, to buy land the size of a whole city quarter in order to build a hospital. They built a wall around the land, and the minister, the architect and the contractor split the rest of money. Now the "hospital" is a meeting ground for dogs, and Hajji Mirza Bey's heirs have been turned into beggars.[28]

Beza'i points out in a commentary on this text that although a script is given, it is most likely that the performance was improvisatory in nature, the performers adding whatever they thought would be appreciated at the time.

Rezvani identifies *baqqal-bazi* as a performance type and mentions having seen a show in Gorgan in 1923.[29] This performance was likewise improvised, but involved the confrontation of a grocer and a clown figure in a scene which essentially replicates many of the basic elements of *Baqqal-bazi dar Hozur* mentioned above. The play ends in argumentation and a fight between the two principal characters who chase and beat each other. This basic play is still presented in various different forms throughout Iran today, and though each performing group varies their presentation, it is received very well.

As with *ta'ziyeh*, comic improvisatory theatre suffered a decline at the close of the Qajar era due to two factors: the first was the decline of the court and upper classes, who set the tone in popular entertainment; the second was the rise of Western-style scripted theatre in the large cities of the country, particularly Tabriz, Rasht, and Tehran, which had already begun to make inroads in Iran by the late nineteenth century.[30]

Nevertheless, troupes of entertainers continued to perform in the old improvisatory style in cities and small towns where they were engaged primarily for weddings and village celebrations. A few of the best clowns and performing troupes were able to continue to be accepted in legitimate theatres throughout the country, particularly in Tehran, Isfahan and Mashhad.

Traditional improvisatory performance also attracted the attention of modern authors and playwrights. Ali Nassirian, head of the Ministry of Culture's Office of Theatre in Tehran until 1978 has been one of the most loyal supporters of the traditional theatre form. His production *Bongah-e Theatral* (The Theatre Company), presented first at the Festival of Arts in Shiraz in 1974, is a straight scripted version of a comic improvisatory performance. It was popular at its original showing, and was reproduced several times with great success. Another of his plays, *Siah* (The Black), explores the troubled thoughts of the blackface clown, looking for meaning in life. Bizhan Mofid's wildly popular *Jan-Nessar* (Soul-sacrificer) preserves the form and spirit of traditional improvisatory comedy, and adds the biting satire present in the Qajar court comedy.

Most recently, the Festival of Arts in Shiraz staged performances in 1977 from traditional troupes drawn from Khorassan, Kerman, and Fars provinces. Performances were held outdoors in a garden in Shiraz, and were the hit of the festival—widely attended by middle and working class citizens of Shiraz, who would never have attended other events of the festival.

Nevertheless, the bulk of comic improvisatory performance today is enacted by small troupes of entertainers based in small towns performing for village weddings. The number of troupes has diminished greatly in just the last ten or twenty years. One reason is the public feeling that this type of entertainment is no longer modern. Another reason has to do with a basic change in the form and method of financing rural weddings in Iran.[31] The third difficulty concerns the direct interference of officials of the former Iranian regime, particular of the Ministry of Culture and Art under the direction of Mehrdad Pahlbod.

Despite the support of a few officials in the ministry, such as Ali Nassirian, for the promotion of *ru-hauzi* type theatre in rural areas, provincial officials of the Ministry of Culture often attempted to interfere with the activities of the various performing troupes, demanding that they have "licenses" to perform, but not telling them how to obtain licenses (in fact, no licenses existed). Many instances of extortion by officials have also been cited by the troupes. The silliest restriction placed on these groups in recent years was the demand that they submit their "scripts" for censorship to relevant officials. For an improvisatory theatre form, this is clearly an absurd demand. However, to satisfy the officials a number of troupes dutifully wrote some rendering of their plays down on paper to be blue-penciled.

The pattern today is all too clear. The change in public taste, the spread of urban lifestyles to the provinces, and the harassment of officials have all worked together to drive the traditional troupes farther and farther into remote regions of the country. Many have disbanded during the last ten years, and still others are only barely able to make a living from their craft.

In research carried out in 1976–79, it was found that there were still several regions in Iran where the tradition was, fortunately, alive and strong. Studies of troupes in these regions for the basis of discussion which follows.

Performances of *ru-hauzi* type theatre in rural areas of Iran take place exclusively in the context of a total program of entertainment provided for a wedding or circumcision ceremony. The entertainers who enact the performance are also musicians, and during the other hours of the celebration provide music and, occasionally, other kinds of entertainment, such as acrobatics, for the enjoyment of the guests.

Fees paid to performers vary in different parts of the country and at different times of the year. In general, celebrations increase just before the religious months of Ramazan, Moharram, and Safar, and prices go up with demand.[32] As with *ta'ziyeh*, performers are housed and fed throughout the course of the wedding.

All the wedding entertainment takes place in a convenient court-yard, or other open space in the village. Occasionally, the only available place is on the village outskirts. Rugs are spread in the center of the playing area for the performers, and the guests at the celebration arrange themselves in a circle around the playing area. Many people sit on flat roofs of surrounding houses to get a better view of the proceedings. In villages which have electricity, electric lights are strung on trees or poles to light the playing areas. Where there is no electricity, or it is inconvenient to provide electric light, pressure lamps are the usual lighting medium.

As with *ta'ziyeh*, the first rank of spectators is always children. They sit as close to the playing area as possible and are a continual problem for the performers because they tend to move closer and closer to the players as the performance progresses. All celebrations have two or three men who work fulltime keeping the children in their place. If the crowd is large, the voices of the performers may not carry to the edges of the crowd. This means that those farther back may see primarily the actions of the players without hearing exactly what they are saying. Additionally, the performance may be interrupted at any minute for a variety of reasons. In Shiraz hardly a performance seen during the course of research was allowed to run to completion, because those sponsoring the celebrations seemed to insist on serving dinner halfway through the plays. Fights and arguments were another common source of disturbance. On one occasion a performance was interrupted when two trucks wanted to drive through the playing area. Occasionally, the performance loses the interest of the spectators, and the sponsor of the celebration, or the players themselves stop it before the normal conclusion.

The central figure in *ru-hauzi* performances is the clown. To him falls the burden of comedy production. He also has the most distinctive makeup and clothing of all the performers. In some areas of the

country he is dressed in a red-patterned costume and made up in blackface.[33] In other areas he wears ragged peasant clothing and uses whiteface makeup, usually simple flour.[34]

In addition to the clown figure, other role specializations in this tradition include the *hajji,* a traditional merchant in turban and beard;[35] a woman, often played by a male; a youth; a king or ruler; courtiers; and occasional specialized characters such as a doctor, witch, or angel. Performers usually develop into playing only one type of role, although they may play several different types of roles over the whole of their career. As in *ta'ziyeh,* performers graduate to older roles. It is common for a young boy to begin playing women's roles, work up to juvenile roles, eventually playing the king, *hajji,* or clown.

Stories are generally uncomplicated and may be loose paraphrases of stories from Iranian folklore, or even classic literature already known to the audience. The difficult performance conditions are thus compensated for, since the audience need not hear every single word in order to enjoy themselves; one can slip in and out of attention throughout the performance without losing the thread of the action. In contrast to the broad, loose plot structure of the performances are the individual pieces of humor which may be finegrained—turning on a single word or phrase, and coming one after another in rapid succession. Because the jokes are largely verbal and physical slapstick routines, they can be heard out of context and still be funny. This assures that when the audience members are able to pay attention, they will always find something humorous which they will be able to understand or react to.

Performers are unanimous in affirming the clown's principal role as the carrier of the burden of production of humor. Since the performances are done without any written script, the success of the humor depends on the ease with which the performers can interact, particularly with the clown. The normal pattern for this interaction involves the clown answering, restating, or reacting to statements made by others. Because the clown carries out his performance by "bounding off" the other characters, he is often peripheral to the main story line. Paradoxically, although he is seen more then any other character by the audience and is the principal vehicle for their enjoyment, he is often not mentioned in story synopses given by the players themselves. This suggests that in this theatrical form it may be the story line itself

---

Figure 10. Popular Theatre *(ru-hauzi)* in Shiraz.

which is peripheral, serving as a skeleton on which comic episodes are arranged.

Much of the humor generated by the clown in traditional improvisatory performance revolves around improper behavior toward authority figures: the wealthy *hajji*, often serving as the master of the clown-servant; the juvenile, often son of the king or *hajji* with whom the clown often has a bantering friendly relationship; and the king, sultan or court minister, who are often subject to indirect insult in the form of puns and malapropisms. When there is a villain, he is always an authority figure of some sort, able to hide his bad deeds behind the prerogatives of his social status. The wife of the *hajji* is also treated as an authority figure when the clown is a household servant, and some of the most humorous banter occurs between these two characters.

The force of the humor in these situations comes from two sources of paradox pertaining to the role of the clown *vis-à-vis* both the authority characters he is dealing with in the playing arena and the audience itself. The first is the paradox involved in the seeming motivation of the clown. He seems to be acting with no knowledge that he is mocking or insulting the other characters. He speaks with distorted speech and his insults are cast in the form of mistakes, mispronunciations, mishearings, and lack of complete understanding of the situation. For example, instead of using an honorific phrase to address the king, he will call him "the head of my donkey" which sounds similar to the intended phrase in Persian. The important point here is that the clown, acting in ignorance, cannot be blamed for his actions, precisely because they are a result of his low social condition *vis-à-vis* his superiors.

In exhibiting humor in this way the clown is, in effect, thwarting the system of social and linguistic hierarchy;[36] and, what is more important, he is "getting away with" what he is doing, since he seems not to be doing it on purpose, but rather out of inability or ignorance. The audience reaction is a combination of delight and disbelief mingled with a sense of outrage, and the result of this reaction is violent laughter. Children, as perhaps the most restricted members of village society, are the ones most affected by this, and they delight in the clown's every mocking insult.

The humor of the clown can also be ribald in the extreme. In some areas of the country the sexual and scatalogical references are so clear as to be unmistakable. Troupes in other regions prefer *double entendre* and puns of a more covert nature. There seems to be good historical precedent in this sort of humor as well. The humor of Karim Shire'i contained a good deal of highly explicit language, judging from the interchange below:

Karim: My dear fellow what might your good name be?
Chordaki: What do you want to do with it?
Karim: Write it on my (asshole)!
Chordaki: Donkey's (cock)![37]

Sexual reference is just as popular with the audience as mocking of authority, and inspires the same kind of raucous laughter. The formulae for the production of this kind of humor involves the same pattern of linguistic distortion, misunderstandings and "sight gags."

As in the mocking of authority, the clown plays on the community's sense of delight, disbelief, and outrage in his overt use of sexual reference. Though in normal circumstances family members are too embarrassed to discuss or even refer to sexual matters,[38] the most impossibly ribald scenes are witnessed and enjoyed by all spectators: the clown and the *hajji's* wife together ("mistakenly") under the bed covers; the clown and women talking about vegetables in ways which suggest that they are really talking about sexual organs; the clown and the *hajji* or sultan juxtaposed in physical situations with obvious homosexual overtones. As always, however, the clown undertakes these actions in total innocence, seemingly unaware of the nature of his actions.

In general, then, we see that comic improvisatory theatre has had a chronological history not dissimilar to that of *ta'ziyeh*. It had historical roots corresponding roughly to the same time frame as *ta'ziyeh*, reaching a point of rapid development during the Safavid era, being protected and encouraged by the court during the Qajar period, and suffering a decline and a rapid movement into rural areas of the country during the reigns of Reza Shah and Mohammad Reza Pahlavi. Like *ta'ziyeh*, *ru-hauzi*-type theatre was hindered by government officials in its free development, despite some limited, belated encouragement by a small group of intellectuals just prior to the revolutionary events of 1979.

Like *ta'ziyeh*, *ru-hauzi* continues to carry out a set of important social and emotional functions for persons who patronize it. It presents a whole range of familiar characters, stories and settings for the audience, but its ostensible purpose is different. It mocks and attacks the whole fabric of social and sexual structures which bind the spectators in their everyday life, and rather than washing the pressures of life away in a sea of tears, it aims to dispel those pressures in gales of laughter—the louder and longer the better.

Traditional Performance as Symbolic Communication

I have decided to deal with *ta'ziyeh* and *ru-hauzi* in a comparative way because in many ways they cannot be treated separately within the context of Iranian society. The characteristics of the two performance forms place them in almost total complementary distribution to each other in terms of their cultural and communicative characteristics. In linguistic analysis, complementarity of distinctive features signals that the two elements may, in fact, be different forms of the same basic underlying structure, and this may be the case for these two performance forms.

One of the most obvious points of complementarity lies in the fact that one performance type is viewed as sacred, and the other secular; and this leads to the observation that they take place at complementary, mutually exclusive, times of the year. Because weddings and other celebrations cannot be held during the months of Moharram and Safar, and are rarely held during the fasting month of Ramazan, musicial entertainers and comic performers are out of work during these periods. Except for rare occasions, when a special commemorative performance is commissioned, *ta'ziyeh* performers rarely perform outside of the traditional months of mourning.

The performance functions for players are likewise mutually exclusive. No *ta'ziyeh* performers also serve as entertainer in *ru-hauzi* theatre. Likewise, in three years of research I found only one comic actor who had ever participated as a player in a *ta'ziyeh* performance, and then only in a minor "crowd" role.

The more striking contrast has to do with the reaction each performance form is supposed to elicit from spectators, and the ways in which each form is able to achieve that reaction. Laughter and tears, though seemingly opposite emotional expressions, may indicate alternate, but equivalent ways of dealing with similar emotional and social situations. The common dynamic in both reactions is the factor of emotional release.

More important than these overt signs of complementarity, however, are the ways in which *ta'ziyeh* and *ru-hauzi* theatre complement each other in the presentation of the Iranian moral and ideological universe. *Ta'ziyeh* presents Iranians with a symbolic statement of the essential Iranian moral order—the beliefs, ideals, and behavior at the core of a society's ideological system must consist of a clear determination of the principles for separating good from bad. In this formulation "bad" is clearly "bad," and "good" is clearly "good."

Ru-hauzi, in contrast, allows Iranians an encounter with symbolic

380

material which represents the antithesis of core beliefs—an inversion of the normal principles of social order; the clown's actions are "bad," but in the context of the play they become "good." The "good" actions of those characters representing normal, upstanding citizens are likewise held up to ridicule and mocked: they become "bad." Removed from clear distinctions between good and bad, the actions of the clown, while teetering on the edge of acceptability, are ambiguous in their indication of the personal culpability of their perpetrator.

The distinction between "core" and "periphery" has become a dominant theme in contemporary study of society and culture.[39] Probably all societies have symbolic means for presenting core beliefs central to moral order and their antithesis. Both are necessary: presentation of the core to reinforce the principles of order which hold a society together, and the antithesis to make man aware of the possibilities for altering that order.

This point is well developed in Natalie Davis' brilliant essay on ludic carnival performance in the popular festivals of early sixteenth century France, cited at the beginning of this discussion.[40] She maintains that as the "truth" of the absurdities of the structure of society are revealed through the clear contrast of the inverted social order of the comic performance, laughter is produced. This paradoxically serves to reinforce the moral order as it is; but in presenting an alternative view, the seeds for change are also sown. It is true that the world of the clown is an impossible one. But what if one *could* in fact effect the changes shown in fantasy here?

Following this possibility, we see that both of the Iranian performance forms discussed here lead to the sowing of the seeds of change. *Ta'ziyeh* by holding up the ideal moral order for all to see, reminds everyone of the terrible degree to which society falls short of its high and uncompromising standards; it thus compels man to change, urging him to move closer to the core of the moral order.

Ru-hauzi in contrast, like all comic theatre, by presenting alternatives to the moral order, always holds forth the tantalizing possibility as it did in seventeenth century England in the words of Christopher Hill:

> . . . that the world might be permanently turned upside down; that the dream world of the land of Cokayne or the kingdom of heaven might be attainable on earth now.[41]

20

Chairs and Change in Qajar Times

Samuel R. Peterson

Being offered a seat in a Western chair in Iran today is as ordinary a custom as it is in most of the modern world.[1] However, the chair which is taken for granted as appropriate and comfortable seating in contemporary, urban Iranian communities was assimilated only gradually into the living habits of Iranians during the Qajar period. Like many other imports to Iran during the late eighteenth and nineteenth centuries, it inevitably changed aspects of Iranian life. What distinguishes its history from those of other imports, such as the printing press and photography, is its challenge to some of the most established customs and manners of everyday Iranian life. It took nearly a century to resolve fully the problem of when and where the chair might be adapted within the strict rules of Iranian protocol and social habits. Its eventual success represents a case of a Middle Eastern nation adjusting its traditional customs to accommodate those of the modern world.

Although not widely adopted in Iran until the Qajar era, the chair with a high back and a seat supported by four upright legs was not unknown to Iranian peoples. Such seating is represented in prehistoric, Achaemenian, and Parthian art, most notably in reliefs at Persepolis where in depicting Nau Ruz processions of vassals offering tribute to their Achaemenian ruler it is only the monarch who is represented seated. Accordingly, his seat with footrest—to be classified properly as an Iranian throne—is the most ancient of Iranian seats to offer conspicuous social status to eminent individuals.

After the Arab conquest of Iran in the seventh century, the pre-Islamic throne was abandoned by the new Muslim rulers for the imperial *takht*, the richly decorated large platform-throne low to the ground and wider than any chair, and the *korsi,* the simple stool occasionally overlaid with precious metals and studded with jewels. It was also customary for Muslim rulers to seat themselves directly on a carpeted floor with large brocaded bolsters behind their backs or at their sides. Such a seating position, which perhaps seems informal for a dignified monarch, had its own terms defined by protocol: the right to sit cross-legged was a prerogative of the shah.[2]

The earliest evidence of the chair being introduced to Islamic Iran occurs in several miniatures dating from the Safavid period. In one dated ca. 1560–70 an Iranian musician, represented alone and playing a flute in a stylized landscape, is seated in a wooden X chair, a "Savonarola" chair such as were common in contemporary Renaissance Europe, particularly in Italy.[3] In a miniature dated 1663 and attributed to the court artist reputedly trained in Italy, Mohammad Zaman, a European lady accompanied by Western companions is seated in a landscape in a frail chair with low arms and a low back.[4] In another miniature attributed to Mohammad Zaman, Princes Tur and Salm are seated outdoors in front of a colonnaded hall in chairs with high backs and arms while numerous attendants stand formally at a respectul distance.[5] Little can be specifically determined of the social significance of these chairs which are represented in each case in an outdoor setting. The flute player is represented without any social context and the European lady entirely within a European one. It is only in the formal representation of Tur and Salm that there is indication of the chair being adopted by Iranian princes as a seat of special status. On the whole, chair representations occur seldom in Safavid arts, the traditional *takht,* the *korsi* or the floor more often being the seating for important personages. For example, represented on the walls of Chehel Sotun at state banquets for visiting Oriental dignitaries, both Iranian rulers and their royal guests are seated on a carpet on the floor while being entertained by musicians and dancers. Because the chair was only recently imported to Iran and thereby attracted only moderate interest among the Safavids, its controversial role in the history of Iranian protocol had not yet developed.

About mid-eighteenth century there begins a series of comments by Western travelers on chairs in Iran, which is followed at the end of the century by a series of representations of chairs in Qajar paintings. Both demonstrate that chairs were used by Iranian princes and Westerners. In the 1740s Hanway reports that at a reception with the governor of Astrabad and local dignitaries a chair was ordered for him since he could not "accomodate (himself) to their manner."[6]

Elsewhere in his accounts he mentions Nader Shah "sometimes sits upon a large sofa, or chair, cross-legged."[7]

Like many subsequent travelers, Hanway restricts his comments to the practice and omits any thorough description of the chair itself. Nevertheless, from several detailed, early nineteenth century descriptions and representations by Qajar artists, it seems the chair adopted by the Qajar court was more elaborate than those depicted in the Safavid miniatures mentioned above. Most early Qajar chairs represented as the formal seat for Iranian rulers or observed on formal occasions at the palace are to be classified as chairs of state. Besides their occupant being royalty, their special status is additionally enhanced, like the traditional *takht* and *korsi,* by gilding, encrustation, painted decoration and the high back rising to a point.

During his travels in Iran in 1810–12, Ouseley describes chairs at a Tehran palace as "much (resembling) those . . . fashionable some centuries ago in France and England."[8] His contemporary Morier describes chairs provided the English delegation at an outdoor reception given by the governor of Isfahan in a tent as "old-fashioned, like those in the sculptures at Persepolis."[9] The prototype for the Qajar chair of state, however, seems to be neither the Persepolis throne nor any European model but instead a chair of state which was known to Safavid Iran and Mughal India. Several were given to Russian tsars by Safavids in the sixteenth and seventeenth century;[10] and as many as six appear in a seventeenth century formal portrait of sons of Shah Jehan, the royal progeny being seated under a canopy each in a chair of state which is simply constructed and, characteristic of Mughal minor arts, heavily studded with jewels.[11]

An early Qajar to make frequent use of the chair of state for formal and state occasions was Fath Ali Shah. Besides its examples in various portraits of him, he is mentioned in 1809 at races outside Tehran seated "on a high chair under a canopy, the sides of which were formed of gold cloth, and of looking glasses."[12] Again at the races twenty-five years later, he sits "upon a throne, or chair of state, high-backed and ample, enamelled with gold, and jewelled all over."[13] His son, the crown prince Abbas Mirza, is described in 1808 holding audience outside Tabriz "in his tent . . . seated in the European fashion on an arm chair of gild wood."[14] Fath Ali Shah's eldest son and governor of Kermanshah in the second decade of the century, Mohammad Ali Mirza, is twice portrayed seated in a chair of state, the arms of which are carved in the shape of a lion, an ancient Iranian imperial symbol.[15] Thus, the chair of state which was used for both formal portraits and official audiences of prince governors is defined by Qajar terms as the seat of ruling power in the provinces. Occupied exclusively by the shah or princes, it was also a practical substitute for the more imposing larger *takht*. Easily portable, the chair of state which is consistently portrayed or mentioned in an outdoor setting was used in place of larger thrones, on the one hand, for events attended by the shah held outside the Tehran palace and, on the other, in provincial capitals as the seat of imperial authority. Accordingly, its status approximates that of the traditional *takht* while the occasion where it is used is as formal as state functions held within the palace itself.

After the chair of state was incorporated into Iranian protocol, Qajar princes began to adopt the Western chair. In comparison to the chair of state, it was smaller, of lighter construction, and with a lower back. Its initial appearance and subsequent use, as indicated by Hanway and later travelers, was in part to provide comfort and convenience to Europeans. While being adopted as a privileged seat for Iranians, it was on certain occasions reserved exclusively for princes, thus promoting its status within the hierarchy of Qajar seats. Whether the favor might still be granted to the *farangi* was determined by the formality of the occasion or left to the personal dictates of the individual prince. If the same privilege was granted to an Iranian subject, it was not as a gesture of hospitality to make one feel at home in a foreign land but instead a clear indication of the Iranian's rank.

Travelers' comments indicate that the controversy of the Western chair which arose from the problem of when it was to be used and by whom was not resolved until mid-nineteenth century. In 1808 the English ambassador and his party were offered chairs in Bushehr at a reception held by a local khan.[16] In the 1820s in a nobleman's house in Hamadan chairs were kept for "the accomodation of Europeans."[17] The early Qajar custom of the *farangi* seated in a chair and not the Iranian host is described when Lady Ouseley visited the harem in Shiraz and was provided a chair while "the queen, supported by cushions, sat on a nammed (*sic*) on the floor."[18] If the shah was seated conspicuously on a throne, seating European guests in chairs did not challenge the traditional hierarchy. Arrangements for a reception for the Imperial Russian Embassy held in Soltaniyeh in 1817 included three types of seating accommodations: the throne for the shah, a chair opposite for the ambassador, and chairs upholstered in red velvet, presumably for the ambassador's counselors.[19] A comment made on Fath Ali Shah's court in the 1820s indicates how restricted the privilege of sitting at royal receptions was: "None is allowed to sit excepting poets, persons of extraordinary sanctity and ambassadors; the king's ministers never enjoy this privilege."[20] Yet, in contrast to such practices is a representation of Fath Ali Shah's formal audience in which the entire European delegation, along with the Iranian attendants, is portrayed standing while the shah conspicuously occupies the only seat depicted, the large Peacock Throne.[21] Perhaps the extreme formality of this particular occasion precluded the convenience of chairs for guests. To judge by a comment made by J. B. Fraser, policy seems to have eased during Mohammad Shah's reign (1834–48):

"... a little bit of state which the princes of Persia have of late assumed in consequence of the English having permission to sit in their presence. It became a matter of courtesy to offer them chairs, and, of course, the prince receiving them felt it not consistent with his dignity to sit lower than his visitors, so he perched himself in a chair also; now, whether their guests have chairs given them or not, I observe they commonly make use of one."[22]

Even this policy, however, was altered as late as the early twentieth century when only one armchair for an outdoor reception held in a tent was needed since "no one can sit in the presence of the Shah."[23]

As suggested by Fraser, it was in the 1830s that the Western chair makes its way substantially into the seating habits and state protocol of Iran. Besides a velvet chair, along with a gold watch, being presented in the early 1830s by a foreign embassy to the heir apparent,[24] a Western-type armchair overlaid with gold and inset with turquoise was, according to its inscriptions, used by Mohammad Shah, who preferred the Western chair because he suffered from gout and could not "kneel in the Persian fashion."[25] It is also in the 1830s that there begins a series of portraits of Qajar princes seated in Western chairs, which in type most frequently compare with the drawing room or parlor chairs of Sheraton and Hepplewhite.

Both sexes of the Iranian court evidently adopted the imported custom about the same time. An oil painting attributed to the period of Mohammad Shah portrays an Iranian lady smoking a *qalian* seated in a Western-type chair.[26] When Lady Sheil went to the palace in 1850 for an audience with Naser od-Din Shah's mother, she was first seated in a chair in a waiting room and then escorted into a reception room where, unlike the queen at Lady Ouseley's visit, the dowager sat in a chair at a table. In two chairs at her side sat "the Shah's two principal wives and cousins," still as statues never uttering a word.[27]

During the third quarter of the nineteenth century chairs become more commonplace, and in single rooms their number increases. A reception room in Bushehr is described in the 1850s as having "two dozen arm-chairs distributed along the walls that contain many engravings from Sir Joshua Reynold's paintings."[28] This arrangement of chairs is remarkably similar to that of Naser od-Din Shah's audience hall at the Golestan Palace, a room which defined, of course, tastes and standards in the capital and provinces alike and was in itself totally in keeping with the proper English drawing room as recommended in Sheraton's manual on furniture styles. Western embassies in Iran provided the court and the elite with their models, but as Iranians, including Naser od-Din Shah, made trips to Europe, their knowledge became more firsthand. As furnishings of Iranian homes became sufficiently Westernized that they received only random observation from travelers, by the 1880s the chair is seldom remarked upon as the curiosity it once had been.

In spite of its acceptance by Qajar princes and the elite, the Western chair popularly was identified throughout its history in Iran as a peculiarly *farangi* object. Few of the travelers who witnessed the *ta'ziyeh* production relating the story of the *farangi* ambassadors' conversion to Shi'ism upon seeing the plight of the Kerbala survivors at Yazid's court fail to mention that the ambassadors were seated in Western chairs. Both on stage and in representations of the scene in the popular *qahvehkhaneh* school of painting, the Western chair and European costuming were means for identifying the *farangi* ambassadors.[29] Westerners residing in Qajar Iran customarily were asked to provide both chairs and costumes for this particular *ta'ziyeh* production and, according to Lady Sheil, for accommodating European guests who attended the performance.[30] The distinction which the chair provided its occupant is witnessed by Gobineau who mentions its role in *ta'ziyeh* productions: "There is always an armchair on stage where the Imam Hosain and particular heroes of the *ta'ziyeh* sit; other persons cannot take their place. It is a way to show a person particular respect in public."[31]

It seems the ulama had little or no objection to the use of the Western chair. For an audience at which the *Imam Jom'eh* of Isfahan received foreigners in the 1860s, three chairs were provided for the traveler's party and a fourth for the *Imam*.[32] What might seem an instance of Iranians viewing the chair with skepticism is, in fact, a matter of ritual. When the gold watch and velvet chair mentioned earlier were presented to the heir apparent, both were immersed in water to purify what was impure from the hands of infidels. A response to a rocking chair in the provinces, however, can be attributed to skepticism. When a village woman was seated in a rocking chair in a missionary's home and was rocked forward and onto the floor, she fled from the room crying she had been put into "one of the conversion machines."[33] During its period of adoption in Iran, however, the general controversy over the Western chair was the practical consideration of how it could be adapted to the strict practices of Iranian protocol. Although its resolution was long in coming, the chair throughout its history in Iran always retained its position as a seat of honor and authority.

The assimilation of Western chairs and furnishings in Iran in the course of the nineteenth century was part of a more general assimilation of Western culture and customs. At first it was largely limited to the Qajar court and then included the elite, but as other groups of Iranian society in turn imitated the modern custom of sitting in chairs, the assimilation in the twentieth century continued apace, increasing both the demand and production in Iran of Western-type furniture. Today the furniture store to be found on the main street of the modern Iranian city is as common as the drugstore and supermarket, which also, significantly, are not to be found in the traditional bazaar.

Chairs in middle class homes and in business and government offices are still frequently arranged along the sides of a room, repeating the arrangement noted in the Golestan audience hall. Unless there are particularly eminent guests, the traditional, often provincial, homeowner or official takes his seat in the middle of one side of the room and receives all his guests simultaneously. In the most Westernized homes and offices chairs are likely to be arranged less formally and to be fewer in number since guests, as in the West, are received separately. The ulama, including the highest ranks, receive any number of visitors at the same time; and—as demonstrated by Ayatollah Ruhollah Khomani, even when granting interviews to Westerners in France in 1978—in preference to chairs they are likely to sit on carpets with bolsters at their backs or sides. Finally, among groups neither affluent nor Westernized—i.e., conservative families, particularly in rural areas, and nomads—seating customarily is on carpets. Hence, today there are three major patterns to be found: chairs used as in the West in Westernized homes and offices; chairs used in an adaptation of traditional patterns in more conservative homes; and traditional customs without any use of the chair in rural, religious, and less affluent homes. Accordingly, the chair has become one of the most conspicuous of the sociocultural phenomena which both distinguishes and separates the Westernized elite from traditional classes of Iranian society.

As ubiquitous as the chair is in modern Iran, and in spite of its historical challenge to established conventions, the chair in itself has not trully altered traditional Iranian protocol. Although seating customs have been modified by the chair, the established protocol for receptions with eminent persons being seated in the center and lesser persons to the side has not significantly changed except in extreme examples of Westernized homes and offices. Indeed, rather than Iranian protocol being changed by its occurence, it is the modern chair which has been modified by Iranian use. Besides being treated to veneers of indigenous design, it has continuously been adapted to conform to traditional seating practices. To what extent the chair will be retained in the Islamic Republic may well become one measure of the revival of traditional Islam in Iran.

Notes

1. Religion, Society, and Revolution in Modern Iran

1. The role of the religious opposition was noted in Hamid Algar, "The Oppositional Role of the Ulama in Twentieth Century Iran," in Nikki R. Keddie, ed., *Scholars, Saints, and Sufis* (Berkeley: University of California Press, 1972); and by Nikki R. Keddie's article on religion and politics in Iran in *Le Monde Diplomatique*, August, 1977.

2. In addition to the above cited articles see the articles by G. Thaiss and N. Keddie ed., *Scholars, Saints, and Sufis* (Berkeley: University of California 1785–1906 (Berkeley: University of California Press, 1969; N. Keddie, *Religion and Rebellion in Iran* (London: Frank Cass, 1966), and idem, "Religion and Irreligion in Early Iranian Nationalism," and "The Origins of the Religious-Radical Alliance in Iran," reprinted in *Iran: Religion, Politics and Society* (London: Frank Cass, 1980); and in articles by A. K. S. Lambton, notably, "A Reconsideration of the Position of the Marja' al-Taqlīd and the Religious Institution," *Studia Islamica* 20 (1964): 115–135.

3. N. Keddie, "Roots of the Ulama's Power in Modern Iran," *Scholars, Saints, and Sufis*.

4. Joseph Eliash, "Misconceptions Regarding the Juridical Status of the Iranian 'Ulama'," *International Journal of Middle East Studies* 10: 1 (1979): 9–25; and Said Amir Arjomand, "Political Action and Legitimate Domination in Shi'ite Iran: fourteenth to eighteenth centuries A.D.," *Archives Européennes de Sociologie* 20: 1 (1979): 59–109.

5. Both Eliash and Arjomand have done much research, and many of their points are convincing. Eliash, however, seems to think that only the literal law and doctrines of the first centuries after the occultation may be regarded as true Shi'ism; and says "The establishment of the Safavid state in the sixteenth century was too late to modify any of the politico-theological doctrines of the Imamate" ("Misconceptions," p. 24). In fact, doctrinal changes concerning such matters have continued until now. As to Arjomand, one must reserve judgment about his treatment of unquoted sources when one sees how he misinterprets Algar and Keddie ("Political Action," pp. 60–61) as attributing to the ulama the charisma of the Imams, which is not mentioned or implied by any of the passages he quotes.

6. *Monsieur le Chavalier Chardin en Perse*, Vol. 2 (Amsterdam, 1711), pp. 337–338 and passim.

7. Algar, *Religion and State*, pp. 3–4 is one of those to recognize this early

theoretical and practical quietism stressed by Arjomand. On the double edged potential of Shi'i doctrine see, however, W. Montgomery Watt, "The Reappraisal of 'Abbasid Shi'ism," in *Arabic and Islamic Studies in Honour of Hamilton A. R. Gibb* (Leiden: E. J. Brill, 1966), p. 167.

8. An important contribution to the study of twentieth century religio-political doctrine on this and other matters is Shahrough Akhavi, *Religion and Politics in Contemporary Iran* (Albany: SUNY Press, 1980).

9. Algar, *Religion and State,* passim.

10. A book by the constitutionalist *alim,* Mohammad Hosain Na'ini has been cited by Algar, in "Oppositional Role of the Ulama," and in a book by A. H. Hairi to suggest the high level of ulama understanding of con-stitutionalism early in the century. There is no evidence that Na'ini was widely read during the revolution of 1906. His appeal seems to have been limited until his book was reprinted with an introduction by the oppositional Ayatollah Taleqani in 1955. It seems reasonable to see him more as an influence on recent movements than as representing an important trend at the time he wrote. On the other side, Said Arjomand at a congress at Babolsar, Iran, 1978, presented as an important theorist a nineteenth century *alim* who held views at odds with those of engagé ulama—again no proof of the influence of this *alim* was given.

11. Gad S. Gilbar, "The Big Merchants (tujjār) and the Persian Constitu-tional Revolution of 1906," *Asian and African Studies* 11: 3 (1977): 275–303.

12. N. Keddie, *Religion and Rebellion in Iran,* and the Persian and Western sources cited therein.

13. The Persian literature on the revolution is enormous, but the best general works are probably still Ahmad Kasravi, *Tarikh-e mashruteh-ye Iran,* 4th ed. (Tehran, n.d.); and Mehdi Malekzadeh, *Tarikh-e enqelab-e mashrutiyat-e Iran* (Tehran, 1959); in English the most useful general works are E. G. Browne, *The Persian Revolution of 1905–1909* (Cambridge: Cambridge University Press, 1910); and W. Morgan Shuster, *The Strangling of Persia* (New York: The Century Co., 1912).

14. See Algar, "Oppositional Role," and Lambton, "Reconsideration." Regarding Khomaini, Algar wrote (in 1972), "His fame and popularity rest, however, not so much upon his learning—in which Shari'atmadari and others are acknowledged to excel him—as upon his forthright and uncom-promising hostility to the Shah's regime." (p. 245).

15. Ruhollah Khomaini, *Hokumat-e Islami* (n.p., n.d.). According to the version translated into English by the U. S. Joint Publications Research Service, *Islamic Government* (Washington, 1979), these are lessons in jurispru-dence given by Khomaini in Najaf in 1969–70 under the title "Governance of Jurisprudent" (a title by which the same book is sometimes, confusingly, called in Persian). The early book, *Kashf al-Asrar,* dates from 1943–44.

16. In addition to the above work, see Khomaini, *Nahzat-e Eslami, 3: Tazad-e Eslam ba Shahanshahan va rezhim-e Shahanshahi* (n.d., n.p.) (A June, 1971 speech, Najaf), a work directed particularly against the shah's mythomaniac and wasteful celebration of an alleged 2,500 years of Persian monarchy in 1971.

17. Algar's version is in "Oppositional Role." Willem Floor has sent me copies of open letters from Khomaini in 1963 attacking the electoral law and votes for women, and extensive contacts with Iranians leads Floor, like

Lambton and myself, to believe that many of the ulama, who might own land personally and/or gain income from it as *vaqf*, opposed the land reform, even if there was no official decree after Borujerdi's.

18. See the works cited in ns. 15 and 16, above.

19. Ruhollah Khomaini, *Resaleh-ye Tauzih al-Masa'el* (Najaf: Chapkhaneh-ye Adab, n.d.). This work mainly reprints the words of Borujerdi, but the parts on the Family Protection Law must be Khomaini's.

20. I have been struck in the U. S. and Europe at how little antishah students had read of Khomaini's publications. Those who had read some material tend, as often happens, to stress only the words they like, notably Khomaini's attacks on monarchy, on imperialists, especially Israel and the U. S.; on corruption, profiteering, waste, and the dishonest rich. His views on literal holy law and rule by the ulama were often ignored; subsequent events suggest they should have been taken seriously.

21. The *Mojahedin* and Taleqani have numerous Persian publications, and there are a few translations from the voluminous writings of Shariati, on whose life and ideas see Mangol Bayat-Philipp's article in this volume and the works she cites. Since Shariati's death, proregime forces have sometimes tried to appropriate him, although recently ulama statements against him have been reprinted, possibly to discredit the pro-Shariati *Mojahedin*.

22. Interview with Ayatollah Kazem Shariatmadari, Sept., 1979, Qom. Shariatmadari's criticisms of the regime have been reported in the press. Ayatollah Taleqani suspended criticism of the regime between the spring of 1979 and the last statement of his life, in September 1979, when he criticized the regime and himself for promoting fighting against the Kurds. Between these dates, Khomaini picked Taleqani to lead the massive open air Friday prayers at the University of Tehran that began with the first Friday of Ramazan. At these prayers (which I attended) Taleqani supported the regime's views and said that Kurdish and Arab unrest had been instigated by leftists; minorities had the same rights as all Iranians and hence had no grounds for complaint. On oppositional Shi'ism see Nikki R. Keddie (and Yann Richard), *Roots of Revolution: An Interpretive History of Modern Iran* (New Haven: Yale University Press, 1981).

2. Tradition and Change in Iranian Socio-Religious Thought

1. Henry Corbin, *En Islam Iranien: aspects spirituels et philosophiques,* vol. 1 (Paris, 1971), pp. 7, 15.

2. This idea I discuss further in a forthcoming work on socioreligious thought in nineteenth century Iran.

3. Hamid Algar, *Religion and State in Iran, 1785–1906: The Role of the Ulama in the Qajar Period* (Berkeley and Los Angeles, 1969), p. 10.

4. R. A. Nicholson, *Studies in Islamic Mysticism* (Cambridge, 1922), p. 18; R. Landau, *The Philosophy of Ibn Arabi* (London, 1959), pp. 33, 38, 58.

5. W. Ivanow, *Studies in Early Persian Ismailism* (London, 1948), pp. 5, 6, 8; and idem, *Kalami Pir: A treatise on Ismaili doctrine* (Bombay, 1935), pp. xliii, 21.

6. Fazlur Rahman, *The Philosophy of Mulla Sadra* (Albany, 1975), pp. 169–179, 180–185.

7. Ivanow, *Kalami Pir,* pp. xxxiii, 70; Paul E. Walker, "Eternal Cosmos and

the Womb of History: Time in Early Ismaili Thought," *International Journal of Middle Eastern Studies* 9:3 (1978): 355–366.

8. Landau, *The Philosophy of Mulla Sadra,* pp. 97, 117, 206.

9. In this paper I am using the terms mystics and *urafa* in their broadest possible meaning as a group, comprising the *hukama* (theosophers) as well as the gnostics, distinct from the *fuqaha*.

10. Abol Qasim Ibrahimi, *Fehrest-e kotob-e marhum Ahmad-e Ahsa'i va sayer-e mashayekh-e 'ezam,* 2 vol. in one (Kerman, 1957); Morteza Modarresi, *Shaikhigari va babigari* (Tehran, 1972); H. Corbin, *L'ecole shaykhie en theologie Shi'ite* (Tehran, 1959); and idem, *En Islam iranien,* vol. 4; A.L.M. Nicolas, *Essai sur le Sheikhisme,* 4 vol. (Paris, 1910).

11. Nicolas, *Essai sur le Sheikhisme,* vol. 2, pp. 52–55.

12. *Ershad al-awwam,* Kerman, vol. 1, pp. 81–82, 164–167, 170–171; vol. 3, pp. 186–187, 3–5, 13; vol. 4, pp. 44–49.

13. Ibid., vol. 2, pp. 201–204; vol. 3, pp. 7–10, 14; vol. 4, pp. 11–14, 17–18.

14. Ibid., vol. 4, pp. 116–138, 258–276, 279–287.

15. H. M. Balyuzi, *The Bab* (Oxford, 1973); A. L. M. Nicolas, *Seyyed Ali Mohammad dit le Bab* (Paris, 1905), p. 230.

16. *Selections from the Writings of the Bab* (London, 1976), p. 106.

17. A. L. M. Nicolas, *Le Beyan Persan,* Paris, Part IV, pp. 164–166.

18. Ibid., p. 13.

19. Ibid., p. 117.

20. Ibid., Part III, pp. 74–79.

21. Texts translated by Nikki R. Keddie, *An Islamic Response to Imperialism* (Berkeley and Los Angeles, 1968), p. 125.

22. Ibid., p. 173.

23. Ibid., p. 172.

24. Ibid., p. 173, footnote no. 24.

25. Ibid., p. 182.

26. Ibid., p. 169.

27. Ibid., p. 182.

28. Ibid., pp. 183–184.

29. Ibid., p. 187.

30. *Seh Maktub,* unpublished manuscript, courtesy of Nikki R. Keddie.

31. *Hasht Behesht* (Tehran, n.d.), p. 154; *Seh maktub,* pp. 98–99.

32. Ibid., p. 88.

33. See his "Charand-parand" in S. Nafisi, *Shahkarha-ye nathr-e farsi,* vol. 1 (Tehran, 1957).

34. Parts of his operetta *Rasthakhiz* are translated by M. Ishaque, *Modern Persian Poetry* (Calcutta, 1943).

35. See my own "Shi'ism in contemporary Iranian politics: the case of Ali Shari'ati," in *Iran: Toward Modernity,* ed. by Haim and Kedourie (London, 1980); and "The concept of historical continuity in modern Iranian thought," in *Asian and African Studies,* 1980.

36. E. P. Elwell-Sutton, *Modern Iran* (London, 1941), p. 75.

37. Alireza Maibadi, *Raushanfekran . . . tarek-e donya* (Shiraz, 1973).

38. Jalal Al-e Ahmad, *Arzyabi-ye shattabzadeh* (Tabriz, 1965), p. 164.

39. *Safarnameh: Khasi dar miqat* (Tehran, 1966), p. 19.

40. Ibid., p. 98.

41. *Entezar mazhab-e e'teraz,* Tehran, p. 19.

42. Ibid., pp. 20–21; *Ommat va Emamat* (Tehran, 1968), pp. 5–6.
43. See especially his *Mas'uliyat-e Shi'eh budan* (Tehran, 1971).
44. *Entezar*, pp. 32–39, 41, 45.
45. *Arzyabi*, p. 127.
46. *Az Koja aghaz konim* (Tehran, n.d.), pp. 10–11, 38.
47. *Ommat*, p. 182.
48. Ibid., p. 162.
49. Michael M. J. Fischer, *Iran: From Religious Disputes to Revolution* (Cambridge: Harvard University Press, 1980).

3. *The Transformation of Health Care in Modern Iranian History*

1. Research for this paper was carried out jointly with my wife, Mary-Jo DelVecchio Good, from 1972 to 1974 in Maragheh, East Azerbaijan, Iran. Support was provided by a United States Public Health Service Traineeship and the Pathfinder Fund. Writing and analysis was supported, in part, by NIMH-Psychiatry Education Branch, grant No. MH 14022.
2. Clyde M. Woods and Theodore D. Graves, *The Process of Medical Change in a Highland Guatemalan Town* (Los Angeles: Latin American Center, University of California, 1973).
3. David Landy, "Role Adaptation: Traditional Curers Under the Impact of Western Medicine," *American Ethnologist* 1 (1974): 102–127.
4. See, for example, Harold A. Gould, "Modern Medicine and Folk Cognition in Rural India," *Human Organization* 24 (1965): 201–208; Michael H. Logan, "Humoral Medicine in Guatemala and Peasant Acceptance of Modern Medicine," *Human Organization* 32 (1973): 385–395; Benjamin D. Paul, ed., *Health, Culture, and Community* (New York: Russell Sage Foundation, 1955); and Ozzie G. Simmons, "Popular and Modern Medicine in Mestizo Communities of Costal Peru and Chile," *Journal of American Folklore* 68 (1955): 57–71.
5. Lola Romanucci-Ross, "The Hierarchy of Resort in Curative Practices: The Admiralty Islands, Melanesia," *Journal of Health and Social Behavior* 10 (1969): 201–209.
6. Edward H. Kass, "Infectious Diseases and Social Change," *Journal of Infectious Diseases* 123 (1971): 110–114; and Thomas McKeown, *The Rise of Population* (New York: Academic Press, 1977).
7. Walsh McDermott *et al.*, "Health Care Experiment at Many Farms," *Science* 175 (1972): 23–31.
8. Michel Foucault, *Madness and Civilization* (New York: Random House, 1965); idem, *The Birth of the Clinic: An Archaeology of Medical Perception* (New York: Vintage Books, 1973); cf. Everret Mendelsohn, "The Social Construction of Scientific Reality," *Sociology of the Sciences* 1 (1977): 3–26.
9. Diane Flaherty *et al.*, *The Political Economy of Health*, special volume of *The Review of Radical Political Economics* 9:1 (1977); Vincente Navarro, "The Political and Economic Origin of the Underdevelopment of Health in Latin America," in *Medicine Under Capitalism*, ed. Vincente Navarro (New York: Prodist, 1976), pp. 3–32.
10. Peter Kong-ming New and Mary Louie New, "The Links Between Health and the Political Structure in New China," *Human Organization* 34

(1975): 237–251; Vincente Navarro, "Health, Health Services, and Health Planning in Cuba," *International Journal of Health Services* 2 (1972): 397–432.

11. This analysis was stimulated by a lecture in the Harvard University Department of History of Science by Jean-Claude Guedon, "Althusser, Foucault, and the History of Science," April 16, 1976. See Louis Althusser, *For Marx* (New York: Vintage Books, 1970) for an elaboration of this position.

12. On Abbasid medicine see, for example, Donald Campbell, *Arabian Medicine and its Influence on the Middle Ages* (London: Kegan Paul, Trench, Trubner & Co., 1926); Cyril Elgood, *A Medical History of Persia* (Cambridge: Cambridge University Press, 1951); Dr. Ahmed Issa Bey, *Histoire des Bimaristans (Hopitaux): a l'Epoque Islamique* (Cairo: Imprimerie Paul Barbey, 1928); Amin A. Khairallah, *Outline of Arabic Contributors to Medicine* (Beirut: American Press, 1946); Seyyed Hossein Nasr, *Science and Civilization in Islam* (New York: New American Library, 1968); and Allen O. Whipple, *The Role of the Nestorians and Muslims in the History of Medicine* (Princeton: Princeton University Press, 1967). The classic treatment of Safavid medicine in Iran is Cyril Elgood, *A Medical History of Persia* (Cambridge: Cambridge University Press, 1951); cf. Elgood, *Safavid Surgery* (Oxford: Pergamon Press, 1966).

13. Cyril Elgood, "*Tibb-ul-Nabbi* or *Medicine of the Prophet:* Being a translation of Two Works of the Same Name," *Osiris* 13 (1962): 33–192.

14. Nikki R. Keddie, "The Iranian Power Structure and Social Change 1800–1969: An Overview," *International Journal of Middle Eastern Studies* 2 (1971): 3–20; idem. "Stratification, Social Control and Capitalism in Iranian Villages: Before and After Land Reform," in *Rural Politics and Social Change in the Middle East*, eds. Richard Antoun and Iliya Harik (Bloomington: Indiana University Press, 1971), pp. 364–402. The quotation is from Marx and Engels, in Robert C. Tucker, *The Marx-Engels Reader* (New York: W. W. Norton, 1972), p. 388.

15. See Keddie, "Stratification," pp. 365–370 for a fuller discussion; cf. Robert A. McDaniel, *The Shuster Mission and the Persian Constitutional Revolution* (Minneapolis: Bibliotheca Islamica, 1974).

16. Peter Avery, *Modern Iran* (London: Ernest Benn Ltd., 1965), p. 46.

17. MERIP, "Iranian Nationalism and the Great Powers: 1872–1954," *MERIP Reports*, no. 37 (1975).

18. As described for Morocco by Jim Paul, "Medicine and Imperialism in Morocco," *MERIP Reports*, no. 60 (1977), pp. 3–12.

19. As described for the Ivory Coast by Judith N. Lasker, "The Role of Health Services in Colonial Rule: The Case of the Ivory Coast," *Culture, Medicine and Psychiatry* 1 (1977):277–297.

20. Elgood, *Medical History of Persia*, p. 472.

21. Ibid., p. 501.

22. Of the five major epidemics of cholera in Europe in the nineteenth century, four (1823, 1830, 1847, 1892) passed through Afghanistan, Iran, the Caspian Sea area and Russia, and into Europe. European nations thus sought to control cholera by preventing its spread through Iran and the Persian Gulf. See John Gilmour, *Report on an Investigation into the Sanitary Conditions in Persia* (Geneva: League of Nations, Health Organization, 1925), p. 37.

23. Elgood, *Medical History of Persia*, p. 528.

24. See Gilmour, *Report*, pp. 32–36 for translations.

25. By 1925, when the League of Nations undertook an investigation into

sanitary conditions in Iran, 253 of the 905 licensed physicians had diplomas in Western medicine. Of the total, 323 practiced in Tehran. The ratio of physicians to population was one doctor for every 680 persons in Tehran, but one doctor for every 16,800 inhabitants in the rest of the country. Ibid., p. 32.

26. Mary-Jo DelVecchio Good, "Social Hierarchy and Social Change in a Provincial Iranian Town" (Ph.D. diss., Harvard University, 1976); and idem, "Social Hierarchy in Provincial Iran: The Case of Qajar Maragheh," *Iranian Studies* 10 (1977): 129–163.

27. This mode of treatment is much like the style of practice of some *du'a nevis* today, although women readily come as clients. Receiving several people at the same time to discuss their problems is traditional in Iran.

28. This quotation and similar quotations are taken from my field notes.

29. At times in Persian history in the large cities here were *hakim bashis* (chief or head physicians) or *muhtasibs* (inspectors-general) who examined apprentices and declared them ready for practice. Elgood, *History of Persian Medicine*, pp. 244–278.

30. This oral history of medical care in Maragheh is based on pieces of history from stories people told me or memories they had of practitioners. Each physician was then listed on a card and an estimate made—from cumulated accounts—of when he practiced in Maragheh. I then calculated how many physicians practiced at each time, and what their characteristics were. While these figures are estimates, much effort was taken to make them as accurate as possible.

31. Of the 13 hakims, nine were Muslim (three trained as mullas), one a Bahai, and two Armenian Christians. An Assyrian Catholic surgeon, trained in the Dar ol-Fonun and America, practiced in Maragheh with mission support until he died in 1919.

32. For example, a missionary in Urumiyeh, Dr. Cochrane, became famous for surgery, especially for cataracts. His patients include wealthy aristocrats who traveled with their retinue to seek his care because they were too sick to make the journey to Europe. R. E. Speer, *A Biography of Joseph Plumb Cochrane, M.D. of Persia* (New York: Revell, 1911).

33. Elgood, *Medical History of Persia*, pp. 545–558.

34. Ibid., pp. 559–583.

35. Gilmour, *Report*, pp. 49–62.

36. Quoted in Gilmour, *Report*, p. 55.

37. Elgood, *Medical History of Persia*, p. 564.

38. Calculated from budget estimates given in Julian Bharier, *Economic Development in Iran, 1900–1970* (London: Oxford University Press, 1971), p. 65. It is possible that various public health expenditures—water supplies, sewage systems, etc.—are not included in this estimate.

39. Harry C. Sinderson, *Ten Thousand and One Nights: Memories of Iraq's Sherifan Dynasty* (London: Hodder and Stoughton, 1973), p. 132.

40. Ibid., p. 140.

41. One of these, Hakim Mirza Yusef Tibiyani, was son of a Maragheh *mujtahid*, an *alim* (learned man), preacher, performer of weddings, legal specialist, and also a hakim. Shortly after licensing requirements were instituted, he gave up medical practice and used his office for fulltime legal practice.

42. It is significant that hakims in Maragheh and elsewhere in Iran never

banded together to resist the suppression of Galenic-Islamic medicine as did traditional physicians in India and China. By the time licensing took effect in Maragheh, the use of Western drugs was common, and many of the hakims were able to pass the examination to be licensed. They thus did not strongly oppose the suppression of the formal practice of Galenic-Islamic medicine and the elevation of Western medicine to orthodoxy.

43. I distinguish physicians who were called "hakim" from those called "doktor" by my informants. "Doktor" seems to have been used by physicians trained in cosmopolitan medical institutions. I put "surgeon" in quotations to indicate traditional surgeons who did not carry out modern procedures. Of the six called "doktor" in 1935, two were trained in the Tehran Medical School, two in Russia, one in Europe, and one in the American Presbyterian hospital in Urumiyeh. Three of the six were Muslims, three Armenians. The six came from Tabriz, Ardebil, Khoy and Maragheh, all in Azerbaijan.

44. Byron J. Good, "Medical Change and the Doctor-Patient Relationship in an Iranian Provincial Town," in *Social Sciences and Problems of Development,* ed. Khodadad Farmanfarmaian (Princeton: Princeton University Program in Near Eastern Studies, 1976), pp. 244–259.

45. Physicians and druggists in Iran today often describe the evolution of medicine as a change from herbal medicine *(alafiyat)* to "powders" to synthesized drugs. The powders, called *protoshimi, majestral, resepsiyon,* or simply *toz* ("powder" in Turki), were chemicals that were mixed by formulae to prepare drugs. The proportion of packaged synthetic drugs to mixed chemical drugs used in Maragheh increased from perhaps 30/70 in the 1930s to 50/50 in the mid-1940s, to 80/20 by the early 1950s. Throughout the 1950s druggists in Maragheh needed to know how to mix drugs from formulae, and several of the druggists in town still know how.

46. Byron J. Good, "The Professionalization of Medicine in a Provincial Iranian Town," in *Transcultural Health Care Issues and Conditions,* ed. Madeleine Leininger (Philadelphia: F. A. Davis Co., 1976); idem, "The Heart of What's the Matter: The Structure of Medical Discourse in a Provincial Iranian Town" (Ph.D. diss., University of Chicago, 1977).

47. Overseas Consultants, Inc., *Report on Seven Year Development Plan for the Plan Organization of the Imperial Government of Iran,* 5 vols. (New York: Overseas Consultants, Inc., 1949) 2:5–6.

48. Ibid., 1:14.

49. These figures are taken from Imperial Organization for Social Services, *Report of the Commission on the Study of Health and Medical Problems: A Summary* (Tehran: Imperial Organization for Social Services, 1975).

50. The Ministry of Health primary care clinic was staffed with a physician, a dentist, a midwife, and a pharmacist. The Malaria Office operated primarily in the villages in the subprovince, controlling mosquitoes and searching for cases of malaria. The Public Health Center provided vaccination teams, sanitary inspectors, a family planning clinic and mobile unit, and a maternal-child health care clinic.

51. In about 1950, besides the physicians in the Public Health Office and the hospital, one *mojaz* hakim practiced alongside five physicians with diplomas in Western medicine. A physician trained in the old Presbyterian mission practiced with an apprentice; an elderly Armenian, Dr. Rustamiyan,

trained in Russia, and another Armenian, trained in Europe, remained; and two physicians, trained in Tehran, practiced. In addition, an Armenian who had apprenticed with a "surgeon" trained in Russia continued to practice occasionally; and several *pezeshkiyars* trained by physicians and two new druggists trained by pharmacists (not by hakims) had begun to practice.

52. Of these, six were employed by the Red Lion and Sun, four by the Ministry of Health, three by employee insurance programs, and four by the military. Eleven of Maragheh's physicians studied medicine in Tehran University, eight in Tabriz University, and Dr. Rustamiyan, who still practices parttime at nearly 80 years of age, was trained in Russia almost 50 years ago. Of these 20, 15 were general practitioners, three were surgeons, one a radiologist, and one an ophthalmologist.

53. On at least one occasion of which I heard, the Health Office had a *pezeshkiyar*, who was the only health care provider in a series of remote villages, and he was arrested for practicing medicine.

54. Vincente Navarro, *Medicine Under Capitalism* (New York: Prodist, 1976).

55. W. W. Rostow, *The Stages of Economic Growth* (Cambridge: Cambridge University Press, 1962).

56. Navarro, *Medicine Under Capitalism*, p. 7.

57. Tucker, *Marx-Engels Reader*, pp. 338–339.

58. For example, the director of the Commission on the Study of Health and Medical Problems for the Imperial Organization of Social Services, Majid Rahnema, first presented the outline of the recommendations to be made in the report at a conference on the training of rural health care workers in 1974 in Shiraz. When his recommendations for radical reorganization of medical education were heard, members of the faculty at Pahlavi University Medical School immediately telephoned the deans of all other medical schools, urging them to use their influence to fight Rahnema's suggestions.

59. Further research, based on models provided by Navarro (Vincente Navarro, "The Political and Economic Origins of the Underdevelopment of Health in Latin America," in *Medicine Under Capitalism,* ed. Vincente Navarro (New York: Prodist, 1976), pp. 3–32), is necessary to document this statement adequately. Such research would need to document the distribution of health care resources (precisely where money was spent for health care—for education, development of hospitals and clinics, and research) and the corresponding social class distribution of those resources.

60. In 1970, nearly one-sixth of all Iranian physicians were practicing in the United States. See H. A. Ronaghy, Kathleen Cahill, and Timothy Baker, "Physician Migration to the United States: One Country's Transfusion is Another Country's Hemorrhage," *Journal of the American Medical Association* 227 (1974): 538–542.

61. A random stratified sample of 771 persons in Maragheh and three villages in the subprovince were interviewed in the fall and winter of 1973. The survey and data analysis were conducted jointly by Byron Good and Mary-Jo DelVecchio Good.

4. *The Political Role of the Lutis in Iran*

1. This chapter is an extended version of an article entitled "The political role of the *lutis* in Qajar Iran," published in G. Schweizer, ed., *Interdisziplinäre*

Iran-Forschung, Beiträge aus Kultur-geographie, Ethnologie, Soziologie und Neuerer Geschichte, Beihefte zum Tübinger Atlas des Vorderen Orients, Reihe B (Geisteswissenschaften) Nr. 40 (Wiesbaden: Dr. Ludwig Reichert, 1979), pp. 179–89.

2. R. Arasteh, "The Character, Organization and Social Role of the Lutis (javanmardan) in the Traditional Iranian Society of the 19th century," *Journal of the Economic and Social History of the Orient* 4 (1962): 47–52; see also A. K. S. Lambton, *Islamic Society in Persia* (Oxford, 1954), pp. 18–19.

The *luti* associations were not dissimilar to the *ayyar* associations which were widespread in Eastern Iran from the ninth to fourteenth centuries. To some extent they had the nature of a popular movement. However, the word *ayyar* also was used as a synonym for robbers and seditious people; Ibid., p. 18; see also Parviz Khanlari, "Ain-e Ayyari," *Sokhan* 18, 19 (1968–69); and Hosain Kashefi, *Fotovvatnameh-ye soltani*, ed. Mohammad Jafar Mahjub (Tehran, Bonyad-e Farhang-e Iran, nr. 112, 1352).

4. E. J. Hobsbawm, *Primitive Rebels, Studies in Archaic Forms of Social Movement in the 19th and 20th Centuries* (Manchester, 1959), idem, *Bandits* (Penguin, London, 1963).

5. A. Blok, "On Brigandage with Special Reference to Peasant Mobilization," *Sociologische Gids* 18 (1971): 208–16.

6. In the preface to the Penguin edition of *Bandits*, Hobsbawm states that he is not convinced by Blok's criticism. Hobsbawm's reaction to Blok's contention that "the noble bandit or Robin Hood is almost wholly mythical, and reflects not how social bandits really act, but how the common people would like them to act" is rather weak, and, in fact, underscores Blok's criticism. "However, there seems to me to be sufficient evidence for genuine Robin Hood behavior by at least some bandits, and I have not claimed that 'noble bandits' are common." Hobsbawm did not understand the point Blok wanted to make; e.g., he states "in a sense, all bandits are 'social' insofar as they, like all human beings, are linked to other people by various ties. What seems wrong with Hobsbawm's perception of brigandage is that it pays too much attention to the peasants and the bandits without reference to other groups, classes, or networks with which bandits form specific configurations or interdependent individuals." Blok, "On Brigandage," p. 211.

7. Ibid., p. 210.

8. Ibid., p. 212.

9. R. Fox, *Kin, Clan, Raja and Rule: State Hinterland Relations in Preindustrial India* (Berkeley, 1971), pp. 8–9.

10. E. Abrahamian, "Oriental Despotism, The Case of Qajar Iran," *International Journal of Middle East Studies* 5 (1974): 3–31.

11. S. G. Wilson, *Persia, Western Mission* (Philadelphia, 1896), p. 241; E. G. Browne, *Letters from Tabriz*, translated by Hasan Javadi, *Namehha-az Tabriz* (Tehran: Khwarazemi, 1351), p. 167; Isma'il Amir Khizi, *Qeyam-e Azerbaijan va Sattar Khan* (Tabriz, 1339), p. 146; Ahmad Kasravi, *Tarikh-e hejdeh saleh-ye Azerbaijan* (Tehran: Amir Kabir, 1350), 5th edition, p. 339.

12. For example, the slum quarters of Tehran: Chalmaidan and Sangalaj, and of Tabriz: Davachi and Sorkhab.

13. K. A. Daneshju, *Khuzestan va Khuzestaniyan* (Tehran, 1326), p. 28.

14. According to several authors the origin of the Haidari-Nemati cleavage dates back from the Safavi-Aq Qoyunlu conflict at the end of the fifteenth

century. The Safavids were followers of Shaikh Haidar, the father of Shah Isma'il Safavi, while the rulers of the Aq Qoyunlu dynasty were followers of Shah Nematollah Vali. When the two parties began their struggle for power in Iran, their partisans were referred to as Haidaris and Nematis, because of the religious overtones of the conflict.

15. R. W. Bulliet, *The Patricians of Nishapur* (Cambridge: Harvard University Press, 1972), pp. 30 ff.

16. R. M. B. Binning, *A Journey of Two Years Travel in Persia, Ceylon, etc.*, vol. 1 (London, 1857), pp. 274–75 (Shiraz); Ahmad Kasravi, *Tarikh-e mashruteh-ye Iran*, vol. 1 (Tehran: Taban, 1320), pp. 183, 269, 270 (Tabriz, Shushtar, Ardebil); *Revue du Monde Musulmane* 34 (1917): 138, 479 (Gilan, Mazanderan); Ibrahim Fakhra'i, *Gilan dar jonbesh-e mashrutiyat* (Tehran: Jibi, 1353), p. 111 (Rasht); Mirza Hosain Khan Tahvildar, *Jughrafiya-ye Isfahan* (Tehran: Daneshgah-e Tehran, 1342), ed. M. Setudeh, p. 89 (Isfahan); Hajj Abd ol-Ghaffar Najm ol-Molk, *Safarnameh-ye Khuzestan*, ed. M. Dabir Siyaqi (Tehran: Elmi, 1341), pp. 23, 131 (Dezful); Manuchehr Mamudi, ed., *Safarnameh-ye Mirza Khanlar Khan E'tesam ol-Molk* (Tehran, 1351), p. 285 (Birjand).

17. Ahmad Kasravi, *Zendegani-ye man*, 1st ed. (Tehran, 1323), p. 13.

18. Idem, *Tarikh-e panj sad sal-e Khuzestan*, 2nd ed. (Tehran: Gutenberg, 1333), pp. 89, 91, 92, 154, 161, 162.

19. W. M. Floor, "The Office of Kalantar in Qajar Persia," *Journal of the Economic and Social History of the Orient* 14 (1971): 252–68; see also the publications by Abol-Fazl Qasemi, *Oligarchi ya khandanha-ye hokumatgar-e Iran*, vol. 1: *Khandan-e Firuz Farmanfarma'yan* (Tehran, 1351), vol. 2: *Khandan-e Esfandiyari* (Tehran, 1354).

20. For a fuller discussion of this problem, see W. M. Floor, "The Lutis, a Social Phenomenon in Qajar Persia—a Reappraisal," *Die Welt des Islams* 13 (1971): 103–20.

21. Ibid., p. 114; they were also referred to as Lot's people or *ahl-e Lut* or homosexuals.

22. Floor, "The Lutis," pp. 103–20; Abdollah Mostaufi, *Sharh-e zendegani-ye man*, vol. 1 (Tehran: Zavvar, 1321), pp. 303–15.

23. C. J. Wills, *In the Land of the Lion and the Sun, etc.* (New York, 1891), p. 381; E. Orsolle, *Le Caucase et la Perse* (Paris, 1885), p. 288.

24. Mostaufi, *Zendegani*, vol. 1, p. 394 (partly trans. by Arasteh, "The Character," p. 48).

25. Ibid., pp. 49–50. It was not so much the keeping and raising of pigeons which was opposed by the religious authorities, but the misuse which was made of this sport by organizing races, betting and the like. See F. Meier, "A Difficult Quantrain of Mashati's," in *Melánges d'Orientalisme offerts à Henri Másse*, ed. by M. Minovi (Tehran: Daneshgah-e Tehran, 1963), pp. 269–81. Meier mentions a newspaper report of 1957 in which it is reported that some men are such slaves to this sport as to neglect their work and family—so much so that the wife may start divorce proceedings (p. 270). This sport could even lead to murder amongst dove sportsmen; see *Ettela'at*, Adhar 5, 1352, p. 22.

26. Mostaufi, *Zendegani*, vol. 1, p. 305. (partly trans. by Arasteh, "The Character," p. 49).

27. Binning, *Two Years Travel*, vol. 1, p. 274; Mostaufi, *Zendegani*, vol. 2, p. 278.

28. Ibid., vol. 1, p. 304; Fakhra'i, *Gilan*, p. 27.

29. Gholam Reza Ensafpur, *Tarikh-e zurkhaneh va goruhha-ye ejtima'i-ye Zurkhanehro* (Tehran: Vezarat-e Farhang va Honar, 1353); Floor, "The Lutis," p. 114; Arasteh, "The Social Life of the Zurkhana (House of Strength) in Iranian Urban Communities during the 19th Century," *Der Islam* 37 (1961): 257.

30. Kasravi, *Tarikh-e mashruteh*, vol. 2, p. 279; vol. 3, pp. 188–89.

31. F. A. Buhse, *Aufzahlung der auf einer Reise durch . . . Persien gesammelten Pflanzen nebst einleitenden Reiseberichte . . .* (Moscow, 1860), p. 58 ff; for an Iranian view of these events see: Mohammad Jafar Khan Muji, *Tarikh-e Qajar, Haqa'iq-e Akhbar-e Naseri* (Tehran: Zavvar, 1344), pp. 55–56, 76.

32. Ensafpur, *Tarikh-e zurkhaneh*, pp. 161–62; Floor, "The lutis," pp. 111–14.

33. Ibid., p. 111; Mostaufi, *Zendegani*, vol. 1, pp. 304–05.

34. Abdollah Bahrami, *Khaterat* (Tehran, 1344), vol. 1, p. 250. These were variously referred to as: *sar jomban, pish dash, patoq dar, pish kesvat, baba nama*, and *baba shamal*. Lambton, *Islamic Society*, p. 19; Mostaufi, *Zendegani*, vol. 1, p. 306; Ali Akbar Siassi, *La Perse au contact de l'Occident* (Paris, 1941), p. 135.

35. Mostaufi, *Zendegani*, vol. 1, pp. 303, 497.

36. The idyllic situation described by Arasteh, "The Character," never existed. I take a rather negative view of the *political* role of the *lutis*, which may have been different from their social role in the community. Although I quote various instances which show that in this respect *lutis* were not one's most popular neighbors, at the same time I wish to draw attention to the fact that some authors make a point of their positive *social* role in the community. Nevertheless, it is my opinion that this social role was restricted to their own neighborhood, where at least some of them were feared. For some interesting folklore on one of the "good guys" in Tehran, Luti Saleh, see the newspaper report on old stories of Tehran in *Rastakhiz*, Dey 29, 1354, p. 14.

37. Napier Malcolm, *Five Years in a Persian Town* (London, 1905), p. 58.

38. For such an example, see Kasravi, *Zendegani*, p. 14.

39. Wills, *In the Land*, p. 99; Abbas Eqbal, ed., *Sharh-e hal-e Abbas Mirza Molkara* (Tehran, 1325), p. 60; Floor, "The lutis," p. 116.

40. Hamid Sayyah, ed., *Khaterat-e Hajj Sayyah* (Tehran: Amir Kabir, 1346), p. 46; J. Perkins, *A Residence of Eight Years in Persia among the Nestorian Christians* (Andover, 1843), p. 389: ". . . infuriated crowds headed by the looties, and the permission of the High Priest . . ."; C. E. Yate, *Khurasan and Sistan* (London, 1900), pp. 231–32; Kasravi, *Zendegani*, pp. 46, 57, 82; J. E. Polak, *Persien, das Land und seine Bewohner* (Leipzig, 1865), vol. 1, p. 327.

41. Kasravi, *Khuzestan*, p. 161; D. Fraser, *Persia and Turkey in Revolt* (London, 1910), p. 243; Siassi, *La Perse*, p. 135; Binning, *Two Years Travel*, vol. 1, p. 273.

42. In English they are variously referred to as: rowdies, cutthroats, hooligans, thugs, bandits, scum, loafers, and the swell-mob of the towns. In Persian the list is longer; here they are called: *luti, mashti, dash, ayyar pashneh kundegan, avbash, rendan, sar keshan, chaqu keshan, ashrar, ajamereh, aradhel, gundeh, gholdor, qumeh zanha, gardan-e koloft* and *bi sar o paha*. Although all these terms are reflecting the very negative opinion about the *lutis*, which according to some was held all over Iran, the word *luti* has various meanings. Apart from the negative aspects (hooligan, sexual deviator), it also has a less

negative and even positive meaning, such as man full of *esprit,* a wise and generous man, a bohemian. On this notion of the word *luti,* see Michael Fischer, "Persian Society: Transformation and Strain," in: *Twentieth Century Iran,* ed. H. Amirsadeghi and R. W. Ferrier (London: Heineman, 1977), p. 180.

43. Sir Harford Jones Brydges, *The Dynasty of the Kajars* (London, 1833), p. 147.

44. H. Brugsch, *Reise der K. Preussischen Gesandschaft nach Persien,* vol. 2 (Leipzig, 1863), pp. 182, 196; J. R. Preece, "Journey from Shiraz to Jashk," *Royal Geographical Society, Suppl. Papers,* 1 (1886), p. 431.

45. Jones Brydges, *The Dynasty,* pp. 31, 71.

46. *Revue de l'Orient,* 2 (Paris, 1855): 250, note 1.

47. Kasravi, *Khuzestan,* pp. 161ff.

48. See notes 41–47; Foreign Office/431, letter May 3, 1880, referring to the situation in Tabriz: "The Monshi Bashi has taken precaution to ingratiate himself with the Ulema and with the looties, in view of the vicissitudes of to which tenure of office in Persia is exposed. It is usual for the Persian Priesthood to have to retain bands of armed ruffians at their beck and call." Very conspicuous among such bands were the sayyeds, who sometimes were referred to as the *alwat-e mu'ammam* or the turbaned *lutis.* This also referred to the *tollab* (religious students).

49. Abbas Eqbal, *Mirza Taqi Khan Amir Kabir* (Tehran, 1340), p. 172.

50. Najm ol-Molk, *Safarnameh,* pp. 23, 131.

51. A. von Tornauw, "Aus der neuesten Geschichte Persiens: Die Jahre 1833–35," *Zeitschrift der Deutschen Morgenlandische Gesellschaft* 2 (1848): 42–45; J. B. Fraser, *Travels in Koordestan etc.,* vol. 2 (London, 1840), p. 283; C. A. de Bode, *Travels in Luristan and Arabistan,* vol. 1 (London, 1845), p. 49; Mirza Mohammad Taqi Sepehr, Lesan ol-Molk, *Nasekh ot-Tavarikh,* vol. 1 (Tehran, n.d.), pp. 358, 385; Mirza Hasan Khan E'temad os-Saltaneh, *Tarikh-e montazam-e Naseri,* vol. 3 (Tehran, 1300), pp. 172–73.

52. H. Busse, *History of Persia under Qajar Rule* (New York: Columbia, 1972), pp. 170–71.

53. Kasravi, *Khuzestan,* pp. 161, 62, 65, 75, 88; Fraser, *Persia and Turkey,* p. 243; for other examples see note 51.

54. Perkins, *A Residence,* p. 92, 259.

55. de Bode, *Travels in Luristan,* vol. 1, p. 49.

56. Floor, "The lutis", pp. 116–17.

57. Yahya Daulatabadi, *Hayat-e Yahya,* vol. 2 (Tehran: Ibn-e Sina, 1332), pp. 83, 168; H. Rabino, *Mashruteh-ye Gilan beh inzeman-e vaqaye-ye Mashhad 1912,* ed. Mohammad Roshan (Tehran: Ta'ati, 1352), p. 22.

58. Kazem Beg, "Bab et les Babis," *Journal Asiatique* 7 (1866): 351.

59. A. H. Mounsey, *A Journey through the Caucasus and the Interior of Persia* (London, 1872), p. 218.

60. Iraj Afshar, ed., *Ruznameh-ye mashruteh va enqelab-e Iran* (Tehran: Amir Kabir, 1351), p. 272.

61. Kasravi, *Mashruteh;* Amir Khizi, *Qeyam-e Azerbaijan.*

62. Kasravi, *Mashruteh,* vol. 2, pp. 152, 281 ff; *Revue de Monde Musulmane* 5 (1908): 691–93; Amir Khizi, *Qeyam-e Azerbaijan,* pp. 26, 93.

63. Rabino, *Mashruteh-ye Gilan,* pp. 22, 23, 28, 29.

64. Siassi, *La Perse,* p. 135; Kasravi, *Mashruteh,* vol. 2, p. 299.

65. Fraser, *Persia and Turkey*, p. 243; *Revue du Monde Musulmane* 10 (1910): 428.

66. Ibid., p. 585; also in Shiraz, p. 257.

67. Great Britain, Foreign Office, *Correspondence respecting the Affairs of Persia*, nr. 5 (London: HMSO, 1912), p. 79.

68. Rabino, *Mashruteh-ye Gilan*, pp. 127–31.

69. Kasravi, *Zendegani*, pp. 97–98.

70. There is as yet no good analysis of the Reza Shah period, especially concerning social life in Iran.

71. R. Cottam, *Nationalism in Iran* (University of Pittsburgh Press, 1964).

72. Ibid., p. 308.

73. On these events see W. M. Floor, "The Revolutionary Role of the Shi'ite Ulama: Wishful Thinking or Reality" (forthcoming); E. A. Doroshenko, *Shi'itskoje Dukhovenstvo v sovrennom Irane* (Moscow: Nauka, 1975).

74. Michael Fischer, "Persian Society," p. 193; The Echo of Iran, *For Your Information*, no. 397, August 26, 1963, Tehran Riot Trials, pp. 5–6.

75. Groupe d'Etudes Sociologiques, *Origine des Ouvriers de Teheran* (Tehran: Universite de Teheran, 1965), roneo, p. 44.

76. Personal communication from Iranian friends. See also the pamphlet by the Hezb-e Zahmatkeshan-e Mellat-e Iran, Aban 2, 1357, p. 4 on government activities to sow sedition among the population of Kerman.

77. At this time I stayed in Tehran, and this issue was the talk of the town.

78. See note 29.

79. Busse, *History of Persia*, p. 357; Brugsch, *Reise*, vol. 2, p. 332.

80. Fakhra'i, *Gilan*, p. 77; Fraser, *Persia and Turkey*, p. 201; Daulatabadi, *Hayat-e Yahya*, vol. 2, pp. 189, 232; Amir Khizi, *Qeyam-e Azerbaijan*, pp. 26, 93, 106, 92.

81. Kasravi, *Mashruteh*, vol. 2, p. 152.

82. *International Herald Tribune*, January 16, 1979, p. 1.

5. *Economic Transformations Among Qashqa'i Nomads, 1962–1978*

1. This paper discusses nonelite Qashqa'i, unless otherwise indicated. Field research was conducted during eighteen months in 1970–71, three months in 1977, and a short visit in September 1979. Most of the research was conducted in one Qashqa'i subtribe, consisting of fully nomadic, sedentary, and settling households. Some research was conducted with one tribe's ruling elite. Extensive travel and interviewing throughout Qashqa'i territory and with Qashqa'i settled in towns helped to verify data as well as to provide new perspectives. A Fulbright-Hays Fellowship and a University of Utah Faculty Research Grant helped to support the research. Nikki Keddie, Michael Bonine, Gene Garthwaite, Richard Tapper, Jane Bestor, Michael Fischer, Daniel Bradburd, and Paul Barker offered helpful comments on previous drafts.

2. See Lois Beck, "Iran and the Qashqa'i Tribal Confederacy," in *Tribe and State in Afghanistan and Iran from 1800 to 1980*, ed. Richard Tapper (forthcoming).

3. Ann K. S. Lambton, *The Persian Land Reform, 1962–1966* (Oxford: Clarendon Press, 1969), p. 113.

4. Ibid., p. 351.

5. For an example of how land reform affected the khans of the Qashqa'i tribe of Kashkuli Kuchek, see Richard Salzer, "Social Organization of a Nomadic Pastoral Nobility in Southern Iran: The Kashkuli Kuchek of the Qashqa'i" (Ph.D. diss., University of California, Berkeley, 1974).

6. Since the gendarmerie had been given the authority to enforce land reform, it would have conflicted with the army in the countryside.

7. The 1971 celebration near Shiraz of the 2,500 years of the Iranian monarchy, which delayed the departure of the Qashqa'i from summer pastures by six weeks, caused many animal deaths.

8. Some villagers received deeds to pastureland near their villages, which had traditionally been used by them. However, by 1966 no regulations had been issued governing pasturelands; see Lambton, *The Persian Land Reform,* pp. 235–36, 247, 342.

9. Ibid.; Nikki Keddie, "Stratification, Social Control, and Capitalism in Iranian Villages: Before and After Land Reform," in *Rural Politics and Social Change in the Middle East,* ed. Richard Antoun and Iliya Harik (Bloomington: Indiana University Press, 1972); Eric J. Hooglund, "The Khwushnishin Population of Iran," *Iranian Studies* 6(1973):229–45; Robert Dillon, "Carpet Capitalism and Craft Involution in Kirman, Iran" (Ph.D. diss., Columbia University, 1976).

10. Some Sangsari in north-central Iran moved in 1963 into the traditional rangeland of the Chubdari, who had recently settled, and received official grazing permits to it. "The Chubdari, who were unlettered and had little knowledge of official procedures, did not contest this process until too late"; Brian Spooner, "Flexibility and Interdependence in Traditional Pastoral Land Use Systems," in *Papers and Proceedings of Ecological Guidelines for the Use of Natural Resources in the Middle East and South West Asia* (Morges, Switzerland, 1976), p. 89. Fazel and Afshar Naderi report that some Boir Ahmad settled in order to guard land claims until the registration of land title was established, and "once the security of title was assured there was at least a partial return to nomadism"; see Golamreza Fazel and Nader Afshar Naderi, "Rich Nomad, Poor Nomad, Settled Nomad: A Critique of Barth's Sedentarization Model" (Unpublished manuscript, 1976), p. 39.

11. Lambton, *The Persian Land Reform,* provides some evidence for bribery and corruption, but her general view is that most land reform officials were honest and genuinely concerned with the law's intention. However, her book lacks information on land reform in areas occupied by pastoral nomads. She does state that land reform was more difficult to implement in Fars and in the south than in other areas.

12. In Qashqa'i areas the landholders were usually non-Qashqa'i, but some Qashqa'i khans also engaged in such practices.

13. Golamreza Fazel, "Economic Organization and Change among the Boir Ahmad: A Nomadic Pastoral Tribe of Southwest Iran" (Ph.D. diss., University of California, Berkeley, 1971), p. 219.

14. These were the first two principles of the shah's White Revolution.

15. Village rangelands were defined as twice the size of a village's cultivated lands.

16. Stephen Sandford, "Pastoralism and Development in Iran," *Pastoral Network Paper* 3c (London: Overseas Development Institute, 1977), pp. 6–11.

17. Ibid., p. 10.

18. See A.K.S. Lambton, *Landlord and Peasant in Persia: A Study of Land Tenure and Land Revenue Administration* (London: Oxford University Press, 1953), chs. 15, 20.

19. The licensing system, although in theory universal, was said to cover about 40 percent of Iran's range and pasturelands in 1977; Sandford, "Pastoralism and Development in Iran," p. 5. I would suspect that the actual percentage was less than this.

20. Ibid.

21. Those who had done this prior to 1962 were likely to have been entitled to the land under land reform.

22. Sandford, "Pastoralism and Development"; *Case Study on Desertification, Iran: Turan* (Tehran: Department of the Environment, 1977).

23. *Case Study*, p. 57.

24. Ibid., p. 14.

25. Dillon, "Carpet Capitalism," also notes the conflict between family economy pastoralism and commercial herding in the Kerman area.

26. Lois Beck, "Women among Qashqa'i Nomadic Pastoralists in Iran," in *Women in the Muslim World*, ed. Lois Beck and Nikki Keddie (Cambridge: Harvard University Press, 1978), pp. 351–373.

27. See Fredrik Barth, "Capital, Investment and the Social Structure of a Pastoral Nomad Group in South Persia," in *Capital, Saving and Credit in Peasant Societies*, ed. Raymond Firth and B. S. Yamey (Chicago: Aldine, 1964); Thomas Stauffer, "The Economics of Nomadism in Iran," *The Middle East Journal* 19(1965):284–302.

28. Fazel, "Economic Organization," p. 96, reports the spread of animal contracts among the Boir Ahmad in the 1960s. Afshar Naderi estimates that by the early 1970s a third of the flocks in Kuhgiluyeh were no longer owned by pastoralists but by urban traders; see Nader Afshar Naderi, "The Settlement of Nomads and its Social and Economic Implications," (Tehran: Institute for Social Studies and Research, 1971), p. 7.

29. Herd owners with two or more flocks occasionally separated them, which gave greater independence to some shepherds.

30. The most frequent explanation given by Qashqa'i in 1977 for their rapid sedentarization was that shepherds could no longer be found (despite many other factors). See also *Case Study*, p. 13; Reinhold Loeffler, "Recent Economic Changes in Boir Ahmad: Regional Growth without Development," *Iranian Studies* 9 (1976):266–87.

31. Lois Beck, "Herd Owners and Hired Shepherds: The Qashqa'i of Iran," *Ethnology* 19 (1980):327–51.

32. See Jacob Black, "Tyranny as a Strategy for Survival in an 'Egalitarian' Society: Luri Facts versus an Anthropological Mystique," *Man* 7(1972):614–34.

33. "The buoyancy of the pastoral sector in [the economy of households with mixed economies] may make . . . mixed-economy farmers more prosperous than their more purely agricultural fellows, even if they tend to occupy much more marginal areas"; Fredrik Barth, "A General Perspective on Nomad-Sedentary Relations in the Middle East," in *The Desert and the Sown*, ed. Cynthia Nelson (Berkeley: Institute of International Studies, University of California, 1973), p. 15.

34. Loeffler, "Recent Economic Changes"; Jane Bestor, "The Kurds of

Iranian Baluchistan: A Regional Elite" (M.A. thesis, McGill University, 1979); Emily McIntire, "The Impact of State Consolidation on a Regional System in Southwestern Iran" (Paper presented at the Annual Meeting of the American Anthropological Association, Los Angeles, 1978).

35. See Paul Barker (this volume).

36. Such as ministry offices, gendarme and army posts, tribal settlement office, banks, courts, education offices, tribal education headquarters, secondary schools, khans' residence, health services, shrines, religious practitioners, bathhouses, barbershops, teahouses, and restaurants.

37. They were usually titled *hajji;* most had made the pilgrimage to Mecca. They were able to charge higher prices and interest rates because of the respect the pilgrimage conferred on them.

38. Afshar Naderi, "The Settlement of Nomads," p. 3.

39. The government collected taxes on animals sold to slaughterhouses.

40. Sandford, "Pastoralism and Development in Iran," p. 17.

41. *Case Study,* p. 46.

42. Abraham Rosman and Paula Rubel, "Nomad-Sedentary Interethnic Relations in Iran and Afghanistan," *International Journal of Middle East Studies* 7 (1976): 545–70; Fazel, "Economic Organization."

43. Morton Fried, *The Notion of Tribe* (Menlo Park, Cal.: Cummings Publishing Co., 1975), pp. 99–105.

44. Fredrik Barth, *Nomads of South Persia* (London: Allen and Unwin, 1961), pp. 101–11.

45. For example, Daniel Bates, *Nomads and Farmers: A Study of the Yörük of Southeastern Turkey* (Ann Arbor: University of Michigan, Museum of Anthropology, 1973); Daniel Bradburd, "Never Give a Shepherd an Even Break: Class and Labor Among the Komachi" (Unpublished manuscript, 1980); Beck, "Herd Owners and Hired Shepherds."

46. Surveys by the Shiraz University Population Center of squatter settlements on the outskirts of Shiraz showed a high proportion of Qashqa'i, Arab, Basseri, and gypsy residents (Drs. Momeni and Ayatollahi, personal communication, July 1977).

47. If the Qashqa'i had waited for the lower prices of government redistribution, they would not have been entitled to the land.

48. An indication of the extent and rapidity of sedentarization was the many donkeys abandoned to wander in the countryside. Their market prices were so low, because of the glut on the market, that many individuals did not attempt to sell them. Transport camels were sold to urban butchers for meat.

49. See Lois Beck, "Revolutionary Iran and its Tribal Peoples," *MERIP Reports,* No. 87 (May 1980), pp. 14–20.

50. For example, the Yörük of Turkey; see Daniel Bates, *Nomads and Farmers.*

6. Size and Success: Komachi Adaptation to a Changing Iran

1. Data concerning the Komachi is based upon field research conducted in Iran in 1974 and 1975, which was supported by grants from the National Science Foundation and the National Institute of Mental Health.

2. See for example: Fredrik Barth, *Nomads of South Persia* (Boston: Little Brown, 1966); idem, "Socio-Economic Changes in Pastoral Lands" (Paper

presented at the Meeting on Ecological Guidelines for the Use of Natural Resources in the Middle East and South West Asia, Persepolis, Iran, 1975); Daniel Bates, "The Role of the State in Peasant-Nomad Mutualism" *Anthropological Quarterly* 44 (1971): 109–131; idem, *Nomads and Farmers: A Study of the Yörük of Southeastern Turkey* (Ann Arbor: The University of Michigan, Museum of Anthropology, 1973); Vincent Cronin, *The Last Migration*, (London: Rupert, Hard-Davies, 1957); Philip Salzman, "National Integration of the Tribes in Modern Iran," *Middle East Journal* 25 (1971): 325–36; idem, "Multi-Resource Nomadism in Iranian Baluchistan" in *Perspectives on Nomadism*, ed. William Irons and Neville Dyson-Hudson (Leiden: E. J. Brill, 1972); Thomas Stauffer, "The Qashqa'i Nomads, A Contemporary Appraisal" *The Harvard Review* I (1967): 28–39.

3. Sir Percy Sykes, *10,000 Miles in Persia* (London, 1902) pp. 210, 428, 430; Henry Field, "Contributions to the Anthropology of Iran," *Anthropological Series of the Field Museum of Natural History*, Vol. 29 (Chicago, 1939).

4. Gholamhossein Abusaidi, personal communication, 1975.

5. See Pierre Oberling, *The Qashqa'i Nomads of Fars*, (The Hague: Mouton, 1974) pp. 281–6.

6. Barth, *Nomads of South Persia*, p. 119.

7. Sykes, *10,000 Miles in Persia,* makes mention of a Mehni confederation in Kerman in the late nineteenth century, and Gholamhossein Abusaidi, personal communication, 1974, suggests that his family, which was nontribal, were the former heads of that confederation. It certainly does not exist at the present time, and there is little evidence that it was politically effective when it did exist.

8. Fredrik Barth, "Nomadism in the Middle East and Plateau Areas of Southwest Asia" *Paris Symposium on the Problems of the Arid Zone* (New York: UNESCO, 1960); idem, *Nomads of South Persia*; Philip Salzman, "Political Organization Among Nomadic Peoples," *Proceedings of the American Philosophical Society* 111 (1967): 115–31.

9. Gene Garthwaite, "The Bakhtiari Ilkhans: An Historical View" (Paper presented at the 70th Annual Meeting of the American Anthropological Association, New York, 1971).

10. Oberling, *The Qashqa'i Nomads of Fars*; Richard Cottam, *Nationalism in Iran* (Pittsburgh: University of Pittsburgh Press, 1964); Sir Percy Sykes, *History of Persia* (London: MacMillan, 1930).

11. Daniel Bradburd, "Shepherding Contracts, Conflict and Systemic Collapse in Kerman, Iran," (Paper presented at the Annual Meeting of the Middle East Studies Association (New York, 1977).

12. See Marshall Sahlins, *Stone Age Economics* (Chicago: Aldine, 1972).

13. See Brian Spooner, "Politics, Kinship and Ecology in Southeastern Persia," *Ethnology* 7 (1969): 139–52; and Philip Salzman, "Adaptation and Political Organization in Iranian Baluchistan," *Ethnology* 10 (1971): 433–45, for discussions of political leaders, *hakomzat*, in Baluchistan, who appear quite similar to the men with whom the Komachi had to contend.

14. Note that in this case expanded state control is allowing the expansion of pastoralism into the hinterland. This reverses Lattimore's projections (for a larger scale) of nomad/state interactions. See Owen Lattimore, *Studies of the Frontier in History* (The Hague: Mouton, 1962).

15. Barth, "Nomadism;" idem, *Nomads of South Persia*.

16. Individuals were reticent about how much they used to give. My impression is that the wealthy men would give gifts of several animals and several kilograms of dairy products each year. They would, in turn, collect some of these items from poorer nomads.

17. Lois Beck (this volume).

18. The herds, for example, do not stay in the summer quarters more than a few months. They arrive in May and leave in early August, long before the tribe itself returns to winter quarters. In addition, animals being fattened for market are extensively fed with fodder. It is tempting to speculate that the reason the Komachi do not attempt to restrict access to resources is their very scarcity and variability. One might construct an argument here parallel to Steward's argument for hunters and gatherers. See Julian Steward, *Theory of Culture Change* (Urbana: University of Illinois Press, 1955).

19. These particular ties were largely defunct by 1974–5. The former khans were deferred to if they passed through the area and their advice was occasionally sought. In general, however, the Komachi were seeking and using other patrons. See Daniel Bradburd, "Patron-Client Relations in Kerman: An Inversion of the Stereotype" (Paper presented at the Annual Meetings of the Middle East Studies Association, Ann Arbor, 1978).

20. The Komachi appear to have purchased these pieces of property during the 1940s—a time of extreme unrest. I speculate that it was this unrest which made rural property unattractive to normal purchasers; the lands were, therefore, available to the Komachi.

21. See Nikki Keddie, "Stratification, Social Control and Capitalism in Iranian Villages Before and After Land Reform" in *Rural Politics and Social Change in the Middle East,* ed. Richard Antoun and Iliya Harik (Bloomington: University of Indiana Press, 1972); and Lambton, *Persian Land Reform, 1962–66* (Oxford, Clarendon Press, 1969).

22. Robert Dillon, "Carpet Capitalism and Craft Involution in Iran" (Ph.D. diss., Columbia University, 1976), pp. 160–83, particularly p. 181.

23. Barth, *Nomads.*

24. Bradburd, "Shepherding Contracts;" idem, "Kinship and Contract: The Social Organization of the Komachi of Kerman, Iran" (Ph.D. diss., City University of New York, 1979).

25. See Bates, *Nomads and Farmers,* for a discussion of a somewhat parallel situation with similar effects.

26. In fact, the Komachi suggested that some nomads switched from *kork* to wool production when the price of the former plummeted. The transition is difficult, for sheep are harder to keep and require a greater capital outlay (esp. for fodder).

27. For the Komachi, for example, a "real" meal is one with meat. Visitors have meat prepared for them, and at all ceremonial occasions large amounts of meat are conspicuously consumed.

28. Butchers occasionally told me that live animals were imported from other regions of the country by the government. This, however, was quite rare.

29. Meat prices rose nearly 75 percent during 1974–75 while national inflation ran at a rate of roughly 30 percent. See "Special Report on Iran," *The Economist* (August 28, 1976): 21ff.

30. That is, a broker might show an apparent profit due to an inflationary price increase rather than a real profit in excess of the rate of inflation.

31. Dillon, "Carpet Capitalism."

32. That is, roughly the cash salary of a camel herder or a shepherd: $200–$225 per year.

33. Komachi women do not traditionally produce either tribal carpets or *gelims* which their husbands or fathers might sell.

34. Cf. Salzman, "Multi-Resource Nomadism," and Abraham Rosman and Paula Rubel, "Nomad Sedentary Interethnic Relations in Iran," *International Journal of Middle Eastern Studies* 7 (1976): 545–70.

7. Tent Schools of the Qashqa'i: A Paradox of Local Initiative and State Control

1. From 1973 to 1975 I was a teacher in Tribal High School in Shiraz. During school vacations I traveled extensively in Qashqa'i and other tribal areas of Fars Province. My conclusions are drawn largely from my observations, conversations, and experiences of those years. My close association with Mohammad Bahmanbegi and the Office of Tribal Education has doubtlessly biased my interpretation of those events. I would like to express my deep appreciation to Lois Beck, Michael Bonine, Brad Hanson and Nikki Keddie, whose insightful criticisms have contributed much to this essay.

2. Anecdote related by Bahmanbegi, 1974.

3. The Qashqa'i are really a confederation of five major and several minor tribes, mostly located in Fars Province of southern Iran. Most Qashqa'i are Turkish speaking nomadic pastoralists who make semiannual migrations between their winter quarters south and west of Shiraz to summer pastures high in the Zagros mountains north of Shiraz. The tent schools under Bahmanbegi's authority, even from the earliest years, were scattered among other tribes of Fars as well (Basseri, Boir Ahmad, Arab, Mamasani, etc.) After 1970 Bahmanbegi was given responsibility to develop his schools among all of the tribal populations of Iran. This paper, however, is limited to a discussion of the development of the schools within and their impact on the Qashqa'i.

4. Mohammad Bahmanbegi, *Orf va adat dar ashayer-e Fars* (Tehran: Bongah-e Azar, 1324/1945), pp. 15, 74.

5. Lynn Cubstead, "Madares-e ashayeri-ye Mohammad Bahmanbegi," *Marzha-ye Nau* (Bahman 1354/February 1976), p. 2.

6. While visiting Dadin, winter quarters for part of the Farsimadan *tayafeh* (tribe), my host pointed out a tree called "Konar-e Maktab," a konar tree under which a mulla, himself not a Qashqa'i, used to run a Qoran school.

7. Jean and Franc Shor, "We Dwelt in Kashgai Tents," *National Geographic* 51 (1952): 829.

8. Berthold Schulze-Holthus, *Daybreak in Iran, A Story of the German Intelligence Service*, tr. Mervyn Savill (London: Staples Press Ltd., 1954), p. 196; General Hasan Arfa, *Under Five Shahs* (New York: William Morrow & Co., 1965), pp. 358–9.

9. Pierre Oberling, *The Qashqa'i Nomads of Fars* (The Hague: Mouton, 1974), pp. 77–80.

10. Richard Cottam, *Nationalism in Iran* (Pittsburgh: University of Pittsburgh Press, 1964), p. 56.

11. Oberling, *Qashqa'i Nomads*, p. 93.

12. Sir Percy Sykes, *A History of Persia*, Vol. 2 (London: MacMillan & Co., 1930), p. 502.

13. Oberling, *Qashqa'i Nomads*, p. 153; Bahmanbegi, *Orf va adat*, p. 62; Abdullah Gashgai, "The Gashgais of Iran," *Land Reborn* (1954), p. 6.

14. Bahmanbegi, *Orf va adat*, p. 62; William O. Douglas, *Strange Lands and Friendly People* (New York: Harper, 1951), pp. 138–41; Thomas Stauffer, "The Qashqa'i Nomads: A Contemporary Appraisal," *The Harvard Review* 1 (1963): 35; Cottam, *Nationalism*, p. 149.

15. Cottam, *Nationalism*, p. 62; Stauffer, "The Qashqa'i Nomads," p. 36; Douglas, *Strange Lands*, pp. 142–4; Schulze-Holthus, *Daybreak*.

16. Douglas, *Strange Lands*, pp. 134–5; Arfa, *Under Five Shahs*, pp. 373–7.

17. William E. Warne, *Mission for Peace: Point Four in Iran* (New York: Bobbs-Merrill, 1956), pp. 50, 127–31.

18. Glen S. Gagon, "A Study of the Development and Implementation of a System of Elementary Education for the Ghasghi (sic) and Basseri Nomadic Tribes of Fars Ostan, Iran" (M.A. thesis, Brigham Young University, 1956), pp. 91–2.

19. Clarence Hendershot, *Politics, Polemics and Progress: A Study of United States Technical Assistance in Education to Iran* (N.Y.: Vantage Press, 1975), pp. 14–21.

20. Clarence Hendershot, *White Tents in the Mountains: A Report on the Tribal Schools of Fars Province* (Tehran: U.S. AID, 1965), p. 6. The exact status of Bahmanbegi's father is disputed; Bahmanbegi claims he was a *kadkhoda* (headman), others claim he was the *Ilkhani's* cook or stablemaster. The latter claims tend to be made by sons of khans.

21. Vincent Monteil, *Les Tribus du Fārs et la sédentarisation des nomads* (Paris: Mouton & Co., 1966), p. 15. There are several inaccuracies in Monteil's account, but his claim does at least seem plausible. Schulze-Holthus claims that he was met in Tehran by Naser Khan's chauffeur-secretary, Mohammad, who greeted him in "the perfect French of the Comédie Française." Schulze-Holthus, *Daybreak*, p. 152.

22. Bahmanbegi, *Orf va adat*, pp. 56–7, 65–6.

23. Ibid., pp. 10–11, 16–17, 56, 75.

24. Mohammad Bahmanbegi, "Hardy Shepherds Build a Future through Tent School Education," in *Nomads of the World*, ed. Gilbert Grosvenor (Washington, D.C.: National Geographic Society, 1971), p. 100.

25. Gagon, *A Study*, p. 75.

26. Hendershot, *White Tents*, pp. 7–9. The latrine tent and student desks were later dropped from the standard equipment list and a small science kit added.

27. Ministry of Education, *Tribal Education in Iran* (Tehran: Kayhan Press, 1965), p. 5; Gagon, *A Study*, p. 70.

28. Informants were reluctant to mention specific names, but one infers that the Four Brothers were more eager to impress foreigners with a progressive image than they were to help finance the schools.

29. Gagon, *A Study*, pp. 75–79.

30. Ibid., pp. 89–94.

31. Ibid., p. 70.

32. Hendershot, *White Tents*, p. 12. When Bahmanbegi was transfered from the Point Four payroll to that of the Ministry of Education, he suffered a 50 percent reduction in pay.

33. Ibid., p. 14.

34. Hendershot, *Politics*, p. 90.

35. For more information on economic and ecological problems faced by the Qashqa'i in the past two decades, see Lois Beck (this volume).

36. In 1977 females made up roughly a quarter of the enrollment of the tribal primary schools and one tenth of the enrollment at Tribal High School and Tribal Teacher Training School.

37. Brad Hanson, who, like myself, worked in tribal schools through the Peace Corps, reports having heard a poem to this effect at a 1976 *ordu*.

38. Beck (this volume).

39. Hendershot, *White Tents*, p. 14.

40. In violation of official policy, some teachers explained difficult concepts in Turkish and made Iranian history more comprehensible by citing parallels in Qashqa'i history. Lois Beck, personal communication, November 1978.

41. Letter from Abdi Firuzmand, former head of the English Department at Tribal High School, May 1979.

8. Khans and Kings: The Dialectics of Power in Bakhtiyari History

1. Nikki R. Keddie, "The Iranian Power Structure and Social Change 1800–1969: An Overview," *International Journal of Middle East Studies*, 2 (1971): 3–20.

2. My thanks to my Dartmouth colleague, John Major, for his assistance in focusing and phrasing this hypothesis. The whole of this hypothesis is presented in my "The Bakhtiyari and the State" (Paper presented at the Conference on Tribes of Iran and Afghanistan, London, July 1979).

3. Hamdollah Mostaufi Qazvini, *Tarikh-e Gozideh*, ed. Abdol-Hosain Nava'i (Tehran: Amir-e Kabir, 1339/1961), p. 540.

4. Amir Sharaf Khan Badlisi, *Sharafnamah ya tarikh-e mofassel-e Kurdestan*, ed. Mohammad Abbasi (Tehran: Elmi, 1343/1965). J. Chardin, *The Travels of Sir John Chardin into Persia and the East Indies. To Which is Added, the Coronation of This Present King of Persia, Solyman the Third* (London, 1686). Iskandar Baig Turkman, *Tarikh-e alam ara-ye Abbasi*, ed. Iraj Afshar, vols. 1 & 2 (Isfahan: Amir-e Kabir, 1334/1956). *Tadhkirat al-moluk*, ed. V. Minorsky (London: Luzac, 1943).

5. G. R. Garthwaite, "Nomadism and Tribal Power," *Iranian Studies*, 11 (1978): 173–98.

6. Jean-Pierre Digard, "De la nécessité et des inconvénients, pour un Baxtyâri, d'être Baxtyâri," *Pastoral Production and Society/Production Pastorale et Société* (Cambridge: Cambridge University Press, 1979), pp. 127–139.

7. Ibid.

8. Possibly the designations *bakhsh* or *boluk* date only from the 1930s when the central government assumed direct administration of the Bakhtiyari. They have not been found in earlier sources.

9. Jonas Hanway, *The Revolutions of Persia* (London: J. Osborne, 1754), p. 238. Father Krusinski, *The History of the Late Revolutions of Persia*, I (London: J. Osborne, 1740), p. 97.

10. No historical evidence is to be found for a unified Bakhtiyari until the *Ilkhani* of Hosain Qoli Khan, 1867–82. Briefly during the Constitutional Revolution most Bakhtiyari were united.

11. G. R. Garthwaite, "Rivalry and Alliances: Kinship and the Bakhtiyari Khans" (Paper presented at the Annual Meeting of the Middle East Studies Association, Louisville, November 1975).

12. Free translation of Mohammad Kazem, *Nameh-ye alam ara-ye Naderi*, vol. 2 (Moscow: Nauka, 1960–66), pp. 21a–23a.

13. Ann K. S. Lambton, "Quis Custodiet Custodes: Some Reflections of the Persian Theory of Government," *Studia Islamica*, 6 (1956): 125.

14. Abbas III, "Farman" (Isfahan [?], 1144 1731–32).

15. L. Lockhart, *Nadir Shah* (London: Luzac, 1938), p. 99.

16. G. R. Garthwaite, "Khans and Shahs: A Documentary Analysis of the Bakhtiyari in Iran" (forthcoming).

17. *Encyclopaedia of Islam*, 2nd ed., s.v. "Karim Khan Zand."

18. Ahmad Kasravi, *Tarikh-e pansad saleh-ye Khuzestan* (Tehran: Amir Kabir, 1330/1952), pp. 20–1.

19. Marshall G. S. Hodgson, *The Venture of Islam*, vol. 2 (Chicago: University of Chicago Press, 1974), pp. 400–4.

20. Hasan Fasa'i, *History of Persia Under Qajar Rule (Farsnama-ye Naseri)*, tr. by Heribert Busse (New York: Columbia, 1972), p. 160.

21. Naser od-Din Shah, "Farman" (Tehran, Sha'ban 1284/December 1867).

22. Hosain Qoli Khan Ilkhani, "Letter to Naser od-Din Shah," 1295/1878.

23. Hosain Qoli Khan Ilkhani, "Ketabcheh," 1872–82.

24. Digard, "De la nécessité . . . d'être Baxtyari."

25. Jean-Pierre Digard, personal communication.

26. Lois Beck (this volume).

9. *Persian Gulf Trade and the Agricultural Economy of Southern Iran in the Nineteenth Century*

1. This chapter is based primarily on a survey of patterns of production and distribution of major agricultural commodities in southern Iran during the nineteenth century. Among the commodities investigated were wheat, barley, rice, dates, maize, opium, and tobacco. The survey covered an area in Fars Province as far north as the Abadeh district, and the Persian Gulf coast between Bandar-e Dailam and approximately Bandar-e Taheri. The term "southern Iran" as used in this chapter refers to that area. The author wishes to express his appreciation to Professor Thomas Ricks of Georgetown University for his encouragement and assistance.

2. Such developments were not limited to southern Iran. The nineteenth century was a period of profound change throughout Iran as Iranian society sought to adjust to increasing economic and political pressures from without. For the context in which southern Iranian developments took place, see Charles Issawi, ed., *The Economic History of Iran 1800–1914* (Chicago: University of Chicago Press, 1971); and Nikki Keddie, "The Economic History of Iran, 1800–1914, and its Political Impact: An Overview," *Iranian Studies*, 2–3 (1972): 181–96. Vahid F. Nowshirvani, "The Beginnings of Commercial Agriculture in Iran," in an in-press volume, ed. Abraham Udovitch (Princeton:

Darwin Press, 1981), provides a useful overview of agricultural transformations during the second half of the century. A. K. S. Lambton, *Landlord and Peasant in Persia* (London: Oxford University Press, 1953) also has important insights, although the bulk of her work is concerned with other regions. As Nowshirvani notes, poor communications and variations in available resources led different regions to respond differently to external pressures. Consequently, trends found, for example, in Isfahan are not always applicable to areas like southern Iran. General works become more relevant to southern Iran after about 1890 as it became more fully integrated, although as a relatively marginal area, into the emerging national economy.

3. Population figures for southern Iranian villages during that period are scarce and unreliable. The average village may have had as many as 200 families, although "villages" with as few as two families were reported. The most comprehensive estimates are those in Keith E. Abbott, "Notes Taken on a Journey Eastwards from Shiraz to Fessa and Darab, thence Westwards by Jehrum to Kazerun in 1850," *Journal of the Royal Geographic Society*, 27 (1857): 152–3.

4. Persian Gulf Political Residency, *Report on the Administration of the Persian Gulf Political Residency and the Muskat Political Agency for the Year 1879–1880* (Calcutta: Office of the Superintendent of Government Printing, 1880), pp. 68–9. Appendix B to Part III, "List of Productions in the Districts of Fars," gives a detailed list of the crops grown in each district of southern Iran. Numerous travelers' accounts show that except for maize and opium, the distribution of crops changed little between 1800 and 1880.

5. There is no evidence of any village in southern Iran devoting most of its efforts to cultivating anything but its own food supply before midcentury. The cultivation of opium at that time apparently was something of a "backyard" cultivation, similar to that of certain other drugs today.

6. Such simple precise figures were at best no more than theoretical guidelines sanctioned by customary law and precedent. In a rugged area like southern Iran, tribal bonds, varying local customs or measures, and scores of minor claims and rights peculiar to individual groups or valleys gave rise to innumerable variations in crop division. Such variations have yet to be investigated. During this period it appears that southern Iran had an unusually large amount of *divani* land and an unusually small number of religious endowments and peasant proprietors compared to the rest of the country. However, those may have been transitory conditions related to the destruction of the Shiraz-based Zand dynasty by the Qajars in the late eighteenth century. For a general discussion of the problem, see Lambton, *Landlord and Peasant*, pp. 306–29. For observations on southern Iran, see Edward Scott Waring, *A Tour to Sheeraz by the Route of Kazirun and Feerozabad* (New York: Arno Press, 1973), pp. 16–7; John MacDonald Kinneir, *A Geographical Memoir of the Persian Empire* (London: 1813); and Abbott, "Notes," p. 176. For the purposes of this chapter, the key fact is that the peasants retained relatively little of the crop.

7. Most travelers who noticed such things observed that provisions were plentiful in the villages they saw. Signs of chronic shortages did not occur until the 1880s. However, there seldom was much of a surplus. Morier noted that the presence of a party of twelve men and fifteen animals for a period of a few weeks gave rise to a scarcity of food and fodder in the region to the

northwest of Shiraz. See James Morier, *A Second Journey Through Persia, Armenia, and Asia Minor* (London: Longman, 1818), p. 90.

8. For some of the truly amazing number of such imposts, which could include sums levied to ransom prisoners from the Russians, pay indemnities, build ships, finance public works in other provinces, or restore religious properties, see Robert M. Binning, *A Journal of Two Years' Travel in Persia, Ceylon, etc.* (London: W. H. Allen and Company, 1857), pp. 176–7.

9. The government sought to increase its share by demanding taxes before rather than after seed was deducted. See Binning, *Journal*, p. 345. In the early 1800s, the government often preferred to receive taxes in kind so that it could use the produce to feed its tribal levies. Occasionally it would not collect taxes in years when there were no troops in the region. If subsequently it became necessary to quarter troops there, the government would take everything in sight to feed them. See Waring, *Tour*, p. 86.

10. For example, in 1850 the governor of Fars was expected to remit 500,000 tomans to the shah's treasury. See Binning, *Journal*, p. 357.

11. For a general description of the *tuyul* system in Qajar Iran, see Lambton, *Landlord and Peasant*, pp. 471–2. The *tuyul* system in southern Iran was affected by many local customs and peculiarities, as were the methods of crop division. Generally, officials had more freedom of action in assigning *tuyuls* in the settled agricultural districts of the hinterland than in the districts along the Persian Gulf coast where tribal bonds remained strong—much less in districts dominated by major nomadic groups such as the Qashqa'i. However, the main factor involved in granting a *tuyul* remained the ability and willingness of the recipient to pay for it. In that sense, the operation of the system in the south was not entirely typical of the rest of Iran. In areas directly threatened by hostile neighbors or valued by the Qajars as sources of military or political support rather than just revenue, government used *tuyuls* in a less exploitative and more responsible way. For an example of the system at its best, see George Bournoutian, "Husayn Quli Khan Qazvini, Sardar of Erevan: A Portrait of a Qajar Administrator," *Iranian Studies*, 2–3 (1976): 163–79.

12. George N. Curzon, *Persia and the Persian Question*, vol. 2 (London: Longmans, Green and Company, 1892), p. 472.

13. The power and influence of the "local gentry" of the hinterland agricultural towns tended to persist longer in regions like Larestan, which remained relatively isolated from the major southern centers of economic activity than in southern Iran itself. See Edward Stack, *Six Months in Persia* (London: Sampson Low and Company, 1882), pp. 116–8 for observations on Lar. Also Morier, *Second Journey*, p. 123, and J. G. Lorimer, *Gazetteer of the Persian Gulf, Oman and Central Arabia*, vol. 1, 2 (Calcutta: Office of the Superintendent of Government Printing, 1915), pp. 1,846–52, 1,911.

14. Such handicrafts included glassware, ceramics, and some textiles. See Kinneir, *Memoir*, pp. 74–6; Binning, *Journal*, pp. 288–9; and William Ouseley, *Travels in Various Countries of the East: More Particularly Persia* (London, 1821), p. 74.

15. Bandar-e Mahshahr served as the port for the Ram Hormuz district. Hindiyan, Bandar-e Deilam, and Bandar-e Rig served the Behbehan district and parts of the Ram Hormuz and Kazerun districts. Bandar-e Taheri and several smaller ports south of Bushehr served the relatively small, scattered

agricultural valleys south of Shiraz and southwest of Lar. See Waring, *Tour*, pp. 76–7; and W. H. Colville, "Land Journey along the Shores of the Persian Gulf from Bushire to Lingah," *Proceedings of the Royal Geographic Society* 11 (1866–7): 37–8.

16. William Francklin, "Observations Made on a Tour from Bengal to Persia in the Years 1786–7," in *A General Collection of the Best and Most Interesting Voyages and Travels in All Parts of the World*, vol. 11, ed. by John Pinkerton (London, 1811), p. 238.

17. There is little evidence of any direct economic relations among southern Iranian villages during the early nineteenth century; what exists is quite vague. See, for example, Ouseley, *Travels*, pp. 70–1, for the gathering of salt from dry lake beds for distribution in Shiraz and villages southeast of it. Even those activities probably were controlled from the towns. The lack of direct economic relations among the villages is not surprising, as they were left with little to trade.

18. "Trade of Bushire, 1780's," in Issawi, ed., *Economic History*, p. 87; see also Curzon, *Persia*, vol. 2, pp. 552–3. In one year, the Company's sales amounted to only £93.

19. Most of the silk purchased by the East India Company in Persia, as well as much from Bengal and China, was shipped via India to Britain where it was used for silk fabrics. By 1800, however, in Britain metal, not silk, buttons became dominant and cheap mass-produced cotton and worsted products displaced silk thread and stockings. See Ralph Davis, "English Imports from the Middle East 1580–1780," in *Studies in the Economic History of the Middle East*, ed. M. A. Cook (London: Oxford University Press, 1970), pp. 196–201, and Ignatius Durga Parshad, *Some Aspects of Indian Foreign Trade 1757–1893* (London: P. S. King and Son, 1932), pp. 91–109.

20. Estimates of change in Iranian trade patterns during the nineteenth century are complicated by the devaluation of Iranian currency throughout the period and by regional fluctuations in the value of the toman. In 1817, one pound sterling equalled 13 krans in Tehran. By 1823, its value rose only to 13.6 krans. However, between 1823 and 1870, when the bulk of the expansion of trade with India and Europe described in this section occurred, the value of the pound in relation to the kran nearly doubled to 26 kran to the pound. See the exchange tables in Issawi, ed., *Economic History*, pp. 339–40. A provocative discussion of the issue can be found in Nowshirvani, "Beginnings of Commercial Agriculture."

21. Issawi, ed., *Economic History*, pp. 83, 89–90.

22. Abbott, "Notes," pp. 158, 164–5. By 1850, for example, merchants of Jahrom sold between 30,000 and 40,000 tomans worth of British cotton goods per year.

23. Binning, *Journal*, pp. 287–8. By 1857, there were only ten "weaver's factories" in Shiraz, where earlier in the century there had been as many as 500. The trade in good quality cloth for local consumption which Shiraz maintained with Kerman, Yazd, and Kashan also had been ruined.

24. Estimates of the Iranian specie exported to India to pay for imports are very difficult to obtain before 1870, since the figures usually were combined with those of the pearl trade and often represent specie drawn from the entire Gulf area. The drain of specie apparently was perceived to be a significant

problem by the Qajar regime, though. As early as 1800, Qajar officials unsuccessfully sought to reduce the flow by encouraging local weavers to make cloth similar to that imported from India. See Waring, *Tour,* pp. 7–8; for a general discussion of the problem, see Issawi, ed., *Economic History,* pp. 128–35. Nowshirvani, however, argues convincingly that the problem was not caused so much by a loss of specie as by the increasing strains placed on Iranian currency supplies and credit mechanisms by the expanding economy. See Nowshirvani, "Beginnings of Commercial Agriculture."

25. Binning, *Journal,* pp. 156–7, 176–7; Abbott, "Notes," p. 164. Most of the horses exported from Bushehr were raised in northern Iran.

26. "Opium Production and Trade, 1824," in Issawi, ed., *Economic History,* p. 240. For information on the Indian opium monopoly see Durga Parshad, *Indian Foreign Trade,* pp. 71–2.

27. For the figures for 1800, see Waring, *Tour,* p. 17; for 1850, see Binning, *Journal,* p. 150; for 1882 see Stack, *Six Months,* 1, p. 25; for 1889 see Curzon, *Persia,* vol. 2, p. 235. After 1870, the revenues derived from farming the customs at Bandar Abbas and Bandar-e Lengeh also rose dramatically.

28. Between 1800 and 1850, the value of *tuyuls* in the agricultural areas of the interior rose only slightly. Morier cites a figure of 40,000 tomans (which he thought exaggerated) as the amount annually collected by the district governor from 17 villages in the Marv Dasht district in 1816–1820. That averages ca. 2,300 tomans per village. If that was the amount collected, the amount bid was probably about 20 percent lower—about 32,000 tomans for the district or ca. 1,880 tomans per village. By 1845, the revenue derived from a major agricultural village like Abadeh was still only 6,000 tomans while that for smaller villages remained in the 1,000–2,000 toman range. Although such figures must be used with caution, their general order of magnitude is probably correct. See Morier, *Second Journey,* p. 82; and C. A. de Bode, *Travels in Luristan and Arabistan,* vol. 1 (London: J. Madden and Company, 1845), pp. 67, 238.

29. This did not mean that the shaikh of Bushehr actually expanded his rule over the ports. In most small ports, tribal feelings and organization remained strong enough to ensure that only the locally accepted tribal leader could control the port. The shaikh simply was able to interpose himself as a profit-making intermediary between local leaders and provincial authorities.

30. The Qavam ol-Molk for much of this period was the son of Hajji Ebrahim, governor of Shiraz under the last Zand, Loft Ali Khan (1790–95). He inherited a wide variety of political and economic connections—as well as a formidable set of enemies—from his father, who had played a key role in the Qajar conquest of the region. Among other notables who sought to increase their power through much the same means during this period were Mohammad Ali Khan Nezam ol-Molk, and the Moshir ol-Molk, a bitter rival of the Qavam ol-Molk.

31. This was not the first time that powerful figures in Shiraz sought to gain control over the lucrative customs revenues of Bushehr. It was, however, the most successful and enduring such attempt. As early as 1808, two Shirazi landowner-merchants, Mohammad Nabi Khan and his brother Aqa Mohammad Ja'far, successfully cornered the grain trade supplying the city. They used the resulting power and revenue to induce the provincial governor

to grant them the *tuyul* for Bushehr. They maintained themselves there unsteadily until 1811, when they were driven out by a combination of popular unrest and the breakdown of their economic position in Shiraz.

32. The only new crop introduced into southern Iran on a significant scale between 1800 and 1870 was maize. It was grown for local consumption and apparently was adopted by the peasants with little difficulty because of its advantages as a subsistence crop. See Abbott, "Notes," p. 150; and Binning, *Journal*, pp. 306, 335–6. Maize cultivation is no longer mentioned by travelers after 1880.

33. Durga Parshad, *Indian Foreign Trade*, pp. 169–75, 201.

34. The shift in British trade from the Trebizond route to the Bushehr route was aided by several "extraneous" factors such as the Russo-Turkish War of 1877. However, the bulk of British trade shifted to the Suez-Bushehr-Shiraz route and *remained* there because of the concrete economic advantages it offered.

35. Statistics for the trade of Bushehr between 1878 and 1900 can be found in the tables in the Persian Gulf Residency Reports for the years 1878–79 through 1900–01. Supplementary information can be found in Eteocle Lorini, *La Persia economica contemporanea e la sua questionne monetaria* (Rome: Hermanno Lossler, 1900), pp. 410–11.

36. Great Britain, Board of Trade—Intelligence Committee, *Report on the Condition and Prospects of British Trade in Persia* (London: His Majesty's Stationery Office, 1904), p. 26. The opium crop often was sold to a broker or an agent of an Indian firm in advance of the harvest. The landlord could then use part of this cash payment to cover his own financial needs, which were often urgent. He could distribute the rest as advances to the cultivators, thus ensuring their continued dependence on him. How the owners or controllers of opium producing lands were paid and how they used the revenue they received is a crucial question. Unfortunately, little attention has been paid to it in either contemporary or recent works. Sometimes, the need to operate constantly on credit seriously disadvantaged landowners who invested heavily in opium. Iranian opium never constituted more than a small fraction of the total produced in eastern Asia for export to China and Europe. Hence, Iranian producers could not control the market conditions that determined the price they received for opium. In years when, for example, the Bengal harvest was very good, the low price of opium might not provide landowners with enough funds to pay off debts incurred earlier under different conditions. Of course, if part of the Indian opium crop failed, as it often did, Iranian opium producers might benefit substantially.

37. The mere presence of steamships in the Persian Gulf does not appear to have been decisive in stimulating opium production for export in southern Iran—although it did have a significant effect on the growth of grain exports to India. Rather, the change in shipping patterns brought on by the Suez Canal enabled southern Iranian merchants to avoid prohibitive duties imposed on opium at Indian ports without having to assume the great burden and risk of financing a voyage to East Asia and back. See Stack, *Six Months*, pp. 263–4.

38. Persian Gulf Political Residency, *Report*, for the years 1878–79 and 1880–81; see also Great Britain, *British Trade*; and Curzon, *Persia*, vol. 2, p. 559. Curzon's figures for 1889 are particularly interesting. He gives the total

value of all Persian exports for the year as 7,442,000 tomans. Opium exports accounted for 1,900,000 tomans (25.5 percent of the total) and constituted the single largest item of Persian export by value. The next two largest items of export—raw silk which accounted for 17.5 percent of the total (1,300,000 tomans) and rice which accounted for 13.5 percent of the total (1,000,000 tomans)—were exported almost exclusively via Russia or Baghdad. They did not play a significant role in the export trade of southern Iran. When those and similar, smaller items are deducted, the monumental importance of opium in the trade of southern Iran becomes apparent.

39. The ten districts in which opium became a major item were Abad-e Tashk (approximately 100 km ENE of Shiraz); Estahbanat (approximately 150 km ESE of Shiraz); Sarvestan (80 km ESE of Shiraz); Kavar (50 km SSE of Shiraz); Fasa (120 km north of Shiraz); Arsanjan (80 km ENE of Shiraz); Eqlid (150 km north of Shiraz); Ramjerd (60 km north of Shiraz); Korbal (approximately 65 km NNE of Shiraz); and Kamin (approximately 115 km NE of Shiraz). See Persian Gulf Political Residency, *Report for the Year 1879–80*, pp. 68–9.

40. Stack, *Six Months,* pp. 75–6. See also Arnold T. Wilson, *SW Persia. A Political Officer's Diary 1907*–1914 (London: Oxford University Press, 1941), p. 186; and Curzon, *Persia*, 2, p. 406.

41. Stack, *Six Months,* pp. 38, 263. Such inducements were particularly effective in years following severe famines such as that of 1878–80 in the Kazerun district.

42. Iranian landowners and merchants, fully supported by the foreign merchants with whom they dealt, continued to export grain during periods of famine, which intensified the region's economic and social difficulties. British Gulf authorities occasionally sought to restrict the grain trade between India and Iran so as to keep needed food supplies in the region, but their efforts usually were ineffective. The situation is reminiscent of the U.S. Army's attempts to protect Indian lands against the encroachments of speculators and settlers whose safety and "rights" they also were obliged to protect.

43. During the 1879–80 famine, for example, popular unrest forced a few landowners to plough up poppy fields and plant grain. Once the immediate crisis passed, however, opium cultivation quickly was restored. During the same period, provincial authorities decreed that local landowners had to plant one *jarib* of grain for each *jarib* of land planted in opium poppies. They also forced bakers in Shiraz to sell bread at fixed prices in order to reduce unrest in the city and its environs. That, however, greatly reduced the profitability of grain relative to opium and provided landowners with even more incentive to avoid planting restrictions. See Stack, *Six Months*, vol. 2, pp. 36–37; and Persian Gulf Political Residency, *Report for the Year 1880–81*, p. 43.

10. *Rural Socioeconomic Organization in Transition: The Case of Iran's Bonehs*

1. Research for part of this paper was conducted in the summer of 1977. The author wishes to express appreciation for the award of an Iran Bicentennial Fellowship, administered by the American Friends of the Middle East, which enabled the research to be carried out.

2. See Eric J. Hooglund, "The Effects of the Land Reform Program on Rural Iran." (Ph.D. diss., Johns Hopkins University, 1975).

3. The indispensable work on tenure relationships in pre-land reform is A.K.S. Lambton, *Landlord and Peasant in Persia* (London: Oxford University Press, 1953).

4. The share of the harvest kept by the landlord varied from village to village. In most villages it averaged between one-half to two-thirds of the crop, although in rare instances it could be as low as 20 percent or as high as 80 percent.

5. Useful statistics on land holdings are in Oddvar Aresvik, *The Agricultural Development of Iran* (New York: Praeger, 1976), p. 100.

6. The sale of land acquired under the land reform law is not allowed; however, this writer heard considerable oral testimony from both sellers and buyers of such land in various villages in western Iran in the summer of 1977 and in Fars in the summer of 1978.

7. For more detail about the *khoshneshins* see Eric J. Hooglund, "The Khwushnishin Population of Iran," *Iranian Studies* 6 (1973): 229–245.

8. Preliminary research by this writer in the summer of 1978 found that the position of some *khoshneshin* families was changing as a result of male members commuting or migrating to cities for jobs which provide a regular income.

9. Aresvik, *Agricultural Development,* pp. 105–106.

10. Ibid., p. 171.

11. In areas where wheat is dry-farmed and thus its production costs are less, the deficit may amount to the equivalent of only one or two rials per kilo; but in areas where wheat is irrigated the difference is as high as 12 rials a kilogram. These rial sums assume much larger significance when it is noted that wheat production per hectare is measured in tons.

12. The term *boneh* is generally restricted to the area stretching from Qazvin in the west through Varamin to Gamsar in the east. For the use of other terms with the same meaning see discussion in the text below.

13. The most valuable study before the 1960s was Lambton's *Landlord and Peasant.* The Persian translation of this work was for years the most authoritative study available in Iran about villages. However, Lambton's primary concern was with land tenure from an historical perspective rather than with socioeconomic matters.

14. Javad Safi-nezhad, *Talebabad* (Tehran: University of Tehran, 1345/1966–67), pp. 163–324.

15. Javad Safi-nezhad, *Asnad-e Bonehha* (Tehran: University of Tehran, 1978), is a collection of agreements between *bonehs* and landlords dating back to Qajar times. These documents provide evidence of continuity of *bonehs* for at least 80 years preceding land reform.

16. Safi-nezhad initially explained his theory of the pre-Islamic origins of Iran's *bonehs* in conversations with the author during the winter and spring of 1972. He has consistently maintained his views in numerous conversations and personal communications since that time.

17. Mr. Abbas Garrousi, personal interview, Institute for Peasant and Rural Studies, Tehran, 1977. Mr. Garrousi currently is translating the relevant manuscripts into Persian for publication.

18. Safi-nezhad, for example has hypothesized that *boneh* formation

closely paralleled the 300 millimeter rainfall line; that is, *bonehs* generally existed in areas which received less than 300 millimeters of rain per year but were not found in areas which received more. Effectively, this theory would preclude the existence of *bonehs* in western Iran. For more detail see his articles, "Bonehha va Abyari dar Iran," *Jughrafiya*, 2 (1977); and "Ta'avoniha-ye Kohn," *Daneshkadeh*, 1, (1354/1975–76):47–50.

19. Preliminary findings from research in 1971–72 and 1977 indicate that *bonehs* existed in some villages, but were absent in others. *Bonehs* were found, for example, in villages around Mianeh, Mianduab and Mahabad. It is significant that irrigation is practiced for summer crops in all three of these areas.

20. The same 200 hectares, however, were not always cultivated annually; as much as 400 hectares may be cultivable, but half was left fallow each season. Still, less than half of all land associated with the village was ever cultivated.

21. For more detail on the variety of *bonehs,* see Safi-nezhad, *Boneh,* 3rd. ed., pp. 156–168.

22. Safi-nezhad, *Boneh,* 2nd. ed., p. 179f.

23. Ibid., p. 180.

24. For example, a peasant with only three hectares of land may have his holdings scattered in 10 separate plots.

25. Safi-nezhad, *Boneh,* 2nd ed., p. 178.

26. Ibid., pp. 179–180.

27. This writer's own field research in the summer of 1977 and 1978 found in a sample of 35 villages that *bonehs* had completely disappeared in 18 and survived in some form in the other 17.

28. See Safi-nezhad, *Boneh,* 2nd. ed., pp. 180–189; and 3rd. ed., pp. 171–190.

29. Ibid., 3rd. ed., p. 186.

30. Aresvik, *Agricultural Development,* p. 100.

31. In 1978 peasants in the Shiraz area cited conflicts over the sharing of work as typical disputes and the main reason for *boneh* dissolution.

32. See Hushang Aliasian, *Moqaddameh bar tahqiq-e ejtema'i-ye rostaha-ye dasht-e Qazvin,* (Tehran: Qazvin Development Organization, 1348/1969–70), pp. 42–44.

33. Safi-nezhad, *Boneh,* 2nd. ed., pp. 188–189.

34. For the most important work on the survival of *bonehs,* see Mustafa Azkia, "Fardis," *Olum-e Ejtema'i* (1976): 180–188.

35. Much of the information on Fardis was collected on several field trips between February and July, 1972. I wish to acknowledge my gratitude to Professor Azkia for keeping me informed and up-to-date on developments in Fardis since that time.

36. For example, in the Beyza area of Fars province this writer found in the summer of 1978 that *bonehs* still functioned in small villages (under 50 peasants) as well as very large villages (more than 200 farmers).

37. For a detailed study of Iran's agricultural production problems with numerous statistical tables see Aresvik, *Agricultural Development.*

38. Ibid., pp. 169–174; 201–226.

39. For an assessment of the cooperatives see A.K.S. Lambton, "Land Reform and Rural Cooperatives," *Royal Central Asian Journal* 56 (1969): 1–28;

for a detailed comparative study of 79 cooperatives in Ehsan Naraghi, ed., *Sherkatha-ye ta'avoni rosta'i dar shesh manteqeh* (Tehran: University of Tehran, 1348/1969–70).

40. In this regard several senior government officials affirmed to this writer during interviews in 1972 and 1977 their belief that Iranian peasants essentially were lazy and incapable of working together even when compelled.

41. The overwhelming majority of peasants belonged to a cooperative by 1978. However, they provide few services and their main function is the provision of short-term, low-interest credit to members. While this is important, government funding has been limited so that cooperatives are not the major source of total peasant credit; a significant proportion of loans are used for consumption rather than productive purposes. See Hooglund, "Land Reform," pp. 178–186; and Aresvik, *Agricultural Development,* pp. 169–174.

11. The Strengths and Weaknesses of the Labor Movement in Iran, 1941–1953

1. For details on the statistics presented throughout this paper see my forthcoming book, *Iran between Two Revolutions.*

2. British Ambassador to the Foreign Office, 13 June 1946, F.O. 371/Persia 1946/34–52664. Crown copyright records by kind permission of the Controller, Her Majesty's Stationery Office.

3. *Time,* 13 July 1953.

4. For a detailed discussion of the history and politics of the Tudeh Party see S. Zabih, *The Communist Movement in Iran* (Berkeley, 1966).

5. For the early labor movement see S. Mani, *Tarikhcheh-e nahzat-e kargar dar Iran* [A Short History of the Labor Movement in Iran] (Tehran, 1946); M. Nasehi, "Workers' Organization in Iran," *Rahbar,* 10 April 1946; R. Rusta, "The C.C.F.T.U.," *Razm Mahaneh* 1:1 (June 1948): 62–4: M. Ivanov, *The Working Class in Contemporary Iran* [in Russian] (Moscow, 1968), pp. 200–10; A. Ovanessian, "Reminiscences on the Iranian Communist Party," *Donya* 3:1 (Spring 1962): 33–9; A. Sultanzadeh, *Asnad-e tarikh* [Historical Documents] (Paris, 1973).

6. Iranian Government, Ministry of Labor, *Amar-e sana'i-ye Iran* [Industrial Statistics of Iran] (Tehran, 1948).

7. British Minister to the Foreign Office, "Annual Report for 1934," F.O. 371/Persia 1935/34–18995.

8. British Consul in Tabriz, "The Economic Situation in Azerbayjan," F.O. 371/Persia 1937/34–20830.

9. British Consul in Isfahan, "Report on Isfahan," F.O. 371/Persia 1945/34–45446.

10. Biographical information has been obtained from interviews, newspapers, memoirs, and transcripts of political trials.

11. R. Rusta, "Speech to the First Conference of the Union of Railwaymen," *Zafar,* 15 August 1946.

12. The World Federation of Trade Unions, *Report on Iran, October 1945–April 1949* (Milan, 1949), p. 167.

13. International Labour Office, *Provisional Records of the Twenty–Seventh Session* (Paris, 1945).

14. M. Djamalzadeh, "Social and Economic Structure of Iran," *International Labour Review* 43:2 (February 1951): 178–91.

15. U.S. Congress, Committee on Foreign Relations, *The Strategy and Tactics of World Communism* (Washington, D.C., 1949), p. 7.

16. The Military Governor of Tehran, *The Evolution of Communism in Iran* (Tehran, 1956), pp. 8–9.

17. British Ambassador to the Foreign Office, "Report on Labour Conditions in Persia," *F.O. 371/Persia 1944/34-40222.*

18. *Rahbar*, 13 November 1946.

19. British Military Attaché to the Foreign Office, 18 November 1946, *India Office/L/P & S/12–3505.*

20. British Consul in Isfahan, 1 January 1947, *India Office/ L/P & S/12–3529.*

21. British Consul in Isfahan, 30 December 1946, *India Office/ L/P & S/12–3529.*

22. British Labour Attaché to the Foreign Office, "Labour Conditions in the Anglo-Iranian Oil Company," *India Office/ L/P & S/12–3490A.*

23. U.S. Congress, *Strategy and Tactics*, p. 9.

24. Anonymous, "The Crisis in Khuzestan," *Ettela'at-e Haftegi*, 19–30 April 1952.

25. Anonymous, "The Situation in Isfahan," *Ettela'at-e Haftegi*, 19 April 1951.

26. M. Malekzadeh, *Mozakkerat-e Majles* (Parliamentary Proceedings) (Tehran) (Referred below as *Parliamentary Proceedings)*, 20 April 1951.

27. *Ettela'at-e Haftegi*, 20 April 1951.

28. *Tehran Mosavvar*, 6 September 1951.

29. R. Shafaq, *Parliamentary Proceedings*, 1st Senate, 26 June 1951.

30. A. Raji, *Parliamentary Proceedings*, 16th Majlis, 23 May 1951.

31. Kh. Maleki, "Strikes," *Niru-ye Sevvom*, 29 June 1952.

32. *Ettela'at*, 23 October 1952.

33. Sh. Qonatabadi, *Parliamentary Proceedings*, 17th Majlis, 28 October 1952.

34. Banki Melli Iran, "The Cost of Living Index," *Bulletin*, No. 142 (January 1954), pp. 19–20.

35. Data compiled from *Rahbar, Mardom, Zafar, Besu-ye Ayandeh, Bakhtar-e Emruz, Ettela'at,* and *Mard-e Emruz.*

36. Kh. Iraqi, "Secrets from Razmara's Administration: A Survey of the Bazaar," *Khandaniha*, 23 January 1956.

37. M. Azizi, "Speech to the First Conference of the C.C.F.T.U.," *Rahbar*, 1 August 1946.

38. British Consul in Kerman, 30 December 1946, *F.O. 371/Persia 1946/ 34–52749.*

39. British Consul in Bandar Abbas, 30 June 1946, *F.O. 371/Persia 1946/ 34–52699.*

40. British Consul in Shiraz, 30 April 1944, *F.O. 371/Persia 1944/34–40162.*

41. British Consul in Zahedan, 30 June 1946, *F.O. 371/Persia 1944/34– 52756.*

42. For an explanation of rural conservatism, see F. Kazemi and E. Abrahamian, "The Non-Revolutionary Peasantry in Iran," *Iranian Studies* 11 (1978): 259–304.

43. British Ambassador to the Foreign Office, 31 May 1945, *F.O. 371/Persia 1945/34–45448.*

44. British Ambassador to the Foreign Office, "Discussions with the A.I.O.C.," *F.O. 371*/Persia 1945/34–45461.

45. The Anglo-Iranian Oil Company, "Memorandum on Security," *F.O. 371*/Persia 1944/34–40197.

46. British Consul in Khorramshahr, "Report on Tudeh Activities in the Oil Industry," *F.O. 371*/Persia 1946/34–52714.

47. British Ambassador to the Foreign Office, "Memorandum on Tudeh Activities in the A.I.O.C.," *F.O. 371*/Persia 1946/34–52713.

48. *The Times*, 30 July 1946.

49. British Consul in Khorramshahr, "Report on the General Strike," *India Office*/ L/P & S/12–3490A.

50. British Ambassador to the Foreign Office, 20 May 1946, *F.O. 371*/Persia 1946/34–52713.

51. British Consul in Ahwaz, 30 June 1946, *F.O. 371*/Persia 1946/34–52700.

52. M. Audsley, "Report on the Oilfields," *F.O. 371*/Persia 1946/34–52723.

53. British Ambassador to the Foreign Office, "The Tudeh Party in the Oil Industry," *F.O. 371*/Persia 1946/34–52714.

54. British Military Attaché to the Foreign Office, 10 June 1946, *F. O. 371*/1946/34–52710.

55. British Consul in Ahwaz, 1 August 1946, *F.O. 371*/Persia 1946/34–52700.

56. British Consul in Khorramshahr, "Report on the General Strike," *India Office*/ L/P & S/12–3490A.

57. British Military Attaché to the Foreign Office, 23 July 1946, *F.O. 371*/1946/34–52711.

58. British Military Attaché to the Foreign Office, 10 July 1946, *F.O. 371*/Persia 1946/34–52742.

59. British Consul in Khorramshahr, 1 June 1946, *F.O. 371*/Persia 1946/34–52742.

60. British Consul in Khorramshahr, "Report on the General Strike," *India Office*/ L/P & S/12–3490A.

61. Ibid.

62. *Zafar*, 5 July 1946.

63. British Consul in Khorramshahr, "Report on the General Strike," *India Office*/ L/P & S/12–3490A.

64. Ibid.

65. Ibid.

66. British Military Attaché to the Foreign Office, 31 July 1946, *F.O. 371*/Persia 1946/34–52711.

67. N. Baker, 17 July 1946, *F.O. 371*/Persia 1946/34–52719.

68. Anonymous Letter to the Foreign Office, 18 July 1946, *F.O. 371*/Persia 1946/34–52720.

69. British Foreign Office, "Report on the Parliamentary Delegation's Visit to Persia," *F.O. 371*/Persia 1946/34–52718.

70. British Cabinet, "Notes on the Parliamentary Delegation's Visit to Persia," *F.O. 371*/Persia 1946/34–52616.

71. British Consul in Ahwaz, 1 September 1946, *F.O. 371*/Persia 1946/34–52700.

72. F. Halliday, "Iran: Trade Unions and the Working Class Opposition," *MERIP Reports*, No. 71 (October 1978), pp. 7–13.

73. For the role of the labor movement in the Islamic Revolution see: E. Abrahamian, "Iran: The Political Challenge," *MERIP Reports*, No. 69 (July-August 1978); idem, "Iran: The Political Crisis Intensifies," *MERIP Reports*, No. 71 (October 1979).

74. For the role of the left in the oil strike see: *Iran Times* (In Persian), 2 March 1979, 2 February 1979, 12 January 1979, 22 December 1978, 6 December 1978; *Washington Post*, 14 February 1979, 19 January 1979; *Ettela'at*, 7 March 1979; *New York Times*, 5 March 1979.

75. *Iran Times*, 12 January 1979.

12. *Shops and Shopkeepers: Dynamics of an Iranian Provincial Bazaar*

1. The field research for this paper was conducted in 1970–71 with funds by a Fulbright-Hays fellowship and in the summer of 1977 by a grant from the Social Science Research Council. I thank these agencies for their financial support. I also wish to thank my assistants in Yazd, especially for the help of Mr. Mehdi Abedi. Lastly, I must thank the people of Yazd for their kindness and cooperation—especially the bazaaris who endured many hours of strange questions by a foreigner. This study represents conditions in Yazd before the revolution of 1978–79 and the establishment of the Islamic Republic of Iran.

2. For examinations of the morphology of Iranian and other Middle Eastern bazaars see Eugen Wirth, "Zum Problem des Bazars (sūq, çarşi): Versuch einer Begriffsbestimmung und Theorie des traditionellen Wirtschaftszentrums der orientalisch-islamischen Stadt," *Der Islam* 51 (1974): 203–260; 52 (1975): 6–46; and idem, "Strukturwandlungen und Entwicklungstendenzen der orientalischen Stadt," *Erdkunde* 22 (1968): 101–128.

3. The various bazaar officials have been discussed in W. M. Floor, "The Marketpolice in Qajar Iran," *Die Welt des Islams* 13 (1971): 212–229; idem, "The Office of Kalantar in Qajar Persia," *Journal of the Economic and Social History of the Orient* 14 (1971): 253–268; and idem, "The Guilds in Iran: An Overview from the Earliest Beginnings till 1972," *Zeitschrift der Deutschen Morgenländischen Gesellschaft* 125 (1975), 99–116.

4. An example of foreselling and its effect in the Dezful region can be found in Eckart Ehlers, "Dezful and its Hinterland: Observations on the Relationships of Lesser Iranian Cities and Towns to their Hinterland," *Geography: Journal of the Association of Iranian Geographers* 1 (1976), 20–30.

5. James Alban Bill, *The Politics of Iran: Groups, Classes and Modernization* (Columbus, Ohio: Charles E. Merrill, 1972); see Chapter 1: "The Irano-Islamic Social Structure," 1–51.

6. Ibid., p. 11.

7. For a discussion of *vaqf* in the Yazd bazaar and its implications, see Michael E. Bonine, "Vaqf and Commercial Land Use: The Bazaar of Yazd, Iran," in *Economic and Social Aspects of the Muslim Waqf*, ed. Gabriel Baer [forthcoming]. A few other papers in this volume also shed light on the relationship between *waqf* and the central bazaar or *suq*.

8. Michael Fischer, "Persian Society: Transformation and Strain," in *Twentieth Century Iran*, ed. Hossein Amirsadeghi and R. W. Ferrier (London: Heinemann, 1977), 180.

425

9. For the changes in the guilds in much of the Pahlavi era see Floor, "The Guilds in Iran."

10. See Bill, *The Politics of Iran,* Chapter 2: "The Professional-Bureaucratic Intelligentsia: The New Class," 53–72.

11. The political role of the Yazd bazaar was not examined, a topic which could not be investigated openly in the Pahlavi era.

12. For example, in the thirteenth century Marco Polo visited Yazd and remarked on its great silk production. See Sir Henry Yule, *The Book of Marco Polo* (London: John Murray, 1903), Vol. 1, 88. Similarly, in the mid-fifteenth century Josafa Barbaro visited Yazd and talks about the great amount of weaving and silk production. See Josafa Barbaro and Ambrogio Contarini, *Travels to Tana and Persia* (London: Hakluyt Society, 1873), 73–74.

13. The discussion of the traditional weaving relationships results from observations and interviews in 1970–71. Although the patterns described have been similar the last several decades, whether or not the same system existed for earlier periods has not been investigated.

14. The economics of operating one of these electric looms has been discussed by Michael M. J. Fischer, "Zoroastrian Iran Between Myth and Praxis" (Ph.D. diss., University of Chicago, 1973), 138–139 (fn1).

15. Such rough cotton cloth generically is called *karbaf, kishbaf,* or *sha'rbaf;* it includes *chador shab* (woman's outer garment), *toshaki* (for washing), *pilas* (for floor covering), *rui farsh* (for floor covering), and *jem* (black cloth for peasant clothing—although this cloth is now woven with nylon and rayon instead of cotton).

16. In 1977 these large factories employed about 5,200 persons; ten factories had 100 or more employees. The largest factory is Yazd Baft which employs about 1,500 persons and produces 120,000 meters of cloth per day.

17. A. Cecil Edwards, *The Persian Carpet: A Survey of the Carpet-Weaving Industry of Persia* (London: G. Duckworth, 1953), 214.

18. Ibid.

19. The all silk Qom carpet can also be added to the list of patterns woven in Yazd Province. In the village of Zarch, northwest of Yazd, several looms weave this expensive silk carpet. This came about because a family in Zarch had a relative in Qom who was a middleman for these carpets. Through him, a master weaver came to Zarch in the late 1960s and taught several girls how to weave these carpets. For at least one of these carpets, the silk was bought in Yazd, spun in Kashan, dyed in Qom, woven in Zarch, and sold by the Qom middleman in Tehran.

20. Kashan, Kerman, and Isfahan patterns woven in Yazd are not identified by Tehran merchants as being woven in the Yazd region. In one instance a London merchant discovered they were not "genuine" and refused to accept them. Some Yazdi carpet merchants used to have "Yazd," "made in Yazd," or the merchant's name woven in a corner of their carpets. Tehran merchants found that they could not sell these carpets and so the names were removed and the Yazdi merchants were instructed to not identify their carpets.

21. When the Kashan pattern began to be woven in the Yazd region none of the Yazdi dyers could dye the wool properly, which is a complex chemical process. The wool was shipped to Kashan to be dyed and then returned to Yazd. Finally, in the late 1960s one man spent several years as an apprentice

in Kashan, learned the technique, and returned to Yazd to open up a shop. However, in the early 1970s most of the wool for Kashan carpets was still being dyed in Kashan.

22. For a description of *zilu* looms and weaving, see Hans E. Wulff, *The Traditional Crafts of Persia* (Cambridge: M.I.T. Press, 1966), 210–211.

23. To give a few examples: Bafruyeh for rope makers, Nasrabad for carpenters, Behabad for blacksmiths, Mehriz for *givehs* and knives, Sakhhod for porters, Meybod for pottery, Mehrjerd for bakers, and Taft for blacksmiths and pomegranates.

24. The pre-Islamic Republic names of the avenues are used in this paper; names referring to the shah and the Pahlavis have, of course, been changed.

25. The data on the shops were all collected in surveys by the author.

26. John I. Clarke and Brian D. Clark, *Kermanshah: An Iranian Provincial City* (Durham: University of Durham, Department of Geography, Research Paper Series, No. 10, 1969), 73; John I. Clarke, *The Iranian City of Shiraz* (Durham: University of Durham, Department of Geography, Research Paper Series, No. 7, 1963), 27–29; and Günther Schweizer, "Tabriz (Nordwest-Iran) und der Tabrizer Bazar," *Erdkunde* 26 (1972):40.

27. Clarke, *The Iranian City of Shiraz*, 27–29; and Clarke and Clark, *Kermanshah: An Iranian Provincial City*, 73.

28. Schweizer, "Tabriz (Nordwest-Iran) und der Tabrizer Bazar," 40.

29. See Wirth, "Strukturwandlungen und Entwicklungstendenzen der orientalischen Stadt," 105.

30. The workshops (and other factories) are not counted as part of the shop totals because they do not deal directly with the public and are primarily manufacturing or secondary activities instead of part of the tertiary sector. There are difficulties in devising categories for these Iranian cities because of the prevalence of producer-retailers (craftsmen).

31. For a discussion of the morphology of villages and their shops, see Michael E. Bonine, *Yazd and its Hinterland: A Central Place System of Dominance in the Central Iranian Plateau* (Marburg/Lahn: Geographischen Institutes der Universität Marburg, Marburger Geographische Schriften, no. 83, 1980), chapter 3.

32. Difficulties were encountered in dividing the avenues for analysis. Wide streets and the difficulty of crossing them meant that shops on each side of an avenue generally are separated for interaction. What finally was done was to group shops along one side of an avenue between intersections.

33. Besides single types it is also important to note the occurrence of the most common category (foodstuffs, textiles, metalworkers, and so forth). The avenues are the least specialized with almost all of the bazaar branches and even many of the *bazarcheh* having a greater percentage of shops of one category. Most of the bazaars have over 50 percent of their shops within one category and some even over 75 percent. Most bazaars are either primarily textiles or metalworkers. The avenues, on the other hand, have no category over 50 percent and, in nearly every instance, foodstuffs comprise the most common category.

34. However, the great expansion of the Iranian economy in the mid-1970s (until 1978) lessened migration outside of the country for employment.

35. Howard J. Rotblat, "Social Organization and Development in an Iranian Provincial Bazaar," *Economic Development and Cultural Change* 23 (1975):

292–305. *Hajji* also is an honorific title for respect and/or wealth, and may not be related to the actual pilgrimage to Mecca. The data on *hajjis* in Yazd, however, represent those who have gone to Mecca.

36. It should be noted that some wealthy *hajjis* may violate Islamic law (on interest, profits, and so forth) and are not trusted by other merchants. Several responses to the question about being a *hajji* were: "No, I'm not a thief."

37. Key money *(sarqofli)* is a payment for the right to occupy a particular shop. No person can dispossess the shopkeeper of this usufruct—not even the landlord. The payment is made from one shopkeeper to another, and on the avenues and main branches of the bazaar in Yazd the payment is now in the tens of thousands of dollars. The rents and key money are not detailed in this paper; for a discussion of these in the Yazd bazaar, see Bonine, "Vaqf and Commercial Land Use."

38. Also, for some of the 20 percent of the shops which had been permanently closed in the bazaar the former shopkeeper had died at some earlier period.

39. Paul Ward English, "The Traditional City of Herat, Afghanistan," *From Madina to Metropolis*, ed. L. Carl Brown (Princeton: Darwin Press, 1973), 86.

40. The kinship network includes fifteen sets of brothers, four father-son sets, four *amu* (paternal uncle), one *dai* (maternal uncle), three *pesar-e amu* (son of *amu*), two fathers-in-law, one brother-in-law, and at least four sons of other relatives. Actually, there probably are a few more relatives among these bazaari coppersmiths, because several of these individuals answered the author's questions rather hedgingly.

41. The southwestern part of the city is in the upslope direction, and Iranian cities generally expanded in that direction. See Michael E. Bonine, "The Morphogenesis of Iranian Cities," *Annals of the Association of American Geographers* 69 (1979): 208–224.

42. It should be stressed that the residential pattern of bazaari coppersmiths is not typical of other Yazd bazaaris; such localization was not necessarily a common pattern in traditional Iranian cities. Such concentration in a separate quarter was common among minorities, and so when one trade was dominated by a minority group there was a strong association of residence and occupation.

43. In 1971, 7.6 tomans = $1.00; in 1977, 7 tomans = $1.00.

44. The family names of some of these individuals in the bazaar reflect their specialty: Sohankar (filer [of copper]), Aftabehsaz (maker of ewers), and Shastisaz (maker of a type of tray).

45. None of the coppersmiths elsewhere in the bazaar, however, had closed their shops. In 1977 one shop which earlier had been storage for a coppersmith was open as a shop, and one coppertinner had become a coppersmith; hence there were 54 coppersmiths in the bazaar in 1977, five fewer than in 1971.

46. Yet, there is still a market for copper goods. A large cauldron *(dik)* for water or cooking *ash* (stew) is still a common item (often for a religious ceremony or a mosque), while large trays and pots still have no suitable noncopper substitute. A set of copper pots and pans still is part of the traditional dowry for a bride.

47. At this time Bazaar-e Zargari was considered a part of Bazaar-e Khan (Vali), but as more and more goldsmiths opened shops in this branch it began to be referred to as the goldsmith bazaar.

48. The extensive kinship network which sometimes exists is illustrated by one of the older masters in the goldsmith bazaar. His father was a goldsmith in the bazaar and he has the following relatives who are (or were) goldsmiths: four brothers, three sons, one *dai* (maternal uncle), one *amu* (paternal uncle), three sons of *amu,* eight grandsons of *amu,* one son of a brother, two sons of *ameh* (paternal aunt), and one son of a sister.

13. *Petty Traders in Iran*

1. Fieldwork in Mazandaran (1971–72) was sponsored by a grant from the National Institute of Mental Health; fieldwork in Tehran (1973–74) was carried out under the general guidance of Dr. Edward Felton, Jr., and with the aid of the classes of 1973 and 1974, especially Ms. E. Alavi and Mr. E. Maliki, of the Iran Center for Management Studies. Additional field observations were made in 1978 while I was conducting field research in Mazandaran for Daneshgah-e Shomal (Babolsar). Michael Bonine and Nikki Keddie made both extensive and perceptive comments on an earlier draft of this paper for which I am grateful.

2. Since these works are all well known and widely cited, I see no reason to review them at length here. Claude Meillassoux, ed., *The Development of Indigenous Trade and Markets in West Africa* (London: Oxford University Press, 1971); Paul Bohannon and George Dalton, eds., *Markets in Africa* (Evanston: Northwestern University Press, 1962); Sol Tax, *Penny Capitalism: A Guatemalan Indian Economy* (Washington, D.C.: Institute of Social Anthropology, Publication No. 16, Smithsonian Institute, 1953); George Foster, "The Economy of Rural Mexico with Special Reference to Marketing," *The Journal of Marketing* 13 (1948): 153–162; Sidney Mintz, "Internal Market Systems as Mechanisms of Social Articulation," *Proceedings of the American Ethnological Society* (1959): 22–30; Alice Dewey, *Peasant Marketing in Java* (New York: The Free Press of Glencoe, 1962); Clifford Geertz, *Peddlers and Princes: Social Change and Economic Modernization in Two Indonesian Towns* (Chicago: University of Chicago Press, 1963); Cyril Belshaw, *Traditional Exchange and Modern Markets* (Englewood Cliffs, N.J.: Prentice Hall, 1965).

3. J. Clarke and B. Clark, *Kermanshah: An Iranian Provincial City* (Durham: Research Paper Series 10, Dept of Geography, University of Durham, 1969); Paul English, *City and Village in Iran* (Madison: University of Wisconsin Press, 1966); H. Hettinger, "Marketing in Persia," *The Journal of Marketing* 15 (1951): 289–97; Faud Khuri, "The Ettiquette of Bargaining in the Middle East," *American Anthropologist* 70 (1968): 698–706; D. Potter, "The Bazaar Merchant," in *Social Forces in the Middle East,* ed. S. Fisher (Ithaca: Cornell University Press, 1955), pp. 98–115; Howard Rotblat, "Stability and Change in an Iranian Provincial Bazaar" (Ph.D. diss., University of Chicago, 1972); Gustav Thaiss, "The Bazaar as a Case Study of Religion and Social Change," in *Iran Faces the Seventies,* ed. E. Yar-Shater (New York: McGraw-Hill, 1971).

4. W. Fogg, "The Suq: A Study in the Human Geography of Morocco," *Geography* 17 (1932): 257–67; idem, "Village and Suq in the High Atlas Mountains in Morocco," *Scottish Geographical Magazine* 15 (1935): 144–51; idem, "A Tribal Market in the Spanish Zone of Morocco," *Africa* 11 (1938): 428–45; idem, "The Importance of Tribal Markets in the Commercial Life of the Countryside of Northwest Morocco," *Africa* 12 (1939): 445–49; F. Benet,

"Explosive Markets: The Berber Highlands," in *Trade and Market in the Early Empires*, ed. Karl Polanyi, Conrad Arensberg, and H. Pearson (New York: Columbia University Press, 1957), pp 188–217; idem, "Weekly Sugs and City Markets: The Transition from Rural Sug Economy to Market Economy," in *Research for the Mediterranean Basin: A Proposal*, ed. C. Van Nieuwenhuijze (The Hague: Mouton and Co., 1961), pp. 86–97; G. Blake, *Misurata: A Market Town in Tripolotania*, (Durham: Research Paper Series 9, Dept of Geography, University of Durham, 1968); M. Mikesell, "The Role of Tribal Markets in Morocco," *Geographical Review* 48 (1958): 494–511.

5. For a few counterexamples, see J. Keith Thorpe, "Periodic Markets in the Caspian Lowlands of Iran: Temporal and Locational Spacing of Markets in the Gilan Plain," manuscript, 1974 and Charles Thomas Thompson, "Impetus for Change: The Transformation of Peasant Marketing in Mazandaran," in *The Social Sciences and Problems of Development*, ed. K. Farmanfarmian (Princeton: Princeton University Program in Near Eastern Studies, 1976), pp. 226–43.

6. Although there is a tendency to think of petty traders as being male, a significant number of traders are women. This is true throughout the Middle East. Even in Riyadh, Saudi Arabia, women sell nuts and candy on the streets and women traders have special sections in the bazaars; see Tom Thompson, "Whatever Happened to the Denver Zephry?" *AnthroTech* (Summer 1977).

7. Handcrafts here refers to utilitarian items—brooms, reed mats, wood and iron utensils and tools, cloth woven on a hand loom, knitted woolen clothing articles, and the like. The use of handcraft is preferred over handicraft, since the latter has become identified with "art" objects for the tourist trade.

8. See Charles Thomas Thompson and Marilyn Huies, "Peasant and Bazaar Marketing Systems as Distinct Types," *Anthropological Quarterly* 41 (1968): 219–27.

9. Although there is no licensing requirement for petty traders, some estimate of their numbers can be made from other sources. In Tehran, the hand lorries used by many traders (fruit and vegetable vendors in particular) must be registered. In 1973, a municipality official told the researchers that there were about 7,000 vendors using hand lorries which they either owned or rented. Traders who use stalls or have "permanent spots" near religious shrines or in traditional *bazarchehs* usually pay a nominal rent of some kind to the owner of the marketplace. In one *bazarcheh* near Cyrus Avenue, there were 110 traders using stalls and between 75 and 100 traders who sat on the ground or sidewalk. If these numbers are typical, the total number of traders using lorries and/or paying fees for space-use at any one time is huge. Moreover, this number is complemented by an at least equal number of traders *not* using hand lorries or renting space.

10. There seems to be a belief shared by traders and their customers alike that the Qoran admonishes merchants to take only a 10 percent profit. Deals are often concluded by a customer asking a trader: "Are you a Muslim?", meaning, is this only a 10 percent profit for you? Or a trader will say: "I am a Muslim and take only the permitted 10 percent profit."

11. These figures are for 1973. Daily wages for unskilled and semiskilled labor averaged between 300–500 rials per day. With subsequent high inflation, incomes in 1978 were higher but still on a level of unskilled or semiskilled labor.

12. I do not want to deemphasize the importance of "petty credit" among these traders. As a group, the traders are prone to understate their dependence upon small loans and daily credit from wholesalers. In many respects, this kind of credit actually helps to hold the system together. However, while the short-range effect helps individual vendors make a daily wage, the long-range effect is pernicious and serves to perpetuate the exploitative system that keeps petty traders in a subservient position vis-a-vis the larger bazaar system.

13. The example is an actual one and is given to illustrate the small amount of credit that is sometimes essential for these traders to maintain subsistence incomes.

14. Thompson, "Impetus for Change."

15. George Skinner, "Marketing and Social Structure in Rural China," *Journal of Asian Studies* 34, Part 1 (1964): 3–43 and Part 2 (1964):195–228; Brian Berry, *Market Centers and Retail Distribution* (Englewood Cliffs, N.J.: Prentice-Hall, 1967); E. Johnson, *The Organization of Space in Developing Countries* (Cambridge: Harvard University Press, 1970); R. Smith, "West African Market Places: Temporal Periodicity and Locational Spacing," in *The Development of Indigenous Trade and Markets in West Africa* ed. Claude Meillassoux (London: Oxford University Press, 1971), pp 302–31; idem, "The Theory of Periodic Markets: Consumer and Trader Behavior" (Preconference papers, Canadian Association of Geographers, Waterloo, 1971), pp. 183–89; idem, "The Synchronization of Periodic Markets" (Paper presented at the 22nd International Geographical Congress, Montreal, 1972), pp. 591–93.

16. Thorpe, "Periodic Markets," p. 5.

17. H. Rabino, *Mazandaran and Astarabad* (London: Routlege and Kegan Paul, 1928).

18. Thompson, "Impetus for Change," p. 231.

19. Ibid, p. 232.

20. What I am emphasizing is the fragility of the ties—kinship or otherwise. Obviously, traders can have a variety of social ties, but these are not durable and dependable over time. I have found that even in the urban bazaar, kinship ties, while reputed to be strong, are fraught with dissension and weaken as brothers form nuclear households and their respective sons set up competitive businesses. This is a reflection, I feel, of general kinship patterns in Iran which tend to be weaker (excepting tribal people, in some cases) perhaps than in the Arab countries where patrilineal and corporate groups are reported. My own field work in the markets, both urban and rural, and with villagers and lower class urban workers shows a weak kinship link (and not unilineal in any case). This was found to be true also for the Tehran upper classes; see Constance Cronin, "The Effect of Development on the Urban Family," in *The Social Sciences and Development*, ed. K. Farmanfarmian (Princeton: Princeton University Program in Near Eastern Studies, 1976), pp. 261–72. See Mary-Jo DelVecchio Good, "Social Hierarchy and Social Change in a Provincial Iranian Town" (Ph.D. diss., Harvard University, 1976), especially Chapter 5, for a description of urban middle class kinship ties.

21. This is as true for the urban and rural resident of the United States. Witness the phenomenal growth of drive-in "convenience" grocery stores which offer a selectively limited range of items at higher prices than the less conveniently located supermarkets.

22. David Kaplan, "The Mexican Marketplace Then and Now" in *Proceedings of the American Ethnological Society* (1965).

23. In a previous article (Thompson, "Impetus for Change") my eagerness to place role changes in peasant marketing practices within an evolutionary framework led me to gloss over the fact that, while changes were occurring (and perhaps not insignificant changes), these were in the nature of greater participation in the traditional bazaar structure on the part of villagers and not real structural changes in the total marketing system. My 1978 observations show that, while role switching is occurring on the part of villagers who handle their own marketing to a greater degree than previously, real structural changes involving petty traders on the periphery of the bazaar system have not occurred to a significant extent.

24. In 1974, a guild for second-hand goods traders had been formed and it was rumored that middlemen and other petty traders would have to purchase licenses from the municipality.

14. *The Changing Status and Composition of an Iranian Provincial Elite*

1. The data presented in this paper was collected in Maragheh, Iran from 1972–74. Field work was done with my husband, Byron Good. Research was supported by a Foreign Area Fellowship of the Social Science Research Council and by the Pathfinder Fund of Boston. While writing this article the author was partially funded by NIMH—Psychiatry Education Branch grant number MH 14022. The author wishes to thank William Royce, Ervand Abrahamian, and Richard Cottam for additional information on the Moqaddam family.

The names of the elite families are undisguised. Moqaddam and Fotuhi family members who recounted their family histories to us were aware of our intention to include references to their families in our writings. Maragheh was an administrative capital in both Qajar and Pahlavi eras and in theory was subordinate to Tabriz, the seat of the Crown Prince. Because of the awkwardness of calling Maragheh a subprovince, I use the term "region."

2. James Bill, *The Politics of Iran: Groups, Classes, and Modernization* (Columbus, Ohio: Charles E. Merrill, 1972); Marvin Zonis, *The Political Elite of Iran* (Princeton: Princeton University Press, 1971).

3. See Nikki Keddie, "Iran, 1797–1941," in *Commoners, Climbers and Notables*, ed. C. A. O. Van Nieuwenhuijze (Leiden: E. J. Brill); idem, "Class Structure and Political Power in Iran Since 1797," *Iranian Studies* 12 (1979), for a discussion of the impact of these processes on social structure in Iran; and see Mary-Jo DelVecchio Good, "Social Hierarchy and Social Change in a Provincial Iranian Town" (Ph.D. diss., Harvard University, 1976) for a detailed analysis of the relationship of social change and social hierarchy in provincial Maragheh.

4. M. Good, "Social Hierarchy and Change;" idem, "Social Hierarchy in Provincial Iran: The Case of Qajar Maragheh," *Iranian Studies* 10 (1977): 129–63.

5. M. Good, "Social Hierarchy and Change," pp. 225–34.

6. Some politicians in Maragheh were noted for taking advantage of

knowledge gained from their official roles; land speculation in the town and its environs was a common occurrence.

7. Iranians' contacts with members of the Tehran political elite are subject to political changes, and to fluctuating personal relationships. When one's Tehran patron is in power, one's fortunes rise in provincial circles. With recent dismissals of Tehran political officials, the local elite attached to them have probably lost prestige.

8. The Moqaddam governors used to support the Moharram religious rituals (*ta'ziyeh* and street processions) in the late nineteenth and early twentieth centuries. Today, as in the past, merchants of the town sponsor many of the *ta'ziyeh* activities. Public officials, such as the Majlis representative, the mayor, and the *farmandar* (governor) also supported these activities in 1973 and 1974, because they saw it as politically advisable as well as enhancing their prestige. They and other local high officials also hosted special religious meals in the town's mosques during Moharram.

9. The titles used for these governors varied. Morier referred to Ahmad Khan Moqaddam as the "governor" of Maragheh, the "chief," and the "reishsefeed (White Beard)" of Azerbaijan; also "beylerbey" is attached to his name. Khan Malik Sasani refers to Ahmad Khan as a *vali*. The Moqaddam descendents in Maragheh who gave the genealogy of the family refer to Ahmad Khan with the title *"Beylerbey,"* and to him and subsequent Moqaddam rulers as *"vali," "hakem,"* and *"hokumat"* or literally "the government."

10. Khan Malek Sasani, *Siyasatgaran-e daureh-ye Qajar* (Tehran: Tahuri, n.d., ca. 1950s), pp. 168–70.

11. James Morier, *A Second Journey Through Persia, Armenia, and Asia Minor* (London: Paternoster-Row, 1818), pp. 281, 293–94.

12. Ibid., pp. 280–94. See also Ervand Abrahamian, "Oriental Despotism: The Case of Qajar Iran," *International Journal of Middle East Studies* 5 (1974): 3–31 for an analysis of relations between the crown and provincial rulers.

13. Sasani, *Siyasat*, p. 167.

14. Ibid., p. 170. In 1844–48, troops from Maragheh were employed by the governor of Shiraz, Hosain Khan Moqaddam Ajudan Bashi Nazem od-Dauleh, who was related to the "tribe" of the Moqaddams of Zanjan. Sasani also notes that one of Ahmad Khan's sons, Hosain Pasha Khan Fauj, led 400 troops from Maragheh in the seige of Herat with Soltan Morad Mirza, the brother of Mohammad Shah. His son, Eskandar Khan Moqaddam, was killed in Gorgan fighting the Turkomans for the shahs. See also: Hasan-e Fasa'i, *History of Persia Under Qajar Rule*, trans. Heribert Busse (New York: Columbia University Press, 1972), pp. 274–83.

15. For example, Eskander Khan Sardar Naser, the last Moqaddam governor of Maragheh, was married to a Qajar princess, one of Fath Ali Shah's many grandchildren. Eskandar's three brothers also married Qajar descendents.

16. Richard Cottam, *Nationalism in Iran* (Pittsburgh: University of Pittsburgh Press, 1979), pp. 351–53.

17. "Member of Iranian Minority Says Khomeini Charter is 'Not for Us'," *New York Times*, 5 December 1979, sec. 1, p. A18; "Thousands of Azerbaijanis March in Tabriz to Back their Ayatollah," *New York Times*, 8 December 1979, sec. 1, p. A4; "Pro-Khomeini Forces, Rebels Intensify Fight," *Sacramento Bee*,

10 December 1979, p. 1; "Khomeini Rebuffed by Rival Ayatollah," *New York Times*, 11 December 1979, Sec. 1, p. 1, A16; "Iran's President Says Hostages May be Freed Soon" by Eric Rouleau, *New York Times*, 12 February 1980, p. A8; Personal Communication, Richard Cottam, 3 March 1980.

18. Howard Rotblat, "The Patterns of Recruitment into the Iranian Political Elite" (M.A. thesis, University of Chicago, 1968), p. 4. Maragheh's Majlis representatives in recent decades (1960s and 1970s) included Dr. Habib Dadfar, a French educated lawyer who was a client of the former prime minister, Manuchehr Eqbal. His father owned several small orchards but was not of the elite. Engineer Zanjanchi, a former director of the local land reform office but not a native, represented Maragheh in the Twenty-First Majlis. Dr. Pir, a judge in the Tehran Court of First Instance, was elected in 1974. His father had been a noted religious leader of a local Sufi order, but the family had not resided in Maragheh for many years.

15. *The Shirazi Provincial Elite: Status Maintenance and Change*

1. I would like to thank Constance Cronin of the University of Arizona for sharing her data on the Qavam-e Shirazi family with me.

2. Edward G. Browne, *A Year Amongst the Persians* (New York: MacMillan, 1926), pp. 237–359.

3. For details on the Qavam family, also known as the Hashemiyeh, up to 1897, see Henry Philip Picot, *Persia: Biographical Note of Members of the Royal Family, Notables, Merchants, and Clergy* (1897), pp. 76–80; see also Abol-Fazl Qasemi, *Tarikh-e siyah ya hokumat-e khanevadeh-ha dar Iran*, vol. I: *Khanevadeh-ye Qavam ol-Molk* (Tehran: 1329/1951).

4. For biographies of Vesal and his sons see Hajji Mirza Hasan-e Fasa'i, *Farsnameh-ye Naseri* (Tehran, 1895–96), vol. 2, pp. 64–72.

5. For biographies of the Qashqa'i *Ilkhanis* see ibid., vol. 2, pp. 115–17.

6. For the history of the Navvab family see ibid., vol. 2, pp. 122–23.

7. For the descendants of Hosain Ali Mirza, see Heribert Busse, *History of Persia Under Qajar Rule*, trans. from the Persian of Hasan-e Fasa'i's *Farsnameh-ye Naseri* (New York: Columbia University Press, 1972), appendix 3, pp. 423–29; see also Fasa'i, *Farsnameh*, vol. 2, pp. 110–12.

8. Busse, *History of Persia*, p. 96.

9. Picot, *Persia: Biographical Note*, p. 76.

10. Busse, *History of Persia*, pp. 96–7.

11. Ibid., p. 97.

12. For his biography see Siavash Danesh, *Ebrahim-e Kalantar* (Tehran: Vahid-Nia, n.d.).

13. For the office of *kalantar* see W. M. Floor, "The Office of Kalantar in Qajar Persia," *Journal of the Economic and Social History of the Orient* (1971), pp. 53–68; A. K. S. Lambton, "Kalantar," *Encyclopedia of Islam*, 2nd ed., vol. 4, pp. 474–76; A. K. S. Lambton, "The Office of Kalantar under the Safavids and Afshars," in *Mélanges Massé*, ed. Ali Akbar Siassi (Tehran, 1963), pp. 206–18.

14. Busse, *History of Persia*, p. 93.

15. Ibid., pp. 95–6.

16. For his biography see Mehdi Bamdad, *Tarikh-e rejal-e Iran*, vol. 2 (Tehran: Zavvar, 1347/1969), pp. 433–34; Mirza Mohammad Ali Mo'allem-e

Habibabadi, *Makarem al-asar dar ahval-e rejal-e daureh-ye Qajar,* vol. 2 (Isfahan: Mohammadi Press, 1337/1959), pp. 151–52.

17. Busse, *History of Persia,* p. 142.

18. Ibid., p. 196.

19. Ibid., p. 348.

20. For his biography, see Bamdad, *Tarikh-e rejal,* vol. 2, p. 483.

21. Ali Mohammad Khan, the second Qavam ol-Molk extended the family's influence in Fars and obtained military support by forming the Khamseh federation of five tribes of the region with himself as paramount chief. See Fredrik Barth, *Nomads of South Persia: The Basseri Tribe of the Khamseh Confederacy* (New York: Humanities Press, 1961) pp. 86–9.

22. In addition to the two individuals mentioned above, these are Mohammad Reza Khan, Qavam ol-Molk III (1851–2/1907–8), Bamdad, *Tarikh-e rejal,* vol. 3, pp. 401–2; Mohammad Hosain Roknzadeh Adamiyyat, *Daneshmandan va sukhansarayan-e Fars* (Tehran: Eslamiyyeh Press, 1340/1962), vol. IF, pp. 219–220; Habibollah Khan, Qavam ol-Molk IV (1869–70/1917–18), Roknzadeh Adamiyyat, *Daneshmandan,* vol. IF, p. 221; Ebrahim Khan, Qavam ol-Molk V (1892–3/1969), Roknzadeh Adamiyyat, ibid., vol. p. 221.

23. For his biography, see Bamdad, *Tarikh-e rejal,* vol. 3, pp. 70–2.

24. Busse, *History of Persia,* p. 379.

25. For Hasan Ali Khan Daryabegi, Nasir ol-Molk, see ibid., pp. 294, 339–40, 350, 264–7, 387, 417 and 419.

26. Constance Cronin, personal communication, University of Arizona.

27. *Iran Almanac and Book of Facts* (Tehran: Echo of Iran, 1977), p. 102.

28. Mo'allem-e Habibabadi, *Makarem,* vol. 4. pp. 713–14.

29. Picot, *Biographical Note,* p. 81; Moallem-e Habibabadi, *Makarem,* pp. 874–5; Fasa'i, *Farsnameh,* vol. 2, pp. 61–4.

16. *The Religious Dimension of Modernization Among the Jews of Shiraz*

1. My thanks to Lois Beck for her comments on earlier drafts of this paper. Field research conducted in 1967–68 was supported by the Memorial Foundation for Jewish Culture, the Cantors Assembly of America and a New York State Herbert Lehman Fellowship. A short revisit to Shiraz took place in October 1977.

2. Brian Spooner, "Religion and Society Today: An Anthropological Perspective," in *Iran Faces the Seventies,* ed. by Ehsan Yar-Shater (New York: Praeger, 1971); Gustav Thaiss, "The Bazaar as a Case Study of Religion and Social Change," in ibid., pp. 189–216; idem, "Religious Symbolism and Social Change: The Drama of Hussein," in *Scholars, Saints and Sufis,* ed. Nikki Keddie (Berkeley: University of California Press, 1972), pp. 349–66.

3. Laurence D. Loeb, "Kashrut: Permitted and Prohibited Foods in the Jewish Great Tradition" (Paper presented at the Annual Meeting of the American Anthropological Association, New Orleans, 1973).

4. Elkan Nathan Adler, *Jewish Travelers,* 2nd ed. (New York: Herman Press, 1966).

5. Walter J. Fischel, "Isfahan: The Story of a Jewish Community in Persia,"

in *The Joshua Starr Memorial Volume,* Jewish Social Studies Publication, vol. 5 (1953), p. 526.

6. J. de Thevenot, *The Travels of Monsieur de Thevenot into the Levant* (London, 1687), p. 131.

7. Yitzhaq Ben-Zvi, *Okhluse Erez Yisrael. Kitve Yitzhaq ben-Zvi,* vol. 5 (Tel Aviv: Mizpe, 1937), p. 82.

8. Alliance, *Bulletin Mensuel de l'Alliance Israelite Universelle* (1889–1911).

9. Habib Levi, *Tarikh-e Yahud-e Iran,* Volume 3 (Tehran: Berukhim and Sons, 1960); informants.

10. Hanina Misrahi, *Toldot yhude faras umshorrehem* (Jerusalem: Rubin Mass, 1966).

11. Carmelite Chronicles, *A Chronicle of the Carmelites in Persia and the Papal Mission of the XVIIth and XVIIIth Centuries* (London: Eyre and Spottiswoode, 1939).

12. Alliance, *Bulletin Mensuel,* 1903, p. 107; M. Yishay, *Zir blo to'ar: rishme shlihut umassa bfaras* (Tel Aviv: N. Tavarski, 1950), p. 70. Zoroastrians: Napier Malcolm, *Five Years in a Persian Town* (New York: E. P. Dutton, 1905); and Nestorians: Richard Schwartz, "The Structure of Christian-Muslim Relations in Contemporary Iran" (Ph.D. diss., Washington University at St. Louis, 1973), p. 117, were subject to the restrictions of the Covenant of Omar/Jam Abbasi. The former, however, maintaining ties with coreligionists in India, followed the Armenians in pressuring the British to have Naser od-Din Shah waive the poll tax in 1882. Nestorians were also subject to the Law of Apostasy in the Qajar period (ibid. pp. 79–80).

13. Including those cited in Bulletins of the Alliance Israelite Universelle (1889–1911): Israel Joseph Benjamin, III, *Eight Years in Asia and Africa—From 1846 to 1854* (Hanover, 1859); Walter Fischel, *Unknown Jews in Unknown Lands: The Travel of Rabbi David d'Beth Hillel* (New York: Ktav, 1973); Henry Stern, *Dawnings of Light in the East* (London: Purday, 1854); C. J. Wills, *In the Land of the Lion and Sun, or Modern Iran* (London: MacMillan, 1883); and idem, *Persia As It Is* (London: Sampson, Low Marston, Searle and Rivington, 1887).

14. Fischel, *Unknown Jews in Unknown Lands,* p. 107; Benjamin, *Eight Years in Asia and Africa,* p. 229.

15. Alliance, *Bulletin Mensuel,* 1902–1910.

16. Ibid., 1904, pp. 33–34.

17. Ibid., 1903, p. 110.

18. Ibid., 1910.

19. Thevenot, *The Travels of Monsieur de Thevenot,* p. 131.

20. Alliance, *Bulletin Mensuel,* 1904, p. 30.

21. Reuben Levy, *The Social Structure of Islam* (Cambridge: University Press, 1962); H. Z. Hirschberg, "The Oriental Jewish communities," in *Religion in the Middle East,* ed. A. J. Arberry, vol. 1 (Cambridge: Cambridge University Press, 1969), pp. 119–225.

22. Schwartz, "The Structure of Christian-Muslim Relations," p. 127.

23. Laurence D. Loeb, "Dhimmi Status and Jewish Roles in Iranian Society," *Ethnic Groups* 1 (1976): 89–105.

24. Laurence D. Loeb, *Outcaste: Jewish Life in Southern Iran* (London: Gordon and Breach, 1977); idem, "Prestige and Piety in an Iranian Synagogue," *Anthropological Quarterly* 51 (1978): 155–61.

25. Wilhelm Bacher, "Les Juifs en Perse au XVII et au XVIII Siecle d'Apres

des Chroniques Poetiques de Babai Loutf et de Babai b. Farhad," *Revenue des Etudes Juives* 53 (1907): 94.

26. William Francklin, *Observations Made on a Tour from Bengal to Persia in the Year 1786–1787,* 2nd ed. (London: T. Cadell in the Strand, 1790), p. 60.

27. Ezra Melamed, "Hayyhudim bfaras lifne shishim shana," *Sinai* 29 (1951): 359–70.

28. Jews, too, restricted the kinds of food they could take from non-Jews in accordance with Great Tradition dietary laws. Judaism does not view physical contact with gentiles as defiling, but for internally sound structural reasons as well as to reduce the impact of acculturation, Judaism diminishes the intensity of mealtime contact with gentiles outside the Jewish community; see I. Grunfeld, *The Jewish Dietary Laws* (London: Soncino Press, 1972), pp. 161–64). The restrictions alluded to in the text indicate that Islam sometimes views the unbeliever himself as contaminating.

29. Benjamin, *Eight Years in Asia and Africa,* p. 259. Nestorians were likewise forbidden from food-handling occupations and testifying against Muslims in law courts (Schwartz, "The Structure of Christian-Muslim Relations," pp. 79–80, 127). Unlike Jews, however, many were engaged in farming and at least a few were landowners in the Qajar period. Furthermore, they were respected by the local Muslim populace (ibid., p. 121). The status of Zoroastrians too, was not a duplication of the Jewish population. In the contemporary period they enjoy a reputation of scrupulous honesty and their Majlis representative has been able to protest discriminatory legislation in a manner no other minority representative would dare; Michael M. J. Fischer, "Zoroastrian Iran Between Myth and Praxis" (Ph.D. diss., University of Chicago, 1973), pp. 101, 107.

30. Loeb, *The Jews of Southwest Iran: A Study of Cultural Persistence* (New York: Columbia University, 1970); idem, *Outcaste;* Max Weber, *Ancient Judaism* (New York: The Free Press, 1952), pp. 336–55; Gideon Sjoberg, *The Preindustrial City* (New York: The Free Press, 1960), pp. 135–37.

31. Literally, "new Muslims"—actually crypto-Jews converted to Islam in 1839 and 1845.

32. Loeb, *Outcaste.*

33. Ibid.

34. Loeb, *The Jews of Southwest Iran.*

35. One talmudic source explains: "The reason for the primacy of the *halakha* (law) is that conduct is the only gauge of a person's belief" (Rosh Hashana 13a).

36. Loeb, *Outcaste.*

37. The ritual bath was attended mainly by women after completion of menses. Men visited when polluted ritually, e.g. by nocturnal emission, and on the eve of the Day of Atonement.

38. Many who are considered "observers" but living outside the old Jewish quarter, drive their cars to synagogue on the Sabbath, though technically forbidden by Great Tradition law.

39. Loeb, "The Jewish Wedding in Modern Shiraz," in *Studies in Marriage Customs,* vol. 4 (Jerusalem: Folklore Research Center Studies, 1974), pp. 167–76.

40. This laxity is viewed by Jewish pietists as extremely dangerous, bringing into question not only the proper relationship of spouses but even the

honor of children. A few women have had a private ritual bath built, but most have retreated to the privacy of their newly acquired bathtubs—a totally inadequate ritual substitute.

41. Jewish law requires it on all doorposts, but the scrolls have traditionally been in short supply, and most Jews remain afraid to identify their houses from the outside.

17. Language and Social Distinctions in Iran

1. This essay is a revision of papers presented at the Conference on Symbols of Social Differentiation sponsored by the Joint Committee on the Near and Middle East of the Social Science Research Council and the American Council of Learned Societies at the Belmont Conference Center in Elkridge, Maryland, in May, 1978, and at the Southwest Branch Meeting of the American Oriental Society held at The University of Texas at Austin in October, 1978.

2. A translation of "Persian Is Sugar" appears in Michael C. Hillmann, comp. and ed., *Major Voices in Contemporary Persian Literature—Literature East and West* 20 (1976), a volume that features a comprehensive and partially annotated bibliography on contemporary Iran, including sociolinguistic studies and literature in translation.

3. Ali Banuazizi, "Iranian 'National Character': A Critique of Some Western Perspectives," *Psychological Dimensions of Near Eastern Studies*, eds. L. Carl Brown and Norman Itzkowitz (Princeton, N. J.: Darwin, 1977): 210–239.

4. For example, Hamid Enayat, "The Politics of Iranology," *Iranian Studies* 6(1973): 13, cites "negative traits in our national character, such as fatalism, love of superstition, submission in the face of oppression and dissimulation."

5. For example, Ahmad Shaml's *Pariya* "The Fairies" and Sadeq Chubak's *Sang-e Sabur* "The Patient Stone" are translated and summarized, respectively, in *Major Voices*.

6. M. A. Jazayery, "Western Loan Words in Persian, with Reference to Westernization," *Islamic Culture* 31 (1967): 11–13.

7. Carleton Hodge, "Some Aspects of Persian Style," *Language* 33 (1957): 355–369.

8. Ibid., p. 369.

9. Donald Wilber, "Language and Society: The Case of Iran," *Behavior Sciences Notes* 2 (1967): 22–30.

10. William Beeman, "Status, Style and Strategy in Iranian Interaction," *Anthropological Linguistics* 18 (1976): 305–322; and idem, "The Hows and Whys of Persian Style: A Pragmatic Approach," *Studies in Language Variation*, ed. Ralph W. Fasold and Roger W. Shuy (Washington, D.C.: Georgetown University Press, 1977), pp. 269–282.

11. Idem, "Status, Style and Strategy," p. 307; and "The Hows and Whys of Persian Style," passim.

12. Hodge, "Some Aspects of Persian Style," pp. 364–366.

13. Beeman, "Status, Style and Strategy," p. 313.

14. Ibid., pp. 307–314.

15. Abbas and Manuchehr Aryanpur. *The Concise Persian English Dictionary*

(Tehran: Amir Kabir, 1976), p. 306; Beeman, "Status, Style and Strategy," p. 312; Solaiman Ha'im, *The One-Volume Persian English Dictionary* (Tehran: Berukhim, 1969), p. 190; Mohammad Mo'in, *A Persian Dictionary* (Tehran: Amir Kabir, 1963–1975), p. 1096; and Wilber, "Language and Society."

16. M. C. Bateson, J. W. Clinton, J. B. M. Kassarjian, H. Safavi, and M. Soraya, "Safa-ye Baten: A Study of the Interrelations of a Set of Iranian Ideal Character Types," *Psychological Dimensions of New Eastern Studies*, pp. 261–262.

17. Ibid., pp. 262–270.

18. Heshmat Moayyad, in a letter dated November 17, 1978.

19. For example, Marvin Zonis, *The Political Elite of Iran* (Princeton: Princeton University Press, 1971).

20. Wilber, "Language and Society."

21. According to Mo'in, *A Persian Dictionary*, pp. 346–347, the word *Imam* has three denotations: (1) *pishva* "leader, lord" or *pishrow* "precursor, pioneer"; (2) in Twelver Shi'i Islam, each of the 12 leaders beginning with Ali (Mohammad's nephew and son-in-law) and ending with the *Mahdi* (who disappeared in A.D. 874 and will return at the end of time); and (3) *qotb* pole, axis or *shaykh* elder, learned man. In referring to Ayatollah Khomeini as *Imam*, his followers are implying that his rank is or approaches that of the historical Twelve *Imams*.

18. Cinema as a Political Instrument

1. For a detailed critical history of feature films in Iran, see Hamid Naficy, "Iranian Feature Film: A Brief Critical History," *Quarterly Review of Film Studies* 4 (1979): 443–64.

2. Mohammad Tahami Nezhad, "Risheh yabi-ye yas: tarikh-e sinema dar Iran, 2," *Dar bareh-ye sinema va teatr* (Dai 1352/1974): 13.

3. For further information on the documentary films produced by these early pioneers of cinema, see Hamid Naficy, "Non-fiction Film in Iran," *Jump Cut* (to be published in summer of 1980).

4. Naficy, "Iranian Feature Film," pp. 450, 456.

5. Mohammad Tahami Nezhad, "Risheh yabi-ye yas dar sinema-ye 1308 ta 1315 Iran," *Vizheh-ye Sinema va Teatr* 2 & 3 (no date): 116.

6. Ali Asadi, "Dar amadi bar jame'eh shenasi-ye sinema dar Iran," *Farhang va zendegi* 13 & 14 (Zemestan 1352–Bahar 1353/1975): 13.

7. Ali Akbar Hakami Zadeh, "Tablighat," *Homayun* 6 (Esfand 1313/1935): 30–31.

8. Ali Asgar Hedayati, *Farhang va jame'eh-ye ma* (Tehran: Naqsh-e Jahan, 1331/1953), pp. 44–46.

9. "Qaichi-ye sansur baraye badanha-ye lokht lebas miduzad," *Kayhan*, #10384, 16 Bahman 2536/5 February 1978, p. 5.

10. Tahami Nezhad, "Tarikh-e sinema dar Iran," pp. 9–10.

11. For more details on the reaction of Iranians to foreign documentaries about Iran, see, Hamid Naficy, "Non-fiction Fiction: Documentaries on Iran," *Iranian Studies*, 3–4 (1979): 217–238.

12. For an interesting and extensive documentation of this trend, see Homa Nateq, "Farang va farang maabi," *Alefba* 6 (2536/1977): 56–72; and Jalal

Al-e Ahmad, *Gharbzadegi* (Tehran: Azad, 1341/1962).

13. Mohammad Tahami Nezhad, "43 sal naqd-e film dar Iran," *Vizheh-ye sinema va teatr* 6 (1353/1975):10.

14. Ibid., p. 11.

15. U.S. Department of Commerce, Office of International Trade, "World Trade in Commodities-Iran," no page number, February 1949.

16. "Iranian Film Industry Blasts Government Ruling that Bans Slums, Sex Scenes," *Variety* (weekly), 26 July 1972.

17. Asadi, "Jam-e shenasi-ye sinema," p. 12.

18. Ali Asghar Hadj Seyyd Javadi, "On the Eve of His Majesty's Trip to America," *Letters from the Great Prison: An Eyewitness Account of Human and Social Conditions in Iran* (Washington D.C.: Committee for Human Rights in Iran, 1978); pp. 10–11.

19. "First Open Letter of the Writers," *Index On Censorship* 7:1 (January/February 1978): 19–20.

20. "Miz-e gerd-e sinema-ye Iran, 1," *Farhang va zendegi* 18 (Tabestan 1354/1976): 57–58.

21. Ali Asadi and Farhad Hakimzadeh, *Social Attitudes and Modernization in Iran*, Part I (Tehran: Iran Communications and Development Institute, 1975), p. 18.

22. Ibid.

23. Elihue Katz and George Wedell, *Broadcasting in the Third World: Promise and Performance* (Cambridge: Harvard University Press, 1977), p. 156.

24. Elihue Katz and Dov Shinar, *The Role of Broadcasting in National Development, Iran Case Study* [draft copy] (Jerusalem: Hebrew University, July 1974), p. 58.

25. Ali Asadi, "Gozaran-e auqat-e faraqat dar Rezaiyeh," *Farhang va zendegi* 12 (Pa'iz 1352/1974): 44.

26. Manuchehr Mohseni, "Tahqiqi piramun-e auqat-e faraqat dar miyan-e daneshjuyan-e daneshgah," *Farhang va zendegi* 12 (Pa'iz 1352/1974): p. 41.

27. *Barresi-ye moshakhasat va nazarat-e tamashagaran-e sinema dar Tehran* (Tehran: Vezarat-e Farhang va Honar, Shahrivar 2536/1977), p. 22.

28. It is worthwhile to note that the heavy burden of responsibility incurred by the role of media in Iran during the Pahlavi regime is also indicated by the fact that two of the most visible and high ranking broadcast media officials of that regime were among the earliest to be convicted and executed by the new Islamic Republic. They were, Mahmud Jafarian, deputy director of National Iranian Radio and Television and the director of the Pars news agency, and Parviz Nikkhah, the head of NIRT's research (propaganda) department.

19. A Full Arena: The Development and Meaning of Popular Performance Traditions in Iran

1. Research on popular performance traditions was carried out from 1976–1979 in Iran. Initial funding for the project came from one of several grants provided for research in Iran in honor of the American Bicentennial by the Iranian Bicentennial Committee. Grantees were selected by a committee of scholars teaching at United States universities after open competition. Grants

were administered through the American Friends of the Middle East (Now American-Mideast Training Services) and the Council for International Exchange of Scholars. The help from this grant is gratefully acknowledged. Additional help was provided by National Iranian Radio Television, and the Center for Traditional Performing Arts affiliated with the Festival of Arts Center, Tehran. Individuals connected with the Center, particularly the director, Farrokh Ghaffary, Mohammad Bagher Ghaffari, Reza Khaki and Khosro Shayesteh, were invaluable in the process of field research. Thanks also to Mr. Hosain Meisami and many individuals from the Office of Iranian Anthropology of the Ministry of Culture and Arts, especially Dr. Mahmoud Khaliqi, director, Ali Bolukbashi and Mohammad Mir-Shokra'i. Valuable comments on this paper have been made by Nikki Keddie, E. T. Kirby, Daniel Neumann, William Royce, Renee Shields, Brian Spooner, Farley Richmond, and Farrokh Ghaffary.

2. Natalie Zemon Davis, "The Reasons of Misrule" in her *Society and Culture in Early Modern France* (Stanford: Stanford University Press, 1975).

3. Cf. Hafizullah Baghban, "The Context and Concept of Humor in Magadi Theatre" (Ph.D. diss., Indiana University, 1977), pp. 6–9, 41–44.

4. Cf. Peter J. Chelkowski, "Dramatic and Literary Aspects of Ta'ziyehkhani-Iranian Passion Play," *Review of National Literatures* 2 (1971): 121–138; idem, *Ta'ziyeh: Indigenous Avant-Garde Theater of Iran* (Tehran: Festival of Arts Series, 1975); idem, Peter J. Chelkowski, ed., *Ta'ziyeh: Ritual and Drama in Iran* (New York: New York University Press and Sorush Press, 1979).

5. Cf. William O. Beeman, "Cultural Dimensions of Performance Conventions in Iranian Ta'ziyeh," in Chelkowski, *Ta'ziyeh*, pp. 24–31.

6. Although *ta'ziyeh* performances are most often held during the Islamic lunar months of Moharram and Safar, they are also held in commemoration of other Islamic martyrs, and religious personages such as Imam Reza, the eighth Shi'i Imam, or Fatemah, mother of Imam Hosain. *Ta'ziyeh* is also held on rare occasions in commemoration of a deceased relative.

7. *Ru-hauzi* or *takht-e hauzi* theatre is so designated because in urban areas, players often performed in the courtyard of private homes on a platform *(takht)* placed over *(ru)* the central courtyard pool *(hauz)* of the home. I do not use the term *ru-hauzi* here as a classificatory term, but only for convenience to designate the many variant forms of comic improvisatory theatre in Iran.

8. See Chelkowski, *Ta'ziyeh*, for a glimpse at the variety of theories existing on this point. This work is also a good source for general bibliography on *ta'ziyeh* which I do not include here.

9. Adrian Dupré, 2 vols., *Voyage en Perse fait dans les annees 1807, 1808, et 1809.* (Paris: Dentu, 1819). The usual argument about the emergence of *ta'ziyeh* as a dramatic form hinges on determining the point in its "evolution" when it changed from being a processional form to a drama presented in a fixed location. This may be a somewhat arbitrary criterion since the processional form continues today. Peter J. Chelkowski, "Bibliographical Spectrum," in Chelkowski, *Ta'ziyeh*, p. 258, cites William Franklin writing in 1787 under the reign of Ja'far Khan Zand, who gives a narrative account of what appears to be very close to dramatic representation. Francklin seems to have observed a procession, albiet one with dramatic elements, and this for many experts does not allow *ta'ziyeh* full dramatic status at this period.

10. One of the most remarkable finds in recent years is a bound collection of handwritten *ta'ziyeh* manuscripts which, though bearing no date, have been dated by experts at the Tehran central library as being from the Zand period. The book is owned by Professor Mayel Baktash of the School of Dramatic Arts of the Ministry of Culture and Arts, Tehran.

11. During this period the tenth day of Moharram, called Ashura, was officially observed by the closing of shops and by mourning ceremonies. Cf. Ahatanhel' Krymsky, *The Persian Theatre: Its Origin and Development.* (Kiev: Ukranian Academy of Sciences, 1925). Translation from the Ukranian by Volodimir Pechenuk. (Unpublished manuscript, Center for Traditional Performing Arts, Festival of Arts Center, Tehran, 1978), pp. 7–10.

12. Jean Calmard, "Le Mécénat des représentations de ta'ziyè. 2: Les débuts de Règne de Nâseroddin Chah." *Le Monde Iranian et L'Islam* 4 (1976–77): 133–162.

13. Krymsky, *The Persian Theatre*, p. 89.

14. Indeed, a number of *ta'ziyeh* manuscripts exist which have little or nothing to do with the martyrdom of Imam Hosain. These often concern other religious and historical figures, and are occasionally drawn from classic literature.

15. K. Smirnov, *Persy* (Tblisi, 1916), pp. 91, 96, in Krymsky, *The Persian Theatre*, p. 92.

16. Krymsky, *The Persian Theatre*, pp. 79–80.

17. An international scholarly conference on *ta'ziyeh* under the direction of Peter J. Chelkowski was also held in conjunction with the performances; cf. Chelkowski, *Ta'ziyeh*.

18. Most professional troupes are urban-based, making tours to rural areas during Moharram and Safar.

19. The *rauzeh-khan* need not be a clergyman, and, indeed, there are many persons, particularly in villages, who earn some small income by this means without any formal religious training. During the Safavid era, *rauzeh-khans* and other eulogizers were treated as entertainers, much as jugglers and musicians, within the general guild structure.

20. Cf. James Brandon, *Theatre in Southeast Asia* (Cambridge: Harvard University Press, 1967); James Peacock, *Rites of Modernization* (Chicago: University of Chicago Press, 1968); for India: Balwant Gargi, *Folk Theater of India* (Seattle: University of Washington Press, 1967); J.C. Mathur, *Drama in Rural India* (Bombay: Asia Publishing House, 1964); Shyam Parmar, *Traditional Folk Media in India* (New Delhi: Geka Books, 1975); for Afghanistan: Baghban, "Magadi Theatre;" and for Turkey: Metin And, *A History of Theatre and Popular Entertainment in Turkey* (Ankara: Forum Yayinlari, 1963–4).

21. Sekandar Amanallahi, *Pezhuheshi dar bare-ye navazandegan-e sunnati-ye Iran* (Shirazi: Pahlavi University, 1356/1977), pp. 10–16).

22. Abol-Qasem Jannati-Ata'i, *Bonyad-e nameyesh dar Iran* (Tehran: Chap-e Mihan, 1333/1955), p. 16.

23. Reproduced in Bahram Beza'i, *Namayesh dar Iran* (Tehran: Chap-e Kavian), p. 55.

24. Ibid., p. 168.

25. Cf. Hosain Nurbakhsh, *Karim Shire'i* (Tehran: Ketabkhaneh-ye Sina'i, 1348/1968).

26. Jannati-Ata'i, *Bonyad-e, namayesh dar Iran*, pp. 30-50.

27. Ibid, p. 19.

28. Ibid, p. 40.

29. Medjid Rezvani, *Le Theatre et la danse en Iran* (Paris: Maisonneuve, 1962), pp. 112–114.

30. Legitimate Western-style theatre was eventually partially reabsorbed into the improvisatory style. Farrokh Ghaffary reports seeing Hamlet done in this style, and troupes in Shiraz do quite a funny and recognizable version of Moliere's *The Doctor in Spite of Himself.*

31. In general, this involves shortening the celebration to a single afternoon or evening, having guests bring tangible presents rather than cash gifts, and the use of Western instruments (saxophone, "jazz" drums, etc.) or cassette tapes of current popular tunes instead of traditional musicians and instruments.

32. Because celebrations of weddings are prohibited during Moharram and Safar, families will try to speed up preparations for marriage to avoid having to wait for one or two months to have the wedding celebration. The result is that there are a great number of weddings in the two or three preceeding months. Fees paid to performers in 1977 ranged between $100 and $750, to which tips from guests were often added.

33. Blackface makeup here is usually simple pot-black mixed with vegetable fat. The clown in blackface is generally identified as having come from Africa. This designation is of unclear origin, since blackface makeup is found in improvisatory traditions in countries neighboring Iran. Probably the black makeup preceeded the African designation.

34. Karim Shire'i is shown as using whiteface makeup: "Karim Shire'i enters, his face covered with flour;" Jannati-Ata'i, *Bonyad-e namayeh dar Iran,* p. 37. In some areas of Iran there were in the past two types of clowns, one in whiteface called *sholi (shol-*loose) and the blackface clown, who had various names. Their personal attributes were opposite in nature, the blackface clown being quick and agile, and the whiteface *sholi* being slow and stupid. In performances today the two types are rarely clearly delineated, and often one blackface clown will exhibit both sets of characteristics. Whiteface is more common in northeastern Iran; Baghban cites its exclusive use in the Herat area. Baghban, "Magadi Theatre," p. 16.

35. The *hajji* is an older traditional man who has presumably been to Mecca on the *hajj* pilgrimage. Older, supposedly wealthy traditional men in Iran also are often called *hajji* whether they have actually made the pilgrimage or not.

36. Cf. William Beeman, "Status, Style and Strategy in Iranian Interaction," *Anthropological Linguistics* 18 (1976): 305–322; idem, "What is (Iranian) National Character? A Sociolinguistic Approach," *Iranian Studies* 9 (1976): 22–45; idem, "The Hows and Whys of Persian Style: A Pragmatic Approach," in *Studies in Language Variation,* ed. Ralph W. Fasold and Roger W. Shuy (Washington: Georgetown University Press, 1977), pp. 269–282.

37. Jannati-Ata'i, *Bonyad-e namayesh dar Iran,* p. 39.

38. Cf. William O. Beeman and Amit Bhattacharyya, "Toward an Assessment of the Social Role of Rural Midwives and its Implication for the Family Planning Program: An Iranian Case Study," *Human Organization* 37 (1978): 295–300.

39. Cf. Barbara Babcock, ed., *The Reversable World: Symbolic Inversion in Art and Society* (Ithaca, N.Y.: Cornell University Press, 1978); Victor Turner, *The*

Ritual Process (Chicago: Aldine, 1969); idem, Dramas, Fields and Metaphors (Ithaca, N.Y.: Cornell University Press, 1974).

40. Davis, "Reasons of Misrule."

41. Christopher Hill, The World Turned Upside Down (London: Temple Smith, 1972).

20. Chairs and Change in Qajar Times

1. For this volume of social science studies on modern Iran, this article includes only materials of my research on the Iranian chair which deal with the social history of the chair in Iran. In a forthcoming illustrated article, I will present an art historical study of examples, styles and manufacture of Iranian chairs.

2. The prerogative of the shah to sit cross-legged is mentioned by two travelers to Safavid Iran; see S. N. Sanson, Present State of Persia, trans. by J. Savage (London: M. Gilliflower, 1695), p. 45; John Bell, Travels from St. Petersburg in Russia to Diverse Parts of Asia, vol. 1 (Glasgow: University Printers, 1763), p. 105. In the Qajar period it is noted that in the presence of a superior an Iranian sits on his heels; with an equal, cross-legged; and with an inferior, any way he chooses; see James Morier, Journey through Persia (London: Longman, 1812), p. 39.

3. For illustration, see Philip Bamborough, Treasures of Islam (Poole, Dorset: Blandford, 1976), p. 44.

4. For illustration, see B. W. Robinson, Islamic Painting and the Arts of the Book (London: Faber, 1976), ill. 44.VIII.51.

5. For reference and reproductions of the Tur and Salm page and several other late seventeenth century miniatures which include representations of chairs, I am deeply grateful to Eleanor Sims. In each of these miniatures, to be published in Sims's forthcoming study on Mohammad Zaman, the setting is outdoors.

6. Jonas Hanway, Historical Account of British Trade, vol. I (London: T. Osborne, 1754), p. 113. Nearly two centuries earlier Anthony Jenkinson describes a similar situation when he was received by the Iranian governor of Shirvan, but when he had difficulty sitting cross-legged, significantly it was a stool, not a chair, which was provided him; see Anthony Jenkinson, "A Compendious and briefe declaration of the journey of M. Anthony Jenkinson, from the famous citie of London into the land of Persia, Anno 1561," in Principal Navigations, ed. by R. Hakluyt, (Cambridge: Hakluyt Society, 1965), p. 367.

7. Hanway, Account, vol. 1, p. 167.

8. William Ouseley, Travels in Various Countries of the East, vol. 3 (London: Rodwell and Martin, 1819), pp. 128–9.

9. Morier, Journey, p. 162.

10. For two examples of chairs of state presented to Russian tsars by Safavids in the sixteenth and seventeenth century, see Drevnosti rossiiskago gosudarstva, izdannyia po vysochaisehemi povelieniiu, vol. 2 (Moscow: Alexsandra Semena, 1851), pp. 100–5.

11. For illustration, see Edwin Binney, 3rd, Indian Miniature Painting (Portland: Portland Art Association, 1973), cat. no. 68. Although the Mughal Peacock Throne is the most renown example of Nader Shah's plunder of

India, Hanway mentions that he carried off from India nine other thrones; see Hanway, *Account,* vol. 2, p. 383. Likely among them were easily portable gold and bejewelled chairs of state such as those represented in the portrait of Shah Jahan's sons, and which are similar to examples represented in early Qajar painting.

12. Morier, *Journey,* p. 211–2.

13. James B. Fraser, *Winter's Journey,* vol. 2 (London: Richard Bentley, 1838), p. 102.

14. P. J. M. Tancoigne, *Narrative of a Journey into Persia* (London: W. Wright, 1820), p. 317.

15. Representation of Mohammad Ali Mirza seated in the chair of state with lion-shaped arms occurs in a Taq-e Bostan relief and in an oil painting dated 123(0)/181(4); see respectively Roloff Beny, *Persia: Bridge of Turquoise* (Boston: New York Graphic Society, 1965), pl. 215; Sotheby's, *Fine Oriental Miniatures, Manuscripts and Qajar Paintings: April 4, 1978 Sale* (London: Sotheby's, 1978), lot. 86.

16. Morier, *Journey,* p. 72.

17. T. B. Armstrong, *Journal of Travels* (London: A Seguin, 1831), p. 142.

18. Ouseley, *Travels,* vol. 2, p. 52.

19. Moritz von Kotsebue, *Narrative of a Journey into Persia* (London: Longman, 1819), p. 264. For similar arrangements of Qajars and ambassadors seated opposite at formal receptions, see Ouseley, *Travels,* vol. 2, p. 11; John Ussher, *Journey from London to Persepolis* (London: Hurst and Blackett, 1865), p. 521.

20. Frederick Shoberl, *Persia* (Philadelphia: John Grigg, 1828), p. 42.

21. For illustration, see Bernard Lewis, ed., *World of Islam* (London: Thames and Hudson, 1976), p. 272.

22. James B. Fraser, *Travels in Koordistan,* vol. 2 (London: Richard Bentley, 1840), p. 191.

23. Eustache de Lorey and Douglas Saladin, *Queer Things about Persia* (London: Eveleigh Nash, 1907), p. 188.

24. Arthur Conolly, *Journey to the North of India,* vol. 1 (London: Richard Bentley, 1838), p. 116.

25. V. B. Meen and A. D. Tushingham, *Crown Jewels of Iran* (Toronto: University of Toronto Press, 1968), pp. 116, 147, n. 24.

26. For illustration, see S. J. Falk, *Qajar Paintings* (London: Faber, 1972), cat. no. 50.

27. Lady Sheil, *Life and Manners in Persia* (London: John Murray, 1856), p. 131. Lady Sheil also comments that a painting representing Aqa Mohammad Khan and, seated in chairs, "the Chiefs of his tribe . . . seems to be an error . . . for though ancient Persians are supposed to have made use of chairs, the ground is preferred by the modern race" (p. 116).

28. William A. Shepherd, *From Bombay to Bushire* (London: Richard Bentley, 1857), p. 130. The first grouping of armchairs Texier sees during his travels in Iran (1839–40) are in the *divan khaneh* of Karaman Mirza in Tabriz; see Charles Texier, *Description de l'Armenie, la Perse et la Mesopotamie,* vol. 2 (Paris: Didot Freres, 1852), p. 44. Mounsey comments there were 18 "solidly gilded chairs" in the "presence chamber" of the Tehran Palace; see Augustus Mounsey, *Journey through the Caucasus* (London: Smith, Elder and Co., 1872), p. 164.

29. For illustration of a *qahvehkhanch* school example, see Samuel R.

Peterson, "The Ta'ziyeh and Related Arts," in *Ta'ziyeh: Ritual and Drama in Iran*, ed. Peter J. Chelkowski (New York: New York University Press, 1979), p. 80.

30. Sheil, *Life and Manners*, p. 126.

31. Comte de Gobineau, *Religions et philosophies dans l'Asie centrale* (1865; rpt. Paris: Gallimard, 1957), p. 349. For a photograph of a *ta'ziyeh* production with chairs used on stage, see Sven Hedin, *Overland to India*, vol. 2 (London: Methuen and Co., 1910), ill. 160; and for an Iranian drawing of an Imam seated in a chair, Charles Virolleaud, *Le Theatre Persan* (Paris: Adrien-Maisonneuve, 1950), title page.

32. Ussher, *Journey*, p. 591.

33. S. G. Wilson, *Persian Life and Customs* (New York: Fleming Revell, 1899), p. 304.

Contributors

Ervand Abrahamian teaches history at Baruch College, City University of New York. He has written articles on nineteenth and twentieth century Iranian history and presently has in press a book on the history of modern Iran.

Paul Barker taught in Tribal High School in Shiraz in 1973–75 and also two years in a high school in Bidokht, Iran. He taught at Warner Pacific College in Portland before becoming a project manager of the Lalmba Association for Eritrean refugees in the Sudan.

Mangol Bayat-Philipp teaches history at Harvard University. She has completed articles and a book on modern Iran, with a special interest in Iranian socioreligious thought.

Lois Beck teaches anthropology at Washington University, St. Louis. She is co-editor of *Women in the Muslim World* and is completing a book on the Qashqa'i. She spent several years with the Qashqa'i in the 1970s and has written articles on the Qashqa'i, nomadism, and women in the Middle East.

William O. Beeman teaches anthropology at Brown University. From 1976–79 he was with the Center for Traditional Performing Arts in Tehran and the Institute of Social and Cultural Sciences at Reza Shah Kabir University (now University of Northern Iran). He has written articles on Iranian sociolinguistics, theater, and politics.

Michael E. Bonine teaches geography of the Middle East in the Department of Oriental Studies at the University of Arizona. He spent several years conducting research in Yazd and its hinterland in the 1970s. He has written articles on housing and urban development in the Middle East and is working on a book on the Middle Eastern city.

Daniel Bradburd is an anthropologist teaching in the Department of Sociology at Virginia Polytechnic Institute. From 1973–75 he conducted research among the Komachi nomads of Kerman Province and has written articles based upon this research.

Willem M. Floor works for the government of The Netherlands and as an "avocation" has researched and written articles on the socioeconomic history of Iran, as well as serving as the editor of the journal *Persica*. He is currently working on publications about the Dutch East India Company in Iran.

Gene R. Garthwaite teaches history at Dartmouth College. He has made a number of research trips to Iran in the 1970s and has written articles on the

447

Bakhtiyari. He recently has written an extensive history of the Bakhtiyari and their role in Iran, being published by Cambridge University Press.

Byron J. Good is an anthropologist teaching in the Department of Psychiatry and the Department of Family Practice in the School of Medicine of the University of California at Davis. He conducted research in Maragheh in 1972–74 and has written articles on medical systems and psycho-social aspects of medical practices in Iran.

Mary-Jo DelVecchio Good is a sociologist teaching in the Department of Psychiatry and Department of Family Practice in the School of Medicine of the University of California at Davis. She conducted research on social stratification and social change in Maragheh in the 1970s and has written articles based on this research.

Michael C. Hillmann teaches Persian at the University of Texas at Austin. He has translated several major Persian texts and written articles on Persian-sociolinguistics. He has written a book on Hafez.

Eric J. Hooglund teaches political science at Bowdoin College. He has specialized on the problems of Iranian peasants and land reform. He has spent several periods of research in Iran, the latest being during the revolution of 1978–79 and the beginnings of the Islamic Republic.

Nikki R. Keddie teaches history at the University of California, Los Angeles. She has written numerous books and articles on Iran, focusing especially on nineteenth and twentieth century Iranian social history. She recently taught at the Sorbonne in Paris.

Laurence D. Loeb teaches anthropology at the University of Utah. He has conducted field research on the Jewish community in Iran and has written a book on the Jews of Shiraz. More recently he has been investigating the Jewish silversmiths of Yemen.

Hamid Naficy is interested in the history of the film industry. He has written articles on the history and content of films in Iran. He works at UCLA.

Roger T. Olson is a historian interested in nineteenth century Iran, especially the agricultural economy. He has presented papers at the annual meetings of the Middle East Studies Association and the American Historical Association, and has been teaching at West Point.

Samuel R. Peterson teaches Islamic art at Arizona State University. He has resided over ten years in the Middle East, during which he was lecturer at the Center for Arabic Studies at the American University in Cairo and lecturer at Robert College in Istanbul. He has spent several years doing research in Iran and has written articles on Iranian art and architecture.

William R. Royce teaches history and Persian in the Department of Oriental Studies at the University of Arizona. He has been a lecturer and translator in Iran and was executive director of the Iran-American Society. His special interests are Sufis and the social, cultural and political history of eighteenth to twentieth century Iran, as well as Persian language and literature.

C. Tom Thompson is an anthropologist who conducted field work in Iran from 1971–74 and again in 1978–79, the later period as a research associate of Reza Shah Kabir University (University of Northern Iran). He has written articles on peasant marketing in Iran.

INDEX